FEDERAL SENTENCING GUIDELINES MANUAL

Publisher's Notice

November 2017

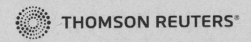

For Customer Assistance Call 1-800-328-4880

Mat #42166192

NOVEMBER 2017 PUBLISHER'S NOTE
RECENT SUPREME COURT DECISIONS
AFFECTING
THE FEDERAL SENTENCING GUIDELINES

by

Thomas W. Hutchison

For the first time in its history, the United States Sentencing Commission did not promulgate amendments to the federal sentencing guidelines in a regular amendment cycle.[1] The Commission lacked a quorum for promulgating amendments from late 2016 until March 21, 2017.[2] The Commission decided that there was not enough time during the 2017 amendment cycle "to schedule a public hearing on the proposed amendments, digest the public comment, deliberate, and hold a public vote by the statutory deadline."[3]

---

[1] A regular amendment cycle starts at the beginning of a regular session of Congress, which occurs in early January, and ends on May 1. The Commission must submit proposed guideline amendments to Congress for review during that period. The proposed amendments take effect on the date designated by the Commission, which cannot be less than 180 days from submission or later than November 1. *See* 28 U.S.C. § 994(p). A quorum of the Commission for that purpose is four voting members. 28 U.S.C.A. § 995(d). The terms of two of the five voting Commissioners serving in late 2016 had expired at the end of the Second Session of the 114th Congress. See Remarks of Chief Judge Patti B. Saris, Chair of the United States Sentencing Commission, December Public Meeting, December 9, 2016, at 1, https://www.ussc.gov/sites/default/files/pdf/amendment-process/public-hearings-and-meetings/20161209/remarks.pdf. The Senate restored a quorum for promulgating amendments when it confirmed two additional Commissioners on March 21, 2017. 163 Cong. Rec. S.1863 (Mar. 21, 2017).

[2] A quorum of the Commission for that purpose is four voting members. 28 U.S.C.A. § 995(d). The terms of two of the five voting Commissioners serving in late 2016 had expired at the end of the Second Session of the 114th Congress. See Remarks of Chief Judge Patti B. Saris, Chair of the United States Sentencing Commission, December Public Meeting, December 9, 2016, at 1, https://www.ussc.gov/sites/default/files/pdf/amendment-process/public-hearings-and-meetings/20161209/remarks.pdf. The Senate restored a quorum for promulgating amendments when it confirmed two additional Commissioners on March 21, 2017. 163 Cong. Rec. S.1863 (Mar. 21, 2017).

[3] Remarks of Circuit Judge William H. Pryor, Jr., Chair of the United States Sentencing Commission, Public Hearing on Alternatives to Incarceration Court Programs & Synthetic Drugs, April 18, 2017, Washington D.C., at 2, https://www.ussc.gov/sites/default/files/pdf/amendment-process/public-hearings-and-meetings/20170418/remarks.pdf.

SUPREME COURT DECISIONS AFFECTING THE FEDERAL SENTENCING GUIDELINES

Dean v. United States, 137 S.Ct. 1170 (2017).

A defendant convicted under 18 U.S.C.A. § 924(c) (use of a firearm in connection with a crime of violence or a drug-trafficking crime) will receive a prison term of not less than five years for a first conviction and not less than 25 years for a second or subsequent conviction. That prison term must run consecutively to "any other term of imprisonment" that the sentencing court imposes on the defendant. This case involved whether a sentencing court could consider the impact of a mandatory minimum prison term under section 924(c) when determining the sentence for other offenses for which the defendant was being sentenced.

Dean and his brother robbed two drug dealers and used a firearm during the robberies. They were convicted of several offenses, including two offenses under section 924(c), subjecting each of them to a mandatory prison term of not less than 30 years under section 924(c). The guideline range on the other offenses was 84-105 months. Dean asked the sentencing court to consider the mandatory prison term when determining the punishment for the other offenses and to impose concurrent one-day prison terms for each of those offenses. Although the sentencing court agreed that such a sentence would be appropriate, the sentencing court held that it "was required to disregard Dean's 30-year mandatory minimum when determining the appropriate sentences for Dean's other counts of conviction."[4] The sentencing court did order a downward variance from the guideline range for the other offenses, sentencing the defendant to 360 months on the section 924(c) offenses and 40 months on the other offenses, a total prison term of 400 months. The defendant appealed, and the Eighth Circuit affirmed.

The Supreme Court reversed the Eighth Circuit. "Sentencing courts have long enjoyed discretion in the sort of information they may consider when setting an appropriate sentence."[5] Under 18 U.S.C.A. § 3553(a), a sentencing court must consider specified factors when imposing sentence. Those factors are used to determine the length of separate prison terms and whether multiple terms of imprisonment are to run concurrently or consecutively.[6] The Court concluded that those statutory provisions "permit a court imposing a sentence on one count of conviction to consider sen-

---

[4] Dean v. United States, 137 S.Ct. 1170, 1175 (2017).

[5] Dean v. United States, 137 S.Ct. at 1175 (citing Pepper v. United States, 562 U.S. 476, 131 S.Ct. 1229, 179 L.Ed. 196 (2011)).

[6] 18 U.S.C.A. § § 3582, 3584. *See* Dean v. United States, 137 S.Ct. at 1176.

tences imposed on other counts."[7]

The government had argued that 18 U.S.C.A. § 924(c) restricted a sentencing court's authority under 18 U.S.C.A. § 3553(a) and related provisions, citing two parts of section 924(c). First, section 924(c)(1)(A) requires that a prison term under section 924(c) must be "in addition to" the sentence imposed on the predicate offense. Second, section 924(c)(1)(D)(ii) prohibits a sentence under section 924(c) from running concurrently "with any other term of imprisonment imposed on the person, including any term of imprisonment imposed for the crime of violence or drug trafficking crime during which the firearm was used, carried, or possessed." The Court responded, "Nothing in § 924(c) restricts the authority conferred on sentencing courts by § 3553(a) and the related provision to consider a sentence imposed under § 924(c) when calculating a just sentence for the predicate count."[8] The first limitation cited by the government "says nothing about the length of a non-§ 924(c) sentence, much less about what information a court may consider in determining that sentence."[9] As for the second limitation, "The bar on imposing concurrent sentences does not affect a court's discretion to consider a mandatory minimum when calculating each individual sentence."[10]

Molina-Martinez v. United States, 136 S.Ct. 1338 (2016).

Rule 52(b) of the Federal Rules of Criminal Procedure provides, "A plain error that affects substantial rights may be considered even though it was not brought to the court's attention." The Supreme Court has interpreted this rule to mean that a reviewing court can grant relief for an error that has not been objected to below if the defendant shows that there has been (1) an error that (2) is plain, (3) affects substantial rights, and (4) "seriously affects the fairness, integrity or public reputation of judicial proceedings."[11]

The issue in this case was whether an error in selecting the appropriate guideline range "affects substantial rights" if the sentence imposed falls within the correct range. The Supreme Court held that it does.

Molina-Martinez had pleaded guilty to being unlawfully in the United States after deportation. The presentence report calculated an applicable guideline range of 77-96 months. The sentencing court accepted the probation office's recommendation for a low-end sentence and imposed a prison term of 77 months. After his attorney submitted an *Anders* brief to the Fifth Circuit, Molina-Martinez submitted a response to the Fifth Circuit

---

[7] Dean v. United States, 137 S.Ct. at 1176.

[8] Dean v. United States, 137 S.Ct. at 1176-77.

[9] Dean v. United States, 137 S.Ct. at 1177.

[10] Dean v. United States, 137 S.Ct. at 1177.

[11] United States v. Olano, 507 U.S. 725, 732, 113 S.Ct. 1770, 1776, 123 L.Ed.2d 508 (1993). *See* Molina-Martinez v. United States, 136 S.Ct. 1338, 1343 (2016).

pointing to an error in the calculation of his criminal history. The Fifth Circuit ordered Molina-Martinez's attorney to file a brief on the merits or a supplemental Anders brief. A brief on the merits was filed.

Molina-Martinez acknowledged that he had not objected below and had to show plain error. He argued that the requirements of Rule 52(b) were met. The Fifth Circuit disagreed, concluding that the defendant's substantial rights had not been affected. If the sentence imposed falls within both the correct guideline range and the incorrect guideline range, the Fifth Circuit said, "we do not assume, in the absence of additional evidence, that the sentence affects a defendant's substantial rights."[12] That the sentencing court imposed a sentence at the bottom of the incorrect guideline range "is insufficient on its own to show that Molina-Martinez would have received a similar low-end sentence had the district court used the correct Guidelines range."[13]

The Supreme Court reversed. "Nothing in the text of Rule 52, its rationale, or the Court's precedents supports a requirement that a defendant seeking appellate review of an unpreserved Guidelines error make some further showing of prejudice beyond the fact that the erroneous, and higher, Guidelines range set the wrong framework for the sentencing proceedings."[14] The government had argued that such a ruling would "require the Government to prove the harmlessness of every Guidelines error raised on appeal regardless of whether it was preserved."[15] The Court disagreed.

> The decision today simply states that courts reviewing sentencing errors cannot apply a categorical rule requiring additional evidence in cases, like this one, where the district court applied an incorrect range but nevertheless sentenced the defendant within the correct range. Rejection of that rule means only that a defendant can rely on the application of an incorrect Guidelines range to show an effect on his substantial rights.[16]

---

[12] United States v. Molina-Martinez, 588 Fed. Appx. 333, 335 (2014) (quoting from United States v. Mudekunye, 646 F.3d 281, 290 (5th Cir. 2011), which in turn was quoting from United States v. Blocker, 612 F.3d 413, 416 (5th Cir. 2010)).

[13] United States v. Molina-Martinez, 588 Fed. Appx. at 335.

[14] Molina-Martinez v. United States, 136 S.Ct. 1338, 1345 (2013).

[15] See Molina-Martinez v. United States, 136 S.Ct. at 1348.

[16] Molina-Martinez v. United States, 136 S.Ct. at 1348.

PUBLISHER'S PREFACE

This 2016 Edition contains the current text of the Sentencing Guidelines, Commentary, and Policy Statements of the United States Sentencing Commission, as most-recently amended.

Features in Volume 1 of this 2016 Edition include:

- Highlights of the 2016 Amendments by Thomas W. Hutchison.

- Statutory index. See Appendix A.

- Selected federal statutes relating to sentencing. See Appendix B.

- Quick-reference "Sentencing Table" on the inside of the front cover.

Features in Volume 2 of this 2016 Edition include:

- Amendments to the Guidelines Manual. See Appendix C.

- Sentencing worksheets. See Appendix D.

- Federal Rules of Criminal Procedure relating to sentencing. See Appendix E.

- Fine and Revocation Tables. See Appendix G.

- Quick-reference "Sentencing Table." See Appendix G and the inside of the front cover.

For further coverage of the federal sentencing guidelines and related sentencing issues, refer to Thomas W. Hutchison, et al., *Federal Sentencing Law and Practice*. This comprehensive publication fully explains and annotates each Guideline and Policy Statement and provides related reference materials not readily available elsewhere.

Retention of Prior Editions

The 2015 Edition of the *Federal Sentencing Guidelines Manual*—along with prior editions—should be retained in the event there is a need to refer to the text of a specific Guidelines, Commentary, or Policy Statement at a particular point in time.

THE PUBLISHER

November, 2016

RELATED PRODUCTS

Courtroom Handbook on Federal Evidence
Steven Goode and Olin Guy Wellborn III

Modern Scientific Evidence
David L. Faigman, David H. Kaye, Michael J. Saks and Joseph Sanders

Federal Jury Practice and Instruction
Kevin F. O'Malley, Jay E. Grenig and William C. Lee
[Instructions available in CD-ROM]

Federal Trial Objections
Charles B. Gibbons

Federal Practice and Procedure
Charles Alan Wright, Arthur R. Miller, Mary Kay Kane, Edward H. Cooper, Richard L. Marcus, Kenneth W. Graham, Victor James Gold, Richard D. Freer, Vikram David Amar, Joan E. Steinman, Nancy J. King, Susan R. Klein, Andrew D. Leipold, Peter J. Henning, Sarah N. Welling, Charles H. Koch, Jr., Catherine T. Struve and Michael H. Graham
[Also available in CD-ROM]

Multidistrict Litigation Manual
David F. Herr

Legal Ethics: The Lawyer's Deskbook on Professional Responsibility
Ronald D. Rotunda and John S. Dzienkowski
[In joint venture with the American Bar Association]

West's Federal Administrative Practice
Federal Practice Experts

West's Federal Forms
Federal Practice Experts
[Also available in CD-ROM]

Federal Court of Appeals Manual
David G. Knibb

Federal Practice Deskbook
Charles Alan Wright and Mary Kay Kane

Handbook of Federal Evidence
Michael H. Graham

Treatise on Constitutional Law
Ronald D. Rotunda and John E. Nowak

Handbook of Federal Civil Discovery and Disclosure
Jay E. Grenig and Jeffrey S. Kinsler
[Includes Forms on Disk]

Annotated Manual for Complex Litigation
David F. Herr

Federal Sentencing Law and Practice
Thomas W. Hutchison, Peter B. Hoffman, Deborah Young, and Sigmund G. Popko

Federal Criminal Restitution
Catharine M. Goodwin, Jay E. Grenig, Nathan A. Fishbach

Administrative Law and Practice
Charles H. Koch, Jr.

Federal Case News

Federal Civil Judicial Procedure and Rules
Federal Sentencing Guidelines Manual
Manual for Complex Litigation
Reference Manual on Scientific Evidence
USCA

US Code Congressional and Administrative News

Westlaw®

West Books, CD-ROM Libraries, Disk Products and Westlaw
The Ultimate Research System

Thomson Reuters thanks you for subscribing to this product. Should you have any questions regarding this product please contact Customer Service at 1-800-328-4880 or by fax at 1-800-340-9378. If you would like to inquire about related publications or place an order, please contact us at 1-800-344-5009.

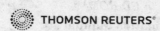 THOMSON REUTERS®   Thomson Reuters
                          610 Opperman Drive
                          Eagan, MN 55123

legalsolutions.thomsonreuters.com

Summary Table of Contents

HIGHLIGHTS OF THE 2016 AMENDMENTS

by

Thomas W. Hutchison

On April 28, 2016, the Sentencing Commission promulgated several amendments to the guidelines, setting November 1, 2016 as the effective date of those amendments.[1] Here is a synopsis of the more noteworthy changes made by the amendments.

§ 1B1.13. Reduction in Term of Imprisonment Under 18 U.S.C. § 3582(c)(1)(A) (Policy Statement).

A federal court, under 18 U.S.C. § 3582(c)(1)(A), can reduce a term of imprisonment if there are "extraordinary and compelling reasons" or if the defendant is at least 70 years old, has served at least 30 years in prison for the offense, and the Director of the Federal Bureau of Prisons determines that the defendant "is not a danger to any other person or to the community." The court can act, however, only upon motion of the Director of the Federal Bureau of Prisons.[2] The Commission promulgated this policy statement, effective November 1, 2006, in response to 28 U.S.C. § 994(t), which directs the Commission to "describe what should be considered extraordinary and compelling reasons for sentence reduction" under 18 U.S.C. § 3582(c)(1)(A).[3]

The Commission conducted an "in-depth review" of how this policy statement is being utilized. As a result of its review, the Commission made a number of changes to this policy statement that address the criteria for a motion under section 3582(c). In addition, the Commission has added an application note that "encourages the Director of the Federal Bureau of Prisons to file a motion under 18 U.S.C. § 3582(c)(1)(A) if the defendant meets any of the circumstances listed as 'extraordinary and compelling reasons' in § 1B1.13."[4]

---

[1] 81 Fed. Reg. 27,261 (May 5, 2016). Under 28 U.S.C. § 994(p), the Commission specifies an effective date, which must be no sooner than 180 days after promulgation and no later than November 1 of the year of promulgation.

[2] 18 U.S.C. § 3582(c)(1)(A). The Federal Bureau of Prisons has developed criteria for carrying out its responsibilities under section 3582(c)(1)(A). *See* U.S. Dep't of Justice, Fed. Bur. of Prisons, Compassionate Release/Reduction in Sentence: Procedures for Implementation of 18 U.S.C. §§ 3582(c)(1)(A) and 4205(g) (Program Statement 5050.49, CN-1).

[3] U.S.S.G. App. C, amend. 683.

[4] U.S.S.G. App. C, amend. 799. The new application note also points out that "The Commission's policy statement is not legally binding on the Bureau of Prisons and does not confer any rights on the defendant . . . ."

Application note 1 addresses what constitutes "extraordinary and compelling reasons." As originally drafted, application note 1 identified three types of reasons – medical condition, family circumstances, and a catchall ("an extraordinary and compelling reason other than, or in combination with," the other two types). Amendment 799 broadens the existing reasons and adds a fourth reason.[5]

Application note 1(A) as originally promulgated covered two types of medical conditions — a terminal illness, and a permanent physical or medical condition, or deteriorating physical or mental health because of the aging process that substantially diminishes the defendant's ability to provide self-care within a prison environment, and for which conventional treatment promises no substantial improvement in defendant's condition. Amendment 799 adds language to the application note to specify that "terminal illness" means a "serious and advanced illness with an end of life trajectory" and to provide that "a probability of death within a specific time period" is not required. The amendment gives as examples of terminal illness metastatic solid-tumor cancer, Lou Gehrig's disease (ALS), end-stage organ disease, and advanced dementia. For nonterminal medical conditions, the amendment drops the requirement that the condition be "permanent," requiring instead that it be "serious." The amendment also expands the medical conditions to include a "serious functional or cognitive impairment." Finally, amendment 799 changes the requirement that conventional treatment promise no substantial improvement in the defendant's condition. The standard now is that the condition is one from which the defendant is not expected to recover.

The only family condition covered by application note 1(A) as originally promulgated was the death or incapacitation of the defendant's only family member capable of caring for the defendant's minor child or minor children. Amendment 799 broadens this provision in two ways. First, the application note provides that caregiver who dies or becomes incapacitated does not have to be a family member. Second, the application note now provides that the incapacitation of the defendant's spouse or registered partner is an extraordinary and compelling reason if the defendant would be the only available caregiver for that person.

Amendment 799 also broadens application note 1 by adding a fourth type of extraordinary and compelling reason – age. Application note 1 now provides that there is an extraordinary and compelling reason if the defendant is at least 65 years old, is experiencing a serious deterioration in physical or mental health because of the aging process, and has served the lesser of 10 years or 75 percent of the term of imprisonment.

The Commission added a new application note that provides that the extraordinary and compelling reason need not have been unforeseen at the

---

[5] The amendment also redesignates the provisions of application note 1. References in text are to the application note before the redesignation.

time of sentencing. That the sentencing court reasonably could have known or anticipated defendant's condition, therefore, does not preclude consideration for a reduction under this policy statement.

§ 2E3.1. Gambling Offenses; Animal Fighting Offenses.

Amendment 800 makes several changes to this guideline in response to congressional changes to the Animal Welfare Act (codified at 7 U.S.C. § 2156).[6] First, because Congress increased the maximum prison term from three to five years for an offense involving an animal-fighting venture, the amendment increases the base offense level for such an offense from 10 to 16.[7] There is an exception to address a new offense with a three-year maximum term of imprisonment.[8] Amendment 800 also adds an application note indicating that a departure may be warranted if the offense involved extraordinary cruelty to an animal beyond the violence inherent in such a venture or if the offense involved animal fighting on an exceptional scale.

§ 2G2.1. Sexually Exploiting a Minor by Production of Sexually Explicit Visual or Printed Material; Custodian Permitting Minor to Engage in Sexually Explicit Conduct; Advertisement for Minors to Engage in Production.

This guideline applies to offenses involving the production of child pornography. Amendment 801 revises the guideline to address offenses involving material that portrays very young children (infants and toddlers) and to clarify the meaning of "distribution."

Subsection (b)(1)(A) calls for a four-level enhancement if the offense involved a minor less than 12 years old, and subsection (b)(1)(B) calls for a two-level enhancement if the offense involved a minor who was at least 12 years old but not 16 years old. For an offense involving very young persons (infants and toddlers), circuits were divided about whether the vulnerable victim adjustment of § 3A1.1(b) also applied.[9] The Commission resolved the conflict by adding a four-level enhancement that applies if the offense involves material that portrays "an infant or toddler."[10] A new application note provides that if the infant or toddler enhancement is applied, the vulnerable victim adjustment of § 3A1.1(b) does not apply.

---

[6] *See* U.S.S.G. App. C, amend. 800 (reason for amendment).

[7] *See* U.S.S.G. App. C, amend. 800 (reason for amendment).

[8] The new offense is set forth in 7 U.S.C. § 2156(a)(2)(B), which has a base offense level of 10. *See* U.S.S.G. App. C, amend. 800 (reason for amendment).

[9] Two circuits, the Fifth and Ninth, held that it was permissible to apply both. The Fourth Circuit held that both could not be applied. See U.S.S.G. App. C, amend. 801 (reason for amendment). *See also* Hutchison, Popko et al, Federal Sentencing Law and Practice § 2G2.1 Authors' Cmt. 2 (2016).

[10] The new provision was added to subsection (b)(4).

Amendment 801 also addresses what constitutes "distribution." Subsection (b)(3) calls for a two-level enhancement "if the offense involved distribution." Application note 1 defines the term "distribution" to mean "any act, including possession with intent to distribute, production, transmission, advertisement, and transportation, related to the transfer of material involving the sexual exploitation of a minor." That definition does not require scienter.[11] Amendment 801 revises subsection (b)(3) to require that "the defendant knowingly engaged in distribution." New application note 3 defines the term "knowingly engaged in distribution" to mean "the defendant (A) knowingly committed the distribution, (B) aided, abetted, counseled, commanded, induced, procured, or willfully caused the distribution, or (C) conspired to distribute."

§ 2G2.2. Trafficking in Material Involving the Sexual Exploitation of a Minor; Receiving, Transporting, Shipping, Soliciting, or Advertising Material Involving the Sexual Exploitation of a Minor; Possessing Material Involving the Sexual Exploitation of a Minor with Intent to Traffic; Possessing Material Involving the Sexual Exploitation of a Minor.

This guideline applies to offenses involving trafficking in child pornography. Amendment 801 addresses two matters, offenses involving very young children (infants and toddlers) and what constitutes "distribution."

Subsection (b)(2) calls for a two-level enhancement "if the material involved a prepubescent minor or a minor who had not attained the age of 12 years." The Commission has amended the guideline to call for a four-level enhancement "if the offense involved material that portrays . . . sexual abuse or exploitation of an infant or toddler." A new application note provides that if the infant or toddler enhancement is applied, the vulnerable victim adjustment of § 3A1.1(b) does not apply.

If the offense involved distribution, subsection (b)(3) calls for a range of enhancements (two to seven levels) based upon the nature of the distribution. Application note 1 defines the term "distribution" to mean "any act, including possession with intent to distribute, production, transmission, advertisement, and transportation, related to the transfer of material involving the sexual exploitation of a minor." There is no scienter requirement.[12]

There has been conflict among circuits involving the scienter requirement for subsections (b)(3)(B) and (b)(3)(F). Subsection (b)(3)(B) calls for a

---

[11] The Commission's approach has been that if scienter is not required, strict liability applies. See Hutchison, Popko et al, Federal Sentencing Law and Practice § 1B1.3 Authors' Cmt. 10, § 2G2.2 Authors' Cmt. 7(h) (2016).

[12] The Commission's approach has been that if scienter is not required, strict liability applies. See Hutchison, Popko et al, Federal Sentencing Law and Practice § 1B1.3 Authors' Cmt. 10, § 2G2.2 Authors' Cmt. 7(h) (2016).

five-level enhancement if the offense involved "distribution for the receipt, or expectation of receipt, of a thing of value, but not for pecuniary gain." Subsection (b)(3)(F) is a catchall provision that calls for a two-level enhancement for "distribution" not covered by subsections (b)(3)(A) through (E). The Commission notes that the circuit conflicts "have arisen frequently, although not exclusively, in cases involving the use of peer-to-peer file-sharing programs or networks."[13]

Peer-to-peer file sharing permits computer users to share files over the Internet without going through a central server or using email. A program installed on a user's computer permits the user to access a shared file in the computer of any other person who has installed the program. Programs vary on the extent of control that a user has over what goes into the shared folder.

Some circuits have held that subsection (b)(3)(F) applies if the defendant used a file-sharing program, whether the defendant did so purposefully, knowingly, or negligently. Some circuits have required that the defendant know of the file-sharing properties of the program. One circuit has held that knowledge is necessary, but that knowledge can be inferred from use of the program, absent "concrete evidence" of ignorance of the file-sharing properties of the program. One circuit has held that there is a presumption that a defendant who uses a file-sharing program understands that others can access the defendant's files.[14] The Commission has resolved the differences by amending subsection (b)(3)(F) to apply "if the defendant knowingly engaged in distribution." New application note 2 defines the term "knowingly engaged in distribution" to mean "the defendant (A) knowingly committed the distribution, (B) aided, abetted, counseled, commanded, induced, procured, or willfully caused the distribution, or (C) conspired to distribute."

The Commission also has amended subsection (b)(3)(B) to require knowledge. Subsection (b)(3)(B) now applies "if the defendant distributed in exchange for any valuable consideration, but not for pecuniary gain." Application note 1 now defines that term to mean "the defendant (A) knowingly committed the distribution, (B) aided, abetted, counseled, commanded, induced, procured, or willfully caused the distribution, or (C) conspired to distribute."

§ 2G3.1. Importing, Mailing, or Transporting Obscene Matter; Transferring Obscene Matter to a Minor; Misleading Domain Names.

Subsection (b)(1) of this guideline, like § 2G2.1(b)(3), calls for a range of enhancements (two to seven levels) based upon the nature of the distribution. Subsection (b)(1)(F) is a catchall provision that calls for a two-level enhancement for "distribution" not covered by subsections

---

[13] U.S.S.G. App. C, amend. 801 (reason for amendment).

[14] *See* U.S.S.G. App. C, amend. 801 (reason for amendment).

(b)(3)(A) through (E). Amendment 801 revises this subsection to conform to § 2G2.3(b)(3). Subsection (b)(1)(F) now applies "if the defendant knowingly engaged in distribution." A new application note defines the term "knowingly engaged in distribution" to mean "the defendant (A) knowingly committed the distribution, (B) aided, abetted, counseled, commanded, induced, procured, or willfully caused the distribution, or (C) conspired to distribute."

Subsection (b)(1)(B) calls for a five-level enhancement if the offense involved "distribution for the receipt, or expectation of receipt, of a thing of value, but not for pecuniary gain." The Commission has amended subsection (b)(1)(B) to require knowledge. Subsection (b)(1)(B) now applies "if the defendant distributed in exchange for any valuable consideration, but not for pecuniary gain." Application note 1 was amended to define that term to mean "the defendant (A) knowingly committed the distribution, (B) aided, abetted, counseled, commanded, induced, procured, or willfully caused the distribution, or (C) conspired to distribute."

§ 2L1.1. Smuggling, Transporting, or Harboring an Illegal Alien.

Amendment 802 makes several changes to subsection (b)(4). Subsection (b)(4) had called for a two-level enhancement "if the defendant smuggled, transported, or harbored a minor who was unaccompanied by the minor's parent or grandparent." Amendment 802 increases the enhancement from two levels to four levels and both expands and narrows the enhancement. The amendment expands the enhancement by making it applicable based upon the full range of relevant conduct, not just the defendant's conduct. The amendment also expands it by increasing the maximum age for a minor from 16 to 18. The amendment narrows the scope of the enhancement by limiting who qualifies as an unaccompanied minor. Before the amendment, the enhancement considered an unaccompanied minor to be a minor who was not with a parent or grandparent. The enhancement now considers an unaccompanied minor to be a minor who is not with a parent, adult relative, or legal guardian.

§ 2L1.2. Unlawfully Entering or Remaining in the United States.

The Commission carried out over several years a review of how the guidelines handle immigration offenses. Based upon that review, the Commission concluded that there were three main concerns with this guideline. First, "the 'categorical approach' used to determine the particular level of enhancement under the existing guideline is overly complex and resource-intensive and often leads to litigation and uncertainty." Second, "the existing 16- and 12- level enhancements for certain prior felonies committed before a defendant's deportation were overly severe." Third, "the existing guideline did not account for other types of criminal conduct committed by illegal reentry offenders."[15]

In response to those concerns, the Commission significantly revised this guideline. The Commission has largely abandoned use of categories of offenses to determine the extent of an enhancement and now is relying on the prison term imposed to determine the extent of an enhancement for a prior conviction.[16]

The revised guideline divides prior convictions into three classes — conviction for an illegal reentry offense (dealt with in new subsection (b)(1)), conviction for an offense committed before the defendant was first deported or ordered removed from the United States (addressed in new subsection (b)(2)), and conviction for an offense committed after the defendant was first deported or ordered removed (dealt with in new subsection (b)(3)).

New subsection (b)(1)(A) calls for an enhancement of four levels if the defendant committed the instant offense after having been convicted of an illegal reentry felony. Application note 2 defines "illegal reentry offense" to mean an offense under 8 U.S.C. §§ 1253 or 1326 or a second or subsequent offense under 8 U.S.C. § 1325(a). Subsection (b)(1)(B) calls for an enhancement of two levels if the defendant committed the instant offense after having been convicted of two illegal reentry misdemeanors.

New subsection (b)(2) calls for an enhancement based upon conviction of an offense committed before the defendant was deported or ordered removed from the United States for the first time. If the prior offense was—

- a felony (other than an illegal reentry felony) for which the prison term imposed was five years or more, the enhancement is 10 levels;
- a felony (other than an illegal reentry felony) for which the prison term imposed was two years or more, the enhancement is 8 levels;
- a felony (other than an illegal reentry felony) for which the prison term imposed was 13 months or more, the enhancement is 6 levels;
- any other felony (other than an illegal reentry felony), the enhancement is 4 levels.

If the defendant was convicted of three or more misdemeanors that are crimes of violence or drug trafficking offenses, the enhancement under subsection (b)(2)(E) is 2 levels. The sentencing court is to apply the greatest applicable enhancement.

---

[15] U.S.S.G. App. C, amend. 802 (reason for amendment).

[16] Because of "a congressional directive requiring inclusion of an enhancement for certain types of misdemeanor offenses," the Commission did not completely abandon the use of categories of offenses U.S.S.G. App. 802 (reason for amendment). The Commission retained two categories of offenses, "drug trafficking offense" and "crime of violence." The Commission carried forward the definition of "drug trafficking offense" but revised the definition of "crime of violence" to conform to the definition of that term in § 4B1.2(a).

New subsection (b)(3) calls for an enhancement based upon conviction for an offense committed after the defendant was deported or ordered removed from the United States for the first time. If that offense was -

- a felony (other than an illegal reentry felony) for which the prison term imposed was five years or more, the enhancement is 10 levels;
- a felony (other than an illegal reentry felony) for which the prison term imposed was two years or more, the enhancement is 8 levels;
- a felony (other than an illegal reentry felony) for which the prison term imposed was 13 months or more, the enhancement is 6 levels;
- a felony (other than an illegal reentry felony) for which the prison term imposed was 13 months or more, the enhancement is 4 levels.

If the defendant was convicted of three or more misdemeanors that are crimes of violence or drug trafficking offenses, the enhancement under subsection (b)(3)(E) is 2 levels. The sentencing court is to apply the greatest applicable enhancement.

New application note 3 provides that to be used to apply any provision of subsection (b), a prior conviction must receive criminal history points under § 4A1.1(a), (b), or (c). New application note 3 also requires that a prior misdemeanor conviction, to be used to apply (b)(1)(B), (b)(2)(E), or (b)(3)(E), must be counted separately under § 4A1.2(a)(2). New application note 4 addresses the situation in which a sentence for an illegal reentry offense and another felony offense are imposed at the same time and treated as a single offense. The application note calls for use of the illegal reentry conviction to apply subsection (b)(1) if that offense "independently would have received criminal history points," and use of the other felony offense to apply subsection (b)(3) if that offense "independently would have received criminal history points."

A new application note addresses departing on the basis of the seriousness of a prior offense. The note provides that a departure may be warranted if

an enhancement in subsection (b)(2) or (b)(3) substantially understates or overstates the seriousness of the conduct underlying the prior offense, because (A) the length of the sentence imposed does not reflect the seriousness of the prior offense; (B) the prior conviction is too remote to receive criminal history points (see § 4A1.2(e)); or (C) the time actually served was substantially less than the length of the sentence imposed for the prior offense.

§ 5B1.3. Conditions of Probation.

After a "multi-year review of sentencing practices relating to federal probation and supervised release," the Commission amended the conditions set forth in this guideline "to make them easier for defendants to understand and probation officers to enforce."[17] To accomplish this, the Commission revised the wording of the conditions and reordered them while retaining the previous structure of the guideline.[18] Subsection (a) sets forth mandatory conditions (conditions required by statute) and subsection (b) restates the statutory authority for imposing discretionary conditions of probation.[19] Subsections (c), (d), and (e), which are designated policy statements, provide guidance about imposing discretionary conditions.

The Commission revised subsection (c)(1) in the prior guideline – the standard condition requiring a defendant not to leave the judicial district or specified geographical area without permission – to require that the defendant not knowingly leave the district or specified area. The Commission also amended subsection (c)(9) in the prior guideline – the standard condition prohibiting associating with persons engaged in criminal activity – to require that the defendant not communicate or interact with someone the defendant knows to be engaged in criminal activity. The Commission deleted the standard conditions addressing excessive use of alcohol and refraining from visiting places where controlled substances are illegally sold or used (subsections (c)(7) and (8) in the prior guideline).[20] The Commission also added an application note providing that the standard condition requiring a defendant to answer truthfully inquiries from the probation officer (subsection (c)(3) in the prior guideline) is not violated by a defendant's invocation of the Fifth Amendment privilege against self-incrimination.

§ 5D1.3. Conditions of Supervised Release.

The Commission's amendment of this guideline is based upon a "multi-year review of sentencing practices relating to federal probation and supervised release."[21] The Commission's intention is to make the conditions set forth in the guideline "easier for defendants to understand and probation officers to enforce."[22] Although the Commission revised the wording of the conditions and reordered them, the Commission retained the previous structure of the guideline. Subsection (a) sets forth mandatory conditions (conditions required by statute) and subsection (b) restates the statutory authority for imposing discretionary conditions of probation.[23] Subsections (c), (d), and (e), which are designated policy statements, provide guidance about imposing discretionary conditions.

---

[17] U.S.S.G. App. C, amend. 803 (reason for amendment).

[18] U.S.S.G. App. C, amend. 803.

[19] See 18 U.S.C. § 3563(b).

[20] "The Commission determined that these conditions are either best dealt with as special conditions or are redundant with other conditions." U.S.S.G. App. C, amend. 803 (reason for amendment).

[21] U.S.S.G. App. C, amend. 803 (reason for amendment).

[22] U.S.S.G. App. C, amend. 803 (reason for amendment).

[23] See 18 U.S.C. § 3583(d).

The Commission revised subsection (c)(1) in the prior guideline – the standard condition requiring a defendant not to leave the judicial district or specified geographical area without permission – to require that the defendant not knowingly leave the district or specified area. The Commission also amended subsection (c)(9) in the prior guideline – the standard condition prohibiting associating with persons engaged in criminal activity – to require that the defendant not communicate or interact with someone the defendant knows to be engaged in criminal activity. The Commission deleted the standard conditions addressing excessive use of alcohol and refraining from visiting places where controlled substances are illegally sold or used (subsections (c)(7) and (8) in the prior guideline).[24] The Commission also added an application note providing that the standard condition requiring a defendant to answer truthfully inquiries from the probation officer (subsection (c)(3) in the prior guideline) is not violated by a defendant's invocation of the Fifth Amendment privilege against self-incrimination.

---

[24] "The Commission determined that these conditions are either best dealt with as special conditions or are redundant with other conditions." U.S.S.G. App. C, amend. 803 (reason for amendment).

UNITED STATES SENTENCING COMMISSION
GUIDELINES MANUAL
2016

PATTI B. SARIS
Chair

CHARLES R. BREYER
Vice Chair

DABNEY L. FRIEDRICH
Commissioner

RACHEL E. BARKOW
Commissioner

WILLIAM H. PRYOR, JR.
Commissioner

MICHELLE MORALES
Commissioner, *Ex-officio*

J. PATRICIA WILSON SMOOT
Commissioner, *Ex-officio*

This document contains the text of the *Guidelines Manual* incorporating amendments effective November 1, 2016, and earlier.

RECOMMENDED CITATION FORM

United States Sentencing Commission Guidelines, Policy Statements, and Commentary may be cited as follows:

I. Full citation form

United States Sentencing Commission, *Guidelines Manual*, §3E1.1 (Nov. 2016)

II. Abbreviated citation form
[using USSG as the designated short form for United States Sentencing Guidelines]

◆   a guideline —

USSG §2D1.1

◆   a policy statement —

USSG §6A1.1, p.s.

◆   commentary designated as an application note —

USSG §2B1.1, comment. (n.1)

◆   commentary designated as background —

USSG §2B1.1, comment. (backg'd.)

◆   commentary designated as an introduction —

USSG Ch.3, Pt.D, intro. comment.

◆   commentary designated as a conclusion —

USSG Ch.3, Pt.D, concl. comment.

◆   an appendix to the Guidelines Manual —

USSG App. C

TABLE OF CONTENTS

TABLE OF CONTENTS

SUPPLEMENTARY VOLUMES

CHAPTER ONE

INTRODUCTION, AUTHORITY, AND GENERAL APPLICATION PRINCIPLES

PART A — INTRODUCTION AND AUTHORITY

Introductory Commentary

Subparts 1 and 2 of this Part provide an introduction to the Guidelines Manual describing the historical development and evolution of the federal sentencing guidelines. Subpart 1 sets forth the original introduction to the Guidelines Manual as it first appeared in 1987, with the inclusion of amendments made occasionally thereto between 1987 and 2000. The original introduction, as so amended, explained a number of policy decisions made by the United States Sentencing Commission ("Commission") when it promulgated the initial set of guidelines and therefore provides a useful reference for contextual and historical purposes. Subpart 2 further describes the evolution of the federal sentencing guidelines after the initial guidelines were promulgated.

Subpart 3 of this Part states the authority of the Commission to promulgate federal sentencing guidelines, policy statements, and commentary.

1. ORIGINAL INTRODUCTION TO THE GUIDELINES MANUAL

The following provisions of this Subpart set forth the original introduction to this manual, effective November 1, 1987, and as amended through November 1, 2000:

1. Authority

The United States Sentencing Commission ("Commission") is an independent agency in the judicial branch composed of seven voting and two non-voting, *ex officio* members. Its principal purpose is to establish sentencing policies and practices for the federal criminal justice system that will assure the ends of justice by promulgating detailed guidelines prescribing the appropriate sentences for offenders convicted of federal crimes.

The guidelines and policy statements promulgated by the Commission are issued pursuant to Section 994(a) of Title 28, United States Code.

2. The Statutory Mission

The Sentencing Reform Act of 1984 (Title II of the Comprehensive Crime Control Act of 1984) provides for the development of guidelines that will further the basic purposes of criminal punishment: deterrence, incapacitation, just punishment, and rehabilitation. The Act delegates broad authority to the Commission to review and rationalize the federal sentencing process.

The Act contains detailed instructions as to how this determination should be made, the most important of which directs the Commission to create categories of offense behavior and offender characteristics. An offense behavior category might consist, for example, of "bank robbery/committed with a gun/$2500 taken." An offender characteristic category might be "offender with one prior conviction not resulting in imprisonment." The Commission is required to prescribe guideline ranges that specify an appropriate sentence for each class of convicted persons determined by coordinating the offense behavior categories with the offender characteristic categories. Where the guidelines call for imprisonment, the range must be narrow: the maximum of the range cannot exceed the minimum by more than the greater of 25 percent or six months. 28 U.S.C. § 994(b)(2).

Pursuant to the Act, the sentencing court must select a sentence from within the guideline range. If, however, a particular case presents atypical features, the Act allows the court to depart from the guidelines and sentence outside the prescribed range. In that case, the court must specify reasons for departure. 18 U.S.C. § 3553(b). If the court sentences within the guideline range, an appellate court may review the sentence to determine whether the guidelines were correctly applied. If the court departs from the guideline range, an appellate court may review the reasonableness of the departure. 18 U.S.C. § 3742. The Act also abolishes parole, and substantially reduces and restructures good behavior adjustments.

The Commission's initial guidelines were submitted to Congress on April 13, 1987. After the prescribed period of Congressional review, the guidelines took effect on November 1, 1987, and apply to all offenses committed on or after that date. The Commission has the authority to submit guideline amendments each year to Congress between the beginning of a regular Congressional session and May 1. Such amendments automatically take effect 180 days after submission unless a law is enacted to the contrary. 28 U.S.C. § 994(p).

The initial sentencing guidelines and policy statements were developed after extensive hearings, deliberation, and consideration of substantial public comment. The Commission emphasizes, however, that it views the guideline-writing process as evolutionary. It expects, and the governing statute anticipates, that continuing research, experience, and analysis will result in modifications and revisions to the guidelines through submission of amendments to Congress. To this end, the Commission is established as a permanent agency to monitor sentencing practices in the federal courts.

3.   The Basic Approach (Policy Statement)

To understand the guidelines and their underlying rationale, it is important to focus on the three objectives that Congress sought to achieve in enacting the Sentencing Reform Act of 1984. The Act's basic objective was to enhance the ability of the criminal justice system to combat crime through an effective, fair sentencing system. To achieve this end, Congress first sought honesty in sentencing. It sought to avoid the confusion and implicit deception that arose out of the pre-guidelines sentencing system which required the court to impose an indeterminate sentence of imprisonment and empowered the parole commission to determine how much of the sentence an offender actually would serve in prison. This practice usually resulted in a substantial reduction in the effective length of the sentence imposed, with defendants often serving only about one-third of the sentence imposed by the court.

Second, Congress sought reasonable uniformity in sentencing by narrowing the wide disparity in sentences imposed for similar criminal offenses committed by similar offenders. Third, Congress sought proportionality in sentencing through a system that imposes appropriately different sentences for criminal conduct of differing severity.

Honesty is easy to achieve: the abolition of parole makes the sentence imposed by the court the sentence the offender will serve, less approximately fifteen percent for good behavior. There is a tension, however, between the mandate of uniformity and the mandate of proportionality. Simple uniformity — sentencing every offender to five years — destroys proportionality. Having only a few simple categories of crimes would make the guidelines uniform and easy to administer, but might lump together offenses that are different in important respects. For example, a single category for robbery that included armed and unarmed robberies, robberies with and without injuries, robberies of a few dollars and robberies of millions, would be far too broad.

A sentencing system tailored to fit every conceivable wrinkle of each case would quickly become unworkable and seriously compromise the certainty of punishment and its deterrent effect. For example: a bank robber with (or without) a gun, which the robber kept hidden (or brandished), might have frightened (or merely warned), injured seriously (or less seriously), tied up (or simply pushed) a guard, teller, or customer, at night (or at noon), in an effort to obtain money for other crimes (or for other purposes), in the company of a few (or many) other robbers, for the first (or fourth) time.

The list of potentially relevant features of criminal behavior is long; the fact that they can occur in multiple combinations means that the list of possible permutations of factors is virtually endless. The appropriate relationships among these different factors are exceedingly difficult to establish, for they are often context specific. Sentencing courts do not treat the occurrence of a simple bruise identically in all cases, irrespective of whether that bruise occurred in the context of a bank robbery or in the context of a breach of peace. This is so, in part, because the risk that such a harm will occur differs depending on the underlying offense with which it is connected; and also because, in part, the relationship between punishment and multiple harms is not simply additive. The relation varies depending on how much other harm has occurred. Thus, it would not be proper to assign points for each kind of harm and simply add them up, irrespective of context and total amounts.

The larger the number of subcategories of offense and offender characteristics included in the guidelines, the greater the complexity and the less workable the system. Moreover, complex combinations of offense and offender characteristics would apply and interact in unforeseen ways to unforeseen situations, thus failing to cure the unfairness of a simple, broad category system. Finally, and perhaps most importantly, probation officers and courts, in applying a complex system having numerous subcategories, would be required to make a host of decisions regarding whether the underlying facts were sufficient to bring the case within a particular subcategory. The greater the number of decisions required and the greater their complexity, the greater the risk that different courts would apply the guidelines differently to situations that, in fact, are similar, thereby reintroducing the very disparity that the guidelines were designed to reduce.

In view of the arguments, it would have been tempting to retreat to the simple, broad category approach and to grant courts the discretion to select the proper point along a broad sentencing range. Granting such broad discretion, however, would have risked correspondingly broad disparity in sentencing, for different courts may exercise their discretionary powers in different ways. Such an approach would have risked a return to the wide disparity that Congress established the Commission to reduce and would have been contrary to the Commission's mandate set forth in the Sentencing Reform Act of 1984.

In the end, there was no completely satisfying solution to this problem. The Commission had to balance the comparative virtues and vices of broad, simple categorization and detailed, complex subcategorization, and within the constraints established by that balance, minimize the discretionary powers of the sentencing court. Any system will, to a degree, enjoy the benefits and suffer from the drawbacks of each approach.

A philosophical problem arose when the Commission attempted to reconcile the differing perceptions of the purposes of criminal punishment. Most observers of the criminal law agree that the ultimate aim of the law itself, and of punishment in particular, is the control of crime. Beyond this point, however, the consensus seems to break down. Some argue that appropriate punishment should be defined primarily on the basis of the principle of "just deserts." Under this principle, punishment should be scaled to the offender's culpability and the resulting harms. Others argue that punishment should be imposed primarily on the basis of practical "crime control" considerations. This theory calls for sentences that most effectively lessen the likelihood of future crime, either by deterring others or incapacitating the defendant.

Adherents of each of these points of view urged the Commission to choose between them and accord one primacy over the other. As a practical matter, however, this choice was unnecessary because in most sentencing decisions the application of either philosophy will produce the same or similar results.

In its initial set of guidelines, the Commission sought to solve both the practical and philosophical problems of developing a coherent sentencing system by taking an empirical approach that used as a starting point data estimating pre-guidelines sentencing practice. It analyzed data drawn from 10,000 presentence investigations, the differing elements of various crimes as distinguished in substantive criminal statutes, the United States Parole Commission's guidelines and statistics, and data from other relevant sources in order to determine which distinctions were important in pre-guidelines practice. After consideration, the Commission accepted, modified, or rationalized these distinctions.

This empirical approach helped the Commission resolve its practical problem by defining a list of relevant distinctions that, although of considerable length, was short enough to create a manageable set of guidelines. Existing categories are relatively broad and omit distinctions that some may believe important, yet they include most of the major distinctions that statutes and data suggest made a significant difference in sentencing decisions. Relevant distinctions not reflected in the guidelines probably will occur rarely and sentencing courts may take such unusual cases into account by departing from the guidelines.

The Commission's empirical approach also helped resolve its philosophical dilemma. Those who adhere to a just deserts philosophy may concede that the lack of consensus might make it difficult to say exactly what punishment is deserved for a particular crime. Likewise, those who subscribe to a philosophy of crime control may acknowledge that the lack of sufficient data might make it difficult to determine exactly the punishment that will best prevent that crime. Both groups might therefore recognize the wisdom of looking to those distinctions that judges and legislators have, in fact, made over the course of time. These established distinctions are ones that the community believes, or has found over time, to be important from either a just deserts or crime control perspective.

The Commission did not simply copy estimates of pre-guidelines practice as revealed by the data, even though establishing offense values on this basis would help eliminate disparity because the data represent averages. Rather, it departed from the data at different points for various important reasons. Congressional statutes, for example, suggested or required departure, as in the case of the Anti-Drug Abuse Act of 1986 that imposed increased and mandatory minimum sentences. In addition, the data revealed inconsistencies in treatment, such as punishing economic crime less severely than other apparently equivalent behavior.

Despite these policy-oriented departures from pre-guidelines practice, the guidelines represent an approach that begins with, and builds upon, empirical data. The guidelines will not please those who wish the Commission to adopt a single philosophical theory and then work deductively to establish a simple and perfect set of categorizations and distinctions. The guidelines may prove acceptable, however, to those who seek more modest, incremental improvements in the status quo, who believe the best is often the enemy of the good, and who recognize that these guidelines are, as the Act contemplates, but the first step in an evolutionary process. After spending considerable time and resources exploring alternative approaches, the Commission developed these guidelines as a practical effort toward the achievement of a more honest, uniform, equitable, proportional, and therefore effective sentencing system.

4. The Guidelines' Resolution of Major Issues (Policy Statement)

The guideline-drafting process required the Commission to resolve a host of important policy questions typically involving rather evenly balanced sets of competing considerations. As an aid to understanding the guidelines, this introduction briefly discusses several of those issues; commentary in the guidelines explains others.

(a) Real Offense vs. Charge Offense Sentencing.

One of the most important questions for the Commission to decide was whether to base sentences upon the actual conduct in which the defendant engaged regardless of the charges for which he was indicted or convicted ("real offense" sentencing), or upon the conduct that constitutes the elements of the offense for which the defendant was charged and of which he was convicted ("charge offense" sentencing). A bank robber, for example, might have used a gun, frightened bystanders, taken $50,000, injured a teller, refused to stop when ordered, and raced away damaging property during his escape. A pure real offense system would sentence on the basis of all identifiable conduct. A pure charge offense system would overlook some of the harms that did not constitute statutory elements of the offenses of which the defendant was convicted.

The Commission initially sought to develop a pure real offense system. After all, the pre-guidelines sentencing system was, in a sense, this type of system. The sentencing court and the parole commission took account of the conduct in which the defendant actually engaged, as determined in a presentence report, at the sentencing hearing, or before a parole commission hearing officer. The Commission's initial efforts in this direction, carried out in the spring and early summer of 1986, proved unproductive, mostly for practical reasons. To make such a system work, even to formalize and rationalize the status quo, would have required the Commission to decide precisely which harms to take into account, how to add them up, and what kinds of procedures the courts should use to determine the presence or absence of disputed factual elements. The Commission found no practical way to combine and account for the large number of diverse harms arising in different circumstances; nor did it find a practical way to reconcile the need for a fair adjudicatory procedure with the need for a speedy sentencing process given the potential existence of hosts of adjudicated "real harm" facts in many typical cases. The effort proposed as a solution to these problems required the use of, for example, quadratic roots and other mathematical operations that the Commission considered too complex to be workable. In the Commission's view, such a system risked return to wide disparity in sentencing practice.

In its initial set of guidelines submitted to Congress in April 1987, the Commission moved closer to a charge offense system. This system, however, does contain a significant number of real offense elements. For one thing, the hundreds of overlapping and duplicative statutory provisions that make up the federal criminal law forced the Commission to write guidelines that are descriptive of generic conduct rather than guidelines that track purely statutory language. For another, the guidelines take account of a number of important, commonly occurring real offense elements such as role in the offense, the presence of a gun, or the amount of money actually taken, through alternative base offense levels, specific offense characteristics, cross references, and adjustments.

The Commission recognized that a charge offense system has drawbacks of its own. One of the most important is the potential it affords prosecutors to influence sentences by increasing or decreasing the number of counts in an indictment. Of course, the defendant's actual conduct (that which the prosecutor can prove in court) imposes a natural limit upon the prosecutor's ability to increase a defendant's sentence. Moreover, the Commission has written its rules for the treatment of multicount convictions with an eye toward eliminating unfair treatment that might flow from count manipulation. For example, the guidelines treat a three-count indictment, each count of which charges sale of 100 grams of heroin or theft of $10,000, the same as a single-count indictment charging sale of 300 grams of heroin or theft of $30,000. Furthermore, a sentencing court may control any inappropriate manipulation of the indictment through use of its departure power. Finally, the Commission will closely monitor charging and plea agreement practices and will make appropriate adjustments should they become necessary.

(b) Departures.

The sentencing statute permits a court to depart from a guideline-specified sentence only when it finds "an aggravating or mitigating circumstance of a kind, or to a degree, not adequately taken into consideration by the Sentencing Commission in formulating the guidelines that should result in a sentence different from that described." 18 U.S.C. § 3553(b). The Commission intends the sentencing courts to treat each guideline as carving out a "heartland," a set of typical cases embodying the conduct that each guideline describes. When a court finds an atypical case, one to which a particular guideline linguistically applies but where conduct significantly differs from the norm, the court may consider whether a departure is warranted. Section 5H1.10 (Race, Sex, National Origin, Creed, Religion, and Socio-Economic Status), §5H1.12 (Lack of Guidance as a Youth and Similar Circumstances), the third sentence of §5H1.4 (Physical Condition, Including Drug or Alcohol Dependence or Abuse), the last sentence of §5K2.12 (Coercion and Duress), and §5K2.19 (Post-Sentencing Rehabilitative Efforts) list several factors that the court cannot take into account as grounds for departure. With those specific exceptions, however, the Commission does not intend to limit the kinds of factors, whether or not mentioned anywhere else in the guidelines, that could constitute grounds for departure in an unusual case.

The Commission has adopted this departure policy for two reasons. First, it is difficult to prescribe a single set of guidelines that encompasses the vast range of human conduct potentially relevant to a sentencing decision. The Commission also recognizes that the initial set of guidelines need not do so. The Commission is a permanent body, empowered by law to write and rewrite guidelines, with progressive changes, over many years. By monitoring when courts depart from the guidelines and by analyzing their stated reasons for doing so and court decisions with references thereto, the Commission, over time, will be able to refine the guidelines to specify more precisely when departures should and should not be permitted.

Second, the Commission believes that despite the courts' legal freedom to depart from the guidelines, they will not do so very often. This is because the guidelines, offense by offense, seek to take account of those factors that the Commission's data indicate made a significant difference in pre-guidelines sentencing practice. Thus, for example, where the presence of physical injury made an important difference in pre-guidelines sentencing practice (as in the case of robbery or assault), the guidelines specifically include this factor to enhance the sentence. Where the guidelines do not specify an augmentation or diminution, this is generally because the sentencing data did not permit the Commission to conclude that the factor was empirically important in relation to the particular offense. Of course, an important factor (*e.g.*, physical injury) may infrequently occur in connection with a particular crime (*e.g.*, fraud). Such rare occurrences are precisely the type of events that the courts' departure powers were designed to cover — unusual cases outside the range of the more typical offenses for which the guidelines were designed.

It is important to note that the guidelines refer to two different kinds of departure. The first involves instances in which the guidelines provide specific guidance for departure by analogy or by other numerical or non-numerical suggestions. The Commission intends such suggestions as policy guidance for the courts. The Commission expects that most departures will reflect the suggestions and that the courts of appeals may prove more likely to find departures "unreasonable" where they fall outside suggested levels.

A second type of departure will remain unguided. It may rest upon grounds referred to in Chapter Five, Part K (Departures) or on grounds not mentioned in the guidelines. While Chapter Five, Part K lists factors that the Commission believes may constitute grounds for departure, the list is not exhaustive. The Commission recognizes that there may be other grounds for departure that are not mentioned; it also believes there may be cases in which a departure outside suggested levels is warranted. In its view, however, such cases will be highly infrequent.

(c) Plea Agreements.

Nearly ninety percent of all federal criminal cases involve guilty pleas and many of these cases involve some form of plea agreement. Some commentators on early Commission guideline drafts urged the Commission not to attempt any major reforms of the plea agreement process on the grounds that any set of guidelines that threatened to change pre-guidelines practice radically also threatened to make the federal system unmanageable. Others argued that guidelines that failed to control and limit plea agreements would leave untouched a "loophole" large enough to undo the good that sentencing guidelines would bring.

The Commission decided not to make major changes in plea agreement practices in the initial guidelines, but rather to provide guidance by issuing general policy statements concerning the acceptance of plea agreements in Chapter Six, Part B (Plea Agreements). The rules set forth in Fed. R. Crim. P. 11(e) govern the acceptance or rejection of such agreements. The Commission will collect data on the courts' plea practices and will analyze this information to determine when and why the courts accept or reject plea agreements and whether plea agreement practices are undermining the intent of the Sentencing Reform Act. In light of this information and analysis, the Commission will seek to further regulate the plea agreement process as appropriate. Importantly, if the policy statements relating to plea agreements are followed, circumvention of the Sentencing Reform Act and the guidelines should not occur.

The Commission expects the guidelines to have a positive, rationalizing impact upon plea agreements for two reasons. First, the guidelines create a clear, definite expectation in respect to the sentence that a court will impose if a trial takes place. In the event a prosecutor and defense attorney explore the possibility of a negotiated plea, they will no longer work in the dark. This fact alone should help to reduce irrationality in respect to actual sentencing outcomes. Second, the guidelines create a norm to which courts will likely refer when they decide whether, under Rule 11(e), to accept or to reject a plea agreement or recommendation.

(d) Probation and Split Sentences.

The statute provides that the guidelines are to "reflect the general appropriateness of imposing a sentence other than imprisonment in cases in which the defendant is a first offender who has not been convicted of a crime of violence or an otherwise serious offense . . . ." 28 U.S.C. § 994(j). Under pre-guidelines sentencing practice, courts sentenced to probation an inappropriately high percentage of offenders guilty of certain economic crimes, such as theft, tax evasion, antitrust offenses, insider trading, fraud, and embezzlement, that in the Commission's view are "serious."

The Commission's solution to this problem has been to write guidelines that classify as serious many offenses for which probation previously was frequently given and provide for at least a short period of imprisonment in such cases. The Commission concluded that the definite prospect of prison, even though the term may be short, will serve as a significant deterrent, particularly when compared with pre-guidelines practice where probation, not prison, was the norm.

More specifically, the guidelines work as follows in respect to a first offender. For offense levels one through eight, the sentencing court may elect to sentence the offender to probation (with or without confinement conditions) or to a prison term. For offense levels nine and ten, the court may substitute probation for a prison term, but the probation must include confinement conditions (community confinement, intermittent confinement, or home detention). For offense levels eleven and twelve, the court must impose at least one-half the minimum confinement sentence in the form of prison confinement, the remainder to be served on supervised release with a condition of community confinement or home detention. The Commission, of course, has not dealt with the single acts of aberrant behavior that still may justify probation at higher offense levels through departures.*

*Note: Although the Commission had not addressed "single acts of aberrant behavior" at the time the Introduction to the Guidelines Manual originally was written, it subsequently addressed the issue in Amendment 603, effective November 1, 2000. (*See* Supplement to Appendix C, amendment 603.)

(e) Multi-Count Convictions.

The Commission, like several state sentencing commissions, has found it particularly difficult to develop guidelines for sentencing defendants convicted of multiple violations of law, each of which makes up a separate count in an indictment. The difficulty is that when a defendant engages in conduct that causes several harms, each additional harm, even if it increases the extent to which punishment is warranted, does not necessarily warrant a proportionate increase in punishment. A defendant who assaults others during a fight, for example, may warrant more punishment if he injures ten people than if he injures one, but his conduct does not necessarily warrant ten times the punishment. If it did, many of the simplest offenses, for reasons that are often fortuitous, would lead to sentences of life imprisonment — sentences that neither just deserts nor crime control theories of punishment would justify.

Several individual guidelines provide special instructions for increasing punishment when the conduct that is the subject of that count involves multiple occurrences or has caused several harms. The guidelines also provide general rules for aggravating punishment in light of multiple harms charged separately in separate counts. These rules may produce occasional anomalies, but normally they will permit an appropriate degree of aggravation of punishment for multiple offenses that are the subjects of separate counts.

These rules are set out in Chapter Three, Part D (Multiple Counts). They essentially provide: (1) when the conduct involves fungible items (*e.g.*, separate drug transactions or thefts of money), the amounts are added and the guidelines apply to the total amount; (2) when nonfungible harms are involved, the offense level for the most serious count is increased (according to a diminishing scale) to reflect the existence of other counts of conviction. The guidelines have been written in order to minimize the possibility that an arbitrary casting of a single transaction into several counts will produce a longer sentence. In addition, the sentencing court will have adequate power to prevent such a result through departures.

(f) Regulatory Offenses.

Regulatory statutes, though primarily civil in nature, sometimes contain criminal provisions in respect to particularly harmful activity. Such criminal provisions often describe not only substantive offenses, but also more technical, administratively-related offenses such as failure to keep accurate records or to provide requested information. These statutes pose two problems: first, which criminal regulatory provisions should the Commission initially consider, and second, how should it treat technical or administratively-related criminal violations?

In respect to the first problem, the Commission found that it could not comprehensively treat all regulatory violations in the initial set of guidelines. There are hundreds of such provisions scattered throughout the United States Code. To find all potential violations would involve examination of each individual federal regulation. Because of this practical difficulty, the Commission sought to determine, with the assistance of the Department of Justice and several regulatory agencies, which criminal regulatory offenses were particularly important in light of the need for enforcement of the general regulatory scheme. The Commission addressed these offenses in the initial guidelines.

In respect to the second problem, the Commission has developed a system for treating technical recordkeeping and reporting offenses that divides them into four categories. First, in the simplest of cases, the offender may have failed to fill out a form intentionally, but without knowledge or intent that substantive harm would likely follow. He might fail, for example, to keep an accurate record of toxic substance transport, but that failure may not lead, nor be likely to lead, to the release or improper handling of any toxic substance. Second, the same failure may be accompanied by a significant likelihood that substantive harm will occur; it may make a release of a toxic substance more likely. Third, the same failure may have led to substantive harm. Fourth, the failure may represent an effort to conceal a substantive harm that has occurred.

The structure of a typical guideline for a regulatory offense provides a low base offense level (*e.g.*, 6) aimed at the first type of recordkeeping or reporting offense. Specific offense characteristics designed to reflect substantive harms that do occur in respect to some regulatory offenses, or that are likely to occur, increase the offense level. A specific offense characteristic also provides that a recordkeeping or reporting offense that conceals a substantive offense will have the same offense level as the substantive offense.

(g) Sentencing Ranges.

In determining the appropriate sentencing ranges for each offense, the Commission estimated the average sentences served within each category under the pre-guidelines sentencing system. It also examined the sentences specified in federal statutes, in the parole guidelines, and in other relevant, analogous sources. The Commission's Supplementary Report on the Initial Sentencing Guidelines (1987) contains a comparison between estimates of pre-guidelines sentencing practice and sentences under the guidelines.

While the Commission has not considered itself bound by pre-guidelines sentencing practice, it has not attempted to develop an entirely new system of sentencing on the basis of theory alone. Guideline sentences, in many instances, will approximate average pre-guidelines practice and adherence to the guidelines will help to eliminate wide disparity. For example, where a high percentage of persons received probation under pre-guidelines practice, a guideline may include one or more specific offense characteristics in an effort to distinguish those types of defendants who received probation from those who received more severe sentences. In some instances, short sentences of incarceration for all offenders in a category have been substituted for a pre-guidelines sentencing practice of very wide variability in which some defendants received probation while others received several years in prison for the same offense. Moreover, inasmuch as those who pleaded guilty under pre-guidelines practice often received lesser sentences, the guidelines permit the court to impose lesser sentences on those defendants who accept responsibility for their misconduct. For defendants who provide substantial assistance to the government in the investigation or prosecution of others, a downward departure may be warranted.

The Commission has also examined its sentencing ranges in light of their likely impact upon prison population. Specific legislation, such as the Anti-Drug Abuse Act of 1986 and the career offender provisions of the Sentencing Reform Act of 1984 (28 U.S.C. § 994(h)), required the Commission to promulgate guidelines that will lead to substantial prison population increases. These increases will occur irrespective of the guidelines. The guidelines themselves, insofar as they reflect policy decisions made by the Commission (rather than legislated mandatory minimum or career offender sentences), are projected to lead to an increase in prison population that computer models, produced by the Commission and the Bureau of Prisons in 1987, estimated at approximately 10 percent over a period of ten years.

(h) The Sentencing Table.

The Commission has established a sentencing table that for technical and practical reasons contains 43 levels. Each level in the table prescribes ranges that overlap with the ranges in the preceding and succeeding levels. By overlapping the ranges, the table should discourage unnecessary litigation. Both prosecution and defense will realize that the difference between one level and another will not necessarily make a difference in the sentence that the court imposes. Thus, little purpose will be served in protracted litigation trying to determine, for example, whether $10,000 or $11,000 was obtained as a result of a fraud. At the same time, the levels work to increase a sentence proportionately. A change of six levels roughly doubles the sentence irrespective of the level at which one starts. The guidelines, in keeping with the statutory requirement that the maximum of any range cannot exceed the minimum by more than the greater of 25 percent or six months (28 U.S.C. § 994(b)(2)), permit courts to exercise the greatest permissible range of sentencing discretion. The table overlaps offense levels meaningfully, works proportionately, and at the same time preserves the maximum degree of allowable discretion for the court within each level.

Similarly, many of the individual guidelines refer to tables that correlate amounts of money with offense levels. These tables often have many rather than a few levels. Again, the reason is to minimize the likelihood of unnecessary litigation. If a money table were to make only a few distinctions, each distinction would become more important and litigation over which category an offender fell within would become more likely. Where a table has many small monetary distinctions, it minimizes the likelihood of litigation because the precise amount of money involved is of considerably less importance.

5. A Concluding Note

The Commission emphasizes that it drafted the initial guidelines with considerable caution. It examined the many hundreds of criminal statutes in the United States Code. It began with those that were the basis for a significant number of prosecutions and sought to place them in a rational order. It developed additional distinctions relevant to the application of these provisions and it applied sentencing ranges to each resulting category. In doing so, it relied upon pre-guidelines sentencing practice as revealed by its own statistical analyses based on summary reports of some 40,000 convictions, a sample of 10,000 augmented presentence reports, the parole guidelines, and policy judgments.

The Commission recognizes that some will criticize this approach as overly cautious, as representing too little a departure from pre-guidelines sentencing practice. Yet, it will cure wide disparity. The Commission is a permanent body that can amend the guidelines each year. Although the data available to it, like all data, are imperfect, experience with the guidelines will lead to additional information and provide a firm empirical basis for consideration of revisions.

Finally, the guidelines will apply to more than 90 percent of all felony and Class A misdemeanor cases in the federal courts. Because of time constraints and the nonexistence of statistical information, some offenses that occur infrequently are not considered in the guidelines. Their exclusion does not reflect any judgment regarding their seriousness and they will be addressed as the Commission refines the guidelines over time.

2. CONTINUING EVOLUTION AND ROLE OF THE GUIDELINES

The Sentencing Reform Act of 1984 changed the course of federal sentencing. Among other things, the Act created the United States Sentencing Commission as an independent agency in the Judicial Branch, and directed it to develop guidelines and policy statements for sentencing courts to use when sentencing offenders convicted of federal crimes. Moreover, it empowered the Commission with ongoing responsibilities to monitor the guidelines, submit to Congress appropriate modifications of the guidelines and recommended changes in criminal statutes, and establish education and research programs. The mandate rested on congressional awareness that sentencing is a dynamic field that requires continuing review by an expert body to revise sentencing policies, in light of application experience, as new criminal statutes are enacted, and as more is learned about what motivates and controls criminal behavior.

This statement finds resonance in a line of Supreme Court cases that, taken together, echo two themes. The first theme is that the guidelines are the product of a deliberative process that seeks to embody the purposes of sentencing set forth in the Sentencing Reform Act, and as such they continue to play an important role in the sentencing court's determination of an appropriate sentence in a particular case. The Supreme Court alluded to this in *Mistretta v. United States*, 488 U.S. 361 (1989), which upheld the constitutionality of both the federal sentencing guidelines and the Commission against nondelegation and separation of powers challenges. Therein the Court stated:

> Developing proportionate penalties for hundreds of different crimes by a virtually limitless array of offenders is precisely the sort of intricate, labor-intensive task for which delegation to an expert body is especially appropriate. Although Congress has delegated significant discretion to the Commission to draw judgments from its analysis of existing sentencing practice and alternative sentencing models, . . . [w]e have no doubt that in the hands of the Commission "the criteria which Congress has supplied are wholly adequate for carrying out the general policy and purpose" of the Act.

Id. at 379 (internal quotation marks and citations omitted).

The continuing importance of the guidelines in federal sentencing was further acknowledged by the Court in *United States v. Booker*, 543 U.S. 220 (2005), even as that case rendered the guidelines advisory in nature. In *Booker*, the Court held that the imposition of an enhanced sentence under the federal sentencing guidelines based on the sentencing judge's determination of a fact (other than a prior conviction) that was not found by the jury or admitted by the defendant violated the Sixth Amendment. The Court reasoned that an advisory guideline system, while lacking the mandatory features that Congress enacted, retains other features that help to further congressional objectives, including providing certainty and fairness in meeting the purposes of sentencing, avoiding unwarranted sentencing disparities, and maintaining sufficient flexibility to permit individualized sentences when warranted. The Court concluded that an advisory guideline system would "continue to move sentencing in Congress' preferred direction, helping to avoid excessive sentencing disparities while maintaining flexibility sufficient to individualize sentences where necessary." *Id.* at 264–65. An advisory guideline system continues to assure transparency by requiring that sentences be based on articulated reasons stated in open court that are subject to appellate review. An advisory guideline system also continues to promote certainty and predictability in sentencing, thereby enabling the parties to better anticipate the likely sentence based on the individualized facts of the case.

The continuing importance of the guidelines in the sentencing determination is predicated in large part on the Sentencing Reform Act's intent that, in promulgating guidelines, the Commission must take into account the purposes of sentencing as set forth in 18 U.S.C. § 3553(a). *See* 28 U.S.C. §§ 994(f), 991(b)(1). The Supreme Court reinforced this view in *Rita v. United States*, 551 U.S. 338 (2007), which held that a court of appeals may apply a presumption of reasonableness to a sentence imposed by a district court within a properly calculated guideline range without violating the Sixth Amendment. In *Rita*, the Court relied heavily on the complementary roles of the Commission and the sentencing court in federal sentencing, stating:

> [T]he presumption reflects the nature of the Guidelines-writing task that Congress set for the Commission and the manner in which the Commission carried out that task. In instructing both the *sentencing judge* and the *Commission* what to do, Congress referred to the basic sentencing objectives that the statute sets forth in 18 U.S.C. § 3553(a) . . . . The provision also tells the sentencing judge to "impose a sentence sufficient, but not greater than necessary, to comply with" the basic aims of sentencing as set out above. Congressional statutes then tell the *Commission* to write Guidelines that will carry out these same § 3553(a) objectives.

Id. at 347–48 (emphasis in original). The Court concluded that "[t]he upshot is that the sentencing statutes envision both the sentencing judge and the Commission as carrying out the same basic § 3553(a) objectives, the one, at retail, the other at wholesale[,]" *id.* at 348, and that the Commission's process for promulgating guidelines results in "a set of Guidelines that seek to embody the § 3553(a) considerations, both in principle and in practice." *Id.* at 350.

Consequently, district courts are required to properly calculate and consider the guidelines when sentencing, even in an advisory guideline system. *See* 18 U.S.C. § 3553(a)(4), (a)(5); *Booker*, 543 U.S. at 264 ("The district courts, while not bound to apply the Guidelines, must . . . take them into account when sentencing."); *Rita*, 551 U.S. at 351 (stating that a district court should begin all sentencing proceedings by correctly calculating the applicable Guidelines range); *Gall v. United States*, 552 U.S. 38, 49 (2007) ("As a matter of administration and to secure nationwide consistency, the Guidelines should be the starting point and the initial benchmark."). The district court, in determining the appropriate sentence in a particular case, therefore, must consider the properly calculated guideline range, the grounds for departure provided in the policy statements, and then the factors under 18 U.S.C. § 3553(a). *See Rita*, 551 U.S. at 351. The appellate court engages in a two-step process upon review. The appellate court "first ensure[s] that the district court committed no significant procedural error, such as failing to calculate (or improperly calculating) the Guidelines range . . . [and] then consider[s] the substantive reasonableness of the sentence imposed under an abuse-of-discretion standard[,] . . . tak[ing] into account the totality of the circumstances, including the extent of any variance from the Guidelines range." *Gall*, 552 U.S. at 51.

The second and related theme resonant in this line of Supreme Court cases is that, as contemplated by the Sentencing Reform Act, the guidelines are evolutionary in nature. They are the product of the Commission's fulfillment of its statutory duties to monitor federal sentencing law and practices, to seek public input on the operation of the guidelines, and to revise the guidelines accordingly. As the Court acknowledged in *Rita*:

> The Commission's work is ongoing. The statutes and the Guidelines themselves foresee continuous evolution helped by the sentencing courts and courts of appeals in that process. The sentencing courts, applying the Guidelines in individual cases may depart (either pursuant to the Guidelines or, since *Booker*, by imposing a non-Guidelines sentence). The judges will set forth their reasons. The Courts of Appeals will determine the reasonableness of the resulting sentence. The Commission will collect and examine the results. In doing so, it may obtain advice from prosecutors, defenders, law enforcement groups, civil liberties associations, experts in penology, and others. And it can revise the Guidelines accordingly.

Rita, 551 U.S. at 350; *see also Booker*, 543 U.S. at 264 ("[T]he Sentencing Commission remains in place, writing Guidelines, collecting information about actual district court sentencing decisions, undertaking research, and revising the Guidelines accordingly."); *Gall*, 552 U.S. at 46 ("[E]ven though the Guidelines are advisory rather than mandatory, they are, as we pointed out in *Rita*, the product of careful study based on extensive empirical evidence derived from the review of thousands of individual sentencing decisions.").

Provisions of the Sentencing Reform Act promote and facilitate this evolutionary process. For example, pursuant to 28 U.S.C. § 994(x), the Commission publishes guideline amendment proposals in the *Federal Register* and conducts hearings to solicit input on those proposals from experts and other members of the public. Pursuant to 28 U.S.C. § 994(o), the Commission periodically reviews and revises the guidelines in consideration of comments it receives from members of the federal criminal justice system, including the courts, probation officers, the Department of Justice, the Bureau of Prisons, defense attorneys and the federal public defenders, and in consideration of data it receives from sentencing courts and other sources. Statutory mechanisms such as these bolster the Commission's ability to take into account fully the purposes of sentencing set forth in 18 U.S.C. § 3553(a)(2) in its promulgation of the guidelines.

Congress retains authority to require certain sentencing practices and may exercise its authority through specific directives to the Commission with respect to the guidelines. As the Supreme Court noted in *Kimbrough v. United States*, 552 U.S. 85 (2007), "Congress has shown that it knows how to direct sentencing practices in express terms. For example, Congress has specifically required the Sentencing Commission to set Guideline sentences for serious recidivist offenders 'at or near' the statutory maximum." *Id.* at 103; 28 U.S.C. § 994(h).

As envisioned by Congress, implemented by the Commission, and reaffirmed by the Supreme Court, the guidelines are the product of a deliberative and dynamic process that seeks to embody within federal sentencing policy the purposes of sentencing set forth in the Sentencing Reform Act. As such, the guidelines continue to be a key component of federal sentencing and to play an important role in the sentencing court's determination of an appropriate sentence in any particular case.

§1A3.1

3. AUTHORITY

---

§1A3.1. Authority

The guidelines, policy statements, and commentary set forth in this Guidelines Manual, including amendments thereto, are promulgated by the United States Sentencing Commission pursuant to: (1) section 994(a) of title 28, United States Code; and (2) with respect to guidelines, policy statements, and commentary promulgated or amended pursuant to specific congressional directive, pursuant to the authority contained in that directive in addition to the authority under section 994(a) of title 28, United States Code.

Historical Note	Effective November 1, 1987. Amended effective November 1, 1989 (amendments 67 and 68); November 1, 1990 (amendment 307); November 1, 1992 (amendment 466); November 1, 1995 (amendment 534); November 1, 1996 (amendment 538); November 1, 2000 (amendments 602 and 603); October 27, 2003 (amendment 651); November 1, 2008 (amendments 717 and 725); November 1, 2014 (amendment 789).

PART B — GENERAL APPLICATION PRINCIPLES

§1B1.1. Application Instructions

(a) The court shall determine the kinds of sentence and the guideline range as set forth in the guidelines (*see* 18 U.S.C. § 3553(a)(4)) by applying the provisions of this manual in the following order, except as specifically directed:

(1) Determine, pursuant to §1B1.2 (Applicable Guidelines), the offense guideline section from Chapter Two (Offense Conduct) applicable to the offense of conviction. *See* §1B1.2.

(2) Determine the base offense level and apply any appropriate specific offense characteristics, cross references, and special instructions contained in the particular guideline in Chapter Two in the order listed.

(3) Apply the adjustments as appropriate related to victim, role, and obstruction of justice from Parts A, B, and C of Chapter Three.

(4) If there are multiple counts of conviction, repeat steps (1) through (3) for each count. Apply Part D of Chapter Three to group the various counts and adjust the offense level accordingly.

(5) Apply the adjustment as appropriate for the defendant's acceptance of responsibility from Part E of Chapter Three.

(6) Determine the defendant's criminal history category as specified in Part A of Chapter Four. Determine from Part B of Chapter Four any other applicable adjustments.

(7) Determine the guideline range in Part A of Chapter Five that corresponds to the offense level and criminal history category determined above.

(8) For the particular guideline range, determine from Parts B through G of Chapter Five the sentencing requirements and options related to probation, imprisonment, supervision conditions, fines, and restitution.

(b) The court shall then consider Parts H and K of Chapter Five, Specific Offender Characteristics and Departures, and any other policy statements or commentary in the guidelines that might warrant consideration in imposing sentence. *See* 18 U.S.C. § 3553(a)(5).

(c)   The court shall then consider the applicable factors in 18 U.S.C. § 3553(a) taken as a whole. *See* 18 U.S.C. § 3553(a).

Commentary

Application Notes:

1.   The following are definitions of terms that are used frequently in the guidelines and are of general applicability (except to the extent expressly modified in respect to a particular guideline or policy statement):

(A)   "*Abducted*" means that a victim was forced to accompany an offender to a different location. For example, a bank robber's forcing a bank teller from the bank into a getaway car would constitute an abduction.

(B)   "*Bodily injury*" means any significant injury; *e.g.*, an injury that is painful and obvious, or is of a type for which medical attention ordinarily would be sought.

(C)   "*Brandished*" with reference to a dangerous weapon (including a firearm) means that all or part of the weapon was displayed, or the presence of the weapon was otherwise made known to another person, in order to intimidate that person, regardless of whether the weapon was directly visible to that person. Accordingly, although the dangerous weapon does not have to be directly visible, the weapon must be present.

(D)   "*Dangerous weapon*" means (i) an instrument capable of inflicting death or serious bodily injury; or (ii) an object that is not an instrument capable of inflicting death or serious bodily injury but (I) closely resembles such an instrument; or (II) the defendant used the object in a manner that created the impression that the object was such an instrument (*e.g.* a defendant wrapped a hand in a towel during a bank robbery to create the appearance of a gun).

(E)   "*Departure*" means (i) for purposes other than those specified in subdivision (ii), imposition of a sentence outside the applicable guideline range or of a sentence that is otherwise different from the guideline sentence; and (ii) for purposes of §4A1.3 (Departures Based on Inadequacy of Criminal History Category), assignment of a criminal history category other than the otherwise applicable criminal history category, in order to effect a sentence outside the applicable guideline range. "*Depart*" means grant a departure.

"*Downward departure*" means departure that effects a sentence less than a sentence that could be imposed under the applicable guideline range or a sentence that is otherwise less than the guideline sentence. "*Depart downward*" means grant a downward departure.

"*Upward departure*" means departure that effects a sentence greater than a sentence that could be imposed under the applicable guideline range or a sentence that is otherwise greater than the guideline sentence. "*Depart upward*" means grant an upward departure.

(F) "**Destructive device**" means any article described in 26 U.S.C. § 5845(f) (including an explosive, incendiary, or poison gas — (i) bomb, (ii) grenade, (iii) rocket having a propellant charge of more than four ounces, (iv) missile having an explosive or incendiary charge of more than one-quarter ounce, (v) mine, or (vi) device similar to any of the devices described in the preceding clauses).

(G) "**Firearm**" means (i) any weapon (including a starter gun) which will or is designed to or may readily be converted to expel a projectile by the action of an explosive; (ii) the frame or receiver of any such weapon; (iii) any firearm muffler or silencer; or (iv) any destructive device. A weapon, commonly known as a "BB" or pellet gun, that uses air or carbon dioxide pressure to expel a projectile is a dangerous weapon but not a firearm.

(H) "**Offense**" means the offense of conviction and all relevant conduct under §1B1.3 (Relevant Conduct) unless a different meaning is specified or is otherwise clear from the context. The term "*instant*" is used in connection with "offense," "federal offense," or "offense of conviction," as the case may be, to distinguish the violation for which the defendant is being sentenced from a prior or subsequent offense, or from an offense before another court (*e.g.*, an offense before a state court involving the same underlying conduct).

(I) "**Otherwise used**" with reference to a dangerous weapon (including a firearm) means that the conduct did not amount to the discharge of a firearm but was more than brandishing, displaying, or possessing a firearm or other dangerous weapon.

(J) "**Permanent or life-threatening bodily injury**" means injury involving a substantial risk of death; loss or substantial impairment of the function of a bodily member, organ, or mental faculty that is likely to be permanent; or an obvious disfigurement that is likely to be permanent. In the case of a kidnapping, for example, maltreatment to a life-threatening degree (*e.g.*, by denial of food or medical care) would constitute life-threatening bodily injury.

(K) "**Physically restrained**" means the forcible restraint of the victim such as by being tied, bound, or locked up.

(L) "**Serious bodily injury**" means injury involving extreme physical pain or the protracted impairment of a function of a bodily member, organ, or mental faculty; or requiring medical intervention such as surgery, hospitalization, or physical rehabilitation. In addition, "serious bodily injury" is deemed to have occurred if the offense involved conduct constituting criminal sexual abuse under 18 U.S.C. § 2241 or § 2242 or any similar offense under state law.

2. Definitions of terms also may appear in other sections. Such definitions are not designed for general applicability; therefore, their applicability to sections other than those expressly referenced must be determined on a case by case basis.

The term "*includes*" is not exhaustive; the term "*e.g.*" is merely illustrative.

3. The list of "Statutory Provisions" in the Commentary to each offense guideline does not necessarily include every statute covered by that guideline. In addition, some statutes may be covered by more than one guideline.

4. (A) **Cumulative Application of Multiple Adjustments within One Guideline.—** The offense level adjustments from more than one specific offense characteristic

within an offense guideline are applied cumulatively (added together) unless the guideline specifies that only the greater (or greatest) is to be used. Within each specific offense characteristic subsection, however, the offense level adjustments are alternative; only the one that best describes the conduct is to be used. For example, in §2A2.2(b)(3), pertaining to degree of bodily injury, the subdivision that best describes the level of bodily injury is used; the adjustments for different degrees of bodily injury (subdivisions (A) – (E)) are not added together.

(B) **Cumulative Application of Multiple Adjustments from Multiple Guidelines.**—Absent an instruction to the contrary, enhancements under Chapter Two, adjustments under Chapter Three, and determinations under Chapter Four are to be applied cumulatively. In some cases, such enhancements, adjustments, and determinations may be triggered by the same conduct. For example, shooting a police officer during the commission of a robbery may warrant an injury enhancement under §2B3.1(b)(3) and an official victim adjustment under §3A1.2, even though the enhancement and the adjustment both are triggered by the shooting of the officer.

5. Where two or more guideline provisions appear equally applicable, but the guidelines authorize the application of only one such provision, use the provision that results in the greater offense level. *E.g.*, in §2A2.2(b)(2), if a firearm is both discharged and brandished, the provision applicable to the discharge of the firearm would be used.

6. **Use of Abbreviated Guideline Titles.**—Whenever a guideline makes reference to another guideline, a parenthetical restatement of that other guideline's heading accompanies the initial reference to that other guideline. This parenthetical is provided only for the convenience of the reader and is not intended to have substantive effect. In the case of lengthy guideline headings, such a parenthetical restatement of the guideline heading may be abbreviated for ease of reference. For example, references to §2B1.1 (Larceny, Embezzlement, and Other Forms of Theft; Offenses Involving Stolen Property; Property Damage or Destruction; Fraud and Deceit; Forgery; Offenses Involving Altered or Counterfeit Instruments Other than Counterfeit Bearer Obligations of the United States) may be abbreviated as follows: §2B1.1 (Theft, Property Destruction, and Fraud).

Background: The court must impose a sentence "sufficient, but not greater than necessary," to comply with the purposes of sentencing set forth in 18 U.S.C. § 3553(a)(2). *See* 18 U.S.C. § 3553(a). Subsections (a), (b), and (c) are structured to reflect the three-step process used in determining the particular sentence to be imposed. If, after step (c), the court imposes a sentence that is outside the guidelines framework, such a sentence is considered a "*variance*". *See Irizarry v. United States*, 553 U.S. 708, 709–16 (2008) (describing within-range sentences and departures as "sentences imposed under the framework set out in the Guidelines").

Historical Note	Effective November 1, 1987. Amended effective January 15, 1988 (amendment 1); November 1, 1989 (amendments 69–72 and 303); November 1, 1990 (amendment 361); November 1, 1991 (amendment 388); November 1, 1993 (amendment 497); November 1, 1997 (amendments 545 and 546); November 1, 2000 (amendments 591 and 601); November 1, 2001 (amendment 617); October 27, 2003 (amendment 651); November 1, 2003 (amendment 661); November 1, 2006 (amendment 684); November 1, 2010 (amendment 741); November 1, 2014 (amendment 789).

§1B1.2.   Applicable Guidelines

(a)   Determine the offense guideline section in Chapter Two (Offense Conduct) applicable to the offense of conviction (*i.e.*, the offense conduct charged in the count of the indictment or information of which the defendant was convicted). However, in the case of a plea agreement (written or made orally on the record) containing a stipulation that specifically establishes a more serious offense than the offense of conviction, determine the offense guideline section in Chapter Two applicable to the stipulated offense.

Refer to the Statutory Index (Appendix A) to determine the Chapter Two offense guideline, referenced in the Statutory Index for the offense of conviction. If the offense involved a conspiracy, attempt, or solicitation, refer to §2X1.1 (Attempt, Solicitation, or Conspiracy) as well as the guideline referenced in the Statutory Index for the substantive offense. For statutory provisions not listed in the Statutory Index, use the most analogous guideline. *See* §2X5.1 (Other Offenses). The guidelines do not apply to any count of conviction that is a Class B or C misdemeanor or an infraction. *See* §1B1.9 (Class B or C Misdemeanors and Infractions).

(b)   After determining the appropriate offense guideline section pursuant to subsection (a) of this section, determine the applicable guideline range in accordance with §1B1.3 (Relevant Conduct).

(c)   A plea agreement (written or made orally on the record) containing a stipulation that specifically establishes the commission of additional offense(s) shall be treated as if the defendant had been convicted of additional count(s) charging those offense(s).

(d)   A conviction on a count charging a conspiracy to commit more than one offense shall be treated as if the defendant had been convicted on a separate count of conspiracy for each offense that the defendant conspired to commit.

Commentary

Application Notes:

1.   This section provides the basic rules for determining the guidelines applicable to the offense conduct under Chapter Two (Offense Conduct). The court is to use the Chapter Two guideline section referenced in the Statutory Index (Appendix A) for the offense of conviction. However, (A) in the case of a plea agreement (written or made orally on the record) containing a stipulation that specifically establishes a more serious offense than the offense of conviction, the Chapter Two offense guideline section applicable to the stipulated offense is to be used; and (B) for statutory provisions not listed in the Statutory Index, the most analogous guideline, determined pursuant to §2X5.1 (Other Offenses), is to be used.

In the case of a particular statute that proscribes only a single type of criminal conduct, the offense of conviction and the conduct proscribed by the statute will coincide, and the Statutory Index will specify only one offense guideline for that offense of conviction. In the case of a particular statute that proscribes a variety of conduct that might constitute the subject of different offense guidelines, the Statutory Index may specify more than one offense guideline for that particular statute, and the court will determine which of the referenced guideline sections is most appropriate for the offense conduct charged in the count of which the defendant was convicted. If the offense involved a conspiracy, attempt, or solicitation, refer to §2X1.1 (Attempt, Solicitation, or Conspiracy) as well as the guideline referenced in the Statutory Index for the substantive offense. For statutory provisions not listed in the Statutory Index, the most analogous guideline is to be used. *See* §2X5.1 (Other Offenses).

As set forth in the first paragraph of this note, an exception to this general rule is that if a plea agreement (written or made orally on the record) contains a stipulation that establishes a more serious offense than the offense of conviction, the guideline section applicable to the stipulated offense is to be used. A factual statement or a stipulation contained in a plea agreement (written or made orally on the record) is a stipulation for purposes of subsection (a) only if both the defendant and the government explicitly agree that the factual statement or stipulation is a stipulation for such purposes. However, a factual statement or stipulation made after the plea agreement has been entered, or after any modification to the plea agreement has been made, is not a stipulation for purposes of subsection (a). The sentence that shall be imposed is limited, however, to the maximum authorized by the statute under which the defendant is convicted. *See* Chapter Five, Part G (Implementing the Total Sentence of Imprisonment). For example, if the defendant pleads guilty to theft, but admits the elements of robbery as part of the plea agreement, the robbery guideline is to be applied. The sentence, however, may not exceed the maximum sentence for theft. *See* H. Rep. 98-1017, 98th Cong., 2d Sess. 99 (1984).

The exception to the general rule has a practical basis. In a case in which the elements of an offense more serious than the offense of conviction are established by a plea agreement, it may unduly complicate the sentencing process if the applicable guideline does not reflect the seriousness of the defendant's actual conduct. Without this exception, the court would be forced to use an artificial guideline and then depart from it to the degree the court found necessary based upon the more serious conduct established by the plea agreement. The probation officer would first be required to calculate the guideline for the offense of conviction. However, this guideline might even contain characteristics that are difficult to establish or not very important in the context of the actual offense conduct. As a simple example, §2B1.1 (Theft, Property Destruction, and Fraud) contains monetary distinctions which are more significant and more detailed than the monetary distinctions in §2B3.1 (Robbery). Then, the probation officer might need to calculate the robbery guideline to assist the court in determining the appropriate degree of departure in a case in which the defendant pled guilty to theft but admitted committing robbery. This cumbersome, artificial procedure is avoided by using the exception rule in guilty or *nolo contendere* plea cases where it is applicable.

As with any plea agreement, the court must first determine that the agreement is acceptable, in accordance with the policies stated in Chapter Six, Part B (Plea Agreements). The limited exception provided here applies only after the court has determined that a plea, otherwise fitting the exception, is acceptable.

2.   Section 1B1.2(b) directs the court, once it has determined the applicable guideline (*i.e.*, the applicable guideline section from Chapter Two) under §1B1.2(a) to determine

any applicable specific offense characteristics (under that guideline), and any other applicable sentencing factors pursuant to the relevant conduct definition in §1B1.3. Where there is more than one base offense level within a particular guideline, the determination of the applicable base offense level is treated in the same manner as a determination of a specific offense characteristic. Accordingly, the "relevant conduct" criteria of §1B1.3 are to be used, unless conviction under a specific statute is expressly required.

3. Subsections (c) and (d) address circumstances in which the provisions of Chapter Three, Part D (Multiple Counts) are to be applied although there may be only one count of conviction. Subsection (c) provides that in the case of a stipulation to the commission of additional offense(s), the guidelines are to be applied as if the defendant had been convicted of an additional count for each of the offenses stipulated. For example, if the defendant is convicted of one count of robbery but, as part of a plea agreement, admits to having committed two additional robberies, the guidelines are to be applied as if the defendant had been convicted of three counts of robbery. Subsection (d) provides that a conviction on a conspiracy count charging conspiracy to commit more than one offense is treated as if the defendant had been convicted of a separate conspiracy count for each offense that he conspired to commit. For example, where a conviction on a single count of conspiracy establishes that the defendant conspired to commit three robberies, the guidelines are to be applied as if the defendant had been convicted on one count of conspiracy to commit the first robbery, one count of conspiracy to commit the second robbery, and one count of conspiracy to commit the third robbery.

4. Particular care must be taken in applying subsection (d) because there are cases in which the verdict or plea does not establish which offense(s) was the object of the conspiracy. In such cases, subsection (d) should only be applied with respect to an object offense alleged in the conspiracy count if the court, were it sitting as a trier of fact, would convict the defendant of conspiring to commit that object offense. Note, however, if the object offenses specified in the conspiracy count would be grouped together under §3D1.2(d) (*e.g.*, a conspiracy to steal three government checks) it is not necessary to engage in the foregoing analysis, because §1B1.3(a)(2) governs consideration of the defendant's conduct.

Historical Note	Effective November 1, 1987. Amended effective January 15, 1988 (amendment 2); November 1, 1989 (amendments 73–75 and 303); November 1, 1991 (amendment 434); November 1, 1992 (amendment 438); November 1, 2000 (amendment 591); November 1, 2001 (amendments 613 and 617).

§1B1.3. Relevant Conduct (Factors that Determine the Guideline Range)

(a) CHAPTERS TWO (OFFENSE CONDUCT) AND THREE (ADJUSTMENTS). Unless otherwise specified, (i) the base offense level where the guideline specifies more than one base offense level, (ii) specific offense characteristics and (iii) cross references in Chapter Two, and (iv) adjustments in Chapter Three, shall be determined on the basis of the following:

    (1) (A) all acts and omissions committed, aided, abetted, counseled, commanded, induced, procured, or willfully caused by the defendant; and

        (B) in the case of a jointly undertaken criminal activity (a criminal plan, scheme, endeavor, or enterprise undertaken by the defendant in concert with others, whether or not charged as a conspiracy), all acts and omissions of others that were—

            (i) within the scope of the jointly undertaken criminal activity,

            (ii) in furtherance of that criminal activity, and

            (iii) reasonably foreseeable in connection with that criminal activity;

        that occurred during the commission of the offense of conviction, in preparation for that offense, or in the course of attempting to avoid detection or responsibility for that offense;

    (2) solely with respect to offenses of a character for which §3D1.2(d) would require grouping of multiple counts, all acts and omissions described in subdivisions (1)(A) and (1)(B) above that were part of the same course of conduct or common scheme or plan as the offense of conviction;

    (3) all harm that resulted from the acts and omissions specified in subsections (a)(1) and (a)(2) above, and all harm that was the object of such acts and omissions; and

    (4) any other information specified in the applicable guideline.

(b) CHAPTERS FOUR (CRIMINAL HISTORY AND CRIMINAL LIVELIHOOD) AND FIVE (DETERMINING THE SENTENCE). Factors in Chapters Four and Five that establish the guideline range shall be determined on the basis of the conduct and information specified in the respective guidelines.

Commentary

Application Notes:

1. **Sentencing Accountability and Criminal Liability.**—The principles and limits of sentencing accountability under this guideline are not always the same as the principles and limits of criminal liability. Under subsections (a)(1) and (a)(2), the focus is on the specific acts and omissions for which the defendant is to be held accountable in determining the applicable guideline range, rather than on whether the defendant is criminally liable for an offense as a principal, accomplice, or conspirator.

2. **Accountability Under More Than One Provision.**—In certain cases, a defendant may be accountable for particular conduct under more than one subsection of this guide-

line. If a defendant's accountability for particular conduct is established under one provision of this guideline, it is not necessary to review alternative provisions under which such accountability might be established.

3.   **Jointly Undertaken Criminal Activity (Subsection (a)(1)(B)).—**

(A)   **In General.**—A "*jointly undertaken criminal activity*" is a criminal plan, scheme, endeavor, or enterprise undertaken by the defendant in concert with others, whether or not charged as a conspiracy.

In the case of a jointly undertaken criminal activity, subsection (a)(1)(B) provides that a defendant is accountable for the conduct (acts and omissions) of others that was:

(i)   within the scope of the jointly undertaken criminal activity;

(ii)   in furtherance of that criminal activity; and

(iii) reasonably foreseeable in connection with that criminal activity.

The conduct of others that meets all three criteria set forth in subdivisions (i) through (iii) (*i.e.*, "within the scope," "in furtherance," and "reasonably foreseeable") is relevant conduct under this provision. However, when the conduct of others does not meet any one of the criteria set forth in subdivisions (i) through (iii), the conduct is not relevant conduct under this provision.

(B)   **Scope.**—Because a count may be worded broadly and include the conduct of many participants over a period of time, the scope of the "jointly undertaken criminal activity" is not necessarily the same as the scope of the entire conspiracy, and hence relevant conduct is not necessarily the same for every participant. In order to determine the defendant's accountability for the conduct of others under subsection (a)(1)(B), the court must first determine the scope of the criminal activity the particular defendant agreed to jointly undertake (*i.e.*, the scope of the specific conduct and objectives embraced by the defendant's agreement). In doing so, the court may consider any explicit agreement or implicit agreement fairly inferred from the conduct of the defendant and others. Accordingly, the accountability of the defendant for the acts of others is limited by the scope of his or her agreement to jointly undertake the particular criminal activity. Acts of others that were not within the scope of the defendant's agreement, even if those acts were known or reasonably foreseeable to the defendant, are not relevant conduct under subsection (a)(1)(B).

In cases involving contraband (including controlled substances), the scope of the jointly undertaken criminal activity (and thus the accountability of the defendant for the contraband that was the object of that jointly undertaken activity) may depend upon whether, in the particular circumstances, the nature of the offense is more appropriately viewed as one jointly undertaken criminal activity or as a number of separate criminal activities.

A defendant's relevant conduct does not include the conduct of members of a conspiracy prior to the defendant joining the conspiracy, even if the defendant knows of that conduct (*e.g.*, in the case of a defendant who joins an ongoing drug distribution conspiracy knowing that it had been selling two kilograms of cocaine per week, the cocaine sold prior to the defendant joining the conspiracy is not included as relevant conduct in determining the defendant's offense level). The Commission does not foreclose the possibility that there may be some unusual set of circumstances in which the exclusion of such conduct may not adequately reflect the defendant's culpability; in such a case, an upward departure may be warranted.

(C) **In Furtherance.**—The court must determine if the conduct (acts and omissions) of others was in furtherance of the jointly undertaken criminal activity.

(D) **Reasonably Foreseeable.**—The court must then determine if the conduct (acts and omissions) of others that was within the scope of, and in furtherance of, the jointly undertaken criminal activity was reasonably foreseeable in connection with that criminal activity.

Note that the criminal activity that the defendant agreed to jointly undertake, and the reasonably foreseeable conduct of others in furtherance of that criminal activity, are not necessarily identical. For example, two defendants agree to commit a robbery and, during the course of that robbery, the first defendant assaults and injures a victim. The second defendant is accountable for the assault and injury to the victim (even if the second defendant had not agreed to the assault and had cautioned the first defendant to be careful not to hurt anyone) because the assaultive conduct was within the scope of the jointly undertaken criminal activity (the robbery), was in furtherance of that criminal activity (the robbery), and was reasonably foreseeable in connection with that criminal activity (given the nature of the offense).

With respect to offenses involving contraband (including controlled substances), the defendant is accountable under subsection (a)(1)(A) for all quantities of contraband with which he was directly involved and, in the case of a jointly undertaken criminal activity under subsection (a)(1)(B), all quantities of contraband that were involved in transactions carried out by other participants, if those transactions were within the scope of, and in furtherance of, the jointly undertaken criminal activity and were reasonably foreseeable in connection with that criminal activity.

The requirement of reasonable foreseeability applies only in respect to the conduct (*i.e.*, acts and omissions) of others under subsection (a)(1)(B). It does not apply to conduct that the defendant personally undertakes, aids, abets, counsels, commands, induces, procures, or willfully causes; such conduct is addressed under subsection (a)(1)(A).

4. **Illustrations of Conduct for Which the Defendant is Accountable under Subsections (a)(1)(A) and (B).**—

(A) **Acts and omissions aided or abetted by the defendant.**—

(i) Defendant A is one of ten persons hired by Defendant B to off-load a ship containing marihuana. The off-loading of the ship is interrupted by law enforcement officers and one ton of marihuana is seized (the amount on the ship as well as the amount off-loaded). Defendant A and the other off-loaders are arrested and convicted of importation of marihuana. Regardless of the number of bales he personally unloaded, Defendant A is accountable for the entire one-ton quantity of marihuana. Defendant A aided and abetted the off-loading of the entire shipment of marihuana by directly participating in the off-loading of that shipment (*i.e.*, the specific objective of the criminal activity he joined was the off-loading of the entire shipment). Therefore, he is accountable for the entire shipment under subsection (a)(1)(A) without regard to the issue of reasonable foreseeability. This is conceptually similar to the case of a defendant who transports a suitcase knowing that it contains a controlled substance and, therefore, is accountable for the controlled substance in the suitcase regardless of his knowledge or lack of knowledge of the actual type or amount of that controlled substance.

In certain cases, a defendant may be accountable for particular conduct under more than one subsection of this guideline. As noted in the preceding paragraph, Defendant A is accountable for the entire one-ton shipment of marihuana under subsection (a)(1)(A). Defendant A also is accountable for the entire one-ton shipment of marihuana on the basis of subsection (a)(1)(B) (applying to a jointly undertaken criminal activity). Defendant A engaged in a jointly undertaken criminal activity and all three criteria of subsection (a)(1)(B) are met. First, the conduct was within the scope of the criminal activity (the importation of the shipment of marihuana). Second, the off-loading of the shipment of marihuana was in furtherance of the criminal activity, as described above. And third, a finding that the one-ton quantity of marihuana was reasonably foreseeable is warranted from the nature of the undertaking itself (the importation of marihuana by ship typically involves very large quantities of marihuana). The specific circumstances of the case (the defendant was one of ten persons off-loading the marihuana in bales) also support this finding. In an actual case, of course, if a defendant's accountability for particular conduct is established under one provision of this guideline, it is not necessary to review alternative provisions under which such accountability might be established. *See* Application Note 2.

(B) **Acts and omissions aided or abetted by the defendant; acts and omissions in a jointly undertaken criminal activity.—**

(i) Defendant C is the getaway driver in an armed bank robbery in which $15,000 is taken and a teller is assaulted and injured. Defendant C is accountable for the money taken under subsection (a)(1)(A) because he aided and abetted the act of taking the money (the taking of money was the specific objective of the offense he joined). Defendant C is accountable for the injury to the teller under subsection (a)(1)(B) because the assault on the teller was within the scope and in furtherance of the jointly undertaken criminal activity (the robbery), and was reasonably foreseeable in connection with that criminal activity (given the nature of the offense).

As noted earlier, a defendant may be accountable for particular conduct under more than one subsection. In this example, Defendant C also is accountable for the money taken on the basis of subsection (a)(1)(B) because the taking of money was within the scope and in furtherance of the jointly undertaken criminal activity (the robbery), and was reasonably foreseeable (as noted, the taking of money was the specific objective of the jointly undertaken criminal activity).

(C) **Requirements that the conduct of others be within the scope of the jointly undertaken criminal activity, in furtherance of that criminal activity, and reasonably foreseeable.—**

(i) Defendant D pays Defendant E a small amount to forge an endorsement on an $800 stolen government check. Unknown to Defendant E, Defendant D then uses that check as a down payment in a scheme to fraudulently obtain

$15,000 worth of merchandise. Defendant E is convicted of forging the $800 check and is accountable for the forgery of this check under subsection (a)(1)(A). Defendant E is not accountable for the $15,000 because the fraudulent scheme to obtain $15,000 was not within the scope of the jointly undertaken criminal activity (*i.e.*, the forgery of the $800 check).

(ii)   Defendants F and G, working together, design and execute a scheme to sell fraudulent stocks by telephone. Defendant F fraudulently obtains $20,000. Defendant G fraudulently obtains $35,000. Each is convicted of mail fraud. Defendants F and G each are accountable for the entire amount ($55,000). Each defendant is accountable for the amount he personally obtained under subsection (a)(1)(A). Each defendant is accountable for the amount obtained by his accomplice under subsection (a)(1)(B) because the conduct of each was within the scope of the jointly undertaken criminal activity (the scheme to sell fraudulent stocks), was in furtherance of that criminal activity, and was reasonably foreseeable in connection with that criminal activity.

(iii)   Defendants H and I engaged in an ongoing marihuana importation conspiracy in which Defendant J was hired only to help off-load a single shipment. Defendants H, I, and J are included in a single count charging conspiracy to import marihuana. Defendant J is accountable for the entire single shipment of marihuana he helped import under subsection (a)(1)(A) and any acts and omissions of others related to the importation of that shipment on the basis of subsection (a)(1)(B) (*see* the discussion in example (A)(i) above). He is not accountable for prior or subsequent shipments of marihuana imported by Defendants H or I because those acts were not within the scope of his jointly undertaken criminal activity (the importation of the single shipment of marihuana).

(iv)   Defendant K is a wholesale distributor of child pornography. Defendant L is a retail-level dealer who purchases child pornography from Defendant K and resells it, but otherwise operates independently of Defendant K. Similarly, Defendant M is a retail-level dealer who purchases child pornography from Defendant K and resells it, but otherwise operates independently of Defendant K. Defendants L and M are aware of each other's criminal activity but operate independently. Defendant N is Defendant K's assistant who recruits customers for Defendant K and frequently supervises the deliveries to Defendant K's customers. Each defendant is convicted of a count charging conspiracy to distribute child pornography. Defendant K is accountable under subsection (a)(1)(A) for the entire quantity of child pornography sold to Defendants L and M. Defendant N also is accountable for the entire quantity sold to those defendants under subsection (a)(1)(B) because the entire quantity was within the scope of his jointly undertaken criminal activity (to distribute child pornography with Defendant K), in furtherance of that criminal activity, and reasonably foreseeable. Defendant L is accountable under subsection (a)(1)(A) only for the quantity of child pornography that he purchased from Defendant K because he is not engaged in a jointly undertaken criminal activity with the other defendants. For the same reason, Defendant M is accountable under subsection (a)(1)(A) only for the quantity of child pornography that he purchased from Defendant K.

(v)   Defendant O knows about her boyfriend's ongoing drug-trafficking activity, but agrees to participate on only one occasion by making a delivery for him at his request when he was ill. Defendant O is accountable under subsection (a)(1)(A) for the drug quantity involved on that one occasion. Defendant O is not accountable for the other drug sales made by her boyfriend because those sales were not within the scope of her jointly undertaken criminal activity (*i.e.*, the one delivery).

(vi) Defendant P is a street-level drug dealer who knows of other street-level drug dealers in the same geographic area who sell the same type of drug as he sells. Defendant P and the other dealers share a common source of supply, but otherwise operate independently. Defendant P is not accountable for the quantities of drugs sold by the other street-level drug dealers because he is not engaged in a jointly undertaken criminal activity with them. In contrast, Defendant Q, another street-level drug dealer, pools his resources and profits with four other street-level drug dealers. Defendant Q is engaged in a jointly undertaken criminal activity and, therefore, he is accountable under subsection (a)(1)(B) for the quantities of drugs sold by the four other dealers during the course of his joint undertaking with them because those sales were within the scope of the jointly undertaken criminal activity, in furtherance of that criminal activity, and reasonably foreseeable in connection with that criminal activity.

(vii) Defendant R recruits Defendant S to distribute 500 grams of cocaine. Defendant S knows that Defendant R is the prime figure in a conspiracy involved in importing much larger quantities of cocaine. As long as Defendant S's agreement and conduct is limited to the distribution of the 500 grams, Defendant S is accountable only for that 500 gram amount (under subsection (a)(1)(A)), rather than the much larger quantity imported by Defendant R. Defendant S is not accountable under subsection (a)(1)(B) for the other quantities imported by Defendant R because those quantities were not within the scope of his jointly undertaken criminal activity (*i.e.*, the 500 grams).

(viii) Defendants T, U, V, and W are hired by a supplier to backpack a quantity of marihuana across the border from Mexico into the United States. Defendants T, U, V, and W receive their individual shipments from the supplier at the same time and coordinate their importation efforts by walking across the border together for mutual assistance and protection. Each defendant is accountable for the aggregate quantity of marihuana transported by the four defendants. The four defendants engaged in a jointly undertaken criminal activity, the object of which was the importation of the four backpacks containing marihuana (subsection (a)(1)(B)), and aided and abetted each other's actions (subsection (a)(1)(A)) in carrying out the jointly undertaken criminal activity (which under subsection (a)(1)(B) were also in furtherance of, and reasonably foreseeable in connection with, the criminal activity). In contrast, if Defendants T, U, V, and W were hired individually, transported their individual shipments at different times, and otherwise operated independently, each defendant would be accountable only for the quantity of marihuana he personally transported (subsection (a)(1)(A)). As this example illustrates, the scope of the jointly undertaken criminal activity may depend upon whether, in the particular circumstances, the nature of the offense is more appropriately viewed as one jointly undertaken criminal activity or as a number of separate criminal activities. *See* Application Note 3(B).

5.   **Application of Subsection (a)(2).—**

(A)   **Relationship to Grouping of Multiple Counts.**—"Offenses of a character for which §3D1.2(d) would require grouping of multiple counts," as used in subsection (a)(2), applies to offenses for which grouping of counts would be required under §3D1.2(d) had the defendant been convicted of multiple counts. Application of this provision does not require the defendant, in fact, to have been convicted of multiple counts. For example, where the defendant engaged in three drug sales of 10, 15, and 20 grams of cocaine, as part of the same course of conduct or common scheme or plan, subsection (a)(2) provides that the total quantity of cocaine involved (45 grams) is to be used to determine the offense level even if the defendant is convicted of a single count charging only one of the sales. If the defendant is convicted of multiple counts for the above noted sales, the grouping rules of Chapter Three, Part D (Multiple Counts) provide that the counts are grouped together. Although Chapter Three, Part D (Multiple Counts) applies to multiple counts of conviction, it does not limit the scope of subsection (a)(2). Subsection (a)(2) merely incorporates by reference the types of offenses set forth in §3D1.2(d); thus, as discussed above, multiple counts of conviction are not required for subsection (a)(2) to apply.

As noted above, subsection (a)(2) applies to offenses of a character for which §3D1.2(d) would require grouping of multiple counts, had the defendant been convicted of multiple counts. For example, the defendant sells 30 grams of cocaine (a violation of 21 U.S.C. § 841) on one occasion and, as part of the same course of conduct or common scheme or plan, attempts to sell an additional 15 grams of cocaine (a violation of 21 U.S.C. § 846) on another occasion. The defendant is convicted of one count charging the completed sale of 30 grams of cocaine. The two offenses (sale of cocaine and attempted sale of cocaine), although covered by different statutory provisions, are of a character for which §3D1.2(d) would require the grouping of counts, had the defendant been convicted of both counts. Therefore, subsection (a)(2) applies and the total amount of cocaine (45 grams) involved is used to determine the offense level.

(B)   **"Same Course of Conduct or Common Scheme or Plan".**—"Common scheme or plan" and "same course of conduct" are two closely related concepts.

(i)   **Common scheme or plan.** For two or more offenses to constitute part of a common scheme or plan, they must be substantially connected to each other by at least one common factor, such as common victims, common accomplices, common purpose, or similar *modus operandi*. For example, the conduct of five defendants who together defrauded a group of investors by computer manipulations that unlawfully transferred funds over an eighteen-month period would qualify as a common scheme or plan on the basis of any of the above listed factors; *i.e.*, the commonality of victims (the same investors were defrauded on an ongoing basis), commonality of offenders (the conduct constituted an ongoing conspiracy), commonality of purpose (to defraud the group of investors), or similarity of *modus operandi* (the same or similar computer manipulations were used to execute the scheme).

(ii)   **Same course of conduct**. Offenses that do not qualify as part of a common scheme or plan may nonetheless qualify as part of the same course of conduct if they are sufficiently connected or related to each other as to warrant the conclusion that they are part of a single episode, spree, or ongoing series of offenses. Factors that are appropriate to the determination of whether offenses are sufficiently connected or related to each other to be considered as part of the same course of conduct include the degree of similarity of the offenses, the regularity (repetitions) of the offenses, and the time interval between the offenses. When one of the above factors is absent, a stronger presence of at least one of the other factors is required. For example, where the conduct alleged to be relevant is relatively remote to the offense of conviction, a stronger showing of similarity or regularity is necessary to compensate for the absence of temporal proximity. The nature of the offenses may also be a relevant consideration (*e.g.*, a defendant's failure to file tax returns in three consecutive years appropriately would be considered as part of the same course of conduct because such returns are only required at yearly intervals).

(C) **Conduct Associated with a Prior Sentence.**—For the purposes of subsection (a)(2), offense conduct associated with a sentence that was imposed prior to the acts or omissions constituting the instant federal offense (the offense of conviction) is not considered as part of the same course of conduct or common scheme or plan as the offense of conviction.

Examples: (1) The defendant was convicted for the sale of cocaine and sentenced to state prison. Immediately upon release from prison, he again sold cocaine to the same person, using the same accomplices and *modus operandi*. The instant federal offense (the offense of conviction) charges this latter sale. In this example, the offense conduct relevant to the state prison sentence is considered as prior criminal history, not as part of the same course of conduct or common scheme or plan as the offense of conviction. The prior state prison sentence is counted under Chapter Four (Criminal History and Criminal Livelihood). (2) The defendant engaged in two cocaine sales constituting part of the same course of conduct or common scheme or plan. Subsequently, he is arrested by state authorities for the first sale and by federal authorities for the second sale. He is convicted in state court for the first sale and sentenced to imprisonment; he is then convicted in federal court for the second sale. In this case, the cocaine sales are not separated by an intervening sentence. Therefore, under subsection (a)(2), the cocaine sale associated with the state conviction is considered as relevant conduct to the instant federal offense. The state prison sentence for that sale is not counted as a prior sentence; *see* §4A1.2(a)(1).

Note, however, in certain cases, offense conduct associated with a previously imposed sentence may be expressly charged in the offense of conviction. Unless otherwise provided, such conduct will be considered relevant conduct under subsection (a)(1), not (a)(2).

6. **Application of Subsection (a)(3).**—

(A) **Definition of "Harm".**—"*Harm*" includes bodily injury, monetary loss, property damage and any resulting harm.

(B) **Risk or Danger of Harm.**—If the offense guideline includes creating a risk or danger of harm as a specific offense characteristic, whether that risk or danger was created is to be considered in determining the offense level. *See, e.g.*, §2K1.4 (Arson; Property Damage by Use of Explosives); §2Q1.2 (Mishandling of Hazardous or Toxic Substances or Pesticides). If, however, the guideline refers only to harm sustained (*e.g.*, §2A2.2 (Aggravated Assault); §2B3.1 (Robbery)) or to actual, attempted or intended harm (*e.g.*, §2B1.1 (Theft, Property Destruction, and Fraud); §2X1.1 (Attempt, Solicitation, or Conspiracy)), the risk created enters into the determination of the offense level only insofar as it is incorporated into the base offense level. Unless clearly indicated by the guidelines, harm that is merely risked is not to be treated as the equivalent of harm that occurred. In a case in which creation of risk is not adequately taken into account by the applicable offense guideline, an upward departure may be warranted. *See generally* §1B1.4 (Information to be Used in Imposing Sentence); §5K2.0 (Grounds for Departure). The extent to which harm that was attempted or intended enters into the determination of the offense level should be determined in accordance with §2X1.1 (Attempt, Solicitation, or Conspiracy) and the applicable offense guideline.

7. **Factors Requiring Conviction under a Specific Statute.**—A particular guideline (in the base offense level or in a specific offense characteristic) may expressly direct that a particular factor be applied only if the defendant was convicted of a particular statute. For example, in §2S1.1 (Laundering of Monetary Instruments; Engaging in Monetary Transactions in Property Derived from Unlawful Activity), subsection (b)(2)(B) applies if the defendant "was convicted under 18 U.S.C. § 1956". Unless such an express direction is included, conviction under the statute is not required. Thus, use of a statutory reference to describe a particular set of circumstances does not require a conviction under the referenced statute. An example of this usage is found in §2A3.4(a)(2) ("if the offense involved conduct described in 18 U.S.C. § 2242").

   Unless otherwise specified, an express direction to apply a particular factor only if the defendant was convicted of a particular statute includes the determination of the offense level where the defendant was convicted of conspiracy, attempt, solicitation, aiding or abetting, accessory after the fact, or misprision of felony in respect to that particular statute. For example, §2S1.1(b)(2)(B) (which is applicable only if the defendant is convicted under 18 U.S.C. § 1956) would be applied in determining the offense level under §2X3.1 (Accessory After the Fact) in a case in which the defendant was convicted of accessory after the fact to a violation of 18 U.S.C. § 1956 but would not be applied in a case in which the defendant is convicted of a conspiracy under 18 U.S.C. § 1956(h) and the sole object of that conspiracy was to commit an offense set forth in 18 U.S.C. § 1957. *See* Application Note 3(C) of §2S1.1.

8. **Partially Completed Offense.**—In the case of a partially completed offense (*e.g.*, an offense involving an attempted theft of $800,000 and a completed theft of $30,000), the offense level is to be determined in accordance with §2X1.1 (Attempt, Solicitation, or Conspiracy) whether the conviction is for the substantive offense, the inchoate offense (attempt, solicitation, or conspiracy), or both. *See* Application Note 4 in the Commentary to §2X1.1. Note, however, that Application Note 4 is not applicable where the offense level is determined under §2X1.1(c)(1).

9. **Solicitation, Misprision, or Accessory After the Fact.**—In the case of solicitation, misprision, or accessory after the fact, the conduct for which the defendant is accountable includes all conduct relevant to determining the offense level for the underlying offense that was known, or reasonably should have been known, by the defendant.

Background: This section prescribes rules for determining the applicable guideline sentencing range, whereas §1B1.4 (Information to be Used in Imposing Sentence) governs the range of information that the court may consider in adjudging sentence once the guideline sentencing range has been determined. Conduct that is not formally charged or is not an element of the offense of conviction may enter into the determination of the applicable guideline sentencing range. The range of information that may be considered at sentencing is broader than the range of information upon which the applicable sentencing range is determined.

   Subsection (a) establishes a rule of construction by specifying, in the absence of more explicit instructions in the context of a specific guideline, the range of conduct that is relevant to determining the applicable offense level (except for the determination of the applicable offense guideline, which is governed by §1B1.2(a)). No such rule of construction is necessary with respect to Chapters Four and Five because the guidelines in those Chapters are explicit as to the specific factors to be considered.

Subsection (a)(2) provides for consideration of a broader range of conduct with respect to one class of offenses, primarily certain property, tax, fraud and drug offenses for which the guidelines depend substantially on quantity, than with respect to other offenses such as assault, robbery and burglary. The distinction is made on the basis of §3D1.2(d), which provides for grouping together (*i.e.*, treating as a single count) all counts charging offenses of a type covered by this subsection. However, the applicability of subsection (a)(2) does not depend upon whether multiple counts are alleged. Thus, in an embezzlement case, for example, embezzled funds that may not be specified in any count of conviction are nonetheless included in determining the offense level if they were part of the same course of conduct or part of the same scheme or plan as the count of conviction. Similarly, in a drug distribution case, quantities and types of drugs not specified in the count of conviction are to be included in determining the offense level if they were part of the same course of conduct or part of a common scheme or plan as the count of conviction. On the other hand, in a robbery case in which the defendant robbed two banks, the amount of money taken in one robbery would *not* be taken into account in determining the guideline range for the other robbery, even if both robberies were part of a single course of conduct or the same scheme or plan. (This is true whether the defendant is convicted of one or both robberies.)

Subsections (a)(1) and (a)(2) adopt different rules because offenses of the character dealt with in subsection (a)(2) (*i.e.*, to which §3D1.2(d) applies) often involve a pattern of misconduct that cannot readily be broken into discrete, identifiable units that are meaningful for purposes of sentencing. For example, a pattern of embezzlement may consist of several acts of taking that cannot separately be identified, even though the overall conduct is clear. In addition, the distinctions that the law makes as to what constitutes separate counts or offenses often turn on technical elements that are not especially meaningful for purposes of sentencing. Thus, in a mail fraud case, the scheme is an element of the offense and each mailing may be the basis for a separate count; in an embezzlement case, each taking may provide a basis for a separate count. Another consideration is that in a pattern of small thefts, for example, it is important to take into account the full range of related conduct. Relying on the entire range of conduct, regardless of the number of counts that are alleged or on which a conviction is obtained, appears to be the most reasonable approach to writing workable guidelines for these offenses. Conversely, when §3D1.2(d) does not apply, so that convictions on multiple counts are considered separately in determining the guideline sentencing range, the guidelines prohibit aggregation of quantities from other counts in order to prevent "double counting" of the conduct and harm from each count of conviction. Continuing offenses present similar practical problems. The reference to §3D1.2(d), which provides for grouping of multiple counts arising out of a continuing offense when the offense guideline takes the continuing nature into account, also prevents double counting.

Subsection (a)(4) requires consideration of any other information specified in the applicable guideline. For example, §2A1.4 (Involuntary Manslaughter) specifies consideration of the defendant's state of mind; §2K1.4 (Arson; Property Damage By Use of Explosives) specifies consideration of the risk of harm created.

Historical Note	Effective November 1, 1987. Amended effective January 15, 1988 (amendment 3); November 1, 1989 (amendments 76–78 and 303); November 1, 1990 (amendment 309); November 1, 1991 (amendment 389); November 1, 1992 (amendment 439); November 1, 1994 (amendment 503); November 1, 2001 (amendments 617 and 634); November 1, 2004 (amendment 674); November 1, 2010 (amendment 746); November 1, 2015 (amendments 790 and 797).

§1B1.4. Information to be Used in Imposing Sentence (Selecting a Point Within the Guideline Range or Departing from the Guidelines)

In determining the sentence to impose within the guideline range, or whether a departure from the guidelines is warranted, the court may consider, without limitation, any information concerning the background, character and conduct of the defendant, unless otherwise prohibited by law. *See* 18 U.S.C. § 3661.

Commentary

Background: This section distinguishes between factors that determine the applicable guideline sentencing range (§1B1.3) and information that a court may consider in imposing sentence within that range. The section is based on 18 U.S.C. § 3661, which recodifies 18 U.S.C. § 3577. The recodification of this 1970 statute in 1984 with an effective date of 1987 (99 Stat. 1728), makes it clear that Congress intended that no limitation would be placed on the information that a court may consider in imposing an appropriate sentence under the future guideline sentencing system. A court is not precluded from considering information that the guidelines do not take into account in determining a sentence within the guideline range or from considering that information in determining whether and to what extent to depart from the guidelines. For example, if the defendant committed two robberies, but as part of a plea negotiation entered a guilty plea to only one, the robbery that was not taken into account by the guidelines would provide a reason for sentencing at the top of the guideline range and may provide a reason for an upward departure. Some policy statements do, however, express a Commission policy that certain factors should not be considered for any purpose, or should be considered only for limited purposes. *See, e.g.*, Chapter Five, Part H (Specific Offender Characteristics).

Historical Note	Effective November 1, 1987. Amended effective January 15, 1988 (amendment 4); November 1, 1989 (amendment 303); November 1, 2000 (amendment 604); November 1, 2004 (amendment 674).

§1B1.5. Interpretation of References to Other Offense Guidelines

    (a)   A cross reference (an instruction to apply another offense guideline) refers to the entire offense guideline (*i.e.*, the base offense level, specific offense characteristics, cross references, and special instructions).

    (b)   (1)   An instruction to use the offense level from another offense guideline refers to the offense level from the entire offense guideline (*i.e.*, the base offense level, specific offense characteristics, cross references, and special instructions), except as provided in subdivision (2) below.

            (2)   An instruction to use a particular subsection or table from another offense guideline refers only to the particular subsection or table referenced, and not to the entire offense guideline.

(c)   If the offense level is determined by a reference to another guideline under subsection (a) or (b)(1) above, the adjustments in Chapter Three (Adjustments) also are determined in respect to the referenced offense guideline, except as otherwise expressly provided.

(d)   A reference to another guideline under subsection (a) or (b)(1) above may direct that it be applied only if it results in the greater offense level. In such case, the greater offense level means the greater Chapter Two offense level, except as otherwise expressly provided.

Commentary

Application Notes:

1.   References to other offense guidelines are most frequently designated "Cross References," but may also appear in the portion of the guideline entitled "Base Offense Level" (*e.g.*, §2D1.2(a)(1) and (2)), or "Specific Offense Characteristics" (*e.g.*, §2A4.1(b)(7)). These references may be to a specific guideline, or may be more general (*e.g.*, to the guideline for the "underlying offense"). Such references incorporate the specific offense characteristics, cross references, and special instructions as well as the base offense level. For example, if the guideline reads "2 plus the offense level from §2A2.2 (Aggravated Assault)," the user would determine the offense level from §2A2.2, including any applicable adjustments for planning, weapon use, degree of injury and motive, and then increase by 2 levels.

   A reference may also be to a specific subsection of another guideline; *e.g.*, the reference in §2D1.10(a)(1) to "3 plus the offense level from the Drug Quantity Table in §2D1.1". In such case, only the specific subsection of that other guideline is used.

2.   A reference to another guideline may direct that such reference is to be used only if it results in a greater offense level. In such cases, the greater offense level means the offense level taking into account only the Chapter Two offense level, unless the offense guideline expressly provides for consideration of both the Chapter Two offense level and applicable Chapter Three adjustments. For situations in which a comparison involving both Chapters Two and Three is necessary, *see* the Commentary to §§2C1.1 (Offering, Giving, Soliciting, or Receiving a Bribe; Extortion Under Color of Official Right; Fraud Involving the Deprivation of the Intangible Right to Honest Services of Public Officials; Conspiracy to Defraud by Interference with Governmental Functions); 2E1.1 (Unlawful Conduct Relating to Racketeer Influenced and Corrupt Organizations); and 2E1.2 (Interstate or Foreign Travel or Transportation in Aid of a Racketeering Enterprise).

3.   A reference may direct that, if the conduct involved another offense, the offense guideline for such other offense is to be applied. Consistent with the provisions of §1B1.3 (Relevant Conduct), such other offense includes conduct that may be a state or local offense and conduct that occurred under circumstances that would constitute a federal offense had the conduct taken place within the territorial or maritime jurisdiction of the United States. Where there is more than one such other offense, the most serious such offense (or group of closely related offenses in the case of offenses that would be grouped together under §3D1.2(d)) is to be used. For example, if a defendant convicted of possession of a firearm by a felon, to which §2K2.1 (Unlawful Receipt, Possession, or Transportation of Firearms or Ammunition; Prohibited Transactions Involving Firearms or Ammunition) applies, is found to have possessed that firearm during commission of a series of offenses,

the cross reference at §2K2.1(c) is applied to the offense resulting in the greatest offense level.

Historical Note	Effective November 1, 1987. Amended effective November 1, 1989 (amendments 79, 80, and 302); November 1, 1991 (amendment 429); November 1, 1992 (amendment 440); November 1, 1995 (amendment 534); November 1, 1997 (amendment 547); November 1, 2001 (amendment 616); November 1, 2004 (amendment 666).

§1B1.6.   Structure of the Guidelines

The guidelines are presented in numbered chapters divided into alphabetical parts. The parts are divided into subparts and individual guidelines. Each guideline is identified by three numbers and a letter corresponding to the chapter, part, subpart and individual guideline.

The first number is the chapter, the letter represents the part of the chapter, the second number is the subpart, and the final number is the guideline. Section 2B1.1, for example, is the first guideline in the first subpart in Part B of Chapter Two. Or, §3A1.2 is the second guideline in the first subpart in Part A of Chapter Three. Policy statements are similarly identified.

To illustrate:

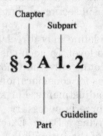

Historical Note	Effective November 1, 1987.

§1B1.7.   Significance of Commentary

The Commentary that accompanies the guideline sections may serve a number of purposes. First, it may interpret the guideline or explain how it is to be applied. Failure to follow such commentary could constitute an incorrect application of the guidelines, subjecting the sentence to possible reversal on appeal. *See* 18 U.S.C. § 3742. Second, the commentary may suggest circumstances which, in the view of the Commission, may warrant departure from the guidelines. Such commentary is to be treated as the legal equivalent of a policy statement. Finally, the commentary may provide background information, including factors considered in promulgating the guideline or reasons underlying promulgation of the guideline. As with a policy statement, such commentary may provide guidance in assessing the reasonableness of any departure from the guidelines.

Commentary

Portions of this document not labeled as guidelines or commentary also express the policy of the Commission or provide guidance as to the interpretation and application of the guidelines. These are to be construed as commentary and thus have the force of policy statements.

"[C]ommentary in the *Guidelines Manual* that interprets or explains a guideline is authoritative unless it violates the Constitution or a federal statute, or is inconsistent with, or a plainly erroneous reading of, that guideline." *Stinson v. United States*, 508 U.S. 36, 38 (1993).

Historical Note	Effective November 1, 1987. Amended effective November 1, 1993 (amendment 498).

§1B1.8.   Use of Certain Information

(a)   Where a defendant agrees to cooperate with the government by providing information concerning unlawful activities of others, and as part of that cooperation agreement the government agrees that self-incriminating information provided pursuant to the agreement will not be used against the defendant, then such information shall not be used in determining the applicable guideline range, except to the extent provided in the agreement.

(b)   The provisions of subsection (a) shall not be applied to restrict the use of information:

(1)   known to the government prior to entering into the cooperation agreement;

(2)   concerning the existence of prior convictions and sentences in determining §4A1.1 (Criminal History Category) and §4B1.1 (Career Offender);

(3)   in a prosecution for perjury or giving a false statement;

(4)   in the event there is a breach of the cooperation agreement by the defendant; or

(5)   in determining whether, or to what extent, a downward departure from the guidelines is warranted pursuant to a government motion under §5K1.1 (Substantial Assistance to Authorities).

Commentary

Application Notes:

1. This provision does not authorize the government to withhold information from the court but provides that self-incriminating information obtained under a cooperation agreement is not to be used to determine the defendant's guideline range. Under this provision, for example, if a defendant is arrested in possession of a kilogram of cocaine and, pursuant to an agreement to provide information concerning the unlawful activities of co-conspirators, admits that he assisted in the importation of an additional three kilograms of cocaine, a fact not previously known to the government, this admission would not be used to increase his applicable guideline range, except to the extent provided in the agreement. Although the guideline itself affects only the determination of the guideline range, the policy of the Commission, as a corollary, is that information prohibited from being used to determine the applicable guideline range shall not be used to depart upward. In contrast, subsection (b)(5) provides that consideration of such information is appropriate in determining whether, and to what extent, a downward departure is warranted pursuant to a government motion under §5K1.1 (Substantial Assistance to Authorities); *e.g.*, a court may refuse to depart downward on the basis of such information.

2. Subsection (b)(2) prohibits any cooperation agreement from restricting the use of information as to the existence of prior convictions and sentences in determining adjustments under §4A1.1 (Criminal History Category) and §4B1.1 (Career Offender). The probation office generally will secure information relevant to the defendant's criminal history independent of information the defendant provides as part of his cooperation agreement.

3. On occasion the defendant will provide incriminating information to the government during plea negotiation sessions before a cooperation agreement has been reached. In the event no agreement is reached, use of such information in a sentencing proceeding is restricted by Rule 11(f) (Admissibility or Inadmissibility of a Plea, Plea Discussions, and Related Statements) of the Federal Rules of Criminal Procedure and Rule 410 (Pleas, Plea Discussions, and Related Statements) of the Rules of Evidence.

4. As with the statutory provisions governing use immunity, 18 U.S.C. § 6002, this guideline does not apply to information used against the defendant in a prosecution for perjury, giving a false statement, or in the event the defendant otherwise fails to comply with the cooperation agreement.

5. This guideline limits the use of certain incriminating information furnished by a defendant in the context of a defendant-government agreement for the defendant to provide information concerning the unlawful activities of other persons. The guideline operates as a limitation on the use of such incriminating information in determining the applicable guideline range, and not merely as a restriction of the government's presentation of such information (*e.g.*, where the defendant, subsequent to having entered into a cooperation agreement, provides such information to the probation officer preparing the presentence report, the use of such information remains protected by this section).

6. Unless the cooperation agreement relates to the provision of information concerning the unlawful activities of others, this guideline does not apply (*i.e.*, an agreement by the defendant simply to detail the extent of his own unlawful activities, not involving an agreement to provide information concerning the unlawful activity of another person, is not covered by this guideline).

Historical Note	Effective June 15, 1988 (amendment 5). Amended effective November 1, 1990 (amendment 308); November 1, 1991 (amendment 390); November 1, 1992 (amendment 441); November 1, 2004 (amendment 674); November 1, 2009 (amendment 736); November 1, 2010 (amendment 746); November 1, 2013 (amendment 778).

§1B1.9. Class B or C Misdemeanors and Infractions

The sentencing guidelines do not apply to any count of conviction that is a Class B or C misdemeanor or an infraction.

Commentary

Application Notes:

1. Notwithstanding any other provision of the guidelines, the court may impose any sentence authorized by statute for each count that is a Class B or C misdemeanor or an infraction. A Class B misdemeanor is any offense for which the maximum authorized term of imprisonment is more than thirty days but not more than six months; a Class C misdemeanor is any offense for which the maximum authorized term of imprisonment is more than five days but not more than thirty days; an infraction is any offense for which the maximum authorized term of imprisonment is not more than five days or for which no imprisonment is authorized. *See* 18 U.S.C. § 3559.

2. The guidelines for sentencing on multiple counts do not apply to counts that are Class B or C misdemeanors or infractions. Sentences for such offenses may be consecutive to or concurrent with sentences imposed on other counts. In imposing sentence, the court should, however, consider the relationship between the Class B or C misdemeanor or infraction and any other offenses of which the defendant is convicted.

Background: For the sake of judicial economy, the Commission has exempted all Class B and C misdemeanors and infractions from the coverage of the guidelines.

Historical Note	Effective June 15, 1988 (amendment 6). Amended effective November 1, 1989 (amendment 81); November 1, 2010 (amendment 746).

§1B1.10. Reduction in Term of Imprisonment as a Result of Amended Guideline Range (Policy Statement)

(a) AUTHORITY.—

    (1) IN GENERAL.—In a case in which a defendant is serving a term of imprisonment, and the guideline range applicable to that defendant has subsequently been lowered as a result of an amendment to the Guidelines Manual listed in subsection (d) below, the court may reduce the defendant's term of imprisonment as provided by 18 U.S.C. § 3582(c)(2). As required by 18 U.S.C. § 3582(c)(2), any such reduction in the defendant's term of imprisonment shall be consistent with this policy statement.

    (2) EXCLUSIONS.—A reduction in the defendant's term of imprisonment is not consistent with this policy statement and therefore is not authorized under 18 U.S.C. § 3582(c)(2) if—

        (A) none of the amendments listed in subsection (d) is applicable to the defendant; or

        (B) an amendment listed in subsection (d) does not have the effect of lowering the defendant's applicable guideline range.

    (3) LIMITATION.—Consistent with subsection (b), proceedings under 18 U.S.C. § 3582(c)(2) and this policy statement do not constitute a full resentencing of the defendant.

(b) DETERMINATION OF REDUCTION IN TERM OF IMPRISONMENT.—

    (1) IN GENERAL.—In determining whether, and to what extent, a reduction in the defendant's term of imprisonment under 18 U.S.C. § 3582(c)(2) and this policy statement is warranted, the court shall determine the amended guideline range that would have been applicable to the defendant if the amendment(s) to the guidelines listed in subsection (d) had been in effect at the time the defendant was sentenced. In making such determination, the court shall substitute only the amendments listed in subsection (d) for the corresponding guideline provisions that were applied when the defendant was sentenced and shall leave all other guideline application decisions unaffected.

    (2)   LIMITATION AND PROHIBITION ON EXTENT OF REDUCTION.—

        (A) LIMITATION.—Except as provided in subdivision (B), the court shall not reduce the defendant's term of imprisonment under 18 U.S.C. § 3582(c)(2) and this policy statement to a term that is less than the minimum of the amended guideline range determined under subdivision (1) of this subsection.

        (B) EXCEPTION FOR SUBSTANTIAL ASSISTANCE.—If the term of imprisonment imposed was less than the term of imprisonment provided by the guideline range applicable to the defendant at the time of sentencing pursuant to a government motion to reflect the defendant's substantial assistance to authorities, a reduction comparably less than the amended guideline range determined under subdivision (1) of this subsection may be appropriate.

        (C) PROHIBITION.—In no event may the reduced term of imprisonment be less than the term of imprisonment the defendant has already served.

(c)   CASES INVOLVING MANDATORY MINIMUM SENTENCES AND SUBSTANTIAL ASSISTANCE.—If the case involves a statutorily required minimum sentence and the court had the authority to impose a sentence below the statutorily required minimum sentence pursuant to a government motion to reflect the defendant's substantial assistance to authorities, then for purposes of this policy statement the amended guideline range shall be determined without regard to the operation of §5G1.1 (Sentencing on a Single Count of Conviction) and §5G1.2 (Sentencing on Multiple Counts of Conviction).

(d)   COVERED AMENDMENTS.—Amendments covered by this policy statement are listed in Appendix C as follows: 126, 130, 156, 176, 269, 329, 341, 371, 379, 380, 433, 454, 461, 484, 488, 490, 499, 505, 506, 516, 591, 599, 606, 657, 702, 706 as amended by 711, 715, 750 (parts A and C only), and 782 (subject to subsection (e)(1)).

(e)   SPECIAL INSTRUCTION.—

    (1)   The court shall not order a reduced term of imprisonment based on Amendment 782 unless the effective date of the court's order is November 1, 2015, or later.

Commentary

Application Notes:

1. **Application of Subsection (a).—**

    (A) **Eligibility.**—Eligibility for consideration under 18 U.S.C. § 3582(c)(2) is triggered only by an amendment listed in subsection (d) that lowers the applicable guideline range (*i.e.*, the guideline range that corresponds to the offense level and criminal history category determined pursuant to §1B1.1(a), which is determined before consideration of any departure provision in the Guidelines Manual or any variance). Accordingly, a reduction in the defendant's term of imprisonment is not authorized under 18 U.S.C. § 3582(c)(2) and is not consistent with this policy statement if: (i) none of the amendments listed in subsection (d) is applicable to the defendant; or (ii) an amendment listed in subsection (d) is applicable to the defendant but the amendment does not have the effect of lowering the defendant's applicable guideline range because of the operation of another guideline or statutory provision (*e.g.*, a statutory mandatory minimum term of imprisonment).

    (B) **Factors for Consideration.—**

        (i) **In General.**—Consistent with 18 U.S.C. § 3582(c)(2), the court shall consider the factors set forth in 18 U.S.C. § 3553(a) in determining: (I) whether a reduction in the defendant's term of imprisonment is warranted; and (II) the extent of such reduction, but only within the limits described in subsection (b).

        (ii) **Public Safety Consideration.**—The court shall consider the nature and seriousness of the danger to any person or the community that may be posed by a reduction in the defendant's term of imprisonment in determining: (I) whether such a reduction is warranted; and (II) the extent of such reduction, but only within the limits described in subsection (b).

        (iii) **Post-Sentencing Conduct.**—The court may consider post-sentencing conduct of the defendant that occurred after imposition of the term of imprisonment in determining: (I) whether a reduction in the defendant's term of imprisonment is warranted; and (II) the extent of such reduction, but only within the limits described in subsection (b).

2. **Application of Subsection (b)(1).**—In determining the amended guideline range under subsection (b)(1), the court shall substitute only the amendments listed in subsection (d) for the corresponding guideline provisions that were applied when the defendant was sentenced. All other guideline application decisions remain unaffected.

3. **Application of Subsection (b)(2).**—Under subsection (b)(2), the amended guideline range determined under subsection (b)(1) and the term of imprisonment already served by the defendant limit the extent to which the court may reduce the defendant's term of imprisonment under 18 U.S.C. § 3582(c)(2) and this policy statement. Specifically, as provided in subsection (b)(2)(A), if the term of imprisonment imposed was within the guideline range applicable to the defendant at the time of sentencing, the court may reduce the defendant's term of imprisonment to a term that is no less than the minimum term of imprisonment provided by the amended guideline range determined under subsection (b)(1). For example, in a case in which: (A) the guideline range applicable to the defendant at the time of sentencing was 70 to 87 months; (B) the term of imprisonment

imposed was 70 months; and (C) the amended guideline range determined under subsection (b)(1) is 51 to 63 months, the court may reduce the defendant's term of imprisonment, but shall not reduce it to a term less than 51 months.

If the term of imprisonment imposed was outside the guideline range applicable to the defendant at the time of sentencing, the limitation in subsection (b)(2)(A) also applies. Thus, if the term of imprisonment imposed in the example provided above was not a sentence of 70 months (within the guidelines range) but instead was a sentence of 56 months (constituting a downward departure or variance), the court likewise may reduce the defendant's term of imprisonment, but shall not reduce it to a term less than 51 months.

Subsection (b)(2)(B) provides an exception to this limitation, which applies if the term of imprisonment imposed was less than the term of imprisonment provided by the guideline range applicable to the defendant at the time of sentencing pursuant to a government motion to reflect the defendant's substantial assistance to authorities. In such a case, the court may reduce the defendant's term, but the reduction is not limited by subsection (b)(2)(A) to the minimum of the amended guideline range. Instead, as provided in subsection (b)(2)(B), the court may, if appropriate, provide a reduction comparably less than the amended guideline range. Thus, if the term of imprisonment imposed in the example provided above was 56 months pursuant to a government motion to reflect the defendant's substantial assistance to authorities (representing a downward departure of 20 percent below the minimum term of imprisonment provided by the guideline range applicable to the defendant at the time of sentencing), a reduction to a term of imprisonment of 41 months (representing a reduction of approximately 20 percent below the minimum term of imprisonment provided by the amended guideline range) would amount to a comparable reduction and may be appropriate.

The provisions authorizing such a government motion are §5K1.1 (Substantial Assistance to Authorities) (authorizing, upon government motion, a downward departure based on the defendant's substantial assistance); 18 U.S.C. § 3553(e) (authorizing the court, upon government motion, to impose a sentence below a statutory minimum to reflect the defendant's substantial assistance); and Fed. R. Crim. P. 35(b) (authorizing the court, upon government motion, to reduce a sentence to reflect the defendant's substantial assistance).

In no case, however, shall the term of imprisonment be reduced below time served. *See* subsection (b)(2)(C). Subject to these limitations, the sentencing court has the discretion to determine whether, and to what extent, to reduce a term of imprisonment under this section.

4. **Application of Subsection (c).**—As stated in subsection (c), if the case involves a statutorily required minimum sentence and the court had the authority to impose a sentence below the statutorily required minimum sentence pursuant to a government motion to reflect the defendant's substantial assistance to authorities, then for purposes of this policy statement the amended guideline range shall be determined without regard to the operation of §5G1.1 (Sentencing on a Single Count of Conviction) and §5G1.2 (Sentencing on Multiple Counts of Conviction). For example:

(A) Defendant A is subject to a mandatory minimum term of imprisonment of 120 months. The original guideline range at the time of sentencing was 135 to 168 months, which is entirely above the mandatory minimum, and the court imposed a sentence of 101 months pursuant to a government motion to reflect the defendant's substantial assistance to authorities. The court determines that the amended guideline range as calculated on the Sentencing Table is 108 to 135 months. Ordinarily, §5G1.1 would operate to restrict the amended guideline range to 120 to 135 months, to reflect the mandatory minimum term of imprisonment. For purposes of this policy statement, however, the amended guideline range remains 108 to 135 months.

To the extent the court considers it appropriate to provide a reduction comparably less than the amended guideline range pursuant to subsection (b)(2)(B), Defendant A's original sentence of 101 months amounted to a reduction of approximately 25 percent below the minimum of the original guideline range of 135 months. Therefore, an amended sentence of 81 months (representing a reduction of approximately 25 percent below the minimum of the amended guideline range of 108 months) would amount to a comparable reduction and may be appropriate.

(B) Defendant B is subject to a mandatory minimum term of imprisonment of 120 months. The original guideline range at the time of sentencing (as calculated on the Sentencing Table) was 108 to 135 months, which was restricted by operation of §5G1.1 to a range of 120 to 135 months. *See* §5G1.1(c)(2). The court imposed a sentence of 90 months pursuant to a government motion to reflect the defendant's substantial assistance to authorities. The court determines that the amended guideline range as calculated on the Sentencing Table is 87 to 108 months. Ordinarily, §5G1.1 would operate to restrict the amended guideline range to precisely 120 months, to reflect the mandatory minimum term of imprisonment. *See* §5G1.1(b). For purposes of this policy statement, however, the amended guideline range is considered to be 87 to 108 months (*i.e.*, unrestricted by operation of §5G1.1 and the statutory minimum of 120 months).

To the extent the court considers it appropriate to provide a reduction comparably less than the amended guideline range pursuant to subsection (b)(2)(B), Defendant B's original sentence of 90 months amounted to a reduction of approximately 25 percent below the original guideline range of 120 months. Therefore, an amended sentence of 65 months (representing a reduction of approximately 25 percent below the minimum of the amended guideline range of 87 months) would amount to a comparable reduction and may be appropriate.

5. **Application to Amendment 750 (Parts A and C Only).**—As specified in subsection (d), the parts of Amendment 750 that are covered by this policy statement are Parts A and C only. Part A amended the Drug Quantity Table in §2D1.1 for crack cocaine and made related revisions to the Drug Equivalency Tables in the Commentary to §2D1.1 (*see* §2D1.1, comment. (n.8)). Part C deleted the cross reference in §2D2.1(b) under which an offender who possessed more than 5 grams of crack cocaine was sentenced under §2D1.1.

6. **Application to Amendment 782.**—As specified in subsection (d) and (e)(1), Amendment 782 (generally revising the Drug Quantity Table and chemical quantity tables across drug and chemical types) is covered by this policy statement only in cases in which the order reducing the defendant's term of imprisonment has an effective date of November 1, 2015, or later.

A reduction based on retroactive application of Amendment 782 that does not comply with the requirement that the order take effect on November 1, 2015, or later is not consistent with this policy statement and therefore is not authorized under 18 U.S.C. § 3582(c)(2).

Subsection (e)(1) does not preclude the court from conducting sentence reduction proceedings and entering orders under 18 U.S.C. § 3582(c)(2) and this policy statement before November 1, 2015, provided that any order reducing the defendant's term of imprisonment has an effective date of November 1, 2015, or later.

7. **Supervised Release.—**

   (A) **Exclusion Relating to Revocation.—**Only a term of imprisonment imposed as part of the original sentence is authorized to be reduced under this section. This section does not authorize a reduction in the term of imprisonment imposed upon revocation of supervised release.

   (B) **Modification Relating to Early Termination.—**If the prohibition in subsection (b)(2)(C) relating to time already served precludes a reduction in the term of imprisonment to the extent the court determines otherwise would have been appropriate as a result of the amended guideline range determined under subsection (b)(1), the court may consider any such reduction that it was unable to grant in connection with any motion for early termination of a term of supervised release under 18 U.S.C. § 3583(e)(1). However, the fact that a defendant may have served a longer term of imprisonment than the court determines would have been appropriate in view of the amended guideline range determined under subsection (b)(1) shall not, without more, provide a basis for early termination of supervised release. Rather, the court should take into account the totality of circumstances relevant to a decision to terminate supervised release, including the term of supervised release that would have been appropriate in connection with a sentence under the amended guideline range determined under subsection (b)(1).

8. **Use of Policy Statement in Effect on Date of Reduction.—**Consistent with subsection (a) of §1B1.11 (Use of Guidelines Manual in Effect on Date of Sentencing), the court shall use the version of this policy statement that is in effect on the date on which the court reduces the defendant's term of imprisonment as provided by 18 U.S.C. § 3582(c)(2).

Background: Section 3582(c)(2) of Title 18, United States Code, provides: "[I]n the case of a defendant who has been sentenced to a term of imprisonment based on a sentencing range that has subsequently been lowered by the Sentencing Commission pursuant to 28 U.S.C. § 994(o), upon motion of the defendant or the Director of the Bureau of Prisons, or on its own motion, the court may reduce the term of imprisonment, after considering the factors set forth in section 3553(a) to the extent that they are applicable, if such a reduction is consistent with applicable policy statements issued by the Sentencing Commission."

This policy statement provides guidance and limitations for a court when considering a motion under 18 U.S.C. § 3582(c)(2) and implements 28 U.S.C. § 994(u), which provides: "If the Commission reduces the term of imprisonment recommended in the guidelines applicable to a particular offense or category of offenses, it shall specify in what circumstances and by what amount the sentences of prisoners serving terms of imprisonment for the offense may be reduced." The Supreme Court has concluded that proceedings under section 3582(c)(2) are not governed by *United States v. Booker*, 543 U.S. 220 (2005), and this policy statement remains binding on courts in such proceedings. *See Dillon v. United States*, 560 U.S. 817 (2010).

Among the factors considered by the Commission in selecting the amendments included in subsection (d) were the purpose of the amendment, the magnitude of the change in the guideline range made by the amendment, and the difficulty of applying the amendment retroactively to determine an amended guideline range under subsection (b)(1).

The listing of an amendment in subsection (d) reflects policy determinations by the Commission that a reduced guideline range is sufficient to achieve the purposes of sentencing and that, in the sound discretion of the court, a reduction in the term of imprisonment may be appropriate for previously sentenced, qualified defendants. The authorization of such a discretionary reduction does not otherwise affect the lawfulness of a previously imposed sentence, does not authorize a reduction in any other component of the sentence, and does not entitle a defendant to a reduced term of imprisonment as a matter of right.

The Commission has not included in this policy statement amendments that generally reduce the maximum of the guideline range by less than six months. This criterion is in accord with the legislative history of 28 U.S.C. § 994(u) (formerly § 994(t)), which states: "It should be noted that the Committee does not expect that the Commission will recommend adjusting existing sentences under the provision when guidelines are simply refined in a way that might cause isolated instances of existing sentences falling above the old guidelines* or when there is only a minor downward adjustment in the guidelines. The Committee does not believe the courts should be burdened with adjustments in these cases." S. Rep. 225, 98th Cong., 1st Sess. 180 (1983).

*So in original. Probably should be "to fall above the amended guidelines".

Historical Note	Effective November 1, 1989 (amendment 306). Amended effective November 1, 1990 (amendment 360); November 1, 1991 (amendment 423); November 1, 1992 (amendment 469); November 1, 1993 (amendment 502); November 1, 1994 (amendment 504); November 1, 1995 (amendment 536); November 1, 1997 (amendment 548); November 1, 2000 (amendment 607); November 5, 2003 (amendment 662); November 1, 2007 (amendment 710); March 3, 2008 (amendments 712 and 713); May 1, 2008 (amendment 716); November 1, 2011 (amendment 759); November 1, 2012 (amendment 770); November 1, 2014 (amendments 780, 788, and 789).

§1B1.11. Use of Guidelines Manual in Effect on Date of Sentencing (Policy Statement)

(a)   The court shall use the Guidelines Manual in effect on the date that the defendant is sentenced.

(b)   (1)   If the court determines that use of the Guidelines Manual in effect on the date that the defendant is sentenced would violate the *ex post facto* clause of the United States Constitution, the court shall use the Guidelines Manual in effect on the date that the offense of conviction was committed.

(2)   The Guidelines Manual in effect on a particular date shall be applied in its entirety. The court shall not apply, for example, one guideline section from one edition of the Guidelines Manual and another guideline section from a different edition of the Guidelines Manual. However, if a court applies an earlier edition of the Guidelines Manual, the court shall consider subsequent amendments, to the extent that such amendments are clarifying rather than substantive changes.

(3) If the defendant is convicted of two offenses, the first committed before, and the second after, a revised edition of the Guidelines Manual became effective, the revised edition of the Guidelines Manual is to be applied to both offenses.

Commentary

Application Notes:

1. Subsection (b)(2) provides that if an earlier edition of the Guidelines Manual is used, it is to be used in its entirety, except that subsequent clarifying amendments are to be considered.

   Example: A defendant is convicted of an antitrust offense committed in November 1989. He is to be sentenced in December 1992. Effective November 1, 1991, the Commission raised the base offense level for antitrust offenses. Effective November 1, 1992, the Commission lowered the guideline range in the Sentencing Table for cases with an offense level of 8 and criminal history category of I from 2–8 months to 0–6 months. Under the 1992 edition of the Guidelines Manual (effective November 1, 1992), the defendant has a guideline range of 4–10 months (final offense level of 9, criminal history category of I). Under the 1989 edition of the Guidelines Manual (effective November 1, 1989), the defendant has a guideline range of 2–8 months (final offense level of 8, criminal history category of I). If the court determines that application of the 1992 edition of the Guidelines Manual would violate the *ex post facto* clause of the United States Constitution, it shall apply the 1989 edition of the Guidelines Manual in its entirety. It shall not apply, for example, the offense level of 8 and criminal history category of I from the 1989 edition of the Guidelines Manual in conjunction with the amended guideline range of 0–6 months for this offense level and criminal history category from the 1992 edition of the Guidelines Manual.

2. Under subsection (b)(1), the last date of the offense of conviction is the controlling date for *ex post facto* purposes. For example, if the offense of conviction (*i.e.*, the conduct charged in the count of the indictment or information of which the defendant was convicted) was determined by the court to have been committed between October 15, 1991 and October 28, 1991, the date of October 28, 1991 is the controlling date for *ex post facto* purposes. This is true even if the defendant's conduct relevant to the determination of the guideline range under §1B1.3 (Relevant Conduct) included an act that occurred on November 2, 1991 (after a revised Guidelines Manual took effect).

Background: Subsections (a) and (b)(1) provide that the court should apply the Guidelines Manual in effect on the date the defendant is sentenced unless the court determines that doing so would violate the *ex post facto* clause in Article I, § 9 of the United States Constitution. Under 18 U.S.C. § 3553, the court is to apply the guidelines and policy statements in effect at the time of sentencing. However, the Supreme Court has held that the *ex post facto* clause applies to sentencing guideline amendments that subject the defendant to increased punishment. *See Peugh v. United States*, 133 S. Ct. 2072, 2078 (2013) (holding that "there is an *ex post facto* violation when a defendant is sentenced under Guidelines promulgated after he committed his criminal acts and the new version provides a higher applicable Guidelines sentencing range than the version in place at the time of the offense").

Subsection (b)(2) provides that the Guidelines Manual in effect on a particular date shall be applied in its entirety.

Subsection (b)(3) provides that where the defendant is convicted of two offenses, the first committed before, and the second after, a revised edition of the Guidelines Manual became effective, the revised edition of the Guidelines Manual is to be applied to both offenses, even if the revised edition results in an increased penalty for the first offense. Because the defendant completed the second offense after the amendment to the guidelines took effect, the *ex post facto* clause does not prevent determining the sentence for that count based on the amended guidelines. For example, if a defendant pleads guilty to a single count of embezzlement that occurred after the most recent edition of the Guidelines Manual became effective, the guideline range applicable in sentencing will encompass any relevant conduct (*e.g.*, related embezzlement offenses that may have occurred prior to the effective date of the guideline amendments) for the offense of conviction. The same would be true for a defendant convicted of two counts of embezzlement, one committed before the amendments were enacted, and the second after. In this example, the *ex post facto* clause would not bar application of the amended guideline to the first conviction; a contrary conclusion would mean that such defendant was subject to a lower guideline range than if convicted only of the second offense. Decisions from several appellate courts addressing the analogous situation of the constitutionality of counting pre-guidelines criminal activity as relevant conduct for a guidelines sentence support this approach. *See United States v. Ykema*, 887 F.2d 697 (6th Cir. 1989) (upholding inclusion of pre-November 1, 1987, drug quantities as relevant conduct for the count of conviction, noting that habitual offender statutes routinely augment punishment for an offense of conviction based on acts committed before a law is passed); *United States v. Allen*, 886 F.2d 143 (8th Cir. 1989) (similar); *see also United States v. Cusack*, 901 F.2d 29 (4th Cir. 1990) (similar).

Moreover, the approach set forth in subsection (b)(3) should be followed regardless of whether the offenses of conviction are the type in which the conduct is grouped under §3D1.2(d). The *ex post facto* clause does not distinguish between groupable and nongroupable offenses, and unless that clause would be violated, Congress's directive to apply the sentencing guidelines in effect at the time of sentencing must be followed. Under the guideline sentencing system, a single sentencing range is determined based on the defendant's overall conduct, even if there are multiple counts of conviction (*see* §§3D1.1–3D1.5, 5G1.2). Thus, if a defendant is sentenced in January 1992 for a bank robbery committed in October 1988 and one committed in November 1991, the November 1991 Guidelines Manual should be used to determine a combined guideline range for both counts. *See generally United States v. Stephenson*, 921 F.2d 438 (2d Cir. 1990) (holding that the Sentencing Commission and Congress intended that the applicable version of the guidelines be applied as a "cohesive and integrated whole" rather than in a piecemeal fashion).

Consequently, even in a complex case involving multiple counts that occurred under several different versions of the Guidelines Manual, it will not be necessary to compare more than two manuals to determine the applicable guideline range — the manual in effect at the time the last offense of conviction was completed and the manual in effect at the time of sentencing.

Historical Note	Effective November 1, 1992 (amendment 442). Amended effective November 1, 1993 (amendment 474); November 1, 2010 (amendment 746); November 1, 2013 (amendment 779); November 1, 2015 (amendment 796).

§1B1.12. Persons Sentenced Under the Federal Juvenile Delinquency Act (Policy Statement)

The sentencing guidelines do not apply to a defendant sentenced under the Federal Juvenile Delinquency Act (18 U.S.C. §§ 5031–5042). However, the sentence imposed upon a juvenile delinquent may not exceed the maximum of the guideline range applicable to an otherwise similarly situated adult defendant unless the court finds an aggravating factor sufficient to warrant an upward departure from that guideline range. *United States v. R.L.C.*, 503 U.S. 291 (1992). Therefore, a necessary step in ascertaining the maximum sentence that may be imposed upon a juvenile delinquent is the determination of the guideline range that would be applicable to a similarly situated adult defendant.

Historical Note	Effective November 1, 1993 (amendment 475).

§1B1.13. Reduction in Term of Imprisonment Under 18 U.S.C. § 3582(c)(1)(A) (Policy Statement)

Upon motion of the Director of the Bureau of Prisons under 18 U.S.C. § 3582(c)(1)(A), the court may reduce a term of imprisonment (and may impose a term of supervised release with or without conditions that does not exceed the unserved portion of the original term of imprisonment) if, after considering the factors set forth in 18 U.S.C. § 3553(a), to the extent that they are applicable, the court determines that—

(1) (A) extraordinary and compelling reasons warrant the reduction; or

   (B) the defendant (i) is at least 70 years old; and (ii) has served at least 30 years in prison pursuant to a sentence imposed under 18 U.S.C. § 3559(c) for the offense or offenses for which the defendant is imprisoned;

(2) the defendant is not a danger to the safety of any other person or to the community, as provided in 18 U.S.C. § 3142(g); and

(3) the reduction is consistent with this policy statement.

§1B1.13

Commentary

Application Notes:

1. **Extraordinary and Compelling Reasons.**—Provided the defendant meets the requirements of subdivision (2), extraordinary and compelling reasons exist under any of the circumstances set forth below:

    (A) **Medical Condition of the Defendant.**—

        (i)   The defendant is suffering from a terminal illness (*i.e.*, a serious and advanced illness with an end of life trajectory). A specific prognosis of life expectancy (*i.e.*, a probability of death within a specific time period) is not required. Examples include metastatic solid-tumor cancer, amyotrophic lateral sclerosis (ALS), end-stage organ disease, and advanced dementia.

        (ii) The defendant is—

            (I)   suffering from a serious physical or medical condition,

            (II)   suffering from a serious functional or cognitive impairment, or

            (III) experiencing deteriorating physical or mental health because of the aging process,

            that substantially diminishes the ability of the defendant to provide self-care within the environment of a correctional facility and from which he or she is not expected to recover.

    (B) **Age of the Defendant.**—The defendant (i) is at least 65 years old; (ii) is experiencing a serious deterioration in physical or mental health because of the aging process; and (iii) has served at least 10 years or 75 percent of his or her term of imprisonment, whichever is less.

    (C) **Family Circumstances.**—

        (i)   The death or incapacitation of the caregiver of the defendant's minor child or minor children.

        (ii) The incapacitation of the defendant's spouse or registered partner when the defendant would be the only available caregiver for the spouse or registered partner.

    (D) **Other Reasons.**—As determined by the Director of the Bureau of Prisons, there exists in the defendant's case an extraordinary and compelling reason other than, or in combination with, the reasons described in subdivisions (A) through (C).

2. **Foreseeability of Extraordinary and Compelling Reasons.**—For purposes of this policy statement, an extraordinary and compelling reason need not have been unforeseen at the time of sentencing in order to warrant a reduction in the term of imprisonment. Therefore, the fact that an extraordinary and compelling reason reasonably could have been known or anticipated by the sentencing court does not preclude consideration for a reduction under this policy statement.

3. **Rehabilitation of the Defendant.**—Pursuant to 28 U.S.C. § 994(t), rehabilitation of the defendant is not, by itself, an extraordinary and compelling reason for purposes of this policy statement.

4. **Motion by the Director of the Bureau of Prisons.**—A reduction under this policy statement may be granted only upon motion by the Director of the Bureau of Prisons pursuant to 18 U.S.C. § 3582(c)(1)(A). The Commission encourages the Director of the Bureau of Prisons to file such a motion if the defendant meets any of the circumstances set forth in Application Note 1. The court is in a unique position to determine whether the circumstances warrant a reduction (and, if so, the amount of reduction), after considering the factors set forth 18 U.S.C. § 3553(a) and the criteria set forth in this policy statement, such as the defendant's medical condition, the defendant's family circumstances, and whether the defendant is a danger to the safety of any other person or to the community.

   This policy statement shall not be construed to confer upon the defendant any right not otherwise recognized in law.

5. **Application of Subdivision (3).**—Any reduction made pursuant to a motion by the Director of the Bureau of Prisons for the reasons set forth in subdivisions (1) and (2) is consistent with this policy statement.

Background: The Commission is required by 28 U.S.C. § 994(a)(2) to develop general policy statements regarding application of the guidelines or other aspects of sentencing that in the view of the Commission would further the purposes of sentencing (18 U.S.C. § 3553(a)(2)), including, among other things, the appropriate use of the sentence modification provisions set forth in 18 U.S.C. § 3582(c). In doing so, the Commission is authorized by 28 U.S.C. § 994(t) to "describe what should be considered extraordinary and compelling reasons for sentence reduction, including the criteria to be applied and a list of specific examples." This policy statement implements 28 U.S.C. § 994(a)(2) and (t).

Historical Note	Effective November 1, 2006 (amendment 683). Amended effective November 1, 2007 (amendment 698); November 1, 2010 (amendment 746); November 1, 2016 (amendment 799).

CHAPTER TWO

OFFENSE CONDUCT

Introductory Commentary

Chapter Two pertains to offense conduct. The chapter is organized by offenses and divided into parts and related sections that may cover one statute or many. Each offense has a corresponding base offense level and may have one or more specific offense characteristics that adjust the offense level upward or downward. Certain factors relevant to the offense that are not covered in specific guidelines in Chapter Two are set forth in Chapter Three, Parts A (Victim-Related Adjustments), B (Role in the Offense), and C (Obstruction and Related Adjustments); Chapter Four, Part B (Career Offenders and Criminal Livelihood); and Chapter Five, Part K (Departures).

Historical Note	Effective November 1, 1987. Amended effective November 1, 2011 (amendment 758).

PART A — OFFENSES AGAINST THE PERSON

1. HOMICIDE

§2A1.1. First Degree Murder

    (a)   Base Offense Level: **43**

Commentary

Statutory Provisions: 18 U.S.C. §§ 1111, 1841(a)(2)(C), 1992(a)(7), 2113(e), 2118(c)(2), 2199, 2282A, 2291, 2332b(a)(1), 2340A; 21 U.S.C. § 848(e). For additional statutory provision(s), *see* Appendix A (Statutory Index).

Application Notes:

1.   **Applicability of Guideline.**—This guideline applies in cases of premeditated killing. This guideline also applies when death results from the commission of certain felonies. For example, this guideline may be applied as a result of a cross reference (*e.g.*, a kidnapping in which death occurs, *see* §2A4.1(c)(1)), or in cases in which the offense level of a guideline is calculated using the underlying crime (*e.g.*, murder in aid of racketeering, *see* §2E1.3(a)(2)).

2.   **Imposition of Life Sentence.**—

    (A)   **Offenses Involving Premeditated Killing.**—In the case of premeditated killing, life imprisonment is the appropriate sentence if a sentence of death is not imposed. A downward departure would not be appropriate in such a case. A downward departure from a mandatory statutory term of life imprisonment is permissible only in cases in which the government files a motion for a downward departure for the defendant's substantial assistance, as provided in 18 U.S.C. § 3553(e).

(B) **Felony Murder.**—If the defendant did not cause the death intentionally or knowingly, a downward departure may be warranted. For example, a downward departure may be warranted if in robbing a bank, the defendant merely passed a note to the teller, as a result of which the teller had a heart attack and died. The extent of the departure should be based upon the defendant's state of mind (*e.g.*, recklessness or negligence), the degree of risk inherent in the conduct, and the nature of the underlying offense conduct. However, departure below the minimum guideline sentence provided for second degree murder in §2A1.2 (Second Degree Murder) is not likely to be appropriate. Also, because death obviously is an aggravating factor, it necessarily would be inappropriate to impose a sentence at a level below that which the guideline for the underlying offense requires in the absence of death.

3. **Applicability of Guideline When Death Sentence Not Imposed.**—If the defendant is sentenced pursuant to 18 U.S.C. § 3591 *et seq.* or 21 U.S.C. § 848(e), a sentence of death may be imposed under the specific provisions contained in that statute. This guideline applies when a sentence of death is not imposed under those specific provisions.

Historical Note	Effective November 1, 1987. Amended effective November 1, 1989 (amendment 82); November 1, 1990 (amendment 310); November 1, 1993 (amendment 476); November 1, 2002 (amendment 637); November 1, 2004 (amendment 663); November 1, 2006 (amendment 685); November 1, 2007 (amendments 699 and 700); November 1, 2010 (amendment 746).

§2A1.2. Second Degree Murder

(a) Base Offense Level: **38**

Commentary

Statutory Provisions: 18 U.S.C. §§ 1111, 1841(a)(2)(C), 2199, 2282A, 2291, 2332b(a)(1), 2340A. For additional statutory provision(s), *see* Appendix A (Statutory Index).

Application Note:

1. **Upward Departure Provision.**—If the defendant's conduct was exceptionally heinous, cruel, brutal, or degrading to the victim, an upward departure may be warranted. *See* §5K2.8 (Extreme Conduct).

Historical Note	Effective November 1, 1987. Amended effective November 1, 2002 (amendment 637); November 1, 2004 (amendment 663); November 1, 2006 (amendment 685); November 1, 2007 (amendments 699 and 700).

§2A1.3. Voluntary Manslaughter

(a) Base Offense Level: **29**

Commentary

Statutory Provisions: 18 U.S.C. §§ 1112, 1841(a)(2)(C), 2199, 2291, 2332b(a)(1). For additional statutory provision(s), *see* Appendix A (Statutory Index).

Historical Note	Effective November 1, 1987. Amended effective November 1, 2002 (amendment 637); November 1, 2004 (amendment 663); November 1, 2006 (amendment 685); November 1, 2007 (amendment 699).

§2A1.4. Involuntary Manslaughter

    (a)   Base Offense Level:

        (1)   **12**, if the offense involved criminally negligent conduct; or

        (2)   (Apply the greater):

            (A)   **18**, if the offense involved reckless conduct; or

            (B)   **22**, if the offense involved the reckless operation of a means of transportation.

    (b)   Special Instruction

        (1)   If the offense involved the involuntary manslaughter of more than one person, Chapter Three, Part D (Multiple Counts) shall be applied as if the involuntary manslaughter of each person had been contained in a separate count of conviction.

Commentary

Statutory Provisions: 18 U.S.C. §§ 1112, 1841(a)(2)(C), 2199, 2291, 2332b(a)(1). For additional statutory provision(s), *see* Appendix A (Statutory Index).

Application Note:

1.   **Definitions.**—For purposes of this guideline:

"*Criminally negligent*" means conduct that involves a gross deviation from the standard of care that a reasonable person would exercise under the circumstances, but which is not reckless. Offenses with this characteristic usually will be encountered as assimilative crimes.

"*Means of transportation*" includes a motor vehicle (including an automobile or a boat) and a mass transportation vehicle. "Mass transportation" has the meaning given that term in 18 U.S.C. § 1992(d)(7).

"*Reckless*" means a situation in which the defendant was aware of the risk created by his conduct and the risk was of such a nature and degree that to disregard that risk constituted a gross deviation from the standard of care that a reasonable person would exercise in such a situation. "Reckless" includes all, or nearly all, convictions for involuntary manslaughter under 18 U.S.C. § 1112. A homicide resulting from driving a means of transportation, or similarly dangerous actions, while under the influence of alcohol or drugs ordinarily should be treated as reckless.

Historical Note	Effective November 1, 1987. Amended effective November 1, 2002 (amendment 637); November 1, 2003 (amendment 652); November 1, 2004 (amendment 663); November 1, 2006 (amendment 685); November 1, 2007 (amendment 699).

§2A1.5. Conspiracy or Solicitation to Commit Murder

(a) Base Offense Level: **33**

(b) Specific Offense Characteristic

    (1) If the offense involved the offer or the receipt of anything of pecuniary value for undertaking the murder, increase by **4** levels.

(c) Cross References

    (1) If the offense resulted in the death of a victim, apply §2A1.1 (First Degree Murder).

    (2) If the offense resulted in an attempted murder or assault with intent to commit murder, apply §2A2.1 (Assault with Intent to Commit Murder; Attempted Murder).

Commentary

Statutory Provisions: 18 U.S.C. §§ 351(d), 371, 373, 1117, 1751(d).

Historical Note	Effective November 1, 1990 (amendment 311). Amended effective November 1, 2004 (amendment 663).

* * * * * *

2. ASSAULT

§2A2.1. Assault with Intent to Commit Murder; Attempted Murder

    (a)   Base Offense Level:

        (1)   **33**, if the object of the offense would have constituted first degree murder; or

        (2)   **27**, otherwise.

    (b)   Specific Offense Characteristics

        (1)   If (A) the victim sustained permanent or life-threatening bodily injury, increase by **4** levels; (B) the victim sustained serious bodily injury, increase by **2** levels; or (C) the degree of injury is between that specified in subdivisions (A) and (B), increase by **3** levels.

        (2)   If the offense involved the offer or the receipt of anything of pecuniary value for undertaking the murder, increase by **4** levels.

Commentary

Statutory Provisions: 18 U.S.C. §§ 113(a)(1), 351(c), 1113, 1116(a), 1751(c), 1841(a)(2)(C), 1992(a)(7), 2199, 2291. For additional statutory provision(s), *see* Appendix A (Statutory Index).

Application Notes:

1.   **Definitions.**—For purposes of this guideline:

"*First degree murder*" means conduct that, if committed within the special maritime and territorial jurisdiction of the United States, would constitute first degree murder under 18 U.S.C. § 1111.

"*Permanent or life-threatening bodily injury*" and "*serious bodily injury*" have the meaning given those terms in Application Note 1 of the Commentary to §1B1.1 (Application Instructions).

2.   **Upward Departure Provision.**—If the offense created a substantial risk of death or serious bodily injury to more than one person, an upward departure may be warranted.

Background: This section applies to the offenses of assault with intent to commit murder and attempted murder. An attempted manslaughter, or assault with intent to commit manslaughter, is covered under §2A2.2 (Aggravated Assault).

Historical Note	Effective November 1, 1987. Amended effective November 1, 1989 (amendments 83 and 84); November 1, 1990 (amendment 311); November 1, 1991 (amendment 391); November 1, 1995 (amendment 534); November 1, 2002 (amendment 637); November 1, 2004 (amendment 663); November 1, 2006 (amendment 685); November 1, 2007 (amendment 699).

§2A2.2. Aggravated Assault

(a) Base Offense Level: **14**

(b) Specific Offense Characteristics

    (1) If the assault involved more than minimal planning, increase by **2** levels.

    (2) If (A) a firearm was discharged, increase by **5** levels; (B) a dangerous weapon (including a firearm) was otherwise used, increase by **4** levels; (C) a dangerous weapon (including a firearm) was brandished or its use was threatened, increase by **3** levels.

    (3) If the victim sustained bodily injury, increase the offense level according to the seriousness of the injury:

DEGREE OF BODILY INJURY	INCREASE IN LEVEL
(A) Bodily Injury	add **3**
(B) Serious Bodily Injury	add **5**
(C) Permanent or Life-Threatening Bodily Injury	add **7**
(D) If the degree of injury is between that specified in subdivisions (A) and (B),	add **4** levels; or
(E) If the degree of injury is between that specified in subdivisions (B) and (C),	add **6** levels.

    However, the cumulative adjustments from application of subdivisions (2) and (3) shall not exceed **10** levels.

    (4) If the offense involved strangling, suffocating, or attempting to strangle or suffocate a spouse, intimate partner, or dating partner, increase by **3** levels.

    However, the cumulative adjustments from application of subdivisions (2), (3), and (4) shall not exceed **12** levels.

    (5) If the assault was motivated by a payment or offer of money or other thing of value, increase by **2** levels.

(6) If the offense involved the violation of a court protection order, increase by **2** levels.

(7) If the defendant was convicted under 18 U.S.C. § 111(b) or § 115, increase by **2** levels.

Commentary

Statutory Provisions: 18 U.S.C. §§ 111, 112, 113(a)(2), (3), (6), (8), 114, 115(a), (b)(1), 351(e), 1751(e), 1841(a)(2)(C), 1992(a)(7), 2199, 2291, 2332b(a)(1), 2340A. For additional statutory provision(s), *see* Appendix A (Statutory Index).

Application Notes:

1. **Definitions.**—For purposes of this guideline:

   "*Aggravated assault*" means a felonious assault that involved (A) a dangerous weapon with intent to cause bodily injury (*i.e.*, not merely to frighten) with that weapon; (B) serious bodily injury; (C) strangling, suffocating, or attempting to strangle or suffocate; or (D) an intent to commit another felony.

   "*Brandished*," "*bodily injury*," "*firearm*," "*otherwise used*," "*permanent or life-threatening bodily injury*," and "*serious bodily injury*," have the meaning given those terms in §1B1.1 (Application Instructions), Application Note 1.

   "*Dangerous weapon*" has the meaning given that term in §1B1.1, Application Note 1, and includes any instrument that is not ordinarily used as a weapon (*e.g.*, a car, a chair, or an ice pick) if such an instrument is involved in the offense with the intent to commit bodily injury.

   "*Strangling*" and "*suffocating*" have the meaning given those terms in 18 U.S.C. § 113.

   "*Spouse*," "*intimate partner*," and "*dating partner*" have the meaning given those terms in 18 U.S.C. § 2266.

2. **Application of Subsection (b)(1).**—For purposes of subsection (b)(1), "*more than minimal planning*" means more planning than is typical for commission of the offense in a simple form. "More than minimal planning" also exists if significant affirmative steps were taken to conceal the offense, other than conduct to which §3C1.1 (Obstructing or Impeding the Administration of Justice) applies. For example, waiting to commit the offense when no witnesses were present would not alone constitute more than minimal planning. By contrast, luring the victim to a specific location or wearing a ski mask to prevent identification would constitute more than minimal planning.

3. **Application of Subsection (b)(2).**—In a case involving a dangerous weapon with intent to cause bodily injury, the court shall apply both the base offense level and subsection (b)(2).

4. **Application of Official Victim Adjustment.**—If subsection (b)(7) applies, §3A1.2 (Official Victim) also shall apply.

Background: This guideline covers felonious assaults that are more serious than other assaults because of the presence of an aggravating factor, *i.e.*, serious bodily injury; the involvement of a dangerous weapon with intent to cause bodily injury; strangling, suffocating, or attempting to strangle or suffocate; or the intent to commit another felony. Such offenses occasionally may involve planning or be committed for hire. Consequently, the structure follows §2A2.1 (Assault with Intent to Commit Murder; Attempted Murder). This guideline also covers attempted manslaughter and assault with intent to commit manslaughter. Assault with intent to commit murder is covered by §2A2.1. Assault with intent to commit rape is covered by §2A3.1 (Criminal Sexual Abuse; Attempt to Commit Criminal Sexual Abuse).

An assault that involves the presence of a dangerous weapon is aggravated in form when the presence of the dangerous weapon is coupled with the intent to cause bodily injury. In such a case, the base offense level and the weapon enhancement in subsection (b)(2) take into account different aspects of the offense, even if application of the base offense level and the weapon enhancement is based on the same conduct.

Subsection (b)(7) implements the directive to the Commission in subsection 11008(e) of the 21st Century Department of Justice Appropriations Act (the "Act"), Public Law 107–273. The enhancement in subsection (b)(7) is cumulative to the adjustment in §3A1.2 (Official Victim) in order to address adequately the directive in section 11008(e)(2)(D) of the Act, which provides that the Commission shall consider "the extent to which sentencing enhancements within the Federal guidelines and the authority of the court to impose a sentence in excess of the applicable guideline range are adequate to ensure punishment at or near the maximum penalty for the most egregious conduct covered by" 18 U.S.C. §§ 111 and 115.

Historical Note	Effective November 1, 1987. Amended effective November 1, 1989 (amendments 85 and 86); November 1, 1990 (amendment 311); November 1, 1995 (amendment 534); November 1, 1997 (amendment 549); November 1, 2001 (amendment 614); November 1, 2002 (amendment 637); November 1, 2004 (amendment 663); November 1, 2006 (amendment 685); November 1, 2007 (amendment 699); November 1, 2014 (amendment 781).

§2A2.3. Assault

    (a)   Base Offense Level:

        (1)   **7**, if the offense involved physical contact, or if a dangerous weapon (including a firearm) was possessed and its use was threatened; or

        (2)   **4**, otherwise.

    (b)   Specific Offense Characteristic

        (1)   If (A) the victim sustained bodily injury, increase by **2** levels; or (B) the offense resulted in substantial bodily injury to a spouse, intimate partner, or dating partner, or an individual under the age of sixteen years, increase by **4** levels.

(c) Cross Reference

(1) If the conduct constituted aggravated assault, apply §2A2.2 (Aggravated Assault).

Commentary

Statutory Provisions: 18 U.S.C. §§ 112, 113(a)(4), (5), (7), 115(a), 115(b)(1), 351(e), 1751(e), 2199, 2291. For additional statutory provision(s), *see* Appendix A (Statutory Index).

Application Notes:

1. **Definitions.**—For purposes of this guideline:

   "*Bodily injury*", "*dangerous weapon*", and "*firearm*" have the meaning given those terms in Application Note 1 of the Commentary to §1B1.1 (Application Instructions).

   "*Spouse*," "*intimate partner*," and "*dating partner*" have the meaning given those terms in 18 U.S.C. § 2266.

   "*Substantial bodily injury*" means "bodily injury which involves (A) a temporary but substantial disfigurement; or (B) a temporary but substantial loss or impairment of the function of any bodily member, organ, or mental faculty." *See* 18 U.S.C. § 113(b)(1).

2. **Application of Subsection (b)(1).**—Conduct that forms the basis for application of subsection (a)(1) also may form the basis for application of the enhancement in subsection (b)(1)(A) or (B).

Background: This section applies to misdemeanor assault and battery and to any felonious assault not covered by §2A2.2 (Aggravated Assault).

Historical Note	Effective November 1, 1987. Amended effective October 15, 1988 (amendment 64); November 1, 1989 (amendments 87 and 88); November 1, 1995 (amendment 510); November 1, 2004 (amendment 663); November 1, 2007 (amendment 699); November 1, 2014 (amendment 781).

§2A2.4. Obstructing or Impeding Officers

(a) Base Offense Level: **10**

(b) Specific Offense Characteristics

(1) If (A) the offense involved physical contact; or (B) a dangerous weapon (including a firearm) was possessed and its use was threatened, increase by **3** levels.

(2) If the victim sustained bodily injury, increase by **2** levels.

(c) Cross Reference

    (1) If the conduct constituted aggravated assault, apply §2A2.2 (Aggravated Assault).

Commentary

Statutory Provisions: 18 U.S.C. §§ 111, 1501, 1502, 2237(a)(1), (a)(2)(A), 3056(d). For additional statutory provision(s), *see* Appendix A (Statutory Index).

Application Notes:

1.   **Definitions.**—For purposes of this guideline, "*bodily injury*", "*dangerous weapon*", and "*firearm*" have the meaning given those terms in Application Note 1 of the Commentary to §1B1.1 (Application Instructions).

2.   **Application of Certain Chapter Three Adjustments.**—The base offense level incorporates the fact that the victim was a governmental officer performing official duties. Therefore, do not apply §3A1.2 (Official Victim) unless, pursuant to subsection (c), the offense level is determined under §2A2.2 (Aggravated Assault). Conversely, the base offense level does not incorporate the possibility that the defendant may create a substantial risk of death or serious bodily injury to another person in the course of fleeing from a law enforcement official (although an offense under 18 U.S.C. § 758 for fleeing or evading a law enforcement checkpoint at high speed will often, but not always, involve the creation of that risk). If the defendant creates that risk and no higher guideline adjustment is applicable for the conduct creating the risk, apply §3C1.2 (Reckless Endangerment During Flight).

3.   **Upward Departure Provision.**—The base offense level does not assume any significant disruption of governmental functions. In situations involving such disruption, an upward departure may be warranted. *See* §5K2.7 (Disruption of Governmental Function).

Historical Note	Effective October 15, 1988 (amendment 64). Amended effective November 1, 1989 (amendments 89 and 90); November 1, 1992 (amendment 443); November 1, 1997 (amendment 550); November 1, 2004 (amendment 663); November 1, 2005 (amendment 679); November 1, 2007 (amendment 699).

*   *   *   *   *

3. CRIMINAL SEXUAL ABUSE AND OFFENSES RELATED TO REGISTRATION AS A SEX OFFENDER

Historical Note	Effective November 1, 1987. Amended effective November 1, 2007 (amendment 701).

§2A3.1. Criminal Sexual Abuse; Attempt to Commit Criminal Sexual Abuse

(a) Base Offense Level:

    (1) **38**, if the defendant was convicted under 18 U.S.C. § 2241(c); or

    (2) **30**, otherwise.

(b) Specific Offense Characteristics

    (1) If the offense involved conduct described in 18 U.S.C. § 2241(a) or (b), increase by **4** levels.

    (2) If subsection (a)(2) applies and (A) the victim had not attained the age of twelve years, increase by **4** levels; or (B) the victim had attained the age of twelve years but had not attained the age of sixteen years, increase by **2** levels.

    (3) If the victim was (A) in the custody, care, or supervisory control of the defendant; or (B) a person held in the custody of a correctional facility, increase by **2** levels.

    (4) (A) If the victim sustained permanent or life-threatening bodily injury, increase by **4** levels; (B) if the victim sustained serious bodily injury, increase by **2** levels; or (C) if the degree of injury is between that specified in subdivisions (A) and (B), increase by **3** levels.

    (5) If the victim was abducted, increase by **4** levels.

    (6) If, to persuade, induce, entice, or coerce a minor to engage in prohibited sexual conduct, or if, to facilitate transportation or travel, by a minor or a participant, to engage in prohibited sexual conduct, the offense involved (A) the knowing misrepresentation of a participant's identity; or (B) the use of a computer or an interactive computer service, increase by **2** levels.

(c)   Cross References

    (1)   If a victim was killed under circumstances that would constitute murder under 18 U.S.C. § 1111 had such killing taken place within the territorial or maritime jurisdiction of the United States, apply §2A1.1 (First Degree Murder), if the resulting offense level is greater than that determined above.

    (2)   If the offense involved causing, transporting, permitting, or offering or seeking by notice or advertisement, a minor to engage in sexually explicit conduct for the purpose of producing a visual depiction of such conduct, apply §2G2.1 (Sexually Exploiting a Minor by Production of Sexually Explicit Visual or Printed Material; Custodian Permitting Minor to Engage in Sexually Explicit Conduct; Advertisement for Minors to Engage in Production), if the resulting offense level is greater than that determined above.

(d)   Special Instruction

    (1)   If the offense occurred in the custody or control of a prison or other correctional facility and the victim was a prison official, the offense shall be deemed to have an official victim for purposes of subsection (c)(2) of §3A1.2 (Official Victim).

Commentary

Statutory Provisions: 18 U.S.C. §§ 2241, 2242. For additional statutory provision(s), *see* Appendix A (Statutory Index).

Application Notes:

1.   **Definitions.**—For purposes of this guideline:

"*Abducted*", "*permanent or life-threatening bodily injury*", and "*serious bodily injury*" have the meaning given those terms in Application Note 1 of the Commentary to §1B1.1 (Application Instructions). However, for purposes of this guideline, "*serious bodily injury*" means conduct other than criminal sexual abuse, which already is taken into account in the base offense level under subsection (a).

"*Custody or control*" and "*prison official*" have the meaning given those terms in Application Note 4 of the Commentary to §3A1.2 (Official Victim).

"*Child pornography*" has the meaning given that term in 18 U.S.C. § 2256(8).

"*Computer*" has the meaning given that term in 18 U.S.C. § 1030(e)(1).

"*Distribution*" means any act, including possession with intent to distribute, production, transportation, and advertisement, related to the transfer of material involving the sexual exploitation of a minor. Accordingly, distribution includes posting material involving the sexual exploitation of a minor on a website for public viewing, but does not include the mere solicitation of such material by a defendant.

"*Interactive computer service*" has the meaning given that term in section 230(e)(2) of the Communications Act of 1934 (47 U.S.C. § 230(f)(2)).

"*Minor*" means (A) an individual who had not attained the age of 18 years; (B) an individual, whether fictitious or not, who a law enforcement officer represented to a participant (i) had not attained the age of 18 years, and (ii) could be provided for the purposes of engaging in sexually explicit conduct; or (C) an undercover law enforcement officer who represented to a participant that the officer had not attained the age of 18 years.

"*Participant*" has the meaning given that term in Application Note 1 of the Commentary to §3B1.1 (Aggravating Role).

"*Prohibited sexual conduct*" (A) means any sexual activity for which a person can be charged with a criminal offense; (B) includes the production of child pornography; and (C) does not include trafficking in, or possession of, child pornography.

"*Victim*" includes an undercover law enforcement officer.

2.　**Application of Subsection (b)(1).—**

(A)　**Definitions.—**For purposes of subsection (b)(1), "***conduct described in 18 U.S.C. § 2241(a) or (b)***" is engaging in, or causing another person to engage in, a sexual act with another person by: (A) using force against the victim; (B) threatening or placing the victim in fear that any person will be subject to death, serious bodily injury, or kidnapping; (C) rendering the victim unconscious; or (D) administering by force or threat of force, or without the knowledge or permission of the victim, a drug, intoxicant, or other similar substance and thereby substantially impairing the ability of the victim to appraise or control conduct. This provision would apply, for example, if any dangerous weapon was used or brandished, or in a case in which the ability of the victim to appraise or control conduct was substantially impaired by drugs or alcohol.

(B)　**Application in Cases Involving a Conviction under 18 U.S.C. § 2241(c).—**If the conduct that forms the basis for a conviction under 18 U.S.C. § 2241(c) is that the defendant engaged in conduct described in 18 U.S.C. § 2241(a) or (b), do not apply subsection (b)(1).

3.　**Application of Subsection (b)(3).—**

(A)　**Care, Custody, or Supervisory Control.—**Subsection (b)(3) is to be construed broadly and includes offenses involving a victim less than 18 years of age entrusted to the defendant, whether temporarily or permanently. For example, teachers, day care providers, baby-sitters, or other temporary caretakers are among those who would be subject to this enhancement. In determining whether to apply this enhancement, the court should look to the actual relationship that existed between the defendant and the minor and not simply to the legal status of the defendant-minor relationship.

(B)　**Inapplicability of Chapter Three Adjustment.—**If the enhancement in subsection (b)(3) applies, do not apply §3B1.3 (Abuse of Position of Trust or Use of Special Skill).

4. **Application of Subsection (b)(6).—**

(A) **Misrepresentation of Participant's Identity.**—The enhancement in subsection (b)(6)(A) applies in cases involving the misrepresentation of a participant's identity to (A) persuade, induce, entice, or coerce a minor to engage in prohibited sexual conduct; or (B) facilitate transportation or travel, by a minor or a participant, to engage in prohibited sexual conduct. Subsection (b)(6)(A) is intended to apply only to misrepresentations made directly to a minor or to a person who exercises custody, care, or supervisory control of the minor. Accordingly, the enhancement in subsection (b)(6)(A) would not apply to a misrepresentation made by a participant to an airline representative in the course of making travel arrangements for the minor.

The misrepresentation to which the enhancement in subsection (b)(6)(A) may apply includes misrepresentation of a participant's name, age, occupation, gender, or status, as long as the misrepresentation was made with the intent to (A) persuade, induce, entice, or coerce a minor to engage in prohibited sexual conduct; or (B) facilitate transportation or travel, by a minor or a participant, to engage in prohibited sexual conduct. Accordingly, use of a computer screen name, without such intent, would not be a sufficient basis for application of the enhancement.

(B) **Use of a Computer or Interactive Computer Service.**—Subsection (b)(6)(B) provides an enhancement if a computer or an interactive computer service was used to (i) persuade, induce, entice, or coerce a minor to engage in prohibited sexual conduct; or (ii) facilitate transportation or travel, by a minor or a participant, to engage in prohibited sexual conduct. Subsection (b)(6)(B) is intended to apply only to the use of a computer or an interactive computer service to communicate directly with a minor or with a person who exercises custody, care, or supervisory control of the minor. Accordingly, the enhancement would not apply to the use of a computer or an interactive computer service to obtain airline tickets for the minor from an airline's Internet site.

5. **Application of Subsection (c)(2).—**

(A) **In General.**—The cross reference in subsection (c)(2) is to be construed broadly and includes all instances where the offense involved employing, using, persuading, inducing, enticing, coercing, transporting, permitting, or offering or seeking by notice or advertisement, a minor to engage in sexually explicit conduct for the purpose of producing any visual depiction of such conduct.

(B) **Definition.**—For purposes of subsection (c)(2), "*sexually explicit conduct*" has the meaning given that term in 18 U.S.C. § 2256(2).

6. **Upward Departure Provision.**—If a victim was sexually abused by more than one participant, an upward departure may be warranted. *See* §5K2.8 (Extreme Conduct).

Historical Note	Effective November 1, 1987. Amended effective November 1, 1989 (amendments 91 and 92); November 1, 1991 (amendment 392); November 1, 1992 (amendment 444); November 1, 1993 (amendment 477); November 1, 1995 (amendment 511); November 1, 1997 (amendment 545); November 1, 2000 (amendments 592 and 601); November 1, 2001 (amendment 615); November 1, 2003 (amendment 661); November 1, 2004 (amendment 664); November 1, 2007 (amendment 701); November 1, 2008 (amendment 725).

§2A3.2. Criminal Sexual Abuse of a Minor Under the Age of Sixteen Years (Statutory Rape) or Attempt to Commit Such Acts

(a) Base Offense Level: **18**

(b) Specific Offense Characteristics

(1) If the minor was in the custody, care, or supervisory control of the defendant, increase by **4** levels.

(2) If (A) subsection (b)(1) does not apply; and (B)(i) the offense involved the knowing misrepresentation of a participant's identity to persuade, induce, entice, or coerce the minor to engage in prohibited sexual conduct; or (ii) a participant otherwise unduly influenced the minor to engage in prohibited sexual conduct, increase by **4** levels.

(3) If a computer or an interactive computer service was used to persuade, induce, entice, or coerce the minor to engage in prohibited sexual conduct, increase by **2** levels.

(c) Cross Reference

(1) If the offense involved criminal sexual abuse or attempt to commit criminal sexual abuse (as defined in 18 U.S.C. § 2241 or § 2242), apply §2A3.1 (Criminal Sexual Abuse; Attempt to Commit Criminal Sexual Abuse). If the victim had not attained the age of 12 years, §2A3.1 shall apply, regardless of the "consent" of the victim.

Commentary

Statutory Provision: 18 U.S.C. § 2243(a). For additional statutory provision(s), *see* Appendix A (Statutory Index).

Application Notes:

1. **Definitions.**—For purposes of this guideline:

"*Computer*" has the meaning given that term in 18 U.S.C. § 1030(e)(1).

"*Interactive computer service*" has the meaning given that term in section 230(e)(2) of the Communications Act of 1934 (47 U.S.C. § 230(f)(2)).

"*Minor*" means (A) an individual who had not attained the age of 16 years; (B) an individual, whether fictitious or not, who a law enforcement officer represented to a participant (i) had not attained the age of 16 years, and (ii) could be provided for the purposes of engaging in sexually explicit conduct; or (C) an undercover law enforcement officer who represented to a participant that the officer had not attained the age of 16 years.

"*Participant*" has the meaning given that term in Application Note 1 of §3B1.1 (Aggravating Role).

"*Prohibited sexual conduct*" has the meaning given that term in Application Note 1 of §2A3.1 (Criminal Sexual Abuse; Attempt to Commit Criminal Sexual Abuse).

2.   **Custody, Care, or Supervisory Control Enhancement.—**

    (A)   **In General.—**Subsection (b)(1) is intended to have broad application and is to be applied whenever the minor is entrusted to the defendant, whether temporarily or permanently. For example, teachers, day care providers, baby-sitters, or other temporary caretakers are among those who would be subject to this enhancement. In determining whether to apply this enhancement, the court should look to the actual relationship that existed between the defendant and the minor and not simply to the legal status of the defendant-minor relationship.

    (B)   **Inapplicability of Chapter Three Adjustment.—**If the enhancement in subsection (b)(1) applies, do not apply subsection (b)(2) or §3B1.3 (Abuse of Position of Trust or Use of Special Skill).

3.   **Application of Subsection (b)(2).—**

    (A)   **Misrepresentation of Identity.**—The enhancement in subsection (b)(2)(B)(i) applies in cases involving the misrepresentation of a participant's identity to persuade, induce, entice, or coerce the minor to engage in prohibited sexual conduct. Subsection (b)(2)(B)(i) is intended to apply only to misrepresentations made directly to the minor or to a person who exercises custody, care, or supervisory control of the minor. Accordingly, the enhancement in subsection (b)(2)(B)(i) would not apply to a misrepresentation made by a participant to an airline representative in the course of making travel arrangements for the minor.

        The misrepresentation to which the enhancement in subsection (b)(2)(B)(i) may apply includes misrepresentation of a participant's name, age, occupation, gender, or status, as long as the misrepresentation was made with the intent to persuade, induce, entice, or coerce the minor to engage in prohibited sexual conduct. Accordingly, use of a computer screen name, without such intent, would not be a sufficient basis for application of the enhancement.

    (B)   **Undue Influence.—**In determining whether subsection (b)(2)(B)(ii) applies, the court should closely consider the facts of the case to determine whether a participant's influence over the minor compromised the voluntariness of the minor's behavior. The voluntariness of the minor's behavior may be compromised without prohibited sexual conduct occurring.

        However, subsection (b)(2)(B)(ii) does not apply in a case in which the only "minor" (as defined in Application Note 1) involved in the offense is an undercover law enforcement officer.

        In a case in which a participant is at least 10 years older than the minor, there shall be a rebuttable presumption that subsection (b)(2)(B)(ii) applies. In such a case, some degree of undue influence can be presumed because of the substantial difference in age between the participant and the minor.

4. **Application of Subsection (b)(3).**—Subsection (b)(3) provides an enhancement if a computer or an interactive computer service was used to persuade, induce, entice, or coerce the minor to engage in prohibited sexual conduct. Subsection (b)(3) is intended to apply only to the use of a computer or an interactive computer service to communicate directly with the minor or with a person who exercises custody, care, or supervisory control of the minor.

5. **Cross Reference.**—Subsection (c)(1) provides a cross reference to §2A3.1 (Criminal Sexual Abuse; Attempt to Commit Criminal Sexual Abuse) if the offense involved criminal sexual abuse or attempt to commit criminal sexual abuse, as defined in 18 U.S.C. § 2241 or § 2242. For example, the cross reference to §2A3.1 shall apply if (A) the victim had not attained the age of 12 years (*see* 18 U.S.C. § 2241(c)); (B) the victim had attained the age of 12 years but not attained the age of 16 years, and was placed in fear of death, serious bodily injury, or kidnapping (*see* 18 U.S.C. § 2241(a),(c)); or (C) the victim was threatened or placed in fear other than fear of death, serious bodily injury, or kidnapping (*see* 18 U.S.C. § 2242(1)).

6. **Upward Departure Consideration.**—There may be cases in which the offense level determined under this guideline substantially understates the seriousness of the offense. In such cases, an upward departure may be warranted. For example, an upward departure may be warranted if the defendant committed the criminal sexual act in furtherance of a commercial scheme such as pandering, transporting persons for the purpose of prostitution, or the production of pornography.

Background: This section applies to offenses involving the criminal sexual abuse of an individual who had not attained the age of 16 years. While this section applies to consensual sexual acts prosecuted under 18 U.S.C. § 2243(a) that would be lawful but for the age of the minor, it also applies to cases, prosecuted under 18 U.S.C. § 2243(a), in which a participant took active measure(s) to unduly influence the minor to engage in prohibited sexual conduct and, thus, the voluntariness of the minor's behavior was compromised. A four-level enhancement is provided in subsection (b)(2) for such cases. It is assumed that at least a four-year age difference exists between the minor and the defendant, as specified in 18 U.S.C. § 2243(a). A four-level enhancement is provided in subsection (b)(1) for a defendant who victimizes a minor under his supervision or care. However, if the minor had not attained the age of 12 years, §2A3.1 (Criminal Sexual Abuse; Attempt to Commit Criminal Sexual Abuse) will apply, regardless of the "consent" of the minor.

Historical Note	Effective November 1, 1987. Amended effective November 1, 1989 (amendment 93); November 1, 1991 (amendment 392); November 1, 1992 (amendment 444); November 1, 1995 (amendment 511); November 1, 2000 (amendment 592); November 1, 2001 (amendment 615); November 1, 2004 (amendment 664); November 1, 2009 (amendment 732); November 1, 2010 (amendment 746).

§2A3.3. Criminal Sexual Abuse of a Ward or Attempt to Commit Such Acts

(a) Base Offense Level: 14

(b) Specific Offense Characteristics

    (1) If the offense involved the knowing misrepresentation of a participant's identity to persuade, induce, entice, or coerce a minor to engage in prohibited sexual conduct, increase by **2** levels.

    (2) If a computer or an interactive computer service was used to persuade, induce, entice, or coerce a minor to engage in prohibited sexual conduct, increase by **2** levels.

Commentary

Statutory Provision: 18 U.S.C. § 2243(b). For additional statutory provision(s), *see* Appendix A (Statutory Index).

Application Notes:

1.   **Definitions.**—For purposes of this guideline:

"*Computer*" has the meaning given that term in 18 U.S.C. § 1030(e)(1).

"*Interactive computer service*" has the meaning given that term in section 230(e)(2) of the Communications Act of 1934 (47 U.S.C. § 230(f)(2)).

"*Minor*" means (A) an individual who had not attained the age of 18 years; (B) an individual, whether fictitious or not, who a law enforcement officer represented to a participant (i) had not attained the age of 18 years; and (ii) could be provided for the purposes of engaging in sexually explicit conduct; or (C) an undercover law enforcement officer who represented to a participant that the officer had not attained the age of 18 years.

"*Participant*" has the meaning given that term in Application Note 1 of the Commentary to §3B1.1 (Aggravating Role).

"*Prohibited sexual conduct*" has the meaning given that term in Application Note 1 of the Commentary to §2A3.1 (Criminal Sexual Abuse; Attempt to Commit Criminal Sexual Abuse).

"*Ward*" means a person in official detention under the custodial, supervisory, or disciplinary authority of the defendant.

2.   **Application of Subsection (b)(1).**—The enhancement in subsection (b)(1) applies in cases involving the misrepresentation of a participant's identity to persuade, induce, entice, or coerce a minor to engage in prohibited sexual conduct. Subsection (b)(1) is intended to apply only to misrepresentations made directly to a minor or to a person who exercises custody, care, or supervisory control of the minor.

The misrepresentation to which the enhancement in subsection (b)(1) may apply includes misrepresentation of a participant's name, age, occupation, gender, or status, as long as the misrepresentation was made with the intent to persuade, induce, entice, or coerce a minor to engage in prohibited sexual conduct. Accordingly, use of a computer screen name, without such intent, would not be a sufficient basis for application of the enhancement.

3. **Application of Subsection (b)(2).**—Subsection (b)(2) provides an enhancement if a computer or an interactive computer service was used to persuade, induce, entice, or coerce a minor to engage in prohibited sexual conduct. Subsection (b)(2) is intended to apply only to the use of a computer or an interactive computer service to communicate directly with a minor or with a person who exercises custody, care, or supervisory control of the minor.

4. **Inapplicability of §3B1.3.**—Do not apply §3B1.3 (Abuse of Position of Trust or Use of Special Skill).

Historical Note	Effective November 1, 1987. Amended effective November 1, 1989 (amendment 94); November 1, 1995 (amendment 511); November 1, 2000 (amendment 592); November 1, 2001 (amendment 615); November 1, 2004 (amendment 664); November 1, 2007 (amendment 701); November 1, 2010 (amendment 746).

§2A3.4. Abusive Sexual Contact or Attempt to Commit Abusive Sexual Contact

(a) Base Offense Level:

    (1) **20**, if the offense involved conduct described in 18 U.S.C. § 2241(a) or (b);

    (2) **16**, if the offense involved conduct described in 18 U.S.C. § 2242; or

    (3) **12**, otherwise.

(b) Specific Offense Characteristics

    (1) If the victim had not attained the age of twelve years, increase by **4** levels; but if the resulting offense level is less than **22**, increase to level **22**.

    (2) If the base offense level is determined under subsection (a)(1) or (2), and the victim had attained the age of twelve years but had not attained the age of sixteen years, increase by **2** levels.

    (3) If the victim was in the custody, care, or supervisory control of the defendant, increase by **2** levels.

    (4) If the offense involved the knowing misrepresentation of a participant's identity to persuade, induce, entice, or coerce a minor to engage in prohibited sexual conduct, increase by **2** levels.

(5) If a computer or an interactive computer service was used to persuade, induce, entice, or coerce a minor to engage in prohibited sexual conduct, increase by **2** levels.

(c) Cross References

(1) If the offense involved criminal sexual abuse or attempt to commit criminal sexual abuse (as defined in 18 U.S.C. § 2241 or § 2242), apply §2A3.1 (Criminal Sexual Abuse; Attempt to Commit Criminal Sexual Abuse).

(2) If the offense involved criminal sexual abuse of a minor or attempt to commit criminal sexual abuse of a minor (as defined in 18 U.S.C. § 2243(a)), apply §2A3.2 (Criminal Sexual Abuse of a Minor Under the Age of Sixteen Years (Statutory Rape) or Attempt to Commit Such Acts), if the resulting offense level is greater than that determined above.

Commentary

Statutory Provision: 18 U.S.C. § 2244. For additional statutory provision(s), *see* Appendix A (Statutory Index).

Application Notes:

1. **Definitions.**—For purposes of this guideline:

    "*Computer*" has the meaning given that term in 18 U.S.C. § 1030(e)(1).

    "*Interactive computer service*" has the meaning given that term in section 230(e)(2) of the Communications Act of 1934 (47 U.S.C. § 230(f)(2)).

    "*Minor*" means (A) an individual who had not attained the age of 18 years; (B) an individual, whether fictitious or not, who a law enforcement officer represented to a participant (i) had not attained the age of 18 years, and (ii) could be provided for the purposes of engaging in sexually explicit conduct; or (C) an undercover law enforcement officer who represented to a participant that the officer had not attained the age of 18 years.

    "*Participant*" has the meaning given that term in Application Note 1 of the Commentary to §3B1.1 (Aggravating Role).

    "*Prohibited sexual conduct*" has the meaning given that term in Application Note 1 of the Commentary to §2A3.1 (Criminal Sexual Abuse; Attempt to Commit Criminal Sexual Abuse).

2. **Application of Subsection (a)(1).**—For purposes of subsection (a)(1), "*conduct described in 18 U.S.C. § 2241(a) or (b)*" is engaging in, or causing sexual contact with, or by another person by: (A) using force against the victim; (B) threatening or placing the victim in fear that any person will be subjected to death, serious bodily injury, or kidnapping; (C) rendering the victim unconscious; or (D) administering by force or threat of force, or without the knowledge or permission of the victim, a drug, intoxicant, or other

similar substance and thereby substantially impairing the ability of the victim to appraise or control conduct.

3. **Application of Subsection (a)(2).**—For purposes of subsection (a)(2), "*conduct described in 18 U.S.C. § 2242*" is: (A) engaging in, or causing sexual contact with, or by another person by threatening or placing the victim in fear (other than by threatening or placing the victim in fear that any person will be subjected to death, serious bodily injury, or kidnapping); or (B) engaging in, or causing sexual contact with, or by another person who is incapable of appraising the nature of the conduct or physically incapable of declining participation in, or communicating unwillingness to engage in, the sexual act.

4. **Application of Subsection (b)(3).**—

    (A) **Custody, Care, or Supervisory Control.**—Subsection (b)(3) is intended to have broad application and is to be applied whenever the victim is entrusted to the defendant, whether temporarily or permanently. For example, teachers, day care providers, baby-sitters, or other temporary caretakers are among those who would be subject to this enhancement. In determining whether to apply this enhancement, the court should look to the actual relationship that existed between the defendant and the victim and not simply to the legal status of the defendant-victim relationship.

    (B) **Inapplicability of Chapter Three Adjustment.**—If the enhancement in subsection (b)(3) applies, do not apply §3B1.3 (Abuse of Position of Trust or Use of Special Skill).

5. **Misrepresentation of a Participant's Identity.**—The enhancement in subsection (b)(4) applies in cases involving the misrepresentation of a participant's identity to persuade, induce, entice, or coerce a minor to engage in prohibited sexual conduct. Subsection (b)(4) is intended to apply only to misrepresentations made directly to a minor or to a person who exercises custody, care, or supervisory control of the minor. Accordingly, the enhancement in subsection (b)(4) would not apply to a misrepresentation made by a participant to an airline representative in the course of making travel arrangements for the minor.

    The misrepresentation to which the enhancement in subsection (b)(4) may apply includes misrepresentation of a participant's name, age, occupation, gender, or status, as long as the misrepresentation was made with the intent to persuade, induce, entice, or coerce a minor to engage in prohibited sexual conduct. Accordingly, use of a computer screen name, without such intent, would not be a sufficient basis for application of the enhancement.

6. **Application of Subsection (b)(5).**—Subsection (b)(5) provides an enhancement if a computer or an interactive computer service was used to persuade, induce, entice, or coerce a minor to engage in prohibited sexual conduct. Subsection (b)(5) is intended to apply only to the use of a computer or an interactive computer service to communicate directly with a minor or with a person who exercises custody, care, or supervisory control of the minor.

Background: This section covers abusive sexual contact not amounting to criminal sexual abuse (criminal sexual abuse is covered under §§2A3.1–3.3). Alternative base offense levels are provided to take account of the different means used to commit the offense.

Historical Note	Effective November 1, 1987. Amended effective November 1, 1989 (amendment 95); November 1, 1991 (amendment 392); November 1, 1992 (amendment 444); November 1, 1995 (amendment 511); November 1, 2000 (amendment 592); November 1, 2001 (amendment 615); November 1, 2004 (amendment 664); November 1, 2007 (amendments 701 and 711).

§2A3.5. Failure to Register as a Sex Offender

    (a)   Base Offense Level (Apply the greatest):

        (1)   **16**, if the defendant was required to register as a Tier III offender;

        (2)   **14**, if the defendant was required to register as a Tier II offender; or

        (3)   **12**, if the defendant was required to register as a Tier I offender.

    (b)   Specific Offense Characteristics

        (1)   (Apply the greatest):

             If, while in a failure to register status, the defendant committed—

            (A)   a sex offense against someone other than a minor, increase by **6** levels;

            (B)   a felony offense against a minor not otherwise covered by subdivision (C), increase by **6** levels; or

            (C)   a sex offense against a minor, increase by **8** levels.

        (2)   If the defendant voluntarily (A) corrected the failure to register; or (B) attempted to register but was prevented from registering by uncontrollable circumstances and the defendant did not contribute to the creation of those circumstances, decrease by **3** levels.

Commentary

Statutory Provision: 18 U.S.C. § 2250(a).

Application Notes:

1.   **Definitions.**—For purposes of this guideline:

"*Minor*" means (A) an individual who had not attained the age of 18 years; (B) an individual, whether fictitious or not, who a law enforcement officer represented to a participant (i) had not attained the age of 18 years; and (ii) could be provided for the purposes of engaging in sexually explicit conduct; or (C) an undercover law enforcement officer who represented to a participant that the officer had not attained the age of 18 years.

"*Sex offense*" has the meaning given that term in 42 U.S.C. § 16911(5).

"*Tier I offender*", "*Tier II offender*", and "*Tier III offender*" have the meaning given the terms "tier I sex offender", "tier II sex offender", and "tier III sex offender", respectively, in 42 U.S.C. § 16911.

2.   **Application of Subsection (b)(2).—**

   (A)   **In General.**—In order for subsection (b)(2) to apply, the defendant's voluntary attempt to register or to correct the failure to register must have occurred prior to the time the defendant knew or reasonably should have known a jurisdiction had detected the failure to register.

   (B)   **Interaction with Subsection (b)(1).**—Do not apply subsection (b)(2) if subsection (b)(1) also applies.

Historical Note   Effective November 1, 2007 (amendments 701 and 711). Amended effective November 1, 2010 (amendment 746).

§2A3.6.   Aggravated Offenses Relating to Registration as a Sex Offender

If the defendant was convicted under—

   (a)   18 U.S.C. § 2250(c), the guideline sentence is the minimum term of imprisonment required by statute; or

   (b)   18 U.S.C. § 2260A, the guideline sentence is the term of imprisonment required by statute.

Chapters Three (Adjustments) and Four (Criminal History and Criminal Livelihood) shall not apply to any count of conviction covered by this guideline.

Commentary

Statutory Provisions: 18 U.S.C. §§ 2250(c), 2260A.

Application Notes:

1.   **In General.**—Section 2250(c) of title 18, United States Code, provides a mandatory minimum term of five years' imprisonment and a statutory maximum term of 30 years' imprisonment. The statute also requires a sentence to be imposed consecutively to any sentence imposed for a conviction under 18 U.S.C. § 2250(a). Section 2260A of title 18,

United States Code, provides a term of imprisonment of 10 years that is required to be imposed consecutively to any sentence imposed for an offense enumerated under that section.

2. **Inapplicability of Chapters Three and Four.**—Do not apply Chapters Three (Adjustments) and Four (Criminal History and Criminal Livelihood) to any offense sentenced under this guideline. Such offenses are excluded from application of those chapters because the guideline sentence for each offense is determined only by the relevant statute. *See* §§3D1.1 (Procedure for Determining Offense Level on Multiple Counts) and 5G1.2 (Sentencing on Multiple Counts of Conviction).

3. **Inapplicability of Chapter Two Enhancement.**—If a sentence under this guideline is imposed in conjunction with a sentence for an underlying offense, do not apply any specific offense characteristic that is based on the same conduct as the conduct comprising the conviction under 18 U.S.C. § 2250(c) or § 2260A.

4. **Upward Departure.**—In a case in which the guideline sentence is determined under subsection (a), a sentence above the minimum term required by 18 U.S.C. § 2250(c) is an upward departure from the guideline sentence. A departure may be warranted, for example, in a case involving a sex offense committed against a minor or if the offense resulted in serious bodily injury to a minor.

Historical Note	Effective November 1, 2007 (amendment 701).

* * * * *

4. KIDNAPPING, ABDUCTION, OR UNLAWFUL RESTRAINT

§2A4.1. Kidnapping, Abduction, Unlawful Restraint

(a)   Base Offense Level: **32**

(b)   Specific Offense Characteristics

(1)   If a ransom demand or a demand upon government was made, increase by **6** levels.

(2)   (A) If the victim sustained permanent or life-threatening bodily injury, increase by **4** levels; (B) if the victim sustained serious bodily injury, increase by **2** levels; or (C) if the degree of injury is between that specified in subdivisions (A) and (B), increase by **3** levels.

(3)   If a dangerous weapon was used, increase by **2** levels.

(4)   (A)   If the victim was not released before thirty days had elapsed, increase by **2** levels.

      (B) If the victim was not released before seven days had elapsed, increase by **1** level.

  (5) If the victim was sexually exploited, increase by **6** levels.

  (6) If the victim is a minor and, in exchange for money or other consideration, was placed in the care or custody of another person who had no legal right to such care or custody of the victim, increase by **3** levels.

  (7) If the victim was kidnapped, abducted, or unlawfully restrained during the commission of, or in connection with, another offense or escape therefrom; or if another offense was committed during the kidnapping, abduction, or unlawful restraint, increase to—

      (A) the offense level from the Chapter Two offense guideline applicable to that other offense if such offense guideline includes an adjustment for kidnapping, abduction, or unlawful restraint, or otherwise takes such conduct into account; or

      (B) **4** plus the offense level from the offense guideline applicable to that other offense, but in no event greater than level **43**, in any other case,

      if the resulting offense level is greater than that determined above.

  (c) Cross Reference

    (1) If the victim was killed under circumstances that would constitute murder under 18 U.S.C. § 1111 had such killing taken place within the territorial or maritime jurisdiction of the United States, apply §2A1.1 (First Degree Murder).

Commentary

Statutory Provisions: 18 U.S.C. §§ 115(b)(2), 351(b), (d), 1201, 1203, 1751(b), 2340A. For additional statutory provision(s), *see* Appendix A (Statutory Index).

Application Notes:

1.   For purposes of this guideline—

Definitions of "***serious bodily injury***" and "***permanent or life-threatening bodily injury***" are found in the Commentary to §1B1.1 (Application Instructions). However, for purposes of this guideline, "***serious bodily injury***" means conduct other than criminal sexual abuse, which is taken into account in the specific offense characteristic under subsection (b)(5).

2. "***A dangerous weapon was used***" means that a firearm was discharged, or a "firearm" or "dangerous weapon" was "otherwise used" (as defined in the Commentary to §1B1.1 (Application Instructions)).

3. "***Sexually exploited***" includes offenses set forth in 18 U.S.C. §§ 2241–2244, 2251, and 2421–2423.

4. In the case of a conspiracy, attempt, or solicitation to kidnap, §2X1.1 (Attempt, Solicitation, or Conspiracy) requires that the court apply any adjustment that can be determined with reasonable certainty. Therefore, for example, if an offense involved conspiracy to kidnap for the purpose of committing murder, subsection (b)(7) would reference first degree murder (resulting in an offense level of 43, subject to a possible 3-level reduction under §2X1.1(b)).

    Similarly, for example, if an offense involved a kidnapping during which a participant attempted to murder the victim under circumstances that would have constituted first degree murder had death occurred, the offense referenced under subsection (b)(7) would be the offense of first degree murder.

Background: Federal kidnapping cases generally encompass three categories of conduct: limited duration kidnapping where the victim is released unharmed; kidnapping that occurs as part of or to facilitate the commission of another offense (often, sexual assault); and kidnapping for ransom or political demand.

The guideline contains an adjustment for the length of time that the victim was detained. The adjustment recognizes the increased suffering involved in lengthy kidnappings and provides an incentive to release the victim.

An enhancement is provided when the offense is committed for ransom (subsection (b)(1)) or involves another federal, state, or local offense that results in a greater offense level (subsections (b)(7) and (c)(1)).

Section 401 of Public Law 101–647 amended 18 U.S.C. § 1201 to require that courts take into account certain specific offense characteristics in cases involving a victim under eighteen years of age and directed the Commission to include those specific offense characteristics within the guidelines. Where the guidelines did not already take into account the conduct identified by the Act, additional specific offense characteristics have been provided.

Subsections (a) and (b)(5), and the deletion of subsection (b)(4)(C), effective May 30, 2003, implement the directive to the Commission in section 104 of Public Law 108–21.

Historical Note	Effective November 1, 1987. Amended effective November 1, 1989 (amendment 96); November 1, 1991 (amendment 363); November 1, 1992 (amendment 445); November 1, 1993 (amendment 478); November 1, 1997 (amendment 545); November 1, 2002 (amendment 637); May 30, 2003 (amendment 650); October 27, 2003 (amendment 651).

§2A4.2. Demanding or Receiving Ransom Money

    (a)   Base Offense Level: **23**

    (b)   Cross Reference

        (1)   If the defendant was a participant in the kidnapping offense, apply §2A4.1 (Kidnapping, Abduction, Unlawful Restraint).

Commentary

Statutory Provisions: 18 U.S.C. §§ 876, 877, 1202. For additional statutory provision(s), *see* Appendix A (Statutory Index).

Application Note:

1.   A "*participant*" is a person who is criminally responsible for the commission of the offense, but need not have been convicted.

Background: This section specifically includes conduct prohibited by 18 U.S.C. § 1202, requiring that ransom money be received, possessed, or disposed of with knowledge of its criminal origins. The actual demand for ransom under these circumstances is reflected in §2A4.1. This section additionally includes extortionate demands through the use of the United States Postal Service, behavior proscribed by 18 U.S.C. §§ 876–877.

Historical Note	Effective November 1, 1987. Amended effective November 1, 1993 (amendment 479).

*   *   *   *   *

5.   AIR PIRACY AND OFFENSES AGAINST MASS TRANSPORTATION SYSTEMS

Historical Note	Effective November 1, 1987. Amended effective November 1, 2002 (amendment 637).

§2A5.1. Aircraft Piracy or Attempted Aircraft Piracy

    (a)   Base Offense Level: **38**

    (b)   Specific Offense Characteristic

        (1)   If death resulted, increase by **5** levels.

Commentary

Statutory Provisions: 49 U.S.C. § 46502(a), (b) (formerly 49 U.S.C. § 1472 (i), (n)). For additional statutory provision(s), *see* Appendix A (Statutory Index).

Background: This section covers aircraft piracy both within the special aircraft jurisdiction of the United States, 49 U.S.C. § 46502(a), and aircraft piracy outside that jurisdiction when the defendant is later found in the United States, 49 U.S.C. § 46502(b). Seizure of control of an aircraft may be by force or violence, or threat of force or violence, or by any other form of intimidation. The presence of a weapon is assumed in the base offense level.

Historical Note	Effective November 1, 1987. Amended effective November 1, 1995 (amendment 534).

§2A5.2. Interference with Flight Crew Member or Flight Attendant; Interference with Dispatch, Navigation, Operation, or Maintenance of Mass Transportation Vehicle

(a) Base Offense Level (Apply the greatest):

    (1) **30**, if the offense involved intentionally endangering the safety of: (A) an airport or an aircraft; or (B) a mass transportation facility or a mass transportation vehicle;

    (2) **18**, if the offense involved recklessly endangering the safety of: (A) an airport or an aircraft; or (B) a mass transportation facility or a mass transportation vehicle;

    (3) if an assault occurred, the offense level from the most analogous assault guideline, §§2A2.1–2A2.4; or

    (4) **9**.

(b) Specific Offense Characteristic

    (1) If (A) subsection (a)(1) or (a)(2) applies; and (B)(i) a firearm was discharged, increase by **5** levels; (ii) a dangerous weapon was otherwise used, increase by **4** levels; or (iii) a dangerous weapon was brandished or its use was threatened, increase by **3** levels. If the resulting offense level is less than level **24**, increase to level **24**.

(c) Cross References

(1) If death resulted, apply the most analogous guideline from Chapter Two, Part A, Subpart 1 (Homicide), if the resulting offense level is greater than that determined above.

(2) If the offense involved possession of, or a threat to use (A) a nuclear weapon, nuclear material, or nuclear byproduct material; (B) a chemical weapon; (C) a biological agent, toxin, or delivery system; or (D) a weapon of mass destruction, apply §2M6.1 (Nuclear, Biological, and Chemical Weapons, and Other Weapons of Mass Destruction), if the resulting offense level is greater than that determined above.

Commentary

Statutory Provisions: 18 U.S.C. § 1992(a)(1), (a)(4), (a)(5), (a)(6); 49 U.S.C. §§ 46308, 46503, 46504 (formerly 49 U.S.C. § 1472(c), (j)). For additional statutory provision(s), *see* Appendix A (Statutory Index).

Application Note:

1. **Definitions.**—For purposes of this guideline:

    "*Biological agent*", "*chemical weapon*", "*nuclear byproduct material*", "*nuclear material*", "*toxin*", and "*weapon of mass destruction*" have the meaning given those terms in Application Note 1 of the Commentary to §2M6.1 (Nuclear, Biological, and Chemical Weapons, and Other Weapons of Mass Destruction).

    "*Brandished*", "*dangerous weapon*", "*firearm*", and "*otherwise used*" have the meaning given those terms in Application Note 1 of the Commentary to §1B1.1 (Application Instructions).

    "*Mass transportation*" has the meaning given that term in 18 U.S.C. § 1992(d)(7).

Historical Note	Effective November 1, 1987. Amended effective November 1, 1989 (amendments 97 and 303); November 1, 1993 (amendment 480); November 1, 1995 (amendment 534); November 1, 2002 (amendment 637); November 1, 2007 (amendment 699).

§2A5.3. Committing Certain Crimes Aboard Aircraft

(a) Base Offense Level: The offense level applicable to the underlying offense.

Commentary

Statutory Provision: 49 U.S.C. § 46506 (formerly 49 U.S.C. § 1472(k)(1)).

Application Notes:

1. "*Underlying offense*" refers to the offense listed in 49 U.S.C. § 46506 of which the defendant is convicted.

2. If the conduct intentionally or recklessly endangered the safety of the aircraft or passengers, an upward departure may be warranted.

Historical Note	Effective October 15, 1988 (amendment 65). Amended effective November 1, 1989 (amendment 98); November 1, 1995 (amendment 534).

*   *   *   *   *

6. THREATENING OR HARASSING COMMUNICATIONS, HOAXES, STALKING, AND DOMESTIC VIOLENCE

Historical Note	Effective November 1, 1987. Amended effective November 1, 1997 (amendment 549); November 1, 2006 (amendment 686).

§2A6.1. Threatening or Harassing Communications; Hoaxes; False Liens

(a) Base Offense Level:

   (1) **12**; or

   (2) **6**, if the defendant is convicted of an offense under 47 U.S.C. § 223(a)(1)(C), (D), or (E) that did not involve a threat to injure a person or property.

(b) Specific Offense Characteristics

   (1) If the offense involved any conduct evidencing an intent to carry out such threat, increase by **6** levels.

   (2) If (A) the offense involved more than two threats; or (B) the defendant is convicted under 18 U.S.C. § 1521 and the offense involved more than two false liens or encumbrances, increase by **2** levels.

   (3) If the offense involved the violation of a court protection order, increase by **2** levels.

(4) If the offense resulted in (A) substantial disruption of public, governmental, or business functions or services; or (B) a substantial expenditure of funds to clean up, decontaminate, or otherwise respond to the offense, increase by **4** levels.

(5) If the defendant (A) is convicted under 18 U.S.C. § 115, (B) made a public threatening communication, and (C) knew or should have known that the public threatening communication created a substantial risk of inciting others to violate 18 U.S.C. § 115, increase by **2** levels.

(6) If (A) subsection (a)(2) and subdivisions (1), (2), (3), (4), and (5) do not apply, and (B) the offense involved a single instance evidencing little or no deliberation, decrease by **4** levels.

(c) Cross Reference

(1) If the offense involved any conduct evidencing an intent to carry out a threat to use a weapon of mass destruction, as defined in 18 U.S.C. § 2332a(c)(2)(B), (C), and (D), apply §2M6.1 (Weapons of Mass Destruction), if the resulting offense level is greater than that determined under this guideline.

Commentary

Statutory Provisions: 18 U.S.C. §§ 32(c), 35(b); 871, 876, 877, 878(a), 879, 1038, 1521, 1992(a)(9), (a)(10), 2291(a)(8), 2291(e), 2292, 2332b(a)(2); 47 U.S.C. § 223(a)(1)(C)–(E); 49 U.S.C. § 46507. For additional statutory provision(s), *see* Appendix A (Statutory Index).

Application Notes:

1. **Scope of Conduct to Be Considered.**—In determining whether subsections (b)(1), (b)(2), and (b)(3) apply, the court shall consider both conduct that occurred prior to the offense and conduct that occurred during the offense; however, conduct that occurred prior to the offense must be substantially and directly connected to the offense, under the facts of the case taken as a whole. For example, if the defendant engaged in several acts of mailing threatening letters to the same victim over a period of years (including acts that occurred prior to the offense), then for purposes of determining whether subsections (b)(1), (b)(2), and (b)(3) apply, the court shall consider only those prior acts of threatening the victim that have a substantial and direct connection to the offense.

2. **Applicability of Chapter Three Adjustments.**—If the defendant is convicted under 18 U.S.C. § 1521, apply §3A1.2 (Official Victim).

3. **Grouping.**—For purposes of Chapter Three, Part D (Multiple Counts), multiple counts involving making a threatening or harassing communication to the same victim are grouped together under §3D1.2 (Groups of Closely Related Counts). Multiple counts involving different victims are not to be grouped under §3D1.2.

4.   **Departure Provisions.—**

   (A)   **In General.**—The Commission recognizes that offenses covered by this guideline may include a particularly wide range of conduct and that it is not possible to include all of the potentially relevant circumstances in the offense level. Factors not incorporated in the guideline may be considered by the court in determining whether a departure from the guidelines is warranted. *See* Chapter Five, Part K (Departures).

   (B)   **Multiple Threats, False Liens or Encumbrances, or Victims; Pecuniary Harm.**—If the offense involved (i) substantially more than two threatening communications to the same victim, (ii) a prolonged period of making harassing communications to the same victim, (iii) substantially more than two false liens or encumbrances against the real or personal property of the same victim, (iv) multiple victims, or (v) substantial pecuniary harm to a victim, an upward departure may be warranted.

Background: These statutes cover a wide range of conduct, the seriousness of which depends upon the defendant's intent and the likelihood that the defendant would carry out the threat. The specific offense characteristics are intended to distinguish such cases.

Subsection (b)(5) implements, in a broader form, the directive to the Commission in section 209 of the Court Security Improvement Act of 2007, Public Law 110–177.

Historical Note	Effective November 1, 1987. Amended effective November 1, 1993 (amendment 480); November 1, 1997 (amendment 549); November 1, 2002 (amendment 637); November 1, 2006 (amendment 686); November 1, 2007 (amendment 699); November 1, 2008 (amendment 718); November 1, 2009 (amendment 729).

§2A6.2.   Stalking or Domestic Violence

   (a)   Base Offense Level: **18**

   (b)   Specific Offense Characteristic

   (1)   If the offense involved one of the following aggravating factors: (A) the violation of a court protection order; (B) bodily injury; (C) strangling, suffocating, or attempting to strangle or suffocate; (D) possession, or threatened use, of a dangerous weapon; or (E) a pattern of activity involving stalking, threatening, harassing, or assaulting the same victim, increase by **2** levels. If the offense involved more than one of subdivisions (A), (B), (C), (D), or (E), increase by **4** levels.

   (c)   Cross Reference

   (1)   If the offense involved the commission of another criminal offense, apply the offense guideline from Chapter Two, Part A (Offenses Against the Person) most applicable to that other

criminal offense, if the resulting offense level is greater than that determined above.

Commentary

Statutory Provisions: 18 U.S.C. §§ 2261–2262.

Application Notes:

1. For purposes of this guideline:

   "*Bodily injury*" and "*dangerous weapon*" are defined in the Commentary to §1B1.1 (Application Instructions).

   "*Pattern of activity involving stalking, threatening, harassing, or assaulting the same victim*" means any combination of two or more separate instances of stalking, threatening, harassing, or assaulting the same victim, whether or not such conduct resulted in a conviction. For example, a single instance of stalking accompanied by a separate instance of threatening, harassing, or assaulting the same victim constitutes a pattern of activity for purposes of this guideline.

   "*Stalking*" means conduct described in 18 U.S.C. § 2261A.

   "*Strangling*" and "*suffocating*" have the meaning given those terms in 18 U.S.C. § 113.

2. Subsection (b)(1) provides for a two-level or four-level enhancement based on the degree to which the offense involved aggravating factors listed in that subsection. If the offense involved aggravating factors more serious than the factors listed in subsection (b)(1), the cross reference in subsection (c) most likely will apply, if the resulting offense level is greater, because the more serious conduct will be covered by another offense guideline from Chapter Two, Part A. For example, §2A2.2 (Aggravated Assault) most likely would apply pursuant to subsection (c) if the offense involved assaultive conduct in which injury more serious than bodily injury occurred or if a dangerous weapon was used rather than merely possessed.

3. In determining whether subsection (b)(1)(E) applies, the court shall consider, under the totality of the circumstances, any conduct that occurred prior to or during the offense; however, conduct that occurred prior to the offense must be substantially and directly connected to the offense. For example, if a defendant engaged in several acts of stalking the same victim over a period of years (including acts that occurred prior to the offense), then for purposes of determining whether subsection (b)(1)(E) applies, the court shall look to the totality of the circumstances, considering only those prior acts of stalking the victim that have a substantial and direct connection to the offense.

   Prior convictions taken into account under subsection (b)(1)(E) are also counted for purposes of determining criminal history points pursuant to Chapter Four, Part A (Criminal History).

4. For purposes of Chapter Three, Part D (Multiple Counts), multiple counts involving stalking, threatening, or harassing the same victim are grouped together (and with counts of other offenses involving the same victim that are covered by this guideline) under §3D1.2 (Groups of Closely Related Counts). For example, if the defendant is convicted of two counts of stalking the defendant's ex-spouse under 18 U.S.C. § 2261A and

one count of interstate domestic violence involving an assault of the ex-spouse under 18 U.S.C. § 2261, the stalking counts would be grouped together with the interstate domestic violence count. This grouping procedure avoids unwarranted "double counting" with the enhancement in subsection (b)(1)(E) (for multiple acts of stalking, threatening, harassing, or assaulting the same victim) and recognizes that the stalking and interstate domestic violence counts are sufficiently related to warrant grouping.

Multiple counts that are cross referenced to another offense guideline pursuant to subsection (c) are to be grouped together if §3D1.2 (Groups of Closely Related Counts) would require grouping of those counts under that offense guideline. Similarly, multiple counts cross referenced pursuant to subsection (c) are not to be grouped together if §3D1.2 would preclude grouping of the counts under that offense guideline. For example, if the defendant is convicted of multiple counts of threatening an ex-spouse in violation of a court protection order under 18 U.S.C. § 2262 and the counts are cross referenced to §2A6.1 (Threatening or Harassing Communications), the counts would group together because Application Note 3 of §2A6.1 specifically requires grouping. In contrast, if the defendant is convicted of multiple counts of assaulting the ex-spouse in violation of a court protection order under 18 U.S.C. § 2262 and the counts are cross referenced to §2A2.2 (Aggravated Assault), the counts probably would not group together inasmuch as §3D1.2(d) specifically precludes grouping of counts covered by §2A2.2 and no other provision of §3D1.2 would likely apply to require grouping.

Multiple counts involving different victims are not to be grouped under §3D1.2 (Groups of Closely Related Counts).

5. If the defendant received an enhancement under subsection (b)(1) but that enhancement does not adequately reflect the extent or seriousness of the conduct involved, an upward departure may be warranted. For example, an upward departure may be warranted if the defendant stalked the victim on many occasions over a prolonged period of time.

Historical *Note*	Effective November 1, 1997 (amendment 549). Amended effective November 1, 2001 (amendment 616); November 1, 2009 (amendment 737); November 1, 2014 (amendment 781).

PART B — BASIC ECONOMIC OFFENSES

1. THEFT, EMBEZZLEMENT, RECEIPT OF STOLEN PROPERTY, PROPERTY DESTRUCTION, AND OFFENSES INVOLVING FRAUD OR DECEIT

Introductory Commentary

These sections address basic forms of property offenses: theft, embezzlement, fraud, forgery, counterfeiting (other than offenses involving altered or counterfeit bearer obligations of the United States), insider trading, transactions in stolen goods, and simple property damage or destruction. (Arson is dealt with separately in Chapter Two, Part K (Offenses Involving Public Safety)). These guidelines apply to offenses prosecuted under a wide variety of federal statutes, as well as offenses that arise under the Assimilative Crimes Act.

Historical Note	Effective November 1, 1987. Amended effective November 1, 1989 (amendment 303); November 1, 2001 (amendment 617).

§2B1.1. Larceny, Embezzlement, and Other Forms of Theft; Offenses Involving Stolen Property; Property Damage or Destruction; Fraud and Deceit; Forgery; Offenses Involving Altered or Counterfeit Instruments Other than Counterfeit Bearer Obligations of the United States

(a) Base Offense Level:

    (1) **7**, if (A) the defendant was convicted of an offense referenced to this guideline; and (B) that offense of conviction has a statutory maximum term of imprisonment of 20 years or more; or

    (2) **6**, otherwise.

(b) Specific Offense Characteristics

    (1) If the loss exceeded $6,500, increase the offense level as follows:

	Loss (Apply the Greatest)	Increase in Level
(A)	$6,500 or less	no increase
(B)	More than $6,500	add **2**
(C)	More than $15,000	add **4**
(D)	More than $40,000	add **6**
(E)	More than $95,000	add **8**
(F)	More than $150,000	add **10**
(G)	More than $250,000	add **12**
(H)	More than $550,000	add **14**
(I)	More than $1,500,000	add **16**

(J)	More than $3,500,000	add **18**
(K)	More than $9,500,000	add **20**
(L)	More than $25,000,000	add **22**
(M)	More than $65,000,000	add **24**
(N)	More than $150,000,000	add **26**
(O)	More than $250,000,000	add **28**
(P)	More than $550,000,000	add **30**.

(2)   (Apply the greatest) If the offense—

    (A)   (i) involved 10 or more victims; (ii) was committed through mass-marketing; or (iii) resulted in substantial financial hardship to one or more victims, increase by **2** levels;

    (B)   resulted in substantial financial hardship to five or more victims, increase by **4** levels; or

    (C)   resulted in substantial financial hardship to 25 or more victims, increase by **6** levels.

(3)   If the offense involved a theft from the person of another, increase by **2** levels.

(4)   If the offense involved receiving stolen property, and the defendant was a person in the business of receiving and selling stolen property, increase by **2** levels.

(5)   If the offense involved theft of, damage to, destruction of, or trafficking in, property from a national cemetery or veterans' memorial, increase by **2** levels.

(6)   If (A) the defendant was convicted of an offense under 18 U.S.C. § 1037; and (B) the offense involved obtaining electronic mail addresses through improper means, increase by **2** levels.

(7)   If (A) the defendant was convicted of a Federal health care offense involving a Government health care program; and (B) the loss under subsection (b)(1) to the Government health care program was (i) more than $1,000,000, increase by **2** levels; (ii) more than $7,000,000, increase by **3** levels; or (iii) more than $20,000,000, increase by **4** levels.

(8)   (Apply the greater) If—

    (A)   the offense involved conduct described in 18 U.S.C. § 670, increase by **2** levels; or

(B) the offense involved conduct described in 18 U.S.C. § 670, and the defendant was employed by, or was an agent of, an organization in the supply chain for the pre-retail medical product, increase by **4** levels.

(9) If the offense involved (A) a misrepresentation that the defendant was acting on behalf of a charitable, educational, religious, or political organization, or a government agency; (B) a misrepresentation or other fraudulent action during the course of a bankruptcy proceeding; (C) a violation of any prior, specific judicial or administrative order, injunction, decree, or process not addressed elsewhere in the guidelines; or (D) a misrepresentation to a consumer in connection with obtaining, providing, or furnishing financial assistance for an institution of higher education, increase by **2** levels. If the resulting offense level is less than level **10**, increase to level **10**.

(10) If (A) the defendant relocated, or participated in relocating, a fraudulent scheme to another jurisdiction to evade law enforcement or regulatory officials; (B) a substantial part of a fraudulent scheme was committed from outside the United States; or (C) the offense otherwise involved sophisticated means and the defendant intentionally engaged in or caused the conduct constituting sophisticated means, increase by **2** levels. If the resulting offense level is less than level **12**, increase to level **12**.

(11) If the offense involved (A) the possession or use of any (i) device-making equipment, or (ii) authentication feature; (B) the production or trafficking of any (i) unauthorized access device or counterfeit access device, or (ii) authentication feature; or (C)(i) the unauthorized transfer or use of any means of identification unlawfully to produce or obtain any other means of identification, or (ii) the possession of 5 or more means of identification that unlawfully were produced from, or obtained by the use of, another means of identification, increase by **2** levels. If the resulting offense level is less than level **12**, increase to level **12**.

(12) If the offense involved conduct described in 18 U.S.C. § 1040, increase by **2** levels. If the resulting offense level is less than level **12**, increase to level **12**.

(13) (Apply the greater) If the offense involved misappropriation of a trade secret and the defendant knew or intended—

(A) that the trade secret would be transported or transmitted out of the United States, increase by **2** levels; or

(B) that the offense would benefit a foreign government, foreign instrumentality, or foreign agent, increase by **4** levels.

If subparagraph (B) applies and the resulting offense level is less than level **14**, increase to level **14**.

(14) If the offense involved an organized scheme to steal or to receive stolen (A) vehicles or vehicle parts; or (B) goods or chattels that are part of a cargo shipment, increase by **2** levels. If the resulting offense level is less than level **14**, increase to level **14**.

(15) If the offense involved (A) the conscious or reckless risk of death or serious bodily injury; or (B) possession of a dangerous weapon (including a firearm) in connection with the offense, increase by **2** levels. If the resulting offense level is less than level **14**, increase to level **14**.

(16) (Apply the greater) If—

(A) the defendant derived more than $1,000,000 in gross receipts from one or more financial institutions as a result of the offense, increase by **2** levels; or

(B) the offense (i) substantially jeopardized the safety and soundness of a financial institution; or (ii) substantially endangered the solvency or financial security of an organization that, at any time during the offense, (I) was a publicly traded company; or (II) had 1,000 or more employees, increase by **4** levels.

(C) The cumulative adjustments from application of both subsections (b)(2) and (b)(16)(B) shall not exceed **8** levels, except as provided in subdivision (D).

(D) If the resulting offense level determined under subdivision (A) or (B) is less than level **24**, increase to level **24**.

(17) If (A) the defendant was convicted of an offense under 18 U.S.C. § 1030, and the offense involved an intent to obtain personal information, or (B) the offense involved the unauthorized public dissemination of personal information, increase by **2** levels.

(18) (A) (Apply the greatest) If the defendant was convicted of an offense under:

    (i)   18 U.S.C. § 1030, and the offense involved a computer system used to maintain or operate a critical infrastructure, or used by or for a government entity in furtherance of the administration of justice, national defense, or national security, increase by **2** levels.

    (ii)   18 U.S.C. § 1030(a)(5)(A), increase by **4** levels.

    (iii) 18 U.S.C. § 1030, and the offense caused a substantial disruption of a critical infrastructure, increase by **6** levels.

  (B) If subdivision (A)(iii) applies, and the offense level is less than level **24**, increase to level **24**.

(19) If the offense involved—

  (A) a violation of securities law and, at the time of the offense, the defendant was (i) an officer or a director of a publicly traded company; (ii) a registered broker or dealer, or a person associated with a broker or dealer; or (iii) an investment adviser, or a person associated with an investment adviser; or

  (B) a violation of commodities law and, at the time of the offense, the defendant was (i) an officer or a director of a futures commission merchant or an introducing broker; (ii) a commodities trading advisor; or (iii) a commodity pool operator,

increase by **4** levels.

(c) Cross References

(1) If (A) a firearm, destructive device, explosive material, or controlled substance was taken, or the taking of any such item was an object of the offense; or (B) the stolen property received, transported, transferred, transmitted, or possessed was a firearm, destructive device, explosive material, or controlled substance, apply §2D1.1 (Unlawful Manufacturing, Importing, Exporting, or Trafficking (Including Possession with Intent to Commit These Offenses); Attempt or Conspiracy), §2D2.1 (Unlawful Possession; Attempt or Conspiracy), §2K1.3 (Unlawful Receipt, Possession, or Transportation of Explosive Materials;

Prohibited Transactions Involving Explosive Materials), or §2K2.1 (Unlawful Receipt, Possession, or Transportation of Firearms or Ammunition; Prohibited Transactions Involving Firearms or Ammunition), as appropriate.

(2) If the offense involved arson, or property damage by use of explosives, apply §2K1.4 (Arson; Property Damage by Use of Explosives), if the resulting offense level is greater than that determined above.

(3) If (A) neither subdivision (1) nor (2) of this subsection applies; (B) the defendant was convicted under a statute proscribing false, fictitious, or fraudulent statements or representations generally (*e.g.*, 18 U.S.C. § 1001, § 1341, § 1342, or § 1343); and (C) the conduct set forth in the count of conviction establishes an offense specifically covered by another guideline in Chapter Two (Offense Conduct), apply that other guideline.

(4) If the offense involved a cultural heritage resource or a paleontological resource, apply §2B1.5 (Theft of, Damage to, or Destruction of, Cultural Heritage Resources or Paleontological Resources; Unlawful Sale, Purchase, Exchange, Transportation, or Receipt of Cultural Heritage Resources or Paleontological Resources), if the resulting offense level is greater than that determined above.

Commentary

Statutory Provisions: 7 U.S.C. §§ 6, 6b, 6c, 6h, 6o, 13, 23; 15 U.S.C. §§ 50, 77e, 77q, 77x, 78j, 78ff, 80b-6, 1644, 6821; 18 U.S.C. §§ 38, 225, 285–289, 471–473, 500, 510, 553(a)(1), 641, 656, 657, 659, 662, 664, 1001–1008, 1010–1014, 1016–1022, 1025, 1026, 1028, 1029, 1030(a)(4)–(5), 1031, 1037, 1040, 1341–1344, 1348, 1350, 1361, 1363, 1369, 1702, 1703 (if vandalism or malicious mischief, including destruction of mail, is involved), 1708, 1831, 1832, 1992(a)(1), (a)(5), 2113(b), 2282A, 2282B, 2291, 2312–2317, 2332b(a)(1), 2701; 19 U.S.C. § 2401f; 29 U.S.C. § 501(c); 42 U.S.C. § 1011; 49 U.S.C. §§ 14915, 30170, 46317(a), 60123(b). For additional statutory provision(s), *see* Appendix A (Statutory Index).

Application Notes:

1. **Definitions.**—For purposes of this guideline:

   "*Cultural heritage resource*" has the meaning given that term in Application Note 1 of the Commentary to §2B1.5 (Theft of, Damage to, or Destruction of, Cultural Heritage Resources or Paleontological Resources; Unlawful Sale, Purchase, Exchange, Transportation, or Receipt of Cultural Heritage Resources or Paleontological Resources).

   "*Equity securities*" has the meaning given that term in section 3(a)(11) of the Securities Exchange Act of 1934 (15 U.S.C. § 78c(a)(11)).

   "*Federal health care offense*" has the meaning given that term in 18 U.S.C. § 24.

"*Financial institution*" includes any institution described in 18 U.S.C. § 20, § 656, § 657, § 1005, § 1006, § 1007, or § 1014; any state or foreign bank, trust company, credit union, insurance company, investment company, mutual fund, savings (building and loan) association, union or employee pension fund; any health, medical, or hospital insurance association; brokers and dealers registered, or required to be registered, with the Securities and Exchange Commission; futures commodity merchants and commodity pool operators registered, or required to be registered, with the Commodity Futures Trading Commission; and any similar entity, whether or not insured by the federal government. "Union or employee pension fund" and "any health, medical, or hospital insurance association," primarily include large pension funds that serve many persons (*e.g.*, pension funds of large national and international organizations, unions, and corporations doing substantial interstate business), and associations that undertake to provide pension, disability, or other benefits (*e.g.*, medical or hospitalization insurance) to large numbers of persons.

"*Firearm*" and "*destructive device*" have the meaning given those terms in the Commentary to §1B1.1 (Application Instructions).

"*Foreign instrumentality*" and "*foreign agent*" have the meaning given those terms in 18 U.S.C. § 1839(1) and (2), respectively.

"*Government health care program*" means any plan or program that provides health benefits, whether directly, through insurance, or otherwise, which is funded directly, in whole or in part, by federal or state government. Examples of such programs are the Medicare program, the Medicaid program, and the CHIP program.

"*Means of identification*" has the meaning given that term in 18 U.S.C. § 1028(d)(7), except that such means of identification shall be of an actual (*i.e.*, not fictitious) individual, other than the defendant or a person for whose conduct the defendant is accountable under §1B1.3 (Relevant Conduct).

"*National cemetery*" means a cemetery (A) established under section 2400 of title 38, United States Code; or (B) under the jurisdiction of the Secretary of the Army, the Secretary of the Navy, the Secretary of the Air Force, or the Secretary of the Interior.

"*Paleontological resource*" has the meaning given that term in Application Note 1 of the Commentary to §2B1.5 (Theft of, Damage to, or Destruction of, Cultural Heritage Resources or Paleontological Resources; Unlawful Sale, Purchase, Exchange, Transportation, or Receipt of Cultural Heritage Resources or Paleontological Resources).

"*Personal information*" means sensitive or private information involving an identifiable individual (including such information in the possession of a third party), including (A) medical records; (B) wills; (C) diaries; (D) private correspondence, including e-mail; (E) financial records; (F) photographs of a sensitive or private nature; or (G) similar information.

"*Pre-retail medical product*" has the meaning given that term in 18 U.S.C. § 670(e).

"*Publicly traded company*" means an issuer (A) with a class of securities registered under section 12 of the Securities Exchange Act of 1934 (15 U.S.C. § 78l); or (B) that is required to file reports under section 15(d) of the Securities Exchange Act of 1934 (15 U.S.C. § 78o(d)). "Issuer" has the meaning given that term in section 3 of the Securities Exchange Act of 1934 (15 U.S.C. § 78c).

"*Supply chain*" has the meaning given that term in 18 U.S.C. § 670(e).

"*Theft from the person of another*" means theft, without the use of force, of property that was being held by another person or was within arms' reach. Examples include pick-pocketing and non-forcible purse-snatching, such as the theft of a purse from a shopping cart.

"*Trade secret*" has the meaning given that term in 18 U.S.C. § 1839(3).

"*Veterans' memorial*" means any structure, plaque, statue, or other monument described in 18 U.S.C. § 1369(a).

"*Victim*" means (A) any person who sustained any part of the actual loss determined under subsection (b)(1); or (B) any individual who sustained bodily injury as a result of the offense. "Person" includes individuals, corporations, companies, associations, firms, partnerships, societies, and joint stock companies.

2. **Application of Subsection (a)(1).—**

   (A) **"Referenced to this Guideline".—**For purposes of subsection (a)(1), an offense is "*referenced to this guideline*" if (i) this guideline is the applicable Chapter Two guideline determined under the provisions of §1B1.2 (Applicable Guidelines) for the offense of conviction; or (ii) in the case of a conviction for conspiracy, solicitation, or attempt to which §2X1.1 (Attempt, Solicitation, or Conspiracy) applies, this guideline is the appropriate guideline for the offense the defendant was convicted of conspiring, soliciting, or attempting to commit.

   (B) **Definition of "Statutory Maximum Term of Imprisonment".—**For purposes of this guideline, "*statutory maximum term of imprisonment*" means the maximum term of imprisonment authorized for the offense of conviction, including any increase in that maximum term under a statutory enhancement provision.

   (C) **Base Offense Level Determination for Cases Involving Multiple Counts.—**In a case involving multiple counts sentenced under this guideline, the applicable base offense level is determined by the count of conviction that provides the highest statutory maximum term of imprisonment.

3. **Loss Under Subsection (b)(1).—**This application note applies to the determination of loss under subsection (b)(1).

   (A) **General Rule.—**Subject to the exclusions in subdivision (D), loss is the greater of actual loss or intended loss.

       (i) **Actual Loss.—**"*Actual loss*" means the reasonably foreseeable pecuniary harm that resulted from the offense.

       (ii) **Intended Loss.—**"*Intended loss*" (I) means the pecuniary harm that the defendant purposely sought to inflict; and (II) includes intended pecuniary harm that would have been impossible or unlikely to occur (*e.g.*, as in a government sting operation, or an insurance fraud in which the claim exceeded the insured value).

(iii) **Pecuniary Harm.**—"*Pecuniary harm*" means harm that is monetary or that otherwise is readily measurable in money. Accordingly, pecuniary harm does not include emotional distress, harm to reputation, or other non-economic harm.

(iv) **Reasonably Foreseeable Pecuniary Harm.**—For purposes of this guideline, "*reasonably foreseeable pecuniary harm*" means pecuniary harm that the defendant knew or, under the circumstances, reasonably should have known, was a potential result of the offense.

(v) **Rules of Construction in Certain Cases.**—In the cases described in subdivisions (I) through (III), reasonably foreseeable pecuniary harm shall be considered to include the pecuniary harm specified for those cases as follows:

(I) **Product Substitution Cases.**—In the case of a product substitution offense, the reasonably foreseeable pecuniary harm includes the reasonably foreseeable costs of making substitute transactions and handling or disposing of the product delivered, or of retrofitting the product so that it can be used for its intended purpose, and the reasonably foreseeable costs of rectifying the actual or potential disruption to the victim's business operations caused by the product substitution.

(II) **Procurement Fraud Cases.**—In the case of a procurement fraud, such as a fraud affecting a defense contract award, reasonably foreseeable pecuniary harm includes the reasonably foreseeable administrative costs to the government and other participants of repeating or correcting the procurement action affected, plus any increased costs to procure the product or service involved that was reasonably foreseeable.

(III) **Offenses Under 18 U.S.C. § 1030.**—In the case of an offense under 18 U.S.C. § 1030, actual loss includes the following pecuniary harm, regardless of whether such pecuniary harm was reasonably foreseeable: any reasonable cost to any victim, including the cost of responding to an offense, conducting a damage assessment, and restoring the data, program, system, or information to its condition prior to the offense, and any revenue lost, cost incurred, or other damages incurred because of interruption of service.

(B) **Gain.**—The court shall use the gain that resulted from the offense as an alternative measure of loss only if there is a loss but it reasonably cannot be determined.

(C) **Estimation of Loss.**—The court need only make a reasonable estimate of the loss. The sentencing judge is in a unique position to assess the evidence and estimate the loss based upon that evidence. For this reason, the court's loss determination is entitled to appropriate deference. *See* 18 U.S.C. § 3742(e) and (f).

The estimate of the loss shall be based on available information, taking into account, as appropriate and practicable under the circumstances, factors such as the following:

(i) The fair market value of the property unlawfully taken, copied, or destroyed; or, if the fair market value is impracticable to determine or inadequately measures the harm, the cost to the victim of replacing that property.

    (ii)   In the case of proprietary information (*e.g.*, trade secrets), the cost of developing that information or the reduction in the value of that information that resulted from the offense.

    (iii)   The cost of repairs to damaged property.

    (iv)   The approximate number of victims multiplied by the average loss to each victim.

    (v)   The reduction that resulted from the offense in the value of equity securities or other corporate assets.

    (vi)   More general factors, such as the scope and duration of the offense and revenues generated by similar operations.

(D)   **Exclusions from Loss.**—Loss shall not include the following:

    (i)   Interest of any kind, finance charges, late fees, penalties, amounts based on an agreed-upon return or rate of return, or other similar costs.

    (ii)   Costs to the government of, and costs incurred by victims primarily to aid the government in, the prosecution and criminal investigation of an offense.

(E)   **Credits Against Loss.**—Loss shall be reduced by the following:

    (i)   The money returned, and the fair market value of the property returned and the services rendered, by the defendant or other persons acting jointly with the defendant, to the victim before the offense was detected. The time of detection of the offense is the earlier of (I) the time the offense was discovered by a victim or government agency; or (II) the time the defendant knew or reasonably should have known that the offense was detected or about to be detected by a victim or government agency.

    (ii)   In a case involving collateral pledged or otherwise provided by the defendant, the amount the victim has recovered at the time of sentencing from disposition of the collateral, or if the collateral has not been disposed of by that time, the fair market value of the collateral at the time of sentencing.

    (iii)   Notwithstanding clause (ii), in the case of a fraud involving a mortgage loan, if the collateral has not been disposed of by the time of sentencing, use the fair market value of the collateral as of the date on which the guilt of the defendant has been established, whether by guilty plea, trial, or plea of *nolo contendere*.

           In such a case, there shall be a rebuttable presumption that the most recent tax assessment value of the collateral is a reasonable estimate of the fair market value. In determining whether the most recent tax assessment value is a reasonable estimate of the fair market value, the court may consider, among other factors, the recency of the tax assessment and the extent to which the jurisdiction's tax assessment practices reflect factors not relevant to fair market value.

(F)   **Special Rules.**—Notwithstanding subdivision (A), the following special rules shall be used to assist in determining loss in the cases indicated:

(i)   **Stolen or Counterfeit Credit Cards and Access Devices; Purloined Numbers and Codes.**—In a case involving any counterfeit access device or unauthorized access device, loss includes any unauthorized charges made with the counterfeit access device or unauthorized access device and shall be not less than $500 per access device. However, if the unauthorized access device is a means of telecommunications access that identifies a specific telecommunications instrument or telecommunications account (including an electronic serial number/mobile identification number (ESN/MIN) pair), and that means was only possessed, and not used, during the commission of the offense, loss shall be not less than $100 per unused means. For purposes of this subdivision, "*counterfeit access device*" and "*unauthorized access device*" have the meaning given those terms in Application Note 10(A).

(ii)   **Government Benefits.**—In a case involving government benefits (*e.g.*, grants, loans, entitlement program payments), loss shall be considered to be not less than the value of the benefits obtained by unintended recipients or diverted to unintended uses, as the case may be. For example, if the defendant was the intended recipient of food stamps having a value of $100 but fraudulently received food stamps having a value of $150, loss is $50.

(iii)   **Davis–Bacon Act Violations.**—In a case involving a Davis–Bacon Act violation (*i.e.*, a violation of 40 U.S.C. § 3142, criminally prosecuted under 18 U.S.C. § 1001), the value of the benefits shall be considered to be not less than the difference between the legally required wages and actual wages paid.

(iv)   **Ponzi and Other Fraudulent Investment Schemes.**—In a case involving a fraudulent investment scheme, such as a Ponzi scheme, loss shall not be reduced by the money or the value of the property transferred to any individual investor in the scheme in excess of that investor's principal investment (*i.e.*, the gain to an individual investor in the scheme shall not be used to offset the loss to another individual investor in the scheme).

(v)   **Certain Other Unlawful Misrepresentation Schemes.**—In a case involving a scheme in which (I) services were fraudulently rendered to the victim by persons falsely posing as licensed professionals; (II) goods were falsely represented as approved by a governmental regulatory agency; or (III) goods for which regulatory approval by a government agency was required but not obtained, or was obtained by fraud, loss shall include the amount paid for the property, services or goods transferred, rendered, or misrepresented, with no credit provided for the value of those items or services.

(vi)   **Value of Controlled Substances.**—In a case involving controlled substances, loss is the estimated street value of the controlled substances.

(vii)   **Value of Cultural Heritage Resources or Paleontological Resources.**—In a case involving a cultural heritage resource or paleontological resource, loss attributable to that resource shall be determined in accordance with the rules for determining the "value of the resource" set forth in Application Note 2 of the Commentary to §2B1.5.

(viii) **Federal Health Care Offenses Involving Government Health Care Programs.**—In a case in which the defendant is convicted of a Federal health care offense involving a Government health care program, the aggregate dollar amount of fraudulent bills submitted to the Government health care program shall constitute prima facie evidence of the amount of the intended loss, *i.e.*, is evidence sufficient to establish the amount of the intended loss, if not rebutted.

(ix) **Fraudulent Inflation or Deflation in Value of Securities or Commodities.**—In a case involving the fraudulent inflation or deflation in the value of a publicly traded security or commodity, the court in determining loss may use any method that is appropriate and practicable under the circumstances. One such method the court may consider is a method under which the actual loss attributable to the change in value of the security or commodity is the amount determined by—

(I) calculating the difference between the average price of the security or commodity during the period that the fraud occurred and the average price of the security or commodity during the 90-day period after the fraud was disclosed to the market, and

(II) multiplying the difference in average price by the number of shares outstanding.

In determining whether the amount so determined is a reasonable estimate of the actual loss attributable to the change in value of the security or commodity, the court may consider, among other factors, the extent to which the amount so determined includes significant changes in value not resulting from the offense (*e.g.*, changes caused by external market forces, such as changed economic circumstances, changed investor expectations, and new industry-specific or firm-specific facts, conditions, or events).

4. **Application of Subsection (b)(2).**—

(A) **Definition.**—For purposes of subsection (b)(2), "*mass-marketing*" means a plan, program, promotion, or campaign that is conducted through solicitation by telephone, mail, the Internet, or other means to induce a large number of persons to (i) purchase goods or services; (ii) participate in a contest or sweepstakes; or (iii) invest for financial profit. "Mass-marketing" includes, for example, a telemarketing campaign that solicits a large number of individuals to purchase fraudulent life insurance policies.

(B) **Applicability to Transmission of Multiple Commercial Electronic Mail Messages.**—For purposes of subsection (b)(2), an offense under 18 U.S.C. § 1037, or any other offense involving conduct described in 18 U.S.C. § 1037, shall be considered to have been committed through mass-marketing. Accordingly, the defendant shall receive at least a two-level enhancement under subsection (b)(2) and may, depending on the facts of the case, receive a greater enhancement under such subsection, if the defendant was convicted under, or the offense involved conduct described in, 18 U.S.C. § 1037.

(C) **Undelivered United States Mail.**—

(i) **In General.**—In a case in which undelivered United States mail was taken, or the taking of such item was an object of the offense, or in a case in which the stolen property received, transported, transferred, transmitted, or possessed was undelivered United States mail, "*victim*" means (I) any victim as defined in Application Note 1; or (II) any person who was the intended recipient, or addressee, of the undelivered United States mail.

(ii) **Special Rule.**—A case described in subdivision (C)(i) of this note that involved—

(I) a United States Postal Service relay box, collection box, delivery vehicle, satchel, or cart, shall be considered to have involved at least 10 victims.

(II) a housing unit cluster box or any similar receptacle that contains multiple mailboxes, whether such receptacle is owned by the United States Postal Service or otherwise owned, shall, unless proven otherwise, be presumed to have involved the number of victims corresponding to the number of mailboxes in each cluster box or similar receptacle.

(iii) **Definition.**—"*Undelivered United States mail*" means mail that has not actually been received by the addressee or the addressee's agent (*e.g.*, mail taken from the addressee's mail box).

(D) **Vulnerable Victims.**—If subsection (b)(2)(B) or (C) applies, an enhancement under §3A1.1(b)(2) shall not apply.

(E) **Cases Involving Means of Identification.**—For purposes of subsection (b)(2), in a case involving means of identification "*victim*" means (i) any victim as defined in Application Note 1; or (ii) any individual whose means of identification was used unlawfully or without authority.

(F) **Substantial Financial Hardship.**—In determining whether the offense resulted in substantial financial hardship to a victim, the court shall consider, among other factors, whether the offense resulted in the victim—

(i) becoming insolvent;

(ii) filing for bankruptcy under the Bankruptcy Code (title 11, United States Code);

(iii) suffering substantial loss of a retirement, education, or other savings or investment fund;

(iv) making substantial changes to his or her employment, such as postponing his or her retirement plans;

(v) making substantial changes to his or her living arrangements, such as relocating to a less expensive home; and

(vi) suffering substantial harm to his or her ability to obtain credit.

5. **Enhancement for Business of Receiving and Selling Stolen Property under Subsection (b)(4).**—For purposes of subsection (b)(4), the court shall consider the following non-exhaustive list of factors in determining whether the defendant was in the business of receiving and selling stolen property:

(A) The regularity and sophistication of the defendant's activities.

(B)   The value and size of the inventory of stolen property maintained by the defendant.

(C)   The extent to which the defendant's activities encouraged or facilitated other crimes.

(D)   The defendant's past activities involving stolen property.

6.   **Application of Subsection (b)(6).**—For purposes of subsection (b)(6), "*improper means*" includes the unauthorized harvesting of electronic mail addresses of users of a website, proprietary service, or other online public forum.

7.   **Application of Subsection (b)(8)(B).**—If subsection (b)(8)(B) applies, do not apply an adjustment under §3B1.3 (Abuse of Position of Trust or Use of Special Skill).

8.   **Application of Subsection (b)(9).**—

(A)   **In General.**—The adjustments in subsection (b)(9) are alternative rather than cumulative. If, in a particular case, however, more than one of the enumerated factors applied, an upward departure may be warranted.

(B)   **Misrepresentations Regarding Charitable and Other Institutions.**—Subsection (b)(9)(A) applies in any case in which the defendant represented that the defendant was acting to obtain a benefit on behalf of a charitable, educational, religious, or political organization, or a government agency (regardless of whether the defendant actually was associated with the organization or government agency) when, in fact, the defendant intended to divert all or part of that benefit (*e.g.*, for the defendant's personal gain). Subsection (b)(9)(A) applies, for example, to the following:

(i)   A defendant who solicited contributions for a non-existent famine relief organization.

(ii)   A defendant who solicited donations from church members by falsely claiming to be a fundraiser for a religiously affiliated school.

(iii)   A defendant, chief of a local fire department, who conducted a public fundraiser representing that the purpose of the fundraiser was to procure sufficient funds for a new fire engine when, in fact, the defendant intended to divert some of the funds for the defendant's personal benefit.

(C)   **Fraud in Contravention of Prior Judicial Order.**—Subsection (b)(9)(C) provides an enhancement if the defendant commits a fraud in contravention of a prior, official judicial or administrative warning, in the form of an order, injunction, decree, or process, to take or not to take a specified action. A defendant who does not comply with such a prior, official judicial or administrative warning demonstrates aggravated criminal intent and deserves additional punishment. If it is established that an entity the defendant controlled was a party to the prior proceeding that resulted in the official judicial or administrative action, and the defendant had knowledge of that prior decree or order, this enhancement applies even if the defendant was not a specifically named party in that prior case. For example, a defendant whose business previously was enjoined from selling a dangerous product, but who nonetheless engaged in fraudulent conduct to sell the product, is subject to this enhancement. This enhancement does not apply if the same conduct resulted in an enhancement pursuant to a provision found elsewhere in the guidelines (*e.g.*, a violation of a condition of release addressed in §3C1.3 (Commission of Offense While on Release) or a violation of probation addressed in §4A1.1 (Criminal History Category)).

(D) **College Scholarship Fraud.**—For purposes of subsection (b)(9)(D):

"*Financial assistance*" means any scholarship, grant, loan, tuition, discount, award, or other financial assistance for the purpose of financing an education.

"*Institution of higher education*" has the meaning given that term in section 101 of the Higher Education Act of 1954 (20 U.S.C. § 1001).

(E) **Non-Applicability of Chapter Three Adjustments.—**

(i) **Subsection (b)(9)(A).**—If the conduct that forms the basis for an enhancement under subsection (b)(9)(A) is the only conduct that forms the basis for an adjustment under §3B1.3 (Abuse of Position of Trust or Use of Special Skill), do not apply that adjustment under §3B1.3.

(ii) **Subsection (b)(9)(B) and (C).**—If the conduct that forms the basis for an enhancement under subsection (b)(9)(B) or (C) is the only conduct that forms the basis for an adjustment under §3C1.1 (Obstructing or Impeding the Administration of Justice), do not apply that adjustment under §3C1.1.

9. **Application of Subsection (b)(10).—**

(A) **Definition of United States.**—For purposes of subsection (b)(10)(B), "*United States*" means each of the 50 states, the District of Columbia, the Commonwealth of Puerto Rico, the United States Virgin Islands, Guam, the Northern Mariana Islands, and American Samoa.

(B) **Sophisticated Means Enhancement under Subsection (b)(10)(C).**—For purposes of subsection (b)(10)(C), "*sophisticated means*" means especially complex or especially intricate offense conduct pertaining to the execution or concealment of an offense. For example, in a telemarketing scheme, locating the main office of the scheme in one jurisdiction but locating soliciting operations in another jurisdiction ordinarily indicates sophisticated means. Conduct such as hiding assets or transactions, or both, through the use of fictitious entities, corporate shells, or offshore financial accounts also ordinarily indicates sophisticated means.

(C) **Non-Applicability of Chapter Three Adjustment.**—If the conduct that forms the basis for an enhancement under subsection (b)(10) is the only conduct that forms the basis for an adjustment under §3C1.1, do not apply that adjustment under §3C1.1.

10. **Application of Subsection (b)(11).—**

(A) **Definitions.**—For purposes of subsection (b)(11):

"*Authentication feature*" has the meaning given that term in 18 U.S.C. § 1028(d)(1).

"*Counterfeit access device*" (i) has the meaning given that term in 18 U.S.C. § 1029(e)(2); and (ii) includes a telecommunications instrument that has been modified or altered to obtain unauthorized use of telecommunications service.

"*Device-making equipment*" (i) has the meaning given that term in 18 U.S.C. § 1029(e)(6); and (ii) includes (I) any hardware or software that has been configured as described in 18 U.S.C. § 1029(a)(9); and (II) a scanning receiver referred to in 18 U.S.C. § 1029(a)(8). "Scanning receiver" has the meaning given that term in 18 U.S.C. § 1029(e)(8).

"*Produce*" includes manufacture, design, alter, authenticate, duplicate, or assemble. "*Production*" includes manufacture, design, alteration, authentication, duplication, or assembly.

"*Telecommunications service*" has the meaning given that term in 18 U.S.C. § 1029(e)(9).

"*Unauthorized access device*" has the meaning given that term in 18 U.S.C. § 1029(e)(3).

(B) **Authentication Features and Identification Documents.**—Offenses involving authentication features, identification documents, false identification documents, and means of identification, in violation of 18 U.S.C. § 1028, also are covered by this guideline. If the primary purpose of the offense, under 18 U.S.C. § 1028, was to violate, or assist another to violate, the law pertaining to naturalization, citizenship, or legal resident status, apply §2L2.1 (Trafficking in a Document Relating to Naturalization) or §2L2.2 (Fraudulently Acquiring Documents Relating to Naturalization), as appropriate, rather than this guideline.

(C) **Application of Subsection (b)(11)(C)(i).**—

   (i)   **In General.**—Subsection (b)(11)(C)(i) applies in a case in which a means of identification of an individual other than the defendant (or a person for whose conduct the defendant is accountable under §1B1.3 (Relevant Conduct)) is used without that individual's authorization unlawfully to produce or obtain another means of identification.

   (ii) **Examples.**—Examples of conduct to which subsection (b)(11)(C)(i) applies are as follows:

      (I)   A defendant obtains an individual's name and social security number from a source (*e.g.*, from a piece of mail taken from the individual's mailbox) and obtains a bank loan in that individual's name. In this example, the account number of the bank loan is the other means of identification that has been obtained unlawfully.

      (II) A defendant obtains an individual's name and address from a source (*e.g.*, from a driver's license in a stolen wallet) and applies for, obtains, and subsequently uses a credit card in that individual's name. In this example, the credit card is the other means of identification that has been obtained unlawfully.

   (iii) **Non-Applicability of Subsection (b)(11)(C)(i).**—Examples of conduct to which subsection (b)(11)(C)(i) does not apply are as follows:

(I) A defendant uses a credit card from a stolen wallet only to make a purchase. In such a case, the defendant has not used the stolen credit card to obtain another means of identification.

(II) A defendant forges another individual's signature to cash a stolen check. Forging another individual's signature is not producing another means of identification.

(D) **Application of Subsection (b)(11)(C)(ii).**—Subsection (b)(11)(C)(ii) applies in any case in which the offense involved the possession of 5 or more means of identification that unlawfully were produced or obtained, regardless of the number of individuals in whose name (or other identifying information) the means of identification were so produced or so obtained.

11. **Application of Subsection (b)(14).**—Subsection (b)(14) provides a minimum offense level in the case of an ongoing, sophisticated operation (*e.g.*, an auto theft ring or "chop shop") to steal or to receive stolen (A) vehicles or vehicle parts; or (B) goods or chattels that are part of a cargo shipment. For purposes of this subsection, "*vehicle*" means motor vehicle, vessel, or aircraft. A "*cargo shipment*" includes cargo transported on a railroad car, bus, steamboat, vessel, or airplane.

12. **Gross Receipts Enhancement under Subsection (b)(16)(A).**—

(A) **In General.**—For purposes of subsection (b)(16)(A), the defendant shall be considered to have derived more than $1,000,000 in gross receipts if the gross receipts to the defendant individually, rather than to all participants, exceeded $1,000,000.

(B) **Definition.**—"*Gross receipts from the offense*" includes all property, real or personal, tangible or intangible, which is obtained directly or indirectly as a result of such offense. *See* 18 U.S.C. § 982(a)(4).

13. **Application of Subsection (b)(16)(B).**—

(A) **Application of Subsection (b)(16)(B)(i).**—The following is a non-exhaustive list of factors that the court shall consider in determining whether, as a result of the offense, the safety and soundness of a financial institution was substantially jeopardized:

(i) The financial institution became insolvent.

(ii) The financial institution substantially reduced benefits to pensioners or insureds.

(iii) The financial institution was unable on demand to refund fully any deposit, payment, or investment.

(iv) The financial institution was so depleted of its assets as to be forced to merge with another institution in order to continue active operations.

(v) One or more of the criteria in clauses (i) through (iv) was likely to result from the offense but did not result from the offense because of federal government intervention, such as a "bailout".

(B) **Application of Subsection (b)(16)(B)(ii).—**

    (i) **Definition.**—For purposes of this subsection, "*organization*" has the meaning given that term in Application Note 1 of §8A1.1 (Applicability of Chapter Eight).

    (ii) **In General.**—The following is a non-exhaustive list of factors that the court shall consider in determining whether, as a result of the offense, the solvency or financial security of an organization that was a publicly traded company or that had more than 1,000 employees was substantially endangered:

        (I) The organization became insolvent or suffered a substantial reduction in the value of its assets.

        (II) The organization filed for bankruptcy under Chapters 7, 11, or 13 of the Bankruptcy Code (title 11, United States Code).

        (III) The organization suffered a substantial reduction in the value of its equity securities or the value of its employee retirement accounts.

        (IV) The organization substantially reduced its workforce.

        (V) The organization substantially reduced its employee pension benefits.

        (VI) The liquidity of the equity securities of a publicly traded company was substantially endangered. For example, the company was delisted from its primary listing exchange, or trading of the company's securities was halted for more than one full trading day.

        (VII) One or more of the criteria in subclauses (I) through (VI) was likely to result from the offense but did not result from the offense because of federal government intervention, such as a "bailout".

14. **Application of Subsection (b)(18).—**

(A) **Definitions.**—For purposes of subsection (b)(18):

"*Critical infrastructure*" means systems and assets vital to national defense, national security, economic security, public health or safety, or any combination of those matters. A critical infrastructure may be publicly or privately owned. Examples of critical infrastructures include gas and oil production, storage, and delivery systems, water supply systems, telecommunications networks, electrical power delivery systems, financing and banking systems, emergency services (including medical, police, fire, and rescue services), transportation systems and services (including highways, mass transit, airlines, and airports), and government operations that provide essential services to the public.

"*Government entity*" has the meaning given that term in 18 U.S.C. § 1030(e)(9).

(B) **Subsection (b)(18)(A)(iii).**—If the same conduct that forms the basis for an enhancement under subsection (b)(18)(A)(iii) is the only conduct that forms the basis for an enhancement under subsection (b)(16)(B), do not apply the enhancement under subsection (b)(16)(B).

15. **Application of Subsection (b)(19).—**

    (A) **Definitions.—**For purposes of subsection (b)(19):

        "*Commodities law*" means (i) the Commodity Exchange Act (7 U.S.C. § 1 *et seq.*) and 18 U.S.C. § 1348; and (ii) includes the rules, regulations, and orders issued by the Commodity Futures Trading Commission.

        "*Commodity pool operator*" has the meaning given that term in section 1a(11) of the Commodity Exchange Act (7 U.S.C. § 1a(11)).

        "*Commodity trading advisor*" has the meaning given that term in section 1a(12) of the Commodity Exchange Act (7 U.S.C. § 1a(12)).

        "*Futures commission merchant*" has the meaning given that term in section 1a(28) of the Commodity Exchange Act (7 U.S.C. § 1a(28)).

        "*Introducing broker*" has the meaning given that term in section 1a(31) of the Commodity Exchange Act (7 U.S.C. § 1a(31)).

        "*Investment adviser*" has the meaning given that term in section 202(a)(11) of the Investment Advisers Act of 1940 (15 U.S.C. § 80b-2(a)(11)).

        "*Person associated with a broker or dealer*" has the meaning given that term in section 3(a)(18) of the Securities Exchange Act of 1934 (15 U.S.C. § 78c(a)(18)).

        "*Person associated with an investment adviser*" has the meaning given that term in section 202(a)(17) of the Investment Advisers Act of 1940 (15 U.S.C. § 80b-2(a)(17)).

        "*Registered broker or dealer*" has the meaning given that term in section 3(a)(48) of the Securities Exchange Act of 1934 (15 U.S.C. § 78c(a)(48)).

        "*Securities law*" (i) means 18 U.S.C. §§ 1348, 1350, and the provisions of law referred to in section 3(a)(47) of the Securities Exchange Act of 1934 (15 U.S.C. § 78c(a)(47)); and (ii) includes the rules, regulations, and orders issued by the Securities and Exchange Commission pursuant to the provisions of law referred to in such section.

    (B) **In General.—**A conviction under a securities law or commodities law is not required in order for subsection (b)(19) to apply. This subsection would apply in the case of a defendant convicted under a general fraud statute if the defendant's conduct violated a securities law or commodities law. For example, this subsection would apply if an officer of a publicly traded company violated regulations issued by the Securities and Exchange Commission by fraudulently influencing an independent audit of the company's financial statements for the purposes of rendering such financial statements materially misleading, even if the officer is convicted only of wire fraud.

    (C) **Nonapplicability of §3B1.3 (Abuse of Position of Trust or Use of Special Skill).—**If subsection (b)(19) applies, do not apply §3B1.3.

16. **Cross Reference in Subsection (c)(3).—**Subsection (c)(3) provides a cross reference to another guideline in Chapter Two (Offense Conduct) in cases in which the defendant is

convicted of a general fraud statute, and the count of conviction establishes an offense involving fraudulent conduct that is more aptly covered by another guideline. Sometimes, offenses involving fraudulent statements are prosecuted under 18 U.S.C. § 1001, or a similarly general statute, although the offense involves fraudulent conduct that is also covered by a more specific statute. Examples include false entries regarding currency transactions, for which §2S1.3 (Structuring Transactions to Evade Reporting Requirements) likely would be more apt, and false statements to a customs officer, for which §2T3.1 (Evading Import Duties or Restrictions (Smuggling); Receiving or Trafficking in Smuggled Property) likely would be more apt. In certain other cases, the mail or wire fraud statutes, or other relatively broad statutes, are used primarily as jurisdictional bases for the prosecution of other offenses. For example, a state employee who improperly influenced the award of a contract and used the mails to commit the offense may be prosecuted under 18 U.S.C. § 1341 for fraud involving the deprivation of the intangible right of honest services. Such a case would be more aptly sentenced pursuant to §2C1.1 (Offering, Giving, Soliciting, or Receiving a Bribe; Extortion Under Color of Official Right; Fraud involving the Deprivation of the Intangible Right to Honest Services of Public Officials; Conspiracy to Defraud by Interference with Governmental Functions).

17. **Continuing Financial Crimes Enterprise.**—If the defendant is convicted under 18 U.S.C. § 225 (relating to a continuing financial crimes enterprise), the offense level is that applicable to the underlying series of offenses comprising the "continuing financial crimes enterprise".

18. **Partially Completed Offenses.**—In the case of a partially completed offense (*e.g.*, an offense involving a completed theft or fraud that is part of a larger, attempted theft or fraud), the offense level is to be determined in accordance with the provisions of §2X1.1 (Attempt, Solicitation, or Conspiracy) whether the conviction is for the substantive offense, the inchoate offense (attempt, solicitation, or conspiracy), or both. *See* Application Note 4 of the Commentary to §2X1.1.

19. **Multiple-Count Indictments.**—Some fraudulent schemes may result in multiple-count indictments, depending on the technical elements of the offense. The cumulative loss produced by a common scheme or course of conduct should be used in determining the offense level, regardless of the number of counts of conviction. *See* Chapter Three, Part D (Multiple Counts).

20. **Departure Considerations.**—

    (A) **Upward Departure Considerations.**—There may be cases in which the offense level determined under this guideline substantially understates the seriousness of the offense. In such cases, an upward departure may be warranted. The following is a non-exhaustive list of factors that the court may consider in determining whether an upward departure is warranted:

        (i) A primary objective of the offense was an aggravating, non-monetary objective. For example, a primary objective of the offense was to inflict emotional harm.

        (ii) The offense caused or risked substantial non-monetary harm. For example, the offense caused physical harm, psychological harm, or severe emotional trauma, or resulted in a substantial invasion of a privacy interest (through, for example, the theft of personal information such as medical, educational, or financial records). An upward departure would be warranted, for example, in an 18 U.S.C. § 1030 offense involving damage to a protected computer, if, as a result of that offense, death resulted. An upward departure also would be warranted, for example, in a case involving animal enterprise terrorism under 18 U.S.C. § 43, if, in the course of the offense, serious bodily injury or death resulted, or substantial scientific research or information were destroyed. Similarly, an upward departure would be warranted in a case involving conduct described in 18 U.S.C. § 670 if the offense resulted in serious bodily injury or death, including serious bodily injury or death resulting from the use of the pre-retail medical product.

(iii) The offense involved a substantial amount of interest of any kind, finance charges, late fees, penalties, amounts based on an agreed-upon return or rate of return, or other similar costs, not included in the determination of loss for purposes of subsection (b)(1).

(iv) The offense created a risk of substantial loss beyond the loss determined for purposes of subsection (b)(1), such as a risk of a significant disruption of a national financial market.

(v) In a case involving stolen information from a "protected computer", as defined in 18 U.S.C. § 1030(e)(2), the defendant sought the stolen information to further a broader criminal purpose.

(vi) In a case involving access devices or unlawfully produced or unlawfully obtained means of identification:

(I) The offense caused substantial harm to the victim's reputation, or the victim suffered a substantial inconvenience related to repairing the victim's reputation.

(II) An individual whose means of identification the defendant used to obtain unlawful means of identification is erroneously arrested or denied a job because an arrest record has been made in that individual's name.

(III) The defendant produced or obtained numerous means of identification with respect to one individual and essentially assumed that individual's identity.

(B) **Upward Departure for Debilitating Impact on a Critical Infrastructure.**— An upward departure would be warranted in a case in which subsection (b)(18)(A)(iii) applies and the disruption to the critical infrastructure(s) is so substantial as to have a debilitating impact on national security, national economic security, national public health or safety, or any combination of those matters.

(C) **Downward Departure Consideration.**—There may be cases in which the offense level determined under this guideline substantially overstates the seriousness of the offense. In such cases, a downward departure may be warranted.

For example, a securities fraud involving a fraudulent statement made publicly to the market may produce an aggregate loss amount that is substantial but diffuse, with relatively small loss amounts suffered by a relatively large number of victims. In such a case, the loss table in subsection (b)(1) and the victims table in subsection (b)(2) may combine to produce an offense level that substantially overstates the seriousness of the offense. If so, a downward departure may be warranted.

(D) **Downward Departure for Major Disaster or Emergency Victims.**—If (i) the minimum offense level of level 12 in subsection (b)(12) applies; (ii) the defendant sustained damage, loss, hardship, or suffering caused by a major disaster or an emergency as those terms are defined in 42 U.S.C. § 5122; and (iii) the benefits received illegally were only an extension or overpayment of benefits received legitimately, a downward departure may be warranted.

Background: This guideline covers offenses involving theft, stolen property, property damage or destruction, fraud, forgery, and counterfeiting (other than offenses involving altered or counterfeit bearer obligations of the United States).

Because federal fraud statutes often are broadly written, a single pattern of offense conduct usually can be prosecuted under several code sections, as a result of which the offense of conviction may be somewhat arbitrary. Furthermore, most fraud statutes cover a broad range of conduct with extreme variation in severity. The specific offense characteristics and cross references contained in this guideline are designed with these considerations in mind.

The Commission has determined that, ordinarily, the sentences of defendants convicted of federal offenses should reflect the nature and magnitude of the loss caused or intended by their crimes. Accordingly, along with other relevant factors under the guidelines, loss serves as a measure of the seriousness of the offense and the defendant's relative culpability and is a principal factor in determining the offense level under this guideline.

Theft from the person of another, such as pickpocketing or non-forcible purse-snatching, receives an enhanced sentence because of the increased risk of physical injury. This guideline does not include an enhancement for thefts from the person by means of force or fear; such crimes are robberies and are covered under §2B3.1 (Robbery).

A minimum offense level of level 14 is provided for offenses involving an organized scheme to steal vehicles or vehicle parts. Typically, the scope of such activity is substantial, but the value of the property may be particularly difficult to ascertain in individual cases because the stolen property is rapidly resold or otherwise disposed of in the course of the offense. Therefore, the specific offense characteristic of "organized scheme" is used as an alternative to "loss" in setting a minimum offense level.

Use of false pretenses involving charitable causes and government agencies enhances the sentences of defendants who take advantage of victims' trust in government or law enforcement agencies or the generosity and charitable motives of victims. Taking advantage of a victim's self-interest does not mitigate the seriousness of fraudulent conduct; rather, defendants who exploit victims' charitable impulses or trust in government create particular social harm. In a similar vein, a defendant who has been subject to civil or administrative proceedings for the same or similar fraudulent conduct demonstrates aggravated criminal intent and is deserving of additional punishment for not conforming with the requirements of judicial process or orders issued by federal, state, or local administrative agencies.

Offenses that involve the use of financial transactions or financial accounts outside the United States in an effort to conceal illicit profits and criminal conduct involve a particularly high level of sophistication and complexity. These offenses are difficult to detect and require costly investigations and prosecutions. Diplomatic processes often must be used to secure testimony and evidence beyond the jurisdiction of United States courts. Consequently, a minimum offense level of level 12 is provided for these offenses.

Subsection (b)(5) implements the instruction to the Commission in section 2 of Public Law 105–101 and the directive to the Commission in section 3 of Public Law 110–384.

Subsection (b)(7) implements the directive to the Commission in section 10606 of Public Law 111–148.

Subsection (b)(8) implements the directive to the Commission in section 7 of Public Law 112–186.

Subsection (b)(9)(D) implements, in a broader form, the directive in section 3 of the College Scholarship Fraud Prevention Act of 2000, Public Law 106–420.

Subsection (b)(10) implements, in a broader form, the instruction to the Commission in section 6(c)(2) of Public Law 105–184.

Subsections (b)(11)(A)(i) and (B)(i) implement the instruction to the Commission in section 4 of the Wireless Telephone Protection Act, Public Law 105–172.

Subsection (b)(11)(C) implements the directive to the Commission in section 4 of the Identity Theft and Assumption Deterrence Act of 1998, Public Law 105–318. This subsection focuses principally on an aggravated form of identity theft known as "affirmative identity theft" or "breeding", in which a defendant uses another individual's name, social security number, or some other form of identification (the "means of identification") to "breed" (*i.e.*, produce or obtain) new or additional forms of identification. Because 18 U.S.C. § 1028(d) broadly defines "means of identification", the new or additional forms of identification can include items such as a driver's license, a credit card, or a bank loan. This subsection provides a minimum offense level of level 12, in part because of the seriousness of the offense. The minimum offense level accounts for the fact that the means of identification that were "bred" (*i.e.*, produced or obtained) often are within the defendant's exclusive control, making it difficult for the individual victim to detect that the victim's identity has been "stolen." Generally, the victim does not become aware of the offense until certain harms have already occurred (*e.g.*, a damaged credit rating or an inability to obtain a loan). The minimum offense level also accounts for the non-monetary harm associated with these types of offenses, much of which may be difficult or impossible to quantify (*e.g.*, harm to the individual's reputation or credit rating, inconvenience, and other difficulties resulting from the offense). The legislative history of the Identity Theft and Assumption Deterrence Act of 1998 indicates that Congress was especially concerned with providing increased punishment for this type of harm.

Subsection (b)(12) implements the directive in section 5 of Public Law 110–179.

Subsection (b)(13) implements the directive in section 3 of Public Law 112–269.

Subsection (b)(15)(B) implements, in a broader form, the instruction to the Commission in section 110512 of Public Law 103–322.

Subsection (b)(16)(A) implements, in a broader form, the instruction to the Commission in section 2507 of Public Law 101–647.

Subsection (b)(16)(B)(i) implements, in a broader form, the instruction to the Commission in section 961(m) of Public Law 101–73.

Subsection (b)(17) implements the directive in section 209 of Public Law 110–326.

Subsection (b)(18) implements the directive in section 225(b) of Public Law 107–296. The minimum offense level of level 24 provided in subsection (b)(18)(B) for an offense that resulted in a substantial disruption of a critical infrastructure reflects the serious impact such an offense could have on national security, national economic security, national public health or safety, or a combination of any of these matters.

Historical Note	Effective November 1, 1987. Amended effective June 15, 1988 (amendment 7); November 1, 1989 (amendments 99–101 and 303); November 1, 1990 (amendments 312, 317, and 361); November 1, 1991 (amendments 364, and 393); November 1, 1993 (amendments 481 and 482); November 1, 1995 (amendment 512); November 1, 1997 (amendment 551); November 1, 1998 (amendment 576); November 1, 2000 (amendment 596); November 1, 2001 (amendment 617); November 1, 2002 (amendments 637, 638, and 646); January 25, 2003 (amendment 647); November 1, 2003 (amendments 653, 654, 655, and 661); November 1, 2004 (amendments 665, 666, and 674); November 1, 2005 (amendment 679); November 1, 2006 (amendments 685 and 696); November 1, 2007 (amendments 699, 700, and 702); February 6, 2008 (amendment 714); November 1, 2008 (amendments 719 and 725); November 1, 2009 (amendments 726, 733, and 737); November 1, 2010 (amendments 745 and 747); November 1, 2011 (amendment 749); November 1, 2012 (amendment 761); November 1, 2013 (amendments 771, 772, and 777); November 1, 2015 (amendments 791 and 792).

§2B1.2. [Deleted]

Historical Note	Section 2B1.2 (Receiving, Transporting, Transferring, Transmitting, or Possessing Stolen Property), effective November 1, 1987, amended effective January 15, 1988 (amendment 8), June 15, 1988 (amendment 9), November 1, 1989 (amendments 102–104), and November 1, 1990 (amendments 312 and 361), was deleted by consolidation with §2B1.1 effective November 1, 1993 (amendment 481).

§2B1.3. [Deleted]

Historical Note	Section 2B1.3 (Property Damage or Destruction), effective November 1, 1987, amended effective June 15, 1988 (amendment 10), November 1, 1990 (amendments 312 and 313), November 1, 1997 (amendment 551), November 1, 1998 (amendment 576), was deleted by consolidation with §2B1.1 effective November 1, 2001 (amendment 617).

§2B1.4. Insider Trading

(a) Base Offense Level: **8**

(b) Specific Offense Characteristics

    (1) If the gain resulting from the offense exceeded $6,500, increase by the number of levels from the table in §2B1.1 (Theft, Property Destruction, and Fraud) corresponding to that amount.

    (2) If the offense involved an organized scheme to engage in insider trading and the offense level determined above is less than level **14**, increase to level **14**.

Commentary

Statutory Provisions: 15 U.S.C. § 78j and 17 C.F.R. § 240.10b-5. For additional statutory provision(s), *see* Appendix A (Statutory Index).

Application Notes:

1. **Application of Subsection (b)(2).**—For purposes of subsection (b)(2), an "*organized scheme to engage in insider trading*" means a scheme to engage in insider trading that involves considered, calculated, systematic, or repeated efforts to obtain and trade on inside information, as distinguished from fortuitous or opportunistic instances of insider trading.

    The following is a non-exhaustive list of factors that the court may consider in determining whether the offense involved an organized scheme to engage in insider trading:

    (A)   the number of transactions;

    (B)   the dollar value of the transactions;

    (C)   the number of securities involved;

    (D)   the duration of the offense;

    (E)   the number of participants in the scheme (although such a scheme may exist even in the absence of more than one participant);

    (F)   the efforts undertaken to obtain material, nonpublic information;

    (G)   the number of instances in which material, nonpublic information was obtained; and

    (H)   the efforts undertaken to conceal the offense.

2. **Application of §3B1.3.**—Section 3B1.3 (Abuse of Position of Trust or Use of Special Skill) should be applied if the defendant occupied and abused a position of special trust. Examples might include a corporate president or an attorney who misused information regarding a planned but unannounced takeover attempt. It typically would not apply to an ordinary "tippee".

    Furthermore, §3B1.3 should be applied if the defendant's employment in a position that involved regular participation or professional assistance in creating, issuing, buying, selling, or trading securities or commodities was used to facilitate significantly the commission or concealment of the offense. It would apply, for example, to a hedge fund professional who regularly participates in securities transactions or to a lawyer who regularly provides professional assistance in securities transactions, if the defendant's employment in such a position was used to facilitate significantly the commission or concealment of the offense. It ordinarily would not apply to a position such as a clerical worker in an investment firm, because such a position ordinarily does not involve special skill. *See* §3B1.3, comment. (n.4).

Background: This guideline applies to certain violations of Rule 10b-5 that are commonly referred to as "insider trading". Insider trading is treated essentially as a sophisticated fraud. Because the victims and their losses are difficult if not impossible to identify, the gain, *i.e.*, the total increase in value realized through trading in securities by the defendant and persons acting in concert with the defendant or to whom the defendant provided inside information, is employed instead of the victims' losses.

Certain other offenses, *e.g.*, 7 U.S.C. § 13(e), that involve misuse of inside information for personal gain also appropriately may be covered by this guideline.

Subsection (b)(2) implements the directive to the Commission in section 1079A(a)(1)(A) of Public Law 111–203.

Historical Note	Effective November 1, 2001 (amendment 617). Amended effective November 1, 2010 (amendment 746); November 1, 2012 (amendment 761); November 1, 2015 (amendment 791).

§2B1.5. Theft of, Damage to, or Destruction of, Cultural Heritage Resources or Paleontological Resources; Unlawful Sale, Purchase, Exchange, Transportation, or Receipt of Cultural Heritage Resources or Paleontological Resources

(a) Base Offense Level: **8**

(b) Specific Offense Characteristics

   (1) If the value of the cultural heritage resource or paleontological resource (A) exceeded $2,500 but did not exceed $6,500, increase by **1** level; or (B) exceeded $6,500, increase by the number of levels from the table in §2B1.1 (Theft, Property Destruction, and Fraud) corresponding to that amount.

   (2) If the offense involved a cultural heritage resource or paleontological resource from, or that, prior to the offense, was on, in, or in the custody of (A) the national park system; (B) a National Historic Landmark; (C) a national monument or national memorial; (D) a national marine sanctuary; (E) a national cemetery or veterans' memorial; (F) a museum; or (G) the World Heritage List, increase by **2** levels.

   (3) If the offense involved a cultural heritage resource constituting (A) human remains; (B) a funerary object; (C) cultural patrimony; (D) a sacred object; (E) cultural property; (F) designated archaeological or ethnological material; or (G) a pre-Columbian monumental or architectural sculpture or mural, increase by **2** levels.

   (4) If the offense was committed for pecuniary gain or otherwise involved a commercial purpose, increase by **2** levels.

    (5)   If the defendant engaged in a pattern of misconduct involving cultural heritage resources or paleontological resources, increase by **2** levels.

    (6)   If a dangerous weapon was brandished or its use was threatened, increase by **2** levels. If the resulting offense level is less than level **14**, increase to level **14**.

(c)   Cross Reference

    (1)   If the offense involved arson, or property damage by the use of any explosive, explosive material, or destructive device, apply §2K1.4 (Arson; Property Damage by Use of Explosives), if the resulting offense level is greater than that determined above.

Commentary

Statutory Provisions: 16 U.S.C. §§ 470aaa–5, 470ee, 668(a), 707(b); 18 U.S.C. §§ 541–546, 554, 641, 661–662, 666, 668, 1163, 1168, 1170, 1361, 1369, 2232, 2314–2315.

Application Notes:

1.   **Definitions.**—For purposes of this guideline:

    (A)   "*Cultural heritage resource*" means any of the following:

        (i)   A historic property, as defined in 16 U.S.C. § 470w(5) (*see also* section 16(l) of 36 C.F.R. pt. 800).

        (ii)   A historic resource, as defined in 16 U.S.C. § 470w(5).

        (iii) An archaeological resource, as defined in 16 U.S.C. § 470bb(1) (*see also* section 3(a) of 43 C.F.R. pt. 7; 36 C.F.R. pt. 296; 32 C.F.R. pt. 229; 18 C.F.R. pt. 1312).

        (iv) A cultural item, as defined in section 2(3) of the Native American Graves Protection and Repatriation Act, 25 U.S.C. § 3001(3) (*see also* 43 C.F.R. § 10.2(d)).

        (v)   A commemorative work. "*Commemorative work*" (I) has the meaning given that term in 40 U.S.C. § 8902(a)(1); and (II) includes any national monument or national memorial.

        (vi) An object of cultural heritage, as defined in 18 U.S.C. § 668(a)(2).

        (vii) Designated ethnological material, as described in 19 U.S.C. §§ 2601(2)(ii), 2601(7), and 2604.

    (B)   "*Paleontological resource*" has the meaning given such term in 16 U.S.C. § 470aaa.

2.   **Value of the Resource Under Subsection (b)(1).**—This application note applies to the determination of the value of the resource under subsection (b)(1).

(A) **General Rule.**—For purposes of subsection (b)(1), the value of the resource shall include, as applicable to the particular resource involved, the following:

    (i)   The archaeological value. (Archaeological value shall be included in the case of any resource that is an archaeological resource.)

    (ii)   The commercial value.

    (iii)   The cost of restoration and repair.

(B) **Estimation of Value.**—For purposes of subsection (b)(1), the court need only make a reasonable estimate of the value of the resource based on available information.

(C) **Definitions.**—For purposes of this application note:

    (i)   "*Archaeological value*" of a resource means the cost of the retrieval of the scientific information which would have been obtainable prior to the offense, including the cost of preparing a research design, conducting field work, conducting laboratory analysis, and preparing reports, as would be necessary to realize the information potential. (*See, e.g.*, 43 C.F.R. § 7.14(a); 36 C.F.R. § 296.14(a); 32 C.F.R. § 229.14(a); 18 C.F.R. § 1312.14(a).)

    (ii)   "*Commercial value*" of a resource means the fair market value of the resource at the time of the offense. (*See, e.g.*, 43 C.F.R. § 7.14(b); 36 C.F.R. § 296.14(b); 32 C.F.R. § 229.14(b); 18 C.F.R. § 1312.14(b).)

    (iii)   "*Cost of restoration and repair*" includes all actual and projected costs of curation, disposition, and appropriate reburial of, and consultation with respect to, the resource; and any other actual and projected costs to complete restoration and repair of the resource, including (I) its reconstruction and stabilization; (II) reconstruction and stabilization of ground contour and surface; (III) research necessary to conduct reconstruction and stabilization; (IV) the construction of physical barriers and other protective devices; (V) examination and analysis of the resource as part of efforts to salvage remaining information about the resource; and (VI) preparation of reports. (*See, e.g.*, 43 C.F.R. § 7.14(c); 36 C.F.R. § 296.14(c); 32 C.F.R. § 229.14(c); 18 C.F.R. § 1312.14(c).)

(D) **Determination of Value in Cases Involving a Variety of Resources.**—In a case involving a variety of resources, the value of the resources is the sum of all calculations made for those resources under this application note.

3.   **Enhancement in Subsection (b)(2).**—For purposes of subsection (b)(2):

(A)   "*Museum*" has the meaning given that term in 18 U.S.C. § 668(a)(1) except that the museum may be situated outside the United States.

(B)   "*National cemetery*" and "*veterans' memorial*" have the meaning given those terms in Application Note 1 of the Commentary to §2B1.1 (Theft, Property Destruction, and Fraud).

(C)   "*National Historic Landmark*" means a property designated as such pursuant to 16 U.S.C. § 470a(a)(1)(B).

(D) "*National marine sanctuary*" means a national marine sanctuary designated as such by the Secretary of Commerce pursuant to 16 U.S.C. § 1433.

(E) "*National monument or national memorial*" means any national monument or national memorial established as such by Act of Congress or by proclamation pursuant to the Antiquities Act of 1906 (16 U.S.C. § 431).

(F) "*National park system*" has the meaning given that term in 16 U.S.C. § 1c(a).

(G) "*World Heritage List*" means the World Heritage List maintained by the World Heritage Committee of the United Nations Educational, Scientific, and Cultural Organization in accordance with the Convention Concerning the Protection of the World Cultural and Natural Heritage.

4. **Enhancement in Subsection (b)(3).**—For purposes of subsection (b)(3):

(A) "*Cultural patrimony*" has the meaning given that term in 25 U.S.C. § 3001(3)(D) (*see also* 43 C.F.R. 10.2(d)(4)).

(B) "*Cultural property*" has the meaning given that term in 19 U.S.C. § 2601(6).

(C) "*Designated archaeological or ethnological material*" means archaeological or ethnological material described in 19 U.S.C. § 2601(7) (*see also* 19 U.S.C. §§ 2601(2) and 2604).

(D) "*Funerary object*" means an object that, as a part of the death rite or ceremony of a culture, was placed intentionally, at the time of death or later, with or near human remains.

(E) "*Human remains*" (i) means the physical remains of the body of a human; and (ii) does not include remains that reasonably may be determined to have been freely disposed of or naturally shed by the human from whose body the remains were obtained, such as hair made into ropes or nets.

(F) "*Pre-Columbian monumental or architectural sculpture or mural*" has the meaning given that term in 19 U.S.C. § 2095(3).

(G) "*Sacred object*" has the meaning given that term in 25 U.S.C. § 3001(3)(C) (*see also* 43 C.F.R. § 10.2(d)(3)).

5. **Pecuniary Gain and Commercial Purpose Enhancement Under Subsection (b)(4).**—

(A) **"For Pecuniary Gain".**—For purposes of subsection (b)(4), "*for pecuniary gain*" means for receipt of, or in anticipation of receipt of, anything of value, whether monetary or in goods or services. Therefore, offenses committed for pecuniary gain include both monetary and barter transactions, as well as activities designed to increase gross revenue.

(B) **Commercial Purpose.**—The acquisition of resources for display to the public, whether for a fee or donation and whether by an individual or an organization, including a governmental entity, a private non-profit organization, or a private for-profit organization, shall be considered to involve a "commercial purpose" for purposes of subsection (b)(4).

6. **Pattern of Misconduct Enhancement Under Subsection (b)(5).—**

    (A) **Definition.**—For purposes of subsection (b)(5), "*pattern of misconduct involving cultural heritage resources or paleontological resources*" means two or more separate instances of offense conduct involving a resource that did not occur during the course of the offense (*i.e.*, that did not occur during the course of the instant offense of conviction and all relevant conduct under §1B1.3 (Relevant Conduct)). Offense conduct involving a resource may be considered for purposes of subsection (b)(5) regardless of whether the defendant was convicted of that conduct.

    (B) **Computation of Criminal History Points.**—A conviction taken into account under subsection (b)(5) is not excluded from consideration of whether that conviction receives criminal history points pursuant to Chapter Four, Part A (Criminal History).

7. **Dangerous Weapons Enhancement Under Subsection (b)(6).—**For purposes of subsection (b)(6), "*brandished*" and "*dangerous weapon*" have the meaning given those terms in Application Note 1 of the Commentary to §1B1.1 (Application Instructions).

8. **Multiple Counts.**—For purposes of Chapter Three, Part D (Multiple Counts), multiple counts involving offenses covered by this guideline are grouped together under subsection (d) of §3D1.2 (Groups of Closely Related Counts). Multiple counts involving offenses covered by this guideline and offenses covered by other guidelines are not to be grouped under §3D1.2(d).

9. **Upward Departure Provision.**—There may be cases in which the offense level determined under this guideline substantially understates the seriousness of the offense. In such cases, an upward departure may be warranted. For example, an upward departure may be warranted if (A) in addition to cultural heritage resources or paleontological resources, the offense involved theft of, damage to, or destruction of, items that are not cultural heritage resources (such as an offense involving the theft from a national cemetery of lawnmowers and other administrative property in addition to historic gravemarkers or other cultural heritage resources) or paleontological resources; or (B) the offense involved a cultural heritage resource that has profound significance to cultural identity (*e.g.*, the Statue of Liberty or the Liberty Bell).

Historical Note	Effective November 1, 2002 (amendment 638). Amended effective November 1, 2006 (amendment 685); November 1, 2007 (amendment 700); November 1, 2010 (amendments 745 and 746); November 1, 2014 (amendment 781); November 1, 2015 (amendment 791).

§2B1.6. Aggravated Identity Theft

(a) If the defendant was convicted of violating 18 U.S.C. § 1028A, the guideline sentence is the term of imprisonment required by statute. Chapters Three (Adjustments) and Four (Criminal History and Criminal Livelihood) shall not apply to that count of conviction.

§2B2.1

Commentary

Statutory Provision: 18 U.S.C. § 1028A. For additional statutory provision(s), *see* Appendix A (Statutory Index).

Application Notes:

1. **Imposition of Sentence.—**

    (A) **In General.—**Section 1028A of title 18, United State Code, provides a mandatory term of imprisonment. Accordingly, the guideline sentence for a defendant convicted under 18 U.S.C. § 1028A is the term required by that statute. Except as provided in subdivision (B), 18 U.S.C. § 1028A also requires a term of imprisonment imposed under this section to run consecutively to any other term of imprisonment.

    (B) **Multiple Convictions Under Section 1028A.—**Section 1028A(b)(4) of title 18, United State Code, provides that in the case of multiple convictions under 18 U.S.C. § 1028A, the terms of imprisonment imposed on such counts may, in the discretion of the court, run concurrently, in whole or in part, with each other. *See* the Commentary to §5G1.2 (Sentencing on Multiple Counts of Conviction) for guidance regarding imposition of sentence on multiple counts of 18 U.S.C. § 1028A.

2. **Inapplicability of Chapter Two Enhancement.—**If a sentence under this guideline is imposed in conjunction with a sentence for an underlying offense, do not apply any specific offense characteristic for the transfer, possession, or use of a means of identification when determining the sentence for the underlying offense. A sentence under this guideline accounts for this factor for the underlying offense of conviction, including any such enhancement that would apply based on conduct for which the defendant is accountable under §1B1.3 (Relevant Conduct). "*Means of identification*" has the meaning given that term in 18 U.S.C. § 1028(d)(7).

3. **Inapplicability of Chapters Three and Four.—**Do not apply Chapters Three (Adjustments) and Four (Criminal History and Criminal Livelihood) to any offense sentenced under this guideline. Such offenses are excluded from application of those chapters because the guideline sentence for each offense is determined only by the relevant statute. *See* §§3D1.1 (Procedure for Determining Offense Level on Multiple Counts) and 5G1.2.

Historical Note	Effective November 1, 2005 (amendment 677).

* * * * *

2. BURGLARY AND TRESPASS

§2B2.1. Burglary of a Residence or a Structure Other than a Residence

(a) Base Offense Level:

   (1) **17**, if a residence; or

     (2)   **12**, if a structure other than a residence.

  (b)   Specific Offense Characteristics

     (1)   If the offense involved more than minimal planning, increase by **2** levels.

     (2)   If the loss exceeded $5,000, increase the offense level as follows:

	LOSS (APPLY THE GREATEST)	INCREASE IN LEVEL
(A)	$5,000 or less	no increase
(B)	More than $5,000	add **1**
(C)	More than $20,000	add **2**
(D)	More than $95,000	add **3**
(E)	More than $500,000	add **4**
(F)	More than $1,500,000	add **5**
(G)	More than $3,000,000	add **6**
(H)	More than $5,000,000	add **7**
(I)	More than $9,500,000	add **8**.

     (3)   If a firearm, destructive device, or controlled substance was taken, or if the taking of such item was an object of the offense, increase by **1** level.

     (4)   If a dangerous weapon (including a firearm) was possessed, increase by **2** levels.

Commentary

Statutory Provisions: 18 U.S.C. §§ 2113(a), 2115, 2117, 2118(b). For additional statutory provision(s), *see* Appendix A (Statutory Index).

Application Notes:

1.   "*Firearm*," "*destructive device*," and "*dangerous weapon*" are defined in the Commentary to §1B1.1 (Application Instructions).

2.   "*Loss*" means the value of the property taken, damaged, or destroyed.

3.   Subsection (b)(4) does not apply to possession of a dangerous weapon (including a firearm) that was stolen during the course of the offense.

4.   **More than Minimal Planning.—**"*More than minimal planning*" means more planning than is typical for commission of the offense in a simple form. "More than minimal planning" also exists if significant affirmative steps were taken to conceal the offense, other than conduct to which §3C1.1 (Obstructing or Impeding the Administration of Justice) applies. "More than minimal planning" shall be considered to be present in any case involving repeated acts over a period of time, unless it is clear that each instance was purely opportune. For example, checking the area to make sure no witnesses were present would not alone constitute more than minimal planning. By contrast, obtaining

building plans to plot a particular course of entry, or disabling an alarm system, would constitute more than minimal planning.

Background: The base offense level for residential burglary is higher than for other forms of burglary because of the increased risk of physical and psychological injury. Weapon possession, but not use, is a specific offense characteristic because use of a weapon (including to threaten) ordinarily would make the offense robbery. Weapon use would be a ground for upward departure.

Historical Note	Effective November 1, 1987. Amended effective January 15, 1988 (amendment 11); June 15, 1988 (amendment 12); November 1, 1989 (amendments 105 and 106); November 1, 1990 (amendments 315 and 361); November 1, 1993 (amendment 481); November 1, 2001 (amendment 617); November 1, 2014 (amendment 781); November 1, 2015 (amendment 791).

§2B2.2. [Deleted]

Historical Note	Section 2B2.2 (Burglary of Other Structures), effective November 1, 1987, amended effective June 15, 1988 (amendment 13), November 1, 1989 (amendment 107), and November 1, 1990 (amendments 315 and 361), was deleted by consolidation with §2B2.1 effective November 1, 1993 (amendment 481).

§2B2.3. Trespass

    (a)   Base Offense Level: **4**

    (b)   Specific Offense Characteristics

        (1)   (Apply the greater) If—

            (A)   the trespass occurred (i) at a secure government facility; (ii) at a nuclear energy facility; (iii) on a vessel or aircraft of the United States; (iv) in a secure area of an airport or a seaport; (v) at a residence; (vi) at Arlington National Cemetery or a cemetery under the control of the National Cemetery Administration; (vii) at any restricted building or grounds; or (viii) on a computer system used (I) to maintain or operate a critical infrastructure; or (II) by or for a government entity in furtherance of the administration of justice, national defense, or national security, increase by **2** levels; or

            (B)   the trespass occurred at the White House or its grounds, or the Vice President's official residence or its grounds, increase by **4** levels.

        (2)   If a dangerous weapon (including a firearm) was possessed, increase by **2** levels.

(3) If (A) the offense involved invasion of a protected computer; and (B) the loss resulting from the invasion (i) exceeded $2,500 but did not exceed $6,500, increase by 1 level; or (ii) exceeded $6,500, increase by the number of levels from the table in §2B1.1 (Theft, Property Destruction, and Fraud) corresponding to that amount.

(c) Cross Reference

(1) If the offense was committed with the intent to commit a felony offense, apply §2X1.1 (Attempt, Solicitation, or Conspiracy) in respect to that felony offense, if the resulting offense level is greater than that determined above.

Commentary

Statutory Provisions: 18 U.S.C. §§ 1030(a)(3), 1036, 2199; 38 U.S.C. § 2413; 42 U.S.C. § 7270b. For additional statutory provision(s), *see* Appendix A (Statutory Index).

Application Notes:

1. **Definitions.**—For purposes of this guideline:

   "*Airport*" has the meaning given that term in section 47102 of title 49, United States Code.

   "*Critical infrastructure*" means systems and assets vital to national defense, national security, economic security, public health or safety, or any combination of those matters. A critical infrastructure may be publicly or privately owned. Examples of critical infrastructures include gas and oil production, storage, and delivery systems, water supply systems, telecommunications networks, electrical power delivery systems, financing and banking systems, emergency services (including medical, police, fire, and rescue services), transportation systems and services (including highways, mass transit, airlines, and airports), and government operations that provide essential services to the public.

   "*Felony offense*" means any offense (federal, state, or local) punishable by imprisonment for a term exceeding one year, whether or not a criminal charge was brought or a conviction was obtained.

   "*Firearm*" and "*dangerous weapon*" are defined in the Commentary to §1B1.1 (Application Instructions).

   "*Government entity*" has the meaning given that term in 18 U.S.C. § 1030(e)(9).

   "*Protected computer*" means a computer described in 18 U.S.C. § 1030(e)(2)(A) or (B).

   "*Restricted building or grounds*" has the meaning given that term in 18 U.S.C. § 1752.

   "*Seaport*" has the meaning given that term in 18 U.S.C. § 26.

2. **Application of Subsection (b)(3).**—Valuation of loss is discussed in the Commentary to §2B1.1 (Theft, Property Destruction, and Fraud).

Background: Most trespasses punishable under federal law involve federal lands or property. The trespass section provides an enhancement for offenses involving trespass on secure government installations (such as nuclear facilities) and other locations (such as airports and seaports) to protect a significant federal interest. Additionally, an enhancement is provided for trespass at a residence.

Historical Note	Effective November 1, 1987. Amended effective November 1, 1989 (amendments 108 and 109); November 1, 1997 (amendment 551); November 1, 2001 (amendment 617); November 1, 2002 (amendment 637); November 1, 2003 (amendment 654); November 1, 2007 (amendments 699 and 703); November 1, 2013 (amendment 777); November 1, 2015 (amendment 791).

*   *   *   *   *

3.   ROBBERY, EXTORTION, AND BLACKMAIL

§2B3.1.   Robbery

(a)   Base Offense Level: **20**

(b)   Specific Offense Characteristics

(1)   If the property of a financial institution or post office was taken, or if the taking of such property was an object of the offense, increase by **2** levels.

(2)   (A) If a firearm was discharged, increase by **7** levels; (B) if a firearm was otherwise used, increase by **6** levels; (C) if a firearm was brandished or possessed, increase by **5** levels; (D) if a dangerous weapon was otherwise used, increase by **4** levels; (E) if a dangerous weapon was brandished or possessed, increase by **3** levels; or (F) if a threat of death was made, increase by **2** levels.

(3)   If any victim sustained bodily injury, increase the offense level according to the seriousness of the injury:

	DEGREE OF BODILY INJURY	INCREASE IN LEVEL
(A)	Bodily Injury	add **2**
(B)	Serious Bodily Injury	add **4**
(C)	Permanent or Life-Threatening Bodily Injury	add **6**
(D)	If the degree of injury is between that specified in subdivisions (A) and (B),	add **3** levels; or
(E)	If the degree of injury is between that specified in subdivisions (B) and (C),	add **5** levels.

Provided, however, that the cumulative adjustments from (2) and (3) shall not exceed **11** levels.

(4) (A) If any person was abducted to facilitate commission of the offense or to facilitate escape, increase by **4** levels; or (B) if any person was physically restrained to facilitate commission of the offense or to facilitate escape, increase by **2** levels.

(5) If the offense involved carjacking, increase by **2** levels.

(6) If a firearm, destructive device, or controlled substance was taken, or if the taking of such item was an object of the offense, increase by **1** level.

(7) If the loss exceeded $20,000, increase the offense level as follows:

LOSS (APPLY THE GREATEST)	INCREASE IN LEVEL
(A) $20,000 or less	no increase
(B) More than $20,000	add **1**
(C) More than $95,000	add **2**
(D) More than $500,000	add **3**
(E) More than $1,500,000	add **4**
(F) More than $3,000,000	add **5**
(G) More than $5,000,000	add **6**
(H) More than $9,500,000	add **7**.

(c) Cross Reference

(1) If a victim was killed under circumstances that would constitute murder under 18 U.S.C. § 1111 had such killing taken place within the territorial or maritime jurisdiction of the United States, apply §2A1.1 (First Degree Murder).

Commentary

Statutory Provisions: 18 U.S.C. §§ 1951, 2113, 2114, 2118(a), 2119. For additional statutory provision(s), *see* Appendix A (Statutory Index).

Application Notes:

1. "*Firearm*," "*destructive device*," "*dangerous weapon*," "*otherwise used*," "*brandished*," "*bodily injury*," "*serious bodily injury*," "*permanent or life-threatening bodily injury*," "*abducted*," and "*physically restrained*" are defined in the Commentary to §1B1.1 (Application Instructions).

"*Carjacking*" means the taking or attempted taking of a motor vehicle from the person or presence of another by force and violence or by intimidation.

2.   Consistent with Application Note 1(D)(ii) of §1B1.1 (Application Instructions), an object shall be considered to be a dangerous weapon for purposes of subsection (b)(2)(E) if (A) the object closely resembles an instrument capable of inflicting death or serious bodily injury; or (B) the defendant used the object in a manner that created the impression that the object was an instrument capable of inflicting death or serious bodily injury (*e.g.*, a defendant wrapped a hand in a towel during a bank robbery to create the appearance of a gun).

3.   "*Loss*" means the value of the property taken, damaged, or destroyed.

4.   The combined adjustments for weapon involvement and injury are limited to a maximum enhancement of 11 levels.

5.   If the defendant intended to murder the victim, an upward departure may be warranted; *see* §2A2.1 (Assault with Intent to Commit Murder; Attempted Murder).

6.   "A threat of death," as used in subsection (b)(2)(F), may be in the form of an oral or written statement, act, gesture, or combination thereof. Accordingly, the defendant does not have to state expressly his intent to kill the victim in order for the enhancement to apply. For example, an oral or written demand using words such as "Give me the money or I will kill you", "Give me the money or I will pull the pin on the grenade I have in my pocket", "Give me the money or I will shoot you", "Give me your money or else (where the defendant draws his hand across his throat in a slashing motion)", or "Give me the money or you are dead" would constitute a threat of death. The court should consider that the intent of this provision is to provide an increased offense level for cases in which the offender(s) engaged in conduct that would instill in a reasonable person, who is a victim of the offense, a fear of death.

Background: Possession or use of a weapon, physical injury, and unlawful restraint sometimes occur during a robbery. The guideline provides for a range of enhancements where these factors are present.

Although in pre-guidelines practice the amount of money taken in robbery cases affected sentence length, its importance was small compared to that of the other harm involved. Moreover, because of the relatively high base offense level for robbery, an increase of 1 or 2 levels brings about a considerable increase in sentence length in absolute terms. Accordingly, the gradations for property loss increase more slowly than for simple property offenses.

The guideline provides an enhancement for robberies where a victim was forced to accompany the defendant to another location, or was physically restrained by being tied, bound, or locked up.

Historical Note	Effective November 1, 1987. Amended effective June 15, 1988 (amendments 14 and 15); November 1, 1989 (amendments 110 and 111); November 1, 1990 (amendments 314, 315, and 361); November 1, 1991 (amendment 365); November 1, 1993 (amendment 483); November 1, 1997 (amendments 545 and 552); November 1, 2000 (amendment 601); November 1, 2001 (amendment 617); November 1, 2010 (amendment 746); November 1, 2015 (amendment 791).

§2B3.2. Extortion by Force or Threat of Injury or Serious Damage

(a) Base Offense Level: **18**

(b) Specific Offense Characteristics

    (1) If the offense involved an express or implied threat of death, bodily injury, or kidnapping, increase by **2** levels.

    (2) If the greater of the amount demanded or the loss to the victim exceeded $20,000, increase by the corresponding number of levels from the table in §2B3.1(b)(7).

    (3) (A)(i) If a firearm was discharged, increase by **7** levels; (ii) if a firearm was otherwise used, increase by **6** levels; (iii) if a firearm was brandished or possessed, increase by **5** levels; (iv) if a dangerous weapon was otherwise used, increase by **4** levels; or (v) if a dangerous weapon was brandished or possessed, increase by **3** levels; or

    (B) If (i) the offense involved preparation to carry out a threat of (I) death; (II) serious bodily injury; (III) kidnapping; (IV) product tampering; or (V) damage to a computer system used to maintain or operate a critical infrastructure, or by or for a government entity in furtherance of the administration of justice, national defense, or national security; or (ii) the participant(s) otherwise demonstrated the ability to carry out a threat described in any of subdivisions (i)(I) through (i)(V), increase by **3** levels.

    (4) If any victim sustained bodily injury, increase the offense level according to the seriousness of the injury:

DEGREE OF BODILY INJURY	INCREASE IN LEVEL
(A) Bodily Injury	add **2**
(B) Serious Bodily Injury	add **4**
(C) Permanent or Life-Threatening Bodily Injury	add **6**
(D) If the degree of injury is between that specified in subdivisions (A) and (B),	add **3** levels; or
(E) If the degree of injury is between that specified in subdivisions (B) and (C),	add **5** levels.

Provided, however, that the cumulative adjustments from (3) and (4) shall not exceed **11** levels.

(5) (A) If any person was abducted to facilitate commission of the offense or to facilitate escape, increase by **4** levels; or (B) if any person was physically restrained to facilitate commission of the offense or to facilitate escape, increase by **2** levels.

(c) Cross References

(1) If a victim was killed under circumstances that would constitute murder under 18 U.S.C. § 1111 had such killing taken place within the territorial or maritime jurisdiction of the United States, apply §2A1.1 (First Degree Murder).

(2) If the offense was tantamount to attempted murder, apply §2A2.1 (Assault with Intent to Commit Murder; Attempted Murder) if the resulting offense level is greater than that determined above.

Commentary

Statutory Provisions: 18 U.S.C. §§ 875(b), 876, 877, 1030(a)(7), 1951. For additional statutory provision(s), *see* Appendix A (Statutory Index).

Application Notes:

1. **Definitions.**—For purposes of this guideline:

    "*Abducted*," "*bodily injury*," "*brandished*," "*dangerous weapon*," "*firearm*," "*otherwise used*," "*permanent or life-threatening bodily injury*," "*physically restrained*," and "*serious bodily injury*" have the meaning given those terms in Application Note 1 of the Commentary to §1B1.1 (Application Instructions).

    "*Critical infrastructure*" means systems and assets vital to national defense, national security, economic security, public health or safety, or any combination of those matters. A critical infrastructure may be publicly or privately owned. Examples of critical infrastructures include gas and oil production, storage, and delivery systems, water supply systems, telecommunications networks, electrical power delivery systems, financing and banking systems, emergency services (including medical, police, fire, and rescue services), transportation systems and services (including highways, mass transit, airlines, and airports), and government operations that provide essential services to the public.

    "*Government entity*" has the meaning given that term in 18 U.S.C. § 1030(e)(9).

2. This guideline applies if there was any threat, express or implied, that reasonably could be interpreted as one to injure a person or physically damage property, or any comparably serious threat, such as to drive an enterprise out of business. Even if the threat does not in itself imply violence, the possibility of violence or serious adverse consequences may be inferred from the circumstances of the threat or the reputation of the person making it. An ambiguous threat, such as "pay up or else," or a threat to cause labor problems, ordinarily should be treated under this section.

3. Guidelines for bribery involving public officials are found in Part C, Offenses Involving Public Officials. "Extortion under color of official right," which usually is solicitation of a bribe by a public official, is covered under §2C1.1 unless there is use of force or a threat that qualifies for treatment under this section. Certain other extortion offenses are covered under the provisions of Part E, Offenses Involving Criminal Enterprises and Racketeering.

4. The combined adjustments for weapon involvement and injury are limited to a maximum enhancement of 11 levels.

5. "*Loss to the victim*," as used in subsection (b)(2), means any demand paid plus any additional consequential loss from the offense (*e.g.*, the cost of defensive measures taken in direct response to the offense).

6. In certain cases, an extortionate demand may be accompanied by conduct that does not qualify as a display of a dangerous weapon under subsection (b)(3)(A)(v) but is nonetheless similar in seriousness, demonstrating the defendant's preparation or ability to carry out the threatened harm (*e.g.*, an extortionate demand containing a threat to tamper with a consumer product accompanied by a workable plan showing how the product's tamper-resistant seals could be defeated, or a threat to kidnap a person accompanied by information showing study of that person's daily routine). Subsection (b)(3)(B) addresses such cases.

7. If the offense involved the threat of death or serious bodily injury to numerous victims (*e.g.*, in the case of a plan to derail a passenger train or poison consumer products), an upward departure may be warranted.

8. If the offense involved organized criminal activity, or a threat to a family member of the victim, an upward departure may be warranted.

Background: The Hobbs Act, 18 U.S.C. § 1951, prohibits extortion, attempted extortion, and conspiracy to extort. It provides for a maximum term of imprisonment of twenty years. 18 U.S.C. §§ 875–877 prohibit communication of extortionate demands through various means. The maximum penalty under these statutes varies from two to twenty years. Violations of 18 U.S.C. § 875 involve threats or demands transmitted by interstate commerce. Violations of 18 U.S.C. § 876 involve the use of the United States mails to communicate threats, while violations of 18 U.S.C. § 877 involve mailing threatening communications from foreign countries. This guideline also applies to offenses under 18 U.S.C. § 1030(a)(7) involving a threat to impair the operation of a "protected computer."

Historical Note	Effective November 1, 1987. Amended effective November 1, 1989 (amendments 112, 113, and 303); November 1, 1990 (amendment 316); November 1, 1991 (amendment 366); November 1, 1993 (amendment 479); November 1, 1997 (amendment 551); November 1, 1998 (amendment 586); November 1, 2000 (amendment 601); November 1, 2003 (amendment 654); November 1, 2015 (amendment 791).

§2B3.3.   Blackmail and Similar Forms of Extortion

(a)   Base Offense Level: **9**

(b) Specific Offense Characteristic

(1) If the greater of the amount obtained or demanded (A) exceeded $2,500 but did not exceed $6,500, increase by 1 level; or (B) exceeded $6,500, increase by the number of levels from the table in §2B1.1 (Theft, Property Destruction, and Fraud) corresponding to that amount.

(c) Cross References

(1) If the offense involved extortion under color of official right, apply §2C1.1 (Offering, Giving, Soliciting, or Receiving a Bribe; Extortion Under Color of Official Right; Fraud Involving the Deprivation of the Intangible Right to Honest Services of Public Officials; Conspiracy to Defraud by Interference with Governmental Functions).

(2) If the offense involved extortion by force or threat of injury or serious damage, apply §2B3.2 (Extortion by Force or Threat of Injury or Serious Damage).

Commentary

Statutory Provisions: 18 U.S.C. §§ 873, 875–877, 1951. For additional statutory provision(s), *see* Appendix A (Statutory Index).

Application Note:

1. This section applies only to blackmail and similar forms of extortion where there clearly is no threat of violence to person or property. "*Blackmail*" (18 U.S.C. § 873) is defined as a threat to disclose a violation of United States law unless money or some other item of value is given.

Background: Under 18 U.S.C. § 873, the maximum term of imprisonment authorized for blackmail is one year. Extortionate threats to injure a reputation, or other threats that are less serious than those covered by §2B3.2, may also be prosecuted under 18 U.S.C. §§ 875–877, which carry higher maximum sentences.

Historical Note	Effective November 1, 1987. Amended effective November 1, 1989 (amendment 114); November 1, 1993 (amendment 479); November 1, 2001 (amendment 617); November 1, 2005 (amendment 679); November 1, 2015 (amendment 791).

*　　*　　*　　*　　*

4. COMMERCIAL BRIBERY AND KICKBACKS

---

§2B4.1. Bribery in Procurement of Bank Loan and Other Commercial Bribery

(a) Base Offense Level: 8

(b) Specific Offense Characteristics

    (1) If the greater of the value of the bribe or the improper benefit to be conferred (A) exceeded $2,500 but did not exceed $6,500, increase by 1 level; or (B) exceeded $6,500, increase by the number of levels from the table in §2B1.1 (Theft, Property Destruction, and Fraud) corresponding to that amount.

    (2) (Apply the greater) If—

        (A) the defendant derived more than $1,000,000 in gross receipts from one or more financial institutions as a result of the offense, increase by 2 levels; or

        (B) the offense substantially jeopardized the safety and soundness of a financial institution, increase by 4 levels.

    If the resulting offense level determined under subdivision (A) or (B) is less than level 24, increase to level 24.

(c) Special Instruction for Fines — Organizations

    (1) In lieu of the pecuniary loss under subsection (a)(3) of §8C2.4 (Base Fine), use the greatest of: (A) the value of the unlawful payment; (B) the value of the benefit received or to be received in return for the unlawful payment; or (C) the consequential damages resulting from the unlawful payment.

Commentary

Statutory Provisions: 18 U.S.C. §§ 215, 224, 225; 26 U.S.C. §§ 9012(e), 9042(d); 41 U.S.C. §§ 8702, 8707; 42 U.S.C. §§ 1395nn(b)(1), (2), 1396h(b)(1),(2); 49 U.S.C. § 11902. For additional statutory provision(s), *see* Appendix A (Statutory Index).

Application Notes:

1. This guideline covers commercial bribery offenses and kickbacks that do not involve officials of federal, state, or local government, foreign governments, or public international organizations. *See* Part C, Offenses Involving Public Officials, if any such officials are involved.

2. The "*value of the improper benefit to be conferred*" refers to the value of the action to be taken or effected in return for the bribe. *See* Commentary to §2C1.1 (Offering, Giving, Soliciting, or Receiving a Bribe; Extortion Under Color of Official Right; Fraud Involving the Deprivation of the Intangible Right to Honest Services of Public Officials; Conspiracy to Defraud by Interference with Governmental Functions).

3. "*Financial institution*," as used in this guideline, is defined to include any institution described in 18 U.S.C. §§ 20, 656, 657, 1005–1007, and 1014; any state or foreign bank, trust company, credit union, insurance company, investment company, mutual fund, savings (building and loan) association, union or employee pension fund; any health, medical or hospital insurance association; brokers and dealers registered, or required to be registered, with the Securities and Exchange Commission; futures commodity merchants and commodity pool operators registered, or required to be registered, with the Commodity Futures Trading Commission; and any similar entity, whether or not insured by the federal government. "Union or employee pension fund" and "any health, medical, or hospital insurance association," as used above, primarily include large pension funds that serve many individuals (*e.g.*, pension funds of large national and international organizations, unions, and corporations doing substantial interstate business), and associations that undertake to provide pension, disability, or other benefits (*e.g.*, medical or hospitalization insurance) to large numbers of persons.

4. **Gross Receipts Enhancement under Subsection (b)(2)(A).—**

    (A) **In General.**—For purposes of subsection (b)(2)(A), the defendant shall be considered to have derived more than $1,000,000 in gross receipts if the gross receipts to the defendant individually, rather than to all participants, exceeded $1,000,000.

    (B) **Definition.**—"*Gross receipts from the offense*" includes all property, real or personal, tangible or intangible, which is obtained directly or indirectly as a result of such offense. *See* 18 U.S.C. § 982(a)(4).

5. **Enhancement for Substantially Jeopardizing the Safety and Soundness of a Financial Institution under Subsection (b)(2)(B).—**For purposes of subsection (b)(2)(B), an offense shall be considered to have substantially jeopardized the safety and soundness of a financial institution if, as a consequence of the offense, the institution (A) became insolvent; (B) substantially reduced benefits to pensioners or insureds; (C) was unable on demand to refund fully any deposit, payment, or investment; (D) was so depleted of its assets as to be forced to merge with another institution in order to continue active operations; or (E) was placed in substantial jeopardy of any of subdivisions (A) through (D) of this note.

6. If the defendant is convicted under 18 U.S.C. § 225 (relating to a continuing financial crimes enterprise), the offense level is that applicable to the underlying series of offenses comprising the "continuing financial crimes enterprise."

Background: This guideline applies to violations of various federal bribery statutes that do not involve governmental officials. The base offense level is to be enhanced based upon the value of the unlawful payment or the value of the action to be taken or effected in return for the unlawful payment, whichever is greater.

One of the more commonly prosecuted offenses to which this guideline applies is offering or accepting a fee in connection with procurement of a loan from a financial institution in violation of 18 U.S.C. § 215.

As with non-commercial bribery, this guideline considers not only the amount of the bribe but also the value of the action received in return. Thus, for example, if a bank officer agreed to the offer of a $25,000 bribe to approve a $250,000 loan under terms for which the applicant would not otherwise qualify, the court, in increasing the offense level, would use the greater of the $25,000 bribe, and the savings in interest over the life of the loan compared with alternative loan terms. If a gambler paid a player $5,000 to shave points in a nationally televised basketball game, the value of the action to the gambler would be the amount that he and his confederates won or stood to gain. If that amount could not be estimated, the amount of the bribe would be used to determine the appropriate increase in offense level.

This guideline also applies to making prohibited payments to induce the award of subcontracts on federal projects for which the maximum term of imprisonment authorized is ten years. 41 U.S.C. §§ 8702, 8707. Violations of 42 U.S.C. § 1320a-7b involve the offer or acceptance of a payment to refer an individual for services or items paid for under a federal health care program (*e.g.*, the Medicare and Medicaid programs).

This guideline also applies to violations of law involving bribes and kickbacks in expenses incurred for a presidential nominating convention or presidential election campaign. These offenses are prohibited under 26 U.S.C. §§ 9012(e) and 9042(d), which apply to candidates for President and Vice President whose campaigns are eligible for federal matching funds.

This guideline also applies to violations of 18 U.S.C. § 224, sports bribery, as well as certain violations of the Interstate Commerce Act.

Subsection (b)(2)(A) implements, in a broader form, the instruction to the Commission in section 961(m) of Public Law 101–73.

Subsection (b)(2)(B) implements the instruction to the Commission in section 2507 of Public Law 101–647.

Historical Note	Effective November 1, 1987. Amended effective November 1, 1990 (amendment 317); November 1, 1991 (amendments 364 and 422); November 1, 1992 (amendment 468); November 1, 1997 (amendment 553); November 1, 2001 (amendment 617); November 1, 2002 (amendments 639 and 646); November 1, 2004 (amendment 666); November 1, 2010 (amendment 746); November 1, 2015 (amendments 791 and 796).

*   *   *   *   *

5.   COUNTERFEITING AND INFRINGEMENT OF COPYRIGHT OR TRADEMARK

Historical Note	Effective November 1, 1987. Amended effective November 1, 1993 (amendment 481).

§2B5.1.   Offenses Involving Counterfeit Bearer Obligations of the United States

(a)   Base Offense Level: **9**

    (b)   Specific Offense Characteristics

        (1)   If the face value of the counterfeit items (A) exceeded $2,500 but did not exceed $6,500, increase by **1** level; or (B) exceeded $6,500, increase by the number of levels from the table in §2B1.1 (Theft, Property Destruction, and Fraud) corresponding to that amount.

        (2)   If the defendant (A) manufactured or produced any counterfeit obligation or security of the United States, or possessed or had custody of or control over a counterfeiting device or materials used for counterfeiting; or (B) controlled or possessed (i) counterfeiting paper similar to a distinctive paper; (ii) genuine United States currency paper from which the ink or other distinctive counterfeit deterrent has been completely or partially removed; or (iii) a feature or device essentially identical to a distinctive counterfeit deterrent, increase by **2** levels.

        (3)   If subsection (b)(2)(A) applies, and the offense level determined under that subsection is less than level **15**, increase to level **15**.

        (4)   If a dangerous weapon (including a firearm) was possessed in connection with the offense, increase by **2** levels. If the resulting offense level is less than level **13**, increase to level **13**.

        (5)   If any part of the offense was committed outside the United States, increase by **2** levels.

Commentary

Statutory Provisions: 18 U.S.C. §§ 470–474A, 476, 477, 500, 501, 1003. For additional statutory provision(s), *see* Appendix A (Statutory Index).

Application Notes:

1.   **Definitions.**—For purposes of this guideline:

"*Counterfeit*" refers to an instrument that has been falsely made, manufactured, or altered. For example, an instrument that has been falsely made or manufactured in its entirety is "counterfeit", as is a genuine instrument that has been falsely altered (such as a genuine $5 bill that has been altered to appear to be a genuine $100 bill).

"*Distinctive counterfeit deterrent*" and "*distinctive paper*" have the meaning given those terms in 18 U.S.C. § 474A(c)(2) and (1), respectively.

"*United States*" means each of the fifty states, the District of Columbia, the Commonwealth of Puerto Rico, the United States Virgin Islands, Guam, the Northern Mariana Islands, and American Samoa.

2. **Applicability to Counterfeit Bearer Obligations of the United States.**—This guideline applies to counterfeiting of United States currency and coins, food stamps, postage stamps, treasury bills, bearer bonds and other items that generally could be described as bearer obligations of the United States, *i.e.*, that are not made out to a specific payee.

3. **Inapplicability to Certain Obviously Counterfeit Items.**—Subsection (b)(2)(A) does not apply to persons who produce items that are so obviously counterfeit that they are unlikely to be accepted even if subjected to only minimal scrutiny.

Background: Possession of counterfeiting devices to copy obligations (including securities) of the United States is treated as an aggravated form of counterfeiting because of the sophistication and planning involved in manufacturing counterfeit obligations and the public policy interest in protecting the integrity of government obligations. Similarly, an enhancement is provided for a defendant who produces, rather than merely passes, the counterfeit items.

Subsection (b)(4) implements, in a broader form, the instruction to the Commission in section 110512 of Public Law 103–322.

Historical Note	Effective November 1, 1987. Amended effective January 15, 1988 (amendment 16); November 1, 1989 (amendment 115); November 1, 1995 (amendment 513); November 1, 1997 (amendment 554); November 1, 1998 (amendment 587); November 1, 2000 (amendments 595 and 605); November 1, 2001 (amendments 617 and 618); November 1, 2009 (amendment 731); November 1, 2015 (amendment 791).

§2B5.2. [Deleted]

Historical Note	Section 2B5.2 (Forgery; Offenses Involving Altered or Counterfeit Instruments Other than Counterfeit Bearer Obligations of the United States), effective November 1, 1987, amended effective January 15, 1988 (amendment 17) and November 1, 1989 (amendment 116), was deleted by consolidation with §2F1.1 effective November 1, 1993 (amendment 481).

§2B5.3. Criminal Infringement of Copyright or Trademark

(a) Base Offense Level: **8**

(b) Specific Offense Characteristics

   (1) If the infringement amount (A) exceeded **$2,500** but did not exceed **$6,500**, increase by **1** level; or (B) exceeded **$6,500**, increase by the number of levels from the table in §2B1.1 (Theft, Property Destruction, and Fraud) corresponding to that amount.

   (2) If the offense involved the display, performance, publication, reproduction, or distribution of a work being prepared for commercial distribution, increase by **2** levels.

(3) If the (A) offense involved the manufacture, importation, or up-loading of infringing items; or (B) defendant was convicted under 17 U.S.C. §§ 1201 and 1204 for trafficking in circumvention devices, increase by **2** levels. If the resulting offense level is less than level **12**, increase to level **12**.

(4) If the offense was not committed for commercial advantage or private financial gain, decrease by **2** levels, but the resulting offense level shall be not less than level **8**.

(5) If the offense involved a counterfeit drug, increase by **2** levels.

(6) If the offense involved (A) the conscious or reckless risk of death or serious bodily injury; or (B) possession of a dangerous weapon (including a firearm) in connection with the offense, increase by **2** levels. If the resulting offense level is less than level **14**, increase to level **14**.

(7) If the offense involved a counterfeit military good or service the use, malfunction, or failure of which is likely to cause (A) the disclosure of classified information; (B) impairment of combat operations; or (C) other significant harm to (i) a combat operation, (ii) a member of the Armed Forces, or (iii) national security, increase by **2** levels. If the resulting offense level is less than level **14**, increase to level **14**.

Commentary

Statutory Provisions: 17 U.S.C. §§ 506(a), 1201, 1204; 18 U.S.C. §§ 2318–2320, 2511. For additional statutory provision(s), *see* Appendix A (Statutory Index).

Application Notes:

1. **Definitions.**—For purposes of this guideline:

    "*Circumvention devices*" are devices used to perform the activity described in 17 U.S.C. §§ 1201(a)(3)(A) and 1201(b)(2)(A).

    "*Commercial advantage or private financial gain*" means the receipt, or expectation of receipt, of anything of value, including other protected works.

    "*Counterfeit drug*" has the meaning given that term in 18 U.S.C. § 2320(f)(6).

    "*Counterfeit military good or service*" has the meaning given that term in 18 U.S.C. § 2320(f)(4).

    "*Infringed item*" means the copyrighted or trademarked item with respect to which the crime against intellectual property was committed.

    "*Infringing item*" means the item that violates the copyright or trademark laws.

"*Uploading*" means making an infringing item available on the Internet or a similar electronic bulletin board with the intent to enable other persons to (A) download or otherwise copy the infringing item; or (B) have access to the infringing item, including by storing the infringing item as an openly shared file. "Uploading" does not include merely downloading or installing an infringing item on a hard drive on a defendant's personal computer unless the infringing item is an openly shared file.

"*Work being prepared for commercial distribution*" has the meaning given that term in 17 U.S.C. § 506(a)(3).

2. **Determination of Infringement Amount.**—This note applies to the determination of the infringement amount for purposes of subsection (b)(1).

    (A) **Use of Retail Value of Infringed Item.**—The infringement amount is the retail value of the infringed item, multiplied by the number of infringing items, in a case involving any of the following:

        (i) The infringing item (I) is, or appears to a reasonably informed purchaser to be, identical or substantially equivalent to the infringed item; or (II) is a digital or electronic reproduction of the infringed item.

        (ii) The retail price of the infringing item is not less than 75% of the retail price of the infringed item.

        (iii) The retail value of the infringing item is difficult or impossible to determine without unduly complicating or prolonging the sentencing proceeding.

        (iv) The offense involves the illegal interception of a satellite cable transmission in violation of 18 U.S.C. § 2511. (In a case involving such an offense, the "retail value of the infringed item" is the price the user of the transmission would have paid to lawfully receive that transmission, and the "infringed item" is the satellite transmission rather than the intercepting device.)

        (v) The retail value of the infringed item provides a more accurate assessment of the pecuniary harm to the copyright or trademark owner than does the retail value of the infringing item.

        (vi) The offense involves the display, performance, publication, reproduction, or distribution of a work being prepared for commercial distribution. In a case involving such an offense, the "retail value of the infringed item" is the value of that item upon its initial commercial distribution.

        (vii) A case under 18 U.S.C. § 2318 or § 2320 that involves a counterfeit label, patch, sticker, wrapper, badge, emblem, medallion, charm, box, container, can, case, hangtag, documentation, or packaging of any type or nature (I) that has not been affixed to, or does not enclose or accompany a good or service; and (II) which, had it been so used, would appear to a reasonably informed purchaser to be affixed to, enclosing or accompanying an identifiable, genuine good or service. In such a case, the "infringed item" is the identifiable, genuine good or service.

        (viii) A case under 17 U.S.C. §§ 1201 and 1204 in which the defendant used a circumvention device. In such an offense, the "retail value of the infringed item" is the price the user would have paid to access lawfully the copyrighted work, and the "infringed item" is the accessed work.

(B) **Use of Retail Value of Infringing Item.**—The infringement amount is the retail value of the infringing item, multiplied by the number of infringing items, in any case not covered by subdivision (A) of this Application Note, including a case involving the unlawful recording of a musical performance in violation of 18 U.S.C. § 2319A.

(C) **Retail Value Defined.**—For purposes of this Application Note, the "*retail value*" of an infringed item or an infringing item is the retail price of that item in the market in which it is sold.

(D) **Determination of Infringement Amount in Cases Involving a Variety of Infringing Items.**—In a case involving a variety of infringing items, the infringement amount is the sum of all calculations made for those items under subdivisions (A) and (B) of this Application Note. For example, if the defendant sold both counterfeit videotapes that are identical in quality to the infringed videotapes and obviously inferior counterfeit handbags, the infringement amount, for purposes of subsection (b)(1), is the sum of the infringement amount calculated with respect to the counterfeit videotapes under subdivision (A)(i) (*i.e.*, the quantity of the infringing videotapes multiplied by the retail value of the infringed videotapes) and the infringement amount calculated with respect to the counterfeit handbags under subdivision (B) (*i.e.*, the quantity of the infringing handbags multiplied by the retail value of the infringing handbags).

(E) **Indeterminate Number of Infringing Items.**—In a case in which the court cannot determine the number of infringing items, the court need only make a reasonable estimate of the infringement amount using any relevant information, including financial records.

3. **Application of Subsection (b)(7).**—In subsection (b)(7), "*other significant harm to a member of the Armed Forces*" means significant harm other than serious bodily injury or death. In a case in which the offense involved a counterfeit military good or service the use, malfunction, or failure of which is likely to cause serious bodily injury or death, subsection (b)(6)(A) (conscious or reckless risk of serious bodily injury or death) would apply.

4. **Application of §3B1.3.**—If the defendant de-encrypted or otherwise circumvented a technological security measure to gain initial access to an infringed item, an adjustment under §3B1.3 (Abuse of Position of Trust or Use of Special Skill) may apply.

5. **Departure Considerations.**—If the offense level determined under this guideline substantially understates or overstates the seriousness of the offense, a departure may be warranted. The following is a non-exhaustive list of factors that the court may consider in determining whether a departure may be warranted:

(A) The offense involved substantial harm to the reputation of the copyright or trademark owner.

(B) The offense was committed in connection with, or in furtherance of, the criminal activities of a national, or international, organized criminal enterprise.

(C)   The method used to calculate the infringement amount is based upon a formula or extrapolation that results in an estimated amount that may substantially exceed the actual pecuniary harm to the copyright or trademark owner.

(D)   The offense resulted in death or serious bodily injury.

Background: This guideline treats copyright and trademark violations much like theft and fraud. Similar to the sentences for theft and fraud offenses, the sentences for defendants convicted of intellectual property offenses should reflect the nature and magnitude of the pecuniary harm caused by their crimes. Accordingly, similar to the loss enhancement in the theft and fraud guideline, the infringement amount in subsection (b)(1) serves as a principal factor in determining the offense level for intellectual property offenses.

Subsection (b)(1) implements section 2(g) of the No Electronic Theft (NET) Act of 1997, Pub. L. 105–147, by using the retail value of the infringed item, multiplied by the number of infringing items, to determine the pecuniary harm for cases in which use of the retail value of the infringed item is a reasonable estimate of that harm. For cases referred to in Application Note 2(B), the Commission determined that use of the retail value of the infringed item would overstate the pecuniary harm or otherwise be inappropriate. In these types of cases, use of the retail value of the infringing item, multiplied by the number of those items, is a more reasonable estimate of the resulting pecuniary harm.

Subsection (b)(5) implements the directive to the Commission in section 717 of Public Law 112–144.

Section 2511 of title 18, United States Code, as amended by the Electronic Communications Act of 1986, prohibits the interception of satellite transmission for purposes of direct or indirect commercial advantage or private financial gain. Such violations are similar to copyright offenses and are therefore covered by this guideline.

Historical Note	Effective November 1, 1987. Amended effective November 1, 1993 (amendments 481 and 482); May 1, 2000 (amendment 590); November 1, 2000 (amendment 593); November 1, 2001 (amendment 617); October 24, 2005 (amendment 675); September 12, 2006 (amendment 682); November 1, 2006 (amendment 687); November 1, 2007 (amendment 704); November 1, 2009 (amendment 735); November 1, 2013 (amendment 773); November 1, 2015 (amendment 791).

§2B5.4. [Deleted]

Historical Note	Section 2B5.4 (Criminal Infringement of Trademark), effective November 1, 1987, was deleted by consolidation with §2B5.3 effective November 1, 1993 (amendment 481).

*   *   *   *   *

6. MOTOR VEHICLE IDENTIFICATION NUMBERS

§2B6.1. Altering or Removing Motor Vehicle Identification Numbers, or Trafficking in Motor Vehicles or Parts with Altered or Obliterated Identification Numbers

(a) Base Offense Level: **8**

(b) Specific Offense Characteristics

(1) If the retail value of the motor vehicles or parts (A) exceeded $2,500 but did not exceed $6,500, increase by **1** level; or (B) exceeded $6,500, increase by the number of levels from the table in §2B1.1 (Theft, Property Destruction, and Fraud) corresponding to that amount.

(2) If the defendant was in the business of receiving and selling stolen property, increase by **2** levels.

(3) If the offense involved an organized scheme to steal vehicles or vehicle parts, or to receive stolen vehicles or vehicle parts, and the offense level as determined above is less than level **14**, increase to level **14**.

Commentary

Statutory Provisions: 18 U.S.C. §§ 511, 553(a)(2), 2321.

Application Notes:

1. Subsection (b)(3), referring to an "organized scheme to steal vehicles or vehicle parts, or to receive stolen vehicles or vehicle parts," provides an alternative minimum measure of loss in the case of an ongoing, sophisticated operation such as an auto theft ring or "chop shop." "*Vehicles*" refers to all forms of vehicles, including aircraft and watercraft. *See* Commentary to §2B1.1 (Theft, Property Destruction, and Fraud).

2. The term "*increase by the number of levels from the table in §2B1.1 (Theft, Property Destruction, and Fraud) corresponding to that amount*," as used in subsection (b)(1), refers to the number of levels corresponding to the retail value of the motor vehicles or parts involved.

Background: The statutes covered in this guideline prohibit altering or removing motor vehicle identification numbers, importing or exporting, or trafficking in motor vehicles or parts knowing that the identification numbers have been removed, altered, tampered with, or obliterated. Violations of 18 U.S.C. § 511 carry a maximum of five years imprisonment. Violations of 18 U.S.C. §§ 553(a)(2) and 2321 carry a maximum of ten years imprisonment.

Historical Note	Effective November 1, 1987. Amended effective November 1, 1989 (amendments 117–119); November 1, 1993 (amendment 482); November 1, 2001 (amendment 617); November 1, 2010 (amendment 746); November 1, 2015 (amendment 791).

PART C — OFFENSES INVOLVING PUBLIC OFFICIALS AND VIOLATIONS OF FEDERAL ELECTION CAMPAIGN LAWS

Historical Note	Effective November 1, 1987. Amended effective January 25, 2003 (amendment 648). Introductory Commentary to Part C, effective November 1, 1987, was deleted effective January 25, 2003 (amendment 648), and November 1, 2003 (amendment 656).

§2C1.1. Offering, Giving, Soliciting, or Receiving a Bribe; Extortion Under Color of Official Right; Fraud Involving the Deprivation of the Intangible Right to Honest Services of Public Officials; Conspiracy to Defraud by Interference with Governmental Functions

(a) Base Offense Level:

   (1) **14**, if the defendant was a public official; or

   (2) **12**, otherwise.

(b) Specific Offense Characteristics

   (1) If the offense involved more than one bribe or extortion, increase by **2** levels.

   (2) If the value of the payment, the benefit received or to be received in return for the payment, the value of anything obtained or to be obtained by a public official or others acting with a public official, or the loss to the government from the offense, whichever is greatest, exceeded $6,500, increase by the number of levels from the table in §2B1.1 (Theft, Property Destruction, and Fraud) corresponding to that amount.

   (3) If the offense involved an elected public official or any public official in a high-level decision-making or sensitive position, increase by **4** levels. If the resulting offense level is less than level **18**, increase to level **18**.

   (4) If the defendant was a public official who facilitated (A) entry into the United States for a person, a vehicle, or cargo; (B) the obtaining of a passport or a document relating to naturalization, citizenship, legal entry, or legal resident status; or (C) the obtaining of a government identification document, increase by **2** levels.

(c) Cross References

    (1) If the offense was committed for the purpose of facilitating the commission of another criminal offense, apply the offense guideline applicable to a conspiracy to commit that other offense, if the resulting offense level is greater than that determined above.

    (2) If the offense was committed for the purpose of concealing, or obstructing justice in respect to, another criminal offense, apply §2X3.1 (Accessory After the Fact) or §2J1.2 (Obstruction of Justice), as appropriate, in respect to that other offense, if the resulting offense level is greater than that determined above.

    (3) If the offense involved a threat of physical injury or property destruction, apply §2B3.2 (Extortion by Force or Threat of Injury or Serious Damage), if the resulting offense level is greater than that determined above.

(d) Special Instruction for Fines — Organizations

    (1) In lieu of the pecuniary loss under subsection (a)(3) of §8C2.4 (Base Fine), use the greatest of: (A) the value of the unlawful payment; (B) the value of the benefit received or to be received in return for the unlawful payment; or (C) the consequential damages resulting from the unlawful payment.

Commentary

Statutory Provisions: 15 U.S.C. §§ 78dd-1, 78dd-2, 78dd-3; 18 U.S.C. §§ 201(b)(1), (2), 226, 227, 371 (if conspiracy to defraud by interference with governmental functions), 872, 1341 (if the scheme or artifice to defraud was to deprive another of the intangible right of honest services of a public official), 1342 (if the scheme or artifice to defraud was to deprive another of the intangible right of honest services of a public official), 1343 (if the scheme or artifice to defraud was to deprive another of the intangible right of honest services of a public official), 1951. For additional statutory provision(s), *see* Appendix A (Statutory Index).

Application Notes:

1. **Definitions.**—For purposes of this guideline:

"*Government identification document*" means a document made or issued by or under the authority of the United States Government, a State, or a political subdivision of a State, which, when completed with information concerning a particular individual, is of a type intended or commonly accepted for the purpose of identification of individuals.

"*Payment*" means anything of value. A payment need not be monetary.

"Public official" shall be construed broadly and includes the following:

(A) "Public official" as defined in 18 U.S.C. § 201(a)(1).

(B) A member of a state or local legislature. "State" means a State of the United States, and any commonwealth, territory, or possession of the United States.

(C) An officer or employee or person acting for or on behalf of a state or local government, or any department, agency, or branch of government thereof, in any official function, under or by authority of such department, agency, or branch of government, or a juror in a state or local trial.

(D) Any person who has been selected to be a person described in subdivisions (A), (B), or (C), either before or after such person has qualified.

(E) An individual who, although not otherwise covered by subdivisions (A) through (D): (i) is in a position of public trust with official responsibility for carrying out a government program or policy; (ii) acts under color of law or official right; or (iii) participates so substantially in government operations as to possess de facto authority to make governmental decisions (*e.g.*, which may include a leader of a state or local political party who acts in the manner described in this subdivision).

2. **More than One Bribe or Extortion.**—Subsection (b)(1) provides an adjustment for offenses involving more than one incident of either bribery or extortion. Related payments that, in essence, constitute a single incident of bribery or extortion (*e.g.*, a number of installment payments for a single action) are to be treated as a single bribe or extortion, even if charged in separate counts.

   In a case involving more than one incident of bribery or extortion, the applicable amounts under subsection (b)(2) (*i.e.*, the greatest of the value of the payment, the benefit received or to be received, the value of anything obtained or to be obtained by a public official or others acting with a public official, or the loss to the government) are determined separately for each incident and then added together.

3. **Application of Subsection (b)(2).**—"*Loss*", for purposes of subsection (b)(2), shall be determined in accordance with Application Note 3 of the Commentary to §2B1.1 (Theft, Property Destruction, and Fraud). The value of "*the benefit received or to be received*" means the net value of such benefit. **Examples:** (A) A government employee, in return for a $500 bribe, reduces the price of a piece of surplus property offered for sale by the government from $10,000 to $2,000; the value of the benefit received is $8,000. (B) A $150,000 contract on which $20,000 profit was made was awarded in return for a bribe; the value of the benefit received is $20,000. Do not deduct the value of the bribe itself in computing the value of the benefit received or to be received. In the preceding examples, therefore, the value of the benefit received would be the same regardless of the value of the bribe.

4. **Application of Subsection (b)(3).**—

(A) **Definition.**—"*High-level decision-making or sensitive position*" means a position characterized by a direct authority to make decisions for, or on behalf of, a government department, agency, or other government entity, or by a substantial influence over the decision-making process.

(B) **Examples.**—Examples of a public official in a high-level decision-making position include a prosecuting attorney, a judge, an agency administrator, and any other public official with a similar level of authority. Examples of a public official who holds a sensitive position include a juror, a law enforcement officer, an election official, and any other similarly situated individual.

5. **Application of Subsection (c).**—For the purposes of determining whether to apply the cross references in this section, the "*resulting offense level*" means the final offense level (*i.e.*, the offense level determined by taking into account both the Chapter Two offense level and any applicable adjustments from Chapter Three, Parts A–D). *See* §1B1.5(d); Application Note 2 of the Commentary to §1B1.5 (Interpretation of References to Other Offense Guidelines).

6. **Inapplicability of §3B1.3.**—Do not apply §3B1.3 (Abuse of Position of Trust or Use of Special Skill).

7. **Upward Departure Provisions.**—In some cases the monetary value of the unlawful payment may not be known or may not adequately reflect the seriousness of the offense. For example, a small payment may be made in exchange for the falsification of inspection records for a shipment of defective parachutes or the destruction of evidence in a major narcotics case. In part, this issue is addressed by the enhancements in §2C1.1(b)(2) and (c)(1), (2), and (3). However, in cases in which the seriousness of the offense is still not adequately reflected, an upward departure is warranted. *See* Chapter Five, Part K (Departures).

In a case in which the court finds that the defendant's conduct was part of a systematic or pervasive corruption of a governmental function, process, or office that may cause loss of public confidence in government, an upward departure may be warranted. *See* §5K2.7 (Disruption of Governmental Function).

Background: This section applies to a person who offers or gives a bribe for a corrupt purpose, such as inducing a public official to participate in a fraud or to influence such individual's official actions, or to a public official who solicits or accepts such a bribe.

The object and nature of a bribe may vary widely from case to case. In some cases, the object may be commercial advantage (*e.g.*, preferential treatment in the award of a government contract). In others, the object may be issuance of a license to which the recipient is not entitled. In still others, the object may be the obstruction of justice. Consequently, a guideline for the offense must be designed to cover diverse situations.

In determining the net value of the benefit received or to be received, the value of the bribe is not deducted from the gross value of such benefit; the harm is the same regardless of value of the bribe paid to receive the benefit. In a case in which the value of the bribe exceeds the value of the benefit, or in which the value of the benefit cannot be determined, the value of the bribe is used because it is likely that the payer of such a bribe expected something in return that would be worth more than the value of the bribe. Moreover, for deterrence purposes, the punishment should be commensurate with the gain to the payer or the recipient of the bribe, whichever is greater.

Under §2C1.1(b)(3), if the payment was for the purpose of influencing an official act by certain officials, the offense level is increased by 4 levels.

Under §2C1.1(c)(1), if the payment was to facilitate the commission of another criminal offense, the guideline applicable to a conspiracy to commit that other offense will apply if the result is greater than that determined above. For example, if a bribe was given to a law enforcement officer to allow the smuggling of a quantity of cocaine, the guideline for conspiracy to import cocaine would be applied if it resulted in a greater offense level.

Under §2C1.1(c)(2), if the payment was to conceal another criminal offense or obstruct justice in respect to another criminal offense, the guideline from §2X3.1 (Accessory After the Fact) or §2J1.2 (Obstruction of Justice), as appropriate, will apply if the result is greater than that determined above. For example, if a bribe was given for the purpose of concealing the offense of espionage, the guideline for accessory after the fact to espionage would be applied.

Under §2C1.1(c)(3), if the offense involved forcible extortion, the guideline from §2B3.2 (Extortion by Force or Threat of Injury or Serious Damage) will apply if the result is greater than that determined above.

Section 2C1.1 also applies to offenses under 15 U.S.C. §§ 78dd-1, 78dd-2, and 78dd-3. Such offenses generally involve a payment to a foreign public official, candidate for public office, or agent or intermediary, with the intent to influence an official act or decision of a foreign government or political party. Typically, a case prosecuted under these provisions will involve an intent to influence governmental action.

Section 2C1.1 also applies to fraud involving the deprivation of the intangible right to honest services of government officials under 18 U.S.C. §§ 1341–1343 and conspiracy to defraud by interference with governmental functions under 18 U.S.C. § 371. Such fraud offenses typically involve an improper use of government influence that harms the operation of government in a manner similar to bribery offenses.

Offenses involving attempted bribery are frequently not completed because the offense is reported to authorities or an individual involved in the offense is acting in an undercover capacity. Failure to complete the offense does not lessen the defendant's culpability in attempting to use public position for personal gain. Therefore, solicitations and attempts are treated as equivalent to the underlying offense.

Historical Note	Effective November 1, 1987. Amended effective January 15, 1988 (amendment 18); November 1, 1989 (amendments 120–122); November 1, 1991 (amendments 367 and 422); November 1, 1997 (amendment 547); November 1, 2001 (amendment 617); November 1, 2002 (amendment 639); November 1, 2003 (amendment 653); November 1, 2004 (amendment 666); November 1, 2007 (amendment 699); November 1, 2008 (amendment 720); November 1, 2010 (amendment 746); November 1, 2015 (amendment 791).

§2C1.2. Offering, Giving, Soliciting, or Receiving a Gratuity

    (a)   Base Offense Level:

        (1)   **11**, if the defendant was a public official; or

        (2)   **9**, otherwise.

    (b)   Specific Offense Characteristics

        (1)   If the offense involved more than one gratuity, increase by **2** levels.

(2) If the value of the gratuity exceeded $6,500, increase by the number of levels from the table in §2B1.1 (Theft, Property Destruction, and Fraud) corresponding to that amount.

(3) If the offense involved an elected public official or any public official in a high-level decision-making or sensitive position, increase by **4** levels. If the resulting offense level is less than level **15**, increase to level **15**.

(4) If the defendant was a public official who facilitated (A) entry into the United States for a person, a vehicle, or cargo; (B) the obtaining of a passport or a document relating to naturalization, citizenship, legal entry, or legal resident status; or (C) the obtaining of a government identification document, increase by **2** levels.

(c) Special Instruction for Fines — Organizations

(1) In lieu of the pecuniary loss under subsection (a)(3) of §8C2.4 (Base Fine), use the value of the unlawful payment.

Commentary

Statutory Provisions: 18 U.S.C. §§ 201(c)(1), 212–214, 217. For additional statutory provision(s), *see* Appendix A (Statutory Index).

Application Notes:

1. **Definitions.**—For purposes of this guideline:

   "*Government identification document*" means a document made or issued by or under the authority of the United States Government, a State, or a political subdivision of a State, which, when completed with information concerning a particular individual, is of a type intended or commonly accepted for the purpose of identification of individuals.

   "*Public official*" shall be construed broadly and includes the following:

   (A) "Public official" as defined in 18 U.S.C. § 201(a)(1).

   (B) A member of a state or local legislature. "State" means a State of the United States, and any commonwealth, territory, or possession of the United States.

   (C) An officer or employee or person acting for or on behalf of a state or local government, or any department, agency, or branch of government thereof, in any official function, under or by authority of such department, agency, or branch of government, or a juror.

   (D) Any person who has been selected to be a person described in subdivisions (A), (B), or (C), either before or after such person has qualified.

(E) An individual who, although not otherwise covered by subdivisions (A) through (D): (i) is in a position of public trust with official responsibility for carrying out a government program or policy; (ii) acts under color of law or official right; or (iii) participates so substantially in government operations as to possess de facto authority to make governmental decisions (*e.g.*, which may include a leader of a state or local political party who acts in the manner described in this subdivision).

2. **Application of Subsection (b)(1).**—Related payments that, in essence, constitute a single gratuity (*e.g.*, separate payments for airfare and hotel for a single vacation trip) are to be treated as a single gratuity, even if charged in separate counts.

3. **Application of Subsection (b)(3).**—

 (A) **Definition.**—"*High-level decision-making or sensitive position*" means a position characterized by a direct authority to make decisions for, or on behalf of, a government department, agency, or other government entity, or by a substantial influence over the decision-making process.

 (B) **Examples.**—Examples of a public official in a high-level decision-making position include a prosecuting attorney, a judge, an agency administrator, a law enforcement officer, and any other public official with a similar level of authority. Examples of a public official who holds a sensitive position include a juror, a law enforcement officer, an election official, and any other similarly situated individual.

4. **Inapplicability of §3B1.3.**—Do not apply the adjustment in §3B1.3 (Abuse of Position of Trust or Use of Special Skill).

Background: This section applies to the offering, giving, soliciting, or receiving of a gratuity to a public official in respect to an official act. It also applies in cases involving (1) the offer to, or acceptance by, a bank examiner of a loan or gratuity; (2) the offer or receipt of anything of value for procuring a loan or discount of commercial bank paper from a Federal Reserve Bank; and (3) the acceptance of a fee or other consideration by a federal employee for adjusting or cancelling a farm debt.

Historical Note	Effective November 1, 1987. Amended effective November 1, 1989 (amendment 121); November 1, 1991 (amendment 422); November 1, 1995 (amendment 534); November 1, 2001 (amendment 617); November 1, 2004 (amendment 666); November 1, 2010 (amendment 746); November 1, 2015 (amendment 791).

§2C1.3. Conflict of Interest; Payment or Receipt of Unauthorized Compensation

(a) Base Offense Level: **6**

(b) Specific Offense Characteristic

 (1) If the offense involved actual or planned harm to the government, increase by **4** levels.

    (c)   Cross Reference

        (1)   If the offense involved a bribe or gratuity, apply §2C1.1 (Offering, Giving, Soliciting, or Receiving a Bribe; Extortion Under Color of Official Right; Fraud Involving the Deprivation of the Intangible Right to Honest Services of Public Officials; Conspiracy to Defraud by Interference with Governmental Functions) or §2C1.2 (Offering, Giving, Soliciting, or Receiving a Gratuity), as appropriate, if the resulting offense level is greater than the offense level determined above.

Commentary

Statutory Provisions: 18 U.S.C. §§ 203, 205, 207, 208, 209, 1909; 40 U.S.C. § 14309(a), (b). For additional statutory provision(s), *see* Appendix A (Statutory Index).

Application Note:

1.   **Abuse of Position of Trust.**—Do not apply the adjustment in §3B1.3 (Abuse of Position of Trust or Use of Special Skill).

Historical Note	Effective November 1, 1987. Amended effective November 1, 1995 (amendment 534); November 1, 2001 (amendment 619); November 1, 2003 (amendment 661); November 1, 2005 (amendment 679).

---

§2C1.4. [Deleted]

Historical Note	Section 2C1.4 (Payment or Receipt of Unauthorized Compensation), effective November 1, 1987, amended effective November 1, 1998 (amendment 588), was deleted by consolidation with §2C1.3 effective November 1, 2001 (amendment 619).

---

§2C1.5. Payments to Obtain Public Office

    (a)   Base Offense Level: **8**

Commentary

Statutory Provisions: 18 U.S.C. §§ 210, 211.

Application Note:

1.   Do not apply the adjustment in §3B1.3 (Abuse of Position of Trust or Use of Special Skill).

Background: Under 18 U.S.C. § 210, it is unlawful to pay, offer, or promise anything of value to a person, firm, or corporation in consideration of procuring appointive office. Under

18 U.S.C. § 211, it is unlawful to solicit or accept anything of value in consideration of a promise of the use of influence in obtaining appointive federal office. Both offenses are misdemeanors for which the maximum term of imprisonment authorized by statute is one year.

Historical Note	Effective November 1, 1987.

---

§2C1.6. [Deleted]

Historical Note	Effective November 1, 1987. Amended effective November 1, 2001 (amendment 617); was deleted by consolidation with §2C1.2 effective November 1, 2004 (amendment 666).

---

§2C1.7. [Deleted]

Historical Note	Effective November 1, 1991 (amendment 368). Amended effective November 1, 1992 (amendment 468); November 1, 1997 (amendment 547); November 1, 2001 (amendment 617); November 1, 2003 (amendment 653); was deleted by consolidation with §2C1.1 effective November 1, 2004 (amendment 666).

§2C1.8. Making, Receiving, or Failing to Report a Contribution, Donation, or Expenditure in Violation of the Federal Election Campaign Act; Fraudulently Misrepresenting Campaign Authority; Soliciting or Receiving a Donation in Connection with an Election While on Certain Federal Property

(a) Base Offense Level: 8

(b) Specific Offense Characteristics

   (1) If the value of the illegal transactions exceeded $6,500, increase by the number of levels from the table in §2B1.1 (Theft, Property Destruction, and Fraud) corresponding to that amount.

   (2) (Apply the greater) If the offense involved, directly or indirectly, an illegal transaction made by or received from—

      (A) a foreign national, increase by **2** levels; or

      (B) a government of a foreign country, increase by **4** levels.

   (3) If (A) the offense involved the contribution, donation, solicitation, expenditure, disbursement, or receipt of governmental

funds; or (B) the defendant committed the offense for the purpose of obtaining a specific, identifiable non-monetary Federal benefit, increase by **2** levels.

(4)   If the defendant engaged in 30 or more illegal transactions, increase by **2** levels.

(5)   If the offense involved a contribution, donation, solicitation, or expenditure made or obtained through intimidation, threat of pecuniary or other harm, or coercion, increase by **4** levels.

(c)   Cross Reference

(1)   If the offense involved a bribe or gratuity, apply §2C1.1 (Offering, Giving, Soliciting, or Receiving a Bribe; Extortion Under Color of Official Right; Fraud Involving the Deprivation of the Intangible Right to Honest Services of Public Officials; Conspiracy to Defraud by Interference with Governmental Functions) or §2C1.2 (Offering, Giving, Soliciting, or Receiving a Gratuity), as appropriate, if the resulting offense level is greater than the offense level determined above.

Commentary

Statutory Provisions: 18 U.S.C. § 607; 52 U.S.C. §§ 30109(d), 30114, 30116, 30117, 30118, 30119, 30120, 30121, 30122, 30123, 30124(a), 30125, 30126. For additional provision(s), *see* Appendix A (Statutory Index).

Application Notes:

1.   **Definitions.**—For purposes of this guideline:

"*Foreign national*" has the meaning given that term in section 319(b) of the Federal Election Campaign Act of 1971, 52 U.S.C. § 30121(b).

"*Government of a foreign country*" has the meaning given that term in section 1(e) of the Foreign Agents Registration Act of 1938 (22 U.S.C. § 611(e)).

"*Governmental funds*" means money, assets, or property, of the United States government, of a State government, or of a local government, including any branch, subdivision, department, agency, or other component of any such government. "State" means any of the fifty States, the District of Columbia, the Commonwealth of Puerto Rico, the United States Virgin Islands, Guam, the Northern Mariana Islands, or American Samoa. "Local government" means the government of a political subdivision of a State.

"*Illegal transaction*" means (A) any contribution, donation, solicitation, or expenditure of money or anything of value, or any other conduct, prohibited by the Federal Election Campaign Act of 1971, 52 U.S.C. § 30101 *et seq.*; (B) any contribution, donation, solicitation, or expenditure of money or anything of value made in excess of the amount of such contribution, donation, solicitation, or expenditure that may be made under such Act; and (C) in the case of a violation of 18 U.S.C. § 607, any solicitation or receipt of money or anything of value under that section. The terms "***contribution***" and "***expenditure***" have the meaning given those terms in section 301(8) and (9) of the Federal Election Campaign Act of 1971 (52 U.S.C. § 30101(8) and (9)), respectively.

2. **Application of Subsection (b)(3)(B).**—Subsection (b)(3)(B) provides an enhancement for a defendant who commits the offense for the purpose of achieving a specific, identifiable non-monetary Federal benefit that does not rise to the level of a bribe or a gratuity. Subsection (b)(3)(B) is not intended to apply to offenses under this guideline in which the defendant's only motivation for commission of the offense is generally to achieve increased visibility with, or heightened access to, public officials. Rather, subsection (b)(3)(B) is intended to apply to defendants who commit the offense to obtain a specific, identifiable non-monetary Federal benefit, such as a Presidential pardon or information proprietary to the government.

3. **Application of Subsection (b)(4).**—Subsection (b)(4) shall apply if the defendant engaged in any combination of 30 or more illegal transactions during the course of the offense, whether or not the illegal transactions resulted in a conviction for such conduct.

4. **Departure Provision.**—In a case in which the defendant's conduct was part of a systematic or pervasive corruption of a governmental function, process, or office that may cause loss of public confidence in government, an upward departure may be warranted.

| *Historical Note* | Effective January 25, 2003 (amendment 648). Amended effective November 1, 2003 (amendment 656); November 1, 2005 (amendment 679); November 1, 2015 (amendments 791 and 796). |

PART D — OFFENSES INVOLVING DRUGS AND NARCO-TERRORISM

Historical Note	Effective November 1, 1987. Amended effective November 1, 2007 (amendment 711).

1. UNLAWFUL MANUFACTURING, IMPORTING, EXPORTING, TRAFFICKING, OR POSSESSION; CONTINUING CRIMINAL ENTERPRISE

§2D1.1. Unlawful Manufacturing, Importing, Exporting, or Trafficking (Including Possession with Intent to Commit These Offenses); Attempt or Conspiracy

    (a)   Base Offense Level (Apply the greatest):

        (1)   **43**, if the defendant is convicted under 21 U.S.C. § 841(b)(1)(A), (b)(1)(B), or (b)(1)(C), or 21 U.S.C. § 960(b)(1), (b)(2), or (b)(3), and the offense of conviction establishes that death or serious bodily injury resulted from the use of the substance and that the defendant committed the offense after one or more prior convictions for a similar offense; or

        (2)   **38**, if the defendant is convicted under 21 U.S.C. § 841(b)(1)(A), (b)(1)(B), or (b)(1)(C), or 21 U.S.C. § 960(b)(1), (b)(2), or (b)(3), and the offense of conviction establishes that death or serious bodily injury resulted from the use of the substance; or

        (3)   **30**, if the defendant is convicted under 21 U.S.C. § 841(b)(1)(E) or 21 U.S.C. § 960(b)(5), and the offense of conviction establishes that death or serious bodily injury resulted from the use of the substance and that the defendant committed the offense after one or more prior convictions for a similar offense; or

        (4)   **26**, if the defendant is convicted under 21 U.S.C. § 841(b)(1)(E) or 21 U.S.C. § 960(b)(5), and the offense of conviction establishes that death or serious bodily injury resulted from the use of the substance; or

        (5)   the offense level specified in the Drug Quantity Table set forth in subsection (c), except that if (A) the defendant receives an adjustment under §3B1.2 (Mitigating Role); and (B) the base offense level under subsection (c) is (i) level **32**, decrease by **2** levels; (ii) level **34** or level **36**, decrease by **3** levels; or (iii) level **38**, decrease by **4** levels. If the resulting offense level

is greater than level **32** and the defendant receives the 4-level ("minimal participant") reduction in §3B1.2(a), decrease to level **32**.

(b)   Specific Offense Characteristics

(1)   If a dangerous weapon (including a firearm) was possessed, increase by **2** levels.

(2)   If the defendant used violence, made a credible threat to use violence, or directed the use of violence, increase by **2** levels.

(3)   If the defendant unlawfully imported or exported a controlled substance under circumstances in which (A) an aircraft other than a regularly scheduled commercial air carrier was used to import or export the controlled substance, (B) a submersible vessel or semi-submersible vessel as described in 18 U.S.C. § 2285 was used, or (C) the defendant acted as a pilot, copilot, captain, navigator, flight officer, or any other operation officer aboard any craft or vessel carrying a controlled substance, increase by **2** levels. If the resulting offense level is less than level **26**, increase to level **26**.

(4)   If the object of the offense was the distribution of a controlled substance in a prison, correctional facility, or detention facility, increase by **2** levels.

(5)   If (A) the offense involved the importation of amphetamine or methamphetamine or the manufacture of amphetamine or methamphetamine from listed chemicals that the defendant knew were imported unlawfully, and (B) the defendant is not subject to an adjustment under §3B1.2 (Mitigating Role), increase by **2** levels.

(6)   If the defendant is convicted under 21 U.S.C. § 865, increase by **2** levels.

(7)   If the defendant, or a person for whose conduct the defendant is accountable under §1B1.3 (Relevant Conduct), distributed a controlled substance through mass-marketing by means of an interactive computer service, increase by **2** levels.

(8)   If the offense involved the distribution of an anabolic steroid and a masking agent, increase by **2** levels.

(9)   If the defendant distributed an anabolic steroid to an athlete, increase by **2** levels.

    (10) If the defendant was convicted under 21 U.S.C. § 841(g)(1)(A), increase by **2** levels.

    (11) If the defendant bribed, or attempted to bribe, a law enforcement officer to facilitate the commission of the offense, increase by **2** levels.

    (12) If the defendant maintained a premises for the purpose of manufacturing or distributing a controlled substance, increase by **2** levels.

    (13) (Apply the greatest):

        (A) If the offense involved (i) an unlawful discharge, emission, or release into the environment of a hazardous or toxic substance; or (ii) the unlawful transportation, treatment, storage, or disposal of a hazardous waste, increase by **2** levels.

        (B) If the defendant was convicted under 21 U.S.C. § 860a of distributing, or possessing with intent to distribute, methamphetamine on premises where a minor is present or resides, increase by **2** levels. If the resulting offense level is less than level **14**, increase to level **14**.

        (C) If—

            (i) the defendant was convicted under 21 U.S.C. § 860a of manufacturing, or possessing with intent to manufacture, methamphetamine on premises where a minor is present or resides; or

            (ii) the offense involved the manufacture of amphetamine or methamphetamine and the offense created a substantial risk of harm to (I) human life other than a life described in subdivision (D); or (II) the environment,

        increase by **3** levels. If the resulting offense level is less than level **27**, increase to level **27**.

        (D) If the offense (i) involved the manufacture of amphetamine or methamphetamine; and (ii) created a substantial risk of harm to the life of a minor or an incompetent, increase by **6** levels. If the resulting offense level is less than level **30**, increase to level **30**.

(14) If (A) the offense involved the cultivation of marihuana on state or federal land or while trespassing on tribal or private land; and (B) the defendant receives an adjustment under §3B1.1 (Aggravating Role), increase by **2** levels.

(15) If the defendant receives an adjustment under §3B1.1 (Aggravating Role) and the offense involved 1 or more of the following factors:

(A) (i) the defendant used fear, impulse, friendship, affection, or some combination thereof to involve another individual in the illegal purchase, sale, transport, or storage of controlled substances, (ii) the individual received little or no compensation from the illegal purchase, sale, transport, or storage of controlled substances, and (iii) the individual had minimal knowledge of the scope and structure of the enterprise;

(B) the defendant, knowing that an individual was (i) less than 18 years of age, (ii) 65 or more years of age, (iii) pregnant, or (iv) unusually vulnerable due to physical or mental condition or otherwise particularly susceptible to the criminal conduct, distributed a controlled substance to that individual or involved that individual in the offense;

(C) the defendant was directly involved in the importation of a controlled substance;

(D) the defendant engaged in witness intimidation, tampered with or destroyed evidence, or otherwise obstructed justice in connection with the investigation or prosecution of the offense;

(E) the defendant committed the offense as part of a pattern of criminal conduct engaged in as a livelihood,

increase by **2** levels.

(16) If the defendant receives the 4-level ("minimal participant") reduction in §3B1.2(a) and the offense involved all of the following factors:

(A) the defendant was motivated by an intimate or familial relationship or by threats or fear to commit the offense and was otherwise unlikely to commit such an offense;

  (B) the defendant received no monetary compensation from the illegal purchase, sale, transport, or storage of controlled substances; and

  (C) the defendant had minimal knowledge of the scope and structure of the enterprise,

decrease by **2** levels.

(17) If the defendant meets the criteria set forth in subdivisions (1)–(5) of subsection (a) of §5C1.2 (Limitation on Applicability of Statutory Minimum Sentences in Certain Cases), decrease by **2** levels.

[Subsection (c) (Drug Quantity Table) is set forth on the following pages.]

(d) **Cross References**

(1) If a victim was killed under circumstances that would constitute murder under 18 U.S.C. § 1111 had such killing taken place within the territorial or maritime jurisdiction of the United States, apply §2A1.1 (First Degree Murder) or §2A1.2 (Second Degree Murder), as appropriate, if the resulting offense level is greater than that determined under this guideline.

(2) If the defendant was convicted under 21 U.S.C. § 841(b)(7) (of distributing a controlled substance with intent to commit a crime of violence), apply §2X1.1 (Attempt, Solicitation, or Conspiracy) in respect to the crime of violence that the defendant committed, or attempted or intended to commit, if the resulting offense level is greater than that determined above.

(e) **Special Instruction**

(1) If (A) subsection (d)(2) does not apply; and (B) the defendant committed, or attempted to commit, a sexual offense against another individual by distributing, with or without that individual's knowledge, a controlled substance to that individual, an adjustment under §3A1.1(b)(1) shall apply.

(c) DRUG QUANTITY TABLE

CONTROLLED SUBSTANCES AND QUANTITY*	BASE OFFENSE LEVEL

(1)
- 90 KG or more of Heroin;   **Level 38**
- 450 KG or more of Cocaine;
- 25.2 KG or more of Cocaine Base;
- 90 KG or more of PCP, or 9 KG or more of PCP (actual);
- 45 KG or more of Methamphetamine, or
    4.5 KG or more of Methamphetamine (actual), or
    4.5 KG or more of "Ice";
- 45 KG or more of Amphetamine, or
    4.5 KG or more of Amphetamine (actual);
- 900 G or more of LSD;
- 36 KG or more of Fentanyl;
- 9 KG or more of a Fentanyl Analogue;
- 90,000 KG or more of Marihuana;
- 18,000 KG or more of Hashish;
- 1,800 KG or more of Hashish Oil;
- 90,000,000 units or more of Ketamine;
- 90,000,000 units or more of Schedule I or II Depressants;
- 5,625,000 units or more of Flunitrazepam.

(2)
- At least 30 KG but less than 90 KG of Heroin;   **Level 36**
- At least 150 KG but less than 450 KG of Cocaine;
- At least 8.4 KG but less than 25.2 KG of Cocaine Base;
- At least 30 KG but less than 90 KG of PCP, or
    at least 3 KG but less than 9 KG of PCP (actual);
- At least 15 KG but less than 45 KG of Methamphetamine, or
  at least 1.5 KG but less than 4.5 KG of Methamphetamine (actual), or
  at least 1.5 KG but less than 4.5 KG of "Ice";
- At least 15 KG but less than 45 KG of Amphetamine, or
    at least 1.5 KG but less than 4.5 KG of Amphetamine (actual);
- At least 300 G but less than 900 G of LSD;
- At least 12 KG but less than 36 KG of Fentanyl;
- At least 3 KG but less than 9 KG of a Fentanyl Analogue;
- At least 30,000 KG but less than 90,000 KG of Marihuana;
- At least 6,000 KG but less than 18,000 KG of Hashish;
- At least 600 KG but less than 1,800 KG of Hashish Oil;
- At least 30,000,000 units but less than 90,000,000 units of Ketamine;
- At least 30,000,000 units but less than 90,000,000 units of
    Schedule I or II Depressants;
- At least 1,875,000 units but less than 5,625,000 units of Flunitrazepam.

(3)
- At least 10 KG but less than 30 KG of Heroin;   **Level 34**
- At least 50 KG but less than 150 KG of Cocaine;
- At least 2.8 KG but less than 8.4 KG of Cocaine Base;
- At least 10 KG but less than 30 KG of PCP, or
    at least 1 KG but less than 3 KG of PCP (actual);
- At least 5 KG but less than 15 KG of Methamphetamine, or
    at least 500 G but less than 1.5 KG of Methamphetamine (actual), or
    at least 500 G but less than 1.5 KG of "Ice";
- At least 5 KG but less than 15 KG of Amphetamine, or

at least 500 G but less than 1.5 KG of Amphetamine (actual);
- At least 100 G but less than 300 G of LSD;
- At least 4 KG but less than 12 KG of Fentanyl;
- At least 1 KG but less than 3 KG of a Fentanyl Analogue;
- At least 10,000 KG but less than 30,000 KG of Marihuana;
- At least 2,000 KG but less than 6,000 KG of Hashish;
- At least 200 KG but less than 600 KG of Hashish Oil;
- At least 10,000,000 but less than 30,000,000 units of Ketamine;
- At least 10,000,000 but less than 30,000,000 units of Schedule I or II Depressants;
- At least 625,000 but less than 1,875,000 units of Flunitrazepam.

(4)
- At least 3 KG but less than 10 KG of Heroin;   **Level 32**
- At least 15 KG but less than 50 KG of Cocaine;
- At least 840 G but less than 2.8 KG of Cocaine Base;
- At least 3 KG but less than 10 KG of PCP, or
    at least 300 G but less than 1 KG of PCP (actual);
- At least 1.5 KG but less than 5 KG of Methamphetamine, or
    at least 150 G but less than 500 G of Methamphetamine (actual), or
    at least 150 G but less than 500 G of "Ice";
- At least 1.5 KG but less than 5 KG of Amphetamine, or
    at least 150 G but less than 500 G of Amphetamine (actual);
- At least 30 G but less than 100 G of LSD;
- At least 1.2 KG but less than 4 KG of Fentanyl;
- At least 300 G but less than 1 KG of a Fentanyl Analogue;
- At least 3,000 KG but less than 10,000 KG of Marihuana;
- At least 600 KG but less than 2,000 KG of Hashish;
- At least 60 KG but less than 200 KG of Hashish Oil;
- At least 3,000,000 but less than 10,000,000 units of Ketamine;
- At least 3,000,000 but less than 10,000,000 units of Schedule I or II Depressants;
- At least 187,500 but less than 625,000 units of Flunitrazepam.

(5)
- At least 1 KG but less than 3 KG of Heroin;   **Level 30**
- At least 5 KG but less than 15 KG of Cocaine;
- At least 280 G but less than 840 G of Cocaine Base;
- At least 1 KG but less than 3 KG of PCP, or
    at least 100 G but less than 300 G of PCP (actual);
- At least 500 G but less than 1.5 KG of Methamphetamine, or
    at least 50 G but less than 150 G of Methamphetamine (actual), or
    at least 50 G but less than 150 G of "Ice";
- At least 500 G but less than 1.5 KG of Amphetamine, or
    at least 50 G but less than 150 G of Amphetamine (actual);
- At least 10 G but less than 30 G of LSD;
- At least 400 G but less than 1.2 KG of Fentanyl;
- At least 100 G but less than 300 G of a Fentanyl Analogue;
- At least 1,000 KG but less than 3,000 KG of Marihuana;
- At least 200 KG but less than 600 KG of Hashish;
- At least 20 KG but less than 60 KG of Hashish Oil;
- At least 1,000,000 but less than 3,000,000 units of Ketamine;
- At least 1,000,000 but less than 3,000,000 units of Schedule I or II Depressants;
- At least 62,500 but less than 187,500 units of Flunitrazepam.

(6)
- At least 700 G but less than 1 KG of Heroin;
- At least 3,5 KG but less than 5 KG of Cocaine;
- At least 196 G but less than 280 G of Cocaine Base;
- At least 700 G but less than 1 KG of PCP, or
  at least 70 G but less than 100 G of PCP (actual);
- At least 350 G but less than 500 G of Methamphetamine, or
  at least 35 G but less than 50 G of Methamphetamine (actual), or
  at least 35 G but less than 50 G of "Ice";
- At least 350 G but less than 500 G of Amphetamine, or
  at least 35 G but less than 50 G of Amphetamine (actual);
- At least 7 G but less than 10 G of LSD;
- At least 280 G but less than 400 G of Fentanyl;
- At least 70 G but less than 100 G of a Fentanyl Analogue;
- At least 700 KG but less than 1,000 KG of Marihuana;
- At least 140 KG but less than 200 KG of Hashish;
- At least 14 KG but less than 20 KG of Hashish Oil;
- At least 700,000 but less than 1,000,000 units of Ketamine;
- At least 700,000 but less than 1,000,000 units of Schedule I or II Depressants;
- At least 43,750 but less than 62,500 units of Flunitrazepam.

Level 28

(7)
- At least 400 G but less than 700 G of Heroin;
- At least 2 KG but less than 3.5 KG of Cocaine;
- At least 112 G but less than 196 G of Cocaine Base;
- At least 400 G but less than 700 G of PCP, or
  at least 40 G but less than 70 G of PCP (actual);
- At least 200 G but less than 350 G of Methamphetamine, or
  at least 20 G but less than 35 G of Methamphetamine (actual), or
  at least 20 G but less than 35 G of "Ice";
- At least 200 G but less than 350 G of Amphetamine, or
  at least 20 G but less than 35 G of Amphetamine (actual);
- At least 4 G but less than 7 G of LSD;
- At least 160 G but less than 280 G of Fentanyl;
- At least 40 G but less than 70 G of a Fentanyl Analogue;
- At least 400 KG but less than 700 KG of Marihuana;
- At least 80 KG but less than 140 KG of Hashish;
- At least 8 KG but less than 14 KG of Hashish Oil;
- At least 400,000 but less than 700,000 units of Ketamine;
- At least 400,000 but less than 700,000 units of Schedule I or II Depressants;
- At least 25,000 but less than 43,750 units of Flunitrazepam.

Level 26

(8)
- At least 100 G but less than 400 G of Heroin;
- At least 500 G but less than 2 KG of Cocaine;
- At least 28 G but less than 112 G of Cocaine Base;
- At least 100 G but less than 400 G of PCP, or
  at least 10 G but less than 40 G of PCP (actual);
- At least 50 G but less than 200 G of Methamphetamine, or
  at least 5 G but less than 20 G of Methamphetamine (actual), or
  at least 5 G but less than 20 G of "Ice";
- At least 50 G but less than 200 G of Amphetamine, or
  at least 5 G but less than 20 G of Amphetamine (actual);
- At least 1 G but less than 4 G of LSD;
- At least 40 G but less than 160 G of Fentanyl;
- At least 10 G but less than 40 G of a Fentanyl Analogue;

Level 24

- At least 100 KG but less than 400 KG of Marihuana;
- At least 20 KG but less than 80 KG of Hashish;
- At least 2 KG but less than 8 KG of Hashish Oil;
- At least 100,000 but less than 400,000 units of Ketamine;
- At least 100,000 but less than 400,000 units of Schedule I or II Depressants;
- At least 6,250 but less than 25,000 units of Flunitrazepam.

(9)   **Level 22**
- At least 80 G but less than 100 G of Heroin;
- At least 400 G but less than 500 G of Cocaine;
- At least 22.4 G but less than 28 G of Cocaine Base;
- At least 80 G but less than 100 G of PCP, or
  at least 8 G but less than 10 G of PCP (actual);
- At least 40 G but less than 50 G of Methamphetamine, or
  at least 4 G but less than 5 G of Methamphetamine (actual), or
  at least 4 G but less than 5 G of "Ice";
- At least 40 G but less than 50 G of Amphetamine, or
  at least 4 G but less than 5 G of Amphetamine (actual);
- At least 800 MG but less than 1 G of LSD;
- At least 32 G but less than 40 G of Fentanyl;
- At least 8 G but less than 10 G of a Fentanyl Analogue;
- At least 80 KG but less than 100 KG of Marihuana;
- At least 16 KG but less than 20 KG of Hashish;
- At least 1.6 KG but less than 2 KG of Hashish Oil;
- At least 80,000 but less than 100,000 units of Ketamine;
- At least 80,000 but less than 100,000 units of Schedule I or II Depressants;
- At least 5,000 but less than 6,250 units of Flunitrazepam.

(10)   **Level 20**
- At least 60 G but less than 80 G of Heroin;
- At least 300 G but less than 400 G of Cocaine;
- At least 16.8 G but less than 22.4 G of Cocaine Base;
- At least 60 G but less than 80 G of PCP, or
  at least 6 G but less than 8 G of PCP (actual);
- At least 30 G but less than 40 G of Methamphetamine, or
  at least 3 G but less than 4 G of Methamphetamine (actual), or
  at least 3 G but less than 4 G of "Ice";
- At least 30 G but less than 40 G of Amphetamine, or
  at least 3 G but less than 4 G of Amphetamine (actual);
- At least 600 MG but less than 800 MG of LSD;
- At least 24 G but less than 32 G of Fentanyl;
- At least 6 G but less than 8 G of a Fentanyl Analogue;
- At least 60 KG but less than 80 KG of Marihuana;
- At least 12 KG but less than 16 KG of Hashish;
- At least 1.2 KG but less than 1.6 KG of Hashish Oil;
- At least 60,000 but less than 80,000 units of Ketamine;
- At least 60,000 but less than 80,000 units of Schedule I or II Depressants;
- 60,000 units or more of Schedule III substances (except Ketamine);
- At least 3,750 but less than 5,000 units of Flunitrazepam.

(11)   **Level 18**
- At least 40 G but less than 60 G of Heroin;
- At least 200 G but less than 300 G of Cocaine;
- At least 11.2 G but less than 16.8 G of Cocaine Base;
- At least 40 G but less than 60 G of PCP, or
  at least 4 G but less than 6 G of PCP (actual);

- At least 20 G but less than 30 G of Methamphetamine, or
  - at least 2 G but less than 3 G of Methamphetamine (actual), or
  - at least 2 G but less than 3 G of "Ice";
- At least 20 G but less than 30 G of Amphetamine, or
  - at least 2 G but less than 3 G of Amphetamine (actual);
- At least 400 MG but less than 600 MG of LSD;
- At least 16 G but less than 24 G of Fentanyl;
- At least 4 G but less than 6 G of a Fentanyl Analogue;
- At least 40 KG but less than 60 KG of Marihuana;
- At least 8 KG but less than 12 KG of Hashish;
- At least 800 G but less than 1.2 KG of Hashish Oil;
- At least 40,000 but less than 60,000 units of Ketamine;
- At least 40,000 but less than 60,000 units of Schedule I or II Depressants;
- At least 40,000 but less than 60,000 units of Schedule III substances (except Ketamine);
- At least 2,500 but less than 3,750 units of Flunitrazepam.

(12)
- At least 20 G but less than 40 G of Heroin; **Level 16**
- At least 100 G but less than 200 G of Cocaine;
- At least 5.6 G but less than 11.2 G of Cocaine Base;
- At least 20 G but less than 40 G of PCP, or
  - at least 2 G but less than 4 G of PCP (actual);
- At least 10 G but less than 20 G of Methamphetamine, or
  - at least 1 G but less than 2 G of Methamphetamine (actual), or
  - at least 1 G but less than 2 G of "Ice";
- At least 10 G but less than 20 G of Amphetamine, or
  - at least 1 G but less than 2 G of Amphetamine (actual);
- At least 200 MG but less than 400 MG of LSD;
- At least 8 G but less than 16 G of Fentanyl;
- At least 2 G but less than 4 G of a Fentanyl Analogue;
- At least 20 KG but less than 40 KG of Marihuana;
- At least 5 KG but less than 8 KG of Hashish;
- At least 500 G but less than 800 G of Hashish Oil;
- At least 20,000 but less than 40,000 units of Ketamine;
- At least 20,000 but less than 40,000 units of Schedule I or II Depressants;
- At least 20,000 but less than 40,000 units of Schedule III substances (except Ketamine);
- At least 1,250 but less than 2,500 units of Flunitrazepam.

(13)
- At least 10 G but less than 20 G of Heroin; **Level 14**
- At least 50 G but less than 100 G of Cocaine;
- At least 2.8 G but less than 5.6 G of Cocaine Base;
- At least 10 G but less than 20 G of PCP, or
  - at least 1 G but less than 2 G of PCP (actual);
- At least 5 G but less than 10 G of Methamphetamine, or
  - at least 500 MG but less than 1 G of Methamphetamine (actual), or
  - at least 500 MG but less than 1 G of "Ice";
- At least 5 G but less than 10 G of Amphetamine, or
  - at least 500 MG but less than 1 G of Amphetamine (actual);
- At least 100 MG but less than 200 MG of LSD;
- At least 4 G but less than 8 G of Fentanyl;
- At least 1 G but less than 2 G of a Fentanyl Analogue;
- At least 10 KG but less than 20 KG of Marihuana;

- At least 2 KG but less than 5 KG of Hashish;
- At least 200 G but less than 500 G of Hashish Oil;
- At least 10,000 but less than 20,000 units of Ketamine;
- At least 10,000 but less than 20,000 units of Schedule I or II Depressants;
- At least 10,000 but less than 20,000 units of Schedule III substances (except Ketamine);
- At least 625 but less than 1,250 units of Flunitrazepam.

(14)
- Less than 10 G of Heroin;   **Level 12**
- Less than 50 G of Cocaine;
- Less than 2.8 G of Cocaine Base;
- Less than 10 G of PCP, or
    less than 1 G of PCP (actual);
- Less than 5 G of Methamphetamine, or
    less than 500 MG of Methamphetamine (actual), or
    less than 500 MG of "Ice";
- Less than 5 G of Amphetamine, or
    less than 500 MG of Amphetamine (actual);
- Less than 100 MG of LSD;
- Less than 4 G of Fentanyl;
- Less than 1 G of a Fentanyl Analogue;
- At least 5 KG but less than 10 KG of Marihuana;
- At least 1 KG but less than 2 KG of Hashish;
- At least 100 G but less than 200 G of Hashish Oil;
- At least 5,000 but less than 10,000 units of Ketamine;
- At least 5,000 but less than 10,000 units of Schedule I or II Depressants;
- At least 5,000 but less than 10,000 units of Schedule III substances (except Ketamine);
- At least 312 but less than 625 units of Flunitrazepam;
- 80,000 units or more of Schedule IV substances (except Flunitrazepam).

(15)
- At least 2.5 KG but less than 5 KG of Marihuana;   **Level 10**
- At least 500 G but less than 1 KG of Hashish;
- At least 50 G but less than 100 G of Hashish Oil;
- At least 2,500 but less than 5,000 units of Ketamine;
- At least 2,500 but less than 5,000 units of Schedule I or II Depressants;
- At least 2,500 but less than 5,000 units of Schedule III substances (except Ketamine);
- At least 156 but less than 312 units of Flunitrazepam;
- At least 40,000 but less than 80,000 units of Schedule IV substances (except Flunitrazepam).

(16)
- At least 1 KG but less than 2.5 KG of Marihuana;   **Level 8**
- At least 200 G but less than 500 G of Hashish;
- At least 20 G but less than 50 G of Hashish Oil;
- At least 1,000 but less than 2,500 units of Ketamine;
- At least 1,000 but less than 2,500 units of Schedule I or II Depressants;
- At least 1,000 but less than 2,500 units of Schedule III substances (except Ketamine);
- Less than 156 units of Flunitrazepam;
- At least 16,000 but less than 40,000 units of Schedule IV substances (except Flunitrazepam);
- 160,000 units or more of Schedule V substances.

(17)	● Less than 1 KG of Marihuana;	**Level 6**

(17) ● Less than 1 KG of Marihuana;   **Level 6**
     ● Less than 200 G of Hashish;
     ● Less than 20 G of Hashish Oil;
     ● Less than 1,000 units of Ketamine;
     ● Less than 1,000 units of Schedule I or II Depressants;
     ● Less than 1,000 units of Schedule III substances (except
       Ketamine);
     ● Less than 16,000 units of Schedule IV substances (except
       Flunitrazepam);
     ● Less than 160,000 units of Schedule V substances.

---

*Notes to Drug Quantity Table:

(A) Unless otherwise specified, the weight of a controlled substance set forth in the table refers to the entire weight of any mixture or substance containing a detectable amount of the controlled substance. If a mixture or substance contains more than one controlled substance, the weight of the entire mixture or substance is assigned to the controlled substance that results in the greater offense level.

(B) The terms "*PCP (actual)*", "*Amphetamine (actual)*", and "*Methamphetamine (actual)*" refer to the weight of the controlled substance, itself, contained in the mixture or substance. For example, a mixture weighing 10 grams containing PCP at 50% purity contains 5 grams of PCP (actual). In the case of a mixture or substance containing PCP, amphetamine, or methamphetamine, use the offense level determined by the entire weight of the mixture or substance, or the offense level determined by the weight of the PCP (actual), amphetamine (actual), or methamphetamine (actual), whichever is greater.

The terms "*Hydrocodone (actual)*" and "*Oxycodone (actual)*" refer to the weight of the controlled substance, itself, contained in the pill, capsule, or mixture.

(C) "*Ice*," for the purposes of this guideline, means a mixture or substance containing d-methamphetamine hydrochloride of at least 80% purity.

(D) "*Cocaine base*," for the purposes of this guideline, means "crack." "*Crack*" is the street name for a form of cocaine base, usually prepared by processing cocaine hydrochloride and sodium bicarbonate, and usually appearing in a lumpy, rocklike form.

(E) In the case of an offense involving marihuana plants, treat each plant, regardless of sex, as equivalent to 100 grams of marihuana. *Provided*, however, that if the actual weight of the marihuana is greater, use the actual weight of the marihuana.

(F) In the case of Schedule I or II Depressants (except gamma-hydroxybutyric acid), Schedule III substances, Schedule IV substances, and Schedule V substances, one "*unit*" means one pill, capsule, or tablet. If the substance (except gamma-hydroxybutyric acid) is in liquid form, one "*unit*" means 0.5 milliliters. For an anabolic steroid that is not in a pill, capsule, tablet, or liquid form (*e.g.*, patch, topical cream, aerosol), the court shall determine the base offense level using a reasonable estimate of the quantity of anabolic steroid involved in the offense. In making a reasonable estimate, the court shall consider that each 25 milligrams of an anabolic steroid is one "unit".

(G) In the case of LSD on a carrier medium (*e.g.*, a sheet of blotter paper), do not use the weight of the LSD/carrier medium. Instead, treat each dose of LSD on the carrier medium as equal to 0.4 milligrams of LSD for the purposes of the Drug Quantity Table.

(H) *Hashish*, for the purposes of this guideline, means a resinous substance of cannabis that includes (i) one or more of the tetrahydrocannabinols (as listed in 21 C.F.R. § 1308.11(d)(31)), (ii) at least two of the following: cannabinol, cannabidiol, or cannabichromene, and (iii) fragments of plant material (such as cystolith fibers).

(I) *Hashish oil*, for the purposes of this guideline, means a preparation of the soluble cannabinoids derived from cannabis that includes (i) one or more of the tetrahydrocannabinols (as listed in 21 C.F.R. § 1308.11(d)(31)), (ii) at least two of the following: cannabinol, cannabidiol, or cannabichromene, and (iii) is essentially free of plant material (*e.g.*, plant fragments). Typically, hashish oil is a viscous, dark colored oil, but it can vary from a dry resin to a colorless liquid.

Commentary

Statutory Provisions: 21 U.S.C. §§ 841(a), (b)(1)–(3), (7), (g), 860a, 865, 960(a), (b); 49 U.S.C. § 46317(b). For additional statutory provision(s), *see* Appendix A (Statutory Index).

Application Notes:

1. **"Mixture or Substance".**—"*Mixture or substance*" as used in this guideline has the same meaning as in 21 U.S.C. § 841, except as expressly provided. Mixture or substance does not include materials that must be separated from the controlled substance before the controlled substance can be used. Examples of such materials include the fiberglass in a cocaine/ fiberglass bonded suitcase, beeswax in a cocaine/beeswax statue, and waste water from an illicit laboratory used to manufacture a controlled substance. If such material cannot readily be separated from the mixture or substance that appropriately is counted in the Drug Quantity Table, the court may use any reasonable method to approximate the weight of the mixture or substance to be counted.

An upward departure nonetheless may be warranted when the mixture or substance counted in the Drug Quantity Table is combined with other, non-countable material in an unusually sophisticated manner in order to avoid detection.

Similarly, in the case of marihuana having a moisture content that renders the marihuana unsuitable for consumption without drying (this might occur, for example, with a bale of rain-soaked marihuana or freshly harvested marihuana that had not been dried), an approximation of the weight of the marihuana without such excess moisture content is to be used.

2. **"Plant".**—For purposes of the guidelines, a "*plant*" is an organism having leaves and a readily observable root formation (*e.g.*, a marihuana cutting having roots, a rootball, or root hairs is a marihuana plant).

3. **Classification of Controlled Substances.**—Certain pharmaceutical preparations are classified as Schedule III, IV, or V controlled substances by the Drug Enforcement Administration under 21 C.F.R. § 1308.13–15 even though they contain a small amount of a Schedule I or II controlled substance. For example, Tylenol 3 is classified as a Schedule III controlled substance even though it contains a small amount of codeine, a Schedule II opiate. For the purposes of the guidelines, the classification of the controlled substance under 21 C.F.R. § 1308.13–15 is the appropriate classification.

4. **Applicability to "Counterfeit" Substances.**—The statute and guideline also apply to *"counterfeit" substances*, which are defined in 21 U.S.C. § 802 to mean controlled substances that are falsely labeled so as to appear to have been legitimately manufactured or distributed.

5. **Determining Drug Types and Drug Quantities.**—Types and quantities of drugs not specified in the count of conviction may be considered in determining the offense level. *See* §1B1.3(a)(2) (Relevant Conduct). Where there is no drug seizure or the amount seized does not reflect the scale of the offense, the court shall approximate the quantity of the controlled substance. In making this determination, the court may consider, for example, the price generally obtained for the controlled substance, financial or other records, similar transactions in controlled substances by the defendant, and the size or capability of any laboratory involved.

    If the offense involved both a substantive drug offense and an attempt or conspiracy (*e.g.*, sale of five grams of heroin and an attempt to sell an additional ten grams of heroin), the total quantity involved shall be aggregated to determine the scale of the offense.

    In an offense involving an agreement to sell a controlled substance, the agreed-upon quantity of the controlled substance shall be used to determine the offense level unless the sale is completed and the amount delivered more accurately reflects the scale of the offense. For example, a defendant agrees to sell 500 grams of cocaine, the transaction is completed by the delivery of the controlled substance — actually 480 grams of cocaine, and no further delivery is scheduled. In this example, the amount delivered more accurately reflects the scale of the offense. In contrast, in a reverse sting, the agreed-upon quantity of the controlled substance would more accurately reflect the scale of the offense because the amount actually delivered is controlled by the government, not by the defendant. If, however, the defendant establishes that the defendant did not intend to provide or purchase, or was not reasonably capable of providing or purchasing, the agreed-upon quantity of the controlled substance, the court shall exclude from the offense level determination the amount of controlled substance that the defendant establishes that the defendant did not intend to provide or purchase or was not reasonably capable of providing or purchasing.

6.   **Analogues and Controlled Substances Not Referenced in this Guideline.**—Any reference to a particular controlled substance in these guidelines includes all salts, isomers, all salts of isomers, and, except as otherwise provided, any analogue of that controlled substance. Any reference to cocaine includes ecgonine and coca leaves, except extracts of coca leaves from which cocaine and ecgonine have been removed. For purposes of this guideline "*analogue*" has the meaning given the term "controlled substance analogue" in 21 U.S.C. § 802(32). In determining the appropriate sentence, the court also may consider whether the same quantity of analogue produces a greater effect on the central nervous system than the controlled substance for which it is an analogue.

In the case of a controlled substance that is not specifically referenced in this guideline, determine the base offense level using the marihuana equivalency of the most closely related controlled substance referenced in this guideline. In determining the most closely related controlled substance, the court shall, to the extent practicable, consider the following:

(A)   Whether the controlled substance not referenced in this guideline has a chemical structure that is substantially similar to a controlled substance referenced in this guideline.

(B)   Whether the controlled substance not referenced in this guideline has a stimulant, depressant, or hallucinogenic effect on the central nervous system that is substantially similar to the stimulant, depressant, or hallucinogenic effect on the central nervous system of a controlled substance referenced in this guideline.

(C)   Whether a lesser or greater quantity of the controlled substance not referenced in this guideline is needed to produce a substantially similar effect on the central nervous system as a controlled substance referenced in this guideline.

7.   **Multiple Transactions or Multiple Drug Types.**—Where there are multiple transactions or multiple drug types, the quantities of drugs are to be added. Tables for making the necessary conversions are provided below.

8.   **Use of Drug Equivalency Tables.**—

(A)   **Controlled Substances Not Referenced in Drug Quantity Table.**—The Commission has used the sentences provided in, and equivalences derived from, the statute (21 U.S.C. § 841(b)(1)), as the primary basis for the guideline sentences. The statute, however, provides direction only for the more common controlled substances, *i.e.*, heroin, cocaine, PCP, methamphetamine, fentanyl, LSD and marihuana. In the case of a controlled substance that is not specifically referenced in the Drug Quantity Table, determine the base offense level as follows:

(i)   Use the Drug Equivalency Tables to convert the quantity of the controlled substance involved in the offense to its equivalent quantity of marihuana.

(ii)   Find the equivalent quantity of marihuana in the Drug Quantity Table.

(iii)   Use the offense level that corresponds to the equivalent quantity of marihuana as the base offense level for the controlled substance involved in the offense.

(*See also* Application Note 6.) For example, in the Drug Equivalency Tables set forth in this Note, 1 gram of a substance containing oxymorphone, a Schedule I opiate, converts to an equivalent quantity of 5 kilograms of marihuana. In a case involving 100 grams of oxymorphone, the equivalent quantity of marihuana would be 500 kilograms, which corresponds to a base offense level of 26 in the Drug Quantity Table.

(B) **Combining Differing Controlled Substances.**—The Drug Equivalency Tables also provide a means for combining differing controlled substances to obtain a single offense level. In each case, convert each of the drugs to its marihuana equivalent, add the quantities, and look up the total in the Drug Quantity Table to obtain the combined offense level.

For certain types of controlled substances, the marihuana equivalencies in the Drug Equivalency Tables are "capped" at specified amounts (*e.g.*, the combined equivalent weight of all Schedule V controlled substances shall not exceed 2.49 kilograms of marihuana). Where there are controlled substances from more than one schedule (*e.g.*, a quantity of a Schedule IV substance and a quantity of a Schedule V substance), determine the marihuana equivalency for each schedule separately (subject to the cap, if any, applicable to that schedule). Then add the marihuana equivalencies to determine the combined marihuana equivalency (subject to the cap, if any, applicable to the combined amounts).

Note: Because of the statutory equivalences, the ratios in the Drug Equivalency Tables do not necessarily reflect dosages based on pharmacological equivalents.

(C) **Examples for Combining Differing Controlled Substances.**—

(i) The defendant is convicted of selling 70 grams of a substance containing PCP (Level 20) and 250 milligrams of a substance containing LSD (Level 16). The PCP converts to 70 kilograms of marihuana; the LSD converts to 25 kilograms of marihuana. The total is therefore equivalent to 95 kilograms of marihuana, for which the Drug Quantity Table provides an offense level of 22.

(ii) The defendant is convicted of selling 500 grams of marihuana (Level 6) and 10,000 units of diazepam (Level 6). The diazepam, a Schedule IV drug, is equivalent to 625 grams of marihuana. The total, 1.125 kilograms of marihuana, has an offense level of 8 in the Drug Quantity Table.

(iii) The defendant is convicted of selling 80 grams of cocaine (Level 14) and 2 grams of cocaine base (Level 12). The cocaine is equivalent to 16 kilograms of marihuana, and the cocaine base is equivalent to 7.142 kilograms of marihuana. The total is therefore equivalent to 23.142 kilograms of marihuana, which has an offense level of 16 in the Drug Quantity Table.

(iv) The defendant is convicted of selling 76,000 units of a Schedule III substance, 200,000 units of a Schedule IV substance, and 600,000 units of a Schedule V substance. The marihuana equivalency for the Schedule III substance is 76 kilograms of marihuana (below the cap of 79.99 kilograms of marihuana set forth as the maximum equivalent weight for Schedule III substances). The marihuana equivalency for the Schedule IV substance is subject to a cap of 9.99 kilograms of marihuana set forth as the maximum equivalent weight for Schedule IV substances (without the cap it would have been 12.5 kilograms). The marihuana equivalency for the Schedule V substance is subject to the cap of 2.49 kilograms of marihuana set forth as the maximum equivalent weight for Schedule V substances (without the cap it would have been 3.75 kilograms). The combined equivalent weight, determined by adding together the above amounts, is subject to the cap of 79.99 kilograms of marihuana set forth as the maximum combined equivalent weight for Schedule III, IV, and V substances. Without the cap, the combined equivalent weight would have been 88.48 (76 + 9.99 + 2.49) kilograms.

(D) **Drug Equivalency Tables.—**

SCHEDULE I OR II OPIATES*	
1 gm of Heroin =	1 kg of marihuana
1 gm of Alpha-Methylfentanyl =	10 kg of marihuana
1 gm of Dextromoramide =	670 gm of marihuana
1 gm of Dipipanone =	250 gm of marihuana
1 gm of 3-Methylfentanyl =	10 kg of marihuana
1 gm of 1-Methyl-4-phenyl-4-propionoxypiperidine/MPPP =	700 gm of marihuana
1 gm of 1-(2-Phenylethyl)-4-phenyl-4-acetyloxypiperidine/ PEPAP =	700 gm of marihuana
1 gm of Alphaprodine =	100 gm of marihuana
1 gm of Fentanyl (N-phenyl-N-[1-(2-phenylethyl)-4-piperidinyl] Propanamide) =	2.5 kg of marihuana
1 gm of Hydromorphone/Dihydromorphinone =	2.5 kg of marihuana
1 gm of Levorphanol =	2.5 kg of marihuana
1 gm of Meperidine/Pethidine =	50 gm of marihuana
1 gm of Methadone =	500 gm of marihuana
1 gm of 6-Monoacetylmorphine =	1 kg of marihuana
1 gm of Morphine =	500 gm of marihuana
1 gm of Oxycodone (actual) =	6700 gm of marihuana
1 gm of Oxymorphone =	5 kg of marihuana
1 gm of Racemorphan =	800 gm of marihuana
1 gm of Codeine =	80 gm of marihuana
1 gm of Dextropropoxyphene/Propoxyphene-Bulk =	50 gm of marihuana
1 gm of Ethylmorphine =	165 gm of marihuana
1 gm of Hydrocodone (actual) =	6700 gm of marihuana
1 gm of Mixed Alkaloids of Opium/Papaveretum =	250 gm of marihuana
1 gm of Opium =	50 gm of marihuana
1 gm of Levo-alpha-acetylmethadol (LAAM) =	3 kg of marihuana

Provided, that the minimum offense level from the Drug Quantity Table for any of these controlled substances individually, or in combination with another controlled substance, is level 12.

COCAINE AND OTHER SCHEDULE I AND II STIMULANTS (AND THEIR IMMEDIATE PRECURSORS)*	
1 gm of Cocaine =	200 gm of marihuana
1 gm of N-Ethylamphetamine =	80 gm of marihuana
1 gm of Fenethylline =	40 gm of marihuana
1 gm of Amphetamine =	2 kg of marihuana
1 gm of Amphetamine (Actual) =	20 kg of marihuana
1 gm of Methamphetamine =	2 kg of marihuana
1 gm of Methamphetamine (Actual) =	20 kg of marihuana
1 gm of "Ice" =	20 kg of marihuana
1 gm of Khat =	.01 gm of marihuana
1 gm of 4-Methylaminorex ("Euphoria") =	100 gm of marihuana
1 gm of Methylphenidate (Ritalin) =	100 gm of marihuana
1 gm of Phenmetrazine =	80 gm of marihuana
1 gm Phenylacetone/P$_2$P (when possessed for the purpose of manufacturing methamphetamine) =	416 gm of marihuana
1 gm Phenylacetone/P$_2$P (in any other case) =	75 gm of marihuana
1 gm Cocaine Base ("Crack") =	3,571 gm of marihuana
1 gm of Aminorex =	100 gm of marihuana
1 gm of Methcathinone =	380 gm of marihuana
1 gm of N-N-Dimethylamphetamine =	40 gm of marihuana
1 gm of N-Benzylpiperazine =	100 gm of marihuana

Provided, that the minimum offense level from the Drug Quantity Table for any of these controlled substances individually, or in combination with another controlled substance, is level 12.

LSD, PCP, AND OTHER SCHEDULE I AND II HALLUCINOGENS (AND THEIR IMMEDIATE PRECURSORS)*	
1 gm of Bufotenine =	70 gm of marihuana
1 gm of D-Lysergic Acid Diethylamide/Lysergide/LSD =	100 kg of marihuana
1 gm of Diethyltryptamine/DET =	80 gm of marihuana
1 gm of Dimethyltryptamine/DM =	100 gm of marihuana
1 gm of Mescaline =	10 gm of marihuana
1 gm of Mushrooms containing Psilocin and/or Psilocybin (Dry) =	1 gm of marihuana
1 gm of Mushrooms containing Psilocin and/or Psilocybin (Wet) =	0.1 gm of marihuana
1 gm of Peyote (Dry) =	0.5 gm of marihuana
1 gm of Peyote (Wet) =	0.05 gm of marihuana
1 gm of Phencyclidine/PCP =	1 kg of marihuana
1 gm of Phencyclidine (actual) /PCP (actual) =	10 kg of marihuana
1 gm of Psilocin =	500 gm of marihuana
1 gm of Psilocybin =	500 gm of marihuana
1 gm of Pyrrolidine Analog of Phencyclidine/PHP =	1 kg of marihuana
1 gm of Thiophene Analog of Phencyclidine/TCP =	1 kg of marihuana
1 gm of 4-Bromo-2,5-Dimethoxyamphetamine/DOB =	2.5 kg of marihuana
1 gm of 2,5-Dimethoxy-4-methylamphetamine/DOM =	1.67 kg of marihuana
1 gm of 3,4-Methylenedioxyamphetamine/MDA =	500 gm of marihuana
1 gm of 3,4-Methylenedioxymethamphetamine/MDMA =	500 gm of marihuana
1 gm of 3,4-Methylenedioxy-N-ethylamphetamine/MDEA =	500 gm of marihuana
1 gm of Paramethoxymethamphetamine/PMA =	500 gm of marihuana
1 gm of 1-Piperidinocyclohexanecarbonitrile/PCC =	680 gm of marihuana
1 gm of N-ethyl-1-phenylcyclohexylamine (PCE) =	1 kg of marihuana

Provided, that the minimum offense level from the Drug Quantity Table for any of these controlled substances individually, or in combination with another controlled substance, is level 12.

SCHEDULE I MARIHUANA	
1 gm of Marihuana/Cannabis, granulated, powdered, etc. =	1 gm of marihuana
1 gm of Hashish Oil =	50 gm of marihuana
1 gm of Cannabis Resin or Hashish =	5 gm of marihuana
1 gm of Tetrahydrocannabinol, Organic =	167 gm of marihuana
1 gm of Tetrahydrocannabinol, Synthetic =	167 gm of marihuana

FLUNITRAZEPAM **	
1 unit of Flunitrazepam =	16 gm of marihuana

**Provided,* that the minimum offense level from the Drug Quantity Table for flunitrazepam individually, or in combination with any Schedule I or II depressants, Schedule III substances, Schedule IV substances, and Schedule V substances is level 8.

SCHEDULE I OR II DEPRESSANTS (EXCEPT GAMMA-HYDROXYBUTYRIC ACID)	
1 unit of a Schedule I or II Depressant (except gamma-hydroxybutyric acid) =	1 gm of marihuana

GAMMA-HYDROXYBUTYRIC ACID	
1 ml of gamma-hydroxybutyric acid =	8.8 gm of marihuana

SCHEDULE III SUBSTANCES (EXCEPT KETAMINE)***

1 unit of a Schedule III Substance =	1 gm of marihuana

***Provided, that the combined equivalent weight of all Schedule III substances (except ketamine), Schedule IV substances (except flunitrazepam), and Schedule V substances shall not exceed 79.99 kilograms of marihuana.

KETAMINE

1 unit of ketamine =	1 gm of marihuana

SCHEDULE IV SUBSTANCES (EXCEPT FLUNITRAZEPAM)*****

1 unit of a Schedule IV Substance (except Flunitrazepam) =	0.0625 gm of marihuana

*****Provided, that the combined equivalent weight of all Schedule IV (except flunitrazepam) and V substances shall not exceed 9.99 kilograms of marihuana.

SCHEDULE V SUBSTANCES******

1 unit of a Schedule V Substance =	0.00625 gm of marihuana

******Provided, that the combined equivalent weight of Schedule V substances shall not exceed 2.49 kilograms of marihuana.

LIST I CHEMICALS (RELATING TO THE MANUFACTURE OF AMPHETAMINE OR METHAMPHETAMINE)*******

1 gm of Ephedrine =	10 kg of marihuana
1 gm of Phenylpropanolamine =	10 kg of marihuana
1 gm of Pseudoephedrine =	10 kg of marihuana

*******Provided, that in a case involving ephedrine, pseudoephedrine, or phenylpropanolamine tablets, use the weight of the ephedrine, pseudoephedrine, or phenylpropanolamine contained in the tablets, not the weight of the entire tablets, in calculating the base offense level.

DATE RAPE DRUGS (EXCEPT FLUNITRAZEPAM, GHB, OR KETAMINE)

1 ml of 1,4-butanediol =	8.8 gm marihuana
1 ml of gamma butyrolactone =	8.8 gm marihuana

To facilitate conversions to drug equivalencies, the following table is provided:

MEASUREMENT CONVERSION TABLE
1 oz = 28.35 gm
1 lb = 453.6 gm
1 lb = 0.4536 kg
1 gal = 3.785 liters
1 qt = 0.946 liters
1 gm = 1 ml (liquid)
1 liter = 1,000 ml
1 kg = 1,000 gm
1 gm = 1,000 mg
1 grain = 64.8 mg.

9. **Determining Quantity Based on Doses, Pills, or Capsules.**—If the number of doses, pills, or capsules but not the weight of the controlled substance is known, multiply the number of doses, pills, or capsules by the typical weight per dose in the table below to estimate the total weight of the controlled substance (*e.g.*, 100 doses of Mescaline at 500 milligrams per dose = 50 grams of mescaline). The Typical Weight Per Unit Table, prepared from information provided by the Drug Enforcement Administration, displays the typical weight per dose, pill, or capsule for certain controlled substances. Do not use this table if any more reliable estimate of the total weight is available from case-specific information.

TYPICAL WEIGHT PER UNIT (DOSE, PILL, OR CAPSULE) TABLE

HALLUCINOGENS	
MDA	250 mg
MDMA	250 mg
Mescaline	500 mg
PCP*	5 mg
Peyote (dry)	12 gm
Peyote (wet)	120 gm
Psilocin*	10 mg
Psilocybe mushrooms (dry)	5 gm
Psilocybe mushrooms (wet)	50 gm
Psilocybin*	10 mg
2,5-Dimethoxy-4-methylamphetamine (STP, DOM)*	3 mg

MARIHUANA	
1 marihuana cigarette	0.5 gm

STIMULANTS	
Amphetamine*	10 mg
Methamphetamine*	5 mg
Phenmetrazine (Preludin)*	75 mg

*For controlled substances marked with an asterisk, the weight per unit shown is the weight of the actual controlled substance, and not generally the weight of the mixture or substance containing the controlled substance. Therefore, use of this table provides a very conservative estimate of the total weight.

10. **Determining Quantity of LSD.**—LSD on a blotter paper carrier medium typically is marked so that the number of doses ("hits") per sheet readily can be determined. When this is not the case, it is to be presumed that each 1/4 inch by 1/4 inch section of the blotter paper is equal to one dose.

In the case of liquid LSD (LSD that has not been placed onto a carrier medium), using the weight of the LSD alone to calculate the offense level may not adequately reflect the seriousness of the offense. In such a case, an upward departure may be warranted.

11. **Application of Subsections (b)(1) and (b)(2).**—

(A) **Application of Subsection (b)(1).**—Definitions of "*firearm*" and "*dangerous weapon*" are found in the Commentary to §1B1.1 (Application Instructions). The enhancement for weapon possession in subsection (b)(1) reflects the increased danger of violence when drug traffickers possess weapons. The enhancement should be applied if the weapon was present, unless it is clearly improbable that the weapon was connected with the offense. For example, the enhancement would not be applied if the defendant, arrested at the defendant's residence, had an unloaded hunting rifle in the closet. The enhancement also applies to offenses that are referenced to §2D1.1; *see* §§2D1.2(a)(1) and (2), 2D1.5(a)(1), 2D1.6, 2D1.7(b)(1), 2D1.8, 2D1.11(c)(1), and 2D1.12(c)(1).

(B) **Interaction of Subsections (b)(1) and (b)(2).**—The enhancements in subsections (b)(1) and (b)(2) may be applied cumulatively (added together), as is generally the case when two or more specific offense characteristics each apply. *See* §1B1.1 (Application Instructions), Application Note 4(A). However, in a case in which the defendant merely possessed a dangerous weapon but did not use violence, make a credible threat to use violence, or direct the use of violence, subsection (b)(2) would not apply.

12. **Application of Subsection (b)(5).**—If the offense involved importation of amphetamine or methamphetamine, and an adjustment from subsection (b)(3) applies, do not apply subsection (b)(5).

13. **Application of Subsection (b)(7).**—For purposes of subsection (b)(7), "*mass-marketing by means of an interactive computer service*" means the solicitation, by means of an interactive computer service, of a large number of persons to induce those persons to purchase a controlled substance. For example, subsection (b)(7) would apply to a defendant who operated a web site to promote the sale of Gamma-hydroxybutyric Acid (GHB) but would not apply to coconspirators who use an interactive computer service only to communicate with one another in furtherance of the offense. "*Interactive computer service*", for purposes of subsection (b)(7) and this note, has the meaning given that term in section 230(e)(2) of the Communications Act of 1934 (47 U.S.C. § 230(f)(2)).

14. **Application of Subsection (b)(8).**—For purposes of subsection (b)(8), "*masking agent*" means a substance that, when taken before, after, or in conjunction with an anabolic steroid, prevents the detection of the anabolic steroid in an individual's body.

15. **Application of Subsection (b)(9).**—For purposes of subsection (b)(9), "*athlete*" means an individual who participates in an athletic activity conducted by (A) an intercollegiate athletic association or interscholastic athletic association; (B) a professional athletic association; or (C) an amateur athletic organization.

16. **Application of Subsection (b)(11).**—Subsection (b)(11) does not apply if the purpose of the bribery was to obstruct or impede the investigation, prosecution, or sentencing of the defendant. Such conduct is covered by §3C1.1 (Obstructing or Impeding the Administration of Justice) and, if applicable, §2D1.1(b)(15)(D).

17. **Application of Subsection (b)(12).**—Subsection (b)(12) applies to a defendant who knowingly maintains a premises (*i.e.*, a building, room, or enclosure) for the purpose of manufacturing or distributing a controlled substance, including storage of a controlled substance for the purpose of distribution.

Among the factors the court should consider in determining whether the defendant "maintained" the premises are (A) whether the defendant held a possessory interest in (*e.g.*, owned or rented) the premises and (B) the extent to which the defendant controlled access to, or activities at, the premises.

Manufacturing or distributing a controlled substance need not be the sole purpose for which the premises was maintained, but must be one of the defendant's primary or principal uses for the premises, rather than one of the defendant's incidental or collateral uses for the premises. In making this determination, the court should consider how frequently the premises was used by the defendant for manufacturing or distributing a controlled substance and how frequently the premises was used by the defendant for lawful purposes.

18. **Application of Subsection (b)(13).—**

   (A) **Hazardous or Toxic Substances (Subsection (b)(13)(A)).—**Subsection (b)(13)(A) applies if the conduct for which the defendant is accountable under §1B1.3 (Relevant Conduct) involved any discharge, emission, release, transportation, treatment, storage, or disposal violation covered by the Resource Conservation and Recovery Act, 42 U.S.C. § 6928(d); the Federal Water Pollution Control Act, 33 U.S.C. § 1319(c); the Comprehensive Environmental Response, Compensation, and Liability Act, 42 U.S.C. § 9603(b); or 49 U.S.C. § 5124 (relating to violations of laws and regulations enforced by the Department of Transportation with respect to the transportation of hazardous material). In some cases, the enhancement under subsection (b)(13)(A) may not account adequately for the seriousness of the environmental harm or other threat to public health or safety (including the health or safety of law enforcement and cleanup personnel). In such cases, an upward departure may be warranted. Additionally, in determining the amount of restitution under §5E1.1 (Restitution) and in fashioning appropriate conditions of probation and supervision under §§5B1.3 (Conditions of Probation) and 5D1.3 (Conditions of Supervised Release), respectively, any costs of environmental cleanup and harm to individuals or property shall be considered by the court in cases involving the manufacture of amphetamine or methamphetamine and should be considered by the court in cases involving the manufacture of a controlled substance other than amphetamine or methamphetamine. *See* 21 U.S.C. § 853(q) (mandatory restitution for cleanup costs relating to the manufacture of amphetamine and methamphetamine).

   (B) **Substantial Risk of Harm Associated with the Manufacture of Amphetamine and Methamphetamine (Subsection (b)(13)(C)–(D)).—**

       (i) **Factors to Consider.—**In determining, for purposes of subsection (b)(13)(C)(ii) or (D), whether the offense created a substantial risk of harm to human life or the environment, the court shall include consideration of the following factors:

           (I) The quantity of any chemicals or hazardous or toxic substances found at the laboratory, and the manner in which the chemicals or substances were stored.

           (II) The manner in which hazardous or toxic substances were disposed, and the likelihood of release into the environment of hazardous or toxic substances.

           (III) The duration of the offense, and the extent of the manufacturing operation.

           (IV) The location of the laboratory (*e.g.*, whether the laboratory is located in a residential neighborhood or a remote area), and the number of human lives placed at substantial risk of harm.

(ii) **Definitions.**—For purposes of subsection (b)(13)(D):

"*Incompetent*" means an individual who is incapable of taking care of the individual's self or property because of a mental or physical illness or disability, mental retardation, or senility.

"*Minor*" has the meaning given that term in Application Note 1 of the Commentary to §2A3.1 (Criminal Sexual Abuse).

19. **Application of Subsection (b)(14).**—Subsection (b)(14) applies to offenses that involve the cultivation of marihuana on state or federal land or while trespassing on tribal or private land. Such offenses interfere with the ability of others to safely access and use the area and also pose or risk a range of other harms, such as harms to the environment.

The enhancements in subsection (b)(13)(A) and (b)(14) may be applied cumulatively (added together), as is generally the case when two or more specific offense characteristics each apply. *See* §1B1.1 (Application Instructions), Application Note 4(A).

20. **Application of Subsection (b)(15).**—

(A) **Distributing to a Specified Individual or Involving Such an Individual in the Offense (Subsection (b)(15)(B)).**—If the defendant distributes a controlled substance to an individual or involves an individual in the offense, as specified in subsection (b)(15)(B), the individual is not a "vulnerable victim" for purposes of §3A1.1(b).

(B) **Directly Involved in the Importation of a Controlled Substance (Subsection (b)(15)(C)).**—Subsection (b)(15)(C) applies if the defendant is accountable for the importation of a controlled substance under subsection (a)(1)(A) of §1B1.3 (Relevant Conduct (Factors that Determine the Guideline Range)), *i.e.*, the defendant committed, aided, abetted, counseled, commanded, induced, procured, or willfully caused the importation of a controlled substance.

If subsection (b)(3) or (b)(5) applies, do not apply subsection (b)(15)(C).

(C) **Pattern of Criminal Conduct Engaged in as a Livelihood (Subsection (b)(15)(E)).**—For purposes of subsection (b)(15)(E), "*pattern of criminal conduct*" and "*engaged in as a livelihood*" have the meaning given such terms in §4B1.3 (Criminal Livelihood).

21. **Applicability of Subsection (b)(17).**—The applicability of subsection (b)(17) shall be determined without regard to whether the defendant was convicted of an offense that subjects the defendant to a mandatory minimum term of imprisonment. Section §5C1.2(b), which provides a minimum offense level of level 17, is not pertinent to the determination of whether subsection (b)(17) applies.

22. **Application of Subsection (e)(1).**—

(A) **Definition.**—For purposes of this guideline, "*sexual offense*" means a "sexual act" or "sexual contact" as those terms are defined in 18 U.S.C. § 2246(2) and (3), respectively.

(B)   **Upward Departure Provision.**—If the defendant committed a sexual offense against more than one individual, an upward departure would be warranted.

23.   **Interaction with §3B1.3.**—A defendant who used special skills in the commission of the offense may be subject to an adjustment under §3B1.3 (Abuse of Position of Trust or Use of Special Skill). Certain professionals often occupy essential positions in drug trafficking schemes. These professionals include doctors, pilots, boat captains, financiers, bankers, attorneys, chemists, accountants, and others whose special skill, trade, profession, or position may be used to significantly facilitate the commission of a drug offense. Additionally, an enhancement under §3B1.3 ordinarily would apply in a case in which the defendant used his or her position as a coach to influence an athlete to use an anabolic steroid. Likewise, an adjustment under §3B1.3 ordinarily would apply in a case in which the defendant is convicted of a drug offense resulting from the authorization of the defendant to receive scheduled substances from an ultimate user or long-term care facility. *See* 21 U.S.C. § 822(g).

Note, however, that if an adjustment from subsection (b)(3)(C) applies, do not apply §3B1.3 (Abuse of Position of Trust or Use of Special Skill).

24.   **Cases Involving Mandatory Minimum Penalties.**—Where a mandatory (statutory) minimum sentence applies, this mandatory minimum sentence may be "waived" and a lower sentence imposed (including a downward departure), as provided in 28 U.S.C. § 994(n), by reason of a defendant's "substantial assistance in the investigation or prosecution of another person who has committed an offense." *See* §5K1.1 (Substantial Assistance to Authorities). In addition, 18 U.S.C. § 3553(f) provides an exception to the applicability of mandatory minimum sentences in certain cases. *See* §5C1.2 (Limitation on Applicability of Statutory Minimum Sentences in Certain Cases).

25.   **Imposition of Consecutive Sentence for 21 U.S.C. § 860a or § 865.**—Sections 860a and 865 of title 21, United States Code, require the imposition of a mandatory consecutive term of imprisonment of not more than 20 years and 15 years, respectively. In order to comply with the relevant statute, the court should determine the appropriate "total punishment" and divide the sentence on the judgment form between the sentence attributable to the underlying drug offense and the sentence attributable to 21 U.S.C. § 860a or § 865, specifying the number of months to be served consecutively for the conviction under 21 U.S.C. § 860a or § 865. For example, if the applicable adjusted guideline range is 151–188 months and the court determines a "total punishment" of 151 months is appropriate, a sentence of 130 months for the underlying offense plus 21 months for the conduct covered by 21 U.S.C. § 860a or § 865 would achieve the "total punishment" in a manner that satisfies the statutory requirement of a consecutive sentence.

26.   **Cases Involving "Small Amount of Marihuana for No Remuneration".**—Distribution of "a small amount of marihuana for no remuneration", 21 U.S.C. § 841(b)(4), is treated as simple possession, to which §2D2.1 applies.

27.   **Departure Considerations.**—

(A)   **Downward Departure Based on Drug Quantity in Certain Reverse Sting Operations.**—If, in a reverse sting (an operation in which a government agent sells or negotiates to sell a controlled substance to a defendant), the court finds that the government agent set a price for the controlled substance that was substantially below the market value of the controlled substance, thereby leading to the defendant's purchase of a significantly greater quantity of the controlled substance than his available resources would have allowed him to purchase except for the artificially low price set by the government agent, a downward departure may be warranted.

(B) **Upward Departure Based on Drug Quantity.**—In an extraordinary case, an upward departure above offense level 38 on the basis of drug quantity may be warranted. For example, an upward departure may be warranted where the quantity is at least ten times the minimum quantity required for level 38. Similarly, in the case of a controlled substance for which the maximum offense level is less than level 38, an upward departure may be warranted if the drug quantity substantially exceeds the quantity for the highest offense level established for that particular controlled substance.

(C) **Upward Departure Based on Unusually High Purity.**—Trafficking in controlled substances, compounds, or mixtures of unusually high purity may warrant an upward departure, except in the case of PCP, amphetamine, methamphetamine, hydrocodone, or oxycodone for which the guideline itself provides for the consideration of purity (*see* the footnote to the Drug Quantity Table). The purity of the controlled substance, particularly in the case of heroin, may be relevant in the sentencing process because it is probative of the defendant's role or position in the chain of distribution. Since controlled substances are often diluted and combined with other substances as they pass down the chain of distribution, the fact that a defendant is in possession of unusually pure narcotics may indicate a prominent role in the criminal enterprise and proximity to the source of the drugs. As large quantities are normally associated with high purities, this factor is particularly relevant where smaller quantities are involved.

Background: Offenses under 21 U.S.C. §§ 841 and 960 receive identical punishment based upon the quantity of the controlled substance involved, the defendant's criminal history, and whether death or serious bodily injury resulted from the offense.

The base offense levels in §2D1.1 are either provided directly by the Anti-Drug Abuse Act of 1986 or are proportional to the levels established by statute, and apply to all unlawful trafficking. Levels 30 and 24 in the Drug Quantity Table are the distinctions provided by the Anti-Drug Abuse Act; however, further refinement of drug amounts is essential to provide a logical sentencing structure for drug offenses. To determine these finer distinctions, the Commission consulted numerous experts and practitioners, including authorities at the Drug Enforcement Administration, chemists, attorneys, probation officers, and members of the Organized Crime Drug Enforcement Task Forces, who also advocate the necessity of these distinctions. Where necessary, this scheme has been modified in response to specific congressional directives to the Commission.

The base offense levels at levels 24 and 30 establish guideline ranges such that the statutory minimum falls within the range; *e.g.*, level 30 ranges from 97 to 121 months, where the statutory minimum term is ten years or 120 months.

For marihuana plants, the Commission has adopted an equivalency of 100 grams per plant, or the actual weight of the usable marihuana, whichever is greater. The decision to treat each plant as equal to 100 grams is premised on the fact that the average yield from a mature marihuana plant equals 100 grams of marihuana. In controlled substance offenses, an attempt is assigned the same offense level as the object of the attempt. Consequently, the Commission adopted the policy that each plant is to be treated as the equivalent of an attempt to produce 100 grams of marihuana, except where the actual weight of the usable marihuana is greater.

Because the weights of LSD carrier media vary widely and typically far exceed the weight of the controlled substance itself, the Commission has determined that basing offense levels on the entire weight of the LSD and carrier medium would produce unwarranted disparity among offenses involving the same quantity of actual LSD (but different carrier weights), as well as sentences disproportionate to those for other, more dangerous controlled substances, such as PCP. Consequently, in cases involving LSD contained in a carrier medium, the Commission has established a weight per dose of 0.4 milligram for purposes of determining the base offense level.

The dosage weight of LSD selected exceeds the Drug Enforcement Administration's standard dosage unit for LSD of 0.05 milligram (*i.e.*, the quantity of actual LSD per dose) in order to assign some weight to the carrier medium. Because LSD typically is marketed and consumed orally on a carrier medium, the inclusion of some weight attributable to the carrier medium recognizes (A) that offense levels for most other controlled substances are based upon the weight of the mixture containing the controlled substance without regard to purity, and (B) the decision in *Chapman v. United States*, 500 U.S. 453 (1991) (holding that the term "mixture or substance" in 21 U.S.C. § 841(b)(1) includes the carrier medium in which LSD is absorbed). At the same time, the weight per dose selected is less than the weight per dose that would equate the offense level for LSD on a carrier medium with that for the same number of doses of PCP, a controlled substance that comparative assessments indicate is more likely to induce violent acts and ancillary crime than is LSD. (Treating LSD on a carrier medium as weighing 0.5 milligram per dose would produce offense levels equivalent to those for PCP.) Thus, the approach decided upon by the Commission will harmonize offense levels for LSD offenses with those for other controlled substances and avoid an undue influence of varied carrier weight on the applicable offense level. Nonetheless, this approach does not override the applicability of "mixture or substance" for the purpose of applying any mandatory minimum sentence (*see Chapman*; §5G1.1(b)).

Frequently, a term of supervised release to follow imprisonment is required by statute for offenses covered by this guideline. Guidelines for the imposition, duration, and conditions of supervised release are set forth in Chapter Five, Part D (Supervised Release).

The last sentence of subsection (a)(5) implements the directive to the Commission in section 7(1) of Public Law 111–220.

Subsection (b)(2) implements the directive to the Commission in section 5 of Public Law 111–220.

Subsection (b)(3) is derived from Section 6453 of the Anti-Drug Abuse Act of 1988.

Subsection (b)(11) implements the directive to the Commission in section 6(1) of Public Law 111–220.

Subsection (b)(12) implements the directive to the Commission in section 6(2) of Public Law 111–220.

Subsection (b)(13)(A) implements the instruction to the Commission in section 303 of Public Law 103–237.

Subsections (b)(13)(C)(ii) and (D) implement, in a broader form, the instruction to the Commission in section 102 of Public Law 106–310.

Subsection (b)(15) implements the directive to the Commission in section 6(3) of Public Law 111–220.

Subsection (b)(16) implements the directive to the Commission in section 7(2) of Public Law 111–220.

| Historical Note | Effective November 1, 1987. Amended effective January 15, 1988 (amendments 19, 20, and 21); November 1, 1989 (amendments 123–134, 302, and 303); November 1, 1990 (amendment 318); November 1, 1991 (amendments 369–371 and 394–396); November 1, 1992 (amendments 446 and 447); November 1, 1993 (amendments 479, 484–488, and 499); September 23, 1994 (amendment 509); November 1, 1994 (amendment 505); November 1, 1995 (amendments 514–518); November 1, 1997 (amendments 555 and 556); November 1, 2000 (amendments 594 and 605); December 16, 2000 (amendment 608); May 1, 2001 (amendments 609–611); November 1, 2001 (amendments 620–625); November 1, 2002 (amendment 640); November 1, 2003 (amendment 657); November 1, 2004 (amendments 667, 668, and 674); November 1, 2005 (amendment 679); March 27, 2006 (amendment 681); November 1, 2006 (amendments 684 and 688); November 1, 2007 (amendments 705, 706, and 711); May 1, 2008 (amendment 715); November 1, 2009 (amendments 727 and 728); November 1, 2010 (amendments 746 and 748); November 1, 2011 (amendments 750, 751, and 760); November 1, 2012 (amendments 762 and 770); November 1, 2013 (amendment 777); November 1, 2014 (amendments 782 and 783); November 1, 2015 (amendments 793 and 797). |

§2D1.2. Drug Offenses Occurring Near Protected Locations or Involving Underage or Pregnant Individuals; Attempt or Conspiracy

(a)   Base Offense Level (Apply the greatest):

   (1)   **2** plus the offense level from §2D1.1 applicable to the quantity of controlled substances directly involving a protected location or an underage or pregnant individual; or

   (2)   **1** plus the offense level from §2D1.1 applicable to the total quantity of controlled substances involved in the offense; or

   (3)   **26**, if the offense involved a person less than eighteen years of age; or

   (4)   **13**, otherwise.

Commentary

Statutory Provisions: 21 U.S.C. §§ 859 (formerly 21 U.S.C. § 845), 860 (formerly 21 U.S.C, § 845a), 861 (formerly 21 U.S.C. § 845b).

Application Note:

1.   This guideline applies only in a case in which the defendant is convicted of a statutory violation of drug trafficking in a protected location or involving an underage or pregnant individual (including an attempt or conspiracy to commit such a violation) or in a case in which the defendant stipulated to such a statutory violation. *See* §1B1.2(a). In a case involving such a conviction but in which only part of the relevant offense conduct directly involved a protected location or an underage or pregnant individual, subsections (a)(1) and (a)(2) may result in different offense levels. For example, if the defendant, as part of the same course of conduct or common scheme or plan, sold 5 grams of heroin near a protected location and 10 grams of heroin elsewhere, the offense level from subsection

(a)(1) would be level 14 (2 plus the offense level for the sale of 5 grams of heroin, the amount sold near the protected location); the offense level from subsection (a)(2) would be level 15 (1 plus the offense level for the sale of 15 grams of heroin, the total amount of heroin involved in the offense).

Background: This section implements the direction to the Commission in Section 6454 of the Anti-Drug Abuse Act of 1988.

Historical Note	Effective November 1, 1987. Amended effective January 15, 1988 (amendment 22); November 1, 1989 (amendment 135); November 1, 1990 (amendment 319); November 1, 1991 (amendment 421); November 1, 1992 (amendment 447); November 1, 2000 (amendment 591); November 1, 2014 (amendment 782).

§2D1.3. [Deleted]

Historical Note	Section 2D1.3 (Distributing Controlled Substances to Individuals Younger than Twenty-One Years, to Pregnant Women, or Within 1000 Feet of a School or College), effective November 1, 1987, amended effective January 15, 1988 (amendment 23), was deleted by consolidation with §2D1.2 effective November 1, 1989 (amendment 135).

§2D1.4. [Deleted]

Historical Note	Section 2D1.4 (Attempts and Conspiracies), effective November 1, 1987, amended effective November 1, 1989 (amendments 136–138), was deleted by consolidation with the guidelines applicable to the underlying substantive offenses effective November 1, 1992 (amendment 447).

§2D1.5. Continuing Criminal Enterprise; Attempt or Conspiracy

    (a)   Base Offense Level (Apply the greater):

        (1)   **4 plus the offense level from §2D1.1 applicable to the underlying offense; or**

        (2)   **38.**

Commentary

Statutory Provision: 21 U.S.C. § 848.

Application Notes:

1.   Do not apply any adjustment from Chapter Three, Part B (Role in the Offense).

2.   If as part of the enterprise the defendant sanctioned the use of violence, or if the number of persons managed by the defendant was extremely large, an upward departure may be warranted.

3. Under 21 U.S.C. § 848, certain conduct for which the defendant has previously been sentenced may be charged as part of the instant offense to establish a "continuing series of violations." A sentence resulting from a conviction sustained prior to the last overt act of the instant offense is to be considered a prior sentence under §4A1.2(a)(1) and not part of the instant offense.

4. Violations of 21 U.S.C. § 848 will be grouped with other drug offenses for the purpose of applying Chapter Three, Part D (Multiple Counts).

Background: Because a conviction under 21 U.S.C. § 848 establishes that a defendant controlled and exercised authority over one of the most serious types of ongoing criminal activity, this guideline provides a minimum base offense level of 38. An adjustment from Chapter Three, Part B is not authorized because the offense level of this guideline already reflects an adjustment for role in the offense.

Title 21 U.S.C. § 848 provides a 20-year minimum mandatory penalty for the first conviction, a 30-year minimum mandatory penalty for a second conviction, and a mandatory life sentence for principal administrators of extremely large enterprises. If the application of the guidelines results in a sentence below the minimum sentence required by statute, the statutory minimum shall be the guideline sentence. *See* §5G1.1(b).

Historical Note	Effective November 1, 1987. Amended effective October 15, 1988 (amendment 66); November 1, 1989 (amendment 139); November 1, 1992 (amendment 447).

§2D1.6.   Use of Communication Facility in Committing Drug Offense; Attempt or Conspiracy

(a) Base Offense Level: the offense level applicable to the underlying offense.

Commentary

Statutory Provision: 21 U.S.C. § 843(b).

Application Note:

1. Where the offense level for the underlying offense is to be determined by reference to §2D1.1, *see* Application Note 5 of the Commentary to §2D1.1 for guidance in determining the scale of the offense. Note that the Drug Quantity Table in §2D1.1 provides a minimum offense level of 12 where the offense involves heroin (or other Schedule I or II opiates), cocaine (or other Schedule I or II stimulants), cocaine base, PCP, methamphetamine, LSD (or other Schedule I or II hallucinogens), fentanyl, or fentanyl analogue (§2D1.1(c)(14)); a minimum offense level of 8 where the offense involves flunitrazepam (§2D1.1(c)(16)); and a minimum offense level of 6 otherwise (§2D1.1(c)(17)).

Background: This section covers the use of a communication facility in committing a drug offense. A communication facility includes any public or private instrument used in the transmission of writing, signs, signals, pictures, and sound; *e.g.*, telephone, wire, radio.

Historical Note	Effective November 1, 1987. Amended effective November 1, 1990 (amendment 320); November 1, 1992 (amendment 447); November 1, 1994 (amendment 505); November 1, 2009 (amendment 737); November 1, 2012 (amendment 770).

§2D1.7. Unlawful Sale or Transportation of Drug Paraphernalia; Attempt or Conspiracy

(a)   Base Offense Level: **12**

(b)   Cross Reference

   (1)   If the offense involved a controlled substance, apply §2D1.1 (Unlawful Manufacturing, Importing, Exporting, or Trafficking) or §2D2.1 (Unlawful Possession), as appropriate, if the resulting offense level is greater than that determined above.

Commentary

Statutory Provision: 21 U.S.C. § 863 (formerly 21 U.S.C. § 857).

Application Note:

1.   The typical case addressed by this guideline involves small-scale trafficking in drug paraphernalia (generally from a retail establishment that also sells items that are not unlawful). In a case involving a large-scale dealer, distributor, or manufacturer, an upward departure may be warranted. Conversely, where the offense was not committed for pecuniary gain (*e.g.*, transportation for the defendant's personal use), a downward departure may be warranted.

Historical Note	Effective November 1, 1987. Amended effective November 1, 1991 (amendment 397); November 1, 1992 (amendment 447).

§2D1.8. Renting or Managing a Drug Establishment; Attempt or Conspiracy

(a)   Base Offense Level:

   (1)   The offense level from §2D1.1 applicable to the underlying controlled substance offense, except as provided below.

   (2)   If the defendant had no participation in the underlying controlled substance offense other than allowing use of the premises, the offense level shall be **4** levels less than the offense level from §2D1.1 applicable to the underlying controlled substance offense, but not greater than level **26**.

    (b)   Special Instruction

        (1)   If the offense level is determined under subsection (a)(2), do not apply an adjustment under §3B1.2 (Mitigating Role).

Commentary

Statutory Provision: 21 U.S.C. § 856.

Application Note:

1.   Subsection (a)(2) does not apply unless the defendant had no participation in the underlying controlled substance offense other than allowing use of the premises. For example, subsection (a)(2) would not apply to a defendant who possessed a dangerous weapon in connection with the offense, a defendant who guarded the cache of controlled substances, a defendant who arranged for the use of the premises for the purpose of facilitating a drug transaction, a defendant who allowed the use of more than one premises, a defendant who made telephone calls to facilitate the underlying controlled substance offense, or a defendant who otherwise assisted in the commission of the underlying controlled substance offense. Furthermore, subsection (a)(2) does not apply unless the defendant initially leased, rented, purchased, or otherwise acquired a possessory interest in the premises for a legitimate purpose. Finally, subsection (a)(2) does not apply if the defendant had previously allowed any premises to be used as a drug establishment without regard to whether such prior misconduct resulted in a conviction.

Background: This section covers the offense of knowingly opening, maintaining, managing, or controlling any building, room, or enclosure for the purpose of manufacturing, distributing, storing, or using a controlled substance contrary to law (*e.g.*, a "crack house").

Historical Note	Effective November 1, 1987. Amended effective November 1, 1991 (amendment 394); November 1, 1992 (amendments 447 and 448); November 1, 2002 (amendment 640).

---

§2D1.9. Placing or Maintaining Dangerous Devices on Federal Property to Protect the Unlawful Production of Controlled Substances; Attempt or Conspiracy

    (a)   Base Offense Level: **23**

Commentary

Statutory Provision: 21 U.S.C. § 841(d)(1).

Background: This section covers the offense of assembling, placing, or causing to be placed, or maintaining a "booby-trap" on federal property where a controlled substance is being manufactured or distributed.

Historical Note	Effective November 1, 1987. Amended effective November 1, 1992 (amendment 447); November 1, 2002 (amendment 646).

§2D1.10. Endangering Human Life While Illegally Manufacturing a Controlled Substance; Attempt or Conspiracy

    (a) Base Offense Level (Apply the greater):

        (1) **3** plus the offense level from the Drug Quantity Table in §2D1.1; or

        (2) **20**.

    (b) Specific Offense Characteristic

        (1) (Apply the greater):

            (A) If the offense involved the manufacture of amphetamine or methamphetamine, increase by **3** levels. If the resulting offense level is less than level **27**, increase to level **27**.

            (B) If the offense (i) involved the manufacture of amphetamine or methamphetamine; and (ii) created a substantial risk of harm to the life of a minor or an incompetent, increase by **6** levels. If the resulting offense level is less than level **30**, increase to level **30**.

Commentary

Statutory Provision: 21 U.S.C. § 858.

Application Note:

1. **Substantial Risk of Harm Associated with the Manufacture of Amphetamine and Methamphetamine.**—

    (A) **Factors to Consider.**—In determining, for purposes of subsection (b)(1)(B), whether the offense created a substantial risk of harm to the life of a minor or an incompetent, the court shall include consideration of the following factors:

        (i) The quantity of any chemicals or hazardous or toxic substances found at the laboratory, and the manner in which the chemicals or substances were stored.

        (ii) The manner in which hazardous or toxic substances were disposed, and the likelihood of release into the environment of hazardous or toxic substances.

        (iii) The duration of the offense, and the extent of the manufacturing operation.

        (iv) The location of the laboratory (*e.g.*, whether the laboratory is located in a residential neighborhood or a remote area), and the number of human lives placed at substantial risk of harm.

    (B) **Definitions.**—For purposes of subsection (b)(1)(B):

"***Incompetent***" means an individual who is incapable of taking care of the individual's self or property because of a mental or physical illness or disability, mental retardation, or senility.

"***Minor***" has the meaning given that term in Application Note 1 of the Commentary to §2A3.1 (Criminal Sexual Abuse).

Background: Subsection (b)(1) implements the instruction to the Commission in section 102 of Public Law 106–310.

Historical Note	Effective November 1, 1989 (amendment 140). Amended effective November 1, 1992 (amendment 447); December 16, 2000 (amendment 608); November 1, 2001 (amendment 620).

§2D1.11. Unlawfully Distributing, Importing, Exporting or Possessing a Listed Chemical; Attempt or Conspiracy

    (a)   Base Offense Level: The offense level from the Chemical Quantity Table set forth in subsection (d) or (e), as appropriate, except that if (A) the defendant receives an adjustment under §3B1.2 (Mitigating Role); and (B) the base offense level under subsection (d) is (i) level **32**, decrease by **2** levels; (ii) level **34** or level **36**, decrease by **3** levels; or (iii) level **38**, decrease by **4** levels.

    (b)   Specific Offense Characteristics

        (1)   If a dangerous weapon (including a firearm) was possessed, increase by **2** levels.

        (2)   If the defendant is convicted of violating 21 U.S.C. § 841(c)(2) or (f)(1), or § 960(d)(2), (d)(3), or (d)(4), decrease by **3** levels, unless the defendant knew or believed that the listed chemical was to be used to manufacture a controlled substance unlawfully.

        (3)   If the offense involved (A) an unlawful discharge, emission, or release into the environment of a hazardous or toxic substance; or (B) the unlawful transportation, treatment, storage, or disposal of a hazardous waste, increase by **2** levels.

        (4)   If the defendant, or a person for whose conduct the defendant is accountable under §1B1.3 (Relevant Conduct), distributed a listed chemical through mass-marketing by means of an interactive computer service, increase by **2** levels.

(5) If the defendant is convicted under 21 U.S.C. § 865, increase by **2** levels.

(6) If the defendant meets the criteria set forth in subdivisions (1)–(5) of subsection (a) of §5C1.2 (Limitation on Applicability of Statutory Minimum Sentences in Certain Cases), decrease by **2** levels.

(c) Cross Reference

(1) If the offense involved unlawfully manufacturing a controlled substance, or attempting to manufacture a controlled substance unlawfully, apply §2D1.1 (Unlawful Manufacturing, Importing, Exporting, Trafficking) if the resulting offense level is greater than that determined above.

(d) EPHEDRINE, PSEUDOEPHEDRINE, AND PHENYLPROPANOLAMINE QUANTITY TABLE*
(Methamphetamine and Amphetamine Precursor Chemicals)

QUANTITY	BASE OFFENSE LEVEL
(1) 9 KG or more of Ephedrine; 9 KG or more of Phenylpropanolamine; 9 KG or more of Pseudoephedrine.	Level 38
(2) At least 3 KG but less than 9 KG of Ephedrine; At least 3 KG but less than 9 KG of Phenylpropanolamine; At least 3 KG but less than 9 KG of Pseudoephedrine.	Level 36
(3) At least 1 KG but less than 3 KG of Ephedrine; At least 1 KG but less than 3 KG of Phenylpropanolamine; At least 1 KG but less than 3 KG of Pseudoephedrine.	Level 34
(4) At least 300 G but less than 1 KG of Ephedrine; At least 300 G but less than 1 KG of Phenylpropanolamine; At least 300 G but less than 1 KG of Pseudoephedrine.	Level 32
(5) At least 100 G but less than 300 G of Ephedrine; At least 100 G but less than 300 G of Phenylpropanolamine; At least 100 G but less than 300 G of Pseudoephedrine.	Level 30
(6) At least 70 G but less than 100 G of Ephedrine; At least 70 G but less than 100 G of Phenylpropanolamine; At least 70 G but less than 100 G of Pseuodoephedrine.	Level 28

(7)	At least 40 G but less than 70 G of Ephedrine; At least 40 G but less than 70 G of Phenylpropanolamine; At least 40 G but less than 70 G of Pseudoephedrine.	**Level 26**
(8)	At least 10 G but less than 40 G of Ephedrine; At least 10 G but less than 40 G of Phenylpropanolamine; At least 10 G but less than 40 G of Pseudoephedrine.	**Level 24**
(9)	At least 8 G but less than 10 G of Ephedrine; At least 8 G but less than 10 G of Phenylpropanolamine; At least 8 G but less than 10 G of Pseudoephedrine.	**Level 22**
(10)	At least 6 G but less than 8 G of Ephedrine; At least 6 G but less than 8 G of Phenylpropanolamine; At least 6 G but less than 8 G of Pseudoephedrine.	**Level 20**
(11)	At least 4 G but less than 6 G of Ephedrine; At least 4 G but less than 6 G of Phenylpropanolamine; At least 4 G but less than 6 G of Pseudoephedrine.	**Level 18**
(12)	At least 2 G but less than 4 G of Ephedrine; At least 2 G but less than 4 G of Phenylpropanolamine; At least 2 G but less than 4 G of Pseudoephedrine.	**Level 16**
(13)	At least 1 G but less than 2 G of Ephedrine; At least 1 G but less than 2 G of Phenylpropanolamine; At least 1 G but less than 2 G of Pseudoephedrine.	**Level 14**
(14)	Less than 1 G of Ephedrine; Less than 1 G of Phenylpropanolamine; Less than 1 G of Pseudoephedrine.	**Level 12**

(e) CHEMICAL QUANTITY TABLE*
(All Other Precursor Chemicals)

LISTED CHEMICALS AND QUANTITY	BASE OFFENSE LEVEL
(1) **List I Chemicals** 2.7 KG or more of Benzaldehyde; 60 KG or more of Benzyl Cyanide; 600 G or more of Ergonovine; 1.2 KG or more of Ergotamine; 60 KG or more of Ethylamine; 6.6 KG or more of Hydriodic Acid; 3.9 KG or more of Iodine; 960 KG or more of Isosafrole; 600 G or more of Methylamine; 1500 KG or more of N-Methylephedrine; 1500 KG or more of N-Methylpseudoephedrine;	**Level 30**

1.9 KG or more of Nitroethane;
30 KG or more of Norpseudoephedrine;
60 KG or more of Phenylacetic Acid;
30 KG or more of Piperidine;
960 KG or more of Piperonal;
4.8 KG or more of Propionic Anhydride;
960 KG or more of Safrole;
1200 KG or more of 3, 4-Methylenedioxyphenyl-2-propanone;
3406.5 L or more of Gamma-butyrolactone;
2.1 KG or more of Red Phosphorus, White Phosphorus, or Hypophosphorous Acid.

(2) **List I Chemicals** **Level 28**
At least 890 G but less than 2.7 KG of Benzaldehyde;
At least 20 KG but less than 60 KG of Benzyl Cyanide;
At least 200 G but less than 600 G of Ergonovine;
At least 400 G but less than 1.2 KG of Ergotamine;
At least 20 KG but less than 60 KG of Ethylamine;
At least 2.2 KG but less than 6.6 KG of Hydriodic Acid;
At least 1.3 KG but less than 3.9 KG of Iodine;
At least 320 KG but less than 960 KG of Isosafrole;
At least 200 G but less than 600 G of Methylamine;
At least 500 KG but less than 1500 KG of N-Methylephedrine;
At least 500 KG but less than 1500 KG of N-Methylpseudoephedrine;
At least 625 G but less than 1.9 KG of Nitroethane;
At least 10 KG but less than 30 KG of Norpseudoephedrine;
At least 20 KG but less than 60 KG of Phenylacetic Acid;
At least 10 KG but less than 30 KG of Piperidine;
At least 320 KG but less than 960 KG of Piperonal;
At least 1.6 KG but less than 4.8 KG of Propionic Anhydride;
At least 320 KG but less than 960 KG of Safrole;
At least 400 KG but less than 1200 KG of 3, 4-Methylenedioxyphenyl-2-propanone;
At least 1135.5 L but less than 3406.5 L of Gamma-butyrolactone;
At least 714 G but less than 2.1 KG of Red Phosphorus, White Phosphorus, or
    Hypophosphorous Acid.

List II Chemicals
33 KG or more of Acetic Anhydride;
3525 KG or more of Acetone;
60 KG or more of Benzyl Chloride;
3225 KG or more of Ethyl Ether;
3600 KG or more of Methyl Ethyl Ketone;
30 KG or more of Potassium Permanganate;
3900 KG or more of Toluene.

(3) **List I Chemicals** **Level 26**
At least 267 G but less than 890 G of Benzaldehyde;
At least 6 KG but less than 20 KG of Benzyl Cyanide;
At least 60 G but less than 200 G of Ergonovine;
At least 120 G but less than 400 G of Ergotamine;
At least 6 KG but less than 20 KG of Ethylamine;
At least 660 G but less than 2.2 KG of Hydriodic Acid;
At least 376.2 G but less than 1.3 KG of Iodine;
At least 96 KG but less than 320 KG of Isosafrole;

At least 60 G but less than 200 G of Methylamine;
At least 150 KG but less than 500 KG of N-Methylephedrine;
At least 150 KG but less than 500 KG of N-Methylpseudoephedrine;
At least 187.5 G but less than 625 G of Nitroethane;
At least 3 KG but less than 10 KG of Norpseudoephedrine;
At least 6 KG but less than 20 KG of Phenylacetic Acid;
At least 3 KG but less than 10 KG of Piperidine;
At least 96 KG but less than 320 KG of Piperonal;
At least 480 G but less than 1.6 KG of Propionic Anhydride;
At least 96 KG but less than 320 KG of Safrole;
At least 120 KG but less than 400 KG of 3, 4-Methylenedioxyphenyl-2-propanone;
At least 340.7 L but less than 1135.5 L of Gamma-butyrolactone;
At least 214 G but less than 714 G of Red Phosphorus, White Phosphorus, or
    Hypophosphorous Acid;

List II Chemicals

At least 11 KG but less than 33 KG of Acetic Anhydride;
At least 1175 KG but less than 3525 KG of Acetone;
At least 20 KG but less than 60 KG of Benzyl Chloride;
At least 1075 KG but less than 3225 KG of Ethyl Ether;
At least 1200 KG but less than 3600 KG of Methyl Ethyl Ketone;
At least 10 KG but less than 30 KG of Potassium Permanganate;
At least 1300 KG but less than 3900 KG of Toluene.

(4) **List I Chemicals**   **Level 24**

At least 89 G but less than 267 G of Benzaldehyde;
At least 2 KG but less than 6 KG of Benzyl Cyanide;
At least 20 G but less than 60 G of Ergonovine;
At least 40 G but less than 120 G of Ergotamine;
At least 2 KG but less than 6 KG of Ethylamine;
At least 220 G but less than 660 G of Hydriodic Acid;
At least 125.4 G but less than 376.2 G of Iodine;
At least 32 KG but less than 96 KG of Isosafrole;
At least 20 G but less than 60 G of Methylamine;
At least 50 KG but less than 150 KG of N-Methylephedrine;
At least 50 KG but less than 150 KG of N-Methylpseudoephedrine;
At least 62.5 G but less than 187.5 G of Nitroethane;
At least 1 KG but less than 3 KG of Norpseudoephedrine;
At least 2 KG but less than 6 KG of Phenylacetic Acid;
At least 1 KG but less than 3 KG of Piperidine;
At least 32 KG but less than 96 KG of Piperonal;
At least 160 G but less than 480 G of Propionic Anhydride;
At least 32 KG but less than 96 KG of Safrole;
At least 40 KG but less than 120 KG of 3, 4-Methylenedioxyphenyl-2-propanone;
At least 113.6 L but less than 340.7 L of Gamma-butyrolactone;
At least 71 G but less than 214 G of Red Phosphorus, White Phosphorus, or
    Hypophosphorous Acid;

List II Chemicals

At least 3.3 KG but less than 11 KG of Acetic Anhydride;
At least 352.5 KG but less than 1175 KG of Acetone;
At least 6 KG but less than 20 KG of Benzyl Chloride;
At least 322.5 KG but less than 1075 KG of Ethyl Ether;
At least 360 KG but less than 1200 KG of Methyl Ethyl Ketone;

At least 3 KG but less than 10 KG of Potassium Permanganate;
At least 390 KG but less than 1300 KG of Toluene.

(5)   **List I Chemicals**   **Level 22**
At least 62.3 G but less than 89 G of Benzaldehyde;
At least 1.4 KG but less than 2 KG of Benzyl Cyanide;
At least 14 G but less than 20 G of Ergonovine;
At least 28 G but less than 40 G of Ergotamine;
At least 1.4 KG but less than 2 KG of Ethylamine;
At least 154 G but less than 220 G of Hydriodic Acid;
At least 87.8 G but less than 125.4 G of Iodine;
At least 22.4 KG but less than 32 KG of Isosafrole;
At least 14 G but less than 20 G of Methylamine;
At least 35 KG but less than 50 KG of N-Methylephedrine;
At least 35 KG but less than 50 KG of N-Methylpseudoephedrine;
At least 43.8 G but less than 62.5 G of Nitroethane;
At least 700 G but less than 1 KG of Norpseudoephedrine;
At least 1.4 KG but less than 2 KG of Phenylacetic Acid;
At least 700 G but less than 1 KG of Piperidine;
At least 22.4 KG but less than 32 KG of Piperonal;
At least 112 G but less than 160 G of Propionic Anhydride;
At least 22.4 KG but less than 32 KG of Safrole;
At least 28 KG but less than 40 KG of 3, 4-Methylenedioxyphenyl-2-propanone;
At least 79.5 L but less than 113.6 L of Gamma-butyrolactone;
At least 50 G but less than 71 G of Red Phosphorus, White Phosphorus, or
     Hypophosphorous Acid;

List II Chemicals
At least 1.1 KG but less than 3.3 KG of Acetic Anhydride;
At least 117.5 KG but less than 352.5 KG of Acetone;
At least 2 KG but less than 6 KG of Benzyl Chloride;
At least 107.5 KG but less than 322.5 KG of Ethyl Ether;
At least 120 KG but less than 360 KG of Methyl Ethyl Ketone;
At least 1 KG but less than 3 KG of Potassium Permanganate;
At least 130 KG but less than 390 KG of Toluene.

(6)   **List I Chemicals**   **Level 20**
At least 35.6 G but less than 62.3 G of Benzaldehyde;
At least 800 G but less than 1.4 KG of Benzyl Cyanide;
At least 8 G but less than 14 G of Ergonovine;
At least 16 G but less than 28 G of Ergotamine;
At least 800 G but less than 1.4 KG of Ethylamine;
At least 88 G but less than 154 G of Hydriodic Acid;
At least 50.2 G but less than 87.8 G of Iodine;
At least 12.8 KG but less than 22.4 KG of Isosafrole;
At least 8 G but less than 14 G of Methylamine;
At least 20 KG but less than 35 KG of N-Methylephedrine;
At least 20 KG but less than 35 KG of N-Methylpseudoephedrine;
At least 25 G but less than 43.8 G of Nitroethane;
At least 400 G but less than 700 G of Norpseudoephedrine;
At least 800 G but less than 1.4 KG of Phenylacetic Acid;
At least 400 G but less than 700 G of Piperidine;
At least 12.8 KG but less than 22.4 KG of Piperonal;

At least 64 G but less than 112 G of Propionic Anhydride;
At least 12.8 KG but less than 22.4 KG of Safrole;
At least 16 KG but less than 28 KG of 3, 4-Methylenedioxyphenyl-2-propanone;
At least 45.4 L but less than 79.5 L of Gamma-butyrolactone;
At least 29 G but less than 50 G of Red Phosphorus, White Phosphorus, or
    Hypophosphorous Acid;

List II Chemicals
At least 726 G but less than 1.1 KG of Acetic Anhydride;
At least 82.25 KG but less than 117.5 KG of Acetone;
At least 1.4 KG but less than 2 KG of Benzyl Chloride;
At least 75.25 KG but less than 107.5 KG of Ethyl Ether;
At least 84 KG but less than 120 KG of Methyl Ethyl Ketone;
At least 700 G but less than 1 KG of Potassium Permanganate;
At least 91 KG but less than 130 KG of Toluene.

(7)   **List I Chemicals**   **Level 18**
At least 8.9 G but less than 35.6 G of Benzaldehyde;
At least 200 G but less than 800 G of Benzyl Cyanide;
At least 2 G but less than 8 G of Ergonovine;
At least 4 G but less than 16 G of Ergotamine;
At least 200 G but less than 800 G of Ethylamine;
At least 22 G but less than 88 G of Hydriodic Acid;
At least 12.5 G but less than 50.2 G of Iodine;
At least 3.2 KG but less than 12.8 KG of Isosafrole;
At least 2 G but less than 8 G of Methylamine;
At least 5 KG but less than 20 KG of N-Methylephedrine;
At least 5 KG but less than 20 KG of N-Methylpseudoephedrine;
At least 6.3 G but less than 25 G of Nitroethane;
At least 100 G but less than 400 G of Norpseudoephedrine;
At least 200 G but less than 800 G of Phenylacetic Acid;
At least 100 G but less than 400 G of Piperidine;
At least 3.2 KG but less than 12.8 KG of Piperonal;
At least 16 G but less than 64 G of Propionic Anhydride;
At least 3.2 KG but less than 12.8 KG of Safrole;
At least 4 KG but less than 16 KG of 3, 4-Methylenedioxyphenyl-2-propanone;
At least 11.4 L but less than 45.4 L of Gamma-butyrolactone;
At least 7 G but less than 29 G of Red Phosphorus, White Phosphorus, or
    Hypophosphorous Acid;

List II Chemicals
At least 440 G but less than 726 G of Acetic Anhydride;
At least 47 KG but less than 82.25 KG of Acetone;
At least 800 G but less than 1.4 KG of Benzyl Chloride;
At least 43 KG but less than 75.25 KG of Ethyl Ether;
At least 48 KG but less than 84 KG of Methyl Ethyl Ketone;
At least 400 G but less than 700 G of Potassium Permanganate;
At least 52 KG but less than 91 KG of Toluene.

(8)   **List I Chemicals**   **Level 16**
At least 7.1 G but less than 8.9 G of Benzaldehyde;
At least 160 G but less than 200 G of Benzyl Cyanide;
At least 1.6 G but less than 2 G of Ergonovine;

At least 3.2 G but less than 4 G of Ergotamine;
At least 160 G but less than 200 G of Ethylamine;
At least 17.6 G but less than 22 G of Hydriodic Acid;
At least 10 G but less than 12.5 G of Iodine;
At least 2.56 KG but less than 3.2 KG of Isosafrole;
At least 1.6 G but less than 2 G of Methylamine;
At least 4 KG but less than 5 KG of N-Methylephedrine;
At least 4 KG but less than 5 KG of N-Methylpseudoephedrine;
At least 5 G but less than 6.3 G of Nitroethane;
At least 80 G but less than 100 G of Norpseudoephedrine;
At least 160 G but less than 200 G of Phenylacetic Acid;
At least 80 G but less than 100 G of Piperidine;
At least 2.56 KG but less than 3.2 KG of Piperonal;
At least 12.8 G but less than 16 G of Propionic Anhydride;
At least 2.56 KG but less than 3.2 KG of Safrole;
At least 3.2 KG but less than 4 KG of 3, 4-Methylenedioxyphenyl-2-propanone;
At least 9.1 L but less than 11.4 L of Gamma-butyrolactone;
At least 6 G but less than 7 G of Red Phosphorus, White Phosphorus, or
    Hypophosphorous Acid;

List II Chemicals
At least 110 G but less than 440 G of Acetic Anhydride;
At least 11.75 KG but less than 47 KG of Acetone;
At least 200 G but less than 800 G of Benzyl Chloride;
At least 10.75 KG but less than 43 KG of Ethyl Ether;
At least 12 KG but less than 48 KG of Methyl Ethyl Ketone;
At least 100 G but less than 400 G of Potassium Permanganate;
At least 13 KG but less than 52 KG of Toluene.

(9) **List I Chemicals**   **Level 14**
3.6 KG or more of Anthranilic Acid;
At least 5.3 G but less than 7.1 G of Benzaldehyde;
At least 120 G but less than 160 G of Benzyl Cyanide;
At least 1.2 G but less than 1.6 G of Ergonovine;
At least 2.4 G but less than 3.2 G of Ergotamine;
At least 120 G but less than 160 G of Ethylamine;
At least 13.2 G but less than 17.6 G of Hydriodic Acid;
At least 7.5 G but less than 10 G of Iodine;
At least 1.92 KG but less than 2.56 KG of Isosafrole;
At least 1.2 G but less than 1.6 G of Methylamine;
4.8 KG or more of N-Acetylanthranilic Acid;
At least 3 KG but less than 4 KG of N-Methylephedrine;
At least 3 KG but less than 4 KG of N-Methylpseudoephedrine;
At least 3.8 G but less than 5 G of Nitroethane;
At least 60 G but less than 80 G of Norpseudoephedrine;
At least 120 G but less than 160 G of Phenylacetic Acid;
At least 60 G but less than 80 G of Piperidine;
At least 1.92 KG but less than 2.56 KG of Piperonal;
At least 9.6 G but less than 12.8 G of Propionic Anhydride;
At least 1.92 KG but less than 2.56 KG of Safrole;
At least 2.4 KG but less than 3.2 KG of 3, 4-Methylenedioxyphenyl-2-propanone;
At least 6.8 L but less than 9.1 L of Gamma-butyrolactone;
At least 4 G but less than 6 G of Red Phosphorus, White Phosphorus, or
    Hypophosphorous Acid;

List II Chemicals
At least 88 G but less than 110 G of Acetic Anhydride;
At least 9.4 KG but less than 11.75 KG of Acetone;
At least 160 G but less than 200 G of Benzyl Chloride;
At least 8.6 KG but less than 10.75 KG of Ethyl Ether;
At least 9.6 KG but less than 12 KG of Methyl Ethyl Ketone;
At least 80 G but less than 100 G of Potassium Permanganate;
At least 10.4 KG but less than 13 KG of Toluene.

(10)   **List I Chemicals**   **Level 12**
Less than 3.6 KG of Anthranilic Acid;
Less than 5.3 G of Benzaldehyde;
Less than 120 G of Benzyl Cyanide;
Less than 1.2 G of Ergonovine;
Less than 2.4 G of Ergotamine;
Less than 120 G of Ethylamine;
Less than 13.2 G of Hydriodic Acid;
Less than 7.5 G of Iodine;
Less than 1.92 KG of Isosafrole;
Less than 1.2 G of Methylamine;
Less than 4.8 KG of N-Acetylanthranilic Acid;
Less than 3 KG of N-Methylephedrine;
Less than 3 KG of N-Methylpseudoephedrine;
Less than 3.8 G of Nitroethane;
Less than 60 G of Norpseudoephedrine;
Less than 120 G of Phenylacetic Acid;
Less than 60 G of Piperidine;
Less than 1.92 KG of Piperonal;
Less than 9.6 G of Propionic Anhydride;
Less than 1.92 KG of Safrole;
Less than 2.4 KG of 3, 4-Methylenedioxyphenyl-2-propanone;
Less than 6.8 L of Gamma-butyrolactone;
Less than 4 G of Red Phosphorus, White Phosphorus, or Hypophosphorous Acid;

List II Chemicals
Less than 88 G of Acetic Anhydride;
Less than 9.4 KG of Acetone;
Less than 160 G of Benzyl Chloride;
Less than 8.6 KG of Ethyl Ether;
Less than 9.6 KG of Methyl Ethyl Ketone;
Less than 80 G of Potassium Permanganate;
Less than 10.4 KG of Toluene.

*Notes:

(A)   Except as provided in Note (B), to calculate the base offense level in an offense
      that involves two or more chemicals, use the quantity of the single chemical
      that results in the greatest offense level, regardless of whether the chemicals
      are set forth in different tables or in different categories (*i.e.*, list I or list II)
      under subsection (d) or (e) of this guideline, as appropriate.

(B) To calculate the base offense level in an offense that involves two or more chemicals each of which is set forth in the Ephedrine, Pseudoephedrine, and Phenylpropanolamine Quantity Table, (i) aggregate the quantities of all such chemicals, and (ii) determine the base offense level corresponding to the aggregate quantity.

(C) In a case involving ephedrine, pseudoephedrine, or phenylpropanolamine tablets, use the weight of the ephedrine, pseudoephedrine, or phenylpropanolamine contained in the tablets, not the weight of the entire tablets, in calculating the base offense level.

Commentary

Statutory Provisions: 21 U.S.C. §§ 841(c)(1), (2), (f)(1), 865, 960(d)(1), (2), (3), (4).

Application Notes:

1. **Cases Involving Multiple Chemicals.—**

    (A) **Determining the Base Offense Level for Two or More Chemicals.—**Except as provided in subdivision (B), if the offense involves two or more chemicals, use the quantity of the single chemical that results in the greatest offense level, regardless of whether the chemicals are set forth in different tables or in different categories (*i.e.*, list I or list II) under this guideline.

    Example: The defendant was in possession of five kilograms of ephedrine and 300 grams of hydriodic acid. Ephedrine and hydriodic acid typically are used together in the same manufacturing process to manufacture methamphetamine. The base offense level for each chemical is calculated separately and the chemical with the higher base offense level is used. Five kilograms of ephedrine result in a base offense level of level 36; 300 grams of hydriodic acid result in a base offense level of level 24. In this case, the base offense level would be level 36.

    (B) **Determining the Base Offense Level for Offenses involving Ephedrine, Pseudoephedrine, or Phenylpropanolamine.—**If the offense involves two or more chemicals each of which is set forth in the Ephedrine, Pseudoephedrine, and Phenylpropanolamine Quantity Table, (i) aggregate the quantities of all such chemicals, and (ii) determine the base offense level corresponding to the aggregate quantity.

    Example: The defendant was in possession of 80 grams of ephedrine and 50 grams of phenylpropanolamine, an aggregate quantity of 130 grams of such chemicals. The base offense level corresponding to that aggregate quantity is level 30.

    (C) **Upward Departure.—**In a case involving two or more chemicals used to manufacture different controlled substances, or to manufacture one controlled substance by different manufacturing processes, an upward departure may be warranted if the offense level does not adequately address the seriousness of the offense.

2. **Application of Subsection (b)(1).—**"*Firearm*" and "*dangerous weapon*" are defined in the Commentary to §1B1.1 (Application Instructions). The adjustment in subsection

(b)(1) should be applied if the weapon was present, unless it is improbable that the weapon was connected with the offense.

3.   **Application of Subsection (b)(2).**—Convictions under 21 U.S.C. §§ 841(c)(2) and (f)(1), and 960(d)(2), (d)(3), and (d)(4) do not require that the defendant have knowledge or an actual belief that the listed chemical was to be used to manufacture a controlled substance unlawfully. In a case in which the defendant possessed or distributed the listed chemical without such knowledge or belief, a 3-level reduction is provided to reflect that the defendant is less culpable than one who possessed or distributed listed chemicals knowing or believing that they would be used to manufacture a controlled substance unlawfully.

4.   **Application of Subsection (b)(3).**—Subsection (b)(3) applies if the conduct for which the defendant is accountable under §1B1.3 (Relevant Conduct) involved any discharge, emission, release, transportation, treatment, storage, or disposal violation covered by the Resource Conservation and Recovery Act, 42 U.S.C. § 6928(d), the Federal Water Pollution Control Act, 33 U.S.C. § 1319(c), the Comprehensive Environmental Response, Compensation, and Liability Act, 42 U.S.C. § 9603(b), and 49 U.S.C. § 5124 (relating to violations of laws and regulations enforced by the Department of Transportation with respect to the transportation of hazardous material). In some cases, the enhancement under subsection (b)(3) may not adequately account for the seriousness of the environmental harm or other threat to public health or safety (including the health or safety of law enforcement and cleanup personnel). In such cases, an upward departure may be warranted. Additionally, any costs of environmental cleanup and harm to persons or property should be considered by the court in determining the amount of restitution under §5E1.1 (Restitution) and in fashioning appropriate conditions of supervision under §§5B1.3 (Conditions of Probation) and 5D1.3 (Conditions of Supervised Release).

5.   **Application of Subsection (b)(4).**—For purposes of subsection (b)(4), "*mass-marketing by means of an interactive computer service*" means the solicitation, by means of an interactive computer service, of a large number of persons to induce those persons to purchase a controlled substance. For example, subsection (b)(4) would apply to a defendant who operated a web site to promote the sale of Gamma-butyrolactone (GBL) but would not apply to coconspirators who use an interactive computer service only to communicate with one another in furtherance of the offense. "*Interactive computer service*", for purposes of subsection (b)(4) and this note, has the meaning given that term in section 230(e)(2) of the Communications Act of 1934 (47 U.S.C. § 230(f)(2)).

6.   **Imposition of Consecutive Sentence for 21 U.S.C. § 865.**—Section 865 of title 21, United States Code, requires the imposition of a mandatory consecutive term of imprisonment of not more than 15 years. In order to comply with the relevant statute, the court should determine the appropriate "total punishment" and, on the judgment form, divide the sentence between the sentence attributable to the underlying drug offense and the sentence attributable to 21 U.S.C. § 865, specifying the number of months to be served consecutively for the conviction under 21 U.S.C. § 865. For example, if the applicable adjusted guideline range is 151–188 months and the court determines a "total punishment" of 151 months is appropriate, a sentence of 130 months for the underlying offense plus 21 months for the conduct covered by 21 U.S.C. § 865 would achieve the "total punishment" in a manner that satisfies the statutory requirement of a consecutive sentence.

7.   **Applicability of Subsection (b)(6).**—The applicability of subsection (b)(6) shall be determined without regard to the offense of conviction. If subsection (b)(6) applies, §5C1.2(b) does not apply. *See* §5C1.2(b)(2)(requiring a minimum offense level of level 17 if the "statutorily required minimum sentence is at least five years").

8. **Application of Subsection (c)(1).**—"*Offense involved unlawfully manufacturing a controlled substance or attempting to manufacture a controlled substance unlawfully,*" as used in subsection (c)(1), means that the defendant, or a person for whose conduct the defendant is accountable under §1B1.3 (Relevant Conduct), completed the actions sufficient to constitute the offense of unlawfully manufacturing a controlled substance or attempting to manufacture a controlled substance unlawfully.

9. **Offenses Involving Immediate Precursors or Other Controlled Substances Covered Under §2D1.1.**—In certain cases, the defendant will be convicted of an offense involving a listed chemical covered under this guideline, and a related offense involving an immediate precursor or other controlled substance covered under §2D1.1 (Unlawfully Manufacturing, Importing, Exporting, or Trafficking). For example, P2P (an immediate precursor) and methylamine (a listed chemical) are used together to produce methamphetamine. Determine the offense level under each guideline separately. The offense level for methylamine is determined by using §2D1.11. The offense level for P2P is determined by using §2D1.1 (P2P is listed in the Drug Equivalency Table under Cocaine and Other Schedule I and II Stimulants (and their immediate precursors)). Under the grouping rules of §3D1.2(b), the counts will be grouped together. Note that in determining the scale of the offense under §2D1.1, the quantity of both the controlled substance and listed chemical should be considered (*see* Application Note 5 in the Commentary to §2D1.1).

Background: Offenses covered by this guideline involve list I chemicals (including ephedrine, pseudoephedrine, and phenylpropanolamine) and list II chemicals. List I chemicals are important to the manufacture of a controlled substance and usually become part of the final product. For example, ephedrine reacts with other chemicals to form methamphetamine. The amount of ephedrine directly affects the amount of methamphetamine produced. List II chemicals are generally used as solvents, catalysts, and reagents.

Historical Note	Effective November 1, 1991 (amendment 371). Amended effective November 1, 1992 (amendment 447); November 1, 1995 (amendment 519); May 1, 1997 (amendment 541); November 1, 1997 (amendment 557); November 1, 2000 (amendments 605 and 606); May 1, 2001 (amendment 611); November 1, 2001 (amendment 625); November 1, 2002 (amendment 646); November 1, 2003 (amendment 661); November 1, 2004 (amendments 667 and 668); November 1, 2005 (amendment 679); November 1, 2007 (amendments 705 and 707); November 1, 2010 (amendments 745 and 746); November 1, 2012 (amendments 763 and 770); November 1, 2014 (amendment 782); November 1, 2015 (amendment 796).

§2D1.12. Unlawful Possession, Manufacture, Distribution, Transportation, Exportation, or Importation of Prohibited Flask, Equipment, Chemical, Product, or Material; Attempt or Conspiracy

(a) Base Offense Level (Apply the greater):

(1) **12**, if the defendant intended to manufacture a controlled substance or knew or believed the prohibited flask, equipment, chemical, product, or material was to be used to manufacture a controlled substance; or

(2)   **9**, if the defendant had reasonable cause to believe the prohibited flask, equipment, chemical, product, or material was to be used to manufacture a controlled substance.

(b)   Specific Offense Characteristics

(1)   If the defendant (A) intended to manufacture methamphetamine, or (B) knew, believed, or had reasonable cause to believe that prohibited flask, equipment, chemical, product, or material was to be used to manufacture methamphetamine, increase by **2** levels.

(2)   If the offense involved (A) an unlawful discharge, emission, or release into the environment of a hazardous or toxic substance; or (B) the unlawful transportation, treatment, storage, or disposal of a hazardous waste, increase by **2** levels.

(3)   If the defendant, or a person for whose conduct the defendant is accountable under §1B1.3 (Relevant Conduct), distributed any prohibited flask, equipment, chemical, product, or material through mass-marketing by means of an interactive computer service, increase by **2** levels.

(4)   If the offense involved stealing anhydrous ammonia or transporting stolen anhydrous ammonia, increase by **6** levels.

(c)   Cross Reference

(1)   If the offense involved unlawfully manufacturing a controlled substance, or attempting to manufacture a controlled substance unlawfully, apply §2D1.1 (Unlawful Manufacturing, Importing, Exporting, or Trafficking) if the resulting offense level is greater than that determined above.

Commentary

Statutory Provisions: 21 U.S.C. §§ 843(a)(6), (7), 864.

Application Notes:

1.   If the offense involved the large-scale manufacture, distribution, transportation, exportation, or importation of prohibited flasks, equipment, chemicals, products, or material, an upward departure may be warranted.

2.   *"Offense involved unlawfully manufacturing a controlled substance or attempting to manufacture a controlled substance unlawfully,"* as used in subsection (c)(1), means that the defendant, or a person for whose conduct the defendant is accountable

under §1B1.3 (Relevant Conduct), completed the actions sufficient to constitute the offense of unlawfully manufacturing a controlled substance or attempting to manufacture a controlled substance unlawfully.

3. Subsection (b)(2) applies if the conduct for which the defendant is accountable under §1B1.3 (Relevant Conduct) involved any discharge, emission, release, transportation, treatment, storage, or disposal violation covered by the Resource Conservation and Recovery Act, 42 U.S.C. § 6928(d), the Federal Water Pollution Control Act, 33 U.S.C. § 1319(c), the Comprehensive Environmental Response, Compensation, and Liability Act, 42 U.S.C. § 9603(b), and 49 U.S.C. § 5124 (relating to violations of laws and regulations enforced by the Department of Transportation with respect to the transportation of hazardous material). In some cases, the enhancement under subsection (b)(2) may not adequately account for the seriousness of the environmental harm or other threat to public health or safety (including the health or safety of law enforcement and cleanup personnel). In such cases, an upward departure may be warranted. Additionally, any costs of environmental cleanup and harm to persons or property should be considered by the court in determining the amount of restitution under §5E1.1 (Restitution) and in fashioning appropriate conditions of supervision under §§5B1.3 (Conditions of Probation) and 5D1.3 (Conditions of Supervised Release).

4. **Application of Subsection (b)(3).**—For purposes of subsection (b)(3), "***mass-marketing by means of an interactive computer service***" means the solicitation, by means of an interactive computer service, of a large number of persons to induce those persons to purchase a controlled substance. For example, subsection (b)(3) would apply to a defendant who operated a web site to promote the sale of prohibited flasks but would not apply to coconspirators who use an interactive computer service only to communicate with one another in furtherance of the offense. "***Interactive computer service***", for purposes of subsection (b)(3) and this note, has the meaning given that term in section 230(e)(2) of the Communications Act of 1934 (47 U.S.C. § 230(f)(2)).

Historical Note	Effective November 1, 1991 (amendment 371). Amended effective November 1, 1992 (amendment 447); November 1, 1995 (amendment 520); November 1, 1997 (amendment 558); November 1, 2000 (amendment 605); November 1, 2001 (amendment 626); November 1, 2004 (amendment 667); November 1, 2010 (amendment 746).

§2D1.13. Structuring Chemical Transactions or Creating a Chemical Mixture to Evade Reporting or Recordkeeping Requirements; Presenting False or Fraudulent Identification to Obtain a Listed Chemical; Attempt or Conspiracy

(a) Base Offense Level (Apply the greatest):

(1) The offense level from §2D1.11 (Unlawfully Distributing, Importing, Exporting, or Possessing a Listed Chemical) if the defendant knew or believed that the chemical was to be used to manufacture a controlled substance unlawfully; or

(2) The offense level from §2D1.11 (Unlawfully Distributing, Importing, Exporting or Possessing a Listed Chemical) reduced

by **3** levels if the defendant had reason to believe that the chemical was to be used to manufacture a controlled substance unlawfully; or

(3)   **6**, otherwise.

Commentary

Statutory Provisions: 21 U.S.C. §§ 841(c)(3), (f)(1), 843(a)(4)(B), (a)(8).

Application Note:

1.   *"The offense level from §2D1.11"* includes the base offense level and any applicable specific offense characteristic or cross reference; *see* §1B1.5 (Interpretation of References to Other Offense Guidelines).

Historical Note	Effective November 1, 1991 (amendment 371). Amended effective November 1, 1992 (amendment 447); November 1, 2002 (amendment 646).

§2D1.14. Narco-Terrorism

(a)   Base Offense Level:

(1)   The offense level from §2D1.1 (Unlawful Manufacturing, Importing, Exporting, or Trafficking (Including Possession with Intent to Commit These Offenses); Attempt or Conspiracy) applicable to the underlying offense, except that §2D1.1(a)(5)(A), (a)(5)(B), and (b)(17) shall not apply.

(b)   Specific Offense Characteristic

(1)   If §3A1.4 (Terrorism) does not apply, increase by **6** levels.

Commentary

Statutory Provision: 21 U.S.C. § 960a.

Historical Note	Effective November 1, 2007 (amendment 700). Amended effective November 1, 2010 (amendments 746 and 748); November 1, 2011 (amendment 750); November 1, 2014 (amendment 783).

*   *   *   *   *   *

2. UNLAWFUL POSSESSION

---

§2D2.1. Unlawful Possession; Attempt or Conspiracy

    (a)   Base Offense Level:

        (1)   **8**, if the substance is heroin or any Schedule I or II opiate, an analogue of these, or cocaine base; or

        (2)   **6**, if the substance is cocaine, flunitrazepam, LSD, or PCP; or

        (3)   **4**, if the substance is any other controlled substance or a list I chemical.

    (b)   Cross Reference

        (1)   If the offense involved possession of a controlled substance in a prison, correctional facility, or detention facility, apply §2P1.2 (Providing or Possessing Contraband in Prison).

Commentary

Statutory Provision: 21 U.S.C. § 844(a). For additional statutory provision(s), *see* Appendix A (Statutory Index).

Application Note:

1.   The typical case addressed by this guideline involves possession of a controlled substance by the defendant for the defendant's own consumption. Where the circumstances establish intended consumption by a person other than the defendant, an upward departure may be warranted.

Background: Mandatory (statutory) minimum penalties for several categories of cases, ranging from fifteen days' to three years' imprisonment, are set forth in 21 U.S.C. § 844(a). When a mandatory minimum penalty exceeds the guideline range, the mandatory minimum becomes the guideline sentence. *See* §5G1.1(b). Note, however, that 18 U.S.C. § 3553(f) provides an exception to the applicability of mandatory minimum sentences in certain cases. *See* §5C1.2 (Limitation on Applicability of Statutory Minimum Sentences in Certain Cases).

Historical Note	Effective November 1, 1987. Amended effective January 15, 1988 (amendment 24); November 1, 1989 (amendment 304); November 1, 1990 (amendment 321); November 1, 1992 (amendment 447); September 23, 1994 (amendment 509); November 1, 1995 (amendment 514); November 1, 1997 (amendments 556 and 558); November 1, 2010 (amendments 746 and 748); November 1, 2011 (amendment 750).

---

§2D2.2. Acquiring a Controlled Substance by Forgery, Fraud, Deception, or Subterfuge; Attempt or Conspiracy

(a)   Base Offense Level: **8**

Commentary

Statutory Provision: 21 U.S.C. § 843(a)(3).

Historical Note	Effective November 1, 1987. Amended effective November 1, 1992 (amendment 447).

---

§2D2.3. Operating or Directing the Operation of a Common Carrier Under the Influence of Alcohol or Drugs

(a)   Base Offense Level (Apply the greatest):

    (1)   **26**, if death resulted; or

    (2)   **21**, if serious bodily injury resulted; or

    (3)   **13**, otherwise.

(b)   Special Instruction:

    (1)   If the defendant is convicted of a single count involving the death or serious bodily injury of more than one person, apply Chapter Three, Part D (Multiple Counts) as if the defendant had been convicted of a separate count for each such victim.

Commentary

Statutory Provision: 18 U.S.C. § 342.

Background: This section implements the direction to the Commission in Section 6482 of the Anti-Drug Abuse Act of 1988. Offenses covered by this guideline may vary widely with regard to harm and risk of harm. The offense levels assume that the offense involved the operation of a common carrier carrying a number of passengers, *e.g.*, a bus. If no or only a few passengers were placed at risk, a downward departure may be warranted. If the offense resulted in the death or serious bodily injury of a large number of persons, such that the resulting offense level under subsection (b) would not adequately reflect the seriousness of the offense, an upward departure may be warranted.

Historical Note	Effective November 1, 1987. Amended effective January 15, 1988 (amendment 25); November 1, 1989 (amendment 141).

*   *   *   *   *

3. REGULATORY VIOLATIONS

§2D3.1. Regulatory Offenses Involving Registration Numbers; Unlawful Advertising Relating to Scheduled Substances; Attempt or Conspiracy

(a) Base Offense Level: **6**

Commentary

Statutory Provisions: 21 U.S.C. §§ 842(a)(1), 843(a)(1), (2). For additional statutory provision(s), *see* Appendix A (Statutory Index).

Historical Note	Effective November 1, 1987. Amended effective November 1, 1991 (amendment 421); November 1, 1992 (amendment 447); November 1, 1995 (amendment 534); November 1, 2009 (amendment 727).

§2D3.2. Regulatory Offenses Involving Controlled Substances or Listed Chemicals; Attempt or Conspiracy

(a) Base Offense Level: **4**

Commentary

Statutory Provisions: 21 U.S.C. §§ 842(a)(2), (9), (10), (b), 954, 961. For additional statutory provision(s), *see* Appendix A (Statutory Index).

Historical Note	Effective November 1, 1987. Amended effective November 1, 1991 (amendment 421); November 1, 1992 (amendment 447); November 1, 1993 (amendment 481); November 1, 1995 (amendment 534).

§2D3.3. [Deleted]

Historical Note	Section 2D3.3 (Illegal Use of Registration Number to Distribute or Dispense a Controlled Substance to Another Registrant or Authorized Person; Attempt or Conspiracy), effective November 1, 1987, amended effective November 1, 1991 (amendment 421) and November 1, 1992 (amendment 447), was deleted by consolidation with §2D3.2 effective November 1, 1993 (amendment 481).

§2D3.4. [Deleted]

Historical Note	Section 2D3.4 (Illegal Transfer or Transshipment of a Controlled Substance; Attempt or Conspiracy), effective November 1, 1987, amended effective November 1, 1990 (amendment 359) and November 1, 1992 (amendment 447), was deleted by consolidation with §2D3.2 effective November 1, 1993 (amendment 481).

§2D3.5

----

§2D3.5. [Deleted]

Historical Note	Section 2D3.5 (Violation of Recordkeeping or Reporting Requirements for Listed Chemicals and Certain Machines; Attempt or Conspiracy), effective November 1, 1991 (amendment 371), amended effective November 1, 1992 (amendment 447), was deleted by consolidation with §2D3.2 effective November 1, 1993 (amendment 481).

PART E — OFFENSES INVOLVING CRIMINAL ENTERPRISES AND RACKETEERING

1.   RACKETEERING

Introductory Commentary

Because of the jurisdictional nature of the offenses included, this subpart covers a wide variety of criminal conduct. The offense level usually will be determined by the offense level of the underlying conduct.

Historical Note	Effective November 1, 1987.

§2E1.1.   Unlawful Conduct Relating to Racketeer Influenced and Corrupt Organizations

(a)   Base Offense Level (Apply the greater):

(1)   **19**; or

(2)   the offense level applicable to the underlying racketeering activity.

Commentary

Statutory Provisions: 18 U.S.C. §§ 1962, 1963.

Application Notes:

1.   Where there is more than one underlying offense, treat each underlying offense as if contained in a separate count of conviction for the purposes of subsection (a)(2). To determine whether subsection (a)(1) or (a)(2) results in the greater offense level, apply Chapter Three, Parts A, B, C, and D to both (a)(1) and (a)(2). Use whichever subsection results in the greater offense level.

2.   If the underlying conduct violates state law, the offense level corresponding to the most analogous federal offense is to be used.

3.   If the offense level for the underlying racketeering activity is less than the alternative minimum level specified (*i.e.*, 19), the alternative minimum base offense level is to be used.

4.   Certain conduct may be charged in the count of conviction as part of a "pattern of racketeering activity" even though the defendant has previously been sentenced for that conduct. Where such previously imposed sentence resulted from a conviction prior to the last overt act of the instant offense, treat as a prior sentence under §4A1.2(a)(1) and not as part of the instant offense. This treatment is designed to produce a result consistent with

the distinction between the instant offense and criminal history found throughout the guidelines. If this treatment produces an anomalous result in a particular case, a guideline departure may be warranted.

Historical Note	Effective November 1, 1987. Amended effective June 15, 1988 (amendment 26); November 1, 1989 (amendment 142).

§2E1.2. Interstate or Foreign Travel or Transportation in Aid of a Racketeering Enterprise

  (a) Base Offense Level (Apply the greater):

    (1) **6**; or

    (2) the offense level applicable to the underlying crime of violence or other unlawful activity in respect to which the travel or transportation was undertaken.

Commentary

Statutory Provision: 18 U.S.C. § 1952.

Application Notes:

1. Where there is more than one underlying offense, treat each underlying offense as if contained in a separate count of conviction for the purposes of subsection (a)(2). To determine whether subsection (a)(1) or (a)(2) results in the greater offense level, apply Chapter Three, Parts A, B, C, and D to both (a)(1) and (a)(2). Use whichever subsection results in the greater offense level.

2. If the underlying conduct violates state law, the offense level corresponding to the most analogous federal offense is to be used.

3. If the offense level for the underlying conduct is less than the alternative minimum base offense level specified (*i.e.*, 6), the alternative minimum base offense level is to be used.

Historical Note	Effective November 1, 1987. Amended effective June 15, 1988 (amendment 27).

§2E1.3. Violent Crimes in Aid of Racketeering Activity

  (a) Base Offense Level (Apply the greater):

    (1) **12**; or

      (2)   the offense level applicable to the underlying crime or racketeering activity.

Commentary

Statutory Provision: 18 U.S.C. § 1959 (formerly 18 U.S.C. § 1952B).

Application Notes:

1.   If the underlying conduct violates state law, the offense level corresponding to the most analogous federal offense is to be used.

2.   If the offense level for the underlying conduct is less than the alternative minimum base offense level specified (*i.e.*, 12), the alternative minimum base offense level is to be used.

Background: The conduct covered under this section ranges from threats to murder. The maximum term of imprisonment authorized by statute ranges from three years to life imprisonment.

Historical Note	Effective November 1, 1987. Amended effective November 1, 1989 (amendment 143).

---

§2E1.4. Use of Interstate Commerce Facilities in the Commission of Murder-For-Hire

    (a)   Base Offense Level (Apply the greater):

        (1)   **32**; or

        (2)   the offense level applicable to the underlying unlawful conduct.

Commentary

Statutory Provision: 18 U.S.C. § 1958 (formerly 18 U.S.C. § 1952A).

Application Note:

1.   If the underlying conduct violates state law, the offense level corresponding to the most analogous federal offense is to be used.

Background: This guideline and the statute to which it applies do not require that a murder actually have been committed.

Historical Note	Effective November 1, 1987. Amended effective November 1, 1989 (amendment 144); November 1, 1990 (amendment 311); November 1, 1992 (amendment 449).

---
§2E1.5. [Deleted]

Historical Note	Section 2E1.5 (Hobbs Act Extortion or Robbery), effective November 1, 1987, amended effective November 1, 1989 (amendment 145), was deleted by consolidation with §§2B3.1, 2B3.2, 2B3.3, and 2C1.1 effective November 1, 1993 (amendment 481).

*   *   *   *   *

2. EXTORTIONATE EXTENSION OF CREDIT

---
§2E2.1. Making or Financing an Extortionate Extension of Credit; Collecting an Extension of Credit by Extortionate Means
---

(a) Base Offense Level: **20**

(b) Specific Offense Characteristics

    (1) (A) If a firearm was discharged increase by **5** levels; or

        (B) if a dangerous weapon (including a firearm) was otherwise used, increase by **4** levels; or

        (C) if a dangerous weapon (including a firearm) was brandished or possessed, increase by **3** levels.

    (2) If any victim sustained bodily injury, increase the offense level according to the seriousness of the injury:

DEGREE OF BODILY INJURY	INCREASE IN LEVEL
(A) Bodily Injury	add **2**
(B) Serious Bodily Injury	add **4**
(C) Permanent or Life-Threatening Bodily Injury	add **6**
(D) If the degree of injury is between that specified in subdivisions (A) and (B),	add **3** levels; or
(E) If the degree of injury is between that specified in subdivisions (B) and (C),	add **5** levels.

Provided, however, that the combined increase from (1) and (2) shall not exceed **9** levels.

    (3) (A) If any person was abducted to facilitate commission of the offense or to facilitate escape, increase by **4** levels; or

    (B) if any person was physically restrained to facilitate commission of the offense or to facilitate escape, increase by 2 levels.

  (c) Cross Reference

    (1) If a victim was killed under circumstances that would constitute murder under 18 U.S.C. § 1111 had such killing taken place within the territorial or maritime jurisdiction of the United States, apply §2A1.1 (First Degree Murder).

Commentary

Statutory Provisions: 18 U.S.C. §§ 892–894.

Application Notes:

1. Definitions of "*firearm*," "*dangerous weapon*," "*otherwise used*," "*brandished*," "*bodily injury*," "*serious bodily injury*," "*permanent or life-threatening bodily injury*," "*abducted*," and "*physically restrained*" are found in the Commentary to §1B1.1 (Application Instructions).

2. *See also* Commentary to §2B3.2 (Extortion by Force or Threat of Injury or Serious Damage) regarding the interpretation of the specific offense characteristics.

Background: This section refers to offenses involving the making or financing of extortionate extensions of credit, or the collection of loans by extortionate means. These "loan-sharking" offenses typically involve threats of violence and provide economic support for organized crime. The base offense level for these offenses is higher than the offense level for extortion because loan sharking is in most cases a continuing activity. In addition, the guideline does not include the amount of money involved because the amount of money in such cases is often difficult to determine. Other enhancements parallel those in §2B3.2 (Extortion by Force or Threat of Injury or Serious Damage).

Historical Note	Effective November 1, 1987. Amended effective November 1, 1989 (amendments 146–148); November 1, 1991 (amendment 398); November 1, 1993 (amendment 479); November 1, 2000 (amendment 601).

* * * * *

3. GAMBLING

Introductory Commentary

  This subpart covers a variety of proscribed conduct. The adjustments in Chapter Three, Part B (Role in the Offense) are particularly relevant in providing a measure of the scope of the offense and the defendant's participation.

Historical Note	Effective November 1, 1987.

§2E3.1.   Gambling Offenses; Animal Fighting Offenses

(a)   Base Offense Level: (Apply the greatest)

(1)   **16**, if the offense involved an animal fighting venture, except as provided in subdivision (3) below;

(2)   **12**, if the offense was (A) engaging in a gambling business; (B) transmission of wagering information; or (C) committed as part of, or to facilitate, a commercial gambling operation;

(3)   **10**, if the defendant was convicted under 7 U.S.C. § 2156(a)(2)(B); or

(4)   **6**, otherwise.

Commentary

Statutory Provisions: 7 U.S.C. § 2156 (felony provisions only); 15 U.S.C. §§ 1172–1175; 18 U.S.C. §§ 1082, 1301–1304, 1306, 1511, 1953, 1955; 31 U.S.C. § 5363. For additional statutory provision(s), *see* Appendix A (Statutory Index).

Application Notes:

1.   **Definition.**—For purposes of this guideline, "*animal fighting venture*" has the meaning given that term in 7 U.S.C. § 2156(g).

2.   **Upward Departure Provision.**—The base offense levels provided for animal fighting ventures in subsection (a)(1) and (a)(3) reflect that an animal fighting venture involves one or more violent fights between animals and that a defeated animal often is severely injured in the fight, dies as a result of the fight, or is killed afterward. Nonetheless, there may be cases in which the offense level determined under this guideline substantially understates the seriousness of the offense. In such a case, an upward departure may be warranted. For example, an upward departure may be warranted if (A) the offense involved extraordinary cruelty to an animal beyond the violence inherent in such a venture (such as by killing an animal in a way that prolongs the suffering of the animal); or (B) the offense involved animal fighting on an exceptional scale (such as an offense involving an unusually large number of animals).

Historical Note	Effective November 1, 1987. Amended effective November 1, 1993 (amendment 481); November 1, 2007 (amendment 703); November 1, 2008 (amendment 721); November 1, 2016 (amendment 800).

§2E3.2. [Deleted]

Historical Note	Section 2E3.2 (Transmission of Wagering Information), effective November 1, 1987, was deleted by consolidation with §2E3.1 effective November 1, 1993 (amendment 481).

§2E3.3. [Deleted]

Historical Note	Section 2E3.3 (Other Gambling Offenses), effective November 1, 1987, was deleted by consolidation with §2E3.1 effective November 1, 1993 (amendment 481).

* * * * *

4. TRAFFICKING IN CONTRABAND CIGARETTES AND SMOKELESS TOBACCO

Historical Note	Effective November 1, 1987. Amended effective November 1, 2007 (amendment 700).

§2E4.1. Unlawful Conduct Relating to Contraband Cigarettes and Smokeless Tobacco

    (a) Base Offense Level (Apply the greater):

        (1) **9**; or

        (2) the offense level from the table in §2T4.1 (Tax Table) corresponding to the amount of the tax evaded.

Commentary

Statutory Provisions: 18 U.S.C. §§ 2342(a), 2344(a).

Application Note:

1.   "*Tax evaded*" refers to state and local excise taxes.

Background: The conduct covered by this section generally involves evasion of state and local excise taxes. At least 10,000 cigarettes must be involved. Because this offense is basically a tax matter, it is graded by use of the tax table in §2T4.1.

Historical Note	Effective November 1, 1987. Amended effective November 1, 2007 (amendment 700); November 1, 2008 (amendment 724).

* * * * *

5. LABOR RACKETEERING

Introductory Commentary

The statutes included in this subpart protect the rights of employees under the Taft–Hartley Act, members of labor organizations under the Labor-Management Reporting and Disclosure Act of 1959, and participants of employee pension and welfare benefit plans covered under the Employee Retirement Income Security Act.

The base offense levels for many of the offenses in this subpart have been determined by reference to analogous sections of the guidelines. Thus, the base offense levels for bribery, theft, and fraud in this subpart generally correspond to similar conduct under other parts of the guidelines. The base offense levels for bribery and graft have been set higher than the level for commercial bribery due to the particular vulnerability to exploitation of the organizations covered by this subpart.

Historical Note	Effective November 1, 1987.

§2E5.1. **Offering, Accepting, or Soliciting a Bribe or Gratuity Affecting the Operation of an Employee Welfare or Pension Benefit Plan; Prohibited Payments or Lending of Money by Employer or Agent to Employees, Representatives, or Labor Organizations**

    (a) Base Offense Level:

        (1) **10**, if a bribe; or

        (2) **6**, if a gratuity.

    (b) Specific Offense Characteristics

        (1) If the defendant was a fiduciary of the benefit plan or labor organization, increase by **2** levels.

        (2) If the value of the prohibited payment or the value of the improper benefit to the payer, whichever is greater (A) exceeded $2,500 but did not exceed $6,500, increase by **1** level; or (B) exceeded $6,500, increase by the number of levels from the table in §2B1.1 (Theft, Property Destruction, and Fraud) corresponding to that amount.

    (c) Special Instruction for Fines — Organizations

        (1) In lieu of the pecuniary loss under subsection (a)(3) of §8C2.4 (Base Fine), use the greatest of: (A) the value of the unlawful

payment; (B) if a bribe, the value of the benefit received or to be received in return for the unlawful payment; or (C) if a bribe, the consequential damages resulting from the unlawful payment.

Commentary

Statutory Provisions: 18 U.S.C. § 1954; 29 U.S.C. § 186.

Application Notes:

1. "*Bribe*" refers to the offer or acceptance of an unlawful payment with the specific understanding that it will corruptly affect an official action of the recipient.

2. "*Gratuity*" refers to the offer or acceptance of an unlawful payment other than a bribe.

3. "*Fiduciary of the benefit plan*" is defined in 29 U.S.C. § 1002(21)(A) to mean a person who exercises any discretionary authority or control in respect to the management of such plan or exercises authority or control in respect to management or disposition of its assets, or who renders investment advice for a fee or other direct or indirect compensation with respect to any moneys or other property of such plan, or has any authority or responsibility to do so, or who has any discretionary authority or responsibility in the administration of such plan.

4. "*Value of the improper benefit to the payer*" is explained in the Commentary to §2C1.1 (Offering, Giving, Soliciting, or Receiving a Bribe; Extortion Under Color of Official Right; Fraud Involving the Deprivation of the Intangible Right to Honest Services of Public Officials; Conspiracy to Defraud by Interference with Governmental Functions).

5. If the adjustment for a fiduciary at §2E5.1(b)(1) applies, do not apply the adjustment at §3B1.3 (Abuse of Position of Trust or Use of Special Skill).

Background: This section covers the giving or receipt of bribes and other unlawful gratuities involving employee welfare or pension benefit plans, or labor organizations. The seriousness of the offense is determined by several factors, including the value of the bribe or gratuity and the magnitude of the loss resulting from the transaction.

Historical Note	Effective November 1, 1987. Amended effective November 1, 1989 (amendment 149); November 1, 1991 (amendment 422); November 1, 1993 (amendment 481); November 1, 2001 (amendment 617); November 1, 2004 (amendment 666); November 1, 2015 (amendment 791).

---

§2E5.2. [Deleted]

Historical Note	Section 2E5.2 (Theft or Embezzlement from Employee Pension and Welfare Benefit Plans), effective November 1, 1987, amended effective June 15, 1988 (amendment 28), November 1, 1989 (amendment 150), and November 1, 1991 (amendment 399), was deleted by consolidation with §2B1.1 effective November 1, 1993 (amendment 481).

---

§2E5.3. False Statements and Concealment of Facts in Relation to Documents Required by the Employee Retirement Income Security Act; Failure to Maintain and Falsification of Records Required by the Labor Management Reporting and Disclosure Act; Destruction and Failure to Maintain Corporate Audit Records

---

    (a)   Base Offense Level (Apply the greater):

        (1)   **6**; or

        (2)   If the offense was committed to facilitate or conceal (A) an offense involving a theft, a fraud, or an embezzlement; (B) an offense involving a bribe or a gratuity; or (C) an obstruction of justice offense, apply §2B1.1 (Theft, Property Destruction, and Fraud), §2E5.1 (Offering, Accepting, or Soliciting a Bribe or Gratuity Affecting the Operation of an Employee Welfare or Pension Benefit Plan; Prohibited Payments or Lending of Money by Employer or Agent to Employees, Representatives, or Labor Organizations), or §2J1.2 (Obstruction of Justice), as applicable.

Commentary

Statutory Provisions: 18 U.S.C. §§ 1027, 1520; 29 U.S.C. §§ 439, 461, 1131. For additional statutory provision(s), *see* Appendix A (Statutory Index).

Background: This section covers the falsification of documents or records relating to a benefit plan covered by ERISA. It also covers failure to maintain proper documents required by the LMRDA or falsification of such documents. Such violations sometimes occur in connection with the criminal conversion of plan funds or schemes involving bribery or graft. Where a violation under this section occurs in connection with another offense, the offense level is determined by reference to the offense facilitated by the false statements or documents.

Historical Note	Effective November 1, 1987. Amended effective November 1, 1989 (amendment 151); November 1, 1993 (amendment 481); January 25, 2003 (amendment 647); November 1, 2003 (amendment 653).

---

§2E5.4. [Deleted]

Historical Note	Section 2E5.4 (Embezzlement or Theft from Labor Unions in the Private Sector), effective November 1, 1987, amended effective June 15, 1988 (amendment 29) and November 1, 1989 (amendment 152), was deleted by consolidation with §2B1.1 effective November 1, 1993 (amendment 481).

§2E5.5. [Deleted]

Historical Note	Section 2E5.5 (Failure to Maintain and Falsification of Records Required by the Labor Management Reporting and Disclosure Act), effective November 1, 1987, amended effective November 1, 1989 (amendment 153), was deleted by consolidation with §2E5.3 effective November 1, 1993 (amendment 481).

§2E5.6. [Deleted]

Historical Note	Section 2E5.6 (Prohibited Payments or Lending of Money by Employer or Agent to Employees, Representatives, or Labor Organizations), effective November 1, 1987, amended effective November 1, 1991 (amendment 422), was deleted by consolidation with §2E5.1 effective November 1, 1993 (amendment 481).

PART F — [DELETED]

Historical Note	The heading to Part F — Offenses Involving Fraud or Deceit, effective November 1, 1987, was deleted due to the deletion of §§2F1.1 and 2F1.2 effective November 1, 2001 (amendment 617).

§2F1.1. [Deleted]

Historical Note	Section 2F1.1 (Fraud and Deceit; Forgery; Offenses Involving Altered or Counterfeit Instruments Other than Counterfeit Bearer Obligations of the United States), effective November 1, 1987, amended effective June 15, 1988 (amendment 30), November 1, 1989 (amendments 154–156 and 303), November 1, 1990 (amendment 317), November 1, 1991 (amendments 364 and 393), November 1, 1992 (amendment 470), November 1, 1993 (amendments 481 and 482), November 1, 1995 (amendment 513), November 1, 1997 (amendment 551), November 1, 1998 (amendments 577 and 587), November 1, 2000 (amendments 595, 596, and 597), was deleted by consolidation with §2B1.1 effective November 1, 2001 (amendment 617).

§2F1.2. [Deleted]

Historical Note	Section 2F1.2 (Insider Trading), effective November 1, 1987, was deleted by consolidation with §2B1.1 effective November 1, 2001 (amendment 617).

PART G — OFFENSES INVOLVING COMMERCIAL SEX ACTS, SEXUAL EXPLOITATION OF MINORS, AND OBSCENITY

Historical Note	Effective November 1, 1987. Amended effective November 1, 2002 (amendment 641).

1. PROMOTING A COMMERCIAL SEX ACT OR PROHIBITED SEXUAL CONDUCT

Historical Note	Effective November 1, 1987. Amended effective November 1, 2000 (amendment 592); November 1, 2002 (amendment 641).

§2G1.1. Promoting a Commercial Sex Act or Prohibited Sexual Conduct with an Individual Other than a Minor

(a)   Base Offense Level:

    (1)   **34**, if the offense of conviction is 18 U.S.C. § 1591(b)(1); or

    (2)   **14**, otherwise.

(b)   Specific Offense Characteristic

    (1)   If (A) subsection (a)(2) applies; and (B) the offense involved fraud or coercion, increase by **4** levels.

(c)   Cross Reference

    (1)   If the offense involved conduct described in 18 U.S.C. § 2241(a) or (b) or 18 U.S.C. § 2242, apply §2A3.1 (Criminal Sexual Abuse; Attempt to Commit Criminal Sexual Abuse).

(d)   Special Instruction

    (1)   If the offense involved more than one victim, Chapter Three, Part D (Multiple Counts) shall be applied as if the promoting of a commercial sex act or prohibited sexual conduct in respect to each victim had been contained in a separate count of conviction.

Commentary

Statutory Provisions: 8 U.S.C. § 1328 (only if the offense involved a victim other than a minor); 18 U.S.C. §§ 1591 (only if the offense involved a victim other than a minor), 2421 (only if the offense involved a victim other than a minor), 2422(a) (only if the offense involved a victim other than a minor).

Application Notes:

1. **Definitions.**—For purposes of this guideline:

    "*Commercial sex act*" has the meaning given that term in 18 U.S.C. § 1591(e)(3).

    "*Prohibited sexual conduct*" has the meaning given that term in Application Note 1 of §2A3.1 (Criminal Sexual Abuse; Attempt to Commit Criminal Sexual Abuse).

    "*Promoting a commercial sex act*" means persuading, inducing, enticing, or coercing a person to engage in a commercial sex act, or to travel to engage in, a commercial sex act.

    "*Victim*" means a person transported, persuaded, induced, enticed, or coerced to engage in, or travel for the purpose of engaging in, a commercial sex act or prohibited sexual conduct, whether or not the person consented to the commercial sex act or prohibited sexual conduct. Accordingly, "victim" may include an undercover law enforcement officer.

2. **Application of Subsection (b)(1).**—Subsection (b)(1) provides an enhancement for fraud or coercion that occurs as part of the offense and anticipates no bodily injury. If bodily injury results, an upward departure may be warranted. *See* Chapter Five, Part K (Departures). For purposes of subsection (b)(1), "*coercion*" includes any form of conduct that negates the voluntariness of the victim. This enhancement would apply, for example, in a case in which the ability of the victim to appraise or control conduct was substantially impaired by drugs or alcohol. This characteristic generally will not apply if the drug or alcohol was voluntarily taken.

3. **Application of Chapter Three Adjustment.**—For the purposes of §3B1.1 (Aggravating Role), a victim, as defined in this guideline, is considered a participant only if that victim assisted in the promoting of a commercial sex act or prohibited sexual conduct in respect to another victim.

4. **Application of Subsection (c)(1).**—

    (A) **Conduct Described in 18 U.S.C. § 2241(a) or (b).**—For purposes of subsection (c)(1), conduct described in 18 U.S.C. § 2241(a) or (b) is engaging in, or causing another person to engage in, a sexual act with another person by: (i) using force against the victim; (ii) threatening or placing the victim in fear that any person will be subject to death, serious bodily injury, or kidnapping; (iii) rendering the victim unconscious; or (iv) administering by force or threat of force, or without the knowledge or permission of the victim, a drug, intoxicant, or other similar substance and thereby substantially impairing the ability of the victim to appraise or control conduct. This provision would apply, for example, if any dangerous weapon was used or brandished, or in a case in which the ability of the victim to appraise or control conduct was substantially impaired by drugs or alcohol.

    (B) **Conduct Described in 18 U.S.C. § 2242.**—For purposes of subsection (c)(1), conduct described in 18 U.S.C. § 2242 is: (i) engaging in, or causing another person to engage in, a sexual act with another person by threatening or placing the victim in fear (other than by threatening or placing the victim in fear that any person will be subject to death, serious bodily injury, or kidnapping); or (ii) engaging in, or causing another person to engage in, a sexual act with a victim who is incapable of appraising the nature of the conduct or who is physically incapable of declining participation in, or communicating unwillingness to engage in, the sexual act.

5. **Special Instruction at Subsection (d)(1).**—For the purposes of Chapter Three, Part D (Multiple Counts), each person transported, persuaded, induced, enticed, or coerced to engage in, or travel to engage in, a commercial sex act or prohibited sexual conduct is to be treated as a separate victim. Consequently, multiple counts involving more than one victim are not to be grouped together under §3D1.2 (Groups of Closely Related Counts). In addition, subsection (d)(1) directs that if the relevant conduct of an offense of conviction includes the promoting of a commercial sex act or prohibited sexual conduct in respect to more than one victim, whether specifically cited in the count of conviction, each such victim shall be treated as if contained in a separate count of conviction.

6. **Upward Departure Provision.**—If the offense involved more than ten victims, an upward departure may be warranted.

Historical Note	Effective November 1, 1987. Amended effective November 1, 1989 (amendments 157 and 158); November 1, 1990 (amendment 322); November 1, 1996 (amendment 538); November 1, 2000 (amendment 592); May 1, 2001 (amendment 612); November 1, 2001 (amendment 627); November 1, 2002 (amendment 641); November 1, 2004 (amendment 664); November 1, 2007 (amendment 701); November 1, 2009 (amendment 737).

§2G1.2. [Deleted]

Historical Note	Section 2G1.2 (Transportation of a Minor for the Purpose of Prostitution or Prohibited Sexual Conduct), effective November 1, 1987, amended effective November 1, 1989 (amendments 159 and 160), November 1, 1990 (amendment 323), November 1, 1991 (amendment 400), and November 1, 1992 (amendment 444), was deleted by consolidation with §2G1.1 effective November 1, 1996 (amendment 538).

2G1.3. Promoting a Commercial Sex Act or Prohibited Sexual Conduct with a Minor; Transportation of Minors to Engage in a Commercial Sex Act or Prohibited Sexual Conduct; Travel to Engage in Commercial Sex Act or Prohibited Sexual Conduct with a Minor; Sex Trafficking of Children; Use of Interstate Facilities to Transport Information about a Minor

(a) Base Offense Level:

    (1) **34**, if the defendant was convicted under 18 U.S.C. § 1591(b)(1);

    (2) **30**, if the defendant was convicted under 18 U.S.C. § 1591(b)(2);

    (3) **28**, if the defendant was convicted under 18 U.S.C. § 2422(b) or § 2423(a); or

    (4) **24**, otherwise.

(b) Specific Offense Characteristics

    (1) If (A) the defendant was a parent, relative, or legal guardian of the minor; or (B) the minor was otherwise in the custody, care, or supervisory control of the defendant, increase by 2 levels.

    (2) If (A) the offense involved the knowing misrepresentation of a participant's identity to persuade, induce, entice, coerce, or facilitate the travel of, a minor to engage in prohibited sexual conduct; or (B) a participant otherwise unduly influenced a minor to engage in prohibited sexual conduct, increase by 2 levels.

    (3) If the offense involved the use of a computer or an interactive computer service to (A) persuade, induce, entice, coerce, or facilitate the travel of, the minor to engage in prohibited sexual conduct; or (B) entice, encourage, offer, or solicit a person to engage in prohibited sexual conduct with the minor, increase by 2 levels.

    (4) If (A) the offense involved the commission of a sex act or sexual contact; or (B) subsection (a)(3) or (a)(4) applies and the offense involved a commercial sex act, increase by 2 levels.

    (5) If (A) subsection (a)(3) or (a)(4) applies; and (B) the offense involved a minor who had not attained the age of 12 years, increase by 8 levels.

(c) Cross References

    (1) If the offense involved causing, transporting, permitting, or offering or seeking by notice or advertisement, a minor to engage in sexually explicit conduct for the purpose of producing a visual depiction of such conduct, apply §2G2.1 (Sexually Exploiting a Minor by Production of Sexually Explicit Visual or Printed Material; Custodian Permitting Minor to Engage in Sexually Explicit Conduct; Advertisement for Minors to Engage in Production), if the resulting offense level is greater than that determined above.

    (2) If a minor was killed under circumstances that would constitute murder under 18 U.S.C. § 1111 had such killing taken place within the territorial or maritime jurisdiction of the United States, apply §2A1.1 (First Degree Murder), if the resulting offense level is greater than that determined above.

(3) If the offense involved conduct described in 18 U.S.C. § 2241 or § 2242, apply §2A3.1 (Criminal Sexual Abuse; Attempt to Commit Criminal Sexual Abuse), if the resulting offense level is greater than that determined above. If the offense involved interstate travel with intent to engage in a sexual act with a minor who had not attained the age of 12 years, or knowingly engaging in a sexual act with a minor who had not attained the age of 12 years, §2A3.1 shall apply, regardless of the "consent" of the minor.

(d) Special Instruction

(1) If the offense involved more than one minor, Chapter Three, Part D (Multiple Counts) shall be applied as if the persuasion, enticement, coercion, travel, or transportation to engage in a commercial sex act or prohibited sexual conduct of each victim had been contained in a separate count of conviction.

Commentary

Statutory Provisions: 8 U.S.C. § 1328 (only if the offense involved a minor); 18 U.S.C. §§ 1591 (only if the offense involved a minor), 2421 (only if the offense involved a minor), 2422 (only if the offense involved a minor), 2423, 2425.

Application Notes:

1. **Definitions.**—For purposes of this guideline:

"*Commercial sex act*" has the meaning given that term in 18 U.S.C. § 1591(e)(3).

"*Computer*" has the meaning given that term in 18 U.S.C. § 1030(e)(1).

"*Illicit sexual conduct*" has the meaning given that term in 18 U.S.C. § 2423(f).

"*Interactive computer service*" has the meaning given that term in section 230(e)(2) of the Communications Act of 1934 (47 U.S.C. § 230(f)(2)).

"*Minor*" means (A) an individual who had not attained the age of 18 years; (B) an individual, whether fictitious or not, who a law enforcement officer represented to a participant (i) had not attained the age of 18 years, and (ii) could be provided for the purposes of engaging in sexually explicit conduct; or (C) an undercover law enforcement officer who represented to a participant that the officer had not attained the age of 18 years.

"*Participant*" has the meaning given that term in Application Note 1 of the Commentary to §3B1.1 (Aggravating Role).

"*Prohibited sexual conduct*" has the meaning given that term in Application Note 1 of the Commentary to §2A3.1 (Criminal Sexual Abuse; Attempt to Commit Criminal Sexual Abuse).

"*Sexual act*" has the meaning given that term in 18 U.S.C. § 2246(2).

"*Sexual contact*" has the meaning given that term in 18 U.S.C. § 2246(3).

2. **Application of Subsection (b)(1).—**

(A) **Custody, Care, or Supervisory Control.—**Subsection (b)(1) is intended to have broad application and includes offenses involving a victim less than 18 years of age entrusted to the defendant, whether temporarily or permanently. For example, teachers, day care providers, baby-sitters, or other temporary caretakers are among those who would be subject to this enhancement. In determining whether to apply this enhancement, the court should look to the actual relationship that existed between the defendant and the minor and not simply to the legal status of the defendant-minor relationship.

(B) **Inapplicability of Chapter Three Adjustment.—**If the enhancement under subsection (b)(1) applies, do not apply §3B1.3 (Abuse of Position of Trust or Use of Special Skill).

3. **Application of Subsection (b)(2).—**

(A) **Misrepresentation of Participant's Identity.—**The enhancement in subsection (b)(2)(A) applies in cases involving the misrepresentation of a participant's identity to persuade, induce, entice, coerce, or facilitate the travel of, a minor to engage in prohibited sexual conduct. Subsection (b)(2)(A) is intended to apply only to misrepresentations made directly to a minor or to a person who exercises custody, care, or supervisory control of the minor. Accordingly, the enhancement in subsection (b)(2)(A) would not apply to a misrepresentation made by a participant to an airline representative in the course of making travel arrangements for the minor.

The misrepresentation to which the enhancement in subsection (b)(2)(A) may apply includes misrepresentation of a participant's name, age, occupation, gender, or status, as long as the misrepresentation was made with the intent to persuade, induce, entice, coerce, or facilitate the travel of, a minor to engage in prohibited sexual conduct. Accordingly, use of a computer screen name, without such intent, would not be a sufficient basis for application of the enhancement.

(B) **Undue Influence.—**In determining whether subsection (b)(2)(B) applies, the court should closely consider the facts of the case to determine whether a participant's influence over the minor compromised the voluntariness of the minor's behavior. The voluntariness of the minor's behavior may be compromised without prohibited sexual conduct occurring.

However, subsection (b)(2)(B) does not apply in a case in which the only "minor" (as defined in Application Note 1) involved in the offense is an undercover law enforcement officer.

In a case in which a participant is at least 10 years older than the minor, there shall be a rebuttable presumption that subsection (b)(2)(B) applies. In such a case, some degree of undue influence can be presumed because of the substantial difference in age between the participant and the minor.

4. **Application of Subsection (b)(3).—**Subsection (b)(3) is intended to apply only to the use of a computer or an interactive computer service to communicate directly with a minor or with a person who exercises custody, care, or supervisory control of the minor.

Accordingly, the enhancement in subsection (b)(3) would not apply to the use of a computer or an interactive computer service to obtain airline tickets for the minor from an airline's Internet site.

5.   **Application of Subsection (c).—**

(A)   **Application of Subsection (c)(1).—**The cross reference in subsection (c)(1) is to be construed broadly and includes all instances in which the offense involved employing, using, persuading, inducing, enticing, coercing, transporting, permitting, or offering or seeking by notice, advertisement or other method, a minor to engage in sexually explicit conduct for the purpose of producing any visual depiction of such conduct. For purposes of subsection (c)(1), "*sexually explicit conduct*" has the meaning given that term in 18 U.S.C. § 2256(2).

(B)   **Application of Subsection (c)(3).—**For purposes of subsection (c)(3), conduct described in 18 U.S.C. § 2241 means conduct described in 18 U.S.C. § 2241(a), (b), or (c). Accordingly, for purposes of subsection (c)(3):

   (i)   Conduct described in 18 U.S.C. § 2241(a) or (b) is engaging in, or causing another person to engage in, a sexual act with another person: (I) using force against the minor; (II) threatening or placing the minor in fear that any person will be subject to death, serious bodily injury, or kidnapping; (III) rendering the minor unconscious; or (IV) administering by force or threat of force, or without the knowledge or permission of the minor, a drug, intoxicant, or other similar substance and thereby substantially impairing the ability of the minor to appraise or control conduct. This provision would apply, for example, if any dangerous weapon was used or brandished, or in a case in which the ability of the minor to appraise or control conduct was substantially impaired by drugs or alcohol.

   (ii)   Conduct described in 18 U.S.C. § 2241(c) is: (I) interstate travel with intent to engage in a sexual act with a minor who has not attained the age of 12 years; (II) knowingly engaging in a sexual act with a minor who has not attained the age of 12 years; or (III) knowingly engaging in a sexual act under the circumstances described in 18 U.S.C. § 2241(a) and (b) with a minor who has attained the age of 12 years but has not attained the age of 16 years (and is at least 4 years younger than the person so engaging).

   (iii)   Conduct described in 18 U.S.C. § 2242 is: (I) engaging in, or causing another person to engage in, a sexual act with another person by threatening or placing the minor in fear (other than by threatening or placing the minor in fear that any person will be subject to death, serious bodily injury, or kidnapping); or (II) engaging in, or causing another person to engage in, a sexual act with a minor who is incapable of appraising the nature of the conduct or who is physically incapable of declining participation in, or communicating unwillingness to engage in, the sexual act.

6.   **Application of Subsection (d)(1).—**For the purposes of Chapter Three, Part D (Multiple Counts), each minor transported, persuaded, induced, enticed, or coerced to engage in, or travel to engage in, a commercial sex act or prohibited sexual conduct is to be treated as a separate minor. Consequently, multiple counts involving more than one minor are not to be grouped together under §3D1.2 (Groups of Closely Related Counts). In addition, subsection (d)(1) directs that if the relevant conduct of an offense of conviction includes travel or transportation to engage in a commercial sex act or prohibited sexual

conduct in respect to more than one minor, whether specifically cited in the count of conviction, each such minor shall be treated as if contained in a separate count of conviction.

7.   **Upward Departure Provision.**—If the offense involved more than ten minors, an upward departure may be warranted.

| *Historical Note* | Effective November 1, 2004 (amendment 664). Amended effective November 1, 2007 (amendment 701); November 1, 2009 (amendments 732 and 737). |

* * * * * *

2.   SEXUAL EXPLOITATION OF A MINOR

§2G2.1.   Sexually Exploiting a Minor by Production of Sexually Explicit Visual or Printed Material; Custodian Permitting Minor to Engage in Sexually Explicit Conduct; Advertisement for Minors to Engage in Production

(a)   Base Offense Level: **32**

(b)   Specific Offense Characteristics

(1)   If the offense involved a minor who had (A) not attained the age of twelve years, increase by **4** levels; or (B) attained the age of twelve years but not attained the age of sixteen years, increase by **2** levels.

(2)   (Apply the greater) If the offense involved—

(A)   the commission of a sexual act or sexual contact, increase by **2** levels; or

(B)   (i) the commission of a sexual act; and (ii) conduct described in 18 U.S.C. § 2241(a) or (b), increase by **4** levels.

(3)   If the defendant knowingly engaged in distribution, increase by **2** levels.

(4)   If the offense involved material that portrays (A) sadistic or masochistic conduct or other depictions of violence; or (B) an infant or toddler, increase by **4** levels.

(5)   If the defendant was a parent, relative, or legal guardian of the minor involved in the offense, or if the minor was otherwise in the custody, care, or supervisory control of the defendant, increase by **2** levels.

(6) If, for the purpose of producing sexually explicit material or for the purpose of transmitting such material live, the offense involved (A) the knowing misrepresentation of a participant's identity to persuade, induce, entice, coerce, or facilitate the travel of, a minor to engage sexually explicit conduct; or (B) the use of a computer or an interactive computer service to (i) persuade, induce, entice, coerce, or facilitate the travel of, a minor to engage in sexually explicit conduct, or to otherwise solicit participation by a minor in such conduct; or (ii) solicit participation with a minor in sexually explicit conduct, increase by 2 levels.

(c) Cross Reference

(1) If the victim was killed in circumstances that would constitute murder under 18 U.S.C. § 1111 had such killing taken place within the territorial or maritime jurisdiction of the United States, apply §2A1.1 (First Degree Murder), if the resulting offense level is greater than that determined above.

(d) Special Instruction

(1) If the offense involved the exploitation of more than one minor, Chapter Three, Part D (Multiple Counts) shall be applied as if the exploitation of each minor had been contained in a separate count of conviction.

Commentary

Statutory Provisions: 18 U.S.C. §§ 1591, 2251(a)–(c), 2251(d)(1)(B), 2260(a). For additional statutory provision(s), *see* Appendix A (Statutory Index).

Application Notes:

1. **Definitions.**—For purposes of this guideline:

"*Computer*" has the meaning given that term in 18 U.S.C. § 1030(e)(1).

"*Distribution*" means any act, including possession with intent to distribute, production, transmission, advertisement, and transportation, related to the transfer of material involving the sexual exploitation of a minor. Accordingly, distribution includes posting material involving the sexual exploitation of a minor on a website for public viewing but does not include the mere solicitation of such material by a defendant.

"*Interactive computer service*" has the meaning given that term in section 230(e)(2) of the Communications Act of 1934 (47 U.S.C. § 230(f)(2)).

"*Material*" includes a visual depiction, as defined in 18 U.S.C. § 2256.

"*Minor*" means (A) an individual who had not attained the age of 18 years; (B) an individual, whether fictitious or not, who a law enforcement officer represented to a participant (i) had not attained the age of 18 years, and (ii) could be provided for the purposes of engaging in sexually explicit conduct; or (C) an undercover law enforcement officer who represented to a participant that the officer had not attained the age of 18 years.

"*Sexually explicit conduct*" has the meaning given that term in 18 U.S.C. § 2256(2).

2.   **Application of Subsection (b)(2).**—For purposes of subsection (b)(2):

"*Conduct described in 18 U.S.C. § 2241(a) or (b)*" is: (i) using force against the minor; (ii) threatening or placing the minor in fear that any person will be subject to death, serious bodily injury, or kidnapping; (iii) rendering the minor unconscious; or (iv) administering by force or threat of force, or without the knowledge or permission of the minor, a drug, intoxicant, or other similar substance and thereby substantially impairing the ability of the minor to appraise or control conduct. This provision would apply, for example, if any dangerous weapon was used or brandished, or in a case in which the ability of the minor to appraise or control conduct was substantially impaired by drugs or alcohol.

"*Sexual act*" has the meaning given that term in 18 U.S.C. § 2246(2).

"*Sexual contact*" has the meaning given that term in 18 U.S.C. § 2246(3).

3.   **Application of Subsection (b)(3).**—For purposes of subsection (b)(3), the defendant "knowingly engaged in distribution" if the defendant (A) knowingly committed the distribution, (B) aided, abetted, counseled, commanded, induced, procured, or willfully caused the distribution, or (C) conspired to distribute.

4.   **Interaction of Subsection (b)(4)(B) and Vulnerable Victim (§3A1.1(b)).**—If subsection (b)(4)(B) applies, do not apply §3A1.1(b).

5.   **Application of Subsection (b)(5).**—

    (A)   **In General.**—Subsection (b)(5) is intended to have broad application and includes offenses involving a minor entrusted to the defendant, whether temporarily or permanently. For example, teachers, day care providers, baby-sitters, or other temporary caretakers are among those who would be subject to this enhancement. In determining whether to apply this adjustment, the court should look to the actual relationship that existed between the defendant and the minor and not simply to the legal status of the defendant-minor relationship.

    (B)   **Inapplicability of Chapter Three Adjustment.**—If the enhancement in subsection (b)(5) applies, do not apply §3B1.3 (Abuse of Position of Trust or Use of Special Skill).

6.   **Application of Subsection (b)(6).**—

    (A)   **Misrepresentation of Participant's Identity.**—The enhancement in subsection (b)(6)(A) applies in cases involving the misrepresentation of a participant's identity to persuade, induce, entice, coerce, or facilitate the travel of, a minor to engage in sexually explicit conduct for the purpose of producing sexually explicit material or for the purpose of transmitting such material live. Subsection (b)(6)(A) is intended to apply only to misrepresentations made directly to a minor or to a person who exercises custody, care, or supervisory control of the minor. Accordingly, the enhancement in subsection (b)(6)(A) would not apply to a misrepresentation made by a participant to an airline representative in the course of making travel arrangements for the minor.

The misrepresentation to which the enhancement in subsection (b)(6)(A) may apply includes misrepresentation of a participant's name, age, occupation, gender, or status, as long as the misrepresentation was made with the intent to persuade, induce, entice, coerce, or facilitate the travel of, a minor to engage in sexually explicit conduct for the purpose of producing sexually explicit material or for the purpose of transmitting such material live. Accordingly, use of a computer screen name, without such intent, would not be a sufficient basis for application of the enhancement.

(B) **Use of a Computer or an Interactive Computer Service.**—Subsection (b)(6)(B) provides an enhancement if the offense involved the use of a computer or an interactive computer service to persuade, induce, entice, coerce, or facilitate the travel of, a minor to engage in sexually explicit conduct for the purpose of producing sexually explicit material or for the purpose of transmitting such material live or otherwise to solicit participation by a minor in such conduct for such purposes. Subsection (b)(6)(B) is intended to apply only to the use of a computer or an interactive computer service to communicate directly with a minor or with a person who exercises custody, care, or supervisory control of the minor. Accordingly, the enhancement would not apply to the use of a computer or an interactive computer service to obtain airline tickets for the minor from an airline's Internet site.

7. **Application of Subsection (d)(1).**—For the purposes of Chapter Three, Part D (Multiple Counts), each minor exploited is to be treated as a separate minor. Consequently, multiple counts involving the exploitation of different minors are not to be grouped together under §3D1.2 (Groups of Closely Related Counts). Subsection (d)(1) directs that if the relevant conduct of an offense of conviction includes more than one minor being exploited, whether specifically cited in the count of conviction or not, each such minor shall be treated as if contained in a separate count of conviction.

8. **Upward Departure Provision.**—An upward departure may be warranted if the offense involved more than 10 minors.

Historical Note	Effective November 1, 1987. Amended effective November 1, 1989 (amendment 161); November 1, 1990 (amendment 324); November 1, 1991 (amendment 400); November 1, 1996 (amendment 537); November 1, 1997 (amendment 575); November 1, 2000 (amendment 592); May 1, 2001 (amendment 612); November 1, 2001 (amendment 627); November 1, 2003 (amendment 661); November 1, 2004 (amendment 664); November 1, 2009 (amendments 733, 736, and 737); November 1, 2016 (amendment 801).

§2G2.2. Trafficking in Material Involving the Sexual Exploitation of a Minor; Receiving, Transporting, Shipping, Soliciting, or Advertising Material Involving the Sexual Exploitation of a Minor; Possessing Material Involving the Sexual Exploitation of a Minor with Intent to Traffic; Possessing Material Involving the Sexual Exploitation of a Minor

(a) Base Offense Level:

   (1) **18**, if the defendant is convicted of 18 U.S.C. § 1466A(b), § 2252(a)(4), § 2252A(a)(5), or § 2252A(a)(7).

   (2) **22**, otherwise.

(b) Specific Offense Characteristics

   (1) If (A) subsection (a)(2) applies; (B) the defendant's conduct was limited to the receipt or solicitation of material involving the sexual exploitation of a minor; and (C) the defendant did not intend to traffic in, or distribute, such material, decrease by **2** levels.

   (2) If the material involved a prepubescent minor or a minor who had not attained the age of 12 years, increase by **2** levels.

   (3) (Apply the greatest):

      (A) If the offense involved distribution for pecuniary gain, increase by the number of levels from the table in §2B1.1 (Theft, Property Destruction, and Fraud) corresponding to the retail value of the material, but by not less than **5** levels.

      (B) If the defendant distributed in exchange for any valuable consideration, but not for pecuniary gain, increase by **5** levels.

      (C) If the offense involved distribution to a minor, increase by **5** levels.

      (D) If the offense involved distribution to a minor that was intended to persuade, induce, entice, or coerce the minor to engage in any illegal activity, other than illegal activity covered under subdivision (E), increase by **6** levels.

      (E) If the offense involved distribution to a minor that was intended to persuade, induce, entice, coerce, or facilitate the travel of, the minor to engage in prohibited sexual conduct, increase by **7** levels.

(F) If the defendant knowingly engaged in distribution, other than distribution described in subdivisions (A) through (E), increase by **2** levels.

(4) If the offense involved material that portrays (A) sadistic or masochistic conduct or other depictions of violence; or (B) sexual abuse or exploitation of an infant or toddler, increase by **4** levels.

(5) If the defendant engaged in a pattern of activity involving the sexual abuse or exploitation of a minor, increase by **5** levels.

(6) If the offense involved the use of a computer or an interactive computer service for the possession, transmission, receipt, or distribution of the material, or for accessing with intent to view the material, increase by **2** levels.

(7) If the offense involved—

(A) at least 10 images, but fewer than 150, increase by **2** levels;

(B) at least 150 images, but fewer than 300, increase by **3** levels;

(C) at least 300 images, but fewer than 600, increase by **4** levels; and

(D) 600 or more images, increase by **5** levels.

(c) Cross Reference

(1) If the offense involved causing, transporting, permitting, or offering or seeking by notice or advertisement, a minor to engage in sexually explicit conduct for the purpose of producing a visual depiction of such conduct or for the purpose of transmitting a live visual depiction of such conduct, apply §2G2.1 (Sexually Exploiting a Minor by Production of Sexually Explicit Visual or Printed Material; Custodian Permitting Minor to Engage in Sexually Explicit Conduct; Advertisement for Minors to Engage in Production), if the resulting offense level is greater than that determined above.

Commentary

Statutory Provisions: 18 U.S.C. §§ 1466A, 2252, 2252A(a)–(b), 2260(b). For additional statutory provision(s), *see* Appendix A (Statutory Index).

Application Notes:

1. **Definitions.—**For purposes of this guideline:

    "*Computer*" has the meaning given that term in 18 U.S.C. § 1030(e)(1).

    "*Distribution*" means any act, including possession with intent to distribute, production, transmission, advertisement, and transportation, related to the transfer of material involving the sexual exploitation of a minor. Accordingly, distribution includes posting material involving the sexual exploitation of a minor on a website for public viewing but does not include the mere solicitation of such material by a defendant.

    "*Distribution for pecuniary gain*" means distribution for profit.

    "*The defendant distributed in exchange for any valuable consideration*" means the defendant agreed to an exchange with another person under which the defendant knowingly distributed to that other person for the specific purpose of obtaining something of valuable consideration from that other person, such as other child pornographic material, preferential access to child pornographic material, or access to a child.

    "*Distribution to a minor*" means the knowing distribution to an individual who is a minor at the time of the offense.

    "*Interactive computer service*" has the meaning given that term in section 230(e)(2) of the Communications Act of 1934 (47 U.S.C. § 230(f)(2)).

    "*Material*" includes a visual depiction, as defined in 18 U.S.C. § 2256.

    "*Minor*" means (A) an individual who had not attained the age of 18 years; (B) an individual, whether fictitious or not, who a law enforcement officer represented to a participant (i) had not attained the age of 18 years, and (ii) could be provided for the purposes of engaging in sexually explicit conduct; or (C) an undercover law enforcement officer who represented to a participant that the officer had not attained the age of 18 years.

    "*Pattern of activity involving the sexual abuse or exploitation of a minor*" means any combination of two or more separate instances of the sexual abuse or sexual exploitation of a minor by the defendant, whether or not the abuse or exploitation (A) occurred during the course of the offense; (B) involved the same minor; or (C) resulted in a conviction for such conduct.

    "*Prohibited sexual conduct*" has the meaning given that term in Application Note 1 of the Commentary to §2A3.1 (Criminal Sexual Abuse; Attempt to Commit Criminal Sexual Abuse).

    "*Sexual abuse or exploitation*" means any of the following: (A) conduct described in 18 U.S.C. § 2241, § 2242, § 2243, § 2251(a)–(c), § 2251(d)(1)(B), § 2251A, § 2260(b), § 2421, § 2422, or § 2423; (B) an offense under state law, that would have been an offense under any such section if the offense had occurred within the special maritime or territorial jurisdiction of the United States; or (C) an attempt or conspiracy to commit any of the offenses under subdivisions (A) or (B). "Sexual abuse or exploitation" does not include possession, accessing with intent to view, receipt, or trafficking in material relating to the sexual abuse or exploitation of a minor.

2. **Application of Subsection (b)(3)(F).**—For purposes of subsection (b)(3)(F), the defendant "knowingly engaged in distribution" if the defendant (A) knowingly committed the distribution, (B) aided, abetted, counseled, commanded, induced, procured, or willfully caused the distribution, or (C) conspired to distribute.

3. **Application of Subsection (b)(4)(A).**—Subsection (b)(4)(A) applies if the offense involved material that portrays sadistic or masochistic conduct or other depictions of violence, regardless of whether the defendant specifically intended to possess, access with intent to view, receive, or distribute such materials.

4. **Interaction of Subsection (b)(4)(B) and Vulnerable Victim (§3A1.1(b)).**—If subsection (b)(4)(B) applies, do not apply §3A1.1(b).

5. **Application of Subsection (b)(5).**—A conviction taken into account under subsection (b)(5) is not excluded from consideration of whether that conviction receives criminal history points pursuant to Chapter Four, Part A (Criminal History).

6. **Application of Subsection (b)(7).**—

   (A) **Definition of "Images".**—*"Images"* means any visual depiction, as defined in 18 U.S.C. § 2256(5), that constitutes child pornography, as defined in 18 U.S.C. § 2256(8).

   (B) **Determining the Number of Images.**—For purposes of determining the number of images under subsection (b)(7):

      (i) Each photograph, picture, computer or computer-generated image, or any similar visual depiction shall be considered to be one image. If the number of images substantially underrepresents the number of minors depicted, an upward departure may be warranted.

      (ii) Each video, video-clip, movie, or similar visual depiction shall be considered to have 75 images. If the length of the visual depiction is substantially more than 5 minutes, an upward departure may be warranted.

7. **Application of Subsection (c)(1).**—

   (A) **In General.**—The cross reference in subsection (c)(1) is to be construed broadly and includes all instances where the offense involved employing, using, persuading, inducing, enticing, coercing, transporting, permitting, or offering or seeking by notice or advertisement, a minor to engage in sexually explicit conduct for the purpose of producing any visual depiction of such conduct or for the purpose of transmitting live any visual depiction of such conduct.

   (B) **Definition.**—*"Sexually explicit conduct"* has the meaning given that term in 18 U.S.C. § 2256(2).

8. **Cases Involving Adapted or Modified Depictions.**—If the offense involved material that is an adapted or modified depiction of an identifiable minor (*e.g.*, a case in which the

defendant is convicted under 18 U.S.C. § 2252A(a)(7)), the term "material involving the sexual exploitation of a minor" includes such material.

9. **Upward Departure Provision.**—If the defendant engaged in the sexual abuse or exploitation of a minor at any time (whether or not such abuse or exploitation occurred during the course of the offense or resulted in a conviction for such conduct) and subsection (b)(5) does not apply, an upward departure may be warranted. In addition, an upward departure may be warranted if the defendant received an enhancement under subsection (b)(5) but that enhancement does not adequately reflect the seriousness of the sexual abuse or exploitation involved.

Background: Section 401(i)(1)(C) of Public Law 108–21 directly amended subsection (b) to add subdivision (7), effective April 30, 2003.

Historical Note	Effective November 1, 1987. Amended effective June 15, 1988 (amendment 31); November 1, 1990 (amendment 325); November 1, 1991 (amendment 372); November 27, 1991 (amendment 435); November 1, 1996 (amendment 537); November 1, 1997 (amendment 575); November 1, 2000 (amendment 592); November 1, 2001 (amendment 615); April 30, 2003 (amendment 649); November 1, 2003 (amendment 661); November 1, 2004 (amendment 664); November 1, 2009 (amendments 733 and 736); November 1, 2016 (amendment 801).

§2G2.3. Selling or Buying of Children for Use in the Production of Pornography

> (a) Base Offense Level: **38**

Commentary

Statutory Provision: 18 U.S.C. § 2251A.

Background: The statutory minimum sentence for a defendant convicted under 18 U.S.C. § 2251A is thirty years imprisonment.

Historical Note	Effective November 1, 1989 (amendment 162). Amended effective November 1, 2009 (amendment 736).

§2G2.4. [Deleted]

Historical Note	Effective November 1, 1991 (amendment 372). Amended effective November 27, 1991 (amendment 436); November 1, 1996 (amendment 537); November 1, 2000 (amendment 592); April 30, 2003 (amendment 649); was deleted by consolidation with §2G2.2 effective November 1, 2004 (amendment 664).

§2G2.5. Recordkeeping Offenses Involving the Production of Sexually Explicit Materials; Failure to Provide Required Marks in Commercial Electronic Email

    (a)   Base Offense Level: **6**

    (b)   Cross References

         (1)   If the offense reflected an effort to conceal a substantive offense that involved causing, transporting, permitting, or offering or seeking by notice or advertisement, a minor to engage in sexually explicit conduct for the purpose of producing a visual depiction of such conduct, apply §2G2.1 (Sexually Exploiting a Minor by Production of Sexually Explicit Visual or Printed Material; Custodian Permitting Minor to Engage in Sexually Explicit Conduct; Advertisement for Minors to Engage in Production).

         (2)   If the offense reflected an effort to conceal a substantive offense that involved trafficking in material involving the sexual exploitation of a minor (including receiving, transporting, advertising, or possessing material involving the sexual exploitation of a minor with intent to traffic), apply §2G2.2 (Trafficking in Material Involving the Sexual Exploitation of a Minor; Receiving, Transporting, Advertising, or Possessing Material Involving the Sexual Exploitation of a Minor with Intent to Traffic).

Commentary

Statutory Provisions: 15 U.S.C. § 7704(d); 18 U.S.C. §§ 2257, 2257A.

Historical Note	Effective November 1, 1991 (amendment 372). Amended effective November 1, 2006 (amendment 689); November 1, 2007 (amendment 701).

§2G2.6. Child Exploitation Enterprises

    (a)   Base Offense Level: **35**

    (b)   Specific Offense Characteristics

         (1)   If a victim (A) had not attained the age of 12 years, increase by **4** levels; or (B) had attained the age of 12 years but had not attained the age of 16 years, increase by **2** levels.

(2)   If (A) the defendant was a parent, relative, or legal guardian of a minor victim; or (B) a minor victim was otherwise in the custody, care, or supervisory control of the defendant, increase by **2** levels.

(3)   If the offense involved conduct described in 18 U.S.C. § 2241(a) or (b), increase by **2** levels.

(4)   If a computer or an interactive computer service was used in furtherance of the offense, increase by **2** levels.

Commentary

Statutory Provision: 18 U.S.C. § 2252A(g).

Application Notes:

1.   **Definitions.**—For purposes of this guideline:

"*Computer*" has the meaning given that term in 18 U.S.C. § 1030(e)(1).

"*Interactive computer service*" has the meaning given that term in section 230(e)(2) of the Communications Act of 1934 (47 U.S.C. § 230(f)(2)).

"*Minor*" means (A) an individual who had not attained the age of 18 years; (B) an individual, whether fictitious or not, who a law enforcement officer represented to a participant (i) had not attained the age of 18 years; and (ii) could be provided for the purposes of engaging in sexually explicit conduct; or (C) an undercover law enforcement officer who represented to a participant that the officer had not attained the age of 18 years.

2.   **Application of Subsection (b)(2).**—

(A)   **Custody, Care, or Supervisory Control.**—Subsection (b)(2) is intended to have broad application and includes offenses involving a victim less than 18 years of age entrusted to the defendant, whether temporarily or permanently. For example, teachers, day care providers, baby-sitters, or other temporary caretakers are among those who would be subject to this enhancement. In determining whether to apply this enhancement, the court should look to the actual relationship that existed between the defendant and the minor and not simply to the legal status of the defendant-minor relationship.

(B)   **Inapplicability of Chapter Three Adjustment.**—If the enhancement under subsection (b)(2) applies, do not apply §3B1.3 (Abuse of Position of Trust or Use of Special Skill).

3.   **Application of Subsection (b)(3).**—For purposes of subsection (b)(3), "*conduct described in 18 U.S.C. § 2241(a) or (b)*" is: (i) using force against the minor; (ii) threatening or placing the minor in fear that any person will be subject to death, serious bodily injury, or kidnapping; (iii) rendering the minor unconscious; or (iv) administering by force or threat of force, or without the knowledge or permission of the minor, a drug, intoxicant, or other similar substance and thereby substantially impairing the ability of the minor to appraise or control conduct. This provision would apply, for example, if any dangerous

weapon was used or brandished, or in a case in which the ability of the minor to appraise or control conduct was substantially impaired by drugs or alcohol.

Historical Note	Effective November 1, 2007 (amendment 701).

* * * * *

3. OBSCENITY

§2G3.1. Importing, Mailing, or Transporting Obscene Matter; Transferring Obscene Matter to a Minor; Misleading Domain Names

(a) Base Offense Level: **10**

(b) Specific Offense Characteristics

(1) (Apply the Greatest):

(A) If the offense involved distribution for pecuniary gain, increase by the number of levels from the table in §2B1.1 (Theft, Property Destruction, and Fraud) corresponding to the retail value of the material, but by not less than **5** levels.

(B) If the defendant distributed in exchange for any valuable consideration, but not for pecuniary gain, increase by **5** levels.

(C) If the offense involved distribution to a minor, increase by **5** levels.

(D) If the offense involved distribution to a minor that was intended to persuade, induce, entice, or coerce the minor to engage in any illegal activity, other than illegal activity covered under subdivision (E), increase by **6** levels.

(E) If the offense involved distribution to a minor that was intended to persuade, induce, entice, coerce, or facilitate the travel of, the minor to engage in prohibited sexual conduct, increase by **7** levels.

(F) If the defendant knowingly engaged in distribution, other than distribution described in subdivisions (A) through (E), increase by **2** levels.

  (2) If, with the intent to deceive a minor into viewing material that is harmful to minors, the offense involved the use of (A) a misleading domain name on the Internet; or (B) embedded words or digital images in the source code of a website, increase by **2** levels.

  (3) If the offense involved the use of a computer or an interactive computer service, increase by **2** levels.

  (4) If the offense involved material that portrays sadistic or masochistic conduct or other depictions of violence, increase by **4** levels.

 (c) Cross Reference

  (1) If the offense involved transporting, distributing, receiving, possessing, or advertising to receive material involving the sexual exploitation of a minor, apply §2G2.2 (Trafficking in Material Involving the Sexual Exploitation of a Minor; Receiving, Transporting, Shipping, Soliciting, or Advertising Material Involving the Sexual Exploitation of a Minor; Possessing Material Involving the Sexual Exploitation of a Minor with Intent to Traffic; Possessing Material Involving the Sexual Exploitation of a Minor).

Commentary

Statutory Provisions: 18 U.S.C. §§ 1460–1463, 1465, 1466, 1470, 2252B, 2252C. For additional statutory provision(s), *see* Appendix A (Statutory Index).

Application Notes:

1. **Definitions.**—For purposes of this guideline:

"***Computer***" has the meaning given that term in 18 U.S.C. § 1030(e)(1).

"***Distribution***" means any act, including possession with intent to distribute, production, transmission, advertisement, and transportation, related to the transfer of obscene matter. Accordingly, distribution includes posting material involving the sexual exploitation of a minor on a website for public viewing but does not include the mere solicitation of such material by a defendant.

"***Distribution for pecuniary gain***" means distribution for profit.

"***The defendant distributed in exchange for any valuable consideration***" means the defendant agreed to an exchange with another person under which the defendant knowingly distributed to that other person for the specific purpose of obtaining something of valuable consideration from that other person, such as other obscene material, preferential access to obscene material, or access to a child.

"*Distribution to a minor*" means the knowing distribution to an individual who is a minor at the time of the offense.

"*Interactive computer service*" has the meaning given that term in section 230(e)(2) of the Communications Act of 1934 (47 U.S.C. § 230(f)(2)).

"*Material that is harmful to minors*" has the meaning given that term in 18 U.S.C. § 2252B(d).

"*Minor*" means (A) an individual who had not attained the age of 18 years; (B) an individual, whether fictitious or not, who a law enforcement officer represented to a participant (i) had not attained the age of 18 years, and (ii) could be provided for the purposes of engaging in sexually explicit conduct; or (C) an undercover law enforcement officer who represented to a participant that the officer had not attained the age of 18 years.

"*Prohibited sexual conduct*" has the meaning given that term in Application Note 1 of the Commentary to §2A3.1 (Criminal Sexual Abuse; Attempt to Commit Criminal Sexual Abuse).

"*Sexually explicit conduct*" has the meaning given that term in 18 U.S.C. § 2256(2).

2. **Application of Subsection (b)(1)(F).**—For purposes of subsection (b)(1)(F), the defendant "knowingly engaged in distribution" if the defendant (A) knowingly committed the distribution, (B) aided, abetted, counseled, commanded, induced, procured, or willfully caused the distribution, or (C) conspired to distribute.

3. **Inapplicability of Subsection (b)(3).**—If the defendant is convicted of 18 U.S.C. § 2252B or § 2252C, subsection (b)(3) shall not apply.

4. **Application of Subsection (b)(4).**—Subsection (b)(4) applies if the offense involved material that portrays sadistic or masochistic conduct or other depictions of violence, regardless of whether the defendant specifically intended to possess, receive, or distribute such materials.

Background: Most federal prosecutions for offenses covered in this guideline are directed to offenses involving distribution for pecuniary gain. Consequently, the offense level under this section generally will be at least 15.

Historical Note	Effective November 1, 1987. Amended effective November 1, 1989 (amendment 163); November 1, 1990 (amendment 326); November 1, 1991 (amendment 372); November 27, 1991 (amendment 437); November 1, 2000 (amendment 592); November 1, 2001 (amendment 617); November 1, 2004 (amendment 664); November 1, 2007 (amendment 701); November 1, 2009 (amendment 736); November 1, 2010 (amendment 746); November 1, 2016 (amendment 801).

§2G3.2. Obscene Telephone Communications for a Commercial Purpose; Broadcasting Obscene Material

(a) Base Offense Level: **12**

(b)   Specific Offense Characteristics

(1)   If a person who received the telephonic communication was less than eighteen years of age, or if a broadcast was made between six o'clock in the morning and eleven o'clock at night, increase by **4** levels.

(2)   If **6** plus the offense level from the table in §2B1.1 (Theft, Property Destruction, and Fraud) corresponding to the volume of commerce attributable to the defendant is greater than the offense level determined above, increase to that offense level.

Commentary

Statutory Provisions: 18 U.S.C. §§ 1464, 1468; 47 U.S.C. § 223(b)(1)(A).

Background: Subsection (b)(1) provides an enhancement where an obscene telephonic communication was received by a minor less than 18 years of age or where a broadcast was made during a time when such minors were likely to receive it. Subsection (b)(2) provides an enhancement for large-scale "dial-a-porn" or obscene broadcasting operations that results in an offense level comparable to the offense level for such operations under §2G3.1 (Importing, Mailing, or Transporting Obscene Matter; Transferring Obscene Matter to a Minor). The extent to which the obscene material was distributed is approximated by the volume of commerce attributable to the defendant.

Historical Note	Effective November 1, 1989 (amendment 164). Amended effective November 1, 2000 (amendment 592); November 1, 2001 (amendment 617). A former §2G3.2 (Obscene or Indecent Telephone Communications), effective November 1, 1987, was deleted effective November 1, 1989 (amendment 164).

PART H — OFFENSES INVOLVING INDIVIDUAL RIGHTS

1. CIVIL RIGHTS

Historical Note	Introductory Commentary to Part H, Subpart 1, effective November 1, 1987, was deleted effective November 1, 1995 (amendment 521).

§2H1.1. Offenses Involving Individual Rights

    (a)   Base Offense Level (Apply the Greatest):

        (1)   the offense level from the offense guideline applicable to any underlying offense;

        (2)   **12**, if the offense involved two or more participants;

        (3)   **10**, if the offense involved (A) the use or threat of force against a person; or (B) property damage or the threat of property damage; or

        (4)   **6**, otherwise.

    (b)   Specific Offense Characteristic

        (1)   If (A) the defendant was a public official at the time of the offense; or (B) the offense was committed under color of law, increase by **6** levels.

Commentary

Statutory Provisions: 18 U.S.C. §§ 241, 242, 245(b), 246, 247, 248, 249, 1091; 42 U.S.C. § 3631.

Application Notes:

1.   *"Offense guideline applicable to any underlying offense"* means the offense guideline applicable to any conduct established by the offense of conviction that constitutes an offense under federal, state, or local law (other than an offense that is itself covered under Chapter Two, Part H, Subpart 1).

    In certain cases, conduct set forth in the count of conviction may constitute more than one underlying offense (*e.g.*, two instances of assault, or one instance of assault and one instance of arson). In such cases, use the following comparative procedure to determine the applicable base offense level: (i) determine the underlying offenses encompassed within the count of conviction as if the defendant had been charged with a conspiracy to commit multiple offenses. *See* Application Note 4 of §1B1.2 (Applicable Guidelines);

(ii) determine the Chapter Two offense level (*i.e.*, the base offense level, specific offense characteristics, cross references, and special instructions) for each such underlying offense; and (iii) compare each of the Chapter Two offense levels determined above with the alternative base offense level under subsection (a)(2), (3), or (4). The determination of the applicable alternative base offense level is to be based on the entire conduct underlying the count of conviction (*i.e.*, the conduct taken as a whole). Use the alternative base offense level only if it is greater than each of the Chapter Two offense levels determined above. Otherwise, use the Chapter Two offense levels for each of the underlying offenses (with each underlying offense treated as if contained in a separate count of conviction). Then apply subsection (b) to the alternative base offense level, or to the Chapter Two offense levels for each of the underlying offenses, as appropriate.

2. *"**Participant**"* is defined in the Commentary to §3B1.1 (Aggravating Role).

3. The burning or defacement of a religious symbol with an intent to intimidate shall be deemed to involve the threat of force against a person for the purposes of subsection (a)(3)(A).

4. If the finder of fact at trial or, in the case of a plea of guilty or *nolo contendere*, the court at sentencing determines beyond a reasonable doubt that the defendant intentionally selected any victim or any property as the object of the offense because of the actual or perceived race, color, religion, national origin, ethnicity, gender, gender identity, disability, or sexual orientation of any person, an additional 3-level enhancement from §3A1.1(a) will apply. An adjustment from §3A1.1(a) will not apply, however, if a 6-level adjustment from §2H1.1(b) applies. *See* §3A1.1(c).

5. If subsection (b)(1) applies, do not apply §3B1.3 (Abuse of Position of Trust or Use of Special Skill).

Historical Note	Effective November 1, 1987. Amended effective November 1, 1989 (amendment 303); November 1, 1990 (amendments 313 and 327); November 1, 1991 (amendment 430); November 1, 1995 (amendment 521); November 1, 2000 (amendment 591); November 1, 2010 (amendment 743).

§2H1.2. [Deleted]

Historical Note	Section 2H1.2 (Conspiracy to Interfere with Civil Rights), effective November 1, 1987, amended effective November 1, 1989 (amendment 303), was deleted by consolidation with §2H1.1 effective November 1, 1990 (amendment 327).

§2H1.3. [Deleted]

Historical Note	Section 2H1.3 (Use of Force or Threat of Force to Deny Benefits or Rights in Furtherance of Discrimination; Damage to Religious Real Property), effective November 1, 1987, amended effective November 1, 1989 (amendment 165), was deleted by consolidation with §2H1.1 effective November 1, 1995 (amendment 521).

---
§2H1.4. [Deleted]

Historical Note	Section 2H1.4 (Interference with Civil Rights Under Color of Law), effective November 1, 1987, amended effective November 1, 1989 (amendment 166), was deleted by consolidation with §2H1.1 effective November 1, 1995 (amendment 521).

---
§2H1.5. [Deleted]

Historical Note	Section 2H1.5 (Other Deprivations of Rights or Benefits in Furtherance of Discrimination), effective November 1, 1987, amended effective November 1, 1989 (amendment 167) and November 1, 1990 (amendment 328), was deleted by consolidation with §2H1.1 effective November 1, 1995 (amendment 521).

*   *   *   *   *

2.   POLITICAL RIGHTS

§2H2.1.   Obstructing an Election or Registration

(a)   Base Offense Level (Apply the greatest):

(1)   **18**, if the obstruction occurred by use of force or threat of force against person(s) or property; or

(2)   **12**, if the obstruction occurred by forgery, fraud, theft, bribery, deceit, or other means, except as provided in (3) below; or

(3)   **6**, if the defendant (A) solicited, demanded, accepted, or agreed to accept anything of value to vote, refrain from voting, vote for or against a particular candidate, or register to vote, (B) gave false information to establish eligibility to vote, or (C) voted more than once in a federal election.

Commentary

Statutory Provisions: 18 U.S.C. §§ 241, 242, 245(b)(1)(A), 592, 593, 594, 597, 1015(f); 52 U.S.C. §§ 10307, 10308(a), (b). For additional statutory provision(s), *see* Appendix A (Statutory Index).

Application Note:

1.   If the offense resulted in bodily injury or significant property damage, or involved corrupting a public official, an upward departure may be warranted. *See* Chapter Five, Part K (Departures).

Background: Alternative base offense levels cover three major ways of obstructing an election: by force, by deceptive or dishonest conduct, or by bribery. A defendant who is a public official or who directs others to engage in criminal conduct is subject to an enhancement from Chapter Three, Part B (Role in the Offense).

Historical Note	Effective November 1, 1987. Amended effective November 1, 1989 (amendment 168); November 1, 1995 (amendment 534); November 1, 2003 (amendment 661); November 1, 2015 (amendment 796).

* * * * *

3. PRIVACY AND EAVESDROPPING

§2H3.1. Interception of Communications; Eavesdropping; Disclosure of Certain Private or Protected Information

(a)   Base Offense Level (Apply the greater):

  (1)   **9**; or

  (2)   **6**, if the offense of conviction has a statutory maximum term of imprisonment of one year or less but more than six months.

(b)   Specific Offense Characteristics

  (1)   If (A) the defendant is convicted under 18 U.S.C. § 1039(d) or (e); or (B) the purpose of the offense was to obtain direct or indirect commercial advantage or economic gain, increase by **3** levels.

  (2)   (Apply the greater) If—

    (A)   the defendant is convicted under 18 U.S.C. § 119, increase by **8** levels; or

    (B)   the defendant is convicted under 18 U.S.C. § 119, and the offense involved the use of a computer or an interactive computer service to make restricted personal information about a covered person publicly available, increase by **10** levels.

(c)   Cross Reference

  (1)   If the purpose of the offense was to facilitate another offense, apply the guideline applicable to an attempt to commit that

other offense, if the resulting offense level is greater than that determined above.

Commentary

Statutory Provisions: 8 U.S.C. § 1375a(d)(5)(B)(i), (ii); 18 U.S.C. §§ 119, 1039, 1905, 2511; 26 U.S.C. §§ 7213(a)(1)–(3), (a)(5), (d), 7213A, 7216; 42 U.S.C. §§ 16962, 16984; 47 U.S.C. § 605. For additional statutory provision(s), *see* Appendix A (Statutory Index).

Application Notes:

1.   **Satellite Cable Transmissions.**—If the offense involved interception of satellite cable transmissions for purposes of commercial advantage or private financial gain (including avoiding payment of fees), apply §2B5.3 (Criminal Infringement of Copyright) rather than this guideline.

2.   **Imposition of Sentence for 18 U.S.C. § 1039(d) and (e).**—Subsections 1039(d) and (e) of title 18, United States Code, require a term of imprisonment of not more than 5 years to be imposed in addition to any sentence imposed for a conviction under 18 U.S.C. § 1039(a), (b), or (c). In order to comply with the statute, the court should determine the appropriate "total punishment" and divide the sentence on the judgment form between the sentence attributable to the conviction under 18 U.S.C. § 1039(d) or (e) and the sentence attributable to the conviction under 18 U.S.C. § 1039(a), (b), or (c), specifying the number of months to be served for the conviction under 18 U.S.C. § 1039(d) or (e). For example, if the applicable adjusted guideline range is 15–21 months and the court determines a "total punishment" of 21 months is appropriate, a sentence of 9 months for conduct under 18 U.S.C. § 1039(a) plus 12 months for 18 U.S.C. § 1039(d) conduct would achieve the "total punishment" in a manner that satisfies the statutory requirement.

3.   **Inapplicability of Chapter Three (Adjustments).**—If the enhancement under subsection (b)(2) applies, do not apply §3A1.2 (Official Victim).

4.   **Definitions.**—For purposes of this guideline:

"*Computer*" has the meaning given that term in 18 U.S.C. § 1030(e)(1).

"*Covered person*" has the meaning given that term in 18 U.S.C. § 119(b).

"*Interactive computer service*" has the meaning given that term in section 230(e)(2) of the Communications Act of 1934 (47 U.S.C. § 230(f)(2)).

"*Means of identification*" has the meaning given that term in 18 U.S.C. § 1028(d)(7), except that such means of identification shall be of an actual (*i.e.*, not fictitious) individual, other than the defendant or a person for whose conduct the defendant is accountable under §1B1.3 (Relevant Conduct).

"*Personal information*" means sensitive or private information involving an identifiable individual (including such information in the possession of a third party), including (A) medical records; (B) wills; (C) diaries; (D) private correspondence, including e-mail; (E) financial records; (F) photographs of a sensitive or private nature; or (G) similar information.

"*Restricted personal information*" has the meaning given that term in 18 U.S.C. § 119(b).

5.   **Upward Departure.**—There may be cases in which the offense level determined under this guideline substantially understates the seriousness of the offense. In such a case, an upward departure may be warranted. The following are examples of cases in which an upward departure may be warranted:

(A)   The offense involved personal information, means of identification, confidential phone records information, or tax return information of a substantial number of individuals.

(B)   The offense caused or risked substantial non-monetary harm (*e.g.* physical harm, psychological harm, or severe emotional trauma, or resulted in a substantial invasion of privacy interest) to individuals whose private or protected information was obtained.

Historical Note	Effective November 1, 1987. Amended effective November 1, 1989 (amendment 169); November 1, 2001 (amendment 628); May 1, 2007 (amendment 697); November 1, 2007 (amendment 708); November 1, 2008 (amendment 718); November 1, 2009 (amendments 726 and 737); November 1, 2104 (amendment 781).

---

§2H3.2.   Manufacturing, Distributing, Advertising, or Possessing an Eavesdropping Device

(a)   Base Offense Level: **6**

(b)   Specific Offense Characteristic

(1)   If the offense was committed for pecuniary gain, increase by **3** levels.

Commentary

Statutory Provision: 18 U.S.C. § 2512.

Historical Note	Effective November 1, 1987.

---

§2H3.3.   Obstructing Correspondence

(a)   Base Offense Level:

(1)   **6**; or

(2)   if the conduct was theft or destruction of mail, apply §2B1.1 (Theft, Property Destruction, and Fraud).

Commentary

Statutory Provision: 18 U.S.C. § 1702. For additional statutory provision(s), *see* Appendix A (Statutory Index).

Background: The statutory provision covered by this guideline is sometimes used to prosecute offenses more accurately described as theft or destruction of mail. In such cases, §2B1.1 (Theft, Property Destruction, and Fraud) is to be applied.

Historical Note	Effective November 1, 1987. Amended effective November 1, 1990 (amendment 313); November 1, 2001 (amendment 617).

*   *   *   *   *   *

4.   PEONAGE, INVOLUNTARY SERVITUDE, SLAVE TRADE, AND CHILD SOLDIERS

Historical Note	Effective November 1, 1987. Amended effective November 1, 2009 (amendment 733).

§2H4.1.   Peonage, Involuntary Servitude, Slave Trade, and Child Soldiers

(a)   Base Offense Level:

    (1)   **22**; or

    (2)   **18**, if (A) the defendant was convicted of an offense under 18 U.S.C. § 1592, or (B) the defendant was convicted of an offense under 18 U.S.C. § 1593A based on an act in violation of 18 U.S.C. § 1592.

(b)   Specific Offense Characteristics

    (1)   (A) If any victim sustained permanent or life-threatening bodily injury, increase by **4** levels; or (B) if any victim sustained serious bodily injury, increase by **2** levels.

    (2)   If (A) a dangerous weapon was used, increase by **4** levels; or (B) a dangerous weapon was brandished, or the use of a dangerous weapon was threatened, increase by **2** levels.

    (3)   If any victim was held in a condition of peonage or involuntary servitude for (A) more than one year, increase by **3** levels; (B) between 180 days and one year, increase by **2** levels; or

(C) more than 30 days but less than 180 days, increase by **1** level.

(4) If any other felony offense was committed during the commission of, or in connection with, the peonage or involuntary servitude offense, increase to the greater of:

(A) **2** plus the offense level as determined above, or

(B) **2** plus the offense level from the offense guideline applicable to that other offense, but in no event greater than level **43**.

Commentary

Statutory Provisions: 18 U.S.C. §§ 241, 1581–1590, 1592, 1593A, 2442.

Application Notes:

1. For purposes of this guideline—

   "*A dangerous weapon was used*" means that a firearm was discharged, or that a firearm or other dangerous weapon was otherwise used. "*The use of a dangerous weapon was threatened*" means that the use of a dangerous weapon was threatened regardless of whether a dangerous weapon was present.

   Definitions of "*firearm*," "*dangerous weapon*," "*otherwise used*," "*serious bodily injury*," and "*permanent or life-threatening bodily injury*" are found in the Commentary to §1B1.1 (Application Instructions).

   "*Peonage or involuntary servitude*" includes forced labor, slavery, and recruitment or use of a child soldier.

2. Under subsection (b)(4), "*any other felony offense*" means any conduct that constitutes a felony offense under federal, state, or local law (other than an offense that is itself covered by this subpart). When there is more than one such other offense, the most serious such offense (or group of closely related offenses in the case of offenses that would be grouped together under §3D1.2(d)) is to be used. *See* Application Note 3 of §1B1.5 (Interpretation of References to other Offense Guidelines).

3. If the offense involved the holding of more than ten victims in a condition of peonage or involuntary servitude, an upward departure may be warranted.

4. In a case in which the defendant was convicted under 18 U.S.C. §§ 1589(b) or 1593A, a downward departure may be warranted if the defendant benefitted from participating in a venture described in those sections without knowing that (*i.e.*, in reckless disregard of the fact that) the venture had engaged in the criminal activity described in those sections.

Historical Note	Effective November 1, 1987. Amended effective November 1, 1995 (amendment 521); May 1, 1997 (amendment 542); November 1, 1997 (amendment 559); May 1, 2001 (amendment 612); November 1, 2001 (amendment 627); November 1, 2009 (amendments 730 and 733).

---

§2H4.2. Willful Violations of the Migrant and Seasonal Agricultural Worker Protection Act

---

(a) Base Offense Level: **6**

(b) Specific Offense Characteristics

(1) If the offense involved (A) serious bodily injury, increase by **4** levels; or (B) bodily injury, increase by **2** levels.

(2) If the defendant committed any part of the instant offense subsequent to sustaining a civil or administrative adjudication for similar misconduct, increase by **2** levels.

Commentary

Statutory Provision: 29 U.S.C. § 1851.

Application Notes:

1. **Definitions.**—For purposes of subsection (b)(1), "*bodily injury*" and "*serious bodily injury*" have the meaning given those terms in Application Note 1 of the Commentary to §1B1.1 (Application Instructions).

2. **Application of Subsection (b)(2).**—Section 1851 of title 29, United States Code, covers a wide range of conduct. Accordingly, the enhancement in subsection (b)(2) applies only if the instant offense is similar to previous misconduct that resulted in a civil or administrative adjudication under the provisions of the Migrant and Seasonal Agricultural Worker Protection Act (29 U.S.C. § 1801 *et seq.*).

Historical Note	Effective May 1, 2001 (amendment 612). Amended effective November 1, 2001 (amendment 627); November 1, 2010 (amendment 746); November 1, 2015 (amendment 796).

PART I — [NOT USED]

PART J — OFFENSES INVOLVING THE ADMINISTRATION OF JUSTICE

§2J1.1. Contempt

Apply §2X5.1 (Other Offenses).

Commentary

Statutory Provisions: 18 U.S.C. §§ 401, 228. For additional statutory provision(s), *see* Appendix A (Statutory Index).

Application Notes:

1. **In General.**—Because misconduct constituting contempt varies significantly and the nature of the contemptuous conduct, the circumstances under which the contempt was committed, the effect the misconduct had on the administration of justice, and the need to vindicate the authority of the court are highly context-dependent, the Commission has not provided a specific guideline for this offense. In certain cases, the offense conduct will be sufficiently analogous to §2J1.2 (Obstruction of Justice) for that guideline to apply.

2. **Willful Failure to Pay Court-Ordered Child Support.**—For offenses involving the willful failure to pay court-ordered child support (violations of 18 U.S.C. § 228), the most analogous guideline is §2B1.1 (Theft, Property Destruction, and Fraud). The amount of the loss is the amount of child support that the defendant willfully failed to pay. In such a case, do not apply §2B1.1(b)(9)(C) (pertaining to a violation of a prior, specific judicial order). *Note*: This guideline applies to second and subsequent offenses under 18 U.S.C. § 228(a)(1) and to any offense under 18 U.S.C. § 228(a)(2) and (3). A first offense under 18 U.S.C. § 228(a)(1) is not covered by this guideline because it is a Class B misdemeanor.

3. **Violation of Judicial Order Enjoining Fraudulent Behavior.**—In a case involving a violation of a judicial order enjoining fraudulent behavior, the most analogous guideline is §2B1.1. In such a case, §2B1.1(b)(9)(C) (pertaining to a violation of a prior, specific judicial order) ordinarily would apply.

Historical Note	Effective November 1, 1987. Amended effective November 1, 1989 (amendments 170 and 171); November 1, 1993 (amendment 496); November 1, 1998 (amendment 588); November 1, 2001 (amendment 617); November 1, 2003 (amendment 653); November 1, 2009 (amendment 736); November 1, 2011 (amendments 752 and 760).

§2J1.2. Obstruction of Justice

(a) Base Offense Level: **14**

(b) Specific Offense Characteristics

    (1) (Apply the greatest):

        (A) If the (i) defendant was convicted under 18 U.S.C. § 1001; and (ii) statutory maximum term of eight years' imprisonment applies because the matter relates to sex offenses under 18 U.S.C. § 1591 or chapters 109A, 109B, 110, or 117 of title 18, United States Code, increase by **4** levels.

        (B) If the offense involved causing or threatening to cause physical injury to a person, or property damage, in order to obstruct the administration of justice, increase by **8** levels.

        (C) If the (i) defendant was convicted under 18 U.S.C. § 1001 or § 1505; and (ii) statutory maximum term of eight years' imprisonment applies because the matter relates to international terrorism or domestic terrorism, increase by **12** levels.

    (2) If the offense resulted in substantial interference with the administration of justice, increase by **3** levels.

    (3) If the offense (A) involved the destruction, alteration, or fabrication of a substantial number of records, documents, or tangible objects; (B) involved the selection of any essential or especially probative record, document, or tangible object, to destroy or alter; or (C) was otherwise extensive in scope, planning, or preparation, increase by **2** levels.

(c) Cross Reference

    (1) If the offense involved obstructing the investigation or prosecution of a criminal offense, apply §2X3.1 (Accessory After the Fact) in respect to that criminal offense, if the resulting offense level is greater than that determined above.

Commentary

Statutory Provisions: 18 U.S.C. §§ 1001 (when the statutory maximum term of eight years' imprisonment applies because the matter relates to international terrorism or domestic terrorism, or to sex offenses under 18 U.S.C. § 1591 or chapters 109A, 109B, 110, or 117 of title 18, United States Code), 1503, 1505–1513, 1516, 1519. For additional statutory provision(s), *see* Appendix A (Statutory Index).

Application Notes:

1. **Definitions.**—For purposes of this guideline:

    "*Domestic terrorism*" has the meaning given that term in 18 U.S.C. § 2331(5).

    "*International terrorism*" has the meaning given that term in 18 U.S.C. § 2331(1).

    "*Records, documents, or tangible objects*" includes (A) records, documents, or tangible objects that are stored on, or that are, magnetic, optical, digital, other electronic, or other storage mediums or devices; and (B) wire or electronic communications.

    "*Substantial interference with the administration of justice*" includes a premature or improper termination of a felony investigation; an indictment, verdict, or any judicial determination based upon perjury, false testimony, or other false evidence; or the unnecessary expenditure of substantial governmental or court resources.

2. **Chapter Three Adjustments.**—

    (A) **Inapplicability of §3C1.1.**—For offenses covered under this section, §3C1.1 (Obstructing or Impeding the Administration of Justice) does not apply, unless the defendant obstructed the investigation, prosecution, or sentencing of the obstruction of justice count.

    (B) **Interaction with Terrorism Adjustment.**—If §3A1.4 (Terrorism) applies, do not apply subsection (b)(1)(C).

3. **Convictions for the Underlying Offense.**—In the event that the defendant is convicted of an offense sentenced under this section as well as for the underlying offense (*i.e.*, the offense that is the object of the obstruction), *see* the Commentary to Chapter Three, Part C (Obstruction and Related Adjustments), and to §3D1.2(c) (Groups of Closely Related Counts).

4. **Upward Departure Considerations.**—If a weapon was used, or bodily injury or significant property damage resulted, an upward departure may be warranted. *See* Chapter Five, Part K (Departures). In a case involving an act of extreme violence (for example, retaliating against a government witness by throwing acid in the witness's face) or a particularly serious sex offense, an upward departure would be warranted.

5. **Subsection (b)(1)(B).**—The inclusion of "property damage" under subsection (b)(1)(B) is designed to address cases in which property damage is caused or threatened as a means of intimidation or retaliation (*e.g.*, to intimidate a witness from, or retaliate against a witness for, testifying). Subsection (b)(1)(B) is not intended to apply, for example, where the offense consisted of destroying a ledger containing an incriminating entry.

Background: This section addresses offenses involving the obstruction of justice generally prosecuted under the above-referenced statutory provisions. Numerous offenses of varying seriousness may constitute obstruction of justice: using threats or force to intimidate or influence a juror or federal officer; obstructing a civil or administrative proceeding; stealing or altering court records; unlawfully intercepting grand jury deliberations; obstructing a criminal investigation; obstructing a state or local investigation of illegal gambling; using intimidation or force to influence testimony, alter evidence, evade legal process, or obstruct the communication of a judge or law enforcement officer; or causing a witness bodily injury or property damage in retaliation for providing testimony, information or evidence in a federal proceeding. The conduct that gives rise to the violation may, therefore, range from a mere threat to an act of extreme violence.

The specific offense characteristics reflect the more serious forms of obstruction. Because the conduct covered by this guideline is frequently part of an effort to avoid punishment for an offense that the defendant has committed or to assist another person to escape punishment for an offense, a cross reference to §2X3.1 (Accessory After the Fact) is provided. Use of this cross reference will provide an enhanced offense level when the obstruction is in respect to a particularly serious offense, whether such offense was committed by the defendant or another person.

Historical Note	Effective November 1, 1987. Amended effective November 1, 1989 (amendments 172–174); November 1, 1991 (amendment 401); January 25, 2003 (amendment 647); November 1, 2003 (amendment 653); October 24, 2005 (amendment 676); November 1, 2006 (amendment 690); November 1, 2007 (amendment 701); November 1, 2011 (amendment 758); November 1, 2013 (amendment 777).

§2J1.3.   Perjury or Subornation of Perjury; Bribery of Witness

(a)   Base Offense Level: **14**

(b)   Specific Offense Characteristics

   (1)   If the offense involved causing or threatening to cause physical injury to a person, or property damage, in order to suborn perjury, increase by **8** levels.

   (2)   If the perjury, subornation of perjury, or witness bribery resulted in substantial interference with the administration of justice, increase by **3** levels.

(c)   Cross Reference

   (1)   If the offense involved perjury, subornation of perjury, or witness bribery in respect to a criminal offense, apply §2X3.1 (Accessory After the Fact) in respect to that criminal offense, if the resulting offense level is greater than that determined above.

(d)   Special Instruction

   (1)   In the case of counts of perjury or subornation of perjury arising from testimony given, or to be given, in separate proceedings, do not group the counts together under §3D1.2 (Groups of Closely Related Counts).

Commentary

Statutory Provisions: 18 U.S.C. §§ 201(b)(3), (4), 1621–1623. For additional statutory provision(s), *see* Appendix A (Statutory Index).

Application Notes:

1. "*Substantial interference with the administration of justice*" includes a premature or improper termination of a felony investigation; an indictment, verdict, or any judicial determination based upon perjury, false testimony, or other false evidence; or the unnecessary expenditure of substantial governmental or court resources.

2. For offenses covered under this section, §3C1.1 (Obstructing or Impeding the Administration of Justice) does not apply, unless the defendant obstructed the investigation or trial of the perjury count.

3. In the event that the defendant is convicted under this section as well as for the underlying offense (*i.e.*, the offense with respect to which he committed perjury, subornation of perjury, or witness bribery), *see* the Commentary to §3C1.1, and to §3D1.2(c) (Groups of Closely Related Counts).

4. If a weapon was used, or bodily injury or significant property damage resulted, an upward departure may be warranted. *See* Chapter Five, Part K (Departures).

5. "*Separate proceedings*," as used in subsection (d)(1), includes different proceedings in the same case or matter (*e.g.*, a grand jury proceeding and a trial, or a trial and retrial), and proceedings in separate cases or matters (*e.g.*, separate trials of codefendants), but does not include multiple grand jury proceedings in the same case.

Background: This section applies to perjury, subornation of perjury, and witness bribery, generally prosecuted under the referenced statutes. The guidelines provide a higher penalty for perjury than the pre-guidelines practice estimate of ten months imprisonment. The Commission believes that perjury should be treated similarly to obstruction of justice. Therefore, the same considerations for enhancing a sentence are applied in the specific offense characteristics, and an alternative reference to the guideline for accessory after the fact is made.

Historical Note	Effective November 1, 1987. Amended effective November 1, 1989 (amendment 175); November 1, 1991 (amendments 401 and 402); November 1, 1993 (amendment 481); November 1, 2003 (amendment 653); November 1, 2011 (amendment 758); November 1, 2013 (amendment 777).

§2J1.4. Impersonation

(a) Base Offense Level: **6**

(b) Specific Offense Characteristic

(1) If the impersonation was committed for the purpose of conducting an unlawful arrest, detention, or search, increase by **6** levels.

    (c)   Cross Reference

        (1)   If the impersonation was to facilitate another offense, apply the guideline for an attempt to commit that offense, if the resulting offense level is greater than the offense level determined above.

Commentary

Statutory Provisions: 18 U.S.C. §§ 912, 913.

Background: This section applies to impersonation of a federal officer, agent, or employee; and impersonation to conduct an unlawful search or arrest.

Historical Note	Effective November 1, 1987. Amended effective November 1, 1989 (amendment 176).

§2J1.5.   Failure to Appear by Material Witness

    (a)   Base Offense Level:

        (1)   **6**, if in respect to a felony; or

        (2)   **4**, if in respect to a misdemeanor.

    (b)   Specific Offense Characteristic

        (1)   If the offense resulted in substantial interference with the administration of justice, increase by **3** levels.

Commentary

Statutory Provisions: 18 U.S.C. § 3146(b)(1)(B). For additional statutory provision(s), *see* Appendix A (Statutory Index).

Application Notes:

1.   "*Substantial interference with the administration of justice*" includes a premature or improper termination of a felony investigation; an indictment, verdict, or any judicial determination based upon perjury, false testimony, or other false evidence; or the unnecessary expenditure of substantial governmental or court resources.

2.   By statute, a term of imprisonment imposed for an offense under 18 U.S.C. § 3146(b)(1)(B) runs consecutively to any other term of imprisonment imposed. 18 U.S.C. § 3146(b)(2).

Background: This section applies to a failure to appear by a material witness. The base offense level incorporates a distinction as to whether the failure to appear was in respect to a felony or misdemeanor prosecution. The offense under 18 U.S.C. § 3146(b)(1)(B) is a misdemeanor for which the maximum period of imprisonment authorized by statute is one year.

<table>
<tr><td>Historical
Note</td><td>Effective November 1, 1987. Amended effective November 1, 1989 (amendment 177); November 1, 1991 (amendment 401); November 1, 2009 (amendment 737).</td></tr>
</table>

§2J1.6.   Failure to Appear by Defendant

(a)   Base Offense Level:

    (1)   **11**, if the offense constituted a failure to report for service of sentence; or

    (2)   **6**, otherwise.

(b)   Specific Offense Characteristics

    (1)   If the base offense level is determined under subsection (a)(1), and the defendant—

        (A)   voluntarily surrendered within 96 hours of the time he was originally scheduled to report, decrease by **5** levels; or

        (B)   was ordered to report to a community corrections center, community treatment center, "halfway house," or similar facility, and subdivision (A) above does not apply, decrease by **2** levels.

        Provided, however, that this reduction shall not apply if the defendant, while away from the facility, committed any federal, state, or local offense punishable by a term of imprisonment of one year or more.

    (2)   If the base offense level is determined under subsection (a)(2), and the underlying offense is—

        (A)   punishable by death or imprisonment for a term of fifteen years or more, increase by **9** levels; or

        (B)   punishable by a term of imprisonment of five years or more, but less than fifteen years, increase by **6** levels; or

        (C)   a felony punishable by a term of imprisonment of less than five years, increase by **3** levels.

§2J1.6

Statutory Provision: 18 U.S.C. § 3146(b)(1).

Application Notes:

1. "*Underlying offense*" means the offense in respect to which the defendant failed to appear.

2. For offenses covered under this section, §3C1.1 (Obstructing or Impeding the Administration of Justice) does not apply, unless the defendant obstructed the investigation or trial of the failure to appear count.

3. In the case of a failure to appear for service of sentence, any term of imprisonment imposed on the failure to appear count is to be imposed consecutively to any term of imprisonment imposed for the underlying offense. *See* §5G1.3(a). The guideline range for the failure to appear count is to be determined independently and the grouping rules of §§3D1.1–3D1.5 do not apply.

    However, in the case of a conviction on both the underlying offense and the failure to appear, other than a case of failure to appear for service of sentence, the failure to appear is treated under §3C1.1 (Obstructing or Impeding the Administration of Justice) as an obstruction of the underlying offense, and the failure to appear count and the count or counts for the underlying offense are grouped together under §3D1.2(c). (Note that 18 U.S.C. § 3146(b)(2) does not require a sentence of imprisonment on a failure to appear count, although if a sentence of imprisonment on the failure to appear count is imposed, the statute requires that the sentence be imposed to run consecutively to any other sentence of imprisonment. Therefore, unlike a count in which the statute mandates both a minimum and a consecutive sentence of imprisonment, the grouping rules of §§3D1.1–3D1.5 apply. *See* §3D1.1(b)(1), comment. (n.1), and §3D1.2, comment. (n.1).) The combined sentence will then be constructed to provide a "total punishment" that satisfies the requirements both of §5G1.2 (Sentencing on Multiple Counts of Conviction) and 18 U.S.C. § 3146(b)(2). For example, if the combined applicable guideline range for both counts is 30–37 months and the court determines that a "total punishment" of 36 months is appropriate, a sentence of 30 months for the underlying offense plus a consecutive six months' sentence for the failure to appear count would satisfy these requirements. (Note that the combination of this instruction and increasing the offense level for the obstructive, failure to appear conduct has the effect of ensuring an incremental, consecutive punishment for the failure to appear count, as required by 18 U.S.C. § 3146(b)(2).)

4. If a defendant is convicted of both the underlying offense and the failure to appear count, and the defendant committed additional acts of obstructive behavior (*e.g.*, perjury) during the investigation, prosecution, or sentencing of the instant offense, an upward departure may be warranted. The upward departure will ensure an enhanced sentence for obstructive conduct for which no adjustment under §3C1.1 (Obstructing or Impeding the Administration of Justice) is made because of the operation of the rules set out in Application Note 3.

5. In some cases, the defendant may be sentenced on the underlying offense (the offense in respect to which the defendant failed to appear) before being sentenced on the failure to appear offense. In such cases, criminal history points for the sentence imposed on the underlying offense are to be counted in determining the guideline range on the failure to appear offense only where the offense level is determined under subsection (a)(1) (*i.e.*, where the offense constituted a failure to report for service of sentence).

Background: This section applies to a failure to appear by a defendant who was released pending trial, sentencing, appeal, or surrender for service of sentence. Where the base offense level is determined under subsection (a)(2), the offense level increases in relation to the statutory maximum of the underlying offense.

Historical Note	Effective November 1, 1987. Amended effective November 1, 1990 (amendment 329); November 1, 1991 (amendment 403); November 1, 1998 (amendment 579); November 1, 2001 (amendment 636); November 1, 2005 (amendment 680); November 1, 2011 (amendment 758); November 1, 2013 (amendment 777).

§2J1.7. [Deleted]

Historical Note	Effective November 1, 1987. Amended effective January 15, 1988 (amendment 32); November 1, 1989 (amendment 178); November 1, 1991 (amendment 431); was deleted from Chapter Two and replaced by §3C1.3 effective November 1, 2006 (amendment 684).

§2J1.8. [Deleted]

Historical Note	Section 2J1.8 (Bribery of Witness), effective November 1, 1987, amended effective January 15, 1988 (amendment 33), November 1, 1989 (amendment 179), and November 1, 1991 (amendment 401), was deleted by consolidation with §2J1.3 effective November 1, 1993 (amendment 481).

§2J1.9.   Payment to Witness

(a)   Base Offense Level: **6**

(b)   Specific Offense Characteristic

(1)   If the payment was made or offered for refusing to testify or for the witness absenting himself to avoid testifying, increase by 4 levels.

Commentary

Statutory Provisions: 18 U.S.C. § 201(c)(2), (3).

Application Notes:

1.   For offenses covered under this section, §3C1.1 (Obstructing or Impeding the Administration of Justice) does not apply unless the defendant obstructed the investigation or trial of the payment to witness count.

2. In the event that the defendant is convicted under this section as well as for the under-lying offense (*i.e.*, the offense with respect to which the payment was made), *see* the Commentary to §3C1.1, and to §3D1.2(c) (Groups of Closely Related Counts).

Background: This section applies to witness gratuities in federal proceedings.

Historical Note	Effective November 1, 1987. Amended effective November 1, 1989 (amendments 180 and 181); November 1, 2011 (amendment 758); November 1, 2013 (amendment 777).

PART K — OFFENSES INVOLVING PUBLIC SAFETY

1. EXPLOSIVES AND ARSON

§2K1.1. Failure to Report Theft of Explosive Materials; Improper Storage of Explosive Materials

(a) Base Offense Level: **6**

Commentary

Statutory Provisions: 18 U.S.C. §§ 842(j), (k), 844(b). For additional statutory provision(s), *see* Appendix A (Statutory Index).

Background: The above-referenced provisions are misdemeanors. The maximum term of imprisonment authorized by statute is one year.

Historical Note	Effective November 1, 1987. Amended effective November 1, 1991 (amendment 404); November 1, 1993 (amendment 481).

§2K1.2. [Deleted]

Historical Note	Section 2K1.2 (Improper Storage of Explosive Materials), effective November 1, 1987, amended effective November 1, 1991 (amendment 404), was deleted by consolidation with §2K1.1 effective November 1, 1993 (amendment 481).

§2K1.3. Unlawful Receipt, Possession, or Transportation of Explosive Materials; Prohibited Transactions Involving Explosive Materials

(a) Base Offense Level (Apply the Greatest):

(1) **24**, if the defendant committed any part of the instant offense subsequent to sustaining at least two felony convictions of either a crime of violence or a controlled substance offense;

(2) **20**, if the defendant committed any part of the instant offense subsequent to sustaining one felony conviction of either a crime of violence or a controlled substance offense;

(3) **18**, if the defendant was convicted under 18 U.S.C. § 842(p)(2);

(4) **16**, if the defendant (A) was a prohibited person at the time the defendant committed the instant offense; or (B) knowingly distributed explosive materials to a prohibited person; or

(5) **12**, otherwise.

(b) Specific Offense Characteristics

(1) If the offense involved twenty-five pounds or more of explosive materials, increase as follows:

WEIGHT OF EXPLOSIVE MATERIAL	INCREASE IN LEVEL
(A) At least 25 but less than 100 lbs.	add **1**
(B) At least 100 but less than 250 lbs.	add **2**
(C) At least 250 but less than 500 lbs.	add **3**
(D) At least 500 but less than 1000 lbs.	add **4**
(E) 1000 lbs. or more	add **5**.

(2) If the offense involved any explosive material that the defendant knew or had reason to believe was stolen, increase by **2** levels.

Provided, that the cumulative offense level determined above shall not exceed level **29**.

(3) If the defendant (A) was convicted under 18 U.S.C. § 842(p)(2); or (B) used or possessed any explosive material in connection with another felony offense; or possessed or transferred any explosive material with knowledge, intent, or reason to believe that it would be used or possessed in connection with another felony offense, increase by **4** levels. If the resulting offense level is less than level **18**, increase to level **18**.

(c) Cross Reference

(1) If the defendant (A) was convicted under 18 U.S.C. § 842(p)(2); or (B) used or possessed any explosive material in connection with the commission or attempted commission of another offense, or possessed or transferred any explosive material with knowledge or intent that it would be used or possessed in connection with another offense, apply—

(A) §2X1.1 (Attempt, Solicitation, or Conspiracy) in respect to that other offense if the resulting offense level is greater than that determined above; or

(B) if death resulted, the most analogous offense guideline from Chapter Two, Part A, Subpart 1 (Homicide), if the resulting offense level is greater than that determined above.

Commentary

Statutory Provisions: 18 U.S.C. §§ 842(a)–(e), (h), (i), (l)–(o), (p)(2), 844(d), (g), 1716, 2283; 26 U.S.C. § 5685.

Application Notes:

1. "*Explosive material(s)*" include explosives, blasting agents, and detonators. *See* 18 U.S.C. § 841(c). "Explosives" is defined at 18 U.S.C. § 844(j). A destructive device, defined in the Commentary to §1B1.1 (Application Instructions), may contain explosive materials. Where the conduct charged in the count of which the defendant was convicted establishes that the offense involved a destructive device, apply §2K2.1 (Unlawful Receipt, Possession, or Transportation of Firearms or Ammunition; Prohibited Transactions Involving Firearms or Ammunition) if the resulting offense level is greater.

2. For purposes of this guideline:

   "*Controlled substance offense*" has the meaning given that term in §4B1.2(b) and Application Note 1 of the Commentary to §4B1.2 (Definitions of Terms Used in Section 4B1.1).

   "*Crime of violence*" has the meaning given that term in §4B1.2(a) and Application Note 1 of the Commentary to §4B1.2.

   "*Felony conviction*" means a prior adult federal or state conviction for an offense punishable by death or imprisonment for a term exceeding one year, regardless of whether such offense is specifically designated as a felony and regardless of the actual sentence imposed. A conviction for an offense committed at age eighteen years or older is an adult conviction. A conviction for an offense committed prior to age eighteen years is an adult conviction if it is classified as an adult conviction under the laws of the jurisdiction in which the defendant was convicted (*e.g.*, a federal conviction for an offense committed prior to the defendant's eighteenth birthday is an adult conviction if the defendant was expressly proceeded against as an adult).

3. For purposes of subsection (a)(4), "*prohibited person*" means any person described in 18 U.S.C. § 842(i).

4. "*Felony offense*," as used in subsection (b)(3), means any offense (federal, state, or local) punishable by imprisonment for a term exceeding one year, whether or not a criminal charge was brought, or conviction obtained.

5. For purposes of calculating the weight of explosive materials under subsection (b)(1), include only the weight of the actual explosive material and the weight of packaging material that is necessary for the use or detonation of the explosives. Exclude the weight of any other shipping or packaging materials. For example, the paper and fuse on a stick of dynamite would be included; the box that the dynamite was shipped in would not be included.

6. For purposes of calculating the weight of explosive materials under subsection (b)(1), count only those explosive materials that were unlawfully sought to be obtained, unlawfully possessed, or unlawfully distributed, including any explosive material that a defendant attempted to obtain by making a false statement.

7. If the defendant is convicted under 18 U.S.C. § 842(h) (offense involving stolen explosive materials), and is convicted of no other offenses subject to this guideline, do not apply the adjustment in subsection (b)(2) because the base offense level itself takes such conduct into account.

8. Under subsection (c)(1), the offense level for the underlying offense (which may be a federal, state, or local offense) is to be determined under §2X1.1 (Attempt, Solicitation, or Conspiracy) or, if death results, under the most analogous guideline from Chapter Two, Part A, Subpart 1 (Homicide).

9. For purposes of applying subsection (a)(1) or (2), use only those felony convictions that receive criminal history points under §4A1.1(a), (b), or (c). In addition, for purposes of applying subsection (a)(1), use only those felony convictions that are counted separately under §4A1.1(a), (b), or (c). *See* §4A1.2(a)(2).

    Prior felony conviction(s) resulting in an increased base offense level under subsection (a)(1), (a)(2), or (a)(4) are also counted for purposes of determining criminal history points pursuant to Chapter Four, Part A (Criminal History).

10. An upward departure may be warranted in any of the following circumstances: (A) the quantity of explosive materials significantly exceeded 1000 pounds; (B) the explosive materials were of a nature more volatile or dangerous than dynamite or conventional powder explosives (*e.g.*, plastic explosives); (C) the defendant knowingly distributed explosive materials to a person under twenty-one years of age; or (D) the offense posed a substantial risk of death or bodily injury to multiple individuals.

11. As used in subsections (b)(3) and (c)(1), "*another felony offense*" and "*another offense*" refer to offenses other than explosives or firearms possession or trafficking offenses. However, where the defendant used or possessed a firearm or explosive to facilitate another firearms or explosives offense (*e.g.*, the defendant used or possessed a firearm to protect the delivery of an unlawful shipment of explosives), an upward departure under §5K2.6 (Weapons and Dangerous Instrumentalities) may be warranted.

    In addition, for purposes of subsection (c)(1)(A), "*that other offense*" means, with respect to an offense under 18 U.S.C. § 842(p)(2), the underlying Federal crime of violence.

Historical Note	Effective November 1, 1987. Amended effective November 1, 1989 (amendment 183); November 1, 1991 (amendment 373); November 1, 1992 (amendment 471); November 1, 1993 (amendment 478); November 1, 1995 (amendment 534); November 1, 1997 (amendment 568); November 1, 2001 (amendments 629 and 630); November 1, 2002 (amendment 646); November 1, 2003 (amendment 655); November 1, 2007 (amendment 700); November 1, 2010 (amendments 746 and 747).

§2K1.4. Arson; Property Damage by Use of Explosives

(a) Base Offense Level (Apply the Greatest):

(1) **24**, if the offense (A) created a substantial risk of death or serious bodily injury to any person other than a participant in the offense, and that risk was created knowingly; or (B) involved the destruction or attempted destruction of a dwelling, an airport, an aircraft, a mass transportation facility, a mass transportation vehicle, a maritime facility, a vessel, or a vessel's cargo, a public transportation system, a state or government facility, an infrastructure facility, or a place of public use;

(2) **20**, if the offense (A) created a substantial risk of death or serious bodily injury to any person other than a participant in the offense; (B) involved the destruction or attempted destruction of a structure other than (i) a dwelling, or (ii) an airport, an aircraft, a mass transportation facility, a mass transportation vehicle, a maritime facility, a vessel, or a vessel's cargo, a public transportation system, a state or government facility, an infrastructure facility, or a place of public use; or (C) endangered (i) a dwelling, (ii) a structure other than a dwelling, or (iii) an airport, an aircraft, a mass transportation facility, a mass transportation vehicle, a maritime facility, a vessel, or a vessel's cargo, a public transportation system, a state or government facility, an infrastructure facility, or a place of public use;

(3) **16**, if the offense involved the destruction of or tampering with aids to maritime navigation; or

(4) **2** plus the offense level from §2B1.1 (Theft, Property Destruction, and Fraud).

(b) Specific Offense Characteristics

(1) If the offense was committed to conceal another offense, increase by **2** levels.

(2) If the base offense level is not determined under (a)(4), and the offense occurred on a national cemetery, increase by **2** levels.

(c) Cross Reference

(1) If death resulted, or the offense was intended to cause death or serious bodily injury, apply the most analogous guideline from

Chapter Two, Part A (Offenses Against the Person) if the resulting offense level is greater than that determined above.

Commentary

Statutory Provisions: 18 U.S.C. §§ 32(a), (b), 33, 81, 844(f), (h) (only in the case of an offense committed prior to November 18, 1988), (i), 1855, 1992(a)(1), (a)(2), (a)(4), 2275, 2282A, 2282B, 2291, 2332a, 2332f; 49 U.S.C. § 60123(b). For additional statutory provision(s), *see* Appendix A (Statutory Index).

Application Notes:

1. **Definitions.**—For purposes of this guideline:

    "*Aids to maritime navigation*" means any device external to a vessel intended to assist the navigator to determine position or save course, or to warn of dangers or obstructions to navigation.

    "*Explosives*" includes any explosive, explosive material, or destructive device.

    "*Maritime facility*" means any structure or facility of any kind located in, on, under, or adjacent to any waters subject to the jurisdiction of the United States and used, operated, or maintained by a public or private entity, including any contiguous or adjoining property under common ownership or operation.

    "*National cemetery*" means a cemetery (A) established under section 2400 of title 38, United States Code; or (B) under the jurisdiction of the Secretary of the Army, the Secretary of the Navy, the Secretary of the Air Force, or the Secretary of the Interior.

    "*Mass transportation*" has the meaning given that term in 18 U.S.C. § 1992(d)(7).

    "*State or government facility*", "*infrastructure facility*", "*place of public use*", and "*public transportation system*" have the meaning given those terms in 18 U.S.C. § 2332f(e)(3), (5), (6), and (7), respectively.

    "*Vessel*" includes every description of watercraft or other artificial contrivance used, or capable of being used, as a means of transportation on water.

2. **Risk of Death or Serious Bodily Injury.**—Creating a substantial risk of death or serious bodily injury includes creating that risk to fire fighters and other emergency and law enforcement personnel who respond to or investigate an offense.

3. **Upward Departure Provision.**—If bodily injury resulted, an upward departure may be warranted. *See* Chapter Five, Part K (Departures).

Background: Subsection (b)(2) implements the directive to the Commission in section 2 of Public Law 105–101.

Historical Note	Effective November 1, 1987. Amended effective November 1, 1989 (amendments 182, 184, and 185); November 1, 1990 (amendment 330); November 1, 1991 (amendment 404); November 1, 1998 (amendment 576); November 1, 2001 (amendment 617); November 1, 2002 (amendment 637); November 1, 2003 (amendment 655); November 1, 2007 (amendments 699 and 700); November 1, 2014 (amendment 781).

§2K1.5. Possessing Dangerous Weapons or Materials While Boarding or Aboard an Aircraft

(a)   Base Offense Level: **9**

(b)   Specific Offense Characteristics

If more than one applies, use the greatest:

(1)   If the offense was committed willfully and without regard for the safety of human life, or with reckless disregard for the safety of human life, increase by **15** levels.

(2)   If the defendant was prohibited by another federal law from possessing the weapon or material, increase by **2** levels.

(3)   If the defendant's possession of the weapon or material would have been lawful but for 49 U.S.C. § 46505 and he acted with mere negligence, decrease by **3** levels.

(c)   Cross Reference

(1)   If the defendant used or possessed the weapon or material in committing or attempting another offense, apply the guideline for such other offense, or §2X1.1 (Attempt, Solicitation, or Conspiracy), as appropriate, if the resulting offense level is greater than that determined above.

Commentary

Statutory Provision: 49 U.S.C. § 46505 (formerly 49 U.S.C. § 1472(l)).

Background: This guideline provides an enhancement where the defendant was a person prohibited by federal law from possession of the weapon or material. A decrease is provided in a case of mere negligence where the defendant was otherwise authorized to possess the weapon or material.

Historical Note	Effective November 1, 1987. Amended effective November 1, 1989 (amendments 182, 186, 187, and 303); November 1, 1991 (amendment 404); November 1, 1992 (amendment 443); November 1, 1995 (amendment 534); November 1, 1997 (amendment 560).

§2K1.6. Licensee Recordkeeping Violations Involving Explosive Materials

(a)   Base Offense Level: **6**

    (b) Cross Reference

        (1) If a recordkeeping offense reflected an effort to conceal a substantive explosive materials offense, apply §2K1.3 (Unlawful Receipt, Possession, or Transportation of Explosives Materials; Prohibited Transactions Involving Explosive Materials).

Commentary

Statutory Provisions: 18 U.S.C. § 842(f), (g).

Background: The above-referenced provisions are recordkeeping offenses applicable only to "*licensees*," who are defined at 18 U.S.C. § 841(m).

Historical Note	Effective November 1, 1991 (amendment 373). A former §2K1.6 (Shipping, Transporting, or Receiving Explosives with Felonious Intent or Knowledge; Using or Carrying Explosives in Certain Crimes), effective November 1, 1987, amended effective November 1, 1989 (amendment 303) and November 1, 1990 (amendment 331), was deleted by consolidation with §2K1.3 effective November 1, 1991 (amendment 373).

§2K1.7. [Deleted]

Historical Note	Section 2K1.7 (Use of Fire or Explosives to Commit a Federal Felony), effective November 1, 1989 (amendment 188), amended effective November 1, 1990 (amendment 332), was deleted by consolidation with §2K2.4 effective November 1, 1993 (amendment 481).

*   *   *   *   *   *

2. FIREARMS

§2K2.1. Unlawful Receipt, Possession, or Transportation of Firearms or Ammunition; Prohibited Transactions Involving Firearms or Ammunition

    (a) Base Offense Level (Apply the Greatest):

        (1) **26**, if (A) the offense involved a (i) semiautomatic firearm that is capable of accepting a large capacity magazine; or (ii) firearm that is described in 26 U.S.C. § 5845(a); and (B) the defendant committed any part of the instant offense subsequent to sustaining at least two felony convictions of either a crime of violence or a controlled substance offense;

        (2) **24**, if the defendant committed any part of the instant offense subsequent to sustaining at least two felony convictions of either a crime of violence or a controlled substance offense;

(3) **22**, if (A) the offense involved a (i) semiautomatic firearm that is capable of accepting a large capacity magazine; or (ii) firearm that is described in 26 U.S.C. § 5845(a); and (B) the defendant committed any part of the instant offense subsequent to sustaining one felony conviction of either a crime of violence or a controlled substance offense;

(4) **20**, if—

    (A) the defendant committed any part of the instant offense subsequent to sustaining one felony conviction of either a crime of violence or a controlled substance offense; or

    (B) the (i) offense involved a (I) semiautomatic firearm that is capable of accepting a large capacity magazine; or (II) firearm that is described in 26 U.S.C. § 5845(a); and (ii) defendant (I) was a prohibited person at the time the defendant committed the instant offense; (II) is convicted under 18 U.S.C. § 922(d); or (III) is convicted under 18 U.S.C. § 922(a)(6) or § 924(a)(1)(A) and committed the offense with knowledge, intent, or reason to believe that the offense would result in the transfer of a firearm or ammunition to a prohibited person;

(5) **18**, if the offense involved a firearm described in 26 U.S.C. § 5845(a);

(6) **14**, if the defendant (A) was a prohibited person at the time the defendant committed the instant offense; (B) is convicted under 18 U.S.C. § 922(d); or (C) is convicted under 18 U.S.C. § 922(a)(6) or § 924(a)(1)(A) and committed the offense with knowledge, intent, or reason to believe that the offense would result in the transfer of a firearm or ammunition to a prohibited person;

(7) **12**, except as provided below; or

(8) **6**, if the defendant is convicted under 18 U.S.C. § 922(c), (e), (f), (m), (s), (t), or (x)(1), or 18 U.S.C. § 1715.

(b) Specific Offense Characteristics

(1) If the offense involved three or more firearms, increase as follows:

	NUMBER OF FIREARMS	INCREASE IN LEVEL
(A)	3–7	add **2**
(B)	8–24	add **4**
(C)	25–99	add **6**
(D)	100–199	add **8**
(E)	200 or more	add **10**.

(2) If the defendant, other than a defendant subject to subsection (a)(1), (a)(2), (a)(3), (a)(4), or (a)(5), possessed all ammunition and firearms solely for lawful sporting purposes or collection, and did not unlawfully discharge or otherwise unlawfully use such firearms or ammunition, decrease the offense level determined above to level **6**.

(3) If the offense involved—

(A) a destructive device that is a portable rocket, a missile, or a device for use in launching a portable rocket or a missile, increase by **15** levels; or

(B) a destructive device other than a destructive device referred to in subdivision (A), increase by **2** levels.

(4) If any firearm (A) was stolen, increase by **2** levels; or (B) had an altered or obliterated serial number, increase by **4** levels.

The cumulative offense level determined from the application of subsections (b)(1) through (b)(4) may not exceed level **29**, except if subsection (b)(3)(A) applies.

(5) If the defendant engaged in the trafficking of firearms, increase by **4** levels.

(6) If the defendant—

(A) possessed any firearm or ammunition while leaving or attempting to leave the United States, or possessed or transferred any firearm or ammunition with knowledge, intent, or reason to believe that it would be transported out of the United States; or

(B) used or possessed any firearm or ammunition in connection with another felony offense; or possessed or transferred any firearm or ammunition with knowledge, intent, or reason to believe that it would be used or possessed in connection with another felony offense,

increase by **4** levels. If the resulting offense level is less than level **18**, increase to level **18**.

(7) If a recordkeeping offense reflected an effort to conceal a substantive offense involving firearms or ammunition, increase to the offense level for the substantive offense.

(c) Cross Reference

(1) If the defendant used or possessed any firearm or ammunition cited in the offense of conviction in connection with the commission or attempted commission of another offense, or possessed or transferred a firearm or ammunition cited in the offense of conviction with knowledge or intent that it would be used or possessed in connection with another offense, apply—

(A) §2X1.1 (Attempt, Solicitation, or Conspiracy) in respect to that other offense, if the resulting offense level is greater than that determined above; or

(B) if death resulted, the most analogous offense guideline from Chapter Two, Part A, Subpart 1 (Homicide), if the resulting offense level is greater than that determined above.

Commentary

Statutory Provisions: 18 U.S.C. §§ 922(a)–(p), (r)–(w), (x)(1), 924(a), (b), (e)–(i), (k)–(o), 1715, 2332g; 26 U.S.C. § 5861(a)–(l). For additional statutory provisions, *see* Appendix A (Statutory Index).

Application Notes:

1. **Definitions.**—For purposes of this guideline:

    "*Ammunition*" has the meaning given that term in 18 U.S.C. § 921(a)(17)(A).

    "*Controlled substance offense*" has the meaning given that term in §4B1.2(b) and Application Note 1 of the Commentary to §4B1.2 (Definitions of Terms Used in Section 4B1.1).

    "*Crime of violence*" has the meaning given that term in §4B1.2(a) and Application Note 1 of the Commentary to §4B1.2.

"*Destructive device*" has the meaning given that term in 26 U.S.C. § 5845(f).

"*Felony conviction*" means a prior adult federal or state conviction for an offense punishable by death or imprisonment for a term exceeding one year, regardless of whether such offense is specifically designated as a felony and regardless of the actual sentence imposed. A conviction for an offense committed at age eighteen years or older is an adult conviction. A conviction for an offense committed prior to age eighteen years is an adult conviction if it is classified as an adult conviction under the laws of the jurisdiction in which the defendant was convicted (*e.g.*, a federal conviction for an offense committed prior to the defendant's eighteenth birthday is an adult conviction if the defendant was expressly proceeded against as an adult).

"*Firearm*" has the meaning given that term in 18 U.S.C. § 921(a)(3).

2. **Semiautomatic Firearm That Is Capable of Accepting a Large Capacity Magazine.**—For purposes of subsections (a)(1), (a)(3), and (a)(4), a "*semiautomatic firearm that is capable of accepting a large capacity magazine*" means a semiautomatic firearm that has the ability to fire many rounds without reloading because at the time of the offense (A) the firearm had attached to it a magazine or similar device that could accept more than 15 rounds of ammunition; or (B) a magazine or similar device that could accept more than 15 rounds of ammunition was in close proximity to the firearm. This definition does not include a semiautomatic firearm with an attached tubular device capable of operating only with .22 caliber rim fire ammunition.

3. **Definition of "Prohibited Person".**—For purposes of subsections (a)(4)(B) and (a)(6), "*prohibited person*" means any person described in 18 U.S.C. § 922(g) or § 922(n).

4. **Application of Subsection (a)(7).**—Subsection (a)(7) includes the interstate transportation or interstate distribution of firearms, which is frequently committed in violation of state, local, or other federal law restricting the possession of firearms, or for some other underlying unlawful purpose. In the unusual case in which it is established that neither avoidance of state, local, or other federal firearms law, nor any other underlying unlawful purpose was involved, a reduction in the base offense level to no lower than level 6 may be warranted to reflect the less serious nature of the violation.

5. **Application of Subsection (b)(1).**—For purposes of calculating the number of firearms under subsection (b)(1), count only those firearms that were unlawfully sought to be obtained, unlawfully possessed, or unlawfully distributed, including any firearm that a defendant obtained or attempted to obtain by making a false statement to a licensed dealer.

6. **Application of Subsection (b)(2).**—Under subsection (b)(2), "lawful sporting purposes or collection" as determined by the surrounding circumstances, provides for a reduction to an offense level of 6. Relevant surrounding circumstances include the number and type of firearms, the amount and type of ammunition, the location and circumstances of possession and actual use, the nature of the defendant's criminal history (*e.g.*, prior convictions for offenses involving firearms), and the extent to which possession was restricted by local law. Note that where the base offense level is determined under subsections (a)(1)–(a)(5), subsection (b)(2) is not applicable.

7. **Destructive Devices.**—A defendant whose offense involves a destructive device receives both the base offense level from the subsection applicable to a firearm listed in 26 U.S.C. § 5845(a) (*e.g.*, subsection (a)(1), (a)(3), (a)(4)(B), or (a)(5)), and the applicable

enhancement under subsection (b)(3). Such devices pose a considerably greater risk to the public welfare than other National Firearms Act weapons.

Offenses involving such devices cover a wide range of offense conduct and involve different degrees of risk to the public welfare depending on the type of destructive device involved and the location or manner in which that destructive device was possessed or transported. For example, a pipe bomb in a populated train station creates a substantially greater risk to the public welfare, and a substantially greater risk of death or serious bodily injury, than an incendiary device in an isolated area. In a case in which the cumulative result of the increased base offense level and the enhancement under subsection (b)(3) does not adequately capture the seriousness of the offense because of the type of destructive device involved, the risk to the public welfare, or the risk of death or serious bodily injury that the destructive device created, an upward departure may be warranted. *See also* §§5K2.1 (Death), 5K2.2 (Physical Injury), and 5K2.14 (Public Welfare).

8. **Application of Subsection (b)(4).—**

    (A) **Interaction with Subsection (a)(7).—**If the only offense to which §2K2.1 applies is 18 U.S.C. § 922(i), (j), or (u), or 18 U.S.C. § 924(l) or (m) (offenses involving a stolen firearm or stolen ammunition) and the base offense level is determined under subsection (a)(7), do not apply the enhancement in subsection (b)(4)(A). This is because the base offense level takes into account that the firearm or ammunition was stolen. However, if the offense involved a firearm with an altered or obliterated serial number, apply subsection (b)(4)(B).

    Similarly, if the offense to which §2K2.1 applies is 18 U.S.C. § 922(k) or 26 U.S.C. § 5861(g) or (h) (offenses involving an altered or obliterated serial number) and the base offense level is determined under subsection (a)(7), do not apply the enhancement in subsection (b)(4)(B). This is because the base offense level takes into account that the firearm had an altered or obliterated serial number. However, it the offense involved a stolen firearm or stolen ammunition, apply subsection (b)(4)(A).

    (B) **Knowledge or Reason to Believe.—**Subsection (b)(4) applies regardless of whether the defendant knew or had reason to believe that the firearm was stolen or had an altered or obliterated serial number.

9. **Application of Subsection (b)(7).—**Under subsection (b)(7), if a record-keeping offense was committed to conceal a substantive firearms or ammunition offense, the offense level is increased to the offense level for the substantive firearms or ammunition offense (*e.g.*, if the defendant falsifies a record to conceal the sale of a firearm to a prohibited person, the offense level is increased to the offense level applicable to the sale of a firearm to a prohibited person).

10. **Prior Felony Convictions.—**For purposes of applying subsection (a)(1), (2), (3), or (4)(A), use only those felony convictions that receive criminal history points under §4A1.1(a), (b), or (c). In addition, for purposes of applying subsection (a)(1) and (a)(2), use only those felony convictions that are counted separately under §4A1.1(a), (b), or (c). *See* §4A1.2(a)(2).

    Prior felony conviction(s) resulting in an increased base offense level under subsection (a)(1), (a)(2), (a)(3), (a)(4)(A), (a)(4)(B), or (a)(6) are also counted for purposes of determining criminal history points pursuant to Chapter Four, Part A (Criminal History).

11. **Upward Departure Provisions.**—An upward departure may be warranted in any of the following circumstances: (A) the number of firearms substantially exceeded 200; (B) the offense involved multiple National Firearms Act weapons (*e.g.*, machineguns, destructive devices), military type assault rifles, non-detectable ("plastic") firearms (defined at 18 U.S.C. § 922(p)); (C) the offense involved large quantities of armor-piercing ammunition (defined at 18 U.S.C. § 921(a)(17)(B)); or (D) the offense posed a substantial risk of death or bodily injury to multiple individuals (*see* Application Note 7).

12. **Armed Career Criminal.**—A defendant who is subject to an enhanced sentence under the provisions of 18 U.S.C. § 924(e) is an Armed Career Criminal. *See* §4B1.4.

13. **Application of Subsection (b)(5).**—

     (A) **In General.**—Subsection (b)(5) applies, regardless of whether anything of value was exchanged, if the defendant—

          (i)   transported, transferred, or otherwise disposed of two or more firearms to another individual, or received two or more firearms with the intent to transport, transfer, or otherwise dispose of firearms to another individual; and

          (ii) knew or had reason to believe that such conduct would result in the transport, transfer, or disposal of a firearm to an individual—

                (I)   whose possession or receipt of the firearm would be unlawful; or

                (II) who intended to use or dispose of the firearm unlawfully.

     (B) **Definitions.**—For purposes of this subsection:

          "*Individual whose possession or receipt of the firearm would be unlawful*" means an individual who (i) has a prior conviction for a crime of violence, a controlled substance offense, or a misdemeanor crime of domestic violence; or (ii) at the time of the offense was under a criminal justice sentence, including probation, parole, supervised release, imprisonment, work release, or escape status. "Crime of violence" and "controlled substance offense" have the meaning given those terms in §4B1.2 (Definitions of Terms Used in Section 4B1.1). "Misdemeanor crime of domestic violence" has the meaning given that term in 18 U.S.C. § 921(a)(33)(A).

          The term "*defendant*", consistent with §1B1.3 (Relevant Conduct), limits the accountability of the defendant to the defendant's own conduct and conduct that the defendant aided or abetted, counseled, commanded, induced, procured, or willfully caused.

     (C) **Upward Departure Provision.**—If the defendant trafficked substantially more than 25 firearms, an upward departure may be warranted.

     (D) **Interaction with Other Subsections.**—In a case in which three or more firearms were both possessed and trafficked, apply both subsections (b)(1) and (b)(5). If the defendant used or transferred one of such firearms in connection with another felony offense (*i.e.*, an offense other than a firearms possession or trafficking offense) an enhancement under subsection (b)(6)(B) also would apply.

14. **Application of Subsections (b)(6)(B) and (c)(1).—**

(A) **In General.**—Subsections (b)(6)(B) and (c)(1) apply if the firearm or ammunition facilitated, or had the potential of facilitating, another felony offense or another offense, respectively. However, subsection (c)(1) contains the additional requirement that the firearm or ammunition be cited in the offense of conviction.

(B) **Application When Other Offense is Burglary or Drug Offense.**—Subsections (b)(6)(B) and (c)(1) apply (i) in a case in which a defendant who, during the course of a burglary, finds and takes a firearm, even if the defendant did not engage in any other conduct with that firearm during the course of the burglary; and (ii) in the case of a drug trafficking offense in which a firearm is found in close proximity to drugs, drug-manufacturing materials, or drug paraphernalia. In these cases, application of subsections (b)(6)(B) and, if the firearm was cited in the offense of conviction, (c)(1) is warranted because the presence of the firearm has the potential of facilitating another felony offense or another offense, respectively.

(C) **Definitions.—**

"*Another felony offense*", for purposes of subsection (b)(6)(B), means any federal, state, or local offense, other than the explosive or firearms possession or trafficking offense, punishable by imprisonment for a term exceeding one year, regardless of whether a criminal charge was brought, or a conviction obtained.

"*Another offense*", for purposes of subsection (c)(1), means any federal, state, or local offense, other than the explosive or firearms possession or trafficking offense, regardless of whether a criminal charge was brought, or a conviction obtained.

(D) **Upward Departure Provision.**—In a case in which the defendant used or possessed a firearm or explosive to facilitate another firearms or explosives offense (*e.g.*, the defendant used or possessed a firearm to protect the delivery of an unlawful shipment of explosives), an upward departure under §5K2.6 (Weapons and Dangerous Instrumentalities) may be warranted.

(E) **Relationship Between the Instant Offense and the Other Offense.**—In determining whether subsections (b)(6)(B) and (c)(1) apply, the court must consider the relationship between the instant offense and the other offense, consistent with relevant conduct principles. *See* §1B1.3(a)(1)–(4) and accompanying commentary.

In determining whether subsection (c)(1) applies, the court must also consider whether the firearm used in the other offense was a firearm cited in the offense of conviction.

For example:

(i) **Firearm Cited in the Offense of Conviction.** Defendant A's offense of conviction is for unlawfully possessing a shotgun on October 15. The court determines that, on the preceding February 10, Defendant A used the shotgun in connection with a robbery. Ordinarily, under these circumstances, subsection (b)(6)(B) applies, and the cross reference in subsection (c)(1) also applies if it results in a greater offense level.

Ordinarily, the unlawful possession of the shotgun on February 10 will be "part of the same course of conduct or common scheme or plan" as the unlawful possession of the same shotgun on October 15. *See* §1B1.3(a)(2) and accompanying commentary (including, in particular, the factors discussed in Application Note 5(B) to §1B1.3). The use of the shotgun "in connection with" the robbery is relevant conduct because it is a factor specified in subsections (b)(6)(B) and (c)(1). *See* §1B1.3(a)(4) ("any other information specified in the applicable guideline").

(ii) **Firearm Not Cited in the Offense of Conviction.** Defendant B's offense of conviction is for unlawfully possessing a shotgun on October 15. The court determines that, on the preceding February 10, Defendant B unlawfully possessed a handgun (not cited in the offense of conviction) and used the handgun in connection with a robbery.

Subsection (b)(6)(B). In determining whether subsection (b)(6)(B) applies, the threshold question for the court is whether the two unlawful possession offenses (the shotgun on October 15 and the handgun on February 10) were "part of the same course of conduct or common scheme or plan". *See* §1B1.3(a)(2) and accompanying commentary (including, in particular, the factors discussed in Application Note 5(B) to §1B1.3).

If they were, then the handgun possession offense is relevant conduct to the shotgun possession offense, and the use of the handgun "in connection with" the robbery is relevant conduct because it is a factor specified in subsection (b)(6)(B). *See* §1B1.3(a)(4) ("any other information specified in the applicable guideline"). Accordingly, subsection (b)(6)(B) applies.

On the other hand, if the court determines that the two unlawful possession offenses were not "part of the same course of conduct or common scheme or plan," then the handgun possession offense is not relevant conduct to the shotgun possession offense and subsection (b)(6)(B) does not apply.

Subsection (c)(1). Under these circumstances, the cross reference in subsection (c)(1) does not apply, because the handgun was not cited in the offense of conviction.

15. **Certain Convictions Under 18 U.S.C. §§ 922(a)(6), 922(d), and 924(a)(1)(A).**—In a case in which the defendant is convicted under 18 U.S.C. §§ 922(a)(6), 922(d), or 924(a)(1)(A), a downward departure may be warranted if (A) none of the enhancements in subsection (b) apply, (B) the defendant was motivated by an intimate or familial relationship or by threats or fear to commit the offense and was otherwise unlikely to commit such an offense, and (C) the defendant received no monetary compensation from the offense.

Historical Note	Effective November 1, 1987. Amended effective November 1, 1989 (amendment 189); November 1, 1990 (amendment 333); November 1, 1991 (amendment 374); November 1, 1992 (amendment 471); November 1, 1993 (amendment 478); November 1, 1995 (amendment 522); November 1, 1997 (amendments 568 and 575); November 1, 1998 (amendments 578 and 586); November 1, 2000 (amendment 605); November 1, 2001 (amendments 629–631); November 1, 2004 (amendment 669); November 1, 2005 (amendments 679 and 680); November 1, 2006 (amendments 686, 691, and 696); November 1, 2007 (amendment 707); November 1, 2010 (amendment 746); November 1, 2011 (amendment 753); November 1, 2014 (amendment 784); November 1, 2015 (amendments 790 and 797); November 1, 2016 (amendment 804).

§2K2.2. [Deleted]

Historical Note	Section 2K2.2 (Unlawful Trafficking and Other Prohibited Transactions Involving Firearms), effective November 1, 1987, amended effective January 15, 1988 (amendment 34), November 1, 1989 (amendment 189), and November 1, 1990 (amendment 333), was deleted by consolidation with §2K2.1 effective November 1, 1991 (amendment 374).

§2K2.3. [Deleted]

Historical Note	Section 2K2.3 (Receiving, Transporting, Shipping or Transferring a Firearm or Ammunition With Intent to Commit Another Offense, or With Knowledge that It Will Be Used in Committing Another Offense), effective November 1, 1989 (amendment 189), was deleted by consolidation with §2K2.1 effective November 1, 1991 (amendment 374). A former §2K2.3 (Prohibited Transactions in or Shipment of Firearms and Other Weapons), effective November 1, 1987, was deleted by consolidation with §2K2.2 effective November 1, 1989 (amendment 189).

§2K2.4. Use of Firearm, Armor-Piercing Ammunition, or Explosive During or in Relation to Certain Crimes

(a)   If the defendant, whether or not convicted of another crime, was convicted of violating section 844(h) of title 18, United States Code, the guideline sentence is the term of imprisonment required by statute. Chapters Three (Adjustments) and Four (Criminal History and Criminal Livelihood) shall not apply to that count of conviction.

(b)   Except as provided in subsection (c), if the defendant, whether or not convicted of another crime, was convicted of violating section 924(c) or section 929(a) of title 18, United States Code, the guideline sentence is the minimum term of imprisonment required by statute. Chapters Three and Four shall not apply to that count of conviction.

(c)   If the defendant (1) was convicted of violating section 924(c) or section 929(a) of title 18, United States Code; and (2) as a result of that conviction (alone or in addition to another offense of conviction), is determined to be a career offender under §4B1.1 (Career Offender), the guideline sentence shall be determined under §4B1.1(c). Except for §§3E1.1 (Acceptance of Responsibility), 4B1.1, and 4B1.2 (Definitions of Terms Used in Section 4B1.1), Chapters Three and Four shall not apply to that count of conviction.

(d)   Special Instructions for Fines

(1)   Where there is a federal conviction for the underlying offense, the fine guideline shall be the fine guideline that would have

been applicable had there only been a conviction for the underlying offense. This guideline shall be used as a consolidated fine guideline for both the underlying offense and the conviction underlying this section.

Commentary

Statutory Provisions: 18 U.S.C. §§ 844(h), 924(c), 929(a).

Application Notes:

1. **Application of Subsection (a).**—Section 844(h) of title 18, United State Code, provides a mandatory term of imprisonment of 10 years (or 20 years for the second or subsequent offense). Accordingly, the guideline sentence for a defendant convicted under 18 U.S.C. § 844(h) is the term required by that statute. Section 844(h) of title 18, United State Code, also requires a term of imprisonment imposed under this section to run consecutively to any other term of imprisonment.

2. **Application of Subsection (b).**—

    (A) **In General.**—Sections 924(c) and 929(a) of title 18, United States Code, provide mandatory minimum terms of imprisonment (*e.g.*, not less than five years). Except as provided in subsection (c), in a case in which the defendant is convicted under 18 U.S.C. § 924(c) or § 929(a), the guideline sentence is the minimum term required by the relevant statute. Each of 18 U.S.C. §§ 924(c) and 929(a) also requires that a term of imprisonment imposed under that section shall run consecutively to any other term of imprisonment.

    (B) **Upward Departure Provision.**—In a case in which the guideline sentence is determined under subsection (b), a sentence above the minimum term required by 18 U.S.C. § 924(c) or § 929(a) is an upward departure from the guideline sentence. A departure may be warranted, for example, to reflect the seriousness of the defendant's criminal history in a case in which the defendant is convicted of an 18 U.S.C. § 924(c) or § 929(a) offense but is not determined to be a career offender under §4B1.1.

3. **Application of Subsection (c).**—In a case in which the defendant (A) was convicted of violating 18 U.S.C. § 924(c) or 18 U.S.C. § 929(a); and (B) as a result of that conviction (alone or in addition to another offense of conviction), is determined to be a career offender under §4B1.1 (Career Offender), the guideline sentence shall be determined under §4B1.1(c). In a case involving multiple counts, the sentence shall be imposed according to the rules in subsection (e) of §5G1.2 (Sentencing on Multiple Counts of Conviction)

4. **Weapon Enhancement.**—If a sentence under this guideline is imposed in conjunction with a sentence for an underlying offense, do not apply any specific offense characteristic for possession, brandishing, use, or discharge of an explosive or firearm when determining the sentence for the underlying offense. A sentence under this guideline accounts for any explosive or weapon enhancement for the underlying offense of conviction, including any such enhancement that would apply based on conduct for which the defendant is accountable under §1B1.3 (Relevant Conduct). Do not apply any weapon enhancement in the guideline for the underlying offense, for example, if (A) a co-defendant, as part of the jointly undertaken criminal activity, possessed a firearm different from the one for which

the defendant was convicted under 18 U.S.C. § 924(c); or (B) in an ongoing drug trafficking offense, the defendant possessed a firearm other than the one for which the defendant was convicted under 18 U.S.C. § 924(c). However, if a defendant is convicted of two armed bank robberies, but is convicted under 18 U.S.C. § 924(c) in connection with only one of the robberies, a weapon enhancement would apply to the bank robbery which was not the basis for the 18 U.S.C. § 924(c) conviction.

A sentence under this guideline also accounts for conduct that would subject the defendant to an enhancement under §2D1.1(b)(2) (pertaining to use of violence, credible threat to use violence, or directing the use of violence). Do not apply that enhancement when determining the sentence for the underlying offense.

If the explosive or weapon that was possessed, brandished, used, or discharged in the course of the underlying offense also results in a conviction that would subject the defendant to an enhancement under §2K1.3(b)(3) (pertaining to possession of explosive material in connection with another felony offense) or §2K2.1(b)(6)(B) (pertaining to possession of any firearm or ammunition in connection with another felony offense), do not apply that enhancement. A sentence under this guideline accounts for the conduct covered by these enhancements because of the relatedness of that conduct to the conduct that forms the basis for the conviction under 18 U.S.C. § 844(h), § 924(c) or § 929(a). For example, if in addition to a conviction for an underlying offense of armed bank robbery, the defendant was convicted of being a felon in possession under 18 U.S.C. § 922(g), the enhancement under §2K2.1(b)(6)(B) would not apply.

In a few cases in which the defendant is determined not to be a career offender, the offense level for the underlying offense determined under the preceding paragraphs may result in a guideline range that, when combined with the mandatory consecutive sentence under 18 U.S.C. § 844(h), § 924(c), or § 929(a), produces a total maximum penalty that is less than the maximum of the guideline range that would have resulted had there not been a count of conviction under 18 U.S.C. § 844(h), § 924(c), or § 929(a) (*i.e.*, the guideline range that would have resulted if the enhancements for possession, use, or discharge of a firearm had been applied). In such a case, an upward departure may be warranted so that the conviction under 18 U.S.C. § 844(h), § 924(c), or § 929(a) does not result in a decrease in the total punishment. An upward departure under this paragraph shall not exceed the maximum of the guideline range that would have resulted had there not been a count of conviction under 18 U.S.C. § 844(h), § 924(c), or § 929(a).

5. **Chapters Three and Four.**—Except for those cases covered by subsection (c), do not apply Chapter Three (Adjustments) and Chapter Four (Criminal History and Criminal Livelihood) to any offense sentenced under this guideline. Such offenses are excluded from application of those chapters because the guideline sentence for each offense is determined only by the relevant statute. *See* §§3D1.1 (Procedure for Determining Offense Level on Multiple Counts) and 5G1.2. In determining the guideline sentence for those cases covered by subsection (c): (A) the adjustment in §3E1.1 (Acceptance of Responsibility) may apply, as provided in §4B1.1(c); and (B) no other adjustments in Chapter Three and no provisions of Chapter Four, other than §§4B1.1 and 4B1.2, shall apply.

6. **Terms of Supervised Release.**—Imposition of a term of supervised release is governed by the provisions of §5D1.1 (Imposition of a Term of Supervised Release).

7. **Fines.**—Subsection (d) sets forth special provisions concerning the imposition of fines. Where there is also a conviction for the underlying offense, a consolidated fine guideline is determined by the offense level that would have applied to the underlying offense absent a conviction under 18 U.S.C. § 844(h), § 924(c), or § 929(a). This is required because

the offense level for the underlying offense may be reduced when there is also a conviction under 18 U.S.C. § 844(h), § 924(c), or § 929(a) in that any specific offense characteristic for possession, brandishing, use, or discharge of a firearm is not applied (*see* Application Note 4). The Commission has not established a fine guideline range for the unusual case in which there is no conviction for the underlying offense, although a fine is authorized under 18 U.S.C. § 3571.

Background: Section 844(h) of title 18, United States Code, provides a mandatory term of imprisonment. Sections 924(c) and 929(a) of title 18, United States Code, provide mandatory minimum terms of imprisonment. A sentence imposed pursuant to any of these statutes must be imposed to run consecutively to any other term of imprisonment. To avoid double counting, when a sentence under this section is imposed in conjunction with a sentence for an underlying offense, any specific offense characteristic for explosive or firearm discharge, use, brandishing, or possession is not applied in respect to such underlying offense.

Historical Note	Effective November 1, 1987. Amended effective November 1, 1989 (amendment 190); November 1, 1990 (amendment 332); November 1, 1991 (amendment 405); November 1, 1993 (amendments 481 and 489); November 1, 2000 (amendments 598, 599, and 600); November 1, 2002 (amendment 642); November 1, 2006 (amendment 696); November 1, 2010 (amendment 748); November 1, 2011 (amendments 750 and 760).

§2K2.5. Possession of Firearm or Dangerous Weapon in Federal Facility; Possession or Discharge of Firearm in School Zone

(a) Base Offense Level: **6**

(b) Specific Offense Characteristic

(1) If—

(A) the defendant unlawfully possessed or caused any firearm or dangerous weapon to be present in a federal court facility; or

(B) the defendant unlawfully possessed or caused any firearm to be present in a school zone,

increase by **2** levels.

(c) Cross Reference

(1) If the defendant used or possessed any firearm or dangerous weapon in connection with the commission or attempted commission of another offense, or possessed or transferred a firearm or dangerous weapon with knowledge or intent that it would be used or possessed in connection with another offense, apply—

      (A)   §2X1.1 (Attempt, Solicitation, or Conspiracy) in respect to that other offense if the resulting offense level is greater than that determined above; or

      (B)   if death resulted, the most analogous offense guideline from Chapter Two, Part A, Subpart 1 (Homicide), if the resulting offense level is greater than that determined above.

Commentary

Statutory Provisions: 18 U.S.C. §§ 922(q), 930; 40 U.S.C. § 5104(e)(1).

Application Notes:

1.   "*Dangerous weapon*" and "*firearm*" are defined in the Commentary to §1B1.1 (Application Instructions).

2.   "*Federal court facility*" includes the courtroom; judges' chambers; witness rooms; jury deliberation rooms; attorney conference rooms; prisoner holding cells; offices and parking facilities of the court clerks, the United States attorney, and the United States marshal; probation and parole offices; and adjoining corridors and parking facilities of any court of the United States. *See* 18 U.S.C. § 930(g)(3).

3.   "*School zone*" is defined at 18 U.S.C. § 922(q). A sentence of imprisonment under 18 U.S.C. § 922(q) must run consecutively to any sentence of imprisonment imposed for any other offense. *See* 18 U.S.C. § 924(a)(4). In order to comply with the statute, when the guideline range is based on the underlying offense, and the defendant is convicted both of the underlying offense and 18 U.S.C. § 922(q), the court should apportion the sentence between the count for the underlying offense and the count under 18 U.S.C. § 922(q). For example, if the guideline range is 30–37 months and the court determines "total punishment" of 36 months is appropriate, a sentence of 30 months for the underlying offense, plus 6 months under 18 U.S.C. § 922(q) would satisfy this requirement.

4.   Where the firearm was brandished, discharged, or otherwise used, in a federal facility, federal court facility, or school zone, and the cross reference from subsection (c)(1) does not apply, an upward departure may be warranted.

Historical Note	Effective November 1, 1989 (amendment 191). Amended effective November 1, 1991 (amendment 374); November 1, 2003 (amendment 661); November 1, 2010 (amendment 746).

---

§2K2.6.   Possessing, Purchasing, or Owning Body Armor by Violent Felons

    (a)   Base Offense Level: **10**

    (b)   Specific Offense Characteristic

        (1)   If the defendant used the body armor in connection with another felony offense, increase by **4** levels.

Commentary

Statutory Provision: 18 U.S.C. § 931.

Application Notes:

1. **Application of Subsection (b)(1).—**

    (A) **Meaning of "Defendant".—**Consistent with §1B1.3 (Relevant Conduct), the term "*defendant*", for purposes of subsection (b)(1), limits the accountability of the defendant to the defendant's own conduct and conduct that the defendant aided or abetted, counseled, commanded, induced, procured, or willfully caused.

    (B) **Meaning of "Felony Offense".—**For purposes of subsection (b)(1), "*felony offense*" means any offense (federal, state, or local) punishable by imprisonment for a term exceeding one year, regardless of whether a criminal charge was brought, or a conviction obtained.

    (C) **Meaning of "Used".—**For purposes of subsection (b)(1), "*used*" means the body armor was (i) actively employed in a manner to protect the person from gunfire; or (ii) used as a means of bartering. Subsection (b)(1) does not apply if the body armor was merely possessed. For example, subsection (b)(1) would not apply if the body armor was found in the trunk of a car but was not being actively used as protection.

2. **Inapplicability of §3B1.5.—**If subsection (b)(1) applies, do not apply the adjustment in §3B1.5 (Use of Body Armor in Drug Trafficking Crimes and Crimes of Violence).

3. **Grouping of Multiple Counts.—**If subsection (b)(1) applies (because the defendant used the body armor in connection with another felony offense) and the instant offense of conviction includes a count of conviction for that other felony offense, the counts of conviction for the 18 U.S.C. § 931 offense and that other felony offense shall be grouped pursuant to subsection (c) of §3D1.2 (Groups of Closely Related Counts).

Historical Note	Effective November 1, 2004 (amendment 670).

*   *   *   *   *

3. MAILING INJURIOUS ARTICLES

Historical Note	Effective November 1, 1987. Amended effective November 1, 1993 (amendment 481).

§2K3.1. [Deleted]

Historical Note	Section 2K3.1 (Unlawfully Transporting Hazardous Materials in Commerce), effective November 1, 1987, was deleted by consolidation with §2Q1.2 effective November 1, 1993 (amendment 481).

§2K3.2. Feloniously Mailing Injurious Articles

    (a)   Base Offense Level (Apply the greater):

        (1)   If the offense was committed with intent (A) to kill or injure any person, or (B) to injure the mails or other property, apply §2X1.1 (Attempt, Solicitation, or Conspiracy) in respect to the intended offense; or

        (2)   If death resulted, apply the most analogous offense guideline from Chapter Two, Part A, Subpart 1 (Homicide).

Commentary

Statutory Provision: 18 U.S.C. § 1716 (felony provisions only).

Background: This guideline applies only to the felony provisions of 18 U.S.C. § 1716. The Commission has not promulgated a guideline for the misdemeanor provisions of this statute.

Historical Note	Effective November 1, 1990 (amendment 334).

PART L — OFFENSES INVOLVING IMMIGRATION, NATURALIZATION, AND PASSPORTS

1. IMMIGRATION

§2L1.1.   Smuggling, Transporting, or Harboring an Unlawful Alien

(a)   Base Offense Level:

(1)   **25**, if the defendant was convicted under 8 U.S.C. § 1327 of a violation involving an alien who was inadmissible under 8 U.S.C. § 1182(a)(3);

(2)   **23**, if the defendant was convicted under 8 U.S.C. § 1327 of a violation involving an alien who previously was deported after a conviction for an aggravated felony; or

(3)   **12**, otherwise.

(b)   Specific Offense Characteristics

(1)   If (A) the offense was committed other than for profit, or the offense involved the smuggling, transporting, or harboring only of the defendant's spouse or child (or both the defendant's spouse and child), and (B) the base offense level is determined under subsection (a)(3), decrease by **3** levels.

(2)   If the offense involved the smuggling, transporting, or harboring of six or more unlawful aliens, increase as follows:

NUMBER OF UNLAWFUL ALIENS SMUGGLED, TRANSPORTED, OR HARBORED	INCREASE IN LEVEL
(A) 6–24	add **3**
(B) 25–99	add **6**
(C) 100 or more	add **9**.

(3)   If the defendant committed any part of the instant offense after sustaining (A) a conviction for a felony immigration and naturalization offense, increase by **2** levels; or (B) two (or more) convictions for felony immigration and naturalization offenses, each such conviction arising out of a separate prosecution, increase by **4** levels.

(4) If the offense involved the smuggling, transporting, or harboring of a minor who was unaccompanied by the minor's parent, adult relative, or legal guardian, increase by **4** levels.

(5) (Apply the Greatest):

(A) If a firearm was discharged, increase by **6** levels, but if the resulting offense level is less than level **22**, increase to level **22**.

(B) If a dangerous weapon (including a firearm) was brandished or otherwise used, increase by **4** levels, but if the resulting offense level is less than level **20**, increase to level **20**.

(C) If a dangerous weapon (including a firearm) was possessed, increase by **2** levels, but if the resulting offense level is less than level **18**, increase to level **18**.

(6) If the offense involved intentionally or recklessly creating a substantial risk of death or serious bodily injury to another person, increase by **2** levels, but if the resulting offense level is less than level **18**, increase to level **18**.

(7) If any person died or sustained bodily injury, increase the offense level according to the seriousness of the injury:

Death or Degree of Injury	Increase in Level
(A) Bodily Injury	add **2** levels
(B) Serious Bodily Injury	add **4** levels
(C) Permanent or Life-Threatening Bodily Injury	add **6** levels
(D) Death	add **10** levels.

(8) (Apply the greater):

(A) If an alien was involuntarily detained through coercion or threat, or in connection with a demand for payment, (i) after the alien was smuggled into the United States; or (ii) while the alien was transported or harbored in the United States, increase by **2** levels. If the resulting offense level is less than level **18**, increase to level **18**.

(B) If (i) the defendant was convicted of alien harboring, (ii) the alien harboring was for the purpose of prostitution, and (iii) the defendant receives an adjustment under

§3B1.1 (Aggravating Role), increase by **2** levels, but if the alien engaging in the prostitution had not attained the age of 18 years, increase by **6** levels.

(9) If the defendant was convicted under 8 U.S.C. § 1324(a)(4), increase by **2** levels.

(c) Cross Reference

(1) If death resulted, apply the appropriate homicide guideline from Chapter Two, Part A, Subpart 1, if the resulting offense level is greater than that determined under this guideline.

Commentary

Statutory Provisions: 8 U.S.C. §§ 1324(a), 1327. For additional statutory provision(s), *see* Appendix A (Statutory Index).

Application Notes:

1. **Definitions.—**For purposes of this guideline:

"*The offense was committed other than for profit*" means that there was no payment or expectation of payment for the smuggling, transporting, or harboring of any of the unlawful aliens.

"*Number of unlawful aliens smuggled, transported, or harbored*" does not include the defendant.

"*Aggravated felony*" has the meaning given that term in section 101(a)(43) of the Immigration and Nationality Act (8 U.S.C. § 1101(a)(43)), without regard to the date of conviction for the aggravated felony.

"*Child*" has the meaning set forth in section 101(b)(1) of the Immigration and Nationality Act (8 U.S.C. § 1101(b)(1)).

"*Spouse*" has the meaning set forth in 101(a)(35) of the Immigration and Nationality Act (8 U.S.C. § 1101(a)(35)).

"*Immigration and naturalization offense*" means any offense covered by Chapter Two, Part L.

"*Minor*" means an individual who had not attained the age of 18 years.

"*Parent*" means (A) a natural mother or father; (B) a stepmother or stepfather; or (C) an adoptive mother or father.

"*Bodily injury*," "*serious bodily injury*," and "*permanent or life-threatening bodily injury*" have the meaning given those terms in the Commentary to §1B1.1 (Application Instructions).

2. **Prior Convictions Under Subsection (b)(3).**—Prior felony conviction(s) resulting in an adjustment under subsection (b)(3) are also counted for purposes of determining criminal history points pursuant to Chapter Four, Part A (Criminal History).

3. **Application of Subsection (b)(6).**—Reckless conduct to which the adjustment from subsection (b)(6) applies includes a wide variety of conduct (*e.g.*, transporting persons in the trunk or engine compartment of a motor vehicle; carrying substantially more passengers than the rated capacity of a motor vehicle or vessel; harboring persons in a crowded, dangerous, or inhumane condition; or guiding persons through, or abandoning persons in, a dangerous or remote geographic area without adequate food, water, clothing, or protection from the elements). If subsection (b)(6) applies solely on the basis of conduct related to fleeing from a law enforcement officer, do not apply an adjustment from §3C1.2 (Reckless Endangerment During Flight). Additionally, do not apply the adjustment in subsection (b)(6) if the only reckless conduct that created a substantial risk of death or serious bodily injury is conduct for which the defendant received an enhancement under subsection (b)(5).

4. **Application of Subsection (b)(7) to Conduct Constituting Criminal Sexual Abuse.**—Consistent with Application Note 1(L) of §1B1.1 (Application Instructions), "serious bodily injury" is deemed to have occurred if the offense involved conduct constituting criminal sexual abuse under 18 U.S.C. § 2241 or § 2242 or any similar offense under state law.

5. **Inapplicability of §3A1.3.**—If an enhancement under subsection (b)(8)(A) applies, do not apply §3A1.3 (Restraint of Victim).

6. **Interaction with §3B1.1.**—For the purposes of §3B1.1 (Aggravating Role), the aliens smuggled, transported, or harbored are not considered participants unless they actively assisted in the smuggling, transporting, or harboring of others. In large scale smuggling, transporting, or harboring cases, an additional adjustment from §3B1.1 typically will apply.

7. **Upward Departure Provisions.**—An upward departure may be warranted in any of the following cases:

   (A) The defendant smuggled, transported, or harbored an alien knowing that the alien intended to enter the United States to engage in subversive activity, drug trafficking, or other serious criminal behavior.

   (B) The defendant smuggled, transported, or harbored an alien the defendant knew was inadmissible for reasons of security and related grounds, as set forth under 8 U.S.C. § 1182(a)(3).

   (C) The offense involved substantially more than 100 aliens.

Background: This section includes the most serious immigration offenses covered under the Immigration Reform and Control Act of 1986.

Historical Note	Effective November 1, 1987. Amended effective January 15, 1988 (amendments 35, 36, and 37); November 1, 1989 (amendment 192); November 1, 1990 (amendment 335); November 1, 1991 (amendment 375); November 1, 1992 (amendment 450); May 1, 1997 (amendment 543); November 1, 1997 (amendment 561); November 1, 2006 (amendments 686 and 692); November 1, 2007 (amendment 702); November 1, 2009 (amendment 730); November 1, 2014 (amendment 785); November 1, 2016 (amendment 802).

---

§2L1.2.   Unlawfully Entering or Remaining in the United States

---

   (a)   Base Offense Level: 8

   (b)   Specific Offense Characteristics

   (1)   (Apply the Greater) If the defendant committed the instant offense after sustaining—

   (A)   a conviction for a felony that is an illegal reentry offense, increase by **4** levels; or

   (B)   two or more convictions for misdemeanors under 8 U.S.C. § 1325(a), increase by **2** levels.

   (2)   (Apply the Greatest) If, before the defendant was ordered deported or ordered removed from the United States for the first time, the defendant sustained—

   (A)   a conviction for a felony offense (other than an illegal reentry offense) for which the sentence imposed was five years or more, increase by **10** levels;

   (B)   a conviction for a felony offense (other than an illegal reentry offense) for which the sentence imposed was two years or more, increase by **8** levels;

   (C)   a conviction for a felony offense (other than an illegal reentry offense) for which the sentence imposed exceeded one year and one month, increase by **6** levels;

   (D)   a conviction for any other felony offense (other than an illegal reentry offense), increase by **4** levels; or

   (E)   three or more convictions for misdemeanors that are crimes of violence or drug trafficking offenses, increase by **2** levels.

   (3)   (Apply the Greatest) If, at any time after the defendant was ordered deported or ordered removed from the United States for the first time, the defendant engaged in criminal conduct resulting in—

   (A)   a conviction for a felony offense (other than an illegal reentry offense) for which the sentence imposed was five years or more, increase by **10** levels;

(B) a conviction for a felony offense (other than an illegal reentry offense) for which the sentence imposed was two years or more, increase by **8** levels;

(C) a conviction for a felony offense (other than an illegal reentry offense) for which the sentence imposed exceeded one year and one month, increase by **6** levels;

(D) a conviction for any other felony offense (other than an illegal reentry offense), increase by **4** levels; or

(E) three or more convictions for misdemeanors that are crimes of violence or drug trafficking offenses, increase by **2** levels.

Commentary

Statutory Provisions: 8 U.S.C. § 1253, § 1325(a) (second or subsequent offense only), § 1326. For additional statutory provision(s), *see* Appendix A (Statutory Index).

Application Notes:

1. **In General.—**

   (A) **"Ordered Deported or Ordered Removed from the United States for the First Time".—**For purposes of this guideline, a defendant shall be considered "ordered deported or ordered removed from the United States" if the defendant was ordered deported or ordered removed from the United States based on a final order of exclusion, deportation, or removal, regardless of whether the order was in response to a conviction. "For the first time" refers to the first time the defendant was ever the subject of such an order.

   (B) **Offenses Committed Prior to Age Eighteen.—**Subsections (b)(1), (b)(2), and (b)(3) do not apply to a conviction for an offense committed before the defendant was eighteen years of age unless such conviction is classified as an adult conviction under the laws of the jurisdiction in which the defendant was convicted.

2. **Definitions.—**For purposes of this guideline:

   "*Crime of violence*" means any of the following offenses under federal, state, or local law: murder, voluntary manslaughter, kidnapping, aggravated assault, a forcible sex offense, robbery, arson, extortion, the use or unlawful possession of a firearm described in 26 U.S.C. § 5845(a) or explosive material as defined in 18 U.S.C. § 841(c), or any other offense under federal, state, or local law that has as an element the use, attempted use, or threatened use of physical force against the person of another. "Forcible sex offense" includes where consent to the conduct is not given or is not legally valid, such as where consent to the conduct is involuntary, incompetent, or coerced. The offenses of sexual abuse of a minor and statutory rape are included only if the sexual abuse of a minor or statutory rape was (A) an offense described in 18 U.S.C. § 2241(c) or (B) an offense under state law that would have been an offense under section 2241(c) if the offense had occurred within the special maritime and territorial jurisdiction of the United States. "Extortion" is obtaining something of value from another by the wrongful use of (A) force, (B) fear of physical injury, or (C) threat of physical injury.

"**Drug trafficking offense**" means an offense under federal, state, or local law that prohibits the manufacture, import, export, distribution, or dispensing of, or offer to sell a controlled substance (or a counterfeit substance) or the possession of a controlled substance (or a counterfeit substance) with intent to manufacture, import, export, distribute, or dispense.

"**Felony**" means any federal, state, or local offense punishable by imprisonment for a term exceeding one year.

"**Illegal reentry offense**" means (A) an offense under 8 U.S.C. § 1253 or § 1326, or (B) a second or subsequent offense under 8 U.S.C. § 1325(a).

"**Misdemeanor**" means any federal, state, or local offense punishable by a term of imprisonment of one year or less.

"**Sentence imposed**" has the meaning given the term "sentence of imprisonment" in Application Note 2 and subsection (b) of §4A1.2 (Definitions and Instructions for Computing Criminal History). The length of the sentence imposed includes any term of imprisonment given upon revocation of probation, parole, or supervised release.

3. **Criminal History Points.**—For purposes of applying subsections (b)(1), (b)(2), and (b)(3), use only those convictions that receive criminal history points under §4A1.1(a), (b), or (c). In addition, for purposes of subsections (b)(1)(B), (b)(2)(E), and (b)(3)(E), use only those convictions that are counted separately under §4A1.2(a)(2).

A conviction taken into account under subsection (b)(1), (b)(2), or (b)(3) is not excluded from consideration of whether that conviction receives criminal history points pursuant to Chapter Four, Part A (Criminal History).

4. **Cases in Which Sentences for An Illegal Reentry Offense and Another Felony Offense were Imposed at the Same Time.**—There may be cases in which the sentences for an illegal reentry offense and another felony offense were imposed at the same time and treated as a single sentence for purposes of calculating the criminal history score under §4A1.1(a), (b), and (c). In such a case, use the illegal reentry offense in determining the appropriate enhancement under subsection (b)(1), if it independently would have received criminal history points. In addition, use the prior sentence for the other felony offense in determining the appropriate enhancement under subsection (b)(3), if it independently would have received criminal history points.

5. **Departure Based on Seriousness of a Prior Offense.**—There may be cases in which the offense level provided by an enhancement in subsection (b)(2) or (b)(3) substantially understates or overstates the seriousness of the conduct underlying the prior offense, because (A) the length of the sentence imposed does not reflect the seriousness of the prior offense; (B) the prior conviction is too remote to receive criminal history points (*see* §4A1.2(e)); or (C) the time actually served was substantially less than the length of the sentence imposed for the prior offense. In such a case, a departure may be warranted.

6. **Departure Based on Time Served in State Custody.**—In a case in which the defendant is located by immigration authorities while the defendant is serving time in state custody, whether pre- or post-conviction, for a state offense, the time served is not covered

by an adjustment under §5G1.3(b) and, accordingly, is not covered by a departure under §5K2.23 (Discharged Terms of Imprisonment). *See* §5G1.3(a). In such a case, the court may consider whether a departure is appropriate to reflect all or part of the time served in state custody, from the time immigration authorities locate the defendant until the service of the federal sentence commences, that the court determines will not be credited to the federal sentence by the Bureau of Prisons. Any such departure should be fashioned to achieve a reasonable punishment for the instant offense.

Such a departure should be considered only in cases where the departure is not likely to increase the risk to the public from further crimes of the defendant. In determining whether such a departure is appropriate, the court should consider, among other things, (A) whether the defendant engaged in additional criminal activity after illegally reentering the United States; (B) the seriousness of any such additional criminal activity, including (1) whether the defendant used violence or credible threats of violence or possessed a firearm or other dangerous weapon (or induced another person to do so) in connection with the criminal activity, (2) whether the criminal activity resulted in death or serious bodily injury to any person, and (3) whether the defendant was an organizer, leader, manager, or supervisor of others in the criminal activity; and (C) the seriousness of the defendant's other criminal history.

7. **Departure Based on Cultural Assimilation.**—There may be cases in which a downward departure may be appropriate on the basis of cultural assimilation. Such a departure should be considered only in cases where (A) the defendant formed cultural ties primarily with the United States from having resided continuously in the United States from childhood, (B) those cultural ties provided the primary motivation for the defendant's illegal reentry or continued presence in the United States, and (C) such a departure is not likely to increase the risk to the public from further crimes of the defendant.

In determining whether such a departure is appropriate, the court should consider, among other things, (1) the age in childhood at which the defendant began residing continuously in the United States, (2) whether and for how long the defendant attended school in the United States, (3) the duration of the defendant's continued residence in the United States, (4) the duration of the defendant's presence outside the United States, (5) the nature and extent of the defendant's familial and cultural ties inside the United States, and the nature and extent of such ties outside the United States, (6) the seriousness of the defendant's criminal history, and (7) whether the defendant engaged in additional criminal activity after illegally reentering the United States.

| *Historical Note* | Effective November 1, 1987. Amended effective January 15, 1988 (amendment 38); November 1, 1989 (amendment 193); November 1, 1991 (amendment 375); November 1, 1995 (amendment 523); November 1, 1997 (amendment 562); November 1, 2001 (amendment 632); November 1, 2002 (amendment 637); November 1, 2003 (amendment 658); November 1, 2007 (amendment 709); November 1, 2008 (amendment 722); November 1, 2010 (amendment 740); November 1, 2011 (amendment 754); November 1, 2012 (amendment 764); November 1, 2014 (amendment 787); November 1, 2015 (amendment 795); November 1, 2016 (amendment 802). |

§2L1.3. [Deleted]

| *Historical Note* | Section 2L1.3 (Engaging in a Pattern of Unlawful Employment of Aliens), effective November 1, 1987, was deleted effective November 1, 1989 (amendment 194). |

*　　*　　*　　*　　*

2. NATURALIZATION AND PASSPORTS

§2L2.1. **Trafficking in a Document Relating to Naturalization, Citizenship, or Legal Resident Status, or a United States Passport; False Statement in Respect to the Citizenship or Immigration Status of Another; Fraudulent Marriage to Assist Alien to Evade Immigration Law**

(a) Base Offense Level: **11**

(b) Specific Offense Characteristics

(1) If the offense was committed other than for profit, or the offense involved the smuggling, transporting, or harboring only of the defendant's spouse or child (or both the defendant's spouse and child), decrease by **3** levels.

(2) If the offense involved six or more documents or passports, increase as follows:

Number of Documents/Passports	Increase in Level
(A) 6–24	add **3**
(B) 25–99	add **6**
(C) 100 or more	add **9**.

(3) If the defendant knew, believed, or had reason to believe that a passport or visa was to be used to facilitate the commission of a felony offense, other than an offense involving violation of the immigration laws, increase by **4** levels.

(4) If the defendant committed any part of the instant offense after sustaining (A) a conviction for a felony immigration and naturalization offense, increase by **2** levels; or (B) two (or more) convictions for felony immigration and naturalization offenses, each such conviction arising out of a separate prosecution, increase by **4** levels.

(5) If the defendant fraudulently obtained or used (A) a United States passport, increase by **4** levels; or (B) a foreign passport, increase by **2** levels.

Commentary

Statutory Provisions: 8 U.S.C. §§ 1160(b)(7)(A), 1185(a)(3), (4), 1325(c), (d); 18 U.S.C. §§ 1015, 1028, 1425–1427, 1542, 1544, 1546. For additional statutory provision(s), *see* Appendix A (Statutory Index).

Application Notes:

1. For purposes of this guideline—

    "*The offense was committed other than for profit*" means that there was no payment or expectation of payment for the smuggling, transporting, or harboring of any of the unlawful aliens.

    "*Immigration and naturalization offense*" means any offense covered by Chapter Two, Part L.

    "*Child*" has the meaning set forth in section 101(b)(1) of the Immigration and Nationality Act (8 U.S.C. § 1101(b)(1)).

    "*Spouse*" has the meaning set forth in section 101(a)(35) of the Immigration and Nationality Act (8 U.S.C. § 1101(a)(35)).

2. Where it is established that multiple documents are part of a set of documents intended for use by a single person, treat the set as one document.

3. Subsection (b)(3) provides an enhancement if the defendant knew, believed, or had reason to believe that a passport or visa was to be used to facilitate the commission of a felony offense, other than an offense involving violation of the immigration laws. If the defendant knew, believed, or had reason to believe that the felony offense to be committed was of an especially serious type, an upward departure may be warranted.

4. Prior felony conviction(s) resulting in an adjustment under subsection (b)(4) are also counted for purposes of determining criminal history points pursuant to Chapter Four, Part A (Criminal History).

5. If the offense involved substantially more than 100 documents, an upward departure may be warranted.

Historical Note	Effective November 1, 1987. Amended effective November 1, 1989 (amendment 195); November 1, 1992 (amendment 450); November 1, 1993 (amendment 481); November 1, 1995 (amendment 524); May 1, 1997 (amendment 544); November 1, 1997 (amendment 563); November 1, 2006 (amendment 692); November 1, 2010 (amendment 746).

---

§2L2.2. Fraudulently Acquiring Documents Relating to Naturalization, Citizenship, or Legal Resident Status for Own Use; False Personation or Fraudulent Marriage by Alien to Evade Immigration Law; Fraudulently Acquiring or Improperly Using a United States Passport

(a) Base Offense Level: 8

(b) Specific Offense Characteristics

(1) If the defendant is an unlawful alien who has been deported (voluntarily or involuntarily) on one or more occasions prior to the instant offense, increase by **2** levels.

(2) If the defendant committed any part of the instant offense after sustaining (A) a conviction for a felony immigration and naturalization offense, increase by **2** levels; or (B) two (or more) convictions for felony immigration and naturalization offenses, each such conviction arising out of a separate prosecution, increase by **4** levels.

(3) If the defendant fraudulently obtained or used (A) a United States passport, increase by **4** levels; or (B) a foreign passport, increase by **2** levels.

(4) (Apply the Greater):

(A) If the defendant committed any part of the instant offense to conceal the defendant's membership in, or authority over, a military, paramilitary, or police organization that was involved in a serious human rights offense during the period in which the defendant was such a member or had such authority, increase by **2** levels. If the resulting offense level is less than level **13**, increase to level **13**.

(B) If the defendant committed any part of the instant offense to conceal the defendant's participation in (i) the offense of incitement to genocide, increase by **6** levels; or (ii) any other serious human rights offense, increase by **10** levels. If clause (ii) applies and the resulting offense level is less than level **25**, increase to level **25**.

(c) Cross Reference

(1) If the defendant used a passport or visa in the commission or attempted commission of a felony offense, other than an offense involving violation of the immigration laws, apply—

(A) §2X1.1 (Attempt, Solicitation, or Conspiracy) in respect to that felony offense, if the resulting offense level is greater than that determined above; or

(B) if death resulted, the most analogous offense guideline from Chapter Two, Part A, Subpart 1 (Homicide), if the resulting offense level is greater than that determined above.

Commentary

Statutory Provisions: 8 U.S.C. §§ 1160(b)(7)(A), 1185(a)(3), (5), 1325(c), (d); 18 U.S.C. §§ 911, 1015, 1028, 1423–1426, 1542–1544, 1546.

Application Notes:

1. **Definition.**—For purposes of this guideline, "*immigration and naturalization offense*" means any offense covered by Chapter Two, Part L.

2. **Application of Subsection (b)(2).**—Prior felony conviction(s) resulting in an adjustment under subsection (b)(2) are also counted for purposes of determining criminal history points pursuant to Chapter Four, Part A (Criminal History).

3. **Application of Subsection (b)(3).**—The term "*used*" is to be construed broadly and includes the attempted renewal of previously-issued passports.

4. **Application of Subsection (b)(4).**—For purposes of subsection (b)(4):

    "*Serious human rights offense*" means (A) violations of federal criminal laws relating to genocide, torture, war crimes, and the use or recruitment of child soldiers under sections 1091, 2340, 2340A, 2441, and 2442 of title 18, United States Code, *see* 28 U.S.C. § 509B(e); and (B) conduct that would have been a violation of any such law if the offense had occurred within the jurisdiction of the United States or if the defendant or the victim had been a national of the United States.

    "*The offense of incitement to genocide*" means (A) violations of 18 U.S.C. § 1091(c); and (B) conduct that would have been a violation of such section if the offense had occurred within the jurisdiction of the United States or if the defendant or the victim had been a national of the United States.

5. **Multiple Counts.**—For the purposes of Chapter Three, Part D (Multiple Counts), a count of conviction for unlawfully entering or remaining in the United States covered by §2L1.2 (Unlawfully Entering or Remaining in the United States) arising from the same course of conduct as the count of conviction covered by this guideline shall be considered a closely related count to the count of conviction covered by this guideline, and therefore is to be grouped with the count of conviction covered by this guideline.

6. **Upward Departure Provision.**—If the defendant fraudulently obtained or used a United States passport for the purpose of entering the United States to engage in terrorist activity, an upward departure may be warranted. *See* Application Note 4 of the Commentary to §3A1.4 (Terrorism).

Historical Note	Effective November 1, 1987. Amended effective January 15, 1988 (amendment 39); November 1, 1989 (amendment 196); November 1, 1992 (amendment 450); November 1, 1993 (amendment 481); November 1, 1995 (amendment 524); May 1, 1997 (amendment 544); November 1, 1997 (amendment 563); November 1, 2004 (amendment 671); November 1, 2006 (amendment 692); November 1, 2010 (amendment 746); November 1, 2012 (amendment 765).

§2L2.3. [Deleted]

Historical Note	Section 2L2.3 (Trafficking in a United States Passport), effective November 1, 1987, amended effective November 1, 1989 (amendment 197) and November 1, 1992 (amendment 450), was deleted by consolidation with §2L2.1 effective November 1, 1993 (amendment 481).

§2L2.4. [Deleted]

Historical Note	Section 2L2.4 (Fraudulently Acquiring or Improperly Using a United States Passport), effective November 1, 1987, amended effective January 15, 1988 (amendment 40) and November 1, 1989 (amendment 198), was deleted by consolidation with §2L2.2 effective November 1, 1993 (amendment 481).

§2L2.5.   Failure to Surrender Canceled Naturalization Certificate

(a)   Base Offense Level: **6**

Commentary

Statutory Provision: 18 U.S.C. § 1428.

Historical Note	Effective November 1, 1987.

PART M — OFFENSES INVOLVING NATIONAL DEFENSE AND WEAPONS OF MASS DESTRUCTION

Historical Note	Effective November 1, 1987. Amended effective November 1, 2001 (amendment 633).

1. TREASON

§2M1.1. Treason

(a) Base Offense Level:

    (1) **43**, if the conduct is tantamount to waging war against the United States;

    (2) the offense level applicable to the most analogous offense, otherwise.

Commentary

Statutory Provision: 18 U.S.C. § 2381.

Background: Treason is a rarely prosecuted offense that could encompass a relatively broad range of conduct, including many of the more specific offenses in this Part. The guideline contemplates imposition of the maximum penalty in the most serious cases, with reference made to the most analogous offense guideline in lesser cases.

Historical Note	Effective November 1, 1987.

* * * * *

2. SABOTAGE

§2M2.1. Destruction of, or Production of Defective, War Material, Premises, or Utilities

(a) Base Offense Level: **32**

Commentary

Statutory Provisions: 18 U.S.C. § 2153, 2154; 42 U.S.C. § 2284; 49 U.S.C. § 60123(b).

Application Note:

1.   Violations of 42 U.S.C. § 2284 are included in this section where the defendant was con-
     victed of acting with intent to injure the United States or aid a foreign nation.

Historical Note	Effective November 1, 1987. Amended effective November 1, 1993 (amendment 481); November 1, 2002 (amendment 637).

---

§2M2.2.   [Deleted]

Historical Note	Section 2M2.2 (Production of Defective War Material, Premises, or Utilities), effective November 1, 1987, was deleted by consolidation with §2M2.1 effective November 1, 1993 (amendment 481).

---

§2M2.3.   Destruction of, or Production of Defective, National Defense Material, Premises, or Utilities

   (a)   Base Offense Level: **26**

Commentary

Statutory Provisions: 18 U.S.C. §§ 2155, 2156; 42 U.S.C. § 2284; 49 U.S.C. § 60123(b).

Application Note:

1.   Violations of 42 U.S.C. § 2284 not included in §2M2.1 are included in this section.

Historical Note	Effective November 1, 1987. Amended effective November 1, 1993 (amendment 481); November 1, 2002 (amendment 637).

---

§2M2.4.   [Deleted]

Historical Note	Section 2M2.4 (Production of Defective National Defense Material, Premises, or Utilities), effective November 1, 1987, was deleted by consolidation with §2M2.3 effective November 1, 1993 (amendment 481).

*   *   *   *   *

3. ESPIONAGE AND RELATED OFFENSES

---

§2M3.1. Gathering or Transmitting National Defense Information to Aid a Foreign Government

    (a) Base Offense Level:

        (1) **42**, if top secret information was gathered or transmitted; or

        (2) **37**, otherwise.

Commentary

Statutory Provisions: 18 U.S.C. § 794; 42 U.S.C. §§ 2274(a), (b), 2275.

Application Notes:

1.   "***Top secret information***" is information that, if disclosed, "reasonably could be expected to cause exceptionally grave damage to the national security." Executive Order 13526 (50 U.S.C. § 3161 note).

2.   The Commission has set the base offense level in this subpart on the assumption that the information at issue bears a significant relation to the nation's security, and that the revelation will significantly and adversely affect security interests. When revelation is likely to cause little or no harm, a downward departure may be warranted. *See* Chapter Five, Part K (Departures).

3.   The court may depart from the guidelines upon representation by the President or his duly authorized designee that the imposition of a sanction other than authorized by the guideline is necessary to protect national security or further the objectives of the nation's foreign policy.

Background: Offense level distinctions in this subpart are generally based on the classification of the information gathered or transmitted. This classification, in turn, reflects the importance of the information to the national security.

Historical Note	Effective November 1, 1987. Amended effective November 1, 2010 (amendment 746); November 1, 2013 (amendment 778); November 1, 2014 (amendment 789).

---

§2M3.2. Gathering National Defense Information

    (a) Base Offense Level:

        (1) **35**, if top secret information was gathered; or

        (2) **30**, otherwise.

Commentary

Statutory Provisions: 18 U.S.C. §§ 793(a), (b), (c), (d), (e), (g), 1030(a)(1). For additional statutory provision(s), *see* Appendix A (Statutory Index).

Application Notes:

1. *See* Commentary to §2M3.1.

2. If the defendant is convicted under 18 U.S.C. § 793(d) or (e), §2M3.3 may apply. *See* Commentary to §2M3.3.

Background: The statutes covered in this section proscribe diverse forms of obtaining and transmitting national defense information with intent or reason to believe the information would injure the United States or be used to the advantage of a foreign government.

Historical Note	Effective November 1, 1987. Amended effective November 1, 2003 (amendment 654).

§2M3.3. Transmitting National Defense Information; Disclosure of Classified Cryptographic Information; Unauthorized Disclosure to a Foreign Government or a Communist Organization of Classified Information by Government Employee; Unauthorized Receipt of Classified Information

    (a)   Base Offense Level:

         (1)   **29**, if top secret information; or

         (2)   **24**, otherwise.

Commentary

Statutory Provisions: 18 U.S.C. §§ 793(d), (e), (g), 798; 50 U.S.C. § 783.

Application Notes:

1. *See* Commentary to §2M3.1.

2. If the defendant was convicted of 18 U.S.C. § 793(d) or (e) for the willful transmission or communication of intangible information with reason to believe that it could be used to the injury of the United States or the advantage of a foreign nation, apply §2M3.2.

Background: The statutes covered in this section proscribe willfully transmitting or communicating to a person not entitled to receive it a document, writing, code book, signal book, sketch, photograph, photographic negative, blueprint, plan, map, model, instrument, appliance, or note relating to the national defense. Proof that the item was communicated with reason to believe that it could be used to the injury of the United States or the advantage of a foreign nation is required only where intangible information is communicated under 18 U.S.C. § 793(d) or (e).

This section also covers statutes that proscribe the disclosure of classified information concerning cryptographic or communication intelligence to the detriment of the United States or for the benefit of a foreign government, the unauthorized disclosure to a foreign government or a communist organization of classified information by a government employee, and the unauthorized receipt of classified information.

Historical Note	Effective November 1, 1987. Amended effective November 1, 1993 (amendment 481); November 1, 2010 (amendment 746).

§2M3.4. Losing National Defense Information

    (a)   Base Offense Level:

        (1)   **18**, if top secret information was lost; or

        (2)   **13**, otherwise.

Commentary

Statutory Provision: 18 U.S.C. § 793(f).

Application Note:

1.   *See* Commentary to §2M3.1.

Background: Offenses prosecuted under this statute generally do not involve subversive conduct on behalf of a foreign power, but rather the loss of classified information by the gross negligence of an employee of the federal government or a federal contractor.

Historical Note	Effective November 1, 1987.

§2M3.5. Tampering with Restricted Data Concerning Atomic Energy

    (a)   Base Offense Level: **24**

Commentary

Statutory Provision: 42 U.S.C. § 2276.

Application Note:

1.   *See* Commentary to §2M3.1.

Historical Note	Effective November 1, 1987.

§2M3.6. [Deleted]

Historical Note	Section 2M3.6 (Disclosure of Classified Cryptographic Information), effective November 1, 1987, was deleted by consolidation with §2M3.3 effective November 1, 1993 (amendment 481).

§2M3.7. [Deleted]

Historical Note	Section 2M3.7 (Unauthorized Disclosure to Foreign Government or a Communist Organization of Classified Information by Government Employee), effective November 1, 1987, was deleted by consolidation with §2M3.3 effective November 1, 1993 (amendment 481).

§2M3.8. [Deleted]

Historical Note	Section 2M3.8 (Receipt of Classified Information), effective November 1, 1987, was deleted by consolidation with §2M3.3 effective November 1, 1993 (amendment 481).

§2M3.9. Disclosure of Information Identifying a Covert Agent

    (a)   Base Offense Level:

        (1) **30**, if the information was disclosed by a person with, or who had authorized access to classified information identifying a covert agent; or

        (2) **25**, if the information was disclosed by a person with authorized access only to other classified information.

Commentary

Statutory Provision: 50 U.S.C. § 3121.

Application Notes:

1.   *See* Commentary to §2M3.1.

2.   This guideline applies only to violations of 50 U.S.C. § 3121 by persons who have or previously had authorized access to classified information. This guideline does not apply to violations of 50 U.S.C. § 3121 by defendants, including journalists, who disclosed such

information without having or having had authorized access to classified information. Violations of 50 U.S.C. § 3121 not covered by this guideline may vary in the degree of harm they inflict, and the court should impose a sentence that reflects such harm. *See* §2X5.1 (Other Offenses).

3.   A term of imprisonment imposed for a conviction under 50 U.S.C. § 3121 shall be imposed consecutively to any other term of imprisonment. *See* 50 U.S.C. § 3121(d).

Background: The alternative base offense levels reflect a statutory distinction by providing a greater base offense level for a violation of 50 U.S.C. § 3121 by an official who has or had authorized access to classified information identifying a covert agent than for a violation by an official with authorized access only to other classified information. This guideline does not apply to violations of 50 U.S.C. § 3121 by defendants who disclosed such information without having, or having had, authorized access to classified information.

Historical Note	Effective November 1, 1987. Amended effective November 1, 2001 (amendment 636); November 1, 2010 (amendment 746); November 1, 2015 (amendment 796).

*   *   *   *   *

4.   EVASION OF MILITARY SERVICE

§2M4.1.   Failure to Register and Evasion of Military Service

(a)   Base Offense Level: **6**

(b)   Specific Offense Characteristic

(1)   If the offense occurred at a time when persons were being inducted for compulsory military service, increase by **6** levels.

Commentary

Statutory Provision: 50 U.S.C. App. § 462.

Application Note:

1.   Subsection (b)(1) does not distinguish between whether the offense was committed in peacetime or during time of war or armed conflict. If the offense was committed when persons were being inducted for compulsory military service during time of war or armed conflict, an upward departure may be warranted.

Historical Note	Effective November 1, 1987. Amended effective November 1, 1990 (amendment 336).

*   *   *   *   *

5. PROHIBITED FINANCIAL TRANSACTIONS AND EXPORTS, AND PROVIDING MATERIAL SUPPORT TO DESIGNATED FOREIGN TERRORIST ORGANIZATIONS

Historical Note	Effective November 1, 1987. Amended effective November 1, 2002 (amendment 637).

§2M5.1. Evasion of Export Controls; Financial Transactions with Countries Supporting International Terrorism

(a) Base Offense Level (Apply the greater):

    (1) **26**, if (A) national security controls or controls relating to the proliferation of nuclear, biological, or chemical weapons or materials were evaded; or (B) the offense involved a financial transaction with a country supporting international terrorism; or

    (2) **14**, otherwise.

Commentary

Statutory Provisions: 18 U.S.C. § 2332d; 22 U.S.C. § 8512; 50 U.S.C. § 1705; 50 U.S.C. App. §§ 2401–2420.

Application Notes:

1.   In the case of a violation during time of war or armed conflict, an upward departure may be warranted.

2.   In determining the sentence within the applicable guideline range, the court may consider the degree to which the violation threatened a security interest of the United States, the volume of commerce involved, the extent of planning or sophistication, and whether there were multiple occurrences. Where such factors are present in an extreme form, a departure from the guidelines may be warranted. *See* Chapter Five, Part K (Departures).

3.   In addition to the provisions for imprisonment, 50 U.S.C. App. § 2410 contains provisions for criminal fines and forfeiture as well as civil penalties. The maximum fine for individual defendants is $250,000. In the case of corporations, the maximum fine is five times the value of the exports involved or $1 million, whichever is greater. When national security controls are violated, in addition to any other sanction, the defendant is subject to forfeiture of any interest in, security of, or claim against: any goods or tangible items that were the subject of the violation; property used to export or attempt to export that was the subject of the violation; and any proceeds obtained directly or indirectly as a result of the violation.

4.   For purposes of subsection (a)(1)(B), "*a country supporting international terrorism*" means a country designated under section 6(j) of the Export Administration Act (50 U.S.C. App. 2405).

Historical Note	Effective November 1, 1987. Amended effective November 1, 2001 (amendment 633); November 1, 2002 (amendment 637); November 1, 2011 (amendment 753).

§2M5.2. Exportation of Arms, Munitions, or Military Equipment or Services Without Required Validated Export License

    (a)   Base Offense Level:

        (1)   **26**, except as provided in subdivision (2) below;

        (2)   **14**, if the offense involved only (A) non-fully automatic small arms (rifles, handguns, or shotguns), and the number of weapons did not exceed two, (B) ammunition for non-fully automatic small arms, and the number of rounds did not exceed 500, or (C) both.

Commentary

Statutory Provisions: 18 U.S.C. § 554; 22 U.S.C. §§ 2778, 2780, 8512; 50 U.S.C. § 1705.

Application Notes:

1.   Under 22 U.S.C. § 2778, the President is authorized, through a licensing system administered by the Department of State, to control exports of defense articles and defense services that he deems critical to a security or foreign policy interest of the United States. The items subject to control constitute the United States Munitions List, which is set out in 22 C.F.R. Part 121.1. Included in this list are such things as military aircraft, helicopters, artillery, shells, missiles, rockets, bombs, vessels of war, explosives, military and space electronics, and certain firearms.

    The base offense level assumes that the offense conduct was harmful or had the potential to be harmful to a security or foreign policy interest of the United States. In the unusual case where the offense conduct posed no such risk, a downward departure may be warranted. In the case of a violation during time of war or armed conflict, an upward departure may be warranted. *See* Chapter Five, Part K (Departures).

2.   In determining the sentence within the applicable guideline range, the court may consider the degree to which the violation threatened a security or foreign policy interest of the United States, the volume of commerce involved, the extent of planning or sophistication, and whether there were multiple occurrences. Where such factors are present in an extreme form, a departure from the guidelines may be warranted.

Historical Note	Effective November 1, 1987. Amended effective November 1, 1990 (amendment 337); November 1, 2001 (amendment 633); November 1, 2007 (amendment 700); November 1, 2011 (amendment 753).

---

§2M5.3. **Providing Material Support or Resources to Designated Foreign Terrorist Organizations or Specially Designated Global Terrorists, or For a Terrorist Purpose**

(a) Base Offense Level: **26**

(b) Specific Offense Characteristic

    (1) If the offense involved the provision of (A) dangerous weapons; (B) firearms; (C) explosives; (D) funds with the intent, knowledge, or reason to believe such funds would be used to purchase any of the items described in subdivisions (A) through (C); or (E) funds or other material support or resources with the intent, knowledge, or reason to believe they are to be used to commit or assist in the commission of a violent act, increase by **2** levels.

(c) Cross References

    (1) If the offense resulted in death, apply §2A1.1 (First Degree Murder) if the death was caused intentionally or knowingly, or §2A1.2 (Second Degree Murder) otherwise, if the resulting offense level is greater than that determined above.

    (2) If the offense was tantamount to attempted murder, apply §2A2.1 (Assault with Intent to Commit Murder; Attempted Murder), if the resulting offense level is greater than that determined above.

    (3) If the offense involved the provision of (A) a nuclear weapon, nuclear material, or nuclear byproduct material; (B) a chemical weapon; (C) a biological agent, toxin, or delivery system; or (D) a weapon of mass destruction, apply §2M6.1 (Nuclear, Biological, and Chemical Weapons, and Other Weapons of Mass Destruction), if the resulting offense level is greater than that determined above.

Commentary

Statutory Provisions: 18 U.S.C. §§ 2283, 2284, 2339B, 2339C(a)(1)(B), (c)(2)(B) (but only with respect to funds known or intended to have been provided or collected in violation of 18 U.S.C. § 2339C(a)(1)(B)); 22 U.S.C. § 8512; 50 U.S.C. § 1705.

Application Notes:

1. **Definitions.**—For purposes of this guideline:

    "*Biological agent*", "*chemical weapon*", "*nuclear byproduct material*", "*nuclear material*", "*toxin*", and "*weapon of mass destruction*" have the meaning given those terms in Application Note 1 of the Commentary to §2M6.1 (Nuclear, Biological, and Chemical Weapons, and Other Weapons of Mass Destruction).

    "*Dangerous weapon*", "*firearm*", and "*destructive device*" have the meaning given those terms in Application Note 1 of the Commentary to §1B1.1 (Application Instructions).

    "*Explosives*" has the meaning given that term in Application Note 1 of the Commentary to §2K1.4 (Arson; Property Damage by Use of Explosives).

    "*Foreign terrorist organization*" has the meaning given the term "terrorist organization" in 18 U.S.C. § 2339B(g)(6).

    "*Material support or resources*" has the meaning given that term in 18 U.S.C. § 2339B(g)(4).

    "*Specially designated global terrorist*" has the meaning given that term in 31 C.F.R. § 594.513.

2. **Departure Provisions.**—

    (A) **In General.**—In determining the sentence within the applicable guideline range, the court may consider the degree to which the violation threatened a security interest of the United States, the volume of the funds or other material support or resources involved, the extent of planning or sophistication, and whether there were multiple occurrences. In a case in which such factors are present in an extreme form, a departure from the guidelines may be warranted. *See* Chapter Five, Part K (Departures).

    (B) **War or Armed Conflict.**—In the case of a violation during time of war or armed conflict, an upward departure may be warranted.

Historical Note	Effective November 1, 2002 (amendment 637). Amended effective November 1, 2003 (amendment 655); November 1, 2007 (amendment 700); November 1, 2011 (amendment 753).

*　*　*　*　*

6. NUCLEAR, BIOLOGICAL, AND CHEMICAL WEAPONS AND MATERIALS, AND OTHER WEAPONS OF MASS DESTRUCTION

Historical Note	Effective November 1, 1987. Amended effective November 1, 2001 (amendment 633).

§2M6.1. Unlawful Activity Involving Nuclear Material, Weapons, or Facilities, Biological Agents, Toxins, or Delivery Systems, Chemical Weapons, or Other Weapons of Mass Destruction; Attempt or Conspiracy

(a) Base Offense Level (Apply the Greatest):

(1) **42**, if the offense was committed with intent (A) to injure the United States; or (B) to aid a foreign nation or a foreign terrorist organization;

(2) **28**, if subsections (a)(1), (a)(3), and (a)(4) do not apply;

(3) **22**, if the defendant is convicted under 18 U.S.C. § 175b; or

(4) **20**, if (A) the defendant is convicted under 18 U.S.C. § 175(b); or (B) the offense (i) involved a threat to use a nuclear weapon, nuclear material, or nuclear byproduct material, a chemical weapon, a biological agent, toxin, or delivery system, or a weapon of mass destruction; but (ii) did not involve any conduct evidencing an intent or ability to carry out the threat.

(b) Specific Offense Characteristics

(1) If (A) subsection (a)(2) or (a)(4)(A) applies; and (B) the offense involved a threat to use, or otherwise involved (i) a select biological agent; (ii) a listed precursor or a listed toxic chemical; (iii) nuclear material or nuclear byproduct material; or (iv) a weapon of mass destruction that contains any agent, precursor, toxic chemical, or material referred to in subdivision (i), (ii), or (iii), increase by **2** levels.

(2) If (A) subsection (a)(2), (a)(3), or (a)(4)(A) applies; and (B)(i) any victim died or sustained permanent or life-threatening bodily injury, increase by **4** levels; (ii) any victim sustained serious bodily injury, increase by **2** levels; or (iii) the degree of injury is between that specified in subdivisions (i) and (ii), increase by **3** levels.

(3) If (A) subsection (a)(2), (a)(3), or (a)(4) applies; and (B) the offense resulted in (i) substantial disruption of public, governmental, or business functions or services; or (ii) a substantial expenditure of funds to clean up, decontaminate, or otherwise respond to the offense, increase by 4 levels.

(c) Cross References

(1) If the offense resulted in death, apply §2A1.1 (First Degree Murder) if the death was caused intentionally or knowingly, or §2A1.2 (Second Degree Murder) otherwise, if the resulting offense level is greater than that determined above.

(2) If the offense was tantamount to attempted murder, apply §2A2.1 (Assault with Intent to Commit Murder; Attempted Murder), if the resulting offense level is greater than that determined above.

(d) Special Instruction

(1) If the defendant is convicted of a single count involving (A) conduct that resulted in the death or permanent, life-threatening, or serious bodily injury of more than one victim, or (B) conduct tantamount to the attempted murder of more than one victim, Chapter Three, Part D (Multiple Counts) shall be applied as if such conduct in respect to each victim had been contained in a separate count of conviction.

Commentary

Statutory Provisions: 18 U.S.C. §§ 175, 175b, 175c, 229, 831, 832, 842(p)(2) (only with respect to weapons of mass destruction as defined in 18 U.S.C. § 2332a(c)(2)(B), (C), and (D)), 1992(a)(2), (a)(3), (a)(4), (b)(2), 2283, 2291, 2332h; 42 U.S.C. §§ 2077(b), 2122, 2131. For additional statutory provision(s), *see* Appendix A (Statutory Index).

Application Notes:

1. **Definitions.**—For purposes of this guideline:

    "*Biological agent*" has the meaning given that term in 18 U.S.C. § 178(1).

    "*Chemical weapon*" has the meaning given that term in 18 U.S.C. § 229F(1).

    "*Foreign terrorist organization*" (A) means an organization that engages in terrorist activity that threatens the security of a national of the United States or the national security of the United States; and (B) includes an organization designated by the Secretary of State as a foreign terrorist organization pursuant to section 219 of the Immigration and Nationality Act (8 U.S.C. § 1189). "National of the United States" has the meaning given that term in section 101(a)(22) of the Immigration and Nationality Act (8 U.S.C. § 1101(a)(22)).

"*Listed precursor or a listed toxic chemical*" means a precursor or a toxic chemical, respectively, listed in Schedule I of the Annex on Chemicals to the Chemical Weapons Convention. *See* 18 U.S.C. § 229F(6)(B), (8)(B). "Precursor" has the meaning given that term in 18 U.S.C. § 229F(6)(A). "Toxic chemical" has the meaning given that term in 18 U.S.C. § 229F(8)(A).

"*Nuclear byproduct material*" has the meaning given that term in 18 U.S.C. § 831(g)(2).

"*Nuclear material*" has the meaning given that term in 18 U.S.C. § 831(g)(1).

"*Restricted person*" has the meaning given that term in 18 U.S.C. § 175b(d)(2).

"*Select biological agent*" means a biological agent or toxin identified (A) by the Secretary of Health and Human Services on the select agent list established and maintained pursuant to section 351A of the Public Health Service Act (42 U.S.C. § 262a); or (B) by the Secretary of Agriculture on the list established and maintained pursuant to section 212 of the Agricultural Bioterrorism Protection Act of 2002 (7 U.S.C. § 8401).

"*Toxin*" has the meaning given that term in 18 U.S.C. § 178(2).

"*Vector*" has the meaning given that term in 18 U.S.C. § 178(4).

"*Weapon of mass destruction*" has the meaning given that term in 18 U.S.C. § 2332a(c)(2)(B), (C), and (D).

2.   **Threat Cases.**—Subsection (a)(4)(B) applies in cases that involved a threat to use a weapon, agent, or material covered by this guideline but that did not involve any conduct evidencing an intent or ability to carry out the threat. For example, subsection (a)(4)(B) would apply in a case in which the defendant threatened to contaminate an area with anthrax and also dispersed into the area a substance that appeared to be anthrax but that the defendant knew to be harmless talcum powder. In such a case, the dispersal of talcum powder does not evidence an intent on the defendant's part to carry out the threat. In contrast, subsection (a)(4)(B) would not apply in a case in which the defendant threatened to contaminate an area with anthrax and also dispersed into the area a substance that the defendant believed to be anthrax but that in fact was harmless talcum powder. In such a case, the dispersal of talcum powder was conduct evidencing an intent to carry out the threat because of the defendant's belief that the talcum powder was anthrax.

Subsection (a)(4)(B) shall not apply in any case involving both a threat to use any weapon, agent, or material covered by this guideline and the possession of that weapon, agent, or material. In such a case, possession of the weapon, agent, or material is conduct evidencing an intent to use that weapon, agent, or material.

3.   **Application of Special Instruction.**—Subsection (d) applies in any case in which the defendant is convicted of a single count involving (A) the death or permanent, life-threatening, or serious bodily injury of more than one victim, or (B) conduct tantamount to the attempted murder of more than one victim, regardless of whether the offense level is determined under this guideline or under another guideline in Chapter Two (Offense Conduct) by use of a cross reference under subsection (c).

| *Historical Note* | Effective November 1, 1987. Amended effective November 1, 2001 (amendment 633); November 1, 2002 (amendment 637); November 1, 2003 (amendment 655); November 1, 2005 (amendment 679); November 1, 2006 (amendment 686); November 1, 2007 (amendments 699 and 700); November 1, 2010 (amendment 746); November 1, 2016 (amendment 804). |

§2M6.2. Violation of Other Federal Atomic Energy Agency Statutes, Rules, and Regulations

    (a)   Base Offense Level (Apply the greater):

        (1)   **30**, if the offense was committed with intent to injure the United States or to aid a foreign nation; or

        (2)   **6**.

Commentary

Statutory Provision: 42 U.S.C. § 2273.

Background: This section applies to offenses related to nuclear energy not specifically addressed elsewhere. This provision covers, for example, violations of statutes dealing with rules and regulations, license conditions, and orders of the Nuclear Regulatory Commission and the Department of Energy.

| *Historical Note* | Effective November 1, 1987. Amended effective November 1, 1990 (amendment 359). |

PART N — OFFENSES INVOLVING FOOD, DRUGS, AGRICULTURAL PRODUCTS, CONSUMER PRODUCTS, AND ODOMETER LAWS

Historical Note	Effective November 1, 1987. Amended effective November 1, 2009 (amendment 733).

1. TAMPERING WITH CONSUMER PRODUCTS

§2N1.1. Tampering or Attempting to Tamper Involving Risk of Death or Bodily Injury

    (a)   Base Offense Level: **25**

    (b)   Specific Offense Characteristic

        (1)   (A) If any victim sustained permanent or life-threatening bodily injury, increase by **4** levels; (B) if any victim sustained serious bodily injury, increase by **2** levels; or (C) if the degree of injury is between that specified in subdivisions (A) and (B), increase by **3** levels.

    (c)   Cross References

        (1)   If the offense resulted in death, apply §2A1.1 (First Degree Murder) if the death was caused intentionally or knowingly, or §2A1.2 (Second Degree Murder) in any other case.

        (2)   If the offense was tantamount to attempted murder, apply §2A2.1 (Assault with Intent to Commit Murder; Attempted Murder) if the resulting offense level is greater than that determined above.

        (3)   If the offense involved extortion, apply §2B3.2 (Extortion by Force or Threat of Injury or Serious Damage) if the resulting offense level is greater than that determined above.

    (d)   Special Instruction

        (1)   If the defendant is convicted of a single count involving (A) the death or permanent, life-threatening, or serious bodily injury of more than one victim, or (B) conduct tantamount to the attempted murder of more than one victim, Chapter Three,

Part D (Multiple Counts) shall be applied as if the defendant had been convicted of a separate count for each such victim.

Commentary

Statutory Provisions: 18 U.S.C. § 1365(a), (e).

Application Notes:

1. The base offense level reflects that this offense typically poses a risk of death or serious bodily injury to one or more victims; or causes, or is intended to cause, bodily injury. Where the offense posed a substantial risk of death or serious bodily injury to numerous victims, or caused extreme psychological injury or substantial property damage or monetary loss, an upward departure may be warranted. In the unusual case in which the offense did not cause a risk of death or serious bodily injury, and neither caused nor was intended to cause bodily injury, a downward departure may be warranted.

2. The special instruction in subsection (d)(1) applies whether the offense level is determined under subsection (b)(1) or by use of a cross reference in subsection (c).

Historical Note	Effective November 1, 1987. Amended effective November 1, 1990 (amendment 338); November 1, 1991 (amendment 376).

§2N1.2. Providing False Information or Threatening to Tamper with Consumer Products

(a) Base Offense Level: **16**

(b) Cross Reference

(1) If the offense involved extortion, apply §2B3.2 (Extortion by Force or Threat of Injury or Serious Damage).

Commentary

Statutory Provisions: 18 U.S.C. § 1365(c), (d).

Application Note:

1. If death or bodily injury, extreme psychological injury, or substantial property damage or monetary loss resulted, an upward departure may be warranted. *See* Chapter Five, Part K (Departures).

Historical Note	Effective November 1, 1987. Amended effective November 1, 1990 (amendment 339).

§2N1.3. Tampering With Intent to Injure Business

(a)   Base Offense Level: **12**

Commentary

Statutory Provision: 18 U.S.C. § 1365(b).

Application Note:

1.   If death or bodily injury, extreme psychological injury, or substantial property damage or monetary loss resulted, an upward departure may be warranted. *See* Chapter Five, Part K (Departures).

Historical Note	Effective November 1, 1987.

*   *   *   *   *   *

2.   FOOD, DRUGS, AGRICULTURAL PRODUCTS, AND CONSUMER PRODUCTS

Historical Note	Effective November 1, 1987. Amended effective November 1, 2009 (amendment 733).

§2N2.1.   Violations of Statutes and Regulations Dealing With Any Food, Drug, Biological Product, Device, Cosmetic, Agricultural Product, or Consumer Product

(a)   Base Offense Level: **6**

(b)   Specific Offense Characteristic

(1)   If the defendant was convicted under 21 U.S.C. § 331 after sustaining a prior conviction under 21 U.S.C. § 331, increase by 4 levels.

(c)   Cross References

(1)   If the offense involved fraud, apply §2B1.1 (Theft, Property Destruction, and Fraud).

(2)   If the offense was committed in furtherance of, or to conceal, an offense covered by another offense guideline, apply that other offense guideline if the resulting offense level is greater than that determined above.

Commentary

Statutory Provisions: 7 U.S.C. §§ 150bb, 150gg, 6810, 7734, 8313; 21 U.S.C. §§ 115, 117, 122, 134–134e, 151–158, 331, 333(a)(1), (a)(2), (b), 458–461, 463, 466, 610, 611, 614, 617, 619, 620, 642–644, 676; 42 U.S.C. § 262. For additional statutory provision(s), *see* Appendix A (Statutory Index).

Application Notes:

1. This guideline assumes a regulatory offense that involved knowing or reckless conduct. Where only negligence was involved, a downward departure may be warranted. *See* Chapter Five, Part K (Departures).

2. The cross reference at subsection (c)(1) addresses cases in which the offense involved fraud. The cross reference at subsection (c)(2) addresses cases in which the offense was committed in furtherance of, or to conceal, an offense covered by another offense guideline (*e.g.*, bribery).

3. **Upward Departure Provisions.**—The following are circumstances in which an upward departure may be warranted:

   (A) The offense created a substantial risk of bodily injury or death; or bodily injury, death, extreme psychological injury, property damage, or monetary loss resulted from the offense. *See* Chapter Five, Part K (Departures).

   (B) The defendant was convicted under 7 U.S.C. § 7734.

4. The Commission has not promulgated a guideline for violations of 21 U.S.C. § 333(e) (offenses involving human growth hormones). Offenses involving anabolic steroids are covered by Chapter Two, Part D (Offenses Involving Drugs and Narco-Terrorism). In the case of an offense involving a substance purported to be an anabolic steroid, but not containing any active ingredient, apply §2B1.1 (Theft, Property Destruction, and Fraud) with "loss" measured by the amount paid, or to be paid, by the victim for such substance.

Historical Note	Effective November 1, 1987. Amended effective November 1, 1990 (amendment 340); November 1, 1991 (amendment 432); November 1, 1992 (amendment 451); November 1, 2001 (amendment 617); November 1, 2002 (amendment 646); November 1, 2003 (amendment 661); November 1, 2006 (amendment 685); November 1, 2007 (amendment 711); November 1, 2008 (amendment 723); November 1, 2009 (amendment 733).

* * * * *

3. ODOMETER LAWS AND REGULATIONS

§2N3.1. Odometer Laws and Regulations

(a) Base Offense Level: **6**

    (b)   Cross Reference

        (1) If the offense involved more than one vehicle, apply §2B1.1 (Theft, Property Destruction, and Fraud).

Commentary

Statutory Provisions: 49 U.S.C. §§ 32703–32705, 32709(b).

Background: The base offense level takes into account the deceptive aspect of the offense assuming a single vehicle was involved. If more than one vehicle was involved, §2B1.1 (Theft, Property Destruction, and Fraud) is to be applied because it is designed to deal with a pattern or scheme.

Historical Note	Effective November 1, 1987. Amended effective November 1, 1989 (amendment 199); November 1, 1997 (amendment 553); November 1, 2001 (amendment 617).

PART O — [NOT USED]

PART P — OFFENSES INVOLVING PRISONS AND CORRECTIONAL FACILITIES

§2P1.1. Escape, Instigating or Assisting Escape

(a) Base Offense Level:

    (1) **13**, if the custody or confinement is by virtue of an arrest on a charge of felony, or conviction of any offense;

    (2) **8**, otherwise.

(b) Specific Offense Characteristics

    (1) If the use or the threat of force against any person was involved, increase by **5** levels.

    (2) If the defendant escaped from non-secure custody and returned voluntarily within ninety-six hours, decrease the offense level under §2P1.1(a)(1) by **7** levels or the offense level under §2P1.1(a)(2) by **4** levels. *Provided*, however, that this reduction shall not apply if the defendant, while away from the facility, committed any federal, state, or local offense punishable by a term of imprisonment of one year or more.

    (3) If the defendant escaped from the non-secure custody of a community corrections center, community treatment center, "halfway house," or similar facility, and subsection (b)(2) is not applicable, decrease the offense level under subsection (a)(1) by **4** levels or the offense level under subsection (a)(2) by **2** levels. *Provided*, however, that this reduction shall not apply if the defendant, while away from the facility, committed any federal, state, or local offense punishable by a term of imprisonment of one year or more.

    (4) If the defendant was a law enforcement or correctional officer or employee, or an employee of the Department of Justice, at the time of the offense, increase by **2** levels.

Commentary

Statutory Provisions: 18 U.S.C. §§ 751, 752, 755; 28 U.S.C. § 1826. For additional statutory provision(s), *see* Appendix A (Statutory Index).

§2P1.2

Application Notes:

1. "***Non-secure custody***" means custody with no significant physical restraint (*e.g.*, where a defendant walked away from a work detail outside the security perimeter of an institution; where a defendant failed to return to any institution from a pass or unescorted furlough; or where a defendant escaped from an institution with no physical perimeter barrier).

2. "***Returned voluntarily***" includes voluntarily returning to the institution or turning one's self in to a law enforcement authority as an escapee (not in connection with an arrest or other charges).

3. If the adjustment in subsection (b)(4) applies, no adjustment is to be made under §3B1.3 (Abuse of Position of Trust or Use of Special Skill).

4. If death or bodily injury resulted, an upward departure may be warranted. *See* Chapter Five, Part K (Departures).

5. Criminal history points under Chapter Four, Part A (Criminal History) are to be determined independently of the application of this guideline. For example, in the case of a defendant serving a one-year sentence of imprisonment at the time of the escape, criminal history points from §4A1.1(b) (for the sentence being served at the time of the escape) and §4A1.1(d) (custody status) would be applicable.

6. If the adjustment in subsection (b)(1) applies as a result of conduct that involves an official victim, do not apply §3A1.2 (Official Victim).

Historical Note	Effective November 1, 1987. Amended effective November 1, 1989 (amendments 200 and 201); November 1, 1990 (amendment 341); November 1, 1991 (amendment 406); November 1, 2010 (amendment 747).

§2P1.2. Providing or Possessing Contraband in Prison

(a) Base Offense Level:

  (1) **23**, if the object was a firearm or destructive device.

  (2) **13**, if the object was a weapon (other than a firearm or a destructive device), any object that might be used as a weapon or as a means of facilitating escape, ammunition, LSD, PCP, methamphetamine, or a narcotic drug.

  (3) **6**, if the object was an alcoholic beverage, United States or foreign currency, a mobile phone or similar device, or a controlled substance (other than LSD, PCP, methamphetamine, or a narcotic drug).

(4) **4**, if the object was any other object that threatened the order, discipline, or security of the institution or the life, health, or safety of an individual.

(b) Specific Offense Characteristic

(1) If the defendant was a law enforcement or correctional officer or employee, or an employee of the Department of Justice, at the time of the offense, increase by **2** levels.

(c) Cross Reference

(1) If the object of the offense was the distribution of a controlled substance, apply the offense level from §2D1.1 (Unlawful Manufacturing, Importing, Exporting, or Trafficking; Attempt or Conspiracy). *Provided*, that if the defendant is convicted under 18 U.S.C. § 1791(a)(1) and is punishable under 18 U.S.C. § 1791(b)(1), and the resulting offense level is less than level **26**, increase to level **26**.

Commentary

Statutory Provision: 18 U.S.C. § 1791.

Application Notes:

1. In this guideline, the term "*mobile phone or similar device*" means a phone or other device as described in 18 U.S.C. § 1791(d)(1)(F).

2. If the adjustment in §2P1.2(b)(1) applies, no adjustment is to be made under §3B1.3 (Abuse of Position of Trust or Use of Special Skill).

3. In a case in which the defendant is convicted of the underlying offense and an offense involving providing or possessing a controlled substance in prison, group the offenses together under §3D1.2(c). (Note that 18 U.S.C. § 1791(b) does not require a sentence of imprisonment, although if a sentence of imprisonment is imposed on a count involving providing or possessing a controlled substance in prison, section 1791(c) requires that the sentence be imposed to run consecutively to any other sentence of imprisonment for the controlled substance. Therefore, unlike a count in which the statute mandates both a minimum and a consecutive sentence of imprisonment, the grouping rules of §§3D1.1–3D1.5 apply. *See* §3D1.1(b)(1), comment. (n.1), and §3D1.2, comment. (n.1).) The combined sentence will then be constructed to provide a "total punishment" that satisfies the requirements both of §5G1.2 (Sentencing on Multiple Counts of Conviction) and 18 U.S.C. § 1791(c). For example, if the combined applicable guideline range for both counts is 30–37 months and the court determines a "total punishment" of 36 months is appropriate, a sentence of 30 months for the underlying offense plus a consecutive six months' sentence for the providing or possessing a controlled substance in prison count would satisfy these requirements.

§2P1.4

Pursuant to 18 U.S.C. § 1791(c), a sentence imposed upon an inmate for a violation of 18 U.S.C. § 1791 shall be consecutive to the sentence being served by the inmate at the time of the violation.

Historical Note	Effective November 1, 1987. Amended effective November 1, 1989 (amendments 202 and 203); November 1, 1995 (amendment 525); November 1, 1998 (amendment 579); November 1, 2005 (amendment 680); November 1, 2012 (amendment 769).

§2P1.3. Engaging In, Inciting or Attempting to Incite a Riot Involving Persons in a Facility for Official Detention

(a) Base Offense Level:

    (1) **22**, if the offense was committed under circumstances creating a substantial risk of death or serious bodily injury to any person.

    (2) **16**, if the offense involved a major disruption to the operation of an institution.

    (3) **10**, otherwise.

Commentary

Statutory Provision: 18 U.S.C. § 1792.

Application Note:

1. If death or bodily injury resulted, an upward departure may be warranted. *See* Chapter Five, Part K (Departures).

Historical Note	Effective November 1, 1987.

§2P1.4. [Deleted]

Historical Note	Section 2P1.4 (Trespass on Bureau of Prisons Facilities), effective November 1, 1987, was deleted effective November 1, 1989 (amendment 204).

PART Q — OFFENSES INVOLVING THE ENVIRONMENT

1. ENVIRONMENT

§2Q1.1. Knowing Endangerment Resulting From Mishandling Hazardous or Toxic Substances, Pesticides or Other Pollutants

(a) Base Offense Level: **24**

Commentary

Statutory Provisions: 18 U.S.C. § 1992(b)(3); 33 U.S.C. § 1319(c)(3); 42 U.S.C. § 6928(e).

Application Note:

1. If death or serious bodily injury resulted, an upward departure may be warranted. *See* Chapter Five, Part K (Departures).

Background: This section applies to offenses committed with knowledge that the violation placed another person in imminent danger of death or serious bodily injury.

Historical Note	Effective November 1, 1987. Amended effective November 1, 2007 (amendment 699).

§2Q1.2. Mishandling of Hazardous or Toxic Substances or Pesticides; Recordkeeping, Tampering, and Falsification; Unlawfully Transporting Hazardous Materials in Commerce

(a) Base Offense Level: **8**

(b) Specific Offense Characteristics

    (1) (A) If the offense resulted in an ongoing, continuous, or repetitive discharge, release, or emission of a hazardous or toxic substance or pesticide into the environment, increase by **6** levels; or

        (B) if the offense otherwise involved a discharge, release, or emission of a hazardous or toxic substance or pesticide, increase by **4** levels.

    (2) If the offense resulted in a substantial likelihood of death or serious bodily injury, increase by **9** levels.

(3) If the offense resulted in disruption of public utilities or evacuation of a community, or if cleanup required a substantial expenditure, increase by **4** levels.

(4) If the offense involved transportation, treatment, storage, or disposal without a permit or in violation of a permit, increase by **4** levels.

(5) If a recordkeeping offense reflected an effort to conceal a substantive environmental offense, use the offense level for the substantive offense.

(6) If the offense involved a simple recordkeeping or reporting violation only, decrease by **2** levels.

(7) If the defendant was convicted under 49 U.S.C. § 5124 or § 46312, increase by **2** levels.

Commentary

Statutory Provisions: 7 U.S.C. §§ 136j–136l; 15 U.S.C. §§ 2614 and 2615; 33 U.S.C. §§ 1319(c)(1), (2), 1321(b)(5), 1517(b); 42 U.S.C. §§ 300h-2, 6928(d), 7413, 9603(b), (c), (d); 43 U.S.C. §§ 1350, 1816(a), 1822(b); 49 U.S.C. §§ 5124, 46312. For additional statutory provision(s), *see* Appendix A (Statutory Index).

Application Notes:

1.   "*Recordkeeping offense*" includes both recordkeeping and reporting offenses. The term is to be broadly construed as including failure to report discharges, releases, or emissions where required; the giving of false information; failure to file other required reports or provide necessary information; and failure to prepare, maintain, or provide records as prescribed.

2.   "*Simple recordkeeping or reporting violation*" means a recordkeeping or reporting offense in a situation where the defendant neither knew nor had reason to believe that the recordkeeping offense would significantly increase the likelihood of any substantive environmental harm.

3.   This section applies to offenses involving pesticides or substances designated toxic or hazardous at the time of the offense by statute or regulation. A listing of hazardous and toxic substances in the guidelines would be impractical. Several federal statutes (or regulations promulgated thereunder) list toxics, hazardous wastes and substances, and pesticides. These lists, such as those of toxic pollutants for which effluent standards are published under the Federal Water Pollution Control Act (*e.g.*, 33 U.S.C. § 1317) as well as the designation of hazardous substances under the Comprehensive Environmental Response, Compensation and Liability Act (*e.g.*, 42 U.S.C. § 9601(14)), are revised from time to time. "Toxic" and "hazardous" are defined differently in various statutes, but the common dictionary meanings of the words are not significantly different.

4.   Except when the adjustment in subsection (b)(6) for simple recordkeeping offenses applies, this section assumes knowing conduct. In cases involving negligent conduct, a downward departure may be warranted.

5.   Subsection (b)(1) assumes a discharge or emission into the environment resulting in actual environmental contamination. A wide range of conduct, involving the handling of different quantities of materials with widely differing propensities, potentially is covered. Depending upon the harm resulting from the emission, release or discharge, the quantity and nature of the substance or pollutant, the duration of the offense and the risk associated with the violation, a departure of up to two levels in either direction from the offense levels prescribed in these specific offense characteristics may be appropriate.

6.   Subsection (b)(2) applies to offenses where the public health is seriously endangered. Depending upon the nature of the risk created and the number of people placed at risk, a departure of up to three levels upward or downward may be warranted. If death or serious bodily injury results, a departure would be called for. *See* Chapter Five, Part K (Departures).

7.   Subsection (b)(3) provides an enhancement where a public disruption, evacuation or cleanup at substantial expense has been required. Depending upon the nature of the contamination involved, a departure of up to two levels either upward or downward could be warranted.

8.   Subsection (b)(4) applies where the offense involved violation of a permit, or where there was a failure to obtain a permit when one was required. Depending upon the nature and quantity of the substance involved and the risk associated with the offense, a departure of up to two levels either upward or downward may be warranted.

9.   **Other Upward Departure Provisions.—**

   (A)   **Civil Adjudications and Failure to Comply with Administrative Order.—**In a case in which the defendant has previously engaged in similar misconduct established by a civil adjudication or has failed to comply with an administrative order, an upward departure may be warranted. *See* §4A1.3 (Departures Based on Inadequacy of Criminal History Category).

   (B)   **Extreme Psychological Injury.—**If the offense caused extreme psychological injury, an upward departure may be warranted. *See* §5K2.3 (Extreme Psychological Injury).

   (C)   **Terrorism.—**If the offense was calculated to influence or affect the conduct of government by intimidation or coercion, or to retaliate against government conduct, an upward departure would be warranted. *See* Application Note 4 of the Commentary to §3A1.4 (Terrorism).

Background: This section applies both to substantive violations of the statute governing the handling of pesticides and toxic and hazardous substances and to recordkeeping offenses. The first four specific offense characteristics provide enhancements when the offense involved a substantive violation. The fifth and sixth specific offense characteristics apply to recordkeeping offenses. Although other sections of the guidelines generally prescribe a base offense level of 6 for regulatory violations, §2Q1.2 prescribes a base offense level of 8 because of the inherently dangerous nature of hazardous and toxic substances and pesticides. A decrease of 2 levels is provided, however, for "simple recordkeeping or reporting violations" under §2Q1.2(b)(6).

§2Q1.3

| Historical Note | Effective November 1, 1987. Amended effective November 1, 1993 (amendment 481); November 1, 1997 (amendment 553); November 1, 2004 (amendment 672); November 1, 2010 (amendment 746). |

§2Q1.3. Mishandling of Other Environmental Pollutants; Recordkeeping, Tampering, and Falsification

(a)   Base Offense Level: **6**

(b)   Specific Offense Characteristics

   (1)   (A)   If the offense resulted in an ongoing, continuous, or repetitive discharge, release, or emission of a pollutant into the environment, increase by **6** levels; or

   (B)   if the offense otherwise involved a discharge, release, or emission of a pollutant, increase by **4** levels.

   (2)   If the offense resulted in a substantial likelihood of death or serious bodily injury, increase by **11** levels.

   (3)   If the offense resulted in disruption of public utilities or evacuation of a community, or if cleanup required a substantial expenditure, increase by **4** levels.

   (4)   If the offense involved a discharge without a permit or in violation of a permit, increase by **4** levels.

   (5)   If a recordkeeping offense reflected an effort to conceal a substantive environmental offense, use the offense level for the substantive offense.

Commentary

Statutory Provisions: 33 U.S.C. §§ 403, 406, 407, 411, 1319(c)(1), (c)(2), 1415(b), 1907, 1908; 42 U.S.C. § 7413. For additional statutory provision(s), *see* Appendix A (Statutory Index).

Application Notes:

1.   "*Recordkeeping offense*" includes both recordkeeping and reporting offenses. The term is to be broadly construed as including failure to report discharges, releases, or emissions where required; the giving of false information; failure to file other required reports or provide necessary information; and failure to prepare, maintain, or provide records as prescribed.

2.   If the offense involved mishandling of nuclear material, apply §2M6.2 (Violation of Other Federal Atomic Energy Agency Statutes, Rules, and Regulations) rather than this guideline.

3. The specific offense characteristics in this section assume knowing conduct. In cases involving negligent conduct, a downward departure may be warranted.

4. Subsection (b)(1) assumes a discharge or emission into the environment resulting in actual environmental contamination. A wide range of conduct, involving the handling of different quantities of materials with widely differing propensities, potentially is covered. Depending upon the harm resulting from the emission, release or discharge, the quantity and nature of the substance or pollutant, the duration of the offense and the risk associated with the violation, a departure of up to two levels in either direction from that prescribed in these specific offense characteristics may be appropriate.

5. Subsection (b)(2) applies to offenses where the public health is seriously endangered. Depending upon the nature of the risk created and the number of people placed at risk, a departure of up to three levels upward or downward may be warranted. If death or serious bodily injury results, a departure would be called for. *See* Chapter Five, Part K (Departures).

6. Subsection (b)(3) provides an enhancement where a public disruption, evacuation or cleanup at substantial expense has been required. Depending upon the nature of the contamination involved, a departure of up to two levels in either direction could be warranted.

7. Subsection (b)(4) applies where the offense involved violation of a permit, or where there was a failure to obtain a permit when one was required. Depending upon the nature and quantity of the substance involved and the risk associated with the offense, a departure of up to two levels in either direction may be warranted.

8. Where a defendant has previously engaged in similar misconduct established by a civil adjudication or has failed to comply with an administrative order, an upward departure may be warranted. *See* §4A1.3 (Adequacy of Criminal History Category).

Background: This section parallels §2Q1.2 but applies to offenses involving substances which are not pesticides and are not designated as hazardous or toxic.

Historical Note	Effective November 1, 1987. Amended effective November 1, 1989 (amendment 205).

§2Q1.4. Tampering or Attempted Tampering with a Public Water System; Threatening to Tamper with a Public Water System

    (a)   Base Offense Level (Apply the greatest):

        (1) **26**;

        (2) **22**, if the offense involved (A) a threat to tamper with a public water system; and (B) any conduct evidencing an intent to carry out the threat; or

(3) **16**, if the offense involved a threat to tamper with a public water system but did not involve any conduct evidencing an intent to carry out the threat.

(b) Specific Offense Characteristics

(1) If (A) any victim sustained permanent or life-threatening bodily injury, increase by **4** levels; (B) any victim sustained serious bodily injury, increase by **2** levels; or (C) the degree of injury is between that specified in subdivisions (A) and (B), increase by **3** levels.

(2) If the offense resulted in (A) a substantial disruption of public, governmental, or business functions or services; or (B) a substantial expenditure of funds to clean up, decontaminate, or otherwise respond to the offense, increase by **4** levels.

(3) If the offense resulted in an ongoing, continuous, or repetitive release of a contaminant into a public water system or lasted for a substantial period of time, increase by **2** levels.

(c) Cross References

(1) If the offense resulted in death, apply §2A1.1 (First Degree Murder) if the death was caused intentionally or knowingly, or §2A1.2 (Second Degree Murder) in any other case, if the resulting offense level is greater than that determined above.

(2) If the offense was tantamount to attempted murder, apply §2A2.1 (Assault with Intent to Commit Murder; Attempted Murder) if the resulting offense level is greater than that determined above.

(3) If the offense involved extortion, apply §2B3.2 (Extortion by Force or Threat of Injury or Serious Damage) if the resulting offense level is greater than that determined above.

(d) Special Instruction

(1) If the defendant is convicted of a single count involving (A) the death or permanent, life-threatening, or serious bodily injury of more than one victim; or (B) conduct tantamount to the attempted murder of more than one victim, Chapter Three, Part D (Multiple Counts) shall be applied as if the defendant had been convicted of a separate count for each such victim.

Commentary

Statutory Provision: 42 U.S.C. § 300i-1.

Application Notes:

1. **Definitions.**—For purposes of this guideline, "*permanent or life-threatening bodily injury*" and "*serious bodily injury*" have the meaning given those terms in Note 1 of the Commentary to §1B1.1 (Application Instructions).

2. **Application of Special Instruction.**—Subsection (d) applies in any case in which the defendant is convicted of a single count involving (A) the death or permanent, life-threatening, or serious bodily injury of more than one victim; or (B) conduct tantamount to the attempted murder of more than one victim, regardless of whether the offense level is determined under this guideline or under another guideline in Chapter Two (Offense Conduct) by use of a cross reference under subsection (c).

3. **Departure Provisions.**—

    (A) **Downward Departure Provision.**—The base offense level in subsection (a)(1) reflects that offenses covered by that subsection typically pose a risk of death or serious bodily injury to one or more victims, or cause, or are intended to cause, bodily injury. In the unusual case in which such an offense did not cause a risk of death or serious bodily injury, and neither caused nor was intended to cause bodily injury, a downward departure may be warranted.

    (B) **Upward Departure Provisions.**—If the offense caused extreme psychological injury, or caused substantial property damage or monetary loss, an upward departure may be warranted.

    If the offense was calculated to influence or affect the conduct of government by intimidation or coercion, or to retaliate against government conduct, an upward departure would be warranted. *See* Application Note 4 of §3A1.4 (Terrorism).

Historical Note	Effective November 1, 1987. Amended effective November 1, 1989 (amendment 206); November 1, 2003 (amendment 655).

§2Q1.5. [Deleted]

Historical Note	Effective November 1, 1987. Amended effective November 1, 1989 (amendment 207), was deleted by consolidation with §2Q1.4 effective November 1, 2003 (amendment 655).

§2Q1.6. Hazardous or Injurious Devices on Federal Lands

    (a)   Base Offense Level (Apply the greatest):

        (1)   If the intent was to violate the Controlled Substances Act, apply §2D1.9 (Placing or Maintaining Dangerous Devices on Federal Property to Protect the Unlawful Production of Controlled Substances; Attempt or Conspiracy);

        (2)   If the intent was to obstruct the harvesting of timber, and property destruction resulted, apply §2B1.1 (Theft, Property Destruction, and Fraud);

        (3)   If the offense involved reckless disregard to the risk that another person would be placed in danger of death or serious bodily injury under circumstances manifesting extreme indifference to such risk, the offense level from §2A2.2 (Aggravated Assault); or

        (4)   **6**, otherwise.

Commentary

Statutory Provision: 18 U.S.C. § 1864.

Background: The statute covered by this guideline proscribes a wide variety of conduct, ranging from placing nails in trees to interfere with harvesting equipment to placing anti-personnel devices capable of causing death or serious bodily injury to protect the unlawful production of a controlled substance. Subsections (a)(1)–(a)(3) cover the more serious forms of this offense. Subsection (a)(4) provides a minimum offense level of 6 where the intent was to obstruct the harvesting of timber and little or no property damage resulted.

Historical Note	Effective November 1, 1989 (amendment 208). Amended effective November 1, 1990 (amendment 313); November 1, 2001 (amendment 617); November 1, 2002 (amendment 646); November 1, 2010 (amendment 746).

*   *   *   *   *

2.   CONSERVATION AND WILDLIFE

§2Q2.1. Offenses Involving Fish, Wildlife, and Plants

    (a)   Base Offense Level: **6**

(b)   Specific Offense Characteristics

(1)   If the offense (A) was committed for pecuniary gain or otherwise involved a commercial purpose; or (B) involved a pattern of similar violations, increase by **2** levels.

(2)   If the offense (A) involved fish, wildlife, or plants that were not quarantined as required by law; or (B) otherwise created a significant risk of infestation or disease transmission potentially harmful to humans, fish, wildlife, or plants, increase by **2** levels.

(3)   (If more than one applies, use the greater):

(A)   If the market value of the fish, wildlife, or plants (i) exceeded $2,500 but did not exceed $6,500, increase by **1** level; or (ii) exceeded $6,500, increase by the number of levels from the table in §2B1.1 (Theft, Property Destruction, and Fraud) corresponding to that amount; or

(B)   If the offense involved (i) marine mammals that are listed as depleted under the Marine Mammal Protection Act (as set forth in 50 C.F.R. § 216.15); (ii) fish, wildlife, or plants that are listed as endangered or threatened by the Endangered Species Act (as set forth in 50 C.F.R. Part 17); or (iii) fish, wildlife, or plants that are listed in Appendix I to the Convention on International Trade in Endangered Species of Wild Fauna or Flora (as set forth in 50 C.F.R. Part 23), increase by **4** levels.

(c)   Cross Reference

(1)   If the offense involved a cultural heritage resource or paleontological resource, apply §2B1.5 (Theft of, Damage to, or Destruction of, Cultural Heritage Resources or Paleontological Resources; Unlawful Sale, Purchase, Exchange, Transportation, or Receipt of Cultural Heritage Resources or Paleontological Resources), if the resulting offense level is greater than that determined above.

Commentary

Statutory Provisions: 16 U.S.C. §§ 668(a), 707(b), 1174(a), 1338(a), 1375(b), 1540(b), 3373(d); 18 U.S.C. §§ 545, 554. For additional statutory provision(s), *see* Appendix A (Statutory Index).

Application Notes:

1. "*For pecuniary gain*" means for receipt of, or in anticipation of receipt of, anything of value, whether monetary or in goods or services. Thus, offenses committed for pecuniary gain include both monetary and barter transactions. Similarly, activities designed to increase gross revenue are considered to be committed for pecuniary gain.

2. The acquisition of fish, wildlife, or plants for display to the public, whether for a fee or donation and whether by an individual or an organization, including a governmental entity, a private non-profit organization, or a private for-profit organization, shall be considered to involve a "commercial purpose."

3. For purposes of subsection (b)(2), the quarantine requirements include those set forth in 9 C.F.R. Part 92, and 7 C.F.R., Subtitle B, Chapter III. State quarantine laws are included as well.

4. When information is reasonably available, "*market value*" under subsection (b)(3)(A) shall be based on the fair-market retail price. Where the fair-market retail price is difficult to ascertain, the court may make a reasonable estimate using any reliable information, such as the reasonable replacement or restitution cost or the acquisition and preservation (*e.g.*, taxidermy) cost. Market value, however, shall not be based on measurement of aesthetic loss (so called "contingent valuation" methods).

5. If the offense involved the destruction of a substantial quantity of fish, wildlife, or plants, and the seriousness of the offense is not adequately measured by the market value, an upward departure may be warranted.

6. For purposes of subsection (c)(1), "*cultural heritage resource*" has the meaning given that term in Application Note 1 of the Commentary to §2B1.5 (Theft of, Damage to, or Destruction of, Cultural Heritage Resources; Unlawful Sale, Purchase, Exchange, Transportation, or Receipt of Cultural Heritage Resources).

Background: This section applies to violations of the Endangered Species Act, the Bald Eagle Protection Act, the Migratory Bird Treaty, the Marine Mammal Protection Act, the Wild Free-Roaming Horses and Burros Act, the Fur Seal Act, the Lacey Act, and to violations of 18 U.S.C. §§ 545 and 554 if the smuggling activity involved fish, wildlife, or plants.

Historical Note	Effective November 1, 1987. Amended effective January 15, 1988 (amendment 41); November 1, 1989 (amendments 209 and 210); November 1, 1991 (amendment 407); November 1, 1992 (amendment 452); November 1, 1995 (amendment 534); November 1, 2001 (amendment 617); November 1, 2002 (amendment 638); November 1, 2007 (amendment 700); November 1, 2010 (amendment 746); November 1, 2011 (amendment 758); November 1, 2015 (amendment 791).

----

§2Q2.2. [Deleted]

Historical Note	Section 2Q2.2 (Lacey Act; Smuggling and Otherwise Unlawfully Dealing in Fish, Wildlife, and Plants), effective November 1, 1987, was deleted by consolidation with §2Q2.1 effective November 1, 1989 (amendment 209).

PART R — ANTITRUST OFFENSES

§2R1.1. Bid-Rigging, Price-Fixing or Market-Allocation Agreements Among Competitors

(a) Base Offense Level: **12**

(b) Specific Offense Characteristics

(1) If the conduct involved participation in an agreement to submit non-competitive bids, increase by **1** level.

(2) If the volume of commerce attributable to the defendant was more than $1,000,000, adjust the offense level as follows:

VOLUME OF COMMERCE (APPLY THE GREATEST)	ADJUSTMENT TO OFFENSE LEVEL
(A) More than $1,000,000	add **2**
(B) More than $10,000,000	add **4**
(C) More than $50,000,000	add **6**
(D) More than $100,000,000	add **8**
(E) More than $300,000,000	add **10**
(F) More than $600,000,000	add **12**
(G) More than $1,200,000,000	add **14**
(H) More than $1,850,000,000	add **16**.

For purposes of this guideline, the volume of commerce attributable to an individual participant in a conspiracy is the volume of commerce done by him or his principal in goods or services that were affected by the violation. When multiple counts or conspiracies are involved, the volume of commerce should be treated cumulatively to determine a single, combined offense level.

(c) Special Instruction for Fines

(1) For an individual, the guideline fine range shall be from one to five percent of the volume of commerce, but not less than $20,000.

(d) Special Instructions for Fines — Organizations

(1) In lieu of the pecuniary loss under subsection (a)(3) of §8C2.4 (Base Fine), use **20** percent of the volume of affected commerce.

(2) When applying §8C2.6 (Minimum and Maximum Multipliers), neither the minimum nor maximum multiplier shall be less than 0.75.

(3) In a bid-rigging case in which the organization submitted one or more complementary bids, use as the organization's volume of commerce the greater of (A) the volume of commerce done by the organization in the goods or services that were affected by the violation, or (B) the largest contract on which the organization submitted a complementary bid in connection with the bid-rigging conspiracy.

Commentary

Statutory Provisions: 15 U.S.C. §§ 1, 3(b). For additional statutory provision(s), *see* Appendix A (Statutory Index).

Application Notes:

1. **Application of Chapter Three (Adjustments).**—Sections 3B1.1 (Aggravating Role), 3B1.2 (Mitigating Role), 3B1.3 (Abuse of Position of Trust or Use of Special Skill), and 3C1.1 (Obstructing or Impeding the Administration of Justice) may be relevant in determining the seriousness of the defendant's offense. For example, if a sales manager organizes or leads the price-fixing activity of five or more participants, the 4-level increase at §3B1.1(a) should be applied to reflect the defendant's aggravated role in the offense. For purposes of applying §3B1.2, an individual defendant should be considered for a mitigating role adjustment only if he were responsible in some minor way for his firm's participation in the conspiracy.

2. **Considerations in Setting Fine for Individuals.**—In setting the fine for individuals, the court should consider the extent of the defendant's participation in the offense, the defendant's role, and the degree to which the defendant personally profited from the offense (including salary, bonuses, and career enhancement). If the court concludes that the defendant lacks the ability to pay the guideline fine, it should impose community service in lieu of a portion of the fine. The community service should be equally as burdensome as a fine.

3. The fine for an organization is determined by applying Chapter Eight (Sentencing of Organizations). In selecting a fine for an organization within the guideline fine range, the court should consider both the gain to the organization from the offense and the loss caused by the organization. It is estimated that the average gain from price-fixing is 10 percent of the selling price. The loss from price-fixing exceeds the gain because, among other things, injury is inflicted upon consumers who are unable or for other reasons do not buy the product at the higher prices. Because the loss from price-fixing exceeds the gain, subsection (d)(1) provides that 20 percent of the volume of affected commerce is to be used in lieu of the pecuniary loss under §8C2.4(a)(3). The purpose for specifying a percent of the volume of commerce is to avoid the time and expense that would be required for the court to determine the actual gain or loss. In cases in which the actual monopoly overcharge appears to be either substantially more or substantially less than 10 percent, this factor should be considered in setting the fine within the guideline fine range.

4. Another consideration in setting the fine is that the average level of mark-up due to price-fixing may tend to decline with the volume of commerce involved.

5. It is the intent of the Commission that alternatives such as community confinement not be used to avoid imprisonment of antitrust offenders.

6. Understatement of seriousness is especially likely in cases involving complementary bids. If, for example, the defendant participated in an agreement not to submit a bid, or to submit an unreasonably high bid, on one occasion, in exchange for his being allowed to win a subsequent bid that he did not in fact win, his volume of commerce would be zero, although he would have contributed to harm that possibly was quite substantial. The court should consider sentences near the top of the guideline range in such cases.

7. In the case of a defendant with previous antitrust convictions, a sentence at the maximum of the applicable guideline range, or an upward departure, may be warranted. *See* §4A1.3 (Adequacy of Criminal History Category).

Background: These guidelines apply to violations of the antitrust laws. Although they are not unlawful in all countries, there is near universal agreement that restrictive agreements among competitors, such as horizontal price-fixing (including bid-rigging) and horizontal market-allocation, can cause serious economic harm. There is no consensus, however, about the harmfulness of other types of antitrust offenses, which furthermore are rarely prosecuted and may involve unsettled issues of law. Consequently, only one guideline, which deals with horizontal agreements in restraint of trade, has been promulgated.

The agreements among competitors covered by this section are almost invariably covert conspiracies that are intended to, and serve no purpose other than to, restrict output and raise prices, and that are so plainly anticompetitive that they have been recognized as illegal *per se*, *i.e.*, without any inquiry in individual cases as to their actual competitive effect.

Under the guidelines, prison terms for these offenders should be much more common, and usually somewhat longer, than typical under pre-guidelines practice. Absent adjustments, the guidelines require some period of confinement in the great majority of cases that are prosecuted, including all bid-rigging cases. The court will have the discretion to impose considerably longer sentences within the guideline ranges. Adjustments from Chapter Three, Part E (Acceptance of Responsibility) and, in rare instances, Chapter Three, Part B (Role in the Offense), may decrease these minimum sentences; nonetheless, in very few cases will the guidelines not require that some confinement be imposed. Adjustments will not affect the level of fines.

Tying the offense level to the scale or scope of the offense is important in order to ensure that the sanction is in fact punitive and that there is an incentive to desist from a violation once it has begun. The offense levels are not based directly on the damage caused or profit made by the defendant because damages are difficult and time consuming to establish. The volume of commerce is an acceptable and more readily measurable substitute. The limited empirical data available as to pre-guidelines practice showed that fines increased with the volume of commerce and the term of imprisonment probably did as well.

The Commission believes that the volume of commerce is liable to be an understated measure of seriousness in some bid-rigging cases. For this reason, and consistent with pre-guidelines practice, the Commission has specified a 1-level increase for bid-rigging.

Substantial fines are an essential part of the sentence. For an individual, the guideline fine range is from one to five percent of the volume of commerce, but not less than $20,000.

§2R1.1

For an organization, the guideline fine range is determined under Chapter Eight (Sentencing of Organizations), but pursuant to subsection (d)(2), the minimum multiplier is at least 0.75. This multiplier, which requires a minimum fine of 15 percent of the volume of commerce for the least serious case, was selected to provide an effective deterrent to antitrust offenses. At the same time, this minimum multiplier maintains incentives for desired organizational behavior. Because the Department of Justice has a well-established amnesty program for organizations that self-report antitrust offenses, no lower minimum multiplier is needed as an incentive for self-reporting. A minimum multiplier of at least 0.75 ensures that fines imposed in antitrust cases will exceed the average monopoly overcharge.

The Commission believes that most antitrust defendants have the resources and earning capacity to pay the fines called for by this guideline, at least over time on an installment basis.

Historical Note	Effective November 1, 1987. Amended effective November 1, 1989 (amendments 211 and 303); November 1, 1991 (amendments 377 and 422); November 1, 2003 (amendment 661); November 1, 2004 (amendment 674); November 1, 2005 (amendment 678); November 1, 2015 (amendment 791).

PART S — MONEY LAUNDERING AND MONETARY TRANSACTION REPORTING

Historical Note	Introductory Commentary to this Part, effective November 1, 1987, was deleted effective November 1, 1990 (amendment 342).

§2S1.1. Laundering of Monetary Instruments; Engaging in Monetary Transactions in Property Derived from Unlawful Activity

(a) Base Offense Level:

    (1) The offense level for the underlying offense from which the laundered funds were derived, if (A) the defendant committed the underlying offense (or would be accountable for the underlying offense under subsection (a)(1)(A) of §1B1.3 (Relevant Conduct)); and (B) the offense level for that offense can be determined; or

    (2) 8 plus the number of offense levels from the table in §2B1.1 (Theft, Property Destruction, and Fraud) corresponding to the value of the laundered funds, otherwise.

(b) Specific Offense Characteristics

    (1) If (A) subsection (a)(2) applies; and (B) the defendant knew or believed that any of the laundered funds were the proceeds of, or were intended to promote (i) an offense involving the manufacture, importation, or distribution of a controlled substance or a listed chemical; (ii) a crime of violence; or (iii) an offense involving firearms, explosives, national security, or the sexual exploitation of a minor, increase by 6 levels.

    (2) (Apply the Greatest):

        (A) If the defendant was convicted under 18 U.S.C. § 1957, increase by 1 level.

        (B) If the defendant was convicted under 18 U.S.C. § 1956, increase by 2 levels.

        (C) If (i) subsection (a)(2) applies; and (ii) the defendant was in the business of laundering funds, increase by 4 levels.

(3)   If (A) subsection (b)(2)(B) applies; and (B) the offense involved sophisticated laundering, increase by 2 levels.

Commentary

Statutory Provisions: 18 U.S.C. §§ 1956, 1957, 1960 (but only with respect to unlicensed money transmitting businesses as defined in 18 U.S.C. § 1960(b)(1)(C)). For additional statutory provision(s), *see* Appendix A (Statutory Index).

Application Notes:

1.   **Definitions.**—For purposes of this guideline:

"*Crime of violence*" has the meaning given that term in subsection (a)(1) of §4B1.2 (Definitions of Terms Used in Section 4B1.1).

"*Criminally derived funds*" means any funds derived, or represented by a law enforcement officer, or by another person at the direction or approval of an authorized Federal official, to be derived from conduct constituting a criminal offense.

"*Laundered funds*" means the property, funds, or monetary instrument involved in the transaction, financial transaction, monetary transaction, transportation, transfer, or transmission in violation of 18 U.S.C. § 1956 or § 1957.

"*Laundering funds*" means making a transaction, financial transaction, monetary transaction, or transmission, or transporting or transferring property, funds, or a monetary instrument in violation of 18 U.S.C. § 1956 or § 1957.

"*Sexual exploitation of a minor*" means an offense involving (A) promoting prostitution by a minor; (B) sexually exploiting a minor by production of sexually explicit visual or printed material; (C) distribution of material involving the sexual exploitation of a minor, or possession of material involving the sexual exploitation of a minor with intent to distribute; or (D) aggravated sexual abuse, sexual abuse, or abusive sexual contact involving a minor. "Minor" means an individual under the age of 18 years.

2.   **Application of Subsection (a)(1).**—

(A)   **Multiple Underlying Offenses.**—In cases in which subsection (a)(1) applies and there is more than one underlying offense, the offense level for the underlying offense is to be determined under the procedures set forth in Application Note 3 of the Commentary to §1B1.5 (Interpretation of References to Other Offense Guidelines).

(B)   **Defendants Accountable for Underlying Offense.**—In order for subsection (a)(1) to apply, the defendant must have committed the underlying offense or be accountable for the underlying offense under §1B1.3(a)(1)(A). The fact that the defendant was involved in laundering criminally derived funds after the commission of the underlying offense, without additional involvement in the underlying offense, does not establish that the defendant committed, aided, abetted, counseled, commanded, induced, procured, or willfully caused the underlying offense.

(C)   **Application of Chapter Three Adjustments.**—Notwithstanding §1B1.5(c), in cases in which subsection (a)(1) applies, application of any Chapter Three adjustment shall be determined based on the offense covered by this guideline (*i.e.*, the laundering of criminally derived funds) and not on the underlying offense from which the laundered funds were derived.

3.   **Application of Subsection (a)(2).**—

(A)   **In General.**—Subsection (a)(2) applies to any case in which (i) the defendant did not commit the underlying offense; or (ii) the defendant committed the underlying offense (or would be accountable for the underlying offense under §1B1.3(a)(1)(A)), but the offense level for the underlying offense is impossible or impracticable to determine.

(B)   **Commingled Funds.**—In a case in which a transaction, financial transaction, monetary transaction, transportation, transfer, or transmission results in the commingling of legitimately derived funds with criminally derived funds, the value of the laundered funds, for purposes of subsection (a)(2), is the amount of the criminally derived funds, not the total amount of the commingled funds, if the defendant provides sufficient information to determine the amount of criminally derived funds without unduly complicating or prolonging the sentencing process. If the amount of the criminally derived funds is difficult or impracticable to determine, the value of the laundered funds, for purposes of subsection (a)(2), is the total amount of the commingled funds.

(C)   **Non-Applicability of Enhancement.**—Subsection (b)(2)(B) shall not apply if the defendant was convicted of a conspiracy under 18 U.S.C. § 1956(h) and the sole object of that conspiracy was to commit an offense set forth in 18 U.S.C. § 1957.

4.   **Enhancement for Business of Laundering Funds.**—

(A)   **In General.**—The court shall consider the totality of the circumstances to determine whether a defendant who did not commit the underlying offense was in the business of laundering funds, for purposes of subsection (b)(2)(C).

(B)   **Factors to Consider.**—The following is a non-exhaustive list of factors that may indicate the defendant was in the business of laundering funds for purposes of subsection (b)(2)(C):

(i)   The defendant regularly engaged in laundering funds.

(ii)   The defendant engaged in laundering funds during an extended period of time.

(iii)   The defendant engaged in laundering funds from multiple sources.

(iv)   The defendant generated a substantial amount of revenue in return for laundering funds.

(v)   At the time the defendant committed the instant offense, the defendant had one or more prior convictions for an offense under 18 U.S.C. § 1956 or § 1957, or under 31 U.S.C. § 5313, § 5314, § 5316, § 5324 or § 5326, or any similar offense under state law, or an attempt or conspiracy to commit any such federal or state offense. A conviction taken into account under subsection (b)(2)(C) is not excluded from consideration of whether that conviction receives criminal history points pursuant to Chapter Four, Part A (Criminal History).

(vi) During the course of an undercover government investigation, the defendant made statements that the defendant engaged in any of the conduct described in subdivisions (i) through (iv).

5. (A) **Sophisticated Laundering under Subsection (b)(3).**—For purposes of subsection (b)(3), "*sophisticated laundering*" means complex or intricate offense conduct pertaining to the execution or concealment of the 18 U.S.C. § 1956 offense.

Sophisticated laundering typically involves the use of—

(i) fictitious entities;

(ii) shell corporations;

(iii) two or more levels (*i.e.*, layering) of transactions, transportation, transfers, or transmissions, involving criminally derived funds that were intended to appear legitimate; or

(iv) offshore financial accounts.

(B) **Non-Applicability of Enhancement.**—If subsection (b)(3) applies, and the conduct that forms the basis for an enhancement under the guideline applicable to the underlying offense is the only conduct that forms the basis for application of subsection (b)(3) of this guideline, do not apply subsection (b)(3) of this guideline.

6. **Grouping of Multiple Counts.**—In a case in which the defendant is convicted of a count of laundering funds and a count for the underlying offense from which the laundered funds were derived, the counts shall be grouped pursuant to subsection (c) of §3D1.2 (Groups of Closely-Related Counts).

Historical Note	Effective November 1, 1987. Amended effective November 1, 1989 (amendments 212–214); November 1, 1991 (amendments 378 and 422); November 1, 2001 (amendment 634); November 1, 2003 (amendment 655).

- -

§2S1.2. [Deleted]

- -

Historical Note	Section 2S1.2 (Engaging in Monetary Transactions in Property Derived from Specified Unlawful Activity), effective November 1, 1987, amended effective November 1, 1989 (amendment 215), and November 1, 1991 (amendment 422), was deleted by consolidation with §2S1.1 effective November 1, 2001 (amendment 634).

§2S1.3. Structuring Transactions to Evade Reporting Requirements; Failure to Report Cash or Monetary Transactions; Failure to File Currency and Monetary Instrument Report; Knowingly Filing False Reports; Bulk Cash Smuggling; Establishing or Maintaining Prohibited Accounts

(a) Base Offense Level:

    (1) **8**, if the defendant was convicted under 31 U.S.C. § 5318 or § 5318A; or

    (2) **6** plus the number of offense levels from the table in §2B1.1 (Theft, Property Destruction, and Fraud) corresponding to the value of the funds, if subsection (a)(1) does not apply.

(b) Specific Offense Characteristics

    (1) If (A) the defendant knew or believed that the funds were proceeds of unlawful activity, or were intended to promote unlawful activity; or (B) the offense involved bulk cash smuggling, increase by **2** levels.

    (2) If the defendant (A) was convicted of an offense under subchapter II of chapter 53 of title 31, United States Code; and (B) committed the offense as part of a pattern of unlawful activity involving more than $100,000 in a 12-month period, increase by **2** levels.

    (3) If (A) subsection (a)(2) applies and subsections (b)(1) and (b)(2) do not apply; (B) the defendant did not act with reckless disregard of the source of the funds; (C) the funds were the proceeds of lawful activity; and (D) the funds were to be used for a lawful purpose, decrease the offense level to level **6**.

(c) Cross Reference

    (1) If the offense was committed for the purposes of violating the Internal Revenue laws, apply the most appropriate guideline from Chapter Two, Part T (Offenses Involving Taxation) if the resulting offense level is greater than that determined above.

Commentary

Statutory Provisions: 18 U.S.C. § 1960 (but only with respect to unlicensed money transmitting businesses as defined in 18 U.S.C. § 1960(b)(1)(A) and (B)); 26 U.S.C. §§ 7203 (if a violation based upon 26 U.S.C. § 6050I), 7206 (if a violation based upon 26 U.S.C. § 6050I); 31 U.S.C. §§ 5313, 5314, 5316, 5318, 5318A(b), 5322, 5324, 5326, 5331, 5332. For additional statutory provision(s), *see* Appendix A (Statutory Index).

§2S1.4

Application Notes:

1. **Definition of "Value of the Funds".**—For purposes of this guideline, "*value of the funds*" means the amount of the funds involved in the structuring or reporting conduct. The relevant statutes require monetary reporting without regard to whether the funds were lawfully or unlawfully obtained.

2. **Bulk Cash Smuggling.**—For purposes of subsection (b)(1)(B), "*bulk cash smuggling*" means (A) knowingly concealing, with the intent to evade a currency reporting requirement under 31 U.S.C. § 5316, more than $10,000 in currency or other monetary instruments; and (B) transporting or transferring (or attempting to transport or transfer) such currency or monetary instruments into or outside of the United States. "United States" has the meaning given that term in Application Note 1 of the Commentary to §2B5.1 (Offenses Involving Counterfeit Bearer Obligations of the United States).

3. **Enhancement for Pattern of Unlawful Activity.**—For purposes of subsection (b)(2), "*pattern of unlawful activity*" means at least two separate occasions of unlawful activity involving a total amount of more than $100,000 in a 12-month period, without regard to whether any such occasion occurred during the course of the offense or resulted in a conviction for the conduct that occurred on that occasion.

Background: Some of the offenses covered by this guideline relate to records and reports of certain transactions involving currency and monetary instruments. These reports include Currency Transaction Reports, Currency and Monetary Instrument Reports, Reports of Foreign Bank and Financial Accounts, and Reports of Cash Payments Over $10,000 Received in a Trade or Business.

This guideline also covers offenses under 31 U.S.C. §§ 5318 and 5318A, pertaining to records, reporting and identification requirements, prohibited accounts involving certain foreign jurisdictions, foreign institutions, and foreign banks, and other types of transactions and types of accounts.

Historical Note	Effective November 1, 1987. Amended effective November 1, 1989 (amendments 216–218); November 1, 1991 (amendments 379 and 422); November 1, 1993 (amendment 490); November 1, 2001 (amendments 617 and 634); November 1, 2002 (amendment 637); November 1, 2003 (amendment 655).

§2S1.4. [Deleted]

Historical Note	Section 2S1.4 (Failure to File Currency and Monetary Instrument Report), effective November 1, 1991 (amendments 379 and 422), was deleted by consolidation with §2S1.3 effective November 1, 1993 (amendment 490).

PART T — OFFENSES INVOLVING TAXATION

1. INCOME TAXES, EMPLOYMENT TAXES, ESTATE TAXES, GIFT TAXES, AND EXCISE TAXES (OTHER THAN ALCOHOL, TOBACCO, AND CUSTOMS TAXES)

Historical Note	Effective November 1, 1987. Amended effective November 1, 1993 (amendment 491).

Introductory Commentary

The criminal tax laws are designed to protect the public interest in preserving the integrity of the nation's tax system. Criminal tax prosecutions serve to punish the violator and promote respect for the tax laws. Because of the limited number of criminal tax prosecutions relative to the estimated incidence of such violations, deterring others from violating the tax laws is a primary consideration underlying these guidelines. Recognition that the sentence for a criminal tax case will be commensurate with the gravity of the offense should act as a deterrent to would-be violators.

Historical Note	Effective November 1, 1987.

§2T1.1. Tax Evasion; Willful Failure to File Return, Supply Information, or Pay Tax; Fraudulent or False Returns, Statements, or Other Documents

(a) Base Offense Level:

    (1) Level from §2T4.1 (Tax Table) corresponding to the tax loss; or

    (2) **6**, if there is no tax loss.

(b) Specific Offense Characteristics

    (1) If the defendant failed to report or to correctly identify the source of income exceeding $10,000 in any year from criminal activity, increase by **2** levels. If the resulting offense level is less than level **12**, increase to level **12**.

    (2) If the offense involved sophisticated means, increase by **2** levels. If the resulting offense level is less than level **12**, increase to level **12**.

(c)   Special Instructions

For the purposes of this guideline—

(1)   If the offense involved tax evasion or a fraudulent or false return, statement, or other document, the tax loss is the total amount of loss that was the object of the offense (*i.e.*, the loss that would have resulted had the offense been successfully completed).

Notes:

(A)   If the offense involved filing a tax return in which gross income was underreported, the tax loss shall be treated as equal to 28% of the unreported gross income (34% if the taxpayer is a corporation) plus 100% of any false credits claimed against tax, unless a more accurate determination of the tax loss can be made.

(B)   If the offense involved improperly claiming a deduction or an exemption, the tax loss shall be treated as equal to 28% of the amount of the improperly claimed deduction or exemption (34% if the taxpayer is a corporation) plus 100% of any false credits claimed against tax, unless a more accurate determination of the tax loss can be made.

(C)   If the offense involved improperly claiming a deduction to provide a basis for tax evasion in the future, the tax loss shall be treated as equal to 28% of the amount of the improperly claimed deduction (34% if the taxpayer is a corporation) plus 100% of any false credits claimed against tax, unless a more accurate determination of the tax loss can be made.

(D)   If the offense involved (i) conduct described in subdivision (A), B), or (C) of these Notes; and (ii) both individual and corporate tax returns, the tax loss is the aggregate tax loss from the offenses added together.

(2)   If the offense involved failure to file a tax return, the tax loss is the amount of tax that the taxpayer owed and did not pay.

Notes:

(A)   If the offense involved failure to file a tax return, the tax loss shall be treated as equal to 20% of the gross income (25% if the taxpayer is a corporation) less any tax withheld or otherwise paid, unless a more accurate determination of the tax loss can be made.

    (B)   If the offense involved (i) conduct described in subdivision (A) of these Notes; and (ii) both individual and corporate tax returns, the tax loss is the aggregate tax loss from the offenses added together.

(3)   If the offense involved willful failure to pay tax, the tax loss is the amount of tax that the taxpayer owed and did not pay.

(4)   If the offense involved improperly claiming a refund to which the claimant was not entitled, the tax loss is the amount of the claimed refund to which the claimant was not entitled.

(5)   The tax loss is not reduced by any payment of the tax subsequent to the commission of the offense.

Commentary

Statutory Provisions: 26 U.S.C. §§ 7201, 7203 (other than a violation based upon 26 U.S.C. § 6050I), 7206 (other than a violation based upon 26 U.S.C. § 6050I or § 7206(2)), and 7207. For additional statutory provision(s), *see* Appendix A (Statutory Index).

Application Notes:

1.   **Tax Loss.**—"*Tax loss*" is defined in subsection (c). The tax loss does not include interest or penalties, except in willful evasion of payment cases under 26 U.S.C. § 7201 and willful failure to pay cases under 26 U.S.C. § 7203. Although the definition of tax loss corresponds to what is commonly called the "criminal figures," its amount is to be determined by the same rules applicable in determining any other sentencing factor. In some instances, such as when indirect methods of proof are used, the amount of the tax loss may be uncertain; the guidelines contemplate that the court will simply make a reasonable estimate based on the available facts.

Notes under subsections (c)(1) and (c)(2) address certain situations in income tax cases in which the tax loss may not be reasonably ascertainable. In these situations, the "presumptions" set forth are to be used unless the government or defense provides sufficient information for a more accurate assessment of the tax loss. In cases involving other types of taxes, the presumptions in the notes under subsections (c)(1) and (c)(2) do not apply.

Example 1: A defendant files a tax return reporting income of $40,000 when his income was actually $90,000. Under Note (A) to subsection (c)(1), the tax loss is treated as $14,000 ($90,000 of actual gross income minus $40,000 of reported gross income = $50,000 x 28%) unless sufficient information is available to make a more accurate assessment of the tax loss.

Example 2: A defendant files a tax return reporting income of $60,000 when his income was actually $130,000. In addition, the defendant claims $10,000 in false tax credits. Under Note (A) to subsection (c)(1), the tax loss is treated as $29,600 ($130,000 of actual gross income minus $60,000 of reported gross income = $70,000 x 28% = $19,600, plus

$10,000 of false tax credits) unless sufficient information is available to make a more accurate assessment of the tax loss.

Example 3: A defendant fails to file a tax return for a year in which his salary was $24,000, and $2,600 in income tax was withheld by his employer. Under the note to subsection (c)(2), the tax loss is treated as $2,200 ($24,000 of gross income x 20% = $4,800, minus $2,600 of tax withheld) unless sufficient information is available to make a more accurate assessment of the tax loss.

In determining the tax loss attributable to the offense, the court should use as many methods set forth in subsection (c) and this commentary as are necessary given the circumstances of the particular case. If none of the methods of determining the tax loss set forth fit the circumstances of the particular case, the court should use any method of determining the tax loss that appears appropriate to reasonably calculate the loss that would have resulted had the offense been successfully completed.

2.   **Total Tax Loss Attributable to the Offense.**—In determining the total tax loss attributable to the offense (*see* §1B1.3(a)(2)), all conduct violating the tax laws should be considered as part of the same course of conduct or common scheme or plan unless the evidence demonstrates that the conduct is clearly unrelated. The following examples are illustrative of conduct that is part of the same course of conduct or common scheme or plan: (A) there is a continuing pattern of violations of the tax laws by the defendant; (B) the defendant uses a consistent method to evade or camouflage income, *e.g.*, backdating documents or using off-shore accounts; (C) the violations involve the same or a related series of transactions; (D) the violation in each instance involves a false or inflated claim of a similar deduction or credit; and (E) the violation in each instance involves a failure to report or an understatement of a specific source of income, *e.g.*, interest from savings accounts or income from a particular business activity. These examples are not intended to be exhaustive.

3.   **Unclaimed Credits, Deductions, and Exemptions.**—In determining the tax loss, the court should account for the standard deduction and personal and dependent exemptions to which the defendant was entitled. In addition, the court should account for any unclaimed credit, deduction, or exemption that is needed to ensure a reasonable estimate of the tax loss, but only to the extent that (A) the credit, deduction, or exemption was related to the tax offense and could have been claimed at the time the tax offense was committed; (B) the credit, deduction, or exemption is reasonably and practicably ascertainable; and (C) the defendant presents information to support the credit, deduction, or exemption sufficiently in advance of sentencing to provide an adequate opportunity to evaluate whether it has sufficient indicia of reliability to support its probable accuracy (*see* §6A1.3 (Resolution of Disputed Factors) (Policy Statement)).

However, the court shall not account for payments to third parties made in a manner that encouraged or facilitated a separate violation of law (*e.g.*, "under the table" payments to employees or expenses incurred to obstruct justice).

The burden is on the defendant to establish any such credit, deduction, or exemption by a preponderance of the evidence. *See* §6A1.3, comment.

4.   **Application of Subsection (b)(1) (Criminal Activity).**—"*Criminal activity*" means any conduct constituting a criminal offense under federal, state, local, or foreign law.

5. **Application of Subsection (b)(2) (Sophisticated Means).**—For purposes of subsection (b)(2), "*sophisticated means*" means especially complex or especially intricate offense conduct pertaining to the execution or concealment of an offense. Conduct such as hiding assets or transactions, or both, through the use of fictitious entities, corporate shells, or offshore financial accounts ordinarily indicates sophisticated means.

6. **Other Definitions.**—For purposes of this section:

A "*credit claimed against tax*" is an item that reduces the amount of tax directly. In contrast, a "*deduction*" is an item that reduces the amount of taxable income.

"*Gross income*" has the same meaning as it has in 26 U.S.C. § 61 and 26 C.F.R. § 1.61.

7. **Aggregation of Individual and Corporate Tax Loss.**—If the offense involved both individual and corporate tax returns, the tax loss is the aggregate tax loss from the individual tax offense and the corporate tax offense added together. Accordingly, in a case in which a defendant fails to report income derived from a corporation on both the defendant's individual tax return and the defendant's corporate tax return, the tax loss is the sum of (A) the unreported or diverted amount multiplied by (i) 28%; or (ii) the tax rate for the individual tax offense, if sufficient information is available to make a more accurate assessment of that tax rate; and (B) the unreported or diverted amount multiplied by (i) 34%; or (ii) the tax rate for the corporate tax offense, if sufficient information is available to make a more accurate assessment of that tax rate. For example, the defendant, the sole owner of a Subchapter C corporation, fraudulently understates the corporation's income in the amount of $100,000 on the corporation's tax return, diverts the funds to the defendant's own use, and does not report these funds on the defendant's individual tax return. For purposes of this example, assume the use of 34% with respect to the corporate tax loss and the use of 28% with respect to the individual tax loss. The tax loss attributable to the defendant's corporate tax return is $34,000 ($100,000 multiplied by 34%). The tax loss attributable to the defendant's individual tax return is $28,000 ($100,000 multiplied by 28%). The tax loss for the offenses are added together to equal $62,000 ($34,000 + $28,000).

Background: This guideline relies most heavily on the amount of loss that was the object of the offense. Tax offenses, in and of themselves, are serious offenses; however, a greater tax loss is obviously more harmful to the treasury and more serious than a smaller one with otherwise similar characteristics. Furthermore, as the potential benefit from the offense increases, the sanction necessary to deter also increases.

Under pre-guidelines practice, roughly half of all tax evaders were sentenced to probation without imprisonment, while the other half received sentences that required them to serve an average prison term of twelve months. This guideline is intended to reduce disparity in sentencing for tax offenses and to somewhat increase average sentence length. As a result, the number of purely probationary sentences will be reduced. The Commission believes that any additional costs of imprisonment that may be incurred as a result of the increase in the average term of imprisonment for tax offenses are inconsequential in relation to the potential increase in revenue. According to estimates current at the time this guideline was originally developed (1987), income taxes are underpaid by approximately $90 billion annually. Guideline sentences should result in small increases in the average length of imprisonment for most tax cases that involve less than $100,000 in tax loss. The increase is expected to be somewhat larger for cases involving more taxes.

Failure to report criminally derived income is included as a factor for deterrence purposes. Criminally derived income is generally difficult to establish, so that the tax loss in such cases will tend to be substantially understated. An enhancement for offenders who violate the tax laws as part of a pattern of criminal activity from which they derive a substantial portion of their income also serves to implement the mandate of 28 U.S.C. § 994(i)(2).

Although tax offenses always involve some planning, unusually sophisticated efforts to conceal the offense decrease the likelihood of detection and therefore warrant an additional sanction for deterrence purposes.

The guideline does not make a distinction for an employee who prepares fraudulent returns on behalf of his employer. The adjustments in Chapter Three, Part B (Role in the Offense) should be used to make appropriate distinctions.

Historical Note	Effective November 1, 1987. Amended effective November 1, 1989 (amendments 219–223); November 1, 1990 (amendment 343); November 1, 1992 (amendment 468); November 1, 1993 (amendment 491); November 1, 1998 (amendment 577); November 1, 2001 (amendment 617); November 1, 2002 (amendment 646); November 1, 2013 (amendment 774).

§2T1.2. [Deleted]

Historical Note	Section 2T1.2 (Willful Failure To File Return, Supply Information, or Pay Tax), effective November 1, 1987, amended effective November 1, 1989 (amendments 224–227), November 1, 1990 (amendment 343), and November 1, 1991 (amendment 408), was deleted by consolidation with §2T1.1 effective November 1, 1993 (amendment 491).

§2T1.3. [Deleted]

Historical Note	Section 2T1.3 (Fraud and False Statements Under Penalty of Perjury), effective November 1, 1987, amended effective November 1, 1989 (amendments 228–230), November 1, 1990 (amendment 343), and November 1, 1991 (amendment 426), was deleted by consolidation with §2T1.1 effective November 1, 1993 (amendment 491).

§2T1.4. Aiding, Assisting, Procuring, Counseling, or Advising Tax Fraud

(a) Base Offense Level:

    (1) Level from §2T4.1 (Tax Table) corresponding to the tax loss; or

    (2) **6**, if there is no tax loss.

For purposes of this guideline, the "tax loss" is the tax loss, as defined in §2T1.1, resulting from the defendant's aid, assistance, procurance or advice.

(b)   Specific Offense Characteristics

   (1)   If (A) the defendant committed the offense as part of a pattern or scheme from which he derived a substantial portion of his income; or (B) the defendant was in the business of preparing or assisting in the preparation of tax returns, increase by **2** levels.

   (2)   If the offense involved sophisticated means, increase by **2** levels. If the resulting offense level is less than level **12**, increase to level **12**.

Commentary

Statutory Provision: 26 U.S.C. § 7206(2) (other than a violation based upon 26 U.S.C. § 6050I).

Application Notes:

1.   For the general principles underlying the determination of tax loss, *see* §2T1.1(c) and Application Note 1 of the Commentary to §2T1.1 (Tax Evasion; Willful Failure to File Return, Supply Information, or Pay Tax; Fraudulent or False Returns, Statements, or Other Documents). In certain instances, such as promotion of a tax shelter scheme, the defendant may advise other persons to violate their tax obligations through filing returns that find no support in the tax laws. If this type of conduct can be shown to have resulted in the filing of false returns (regardless of whether the principals were aware of their falsity), the misstatements in all such returns will contribute to one aggregate "tax loss."

2.   Subsection (b)(1) has two prongs. The first prong applies to persons who derive a substantial portion of their income through the promotion of tax schemes, *e.g.*, through promoting fraudulent tax shelters. The second prong applies to persons who regularly prepare or assist in the preparation of tax returns for profit. If an enhancement from this subsection applies, do not apply §3B1.3 (Abuse of Position of Trust or Use of Special Skill).

3.   **Sophisticated Means.**—For purposes of subsection (b)(2), "*sophisticated means*" means especially complex or especially intricate offense conduct pertaining to the execution or concealment of an offense. Conduct such as hiding assets or transactions, or both, through the use of fictitious entities, corporate shells, or offshore financial accounts ordinarily indicates sophisticated means.

Background: An increased offense level is specified for those in the business of preparing or assisting in the preparation of tax returns and those who make a business of promoting tax fraud because their misconduct poses a greater risk of revenue loss and is more clearly willful. Other considerations are similar to those in §2T1.1.

Historical Note	Effective November 1, 1987. Amended effective November 1, 1989 (amendments 231 and 303); November 1, 1990 (amendment 343); November 1, 1993 (amendment 491); November 1, 1998 (amendment 577); November 1, 2001 (amendment 617).

---

§2T1.5. [Deleted]

| *Historical Note* | Section 2T1.5 (Fraudulent Returns, Statements, or Other Documents), effective November 1, 1987, was deleted by consolidation with §2T1.1 effective November 1, 1993 (amendment 491). |

§2T1.6. Failing to Collect or Truthfully Account for and Pay Over Tax

(a) Base Offense Level: Level from §2T4.1 (Tax Table) corresponding to the tax not collected or accounted for and paid over.

(b) Cross Reference

(1) Where the offense involved embezzlement by withholding tax from an employee's earnings and willfully failing to account to the employee for it, apply §2B1.1 (Theft, Property Destruction, and Fraud) if the resulting offense level is greater than that determined above.

Commentary

Statutory Provision: 26 U.S.C. § 7202.

Application Note:

1. In the event that the employer not only failed to account to the Internal Revenue Service and pay over the tax, but also collected the tax from employees and did not account to them for it, it is both tax evasion and a form of embezzlement. Subsection (b)(1) addresses such cases.

Background: The failure to collect or truthfully account for the tax must be willful, as must the failure to pay. Where no effort is made to defraud the employee, the offense is a form of tax evasion, and is treated as such in the guidelines.

| *Historical Note* | Effective November 1, 1987. Amended effective November 1, 1989 (amendment 232); November 1, 1991 (amendment 409); November 1, 2001 (amendment 617); November 1, 2016 (amendment 804). |

§2T1.7. Failing to Deposit Collected Taxes in Trust Account as Required After Notice

(a) Base Offense Level (Apply the greater):

(1) 4; or

(2) **5** less than the level from §2T4.1 (Tax Table) corresponding to the amount not deposited.

Commentary

Statutory Provisions: 26 U.S.C. §§ 7215, 7512(b).

Application Notes:

1. If funds are deposited and withdrawn without being paid to the Internal Revenue Service, they should be treated as never having been deposited.

2. It is recommended that the fine be based on the total amount of funds not deposited.

Background: This offense is a misdemeanor that does not require any intent to evade taxes, nor even that taxes have not been paid. The more serious offense is 26 U.S.C. § 7202 (*see* §2T1.6).

This offense should be relatively easy to detect and fines may be feasible. Accordingly, the offense level has been set considerably lower than for tax evasion, although some effort has been made to tie the offense level to the level of taxes that were not deposited.

Historical Note	Effective November 1, 1987.

§2T1.8.   Offenses Relating to Withholding Statements

(a)   Base Offense Level: **4**

Commentary

Statutory Provisions: 26 U.S.C. §§ 7204, 7205.

Application Note:

1. If the defendant was attempting to evade, rather than merely delay, payment of taxes, an upward departure may be warranted.

Background: The offenses are misdemeanors. Under pre-guidelines practice, imprisonment was unusual.

Historical Note	Effective November 1, 1987. Amended effective November 1, 2004 (amendment 674).

---

§2T1.9.   Conspiracy to Impede, Impair, Obstruct, or Defeat Tax

---

(a)   Base Offense Level (Apply the greater):

(1)   Offense level determined from §2T1.1 or §2T1.4, as appropriate; or

(2)   **10**.

(b)   Specific Offense Characteristics

If more than one applies, use the greater:

(1)   If the offense involved the planned or threatened use of violence to impede, impair, obstruct, or defeat the ascertainment, computation, assessment, or collection of revenue, increase by **4 levels**.

(2)   If the conduct was intended to encourage persons other than or in addition to co-conspirators to violate the internal revenue laws or impede, impair, obstruct, or defeat the ascertainment, computation, assessment, or collection of revenue, increase by **2 levels**. Do not, however, apply this adjustment if an adjustment from §2T1.4(b)(1) is applied.

Commentary

Statutory Provision: 18 U.S.C. § 371.

Application Notes:

1.   This section applies to conspiracies to "defraud the United States by impeding, impairing, obstructing and defeating . . . the collection of revenue." *United States v. Carruth*, 699 F.2d 1017, 1021 (9th Cir. 1983), *cert. denied*, 464 U.S. 1038 (1984). *See also United States v. Browning*, 723 F.2d 1544 (11th Cir. 1984); *United States v. Klein*, 247 F.2d 908, 915 (2d Cir. 1957), *cert. denied*, 355 U.S. 924 (1958). It does not apply to taxpayers, such as a husband and wife, who merely evade taxes jointly or file a fraudulent return.

2.   The base offense level is the offense level (base offense level plus any applicable specific offense characteristics) from §2T1.1 or §2T1.4 (whichever guideline most closely addresses the harm that would have resulted had the conspirators succeeded in impeding, impairing, obstructing, or defeating the Internal Revenue Service) if that offense level is greater than 10. Otherwise, the base offense level is 10.

3.   Specific offense characteristics from §2T1.9(b) are to be applied to the base offense level determined under §2T1.9(a)(1) or (2).

4.   Subsection (b)(2) provides an enhancement where the conduct was intended to encourage persons, other than the participants directly involved in the offense, to violate the tax

laws (*e.g.*, an offense involving a "tax protest" group that encourages persons to violate the tax laws, or an offense involving the marketing of fraudulent tax shelters or schemes).

Background: This type of conspiracy generally involves substantial sums of money. It also typically is complex and may be far-reaching, making it quite difficult to evaluate the extent of the revenue loss caused. Additional specific offense characteristics are included because of the potential for these tax conspiracies to subvert the revenue system and the danger to law enforcement agents and the public.

Historical Note	Effective November 1, 1987. Amended effective November 1, 1989 (amendments 233 and 234); November 1, 1993 (amendment 491).

*   *   *   *   *

2.   ALCOHOL AND TOBACCO TAXES

Introductory Commentary

This subpart deals with offenses contained in Parts I–IV of Subchapter J of Chapter 51 of Subtitle E of Title 26, chiefly 26 U.S.C. §§ 5601–5605, 5607, 5608, 5661, 5671, 5691, and 5762, where the essence of the conduct is tax evasion or a regulatory violation. No effort has been made to provide a section-by-section set of guidelines. Rather, the conduct is dealt with by dividing offenses into two broad categories: tax evasion offenses and regulatory offenses.

Historical Note	Effective November 1, 1987. Amended effective November 1, 2010 (amendment 746); November 1, 2016 (amendment 804).

§2T2.1.   Non-Payment of Taxes

(a)   Base Offense Level: Level from §2T4.1 (Tax Table) corresponding to the tax loss.

For purposes of this guideline, the "tax loss" is the amount of taxes that the taxpayer failed to pay or attempted not to pay.

Commentary

Statutory Provisions: 15 U.S.C. § 377, 26 U.S.C. §§ 5601–5605, 5607, 5608, 5661, 5671, 5691, 5762, provided the conduct constitutes non-payment, evasion or attempted evasion of taxes. For additional statutory provision(s), *see* Appendix A (Statutory Index).

Application Notes:

1.   The tax loss is the total amount of unpaid taxes that were due on the alcohol and/or tobacco, or that the defendant was attempting to evade.

2.   Offense conduct directed at more than tax evasion (*e.g.*, theft or fraud) may warrant an upward departure.

| *Historical* *Note* | Effective November 1, 1987. Amended effective November 1, 2012 (amendment 769); November 1, 2016 (amendment 804). |

---

§2T2.2.   Regulatory Offenses

(a)   Base Offense Level: 4

Commentary

Statutory Provisions: 15 U.S.C. § 377, 26 U.S.C. §§ 5601, 5603–5605, 5661, 5671, 5762, provided the conduct is tantamount to a record-keeping violation rather than an effort to evade payment of taxes. For additional statutory provision(s), *see* Appendix A (Statutory Index).

| *Historical* *Note* | Effective November 1, 1987. Amended effective November 1, 1990 (amendment 359); November 1, 2012 (amendment 769); November 1, 2016 (amendment 804). |

*   *   *   *   *

3.   CUSTOMS TAXES

Introductory Commentary

This Subpart deals with violations of 18 U.S.C. §§ 496, 541–545, 547, 548, 550, 551, 1915 and 19 U.S.C. §§ 283, 1436, 1464, 1465, 1586(e), 1708(b), and 3907, and is designed to address violations involving revenue collection or trade regulation. It is intended to deal with some types of contraband, such as certain uncertified diamonds, but is not intended to deal with the importation of other types of contraband, such as drugs, or other items such as obscene material, firearms or pelts of endangered species, the importation of which is prohibited or restricted for non-economic reasons. Other, more specific criminal statutes apply to most of these offenses. Importation of contraband or stolen goods not specifically covered by this Subpart would be a reason for referring to another, more specific guideline, if applicable, or for departing upward if there is not another more specific applicable guideline.

| *Historical* *Note* | Effective November 1, 1987. Amended effective November 1, 1992 (amendment 453); November 1, 2004 (amendment 674); November 1, 2006 (amendment 685). |

---

§2T3.1.   Evading Import Duties or Restrictions (Smuggling); Receiving or Trafficking in Smuggled Property

(a)   Base Offense Level:

(1) The level from §2T4.1 (Tax Table) corresponding to the tax loss, if the tax loss exceeded $1,500; or

(2) **5**, if the tax loss exceeded $200 but did not exceed $1,500; or

(3) **4**, if the tax loss did not exceed $200.

For purposes of this guideline, the "tax loss" is the amount of the duty.

(b) Specific Offense Characteristic

(1) If the offense involved sophisticated means, increase by **2** levels. If the resulting offense level is less than level **12**, increase to level **12**.

(c) Cross Reference

(1) If the offense involves a contraband item covered by another offense guideline, apply that offense guideline if the resulting offense level is greater than that determined above.

Commentary

Statutory Provisions: 18 U.S.C. §§ 496, 541–545, 547, 548, 550, 551, 1915; 19 U.S.C. §§ 283, 1436, 1464, 1465, 1586(e), 1708(b), 3907. For additional statutory provision(s), *see* Appendix A (Statutory Index).

Application Notes:

1. A sentence at or near the minimum of the guideline range typically would be appropriate for cases involving tourists who bring in items for their own use. Such conduct generally poses a lesser threat to revenue collection.

2. Particular attention should be given to those items for which entry is prohibited, limited, or restricted. Especially when such items are harmful or protective quotas are in effect, the duties evaded on such items may not adequately reflect the harm to society or protected industries resulting from their importation. In such instances, an upward departure may be warranted. A sentence based upon an alternative measure of the "duty" evaded, such as the increase in market value due to importation, or 25 percent of the items' fair market value in the United States if the increase in market value due to importation is not readily ascertainable, might be considered.

3. **Sophisticated Means.**—For purposes of subsection (b)(1), "*sophisticated means*" means especially complex or especially intricate offense conduct pertaining to the execution or concealment of an offense. Conduct such as hiding assets or transactions, or both, through the use of fictitious entities, corporate shells, or offshore financial accounts ordinarily indicates sophisticated means.

§2T4.1

Historical Note	Effective November 1, 1987. Amended effective November 1, 1989 (amendment 235); November 1, 1991 (amendment 410); November 1, 1992 (amendment 453); November 1, 1998 (amendment 577); November 1, 2001 (amendment 617); November 1, 2006 (amendment 685); November 1, 2015 (amendment 791).

----
§2T3.2. [Deleted]

Historical Note	Section 2T3.2 (Receiving or Trafficking in Smuggled Property), effective November 1, 1987, amended effective November 1, 1989 (amendment 236) and November 1, 1991 (amendment 410), was deleted by consolidation with §2T3.1 effective November 1, 1992 (amendment 453).

* * * * *

4. TAX TABLE

§2T4.1. Tax Table

Tax Loss (Apply the Greatest)	Offense Level
(A) $2,500 or less	6
(B) More than $2,500	8
(C) More than $6,500	10
(D) More than $15,000	12
(E) More than $40,000	14
(F) More than $100,000	16
(G) More than $250,000	18
(H) More than $550,000	20
(I) More than $1,500,000	22
(J) More than $3,500,000	24
(K) More than $9,500,000	26
(L) More than $25,000,000	28
(M) More than $65,000,000	30
(N) More than $150,000,000	32
(O) More than $250,000,000	34
(P) More than $550,000,000	36.

Historical Note	Effective November 1, 1987. Amended effective November 1, 1989 (amendment 237); November 1, 1993 (amendment 491); November 1, 2001 (amendment 617); January 25, 2003 (amendment 647); November 1, 2003 (amendment 653); November 1, 2015 (amendment 791).

PART U — [NOT USED]

PART V — [NOT USED]

PART W — [NOT USED]

PART X — OTHER OFFENSES

1. CONSPIRACIES, ATTEMPTS, SOLICITATIONS

---

§2X1.1. Attempt, Solicitation, or Conspiracy (Not Covered by a Specific Offense Guideline)

(a) Base Offense Level: The base offense level from the guideline for the substantive offense, plus any adjustments from such guideline for any intended offense conduct that can be established with reasonable certainty.

(b) Specific Offense Characteristics

   (1) If an attempt, decrease by **3** levels, unless the defendant completed all the acts the defendant believed necessary for successful completion of the substantive offense or the circumstances demonstrate that the defendant was about to complete all such acts but for apprehension or interruption by some similar event beyond the defendant's control.

   (2) If a conspiracy, decrease by **3** levels, unless the defendant or a co-conspirator completed all the acts the conspirators believed necessary on their part for the successful completion of the substantive offense or the circumstances demonstrate that the conspirators were about to complete all such acts but for apprehension or interruption by some similar event beyond their control.

   (3) (A) If a solicitation, decrease by **3** levels unless the person solicited to commit or aid the substantive offense completed all the acts he believed necessary for successful completion of the substantive offense or the circumstances demonstrate that the person was about to complete all such acts but for apprehension or interruption by some similar event beyond such person's control.

   (B) If the statute treats solicitation of the substantive offense identically with the substantive offense, do not apply subdivision (A) above; *i.e.*, the offense level for solicitation is the same as that for the substantive offense.

(c) Cross Reference

    (1) When an attempt, solicitation, or conspiracy is expressly covered by another offense guideline section, apply that guideline section.

(d) Special Instruction

    (1) Subsection (b) shall not apply to:

        (A) Any of the following offenses, if such offense involved, or was intended to promote, a federal crime of terrorism as defined in 18 U.S.C. § 2332b(g)(5):

> 18 U.S.C. § 81;
> 18 U.S.C. § 930(c);
> 18 U.S.C. § 1362;
> 18 U.S.C. § 1363;
> 18 U.S.C. § 1992(a)(1)–(a)(7), (a)(9), (a)(10);
> 18 U.S.C. § 2339A;
> 18 U.S.C. § 2340A;
> 49 U.S.C. § 46504;
> 49 U.S.C. § 46505; and
> 49 U.S.C. § 60123(b).

        (B) Any of the following offenses:

> 18 U.S.C. § 32; and
> 18 U.S.C. § 2332a.

Commentary

Statutory Provisions: 18 U.S.C. §§ 371, 372, 2271, 2282A, 2282B. For additional statutory provision(s), *see* Appendix A (Statutory Index).

Application Notes:

1. Certain attempts, conspiracies, and solicitations are expressly covered by other offense guidelines.

Offense guidelines that expressly cover attempts include:

> §§2A2.1, 2A3.1, 2A3.2, 2A3.3, 2A3.4, 2A4.2, 2A5.1;
> §§2C1.1, 2C1.2;
> §§2D1.1, 2D1.2, 2D1.5, 2D1.6, 2D1.7, 2D1.8, 2D1.9, 2D1.10, 2D1.11, 2D1.12, 2D1.13, 2D2.1, 2D2.2, 2D3.1, 2D3.2;
> §2E5.1;
> §2M6.1;
> §2N1.1;
> §2Q1.4.

Offense guidelines that expressly cover conspiracies include:

§2A1.5;
§§2D1.1, 2D1.2, 2D1.5, 2D1.6, 2D1.7, 2D1.8, 2D1.9, 2D1.10, 2D1.11, 2D1.12, 2D1.13, 2D2.1, 2D2.2, 2D3.1, 2D3.2;
§2H1.1;
§2M6.1;
§2T1.9.

Offense guidelines that expressly cover solicitations include:

§2A1.5;
§§2C1.1, 2C1.2;
§2E5.1.

2. "*Substantive offense*," as used in this guideline, means the offense that the defendant was convicted of soliciting, attempting, or conspiring to commit. Under §2X1.1(a), the base offense level will be the same as that for the substantive offense. But the only specific offense characteristics from the guideline for the substantive offense that apply are those that are determined to have been specifically intended or actually occurred. Speculative specific offense characteristics will not be applied. For example, if two defendants are arrested during the conspiratorial stage of planning an armed bank robbery, the offense level ordinarily would not include aggravating factors regarding possible injury to others, hostage taking, discharge of a weapon, or obtaining a large sum of money, because such factors would be speculative. The offense level would simply reflect the level applicable to robbery of a financial institution, with the enhancement for possession of a weapon. If it was established that the defendants actually intended to physically restrain the teller, the specific offense characteristic for physical restraint would be added. In an attempted theft, the value of the items that the defendant attempted to steal would be considered.

3. If the substantive offense is not covered by a specific guideline, *see* §2X5.1 (Other Offenses).

4. In certain cases, the participants may have completed (or have been about to complete but for apprehension or interruption) all of the acts necessary for the successful completion of part, but not all, of the intended offense. In such cases, the offense level for the count (or group of closely related multiple counts) is whichever of the following is greater: the offense level for the intended offense minus 3 levels (under §2X1.1(b)(1), (b)(2), or (b)(3)(A)), or the offense level for the part of the offense for which the necessary acts were completed (or about to be completed but for apprehension or interruption). For example, where the intended offense was the theft of $800,000 but the participants completed (or were about to complete) only the acts necessary to steal $30,000, the offense level is the offense level for the theft of $800,000 minus 3 levels, or the offense level for the theft of $30,000, whichever is greater.

    In the case of multiple counts that are not closely related counts, whether the 3-level reduction under §2X1.1(b)(1), (b)(2), or (b)(3)(A) applies is determined separately for each count.

Background: In most prosecutions for conspiracies or attempts, the substantive offense was substantially completed or was interrupted or prevented on the verge of completion by the intercession of law enforcement authorities or the victim. In such cases, no reduction of the offense level is warranted. Sometimes, however, the arrest occurs well before the defendant or any co-conspirator has completed the acts necessary for the substantive offense. Under such circumstances, a reduction of 3 levels is provided under §2X1.1(b)(1) or (2).

Historical Note	Effective November 1, 1987. Amended effective January 15, 1988 (amendment 42); November 1, 1989 (amendments 238–242); November 1, 1990 (amendments 311 and 327); November 1, 1991 (amendment 411); November 1, 1992 (amendments 444 and 447); November 1, 1993 (amendment 496); November 1, 2001 (amendment 633); November 1, 2002 (amendment 637); November 1, 2004 (amendment 669); November 1, 2007 (amendments 699 and 700).

*   *   *   *   *

2. AIDING AND ABETTING

§2X2.1. Aiding and Abetting

The offense level is the same level as that for the underlying offense.

Commentary

Statutory Provisions: 18 U.S.C. §§ 2, 2284, 2339, 2339A, 2339C(a)(1)(A).

Application Note:

1. **Definition.**—For purposes of this guideline, "*underlying offense*" means the offense the defendant is convicted of aiding or abetting, or in the case of a violation of 18 U.S.C. § 2339A or § 2339C(a)(1)(A), "underlying offense" means the offense the defendant is convicted of having materially supported or provided or collected funds for, prior to or during its commission.

Background: A defendant convicted of aiding and abetting is punishable as a principal. 18 U.S.C. § 2. This section provides that aiding and abetting the commission of an offense has the same offense level as the underlying offense. An adjustment for a mitigating role (§3B1.2) may be applicable.

Historical Note	Effective November 1, 1987. Amended effective November 1, 1990 (amendment 359); November 1, 2002 (amendment 637); November 1, 2003 (amendment 655); November 1, 2007 (amendment 700).

*   *   *   *   *

3. ACCESSORY AFTER THE FACT

§2X3.1. Accessory After the Fact

(a) Base Offense Level:

(1) **6** levels lower than the offense level for the underlying offense, except as provided in subdivisions (2) and (3).

(2) The base offense level under this guideline shall be not less than level **4**.

(3) (A) The base offense level under this guideline shall be not more than level **30**, except as provided in subdivision (B).

   (B) In any case in which the conduct is limited to harboring a fugitive, other than a case described in subdivision (C), the base offense level under this guideline shall be not more than level **20**.

   (C) The limitation in subdivision (B) shall not apply in any case in which (i) the defendant is convicted under 18 U.S.C. § 2339 or § 2339A; or (ii) the conduct involved harboring a person who committed any offense listed in 18 U.S.C. § 2339 or § 2339A or who committed any offense involving or intending to promote a federal crime of terrorism, as defined in 18 U.S.C. § 2332b(g)(5). In such a case, the base offense level under this guideline shall be not more than level **30**, as provided in subdivision (A).

Commentary

Statutory Provisions: 18 U.S.C. §§ 3, 757, 1071, 1072, 2284, 2339, 2339A, 2339C(c)(2)(A), (c)(2)(B) (but only with respect to funds known or intended to have been provided or collected in violation of 18 U.S.C. § 2339C(a)(1)(A)).

Application Notes:

1. **Definition.**—For purposes of this guideline, "*underlying offense*" means the offense as to which the defendant is convicted of being an accessory, or in the case of a violation of 18 U.S.C. § 2339A, "*underlying offense*" means the offense the defendant is convicted of having materially supported after its commission (*i.e.*, in connection with the concealment of or an escape from that offense), or in the case of a violation of 18 U.S.C. § 2339C(c)(2)(A), "*underlying offense*" means the violation of 18 U.S.C. § 2339B with respect to which the material support or resources were concealed or disguised. Apply the base offense level plus any applicable specific offense characteristics that were known, or reasonably should have been known, by the defendant; *see* Application Note 9 of the Commentary to §1B1.3 (Relevant Conduct).

2. **Application of Mitigating Role Adjustment.**—The adjustment from §3B1.2 (Mitigating Role) normally would not apply because an adjustment for reduced culpability is incorporated in the base offense level.

Historical Note	Effective November 1, 1987. Amended effective November 1, 1989 (amendment 243); November 1, 1991 (amendment 380); November 1, 1993 (amendment 496); November 1, 2002 (amendment 637); November 1, 2003 (amendment 655); November 1, 2007 (amendment 700); November 1, 2015 (amendments 790 and 797).

* * * * *

4.   MISPRISION OF FELONY

§2X4.1.   Misprision of Felony

(a)   Base Offense Level: **9** levels lower than the offense level for the underlying offense, but in no event less than **4**, or more than **19**.

Commentary

Statutory Provision: 18 U.S.C. § 4.

Application Notes:

1.   "*Underlying offense*" means the offense as to which the defendant is convicted of committing the misprision. Apply the base offense level plus any applicable specific offense characteristics that were known, or reasonably should have been known, by the defendant; *see* Application Note 9 of the Commentary to §1B1.3 (Relevant Conduct).

2.   The adjustment from §3B1.2 (Mitigating Role) normally would not apply because an adjustment for reduced culpability is incorporated in the base offense level.

Historical Note	Effective November 1, 1987. Amended effective November 1, 1989 (amendment 244); November 1, 1993 (amendment 496); November 1, 2015 (amendments 790 and 797).

*   *   *   *   *

5.   ALL OTHER FELONY OFFENSES AND CLASS A MISDEMEANORS

Historical Note	Effective November 1, 1987. Amended effective November 1, 2006 (amendment 685).

§2X5.1.   Other Felony Offenses

If the offense is a felony for which no guideline expressly has been promulgated, apply the most analogous offense guideline. If there is not a sufficiently analogous guideline, the provisions of 18 U.S.C. § 3553 shall control, except that any guidelines and policy statements that can be applied meaningfully in the absence of a Chapter Two offense guideline shall remain applicable.

If the defendant is convicted under 18 U.S.C. § 1841(a)(1), apply the guideline that covers the conduct the defendant is convicted of having engaged in, as that conduct is described in 18 U.S.C. § 1841(a)(1) and listed in 18 U.S.C. § 1841(b).

Commentary

Statutory Provision: 18 U.S.C. § 1841(a)(1).

Application Notes:

1. **In General.**—Guidelines and policy statements that can be applied meaningfully in the absence of a Chapter Two offense guideline include: §5B1.3 (Conditions of Probation); §5D1.1 (Imposition of a Term of Supervised Release); §5D1.2 (Term of Supervised Release); §5D1.3 (Conditions of Supervised Release); §5E1.1 (Restitution); §5E1.3 (Special Assessments); §5E1.4 (Forfeiture); Chapter Five, Part F (Sentencing Options); §5G1.3 (Imposition of a Sentence on a Defendant Subject to an Undischarged Term of Imprisonment or Anticipated State Term of Imprisonment); Chapter Five, Part H (Specific Offender Characteristics); Chapter Five, Part J (Relief from Disability); Chapter Five, Part K (Departures); Chapter Six, Part A (Sentencing Procedures); Chapter Six, Part B (Plea Agreements).

2. **Convictions under 18 U.S.C. § 1841(a)(1).**—

    (A) **In General.**—If the defendant is convicted under 18 U.S.C. § 1841(a)(1), the Chapter Two offense guideline that applies is the guideline that covers the conduct the defendant is convicted of having engaged in, *i.e.*, the conduct of which the defendant is convicted that violates a specific provision listed in 18 U.S.C. § 1841(b) and that results in the death of, or bodily injury to, a child in utero at the time of the offense of conviction. For example, if the defendant committed aggravated sexual abuse against the unborn child's mother and it caused the death of the child in utero, the applicable Chapter Two guideline would be §2A3.1 (Criminal Sexual Abuse; Attempt to Commit Criminal Sexual Abuse).

    (B) **Upward Departure Provision.**—For offenses under 18 U.S.C. § 1841(a)(1), an upward departure may be warranted if the offense level under the applicable guideline does not adequately account for the death of, or serious bodily injury to, the child in utero.

3. **Application of §2X5.2.**—This guideline applies only to felony offenses not referenced in Appendix A (Statutory Index). For Class A misdemeanor offenses that have not been referenced in Appendix A, apply §2X5.2 (Class A Misdemeanors (Not Covered by Another Specific Offense Guideline)).

Background: Many offenses, especially assimilative crimes, are not listed in the Statutory Index or in any of the lists of Statutory Provisions that follow each offense guideline. Nonetheless, the specific guidelines that have been promulgated cover the type of criminal behavior that most such offenses proscribe. The court is required to determine if there is a sufficiently analogous offense guideline, and, if so, to apply the guideline that is most analogous. In a case in which there is no sufficiently analogous guideline, the provisions of 18 U.S.C. § 3553 control.

The sentencing guidelines apply to convictions under 18 U.S.C. § 13 (Assimilative Crimes Act) and 18 U.S.C. § 1153 (Indian Major Crimes Act); *see* 18 U.S.C. § 3551(a), as amended by section 1602 of Public Law 101–647.

Historical Note	Effective November 1, 1987. Amended effective June 15, 1988 (amendment 43); November 1, 1991 (amendment 412); November 1, 1997 (amendment 569); November 1, 2006 (amendment 685); November 1, 2014 (amendment 787).

§2X5.2. Class A Misdemeanors (Not Covered by Another Specific Offense Guideline)

    (a)   Base Offense Level: **6**

Commentary

Statutory Provisions: 18 U.S.C. §§ 1365(f), 1801; 42 U.S.C. § 14133; 49 U.S.C. § 31310.

Application Note:

1.   **In General.**—This guideline applies to Class A misdemeanor offenses that are specifically referenced in Appendix A (Statutory Index) to this guideline. This guideline also applies to Class A misdemeanor offenses that have not been referenced in Appendix A. Do not apply this guideline to a Class A misdemeanor that has been specifically referenced in Appendix A to another Chapter Two guideline.

Historical Note	Effective November 1, 2006 (amendment 685). Amended effective November 1, 2007 (amendment 699); November 1, 2008 (amendment 721); November 1, 2010 (amendment 746).

*   *   *   *   *

6. OFFENSES INVOLVING USE OF A MINOR IN A CRIME OF VIOLENCE

Historical Note	Effective November 1, 2004 (amendment 674).

§2X6.1. Use of a Minor in a Crime of Violence

    (a)   Base Offense Level: 4 plus the offense level from the guideline applicable to the underlying crime of violence.

Commentary

Statutory Provision: 18 U.S.C. § 25.

Application Notes:

1.   **Definition.**—For purposes of this guideline, "*underlying crime of violence*" means the crime of violence as to which the defendant is convicted of using a minor.

2.   **Inapplicability of §3B1.4.**—Do not apply the adjustment under §3B1.4 (Using a Minor to Commit a Crime).

3. **Multiple Counts.—**

   (A) In a case in which the defendant is convicted under both 18 U.S.C. § 25 and the underlying crime of violence, the counts shall be grouped pursuant to subsection (a) of §3D1.2 (Groups of Closely Related Counts).

   (B) Multiple counts involving the use of a minor in a crime of violence shall not be grouped under §3D1.2.

Historical Note	Effective November 1, 2004 (amendment 674).

* * * * *

7. OFFENSES INVOLVING BORDER TUNNELS AND SUBMERSIBLE AND SEMI-SUBMERSIBLE VESSELS

Historical Note	Effective November 1, 2007 (amendment 700). Amended effective November 1, 2009 (amendment 728).

§2X7.1. Border Tunnels and Subterranean Passages

   (a) Base Offense Level:

   (1) If the defendant was convicted under 18 U.S.C. § 555(c), **4** plus the offense level applicable to the underlying smuggling offense. If the resulting offense level is less than level **16**, increase to level **16**.

   (2) **16**, if the defendant was convicted under 18 U.S.C. § 555(a); or

   (3) **8**, if the defendant was convicted under 18 U.S.C. § 555(b).

Commentary

Statutory Provision: 18 U.S.C. § 555.

Application Note:

1. **Definition.**—For purposes of this guideline, "*underlying smuggling offense*" means the smuggling offense the defendant committed through the use of the tunnel or subterranean passage.

Historical Note	Effective November 1, 2007 (amendment 700). Amended effective November 1, 2008 (amendment 724).

§2X7.2. Submersible and Semi-Submersible Vessels

(a) Base Offense Level: **26**

(b) Specific Offense Characteristic

(1) (Apply the greatest) If the offense involved—

(A) a failure to heave to when directed by law enforcement officers, increase by **2** levels;

(B) an attempt to sink the vessel, increase by **4** levels; or

(C) the sinking of the vessel, increase by **8** levels.

Commentary

Statutory Provision: 18 U.S.C. § 2285.

Application Note:

1. **Upward Departure Provisions.**—An upward departure may be warranted in any of the following cases:

(A) The defendant engaged in a pattern of activity involving use of a submersible vessel or semi-submersible vessel described in 18 U.S.C. § 2285 to facilitate other felonies.

(B) The offense involved use of the vessel as part of an ongoing criminal organization or enterprise.

Background: This guideline implements the directive to the Commission in section 103 of Public Law 110–407.

Historical Note	Effective November 1, 2009 (amendment 728).

PART Y — [NOT USED]

PART Z — [NOT USED]

CHAPTER THREE

ADJUSTMENTS

PART A — VICTIM-RELATED ADJUSTMENTS

Introductory Commentary

The following adjustments are included in this Part because they may apply to a wide variety of offenses.

Historical Note	Effective November 1, 1987. Amended effective November 1, 1990 (amendment 344).

§3A1.1. Hate Crime Motivation or Vulnerable Victim

(a)   If the finder of fact at trial or, in the case of a plea of guilty or *nolo contendere*, the court at sentencing determines beyond a reasonable doubt that the defendant intentionally selected any victim or any property as the object of the offense of conviction because of the actual or perceived race, color, religion, national origin, ethnicity, gender, gender identity, disability, or sexual orientation of any person, increase by **3** levels.

(b)   (1)   If the defendant knew or should have known that a victim of the offense was a vulnerable victim, increase by **2** levels.

     (2)   If (A) subdivision (1) applies; and (B) the offense involved a large number of vulnerable victims, increase the offense level determined under subdivision (1) by **2** additional levels.

(c)   Special Instruction

     (1)   Subsection (a) shall not apply if an adjustment from §2H1.1(b)(1) applies.

Commentary

Application Notes:

1.   Subsection (a) applies to offenses that are hate crimes. Note that special evidentiary requirements govern the application of this subsection.

Do not apply subsection (a) on the basis of gender in the case of a sexual offense. In such cases, this factor is taken into account by the offense level of the Chapter Two offense guideline. Moreover, do not apply subsection (a) if an adjustment from §2H1.1(b)(1) applies.

2. For purposes of subsection (b), "*vulnerable victim*" means a person (A) who is a victim of the offense of conviction and any conduct for which the defendant is accountable under §1B1.3 (Relevant Conduct); and (B) who is unusually vulnerable due to age, physical or mental condition, or who is otherwise particularly susceptible to the criminal conduct.

Subsection (b) applies to offenses involving an unusually vulnerable victim in which the defendant knows or should have known of the victim's unusual vulnerability. The adjustment would apply, for example, in a fraud case in which the defendant marketed an ineffective cancer cure or in a robbery in which the defendant selected a handicapped victim. But it would not apply in a case in which the defendant sold fraudulent securities by mail to the general public and one of the victims happened to be senile. Similarly, for example, a bank teller is not an unusually vulnerable victim solely by virtue of the teller's position in a bank.

Do not apply subsection (b) if the factor that makes the person a vulnerable victim is incorporated in the offense guideline. For example, if the offense guideline provides an enhancement for the age of the victim, this subsection would not be applied unless the victim was unusually vulnerable for reasons unrelated to age.

3. The adjustments from subsections (a) and (b) are to be applied cumulatively. Do not, however, apply subsection (b) in a case in which subsection (a) applies unless a victim of the offense was unusually vulnerable for reasons unrelated to race, color, religion, national origin, ethnicity, gender, gender identity, disability, or sexual orientation.

4. If an enhancement from subsection (b) applies and the defendant's criminal history includes a prior sentence for an offense that involved the selection of a vulnerable victim, an upward departure may be warranted.

5. For purposes of this guideline, "*gender identity*" means actual or perceived gender-related characteristics. *See* 18 U.S.C. § 249(c)(4).

Background: Subsection (a) reflects the directive to the Commission, contained in Section 280003 of the Violent Crime Control and Law Enforcement Act of 1994, to provide an enhancement of not less than three levels for an offense when the finder of fact at trial determines beyond a reasonable doubt that the defendant had a hate crime motivation. To avoid unwarranted sentencing disparity based on the method of conviction, the Commission has broadened the application of this enhancement to include offenses that, in the case of a plea of guilty or *nolo contendere*, the court at sentencing determines are hate crimes. In section 4703(a) of Public Law 111–84, Congress broadened the scope of that directive to include gender identity; to reflect that congressional action, the Commission has broadened the scope of this enhancement to include gender identity.

Subsection (b)(2) implements, in a broader form, the instruction to the Commission in section 6(c)(3) of Public Law 105–184.

Historical Note	Effective November 1, 1987. Amended effective November 1, 1989 (amendment 245); November 1, 1990 (amendment 344); November 1, 1992 (amendment 454); November 1, 1995 (amendment 521); November 1, 1997 (amendment 564); November 1, 1998 (amendment 587); November 1, 2000 (amendment 595); November 1, 2010 (amendment 743).

§3A1.2.   Official Victim

(Apply the greatest):

(a)   If (1) the victim was (A) a government officer or employee; (B) a former government officer or employee; or (C) a member of the immediate family of a person described in subdivision (A) or (B); and (2) the offense of conviction was motivated by such status, increase by **3** levels.

(b)   If subsection (a)(1) and (2) apply, and the applicable Chapter Two guideline is from Chapter Two, Part A (Offenses Against the Person), increase by **6** levels.

(c)   If, in a manner creating a substantial risk of serious bodily injury, the defendant or a person for whose conduct the defendant is otherwise accountable—

   (1)   knowing or having reasonable cause to believe that a person was a law enforcement officer, assaulted such officer during the course of the offense or immediate flight therefrom; or

   (2)   knowing or having reasonable cause to believe that a person was a prison official, assaulted such official while the defendant (or a person for whose conduct the defendant is otherwise accountable) was in the custody or control of a prison or other correctional facility,

increase by **6** levels.

Commentary

Application Notes:

1.   **Applicability to Certain Victims.**—This guideline applies when specified individuals are victims of the offense. This guideline does not apply when the only victim is an organization, agency, or the government.

2.   **Nonapplicability in Case of Incorporation of Factor in Chapter Two.**—Do not apply this adjustment if the offense guideline specifically incorporates this factor. The only offense guideline in Chapter Two that specifically incorporates this factor is §2A2.4 (Obstructing or Impeding Officers).

3.   **Application of Subsections (a) and (b).**—"*Motivated by such status*", for purposes of subsections (a) and (b), means that the offense of conviction was motivated by the fact that the victim was a government officer or employee, or a member of the immediate family thereof. This adjustment would not apply, for example, where both the defendant and victim were employed by the same government agency and the offense was motivated by a personal dispute. This adjustment also would not apply in the case of a robbery of a

postal employee because the offense guideline for robbery contains an enhancement (§2B3.1(b)(1)) that takes such conduct into account.

4.   **Application of Subsection (c).—**

(A)   **In General.—**Subsection (c) applies in circumstances tantamount to aggravated assault (i) against a law enforcement officer, committed in the course of, or in immediate flight following, another offense; or (ii) against a prison official, while the defendant (or a person for whose conduct the defendant is otherwise accountable) was in the custody or control of a prison or other correctional facility. While subsection (c) may apply in connection with a variety of offenses that are not by nature targeted against official victims, its applicability is limited to assaultive conduct against such official victims that is sufficiently serious to create at least a "substantial risk of serious bodily injury".

(B)   **Definitions.—**For purposes of subsection (c):

"*Custody or control*" includes "non-secure custody", *i.e.*, custody with no significant physical restraint. For example, a defendant is in the custody or control of a prison or other correctional facility if the defendant (i) is on a work detail outside the security perimeter of the prison or correctional facility; (ii) is physically away from the prison or correctional facility while on a pass or furlough; or (iii) is in custody at a community corrections center, community treatment center, "halfway house", or similar facility. The defendant also shall be deemed to be in the custody or control of a prison or other correctional facility while the defendant is in the status of having escaped from that prison or correctional facility.

"*Prison official*" means any individual (including a director, officer, employee, independent contractor, or volunteer, but not including an inmate) authorized to act on behalf of a prison or correctional facility. For example, this enhancement would be applicable to any of the following: (i) an individual employed by a prison as a corrections officer; (ii) an individual employed by a prison as a work detail supervisor; and (iii) a nurse who, under contract, provides medical services to prisoners in a prison health facility.

"*Substantial risk of serious bodily injury*" includes any more serious injury that was risked, as well as actual serious bodily injury (or more serious injury) if it occurs.

5.   **Upward Departure Provision.—**If the official victim is an exceptionally high-level official, such as the President or the Vice President of the United States, an upward departure may be warranted due to the potential disruption of the governmental function.

Historical Note	Effective November 1, 1987. Amended effective January 15, 1988 (amendment 44); November 1, 1989 (amendments 246–248); November 1, 1992 (amendment 455); November 1, 2002 (amendment 643); November 1, 2004 (amendment 663); November 1, 2010 (amendment 747).

§3A1.3.   Restraint of Victim

If a victim was physically restrained in the course of the offense, increase by **2** levels.

Commentary

Application Notes:

1.   *"Physically restrained"* is defined in the Commentary to §1B1.1 (Application Instructions).

2.   Do not apply this adjustment where the offense guideline specifically incorporates this factor, or where the unlawful restraint of a victim is an element of the offense itself (*e.g.,* this adjustment does not apply to offenses covered by §2A4.1 (Kidnapping, Abduction, Unlawful Restraint)).

3.   If the restraint was sufficiently egregious, an upward departure may be warranted. *See* §5K2.4 (Abduction or Unlawful Restraint).

Historical Note	Effective November 1, 1987. Amended effective November 1, 1989 (amendments 249 and 250); November 1, 1991 (amendment 413).

§3A1.4.   Terrorism

(a)   If the offense is a felony that involved, or was intended to promote, a federal crime of terrorism, increase by **12** levels; but if the resulting offense level is less than level **32**, increase to level **32**.

(b)   In each such case, the defendant's criminal history category from Chapter Four (Criminal History and Criminal Livelihood) shall be Category VI.

Commentary

Application Notes:

1.   **"Federal Crime of Terrorism" Defined.**—For purposes of this guideline, *"federal crime of terrorism"* has the meaning given that term in 18 U.S.C. § 2332b(g)(5).

2.   **Harboring, Concealing, and Obstruction Offenses.**—For purposes of this guideline, an offense that involved (A) harboring or concealing a terrorist who committed a federal crime of terrorism (such as an offense under 18 U.S.C. § 2339 or § 2339A); or (B) obstructing an investigation of a federal crime of terrorism, shall be considered to have involved, or to have been intended to promote, that federal crime of terrorism.

3.   **Computation of Criminal History Category.**—Under subsection (b), if the defendant's criminal history category as determined under Chapter Four (Criminal History and Criminal Livelihood) is less than Category VI, it shall be increased to Category VI.

4.   **Upward Departure Provision.**—By the terms of the directive to the Commission in section 730 of the Antiterrorism and Effective Death Penalty Act of 1996, the adjustment provided by this guideline applies only to federal crimes of terrorism. However, there may be cases in which (A) the offense was calculated to influence or affect the conduct of government by intimidation or coercion, or to retaliate against government conduct but the offense involved, or was intended to promote, an offense other than one of the offenses specifically enumerated in 18 U.S.C. § 2332b(g)(5)(B); or (B) the offense involved, or was

intended to promote, one of the offenses specifically enumerated in 18 U.S.C. § 2332b(g)(5)(B), but the terrorist motive was to intimidate or coerce a civilian population, rather than to influence or affect the conduct of government by intimidation or coercion, or to retaliate against government conduct. In such cases an upward departure would be warranted, except that the sentence resulting from such a departure may not exceed the top of the guideline range that would have resulted if the adjustment under this guideline had been applied.

Historical Note	Effective November 1, 1995 (amendment 526). Amended effective November 1, 1996 (amendment 539); November 1, 1997 (amendment 565); November 1, 2002 (amendment 637).

§3A1.5. Serious Human Rights Offense

If the defendant was convicted of a serious human rights offense, increase the offense level as follows:

(a) If the defendant was convicted of an offense under 18 U.S.C. § 1091(c), increase by **2** levels.

(b) If the defendant was convicted of any other serious human rights offense, increase by **4** levels. If (1) death resulted, and (2) the resulting offense level is less than level **37**, increase to level **37**.

Commentary

Application Notes:

1. **Definition.**—For purposes of this guideline, "*serious human rights offense*" means violations of federal criminal laws relating to genocide, torture, war crimes, and the use or recruitment of child soldiers under sections 1091, 2340, 2340A, 2441, and 2442 of title 18, United States Code. *See* 28 U.S.C. § 509B(e).

2. **Application of Minimum Offense Level in Subsection (b).**—The minimum offense level in subsection (b) is cumulative with any other provision in the guidelines. For example, if death resulted and this factor was specifically incorporated into the Chapter Two offense guideline, the minimum offense level in subsection (b) may also apply.

Background: This guideline covers a range of conduct considered to be serious human rights offenses, including genocide, war crimes, torture, and the recruitment or use of child soldiers. *See* generally 28 U.S.C. § 509B(e).

Serious human rights offenses generally have a statutory maximum term of imprisonment of 20 years, but if death resulted, a higher statutory maximum term of imprisonment of any term of years or life applies. *See* 18 U.S.C. §§ 1091(b), 2340A(a), 2442(b). For the offense of war crimes, a statutory maximum term of imprisonment of any term of years or life always applies. *See* 18 U.S.C. § 2441(a). For the offense of incitement to genocide, the statutory maximum term of imprisonment is five years. *See* 18 U.S.C. § 1091(c).

Historical Note	Effective November 1, 2012 (amendment 765).

PART B — ROLE IN THE OFFENSE

Introductory Commentary

This Part provides adjustments to the offense level based upon the role the defendant played in committing the offense. The determination of a defendant's role in the offense is to be made on the basis of all conduct within the scope of §1B1.3 (Relevant Conduct), *i.e.*, all conduct included under §1B1.3(a)(1)–(4), and not solely on the basis of elements and acts cited in the count of conviction.

When an offense is committed by more than one participant, §3B1.1 or §3B1.2 (or neither) may apply. Section 3B1.3 may apply to offenses committed by any number of participants.

Historical Note	Effective November 1, 1987. Amended effective November 1, 1990 (amendment 345); November 1, 1992 (amendment 456).

§3B1.1. Aggravating Role

Based on the defendant's role in the offense, increase the offense level as follows:

(a) If the defendant was an organizer or leader of a criminal activity that involved five or more participants or was otherwise extensive, increase by **4** levels.

(b) If the defendant was a manager or supervisor (but not an organizer or leader) and the criminal activity involved five or more participants or was otherwise extensive, increase by **3** levels.

(c) If the defendant was an organizer, leader, manager, or supervisor in any criminal activity other than described in (a) or (b), increase by **2** levels.

Commentary

Application Notes:

1. A "*participant*" is a person who is criminally responsible for the commission of the offense, but need not have been convicted. A person who is not criminally responsible for the commission of the offense (*e.g.*, an undercover law enforcement officer) is not a participant.

2. To qualify for an adjustment under this section, the defendant must have been the organizer, leader, manager, or supervisor of one or more other participants. An upward departure may be warranted, however, in the case of a defendant who did not organize, lead, manage, or supervise another participant, but who nevertheless exercised management responsibility over the property, assets, or activities of a criminal organization.

3. In assessing whether an organization is "otherwise extensive," all persons involved during the course of the entire offense are to be considered. Thus, a fraud that involved only three participants but used the unknowing services of many outsiders could be considered extensive.

4. In distinguishing a leadership and organizational role from one of mere management or supervision, titles such as "kingpin" or "boss" are not controlling. Factors the court should consider include the exercise of decision making authority, the nature of participation in the commission of the offense, the recruitment of accomplices, the claimed right to a larger share of the fruits of the crime, the degree of participation in planning or organizing the offense, the nature and scope of the illegal activity, and the degree of control and authority exercised over others. There can, of course, be more than one person who qualifies as a leader or organizer of a criminal association or conspiracy. This adjustment does not apply to a defendant who merely suggests committing the offense.

Background: This section provides a range of adjustments to increase the offense level based upon the size of a criminal organization (*i.e.*, the number of participants in the offense) and the degree to which the defendant was responsible for committing the offense. This adjustment is included primarily because of concerns about relative responsibility. However, it is also likely that persons who exercise a supervisory or managerial role in the commission of an offense tend to profit more from it and present a greater danger to the public and/or are more likely to recidivate. The Commission's intent is that this adjustment should increase with both the size of the organization and the degree of the defendant's responsibility.

In relatively small criminal enterprises that are not otherwise to be considered as extensive in scope or in planning or preparation, the distinction between organization and leadership, and that of management or supervision, is of less significance than in larger enterprises that tend to have clearly delineated divisions of responsibility. This is reflected in the inclusiveness of §3B1.1(c).

Historical Note	Effective November 1, 1987. Amended effective November 1, 1991 (amendment 414); November 1, 1993 (amendment 500).

§3B1.2. Mitigating Role

Based on the defendant's role in the offense, decrease the offense level as follows:

(a) If the defendant was a minimal participant in any criminal activity, decrease by **4** levels.

(b) If the defendant was a minor participant in any criminal activity, decrease by **2** levels.

In cases falling between (a) and (b), decrease by **3** levels.

Commentary

Application Notes:

1. **Definition.**—For purposes of this guideline, "*participant*" has the meaning given that term in Application Note 1 of §3B1.1 (Aggravating Role).

2. **Requirement of Multiple Participants.**—This guideline is not applicable unless more than one participant was involved in the offense. *See* the Introductory Commentary to this Part (Role in the Offense). Accordingly, an adjustment under this guideline may not apply to a defendant who is the only defendant convicted of an offense unless that offense involved other participants in addition to the defendant and the defendant otherwise qualifies for such an adjustment.

3. **Applicability of Adjustment.**—

    (A) **Substantially Less Culpable than Average Participant.**—This section provides a range of adjustments for a defendant who plays a part in committing the offense that makes him substantially less culpable than the average participant in the criminal activity.

    A defendant who is accountable under §1B1.3 (Relevant Conduct) only for the conduct in which the defendant personally was involved and who performs a limited function in the criminal activity may receive an adjustment under this guideline. For example, a defendant who is convicted of a drug trafficking offense, whose participation in that offense was limited to transporting or storing drugs and who is accountable under §1B1.3 only for the quantity of drugs the defendant personally transported or stored may receive an adjustment under this guideline.

    Likewise, a defendant who is accountable under §1B1.3 for a loss amount under §2B1.1 (Theft, Property Destruction, and Fraud) that greatly exceeds the defendant's personal gain from a fraud offense or who had limited knowledge of the scope of the scheme may receive an adjustment under this guideline. For example, a defendant in a health care fraud scheme, whose participation in the scheme was limited to serving as a nominee owner and who received little personal gain relative to the loss amount, may receive an adjustment under this guideline.

    (B) **Conviction of Significantly Less Serious Offense.**—If a defendant has received a lower offense level by virtue of being convicted of an offense significantly less serious than warranted by his actual criminal conduct, a reduction for a mitigating role under this section ordinarily is not warranted because such defendant is not substantially less culpable than a defendant whose only conduct involved the less serious offense. For example, if a defendant whose actual conduct involved a minimal role in the distribution of 25 grams of cocaine (an offense having a Chapter Two offense level of level 12 under §2D1.1 (Unlawful Manufacturing, Importing, Exporting, or Trafficking (Including Possession with Intent to Commit These Offenses); Attempt or Conspiracy)) is convicted of simple possession of cocaine (an offense having a Chapter Two offense level of level 6 under §2D2.1 (Unlawful Possession; Attempt or Conspiracy)), no reduction for a mitigating role is warranted because the defendant is not substantially less culpable than a defendant whose only conduct involved the simple possession of cocaine.

(C)   **Fact-Based Determination.**—The determination whether to apply subsection (a) or subsection (b), or an intermediate adjustment, is based on the totality of the circumstances and involves a determination that is heavily dependent upon the facts of the particular case.

In determining whether to apply subsection (a) or (b), or an intermediate adjustment, the court should consider the following non-exhaustive list of factors:

(i)   the degree to which the defendant understood the scope and structure of the criminal activity;

(ii)   the degree to which the defendant participated in planning or organizing the criminal activity;

(iii)   the degree to which the defendant exercised decision-making authority or influenced the exercise of decision-making authority;

(iv)   the nature and extent of the defendant's participation in the commission of the criminal activity, including the acts the defendant performed and the responsibility and discretion the defendant had in performing those acts;

(v)   the degree to which the defendant stood to benefit from the criminal activity.

For example, a defendant who does not have a proprietary interest in the criminal activity and who is simply being paid to perform certain tasks should be considered for an adjustment under this guideline.

The fact that a defendant performs an essential or indispensable role in the criminal activity is not determinative. Such a defendant may receive an adjustment under this guideline if he or she is substantially less culpable than the average participant in the criminal activity.

4.   **Minimal Participant.**—Subsection (a) applies to a defendant described in Application Note 3(A) who plays a minimal role in the criminal activity. It is intended to cover defendants who are plainly among the least culpable of those involved in the conduct of a group. Under this provision, the defendant's lack of knowledge or understanding of the scope and structure of the enterprise and of the activities of others is indicative of a role as minimal participant.

5.   **Minor Participant.**—Subsection (b) applies to a defendant described in Application Note 3(A) who is less culpable than most other participants in the criminal activity, but whose role could not be described as minimal.

6.   **Application of Role Adjustment in Certain Drug Cases.**—In a case in which the court applied §2D1.1 and the defendant's base offense level under that guideline was reduced by operation of the maximum base offense level in §2D1.1(a)(5), the court also shall apply the appropriate adjustment under this guideline.

Historical Note	Effective November 1, 1987. Amended effective November 1, 1992 (amendment 456); November 1, 2001 (amendment 635); November 1, 2002 (amendment 640); November 1, 2009 (amendment 737); November 1, 2011 (amendments 749 and 755); November 1, 2014 (amendment 782); November 1, 2015 (amendment 794).

§3B1.3. Abuse of Position of Trust or Use of Special Skill

If the defendant abused a position of public or private trust, or used a special skill, in a manner that significantly facilitated the commission or concealment of the offense, increase by 2 levels. This adjustment may not be employed if an abuse of trust or skill is included in the base offense level or specific offense characteristic. If this adjustment is based upon an abuse of a position of trust, it may be employed in addition to an adjustment under §3B1.1 (Aggravating Role); if this adjustment is based solely on the use of a special skill, it may not be employed in addition to an adjustment under §3B1.1 (Aggravating Role).

Commentary

Application Notes:

1. **Definition of "Public or Private Trust".**—*"Public or private trust"* refers to a position of public or private trust characterized by professional or managerial discretion (*i.e.*, substantial discretionary judgment that is ordinarily given considerable deference). Persons holding such positions ordinarily are subject to significantly less supervision than employees whose responsibilities are primarily non-discretionary in nature. For this adjustment to apply, the position of public or private trust must have contributed in some significant way to facilitating the commission or concealment of the offense (*e.g.*, by making the detection of the offense or the defendant's responsibility for the offense more difficult). This adjustment, for example, applies in the case of an embezzlement of a client's funds by an attorney serving as a guardian, a bank executive's fraudulent loan scheme, or the criminal sexual abuse of a patient by a physician under the guise of an examination. This adjustment does not apply in the case of an embezzlement or theft by an ordinary bank teller or hotel clerk because such positions are not characterized by the above-described factors.

2. **Application of Adjustment in Certain Circumstances.**—Notwithstanding Application Note 1, or any other provision of this guideline, an adjustment under this guideline shall apply to the following:

    (A) An employee of the United States Postal Service who engages in the theft or destruction of undelivered United States mail.

    (B) A defendant who exceeds or abuses the authority of his or her position in order to obtain, transfer, or issue unlawfully, or use without authority, any means of identification. *"Means of identification"* has the meaning given that term in 18 U.S.C. § 1028(d)(7). The following are examples to which this subdivision would apply: (i) an employee of a state motor vehicle department who exceeds or abuses the authority of his or her position by knowingly issuing a driver's license based on false, incomplete, or misleading information; (ii) a hospital orderly who exceeds or abuses the authority of his or her position by obtaining or misusing patient identification information from a patient chart; and (iii) a volunteer at a charitable organization who exceeds or abuses the authority of his or her position by obtaining or misusing identification information from a donor's file.

3. This adjustment also applies in a case in which the defendant provides sufficient indicia to the victim that the defendant legitimately holds a position of private or public trust when, in fact, the defendant does not. For example, the adjustment applies in the case of

a defendant who (A) perpetrates a financial fraud by leading an investor to believe the defendant is a legitimate investment broker; or (B) perpetrates a fraud by representing falsely to a patient or employer that the defendant is a licensed physician. In making the misrepresentation, the defendant assumes a position of trust, relative to the victim, that provides the defendant with the same opportunity to commit a difficult-to-detect crime that the defendant would have had if the position were held legitimately.

4. "*Special skill*" refers to a skill not possessed by members of the general public and usually requiring substantial education, training or licensing. Examples would include pilots, lawyers, doctors, accountants, chemists, and demolition experts.

5. The following additional illustrations of an abuse of a position of trust pertain to theft or embezzlement from employee pension or welfare benefit plans or labor unions:

   (A) If the offense involved theft or embezzlement from an employee pension or welfare benefit plan and the defendant was a fiduciary of the benefit plan, an adjustment under this section for abuse of a position of trust will apply. "*Fiduciary of the benefit plan*" is defined in 29 U.S.C. § 1002(21)(A) to mean a person who exercises any discretionary authority or control in respect to the management of such plan or exercises authority or control in respect to management or disposition of its assets, or who renders investment advice for a fee or other direct or indirect compensation with respect to any moneys or other property of such plan, or has any authority or responsibility to do so, or who has any discretionary authority or responsibility in the administration of such plan.

   (B) If the offense involved theft or embezzlement from a labor union and the defendant was a union officer or occupied a position of trust in the union (as set forth in 29 U.S.C. § 501(a)), an adjustment under this section for an abuse of a position of trust will apply.

Background: This adjustment applies to persons who abuse their positions of trust or their special skills to facilitate significantly the commission or concealment of a crime. The adjustment also applies to persons who provide sufficient indicia to the victim that they legitimately hold a position of public or private trust when, in fact, they do not. Such persons generally are viewed as more culpable.

| *Historical Note* | Effective November 1, 1987. Amended effective November 1, 1990 (amendment 346); November 1, 1993 (amendment 492); November 1, 1998 (amendment 580); November 1, 2001 (amendment 617); November 1, 2005 (amendment 677); November 1, 2009 (amendment 726). |

§3B1.4.   Using a Minor To Commit a Crime

If the defendant used or attempted to use a person less than eighteen years of age to commit the offense or assist in avoiding detection of, or apprehension for, the offense, increase by **2** levels.

Commentary

Application Notes:

1. "*Used or attempted to use*" includes directing, commanding, encouraging, intimidating, counseling, training, procuring, recruiting, or soliciting.

2. Do not apply this adjustment if the Chapter Two offense guideline incorporates this factor. For example, if the defendant receives an enhancement under §2D1.1(b)(15)(B) for involving an individual less than 18 years of age in the offense, do not apply this adjustment.

3. If the defendant used or attempted to use more than one person less than eighteen years of age, an upward departure may be warranted.

Historical Note	Effective November 1, 1995 (amendment 527). Amended effective November 1, 1996 (amendment 540); November 1, 2010 (amendment 748); November 1, 2011 (amendment 750). A former §3B1.4 (untitled), effective November 1, 1987, amended effective November 1, 1989 (amendment 303), was deleted effective November 1, 1995 (amendment 527); November 1, 2014 (amendment 783).

§3B1.5. Use of Body Armor in Drug Trafficking Crimes and Crimes of Violence

If—

(1) the defendant was convicted of a drug trafficking crime or a crime of violence; and

(2) (apply the greater)—

    (A) the offense involved the use of body armor, increase by **2** levels; or

    (B) the defendant used body armor during the commission of the offense, in preparation for the offense, or in an attempt to avoid apprehension for the offense, increase by **4** levels.

Commentary

Application Notes:

1. **Definitions.**—For purposes of this guideline:

    "*Body armor*" means any product sold or offered for sale, in interstate or foreign commerce, as personal protective body covering intended to protect against gunfire, regardless of whether the product is to be worn alone or is sold as a complement to another product or garment. *See* 18 U.S.C. § 921(a)(35).

    "*Crime of violence*" has the meaning given that term in 18 U.S.C. § 16.

    "*Drug trafficking crime*" has the meaning given that term in 18 U.S.C. § 924(c)(2).

"*Offense*" has the meaning given that term in Application Note 1 of the Commentary to §1B1.1 (Application Instructions).

"*Use*" means (A) active employment in a manner to protect the person from gunfire; or (B) use as a means of bartering. "Use" does not mean mere possession (*e.g.*, "use" does not mean that the body armor was found in the trunk of the car but not used actively as protection). "*Used*" means put into "use" as defined in this paragraph.

2. **Application of Subdivision (2)(B).**—Consistent with §1B1.3 (Relevant Conduct), the term "*defendant*", for purposes of subdivision (2)(B), limits the accountability of the defendant to the defendant's own conduct and conduct that the defendant aided or abetted, counseled, commanded, induced, procured, or willfully caused.

3. **Interaction with §2K2.6 and Other Counts of Conviction.**—If the defendant is convicted only of 18 U.S.C. § 931 and receives an enhancement under subsection (b)(1) of §2K2.6 (Possessing, Purchasing, or Owning Body Armor by Violent Felons), do not apply an adjustment under this guideline. However, if, in addition to the count of conviction under 18 U.S.C. § 931, the defendant (A) is convicted of an offense that is a drug trafficking crime or a crime of violence; and (B) used the body armor with respect to that offense, an adjustment under this guideline shall apply with respect to that offense.

Background: This guideline implements the directive in the James Guelff and Chris McCurley Body Armor Act of 2002 (section 11009(d) of the 21st Century Department of Justice Appropriations Authorization Act, Pub. L. 107–273).

Historical Note	Effective November 1, 2003 (amendment 659). Amended effective November 1, 2004 (amendment 670).

PART C — OBSTRUCTION AND RELATED ADJUSTMENTS

Historical Note	Effective November 1, 1987. Amended effective November 1, 2006 (amendment 684).

§3C1.1. Obstructing or Impeding the Administration of Justice

If (1) the defendant willfully obstructed or impeded, or attempted to obstruct or impede, the administration of justice with respect to the investigation, prosecution, or sentencing of the instant offense of conviction, and (2) the obstructive conduct related to (A) the defendant's offense of conviction and any relevant conduct; or (B) a closely related offense, increase the offense level by 2 levels.

Commentary

Application Notes:

1.   **In General.**—This adjustment applies if the defendant's obstructive conduct (A) occurred with respect to the investigation, prosecution, or sentencing of the defendant's instant offense of conviction, and (B) related to (i) the defendant's offense of conviction and any relevant conduct; or (ii) an otherwise closely related case, such as that of a co-defendant.

     Obstructive conduct that occurred prior to the start of the investigation of the instant offense of conviction may be covered by this guideline if the conduct was purposefully calculated, and likely, to thwart the investigation or prosecution of the offense of conviction.

2.   **Limitations on Applicability of Adjustment.**—This provision is not intended to punish a defendant for the exercise of a constitutional right. A defendant's denial of guilt (other than a denial of guilt under oath that constitutes perjury), refusal to admit guilt or provide information to a probation officer, or refusal to enter a plea of guilty is not a basis for application of this provision. In applying this provision in respect to alleged false testimony or statements by the defendant, the court should be cognizant that inaccurate testimony or statements sometimes may result from confusion, mistake, or faulty memory and, thus, not all inaccurate testimony or statements necessarily reflect a willful attempt to obstruct justice.

3.   **Covered Conduct Generally.**—Obstructive conduct can vary widely in nature, degree of planning, and seriousness. Application Note 4 sets forth examples of the types of conduct to which this adjustment is intended to apply. Application Note 5 sets forth examples of less serious forms of conduct to which this enhancement is not intended to apply, but that ordinarily can appropriately be sanctioned by the determination of the particular sentence within the otherwise applicable guideline range. Although the conduct to which this adjustment applies is not subject to precise definition, comparison of the examples set forth in Application Notes 4 and 5 should assist the court in determining whether application of this adjustment is warranted in a particular case.

4.   **Examples of Covered Conduct.**—The following is a non-exhaustive list of examples of the types of conduct to which this adjustment applies:

(A)   threatening, intimidating, or otherwise unlawfully influencing a co-defendant, witness, or juror, directly or indirectly, or attempting to do so;

(B)   committing, suborning, or attempting to suborn perjury, including during the course of a civil proceeding if such perjury pertains to conduct that forms the basis of the offense of conviction;

(C)   producing or attempting to produce a false, altered, or counterfeit document or record during an official investigation or judicial proceeding;

(D)   destroying or concealing or directing or procuring another person to destroy or conceal evidence that is material to an official investigation or judicial proceeding (*e.g.*, shredding a document or destroying ledgers upon learning that an official investigation has commenced or is about to commence), or attempting to do so; however, if such conduct occurred contemporaneously with arrest (*e.g.*, attempting to swallow or throw away a controlled substance), it shall not, standing alone, be sufficient to warrant an adjustment for obstruction unless it resulted in a material hindrance to the official investigation or prosecution of the instant offense or the sentencing of the offender;

(E)   escaping or attempting to escape from custody before trial or sentencing; or willfully failing to appear, as ordered, for a judicial proceeding;

(F)   providing materially false information to a judge or magistrate judge;

(G)   providing a materially false statement to a law enforcement officer that significantly obstructed or impeded the official investigation or prosecution of the instant offense;

(H)   providing materially false information to a probation officer in respect to a presentence or other investigation for the court;

(I)   other conduct prohibited by obstruction of justice provisions under Title 18, United States Code (*e.g.*, 18 U.S.C. §§ 1510, 1511);

(J)   failing to comply with a restraining order or injunction issued pursuant to 21 U.S.C. § 853(e) or with an order to repatriate property issued pursuant to 21 U.S.C. § 853(p);

(K)   threatening the victim of the offense in an attempt to prevent the victim from reporting the conduct constituting the offense of conviction.

This adjustment also applies to any other obstructive conduct in respect to the official investigation, prosecution, or sentencing of the instant offense where there is a separate count of conviction for such conduct.

5.   **Examples of Conduct Ordinarily Not Covered.**—Some types of conduct ordinarily do not warrant application of this adjustment but may warrant a greater sentence within the otherwise applicable guideline range or affect the determination of whether other guideline adjustments apply (*e.g.*, §3E1.1 (Acceptance of Responsibility)). However, if the defendant is convicted of a separate count for such conduct, this adjustment will apply

and increase the offense level for the underlying offense (*i.e.*, the offense with respect to which the obstructive conduct occurred). *See* Application Note 8, below.

The following is a non-exhaustive list of examples of the types of conduct to which this application note applies:

(A) providing a false name or identification document at arrest, except where such conduct actually resulted in a significant hindrance to the investigation or prosecution of the instant offense;

(B) making false statements, not under oath, to law enforcement officers, unless Application Note 4(G) above applies;

(C) providing incomplete or misleading information, not amounting to a material falsehood, in respect to a presentence investigation;

(D) avoiding or fleeing from arrest (*see, however,* §3C1.2 (Reckless Endangerment During Flight));

(E) lying to a probation or pretrial services officer about defendant's drug use while on pre-trial release, although such conduct may be a factor in determining whether to reduce the defendant's sentence under §3E1.1 (Acceptance of Responsibility).

6. **"Material" Evidence Defined.**—"*Material*" evidence, fact, statement, or information, as used in this section, means evidence, fact, statement, or information that, if believed, would tend to influence or affect the issue under determination.

7. **Inapplicability of Adjustment in Certain Circumstances.**—If the defendant is convicted of an offense covered by §2J1.1 (Contempt), §2J1.2 (Obstruction of Justice), §2J1.3 (Perjury or Subornation of Perjury; Bribery of Witness), §2J1.5 (Failure to Appear by Material Witness), §2J1.6 (Failure to Appear by Defendant), §2J1.9 (Payment to Witness), §2X3.1 (Accessory After the Fact), or §2X4.1 (Misprision of Felony), this adjustment is not to be applied to the offense level for that offense except if a significant further obstruction occurred during the investigation, prosecution, or sentencing of the obstruction offense itself (*e.g.*, if the defendant threatened a witness during the course of the prosecution for the obstruction offense).

Similarly, if the defendant receives an enhancement under §2D1.1(b)(15)(D), do not apply this adjustment.

8. **Grouping Under §3D1.2(c).**—If the defendant is convicted both of an obstruction offense (*e.g.*, 18 U.S.C. § 3146 (Penalty for failure to appear); 18 U.S.C. § 1621 (Perjury generally)) and an underlying offense (the offense with respect to which the obstructive conduct occurred), the count for the obstruction offense will be grouped with the count for the underlying offense under subsection (c) of §3D1.2 (Groups of Closely Related Counts). The offense level for that group of closely related counts will be the offense level for the underlying offense increased by the 2-level adjustment specified by this section, or the offense level for the obstruction offense, whichever is greater.

9. **Accountability for §1B1.3(a)(1)(A) Conduct.**—Under this section, the defendant is accountable for the defendant's own conduct and for conduct that the defendant aided or abetted, counseled, commanded, induced, procured, or willfully caused.

Historical Note	Effective November 1, 1987. Amended effective November 1, 1989 (amendments 251 and 252); November 1, 1990 (amendment 347); November 1, 1991 (amendment 415); November 1, 1992 (amendment 457); November 1, 1993 (amendment 496); November 1, 1997 (amendment 566); November 1, 1998 (amendments 579, 581, and 582); November 1, 2002 (amendment 637); November 1, 2004 (amendment 674); November 1, 2006 (amendment 693); November 1, 2010 (amendments 746, 747, and 748); November 1, 2011 (amendments 750 and 758); November 1, 2014 (amendment 783).

§3C1.2. Reckless Endangerment During Flight

If the defendant recklessly created a substantial risk of death or serious bodily injury to another person in the course of fleeing from a law enforcement officer, increase by 2 levels.

Commentary

Application Notes:

1. Do not apply this enhancement where the offense guideline in Chapter Two, or another adjustment in Chapter Three, results in an equivalent or greater increase in offense level solely on the basis of the same conduct.

2. "*Reckless*" is defined in the Commentary to §2A1.4 (Involuntary Manslaughter). For the purposes of this guideline, "reckless" means that the conduct was at least reckless and includes any higher level of culpability. However, where a higher degree of culpability was involved, an upward departure above the 2-level increase provided in this section may be warranted.

3. "*During flight*" is to be construed broadly and includes preparation for flight. Therefore, this adjustment also is applicable where the conduct occurs in the course of resisting arrest.

4. "*Another person*" includes any person, except a participant in the offense who willingly participated in the flight.

5. Under this section, the defendant is accountable for the defendant's own conduct and for conduct that the defendant aided or abetted, counseled, commanded, induced, procured, or willfully caused.

6. If death or bodily injury results or the conduct posed a substantial risk of death or bodily injury to more than one person, an upward departure may be warranted. *See* Chapter Five, Part K (Departures).

Historical Note	Effective November 1, 1990 (amendment 347). Amended effective November 1, 1991 (amendment 416); November 1, 1992 (amendment 457); November 1, 2010 (amendment 747).

§3C1.3. Commission of Offense While on Release

If a statutory sentencing enhancement under 18 U.S.C. § 3147 applies, increase the offense level by 3 levels.

Commentary

Application Note:

1.   Under 18 U.S.C. § 3147, a sentence of imprisonment must be imposed in addition to the sentence for the underlying offense, and the sentence of imprisonment imposed under 18 U.S.C. § 3147 must run consecutively to any other sentence of imprisonment. Therefore, the court, in order to comply with the statute, should divide the sentence on the judgment form between the sentence attributable to the underlying offense and the sentence attributable to the enhancement. The court will have to ensure that the "total punishment" (*i.e.*, the sentence for the offense committed while on release plus the statutory sentencing enhancement under 18 U.S.C. § 3147) is in accord with the guideline range for the offense committed while on release, including, as in any other case in which a Chapter Three adjustment applies (*see* §1B1.1 (Application Instructions)), the adjustment provided by the enhancement in this section. For example, if the applicable adjusted guideline range is 30–37 months and the court determines a "total punishment" of 36 months is appropriate, a sentence of 30 months for the underlying offense plus 6 months under 18 U.S.C. § 3147 would satisfy this requirement. Similarly, if the applicable adjusted guideline range is 30–37 months and the court determines a "total punishment" of 30 months is appropriate, a sentence of 24 months for the underlying offense plus 6 months under 18 U.S.C. § 3147 would satisfy this requirement.

Background: An enhancement under 18 U.S.C. § 3147 applies, after appropriate sentencing notice, when a defendant is sentenced for an offense committed while released in connection with another federal offense.

This guideline enables the court to determine and implement a combined "total punishment" consistent with the overall structure of the guidelines, while at the same time complying with the statutory requirement.

Historical Note	Effective November 1, 2006 (amendment 684). Amended effective November 1, 2009 (amendment 734).

§3C1.4.   False Registration of Domain Name

If a statutory enhancement under 18 U.S.C. § 3559(g)(1) applies, increase by **2** levels.

Commentary

Background: This adjustment implements the directive to the Commission in section 204(b) of Pub. L. 108–482.

Historical Note	Effective November 1, 2006 (amendment 689). Amended effective November 1, 2008 (amendment 724).

PART D — MULTIPLE COUNTS

Introductory Commentary

This Part provides rules for determining a single offense level that encompasses all the counts of which the defendant is convicted. These rules apply to multiple counts of conviction (A) contained in the same indictment or information; or (B) contained in different indictments or informations for which sentences are to be imposed at the same time or in a consolidated proceeding. The single, "combined" offense level that results from applying these rules is used, after adjustment pursuant to the guidelines in subsequent parts, to determine the sentence. These rules have been designed primarily with the more commonly prosecuted federal offenses in mind.

The rules in this Part seek to provide incremental punishment for significant additional criminal conduct. The most serious offense is used as a starting point. The other counts determine how much to increase the offense level. The amount of the additional punishment declines as the number of additional offenses increases.

Some offenses that may be charged in multiple-count indictments are so closely intertwined with other offenses that conviction for them ordinarily would not warrant increasing the guideline range. For example, embezzling money from a bank and falsifying the related records, although legally distinct offenses, represent essentially the same type of wrongful conduct with the same ultimate harm, so that it would be more appropriate to treat them as a single offense for purposes of sentencing. Other offenses, such as an assault causing bodily injury to a teller during a bank robbery, are so closely related to the more serious offense that it would be appropriate to treat them as part of the more serious offense, leaving the sentence enhancement to result from application of a specific offense characteristic.

In order to limit the significance of the formal charging decision and to prevent multiple punishment for substantially identical offense conduct, this Part provides rules for grouping offenses together. Convictions on multiple counts do not result in a sentence enhancement unless they represent additional conduct that is not otherwise accounted for by the guidelines. In essence, counts that are grouped together are treated as constituting a single offense for purposes of the guidelines.

Some offense guidelines, such as those for theft, fraud and drug offenses, contain provisions that deal with repetitive or ongoing behavior. Other guidelines, such as those for assault and robbery, are oriented more toward single episodes of criminal behavior. Accordingly, different rules are required for dealing with multiple-count convictions involving these two different general classes of offenses. More complex cases involving different types of offenses may require application of one rule to some of the counts and another rule to other counts.

Some offenses, *e.g.*, racketeering and conspiracy, may be "composite" in that they involve a pattern of conduct or scheme involving multiple underlying offenses. The rules in this Part are to be used to determine the offense level for such composite offenses from the offense level for the underlying offenses.

Essentially, the rules in this Part can be summarized as follows: (1) If the offense guidelines in Chapter Two base the offense level primarily on the amount of money or quantity of substance involved (*e.g.*, theft, fraud, drug trafficking, firearms dealing), or otherwise contain provisions dealing with repetitive or ongoing misconduct (*e.g.*, many environmental offenses), add the numerical quantities and apply the pertinent offense guideline, including any specific offense characteristics for the conduct taken as a whole. (2) When offenses are closely interrelated, group them together for purposes of the multiple-count rules, and use only the offense level for the most serious offense in that group. (3) As to other offenses (*e.g.*, independent instances of assault or robbery), start with the offense level for the most serious count and use the number and severity of additional counts to determine the amount by which to increase that offense level.

Historical Note	Effective November 1, 1987. Amended effective November 1, 1989 (amendment 121); November 1, 2007 (amendment 707).

§3D1.1. Procedure for Determining Offense Level on Multiple Counts

(a) When a defendant has been convicted of more than one count, the court shall:

(1) Group the counts resulting in conviction into distinct Groups of Closely Related Counts ("Groups") by applying the rules specified in §3D1.2.

(2) Determine the offense level applicable to each Group by applying the rules specified in §3D1.3.

(3) Determine the combined offense level applicable to all Groups taken together by applying the rules specified in §3D1.4.

(b) Exclude from the application of §§3D1.2–3D1.5 the following:

(1) Any count for which the statute (A) specifies a term of imprisonment to be imposed; and (B) requires that such term of imprisonment be imposed to run consecutively to any other term of imprisonment. Sentences for such counts are governed by the provisions of §5G1.2(a).

(2) Any count of conviction under 18 U.S.C. § 1028A. *See* Application Note 2(B) of the Commentary to §5G1.2 (Sentencing on Multiple Counts of Conviction) for guidance on how sentences for multiple counts of conviction under 18 U.S.C. § 1028A should be imposed.

Commentary

Application Notes:

1. **In General.**—For purposes of sentencing multiple counts of conviction, counts can be (A) contained in the same indictment or information; or (B) contained in different indictments or informations for which sentences are to be imposed at the same time or in a consolidated proceeding.

2. Subsection (b)(1) applies if a statute (A) specifies a term of imprisonment to be imposed; and (B) requires that such term of imprisonment be imposed to run consecutively to any other term of imprisonment. *See, e.g.*, 18 U.S.C. § 924(c) (requiring mandatory minimum terms of imprisonment, based on the conduct involved, to run consecutively). The multiple count rules set out under this Part do not apply to a count of conviction covered by subsection (b). However, a count covered by subsection (b)(1) may affect the offense level determination for other counts. For example, a defendant is convicted of one count of bank robbery (18 U.S.C. § 2113), and one count of use of a firearm in the commission of a crime of violence (18 U.S.C. § 924(c)). The two counts are not grouped together pursuant to this guideline, and, to avoid unwarranted double counting, the offense level for the bank robbery count under §2B3.1 (Robbery) is computed without application of the enhancement for weapon possession or use as otherwise required by subsection (b)(2) of that guideline. Pursuant to 18 U.S.C. § 924(c), the mandatory minimum five-year sentence on the weapon-use count runs consecutively to the guideline sentence imposed on the bank robbery count. *See* §5G1.2(a).

Unless specifically instructed, subsection (b)(1) does not apply when imposing a sentence under a statute that requires the imposition of a consecutive term of imprisonment only if a term of imprisonment is imposed (*i.e.*, the statute does not otherwise require a term of imprisonment to be imposed). *See, e.g.*, 18 U.S.C. § 3146 (Penalty for failure to appear); 18 U.S.C. § 924(a)(4) (regarding penalty for 18 U.S.C. § 922(q) (possession or discharge of a firearm in a school zone)); 18 U.S.C. § 1791(c) (penalty for providing or possessing a controlled substance in prison). Accordingly, the multiple count rules set out under this Part do apply to a count of conviction under this type of statute.

Background: This section outlines the procedure to be used for determining the combined offense level. After any adjustments from Chapter 3, Part E (Acceptance of Responsibility) and Chapter 4, Part B (Career Offenders and Criminal Livelihood) are made, this combined offense level is used to determine the guideline sentence range. Chapter Five (Determining the Sentence) discusses how to determine the sentence from the (combined) offense level; §5G1.2 deals specifically with determining the sentence of imprisonment when convictions on multiple counts are involved. References in Chapter Five (Determining the Sentence) to the "offense level" should be treated as referring to the combined offense level after all subsequent adjustments have been made.

| *Historical Note* | Effective November 1, 1987. Amended effective November 1, 1990 (amendment 348); November 1, 1998 (amendment 579); November 1, 2000 (amendment 598); November 1, 2005 (amendments 677 and 680); November 1, 2007 (amendment 707). |

§3D1.2. Groups of Closely Related Counts

All counts involving substantially the same harm shall be grouped together into a single Group. Counts involve substantially the same harm within the meaning of this rule:

(a) When counts involve the same victim and the same act or transaction.

(b) When counts involve the same victim and two or more acts or transactions connected by a common criminal objective or constituting part of a common scheme or plan.

(c) When one of the counts embodies conduct that is treated as a specific offense characteristic in, or other adjustment to, the guideline applicable to another of the counts.

(d) When the offense level is determined largely on the basis of the total amount of harm or loss, the quantity of a substance involved, or some other measure of aggregate harm, or if the offense behavior is ongoing or continuous in nature and the offense guideline is written to cover such behavior.

Offenses covered by the following guidelines are to be grouped under this subsection:

§2A3.5;
§§2B1.1, 2B1.4, 2B1.5, 2B4.1, 2B5.1, 2B5.3, 2B6.1;
§§2C1.1, 2C1.2, 2C1.8;
§§2D1.1, 2D1.2, 2D1.5, 2D1.11, 2D1.13;
§§2E4.1, 2E5.1;
§§2G2.2, 2G3.1;
§2K2.1;
§§2L1.1, 2L2.1;
§2N3.1;
§2Q2.1;
§2R1.1;
§§2S1.1, 2S1.3;
§§2T1.1, 2T1.4, 2T1.6, 2T1.7, 2T1.9, 2T2.1, 2T3.1.

Specifically excluded from the operation of this subsection are:

all offenses in Chapter Two, Part A (except §2A3.5);
§§2B2.1, 2B2.3, 2B3.1, 2B3.2, 2B3.3;
§2C1.5;
§§2D2.1, 2D2.2, 2D2.3;
§§2E1.3, 2E1.4, 2E2.1;
§§2G1.1, 2G2.1;
§§2H1.1, 2H2.1, 2H4.1;
§§2L2.2, 2L2.5;
§§2M2.1, 2M2.3, 2M3.1, 2M3.2, 2M3.3, 2M3.4, 2M3.5, 2M3.9;
§§2P1.1, 2P1.2, 2P1.3;
§2X6.1.

§3D1.2

For multiple counts of offenses that are not listed, grouping under this subsection may or may not be appropriate; a case-by-case determination must be made based upon the facts of the case and the applicable guidelines (including specific offense characteristics and other adjustments) used to determine the offense level.

Exclusion of an offense from grouping under this subsection does not necessarily preclude grouping under another subsection.

Commentary

Application Notes:

1. Subsections (a)–(d) set forth circumstances in which counts are to be grouped together into a single Group. Counts are to be grouped together into a single Group if any one or more of the subsections provide for such grouping. Counts for which the statute (A) specifies a term of imprisonment to be imposed; and (B) requires that such term of imprisonment be imposed to run consecutively to any other term of imprisonment are excepted from application of the multiple count rules. *See* §3D1.1(b)(1); *id.*, comment. (n.1).

2. The term "*victim*" is not intended to include indirect or secondary victims. Generally, there will be one person who is directly and most seriously affected by the offense and is therefore identifiable as the victim. For offenses in which there are no identifiable victims (*e.g.*, drug or immigration offenses, where society at large is the victim), the "victim" for purposes of subsections (a) and (b) is the societal interest that is harmed. In such cases, the counts are grouped together when the societal interests that are harmed are closely related. Where one count, for example, involves unlawfully entering the United States and the other involves possession of fraudulent evidence of citizenship, the counts are grouped together because the societal interests harmed (the interests protected by laws governing immigration) are closely related. In contrast, where one count involves the sale of controlled substances and the other involves an immigration law violation, the counts are not grouped together because different societal interests are harmed. Ambiguities should be resolved in accordance with the purpose of this section as stated in the lead paragraph, *i.e.*, to identify and group "counts involving substantially the same harm."

3. Under subsection (a), counts are to be grouped together when they represent essentially a single injury or are part of a single criminal episode or transaction involving the same victim.

    When one count charges an attempt to commit an offense and the other charges the commission of that offense, or when one count charges an offense based on a general prohibition and the other charges violation of a specific prohibition encompassed in the general prohibition, the counts will be grouped together under subsection (a).

    Examples: (1) The defendant is convicted of forging and uttering the same check. The counts are to be grouped together. (2) The defendant is convicted of kidnapping and assaulting the victim during the course of the kidnapping. The counts are to be grouped together. (3) The defendant is convicted of bid rigging (an antitrust offense) and of mail fraud for signing and mailing a false statement that the bid was competitive. The counts are to be grouped together. (4) The defendant is convicted of two counts of assault on a federal officer for shooting at the same officer twice while attempting to prevent apprehension as part of a single criminal episode. The counts are to be grouped together. (5) The defendant is convicted of three counts of unlawfully bringing aliens into the United States, all counts arising out of a single incident. The three counts are to be grouped together. *But*: (6) The defendant is convicted of two counts of assault on a federal officer for shooting at the officer on two separate days. The counts *are not* to be grouped together.

4.   Subsection (b) provides that counts that are part of a single course of conduct with a single criminal objective and represent essentially one composite harm to the same victim are to be grouped together, even if they constitute legally distinct offenses occurring at different times. This provision does not authorize the grouping of offenses that cannot be considered to represent essentially one composite harm (*e.g.*, robbery of the same victim on different occasions involves multiple, separate instances of fear and risk of harm, not one composite harm).

When one count charges a conspiracy or solicitation and the other charges a substantive offense that was the sole object of the conspiracy or solicitation, the counts will be grouped together under subsection (b).

Examples: (1) The defendant is convicted of one count of conspiracy to commit extortion and one count of extortion for the offense he conspired to commit. The counts are to be grouped together. (2) The defendant is convicted of two counts of mail fraud and one count of wire fraud, each in furtherance of a single fraudulent scheme. The counts are to be grouped together, even if the mailings and telephone call occurred on different days. (3) The defendant is convicted of one count of auto theft and one count of altering the vehicle identification number of the car he stole. The counts are to be grouped together. (4) The defendant is convicted of two counts of distributing a controlled substance, each count involving a separate sale of 10 grams of cocaine that is part of a common scheme or plan. In addition, a finding is made that there are two other sales, also part of the common scheme or plan, each involving 10 grams of cocaine. The total amount of all four sales (40 grams of cocaine) will be used to determine the offense level for each count under §1B1.3(a)(2). The two counts will then be grouped together under either this subsection or subsection (d) to avoid double counting. *But*: (5) The defendant is convicted of two counts of rape for raping the same person on different days. The counts *are not* to be grouped together.

5.   Subsection (c) provides that when conduct that represents a separate count, *e.g.*, bodily injury or obstruction of justice, is also a specific offense characteristic in or other adjustment to another count, the count represented by that conduct is to be grouped with the count to which it constitutes an aggravating factor. This provision prevents "double counting" of offense behavior. Of course, this rule applies only if the offenses are closely related. It is not, for example, the intent of this rule that (assuming they could be joined together) a bank robbery on one occasion and an assault resulting in bodily injury on another occasion be grouped together. The bodily injury (the harm from the assault) would not be a specific offense characteristic to the robbery and would represent a different harm. On the other hand, use of a firearm in a bank robbery and unlawful possession of that firearm are sufficiently related to warrant grouping of counts under this subsection. Frequently, this provision will overlap subsection (a), at least with respect to specific offense characteristics. However, a count such as obstruction of justice, which represents a Chapter Three adjustment and involves a different harm or societal interest than the underlying offense, is covered by subsection (c) even though it is not covered by subsection (a).

Sometimes there may be several counts, each of which could be treated as an aggravating factor to another more serious count, but the guideline for the more serious count provides an adjustment for only one occurrence of that factor. In such cases, only the count representing the most serious of those factors is to be grouped with the other count. For example, if in a robbery of a credit union on a military base the defendant is also convicted of assaulting two employees, one of whom is injured seriously, the assault with serious bodily injury would be grouped with the robbery count, while the remaining assault conviction would be treated separately.

A cross reference to another offense guideline does not constitute "a specific offense characteristic . . . or other adjustment" within the meaning of subsection (c). For example, the guideline for bribery of a public official contains a cross reference to the guideline for a conspiracy to commit the offense that the bribe was to facilitate. Nonetheless, if the defendant were convicted of one count of securities fraud and one count of bribing a public official to facilitate the fraud, the two counts would not be grouped together by virtue of the cross reference. If, however, the bribe was given for the purpose of hampering a criminal investigation into the offense, it would constitute obstruction and under §3C1.1 would result in a 2-level enhancement to the offense level for the fraud. Under the latter circumstances, the counts would be grouped together.

6. Subsection (d) likely will be used with the greatest frequency. It provides that most property crimes (except robbery, burglary, extortion and the like), drug offenses, firearms offenses, and other crimes where the guidelines are based primarily on quantity or contemplate continuing behavior are to be grouped together. The list of instances in which this subsection should be applied is not exhaustive. Note, however, that certain guidelines are specifically excluded from the operation of subsection (d).

A conspiracy, attempt, or solicitation to commit an offense is covered under subsection (d) if the offense that is the object of the conspiracy, attempt, or solicitation is covered under subsection (d).

Counts involving offenses to which different offense guidelines apply are grouped together under subsection (d) if the offenses are of the same general type and otherwise meet the criteria for grouping under this subsection. In such cases, the offense guideline that results in the highest offense level is used; *see* §3D1.3(b). The "same general type" of offense is to be construed broadly.

Examples: (1) The defendant is convicted of five counts of embezzling money from a bank. The five counts are to be grouped together. (2) The defendant is convicted of two counts of theft of social security checks and three counts of theft from the mail, each from a different victim. All five counts are to be grouped together. (3) The defendant is convicted of five counts of mail fraud and ten counts of wire fraud. Although the counts arise from various schemes, each involves a monetary objective. All fifteen counts are to be grouped together. (4) The defendant is convicted of three counts of unlicensed dealing in firearms. All three counts are to be grouped together. (5) The defendant is convicted of one count of selling heroin, one count of selling PCP, and one count of selling cocaine. The counts are to be grouped together. The Commentary to §2D1.1 provides rules for combining (adding) quantities of different drugs to determine a single combined offense level. (6) The defendant is convicted of three counts of tax evasion. The counts are to be grouped together. (7) The defendant is convicted of three counts of discharging toxic substances from a single facility. The counts are to be grouped together. (8) The defendant is convicted on two counts of check forgery and one count of uttering the first of the forged checks. All three counts are to be grouped together. Note, however, that the uttering count is first grouped with the first forgery count under subsection (a) of this guideline, so that the monetary amount of that check counts only once when the rule in §3D1.3(b) is applied. *But*: (9) The defendant is convicted of three counts of bank robbery. The counts *are not* to be grouped together, nor are the amounts of money involved to be added.

7. A single case may result in application of several of the rules in this section. Thus, for example, example (8) in the discussion of subsection (d) involves an application of §3D1.2(a) followed by an application of §3D1.2(d). Note also that a Group may consist of a single count; conversely, all counts may form a single Group.

8. A defendant may be convicted of conspiring to commit several substantive offenses and also of committing one or more of the substantive offenses. In such cases, treat the conspiracy count as if it were several counts, each charging conspiracy to commit one of the substantive offenses. *See* §1B1.2(d) and accompanying commentary. Then apply the ordinary grouping rules to determine the combined offense level based upon the substantive counts of which the defendant is convicted and the various acts cited by the conspiracy count that would constitute behavior of a substantive nature. **Example:** The defendant is convicted of two counts: conspiring to commit offenses A, B, and C, and committing offense A. Treat this as if the defendant was convicted of (1) committing offense A; (2) conspiracy to commit offense A; (3) conspiracy to commit offense B; and (4) conspiracy to commit offense C. Count (1) and count (2) are grouped together under §3D1.2(b). Group the remaining counts, including the various acts cited by the conspiracy count that would constitute behavior of a substantive nature, according to the rules in this section.

Background: Ordinarily, the first step in determining the combined offense level in a case involving multiple counts is to identify those counts that are sufficiently related to be placed in the same Group of Closely Related Counts ("Group"). This section specifies four situations in which counts are to be grouped together. Although it appears last for conceptual reasons, subsection (d) probably will be used most frequently.

A primary consideration in this section is whether the offenses involve different victims. For example, a defendant may stab three prison guards in a single escape attempt. Some would argue that all counts arising out of a single transaction or occurrence should be grouped together even when there are distinct victims. Although such a proposal was considered, it was rejected because it probably would require departure in many cases in order to capture adequately the criminal behavior. Cases involving injury to distinct victims are sufficiently comparable, whether or not the injuries are inflicted in distinct transactions, so that each such count should be treated separately rather than grouped together. Counts involving different victims (or societal harms in the case of "victimless" crimes) are grouped together only as provided in subsection (c) or (d).

Even if counts involve a single victim, the decision as to whether to group them together may not always be clear cut. For example, how contemporaneous must two assaults on the same victim be in order to warrant grouping together as constituting a single transaction or occurrence? Existing case law may provide some guidance as to what constitutes distinct offenses, but such decisions often turn on the technical language of the statute and cannot be controlling. In interpreting this Part and resolving ambiguities, the court should look to the underlying policy of this Part as stated in the Introductory Commentary.

| *Historical Note* | Effective November 1, 1987. Amended effective June 15, 1988 (amendment 45); November 1, 1989 (amendments 121, 253–256, and 303); November 1, 1990 (amendments 309, 348, and 349); November 1, 1991 (amendment 417); November 1, 1992 (amendment 458); November 1, 1993 (amendment 496); November 1, 1995 (amendment 534); November 1, 1996 (amendment 538); November 1, 1998 (amendment 579); November 1, 2001 (amendments 615, 617, and 634); November 1, 2002 (amendment 638); January 25, 2003 (amendment 648); November 1, 2003 (amendment 656); November 1, 2004 (amendment 664); November 1, 2005 (amendments 679 and 680); November 1, 2007 (amendment 701). |

§3D1.3. Offense Level Applicable to Each Group of Closely Related Counts

Determine the offense level applicable to each of the Groups as follows:

(a) In the case of counts grouped together pursuant to §3D1.2(a)–(c), the offense level applicable to a Group is the offense level, determined in accordance with Chapter Two and Parts A, B, and C of Chapter Three, for the most serious of the counts comprising the Group, *i.e.*, the highest offense level of the counts in the Group.

(b) In the case of counts grouped together pursuant to §3D1.2(d), the offense level applicable to a Group is the offense level corresponding to the aggregated quantity, determined in accordance with Chapter Two and Parts A, B and C of Chapter Three. When the counts involve offenses of the same general type to which different guidelines apply, apply the offense guideline that produces the highest offense level.

Commentary

Application Notes:

1. The "*offense level*" for a count refers to the offense level from Chapter Two after all adjustments from Parts A, B, and C of Chapter Three.

2. When counts are grouped pursuant to §3D1.2(a)–(c), the highest offense level of the counts in the group is used. Ordinarily, it is necessary to determine the offense level for each of the counts in a Group in order to ensure that the highest is correctly identified. Sometimes, it will be clear that one count in the Group cannot have a higher offense level than another, as with a count for an attempt or conspiracy to commit the completed offense. The formal determination of the offense level for such a count may be unnecessary.

3. When counts are grouped pursuant to §3D1.2(d), the offense guideline applicable to the aggregate behavior is used. If the counts in the Group are covered by different guidelines, use the guideline that produces the highest offense level. Determine whether the specific offense characteristics or adjustments from Chapter Three, Parts A, B, and C apply based upon the combined offense behavior taken as a whole. Note that guidelines for similar property offenses have been coordinated to produce identical offense levels, at least when substantial property losses are involved. However, when small sums are involved the differing specific offense characteristics that require increasing the offense level to a certain minimum may affect the outcome.

4. Sometimes the rule specified in this section may not result in incremental punishment for additional criminal acts because of the grouping rules. For example, if the defendant commits forcible criminal sexual abuse (rape), aggravated assault, and robbery, all against the same victim on a single occasion, all of the counts are grouped together under §3D1.2. The aggravated assault will increase the guideline range for the rape. The robbery, however, will not. This is because the offense guideline for rape (§2A3.1) includes the most common aggravating factors, including injury, that data showed to be significant in actual practice. The additional factor of property loss ordinarily can be taken into account adequately within the guideline range for rape, which is fairly wide. However,

an exceptionally large property loss in the course of the rape would provide grounds for an upward departure. *See* §5K2.5 (Property Damage or Loss).

Background: This section provides rules for determining the offense level associated with each Group of Closely Related Counts. Summary examples of the application of these rules are provided at the end of the Commentary to this Part.

Historical Note	Effective November 1, 1987. Amended effective November 1, 1989 (amendments 257 and 303); November 1, 2001 (amendment 617); November 1, 2004 (amendment 674).

§3D1.4. Determining the Combined Offense Level

The combined offense level is determined by taking the offense level applicable to the Group with the highest offense level and increasing that offense level by the amount indicated in the following table:

NUMBER OF UNITS	INCREASE IN OFFENSE LEVEL
1	none
1 1/2	add **1** level
2	add **2** levels
2 1/2 – 3	add **3** levels
3 1/2 – 5	add **4** levels
More than 5	add **5** levels.

In determining the number of Units for purposes of this section:

(a)   Count as one Unit the Group with the highest offense level. Count one additional Unit for each Group that is equally serious or from **1** to **4** levels less serious.

(b)   Count as one-half Unit any Group that is **5** to **8** levels less serious than the Group with the highest offense level.

(c)   Disregard any Group that is **9** or more levels less serious than the Group with the highest offense level. Such Groups will not increase the applicable offense level but may provide a reason for sentencing at the higher end of the sentencing range for the applicable offense level.

Commentary

Application Notes:

1.   Application of the rules in §§3D1.2 and 3D1.3 may produce a single Group of Closely Related Counts. In such cases, the combined offense level is the level corresponding to the Group determined in accordance with §3D1.3.

2. The procedure for calculating the combined offense level when there is more than one Group of Closely Related Counts is as follows: First, identify the offense level applicable to the most serious Group; assign it one Unit. Next, determine the number of Units that the remaining Groups represent. Finally, increase the offense level for the most serious Group by the number of levels indicated in the table corresponding to the total number of Units.

Background: When Groups are of roughly comparable seriousness, each Group will represent one Unit. When the most serious Group carries an offense level substantially higher than that applicable to the other Groups, however, counting the lesser Groups fully for purposes of the table could add excessive punishment, possibly even more than those offenses would carry if prosecuted separately. To avoid this anomalous result and produce declining marginal punishment, Groups 9 or more levels less serious than the most serious Group should not be counted for purposes of the table, and that Groups 5 to 8 levels less serious should be treated as equal to one-half of a Group. Thus, if the most serious Group is at offense level 15 and if two other Groups are at level 10, there would be a total of two Units for purposes of the table (one plus one-half plus one-half) and the combined offense level would be 17. Inasmuch as the maximum increase provided in the guideline is 5 levels, departure would be warranted in the unusual case where the additional offenses resulted in a total of significantly more than 5 Units.

In unusual circumstances, the approach adopted in this section could produce adjustments for the additional counts that are inadequate or excessive. If there are several groups and the most serious offense is considerably more serious than all of the others, there will be no increase in the offense level resulting from the additional counts. Ordinarily, the court will have latitude to impose added punishment by sentencing toward the upper end of the range authorized for the most serious offense. Situations in which there will be inadequate scope for ensuring appropriate additional punishment for the additional crimes are likely to be unusual and can be handled by departure from the guidelines. Conversely, it is possible that if there are several minor offenses that are not grouped together, application of the rules in this Part could result in an excessive increase in the sentence range. Again, such situations should be infrequent and can be handled through departure. An alternative method for ensuring more precise adjustments would have been to determine the appropriate offense level adjustment through a more complicated mathematical formula; that approach was not adopted because of its complexity.

Historical Note	Effective November 1, 1987. Amended effective November 1, 1990 (amendment 350).

§3D1.5. Determining the Total Punishment

Use the combined offense level to determine the appropriate sentence in accordance with the provisions of Chapter Five.

Commentary

This section refers the court to Chapter Five (Determining the Sentence) in order to determine the total punishment to be imposed based upon the combined offense level. The combined offense level is subject to adjustments from Chapter Three, Part E (Acceptance of Responsibility) and Chapter Four, Part B (Career Offenders and Criminal Livelihood).

| Historical Note | Effective November 1, 1987. |

* * * * *

Concluding Commentary to Part D of Chapter Three

Illustrations of the Operation of the Multiple-Count Rules

The following examples, drawn from presentence reports in the Commission's files, illustrate the operation of the guidelines for multiple counts. The examples are discussed summarily; a more thorough, step-by-step approach is recommended until the user is thoroughly familiar with the guidelines.

1. Defendant A was convicted of four counts, each charging robbery of a different bank. Each would represent a distinct Group. §3D1.2. In each of the first three robberies, the offense level was 22 (20 plus a 2-level increase because a financial institution was robbed) (§2B3.1(b)). In the fourth robbery $21,000 was taken and a firearm was displayed; the offense level was therefore 28. As the first three counts are 6 levels lower than the fourth, each of the first three represents one-half unit for purposes of §3D1.4. Altogether there are 2 1/2 Units, and the offense level for the most serious (28) is therefore increased by 3 levels under the table. The combined offense level is 31.

2. Defendant B was convicted of four counts: (1) distribution of 230 grams of cocaine; (2) distribution of 150 grams of cocaine; (3) distribution of 75 grams of heroin; (4) offering a DEA agent $20,000 to avoid prosecution. The combined offense level for drug offenses is determined by the total quantity of drugs, converted to marihuana equivalents (using the Drug Equivalency Tables in the Commentary to §2D1.1 (Unlawful Manufacturing, Importing, Exporting, or Trafficking)). The first count translates into 46 kilograms of marihuana; the second count translates into 30 kilograms of marihuana; and the third count translates into 75 kilograms of marihuana. The total is 151 kilograms of marihuana. Under §2D1.1, the combined offense level for the drug offenses is 24. In addition, because of the attempted bribe of the DEA agent, this offense level is increased by 2 levels to 26 under §3C1.1 (Obstructing or Impeding the Administration of Justice). Because the conduct constituting the bribery offense is accounted for by §3C1.1, it becomes part of the same Group as the drug offenses pursuant to §3D1.2(c). The combined offense level is 26 pursuant to §3D1.3(a), because the offense level for bribery (20) is less than the offense level for the drug offenses (26).

3. Defendant C was convicted of four counts arising out of a scheme pursuant to which the defendant received kickbacks from subcontractors. The counts were as follows: (1) The defendant received $1,000 from subcontractor A relating to contract X (Mail Fraud). (2) The defendant received $1,000 from subcontractor A relating to contract X (Commercial Bribery). (3) The defendant received $1,000 from subcontractor A relating to contract Y (Mail Fraud). (4) The defendant received $1,000 from subcontractor B relating to contract Z (Commercial Bribery). The mail fraud counts are covered by §2B1.1 (Theft, Property Destruction, and Fraud). The bribery counts are covered by §2B4.1 (Bribery in Procurement of Bank Loan and Other Commercial Bribery), which treats the offense as a sophisticated fraud. The total money involved is $4,000, which results in an offense level of 9 under either §2B1.1 (assuming the application of the "sophisticated means" enhancement in §2B1.1(b)(10)) or §2B4.1. Since these two guidelines produce identical offense levels, the combined offense level is 9.

§3D1.5

| *Historical Note* | Effective November 1, 1987. Amended effective November 1, 1989 (amendment 303); November 1, 1990 (amendment 350); November 1, 1991 (amendment 417); November 1, 1995 (amendment 534); November 1, 2001 (amendment 617); November 1, 2009 (amendment 737); November 1, 2011 (amendment 760); November 1, 2014 (amendment 782); November 1, 2015 (amendment 796). |

PART E — ACCEPTANCE OF RESPONSIBILITY

§3E1.1. Acceptance of Responsibility

(a) If the defendant clearly demonstrates acceptance of responsibility for his offense, decrease the offense level by **2** levels.

(b) If the defendant qualifies for a decrease under subsection (a), the offense level determined prior to the operation of subsection (a) is level **16** or greater, and upon motion of the government stating that the defendant has assisted authorities in the investigation or prosecution of his own misconduct by timely notifying authorities of his intention to enter a plea of guilty, thereby permitting the government to avoid preparing for trial and permitting the government and the court to allocate their resources efficiently, decrease the offense level by **1** additional level.

Commentary

Application Notes:

1. In determining whether a defendant qualifies under subsection (a), appropriate considerations include, but are not limited to, the following:

(A) truthfully admitting the conduct comprising the offense(s) of conviction, and truthfully admitting or not falsely denying any additional relevant conduct for which the defendant is accountable under §1B1.3 (Relevant Conduct). Note that a defendant is not required to volunteer, or affirmatively admit, relevant conduct beyond the offense of conviction in order to obtain a reduction under subsection (a). A defendant may remain silent in respect to relevant conduct beyond the offense of conviction without affecting his ability to obtain a reduction under this subsection. However, a defendant who falsely denies, or frivolously contests, relevant conduct that the court determines to be true has acted in a manner inconsistent with acceptance of responsibility;

(B) voluntary termination or withdrawal from criminal conduct or associations;

(C) voluntary payment of restitution prior to adjudication of guilt;

(D) voluntary surrender to authorities promptly after commission of the offense;

(E) voluntary assistance to authorities in the recovery of the fruits and instrumentalities of the offense;

(F) voluntary resignation from the office or position held during the commission of the offense;

(G) post-offense rehabilitative efforts (*e.g.*, counseling or drug treatment); and

(H)   the timeliness of the defendant's conduct in manifesting the acceptance of responsibility.

2.   This adjustment is not intended to apply to a defendant who puts the government to its burden of proof at trial by denying the essential factual elements of guilt, is convicted, and only then admits guilt and expresses remorse. Conviction by trial, however, does not automatically preclude a defendant from consideration for such a reduction. In rare situations a defendant may clearly demonstrate an acceptance of responsibility for his criminal conduct even though he exercises his constitutional right to a trial. This may occur, for example, where a defendant goes to trial to assert and preserve issues that do not relate to factual guilt (*e.g.*, to make a constitutional challenge to a statute or a challenge to the applicability of a statute to his conduct). In each such instance, however, a determination that a defendant has accepted responsibility will be based primarily upon pre-trial statements and conduct.

3.   Entry of a plea of guilty prior to the commencement of trial combined with truthfully admitting the conduct comprising the offense of conviction, and truthfully admitting or not falsely denying any additional relevant conduct for which he is accountable under §1B1.3 (Relevant Conduct) (*see* Application Note 1(A)), will constitute significant evidence of acceptance of responsibility for the purposes of subsection (a). However, this evidence may be outweighed by conduct of the defendant that is inconsistent with such acceptance of responsibility. A defendant who enters a guilty plea is not entitled to an adjustment under this section as a matter of right.

4.   Conduct resulting in an enhancement under §3C1.1 (Obstructing or Impeding the Administration of Justice) ordinarily indicates that the defendant has not accepted responsibility for his criminal conduct. There may, however, be extraordinary cases in which adjustments under both §§3C1.1 and 3E1.1 may apply.

5.   The sentencing judge is in a unique position to evaluate a defendant's acceptance of responsibility. For this reason, the determination of the sentencing judge is entitled to great deference on review.

6.   Subsection (a) provides a 2-level decrease in offense level. Subsection (b) provides an additional 1-level decrease in offense level for a defendant at offense level 16 or greater prior to the operation of subsection (a) who both qualifies for a decrease under subsection (a) and who has assisted authorities in the investigation or prosecution of his own misconduct by taking the steps set forth in subsection (b). The timeliness of the defendant's acceptance of responsibility is a consideration under both subsections, and is context specific. In general, the conduct qualifying for a decrease in offense level under subsection (b) will occur particularly early in the case. For example, to qualify under subsection (b), the defendant must have notified authorities of his intention to enter a plea of guilty at a sufficiently early point in the process so that the government may avoid preparing for trial and the court may schedule its calendar efficiently.

Because the Government is in the best position to determine whether the defendant has assisted authorities in a manner that avoids preparing for trial, an adjustment under subsection (b) may only be granted upon a formal motion by the Government at the time of sentencing. *See* section 401(g)(2)(B) of Public Law 108–21. The government should not withhold such a motion based on interests not identified in §3E1.1, such as whether the defendant agrees to waive his or her right to appeal.

If the government files such a motion, and the court in deciding whether to grant the motion also determines that the defendant has assisted authorities in the investigation or prosecution of his own misconduct by timely notifying authorities of his intention to enter a plea of guilty, thereby permitting the government to avoid preparing for trial and permitting the government and the court to allocate their resources efficiently, the court should grant the motion.

Background: The reduction of offense level provided by this section recognizes legitimate societal interests. For several reasons, a defendant who clearly demonstrates acceptance of responsibility for his offense by taking, in a timely fashion, the actions listed above (or some equivalent action) is appropriately given a lower offense level than a defendant who has not demonstrated acceptance of responsibility.

Subsection (a) provides a 2-level decrease in offense level. Subsection (b) provides an additional 1-level decrease for a defendant at offense level 16 or greater prior to operation of subsection (a) who both qualifies for a decrease under subsection (a) and has assisted authorities in the investigation or prosecution of his own misconduct by taking the steps specified in subsection (b). Such a defendant has accepted responsibility in a way that ensures the certainty of his just punishment in a timely manner, thereby appropriately meriting an additional reduction. Subsection (b) does not apply, however, to a defendant whose offense level is level 15 or lower prior to application of subsection (a). At offense level 15 or lower, the reduction in the guideline range provided by a 2-level decrease in offense level under subsection (a) (which is a greater proportional reduction in the guideline range than at higher offense levels due to the structure of the Sentencing Table) is adequate for the court to take into account the factors set forth in subsection (b) within the applicable guideline range.

Section 401(g) of Public Law 108–21 directly amended subsection (b), Application Note 6 (including adding the first sentence of the second paragraph of that application note), and the Background Commentary, effective April 30, 2003.

Historical Note	Effective November 1, 1987. Amended effective January 15, 1988 (amendment 46); November 1, 1989 (amendment 258); November 1, 1990 (amendment 351); November 1, 1992 (amendment 459); April 30, 2003 (amendment 649); November 1, 2010 (amendments 746 and 747); November 1, 2013 (amendment 775).

CHAPTER FOUR

CRIMINAL HISTORY
AND CRIMINAL LIVELIHOOD

PART A — CRIMINAL HISTORY

Introductory Commentary

The Comprehensive Crime Control Act sets forth four purposes of sentencing. (*See* 18 U.S.C. § 3553(a)(2).) A defendant's record of past criminal conduct is directly relevant to those purposes. A defendant with a record of prior criminal behavior is more culpable than a first offender and thus deserving of greater punishment. General deterrence of criminal conduct dictates that a clear message be sent to society that repeated criminal behavior will aggravate the need for punishment with each recurrence. To protect the public from further crimes of the particular defendant, the likelihood of recidivism and future criminal behavior must be considered. Repeated criminal behavior is an indicator of a limited likelihood of successful rehabilitation.

The specific factors included in §4A1.1 and §4A1.3 are consistent with the extant empirical research assessing correlates of recidivism and patterns of career criminal behavior. While empirical research has shown that other factors are correlated highly with the likelihood of recidivism, *e.g.*, age and drug abuse, for policy reasons they were not included here at this time. The Commission has made no definitive judgment as to the reliability of the existing data. However, the Commission will review additional data insofar as they become available in the future.

Historical Note	Effective November 1, 1987.

§4A1.1. Criminal History Category

The total points from subsections (a) through (e) determine the criminal history category in the Sentencing Table in Chapter Five, Part A.

(a)   Add **3** points for each prior sentence of imprisonment exceeding one year and one month.

(b)   Add **2** points for each prior sentence of imprisonment of at least sixty days not counted in (a).

(c)   Add **1** point for each prior sentence not counted in (a) or (b), up to a total of **4** points for this subsection.

(d)   Add **2** points if the defendant committed the instant offense while under any criminal justice sentence, including probation, parole, supervised release, imprisonment, work release, or escape status.

(e)   Add **1** point for each prior sentence resulting from a conviction of a crime of violence that did not receive any points under (a), (b), or (c) above because such sentence was treated as a single sentence, up to a total of **3** points for this subsection.

Commentary

The total criminal history points from §4A1.1 determine the criminal history category (I–VI) in the Sentencing Table in Chapter Five, Part A. The definitions and instructions in §4A1.2 govern the computation of the criminal history points. Therefore, §§4A1.1 and 4A1.2 must be read together. The following notes highlight the interaction of §§4A1.1 and 4A1.2.

Application Notes:

1.   **§4A1.1(a).** Three points are added for each prior sentence of imprisonment exceeding one year and one month. There is no limit to the number of points that may be counted under this subsection. The term "***prior sentence***" is defined at §4A1.2(a). The term "***sentence of imprisonment***" is defined at §4A1.2(b). Where a prior sentence of imprisonment resulted from a revocation of probation, parole, or a similar form of release, *see* §4A1.2(k).

Certain prior sentences are not counted or are counted only under certain conditions:

A sentence imposed more than fifteen years prior to the defendant's commencement of the instant offense is not counted unless the defendant's incarceration extended into this fifteen-year period. *See* §4A1.2(e).

A sentence imposed for an offense committed prior to the defendant's eighteenth birthday is counted under this subsection only if it resulted from an adult conviction. *See* §4A1.2(d).

A sentence for a foreign conviction, a conviction that has been expunged, or an invalid conviction is not counted. *See* §4A1.2(h) and (j) and the Commentary to §4A1.2.

2.   **§4A1.1(b).** Two points are added for each prior sentence of imprisonment of at least sixty days not counted in §4A1.1(a). There is no limit to the number of points that may be counted under this subsection. The term "***prior sentence***" is defined at §4A1.2(a). The term "***sentence of imprisonment***" is defined at §4A1.2(b). Where a prior sentence of imprisonment resulted from a revocation of probation, parole, or a similar form of release, *see* §4A1.2(k).

Certain prior sentences are not counted or are counted only under certain conditions:

A sentence imposed more than ten years prior to the defendant's commencement of the instant offense is not counted. *See* §4A1.2(e).

An adult or juvenile sentence imposed for an offense committed prior to the defendant's eighteenth birthday is counted only if confinement resulting from such sentence extended into the five-year period preceding the defendant's commencement of the instant offense. *See* §4A1.2(d).

Sentences for certain specified non-felony offenses are never counted. *See* §4A1.2(c)(2).

A sentence for a foreign conviction or a tribal court conviction, an expunged conviction, or an invalid conviction is not counted. *See* §4A1.2(h), (i), (j), and the Commentary to §4A1.2.

A military sentence is counted only if imposed by a general or special court-martial. *See* §4A1.2(g).

3.   **§4A1.1(c).** One point is added for each prior sentence not counted under §4A1.1(a) or (b). A maximum of four points may be counted under this subsection. The term "***prior sentence***" is defined at §4A1.2(a).

Certain prior sentences are not counted or are counted only under certain conditions:

A sentence imposed more than ten years prior to the defendant's commencement of the instant offense is not counted. *See* §4A1.2(e).

An adult or juvenile sentence imposed for an offense committed prior to the defendant's eighteenth birthday is counted only if imposed within five years of the defendant's commencement of the current offense. *See* §4A1.2(d).

Sentences for certain specified non-felony offenses are counted only if they meet certain requirements. *See* §4A1.2(c)(1).

Sentences for certain specified non-felony offenses are never counted. *See* §4A1.2(c)(2).

A diversionary disposition is counted only where there is a finding or admission of guilt in a judicial proceeding. *See* §4A1.2(f).

A sentence for a foreign conviction, a tribal court conviction, an expunged conviction, or an invalid conviction, is not counted. *See* §4A1.2(h), (i), (j), and the Commentary to §4A1.2.

A military sentence is counted only if imposed by a general or special court-martial. *See* §4A1.2(g).

4.   **§4A1.1(d).** Two points are added if the defendant committed any part of the instant offense (*i.e.*, any relevant conduct) while under any criminal justice sentence, including probation, parole, supervised release, imprisonment, work release, or escape status. Failure to report for service of a sentence of imprisonment is to be treated as an escape from such sentence. *See* §4A1.2(n). For the purposes of this subsection, a "***criminal justice sentence***" means a sentence countable under §4A1.2 (Definitions and Instructions for Computing Criminal History) having a custodial or supervisory component, although active supervision is not required for this subsection to apply. For example, a term of unsupervised probation would be included; but a sentence to pay a fine, by itself, would not be included. A defendant who commits the instant offense while a violation warrant from

a prior sentence is outstanding (*e.g.*, a probation, parole, or supervised release violation warrant) shall be deemed to be under a criminal justice sentence for the purposes of this provision if that sentence is otherwise countable, even if that sentence would have expired absent such warrant. *See* §4A1.2(m).

5.　**§4A1.1(e).** In a case in which the defendant received two or more prior sentences as a result of convictions for crimes of violence that are treated as a single sentence (*see* §4A1.2(a)(2)), one point is added under §4A1.1(e) for each such sentence that did not result in any additional points under §4A1.1(a), (b), or (c). A total of up to 3 points may be added under §4A1.1(e). For purposes of this guideline, "***crime of violence***" has the meaning given that term in §4B1.2(a). *See* §4A1.2(p).

For example, a defendant's criminal history includes two robbery convictions for offenses committed on different occasions. The sentences for these offenses were imposed on the same day and are treated as a single prior sentence. *See* §4A1.2(a)(2). If the defendant received a five-year sentence of imprisonment for one robbery and a four-year sentence of imprisonment for the other robbery (consecutively or concurrently), a total of 3 points is added under §4A1.1(a). An additional point is added under §4A1.1(e) because the second sentence did not result in any additional point(s) (under §4A1.1(a), (b), or (c)). In contrast, if the defendant received a one-year sentence of imprisonment for one robbery and a nine-month consecutive sentence of imprisonment for the other robbery, a total of 3 points also is added under §4A1.1(a) (a one-year sentence of imprisonment and a consecutive nine-month sentence of imprisonment are treated as a combined one-year-nine-month sentence of imprisonment). But no additional point is added under §4A1.1(e) because the sentence for the second robbery already resulted in an additional point under §4A1.1(a). Without the second sentence, the defendant would only have received two points under §4A1.1(b) for the one-year sentence of imprisonment.

Background: Prior convictions may represent convictions in the federal system, fifty state systems, the District of Columbia, territories, and foreign, tribal, and military courts. There are jurisdictional variations in offense definitions, sentencing structures, and manner of sentence pronouncement. To minimize problems with imperfect measures of past crime seriousness, criminal history categories are based on the maximum term imposed in previous sentences rather than on other measures, such as whether the conviction was designated a felony or misdemeanor. In recognition of the imperfection of this measure however, §4A1.3 authorizes the court to depart from the otherwise applicable criminal history category in certain circumstances.

Subsections (a), (b), and (c) of §4A1.1 distinguish confinement sentences longer than one year and one month, shorter confinement sentences of at least sixty days, and all other sentences, such as confinement sentences of less than sixty days, probation, fines, and residency in a halfway house.

Section 4A1.1(d) adds two points if the defendant was under a criminal justice sentence during any part of the instant offense.

Historical Note	Effective November 1, 1987. Amended effective November 1, 1989 (amendments 259–261); November 1, 1991 (amendments 381 and 382); October 27, 2003 (amendment 651); November 1, 2007 (amendment 709); November 1, 2010 (amendment 742); November 1, 2013 (amendment 777); November 1, 2015 (amendment 795).

§4A1.2. Definitions and Instructions for Computing Criminal History

(a) PRIOR SENTENCE

(1) The term "prior sentence" means any sentence previously imposed upon adjudication of guilt, whether by guilty plea, trial, or plea of *nolo contendere,* for conduct not part of the instant offense.

(2) If the defendant has multiple prior sentences, determine whether those sentences are counted separately or treated as a single sentence. Prior sentences always are counted separately if the sentences were imposed for offenses that were separated by an intervening arrest (*i.e.,* the defendant is arrested for the first offense prior to committing the second offense). If there is no intervening arrest, prior sentences are counted separately unless (A) the sentences resulted from offenses contained in the same charging instrument; or (B) the sentences were imposed on the same day. Treat any prior sentence covered by (A) or (B) as a single sentence. *See also* §4A1.1(e).

For purposes of applying §4A1.1(a), (b), and (c), if prior sentences are treated as a single sentence, use the longest sentence of imprisonment if concurrent sentences were imposed. If consecutive sentences were imposed, use the aggregate sentence of imprisonment.

(3) A conviction for which the imposition or execution of sentence was totally suspended or stayed shall be counted as a prior sentence under §4A1.1(c).

(4) Where a defendant has been convicted of an offense, but not yet sentenced, such conviction shall be counted as if it constituted a prior sentence under §4A1.1(c) if a sentence resulting from that conviction otherwise would be countable. In the case of a conviction for an offense set forth in §4A1.2(c)(1), apply this provision only where the sentence for such offense would be countable regardless of type or length.

"Convicted of an offense," for the purposes of this provision, means that the guilt of the defendant has been established, whether by guilty plea, trial, or plea of *nolo contendere.*

(b) SENTENCE OF IMPRISONMENT DEFINED

(1) The term "sentence of imprisonment" means a sentence of incarceration and refers to the maximum sentence imposed.

(2) If part of a sentence of imprisonment was suspended, "sentence of imprisonment" refers only to the portion that was not suspended.

(c) SENTENCES COUNTED AND EXCLUDED

Sentences for all felony offenses are counted. Sentences for misdemeanor and petty offenses are counted, except as follows:

(1) Sentences for the following prior offenses and offenses similar to them, by whatever name they are known, are counted only if (A) the sentence was a term of probation of more than one year or a term of imprisonment of at least thirty days, or (B) the prior offense was similar to an instant offense:

> Careless or reckless driving
> Contempt of court
> Disorderly conduct or disturbing the peace
> Driving without a license or with a revoked or suspended license
> False information to a police officer
> Gambling
> Hindering or failure to obey a police officer
> Insufficient funds check
> Leaving the scene of an accident
> Non-support
> Prostitution
> Resisting arrest
> Trespassing.

(2) Sentences for the following prior offenses and offenses similar to them, by whatever name they are known, are never counted:

> Fish and game violations
> Hitchhiking
> Juvenile status offenses and truancy
> Local ordinance violations (except those violations that are also violations under state criminal law)
> Loitering
> Minor traffic infractions (*e.g.*, speeding)
> Public intoxication
> Vagrancy.

(d) OFFENSES COMMITTED PRIOR TO AGE EIGHTEEN

(1) If the defendant was convicted as an adult and received a sentence of imprisonment exceeding one year and one month, add **3** points under §4A1.1(a) for each such sentence.

(2) In any other case,

(A) add **2** points under §4A1.1(b) for each adult or juvenile sentence to confinement of at least sixty days if the defendant was released from such confinement within five years of his commencement of the instant offense;

(B) add **1** point under §4A1.1(c) for each adult or juvenile sentence imposed within five years of the defendant's commencement of the instant offense not covered in (A).

(e) APPLICABLE TIME PERIOD

(1) Any prior sentence of imprisonment exceeding one year and one month that was imposed within fifteen years of the defendant's commencement of the instant offense is counted. Also count any prior sentence of imprisonment exceeding one year and one month, whenever imposed, that resulted in the defendant being incarcerated during any part of such fifteen-year period.

(2) Any other prior sentence that was imposed within ten years of the defendant's commencement of the instant offense is counted.

(3) Any prior sentence not within the time periods specified above is not counted.

(4) The applicable time period for certain sentences resulting from offenses committed prior to age eighteen is governed by §4A1.2(d)(2).

(f) DIVERSIONARY DISPOSITIONS

Diversion from the judicial process without a finding of guilt (*e.g.*, deferred prosecution) is not counted. A diversionary disposition resulting from a finding or admission of guilt, or a plea of *nolo contendere*, in a judicial proceeding is counted as a sentence under §4A1.1(c) even if a conviction is not formally entered, except that diversion from juvenile court is not counted.

(g) MILITARY SENTENCES

Sentences resulting from military offenses are counted if imposed by a general or special court-martial. Sentences imposed by a summary court-martial or Article 15 proceeding are not counted.

(h) FOREIGN SENTENCES

Sentences resulting from foreign convictions are not counted, but may be considered under §4A1.3 (Adequacy of Criminal History Category).

(i) TRIBAL COURT SENTENCES

Sentences resulting from tribal court convictions are not counted, but may be considered under §4A1.3 (Adequacy of Criminal History Category).

(j) EXPUNGED CONVICTIONS

Sentences for expunged convictions are not counted, but may be considered under §4A1.3 (Adequacy of Criminal History Category).

(k) REVOCATIONS OF PROBATION, PAROLE, MANDATORY RELEASE, OR SUPERVISED RELEASE

(1) In the case of a prior revocation of probation, parole, supervised release, special parole, or mandatory release, add the original term of imprisonment to any term of imprisonment imposed upon revocation. The resulting total is used to compute the criminal history points for §4A1.1(a), (b), or (c), as applicable.

(2) Revocation of probation, parole, supervised release, special parole, or mandatory release may affect the time period under which certain sentences are counted as provided in §4A1.2(d)(2) and (e). For the purposes of determining the applicable time period, use the following: (A) in the case of an adult term of imprisonment totaling more than one year and one month, the date of last release from incarceration on such sentence (see §4A1.2(e)(1)); (B) in the case of any other confinement sentence for an offense committed prior to the defendant's eighteenth birthday, the date of the defendant's last release from confinement on such sentence (see §4A1.2(d)(2)(A)); and (C) in any other case, the date of the original sentence (see §4A1.2(d)(2)(B) and (e)(2)).

(l) SENTENCES ON APPEAL

Prior sentences under appeal are counted except as expressly provided below. In the case of a prior sentence, the execution of which has been stayed pending appeal, §4A1.1(a), (b), (c), (d), and (e) shall apply as if the execution of such sentence had not been stayed.

(m) EFFECT OF A VIOLATION WARRANT

For the purposes of §4A1.1(d), a defendant who commits the instant offense while a violation warrant from a prior sentence is outstanding (*e.g.*, a probation, parole, or supervised release violation warrant) shall be deemed to be under a criminal justice sentence if that sentence is otherwise countable, even if that sentence would have expired absent such warrant.

(n) FAILURE TO REPORT FOR SERVICE OF SENTENCE OF IMPRISONMENT

For the purposes of §4A1.1(d), failure to report for service of a sentence of imprisonment shall be treated as an escape from such sentence.

(o) FELONY OFFENSE

For the purposes of §4A1.2(c), a "felony offense" means any federal, state, or local offense punishable by death or a term of imprisonment exceeding one year, regardless of the actual sentence imposed.

(p) CRIME OF VIOLENCE DEFINED

For the purposes of §4A1.1(e), the definition of "crime of violence" is that set forth in §4B1.2(a).

Commentary

Application Notes:

1. **Prior Sentence.**—"*Prior sentence*" means a sentence imposed prior to sentencing on the instant offense, other than a sentence for conduct that is part of the instant offense. *See* §4A1.2(a). A sentence imposed after the defendant's commencement of the instant offense, but prior to sentencing on the instant offense, is a prior sentence if it was for conduct other than conduct that was part of the instant offense. Conduct that is part of the instant offense means conduct that is relevant conduct to the instant offense under the provisions of §1B1.3 (Relevant Conduct).

Under §4A1.2(a)(4), a conviction for which the defendant has not yet been sentenced is treated as if it were a prior sentence under §4A1.1(c) if a sentence resulting from such conviction otherwise would have been counted. In the case of an offense set forth in §4A1.2(c)(1) (which lists certain misdemeanor and petty offenses), a conviction for which the defendant has not yet been sentenced is treated as if it were a prior sentence under

§4A1.2(a)(4) only where the offense is similar to the instant offense (because sentences for other offenses set forth in §4A1.2(c)(1) are counted only if they are of a specified type and length).

2.   **Sentence of Imprisonment.**—To qualify as a sentence of imprisonment, the defendant must have actually served a period of imprisonment on such sentence (or, if the defendant escaped, would have served time). *See* §4A1.2(a)(3) and (b)(2). For the purposes of applying §4A1.1(a), (b), or (c), the length of a sentence of imprisonment is the stated maximum (*e.g.*, in the case of a determinate sentence of five years, the stated maximum is five years; in the case of an indeterminate sentence of one to five years, the stated maximum is five years; in the case of an indeterminate sentence for a term not to exceed five years, the stated maximum is five years; in the case of an indeterminate sentence for a term not to exceed the defendant's twenty-first birthday, the stated maximum is the amount of time in pre-trial detention plus the amount of time between the date of sentence and the defendant's twenty-first birthday). That is, criminal history points are based on the sentence pronounced, not the length of time actually served. *See* §4A1.2(b)(1) and (2). A sentence of probation is to be treated as a sentence under §4A1.1(c) unless a condition of probation requiring imprisonment of at least sixty days was imposed.

3.   **Application of "Single Sentence" Rule (Subsection (a)(2)).**—

(A)   **Predicate Offenses.**—In some cases, multiple prior sentences are treated as a single sentence for purposes of calculating the criminal history score under §4A1.1(a), (b), and (c). However, for purposes of determining predicate offenses, a prior sentence included in the single sentence should be treated as if it received criminal history points, if it independently would have received criminal history points. Therefore, an individual prior sentence may serve as a predicate under the career offender guideline (*see* §4B1.2(c)) or other guidelines with predicate offenses, if it independently would have received criminal history points. However, because predicate offenses may be used only if they are counted "separately" from each other (*see* §4B1.2(c)), no more than one prior sentence in a given single sentence may be used as a predicate offense.

For example, a defendant's criminal history includes one robbery conviction and one theft conviction. The sentences for these offenses were imposed on the same day, eight years ago, and are treated as a single sentence under §4A1.2(a)(2). If the defendant received a one-year sentence of imprisonment for the robbery and a two-year sentence of imprisonment for the theft, to be served concurrently, a total of 3 points is added under §4A1.1(a). Because this particular robbery met the definition of a felony crime of violence and independently would have received 2 criminal history points under §4A1.1(b), it may serve as a predicate under the career offender guideline.

Note, however, that if the sentences in the example above were imposed thirteen years ago, the robbery independently would have received no criminal history points under §4A1.1(b), because it was not imposed within ten years of the defendant's commencement of the instant offense. *See* §4A1.2(e)(2). Accordingly, it may not serve as a predicate under the career offender guideline.

(B)   **Upward Departure Provision.**—Treating multiple prior sentences as a single sentence may result in a criminal history score that underrepresents the seriousness of the defendant's criminal history and the danger that the defendant presents to the public. In such a case, an upward departure may be warranted. For example, if a defendant was convicted of a number of serious non-violent offenses committed on different occasions, and the resulting sentences were treated as a single sentence because either the sentences resulted from offenses contained in the same charging instrument or the defendant was sentenced for these offenses on the same day, the assignment of a single set of points may not adequately reflect the seriousness of the defendant's criminal history or the frequency with which the defendant has committed crimes.

4.   **Sentences Imposed in the Alternative.**—A sentence which specifies a fine or other non-incarcerative disposition as an alternative to a term of imprisonment (*e.g.*, $1,000 fine or ninety days' imprisonment) is treated as a non-imprisonment sentence.

5.   **Sentences for Driving While Intoxicated or Under the Influence.**—Convictions for driving while intoxicated or under the influence (and similar offenses by whatever name they are known) are always counted, without regard to how the offense is classified. Paragraphs (1) and (2) of §4A1.2(c) do not apply.

6.   **Reversed, Vacated, or Invalidated Convictions.**—Sentences resulting from convictions that (A) have been reversed or vacated because of errors of law or because of subsequently discovered evidence exonerating the defendant, or (B) have been ruled constitutionally invalid in a prior case are not to be counted. With respect to the current sentencing proceeding, this guideline and commentary do not confer upon the defendant any right to attack collaterally a prior conviction or sentence beyond any such rights otherwise recognized in law (*e.g.*, 21 U.S.C. § 851 expressly provides that a defendant may collaterally attack certain prior convictions).

Nonetheless, the criminal conduct underlying any conviction that is not counted in the criminal history score may be considered pursuant to §4A1.3 (Adequacy of Criminal History Category).

7.   **Offenses Committed Prior to Age Eighteen.**—Section 4A1.2(d) covers offenses committed prior to age eighteen. Attempting to count every juvenile adjudication would have the potential for creating large disparities due to the differential availability of records. Therefore, for offenses committed prior to age eighteen, only those that resulted in adult sentences of imprisonment exceeding one year and one month, or resulted in imposition of an adult or juvenile sentence or release from confinement on that sentence within five years of the defendant's commencement of the instant offense are counted. To avoid disparities from jurisdiction to jurisdiction in the age at which a defendant is considered a "juvenile," this provision applies to all offenses committed prior to age eighteen.

8.   **Applicable Time Period.**—Section 4A1.2(d)(2) and (e) establishes the time period within which prior sentences are counted. As used in §4A1.2(d)(2) and (e), the term "*commencement of the instant offense*" includes any relevant conduct. *See* §1B1.3 (Relevant Conduct). If the court finds that a sentence imposed outside this time period is evidence of similar, or serious dissimilar, criminal conduct, the court may consider this information in determining whether an upward departure is warranted under §4A1.3 (Adequacy of Criminal History Category).

9.   **Diversionary Dispositions.**—Section 4A1.2(f) requires counting prior adult diversionary dispositions if they involved a judicial determination of guilt or an admission of guilt in open court. This reflects a policy that defendants who receive the benefit of a rehabilitative sentence and continue to commit crimes should not be treated with further leniency.

10. **Convictions Set Aside or Defendant Pardoned.**—A number of jurisdictions have various procedures pursuant to which previous convictions may be set aside or the defendant may be pardoned for reasons unrelated to innocence or errors of law, *e.g.*, in order to restore civil rights or to remove the stigma associated with a criminal conviction. Sentences resulting from such convictions are to be counted. However, expunged convictions are not counted. §4A1.2(j).

11. **Revocations to be Considered.**—Section 4A1.2(k) covers revocations of probation and other conditional sentences where the original term of imprisonment imposed, if any, did not exceed one year and one month. Rather than count the original sentence and the resentence after revocation as separate sentences, the sentence given upon revocation should be added to the original sentence of imprisonment, if any, and the total should be counted as if it were one sentence. By this approach, no more than three points will be assessed for a single conviction, even if probation or conditional release was subsequently revoked. If the sentence originally imposed, the sentence imposed upon revocation, or the total of both sentences exceeded one year and one month, the maximum three points would be assigned. If, however, at the time of revocation another sentence was imposed for a new criminal conviction, that conviction would be computed separately from the sentence imposed for the revocation.

   Where a revocation applies to multiple sentences, and such sentences are counted separately under §4A1.2(a)(2), add the term of imprisonment imposed upon revocation to the sentence that will result in the greatest increase in criminal history points. **Example:** A defendant was serving two probationary sentences, each counted separately under §4A1.2(a)(2); probation was revoked on both sentences as a result of the same violation conduct; and the defendant was sentenced to a total of 45 days of imprisonment. If one sentence had been a "straight" probationary sentence and the other had been a probationary sentence that had required service of 15 days of imprisonment, the revocation term of imprisonment (45 days) would be added to the probationary sentence that had the 15-day term of imprisonment. This would result in a total of 2 criminal history points under §4A1.1(b) (for the combined 60-day term of imprisonment) and 1 criminal history point under §4A1.1(c) (for the other probationary sentence).

12. **Application of Subsection (c).**—

   (A) **In General.**—In determining whether an unlisted offense is similar to an offense listed in subsection (c)(1) or (c)(2), the court should use a common sense approach that includes consideration of relevant factors such as (i) a comparison of punishments imposed for the listed and unlisted offenses; (ii) the perceived seriousness of the offense as indicated by the level of punishment; (iii) the elements of the offense; (iv) the level of culpability involved; and (v) the degree to which the commission of the offense indicates a likelihood of recurring criminal conduct.

   (B) **Local Ordinance Violations.**—A number of local jurisdictions have enacted ordinances covering certain offenses (*e.g.*, larceny and assault misdemeanors) that are also violations of state criminal law. This enables a local court (*e.g.*, a municipal court) to exercise jurisdiction over such offenses. Such offenses are excluded from the definition of local ordinance violations in §4A1.2(c)(2) and, therefore, sentences for such offenses are to be treated as if the defendant had been convicted under state law.

   (C) **Insufficient Funds Check.**—"*Insufficient funds check*," as used in §4A1.2(c)(1), does not include any conviction establishing that the defendant used a false name or non-existent account.

Background: Prior sentences, not otherwise excluded, are to be counted in the criminal history score, including uncounseled misdemeanor sentences where imprisonment was not imposed.

Historical Note	Effective November 1, 1987. Amended effective November 1, 1989 (amendments 262–265); November 1, 1990 (amendments 352 and 353); November 1, 1991 (amendments 381 and 382); November 1, 1992 (amendment 472); November 1, 1993 (amendment 493); November 1, 2007 (amendment 709); November 1, 2010 (amendment 742); November 1, 2011 (amendment 758); November 1, 2012 (amendment 766); November 1, 2013 (amendment 777); November 1, 2015 (amendment 795).

§4A1.3. Departures Based on Inadequacy of Criminal History Category (Policy Statement)

(a) UPWARD DEPARTURES.—

    (1) STANDARD FOR UPWARD DEPARTURE.—If reliable information indicates that the defendant's criminal history category substantially under-represents the seriousness of the defendant's criminal history or the likelihood that the defendant will commit other crimes, an upward departure may be warranted.

    (2) TYPES OF INFORMATION FORMING THE BASIS FOR UPWARD DEPARTURE.—The information described in subsection (a) may include information concerning the following:

        (A) Prior sentence(s) not used in computing the criminal history category (*e.g.*, sentences for foreign and tribal offenses).

        (B) Prior sentence(s) of substantially more than one year imposed as a result of independent crimes committed on different occasions.

        (C) Prior similar misconduct established by a civil adjudication or by a failure to comply with an administrative order.

        (D) Whether the defendant was pending trial or sentencing on another charge at the time of the instant offense.

        (E) Prior similar adult criminal conduct not resulting in a criminal conviction.

    (3) PROHIBITION.—A prior arrest record itself shall not be considered for purposes of an upward departure under this policy statement.

(4) DETERMINATION OF EXTENT OF UPWARD DEPARTURE.—

    (A) IN GENERAL.—Except as provided in subdivision (B), the court shall determine the extent of a departure under this subsection by using, as a reference, the criminal history category applicable to defendants whose criminal history or likelihood to recidivate most closely resembles that of the defendant's.

    (B) UPWARD DEPARTURES FROM CATEGORY VI.—In a case in which the court determines that the extent and nature of the defendant's criminal history, taken together, are sufficient to warrant an upward departure from Criminal History Category VI, the court should structure the departure by moving incrementally down the sentencing table to the next higher offense level in Criminal History Category VI until it finds a guideline range appropriate to the case.

(b) DOWNWARD DEPARTURES.—

(1) STANDARD FOR DOWNWARD DEPARTURE.—If reliable information indicates that the defendant's criminal history category substantially over-represents the seriousness of the defendant's criminal history or the likelihood that the defendant will commit other crimes, a downward departure may be warranted.

(2) PROHIBITIONS.—

    (A) CRIMINAL HISTORY CATEGORY I.—A departure below the lower limit of the applicable guideline range for Criminal History Category I is prohibited.

    (B) ARMED CAREER CRIMINAL AND REPEAT AND DANGEROUS SEX OFFENDER.—A downward departure under this subsection is prohibited for (i) an armed career criminal within the meaning of §4B1.4 (Armed Career Criminal); and (ii) a repeat and dangerous sex offender against minors within the meaning of §4B1.5 (Repeat and Dangerous Sex Offender Against Minors).

(3) LIMITATIONS.—

    (A) LIMITATION ON EXTENT OF DOWNWARD DEPARTURE FOR CAREER OFFENDER.—The extent of a downward departure under this subsection for a career offender within the meaning of §4B1.1 (Career Offender) may not exceed one criminal history category.

(B) LIMITATION ON APPLICABILITY OF §5C1.2 IN EVENT OF DOWNWARD DEPARTURE TO CATEGORY I.—A defendant whose criminal history category is Category I after receipt of a downward departure under this subsection does not meet the criterion of subsection (a)(1) of §5C1.2 (Limitation on Applicability of Statutory Maximum Sentences in Certain Cases) if, before receipt of the downward departure, the defendant had more than one criminal history point under §4A1.1 (Criminal History Category).

(c) WRITTEN SPECIFICATION OF BASIS FOR DEPARTURE.—In departing from the otherwise applicable criminal history category under this policy statement, the court shall specify in writing the following:

(1) In the case of an upward departure, the specific reasons why the applicable criminal history category substantially under-represents the seriousness of the defendant's criminal history or the likelihood that the defendant will commit other crimes.

(2) In the case of a downward departure, the specific reasons why the applicable criminal history category substantially over-represents the seriousness of the defendant's criminal history or the likelihood that the defendant will commit other crimes.

Commentary

Application Notes:

1. **Definitions.**—For purposes of this policy statement, the terms "*depart*", "*departure*", "*downward departure*", and "*upward departure*" have the meaning given those terms in Application Note 1 of the Commentary to §1B1.1 (Application Instructions).

2. **Upward Departures.—**

(A) **Examples.**—An upward departure from the defendant's criminal history category may be warranted based on any of the following circumstances:

(i) A previous foreign sentence for a serious offense.

(ii) Receipt of a prior consolidated sentence of ten years for a series of serious assaults.

(iii) A similar instance of large scale fraudulent misconduct established by an adjudication in a Securities and Exchange Commission enforcement proceeding.

(iv) Commission of the instant offense while on bail or pretrial release for another serious offense.

(B) **Upward Departures from Criminal History Category VI.**—In the case of an egregious, serious criminal record in which even the guideline range for Criminal History Category VI is not adequate to reflect the seriousness of the defendant's criminal history, a departure above the guideline range for a defendant with Criminal History Category VI may be warranted. In determining whether an upward departure from Criminal History Category VI is warranted, the court should consider that the nature of the prior offenses rather than simply their number is often more indicative of the seriousness of the defendant's criminal record. For example, a defendant with five prior sentences for very large-scale fraud offenses may have 15 criminal history points, within the range of points typical for Criminal History Category VI, yet have a substantially more serious criminal history overall because of the nature of the prior offenses.

3. **Downward Departures.**—A downward departure from the defendant's criminal history category may be warranted if, for example, the defendant had two minor misdemeanor convictions close to ten years prior to the instant offense and no other evidence of prior criminal behavior in the intervening period. A departure below the lower limit of the applicable guideline range for Criminal History Category I is prohibited under subsection (b)(2)(B), due to the fact that the lower limit of the guideline range for Criminal History Category I is set for a first offender with the lowest risk of recidivism.

Background: This policy statement recognizes that the criminal history score is unlikely to take into account all the variations in the seriousness of criminal history that may occur. For example, a defendant with an extensive record of serious, assaultive conduct who had received what might now be considered extremely lenient treatment in the past might have the same criminal history category as a defendant who had a record of less serious conduct. Yet, the first defendant's criminal history clearly may be more serious. This may be particularly true in the case of younger defendants (*e.g.*, defendants in their early twenties or younger) who are more likely to have received repeated lenient treatment, yet who may actually pose a greater risk of serious recidivism than older defendants. This policy statement authorizes the consideration of a departure from the guidelines in the limited circumstances where reliable information indicates that the criminal history category does not adequately reflect the seriousness of the defendant's criminal history or likelihood of recidivism, and provides guidance for the consideration of such departures.

Historical Note	Effective November 1, 1987. Amended effective November 1, 1991 (amendment 381); November 1, 1992 (amendment 460); October 27, 2003 (amendment 651).

PART B — CAREER OFFENDERS AND CRIMINAL LIVELIHOOD

§4B1.1. Career Offender

(a) A defendant is a career offender if (1) the defendant was at least eighteen years old at the time the defendant committed the instant offense of conviction; (2) the instant offense of conviction is a felony that is either a crime of violence or a controlled substance offense; and (3) the defendant has at least two prior felony convictions of either a crime of violence or a controlled substance offense.

(b) Except as provided in subsection (c), if the offense level for a career offender from the table in this subsection is greater than the offense level otherwise applicable, the offense level from the table in this subsection shall apply. A career offender's criminal history category in every case under this subsection shall be Category VI.

OFFENSE STATUTORY MAXIMUM	OFFENSE LEVEL*
(1) Life	37
(2) 25 years or more	34
(3) 20 years or more, but less than 25 years	32
(4) 15 years or more, but less than 20 years	29
(5) 10 years or more, but less than 15 years	24
(6) 5 years or more, but less than 10 years	17
(7) More than 1 year, but less than 5 years	12.

*If an adjustment from §3E1.1 (Acceptance of Responsibility) applies, decrease the offense level by the number of levels corresponding to that adjustment.

(c) If the defendant is convicted of 18 U.S.C. § 924(c) or § 929(a), and the defendant is determined to be a career offender under subsection (a), the applicable guideline range shall be determined as follows:

(1) If the only count of conviction is 18 U.S.C. § 924(c) or § 929(a), the applicable guideline range shall be determined using the table in subsection (c)(3).

(2) In the case of multiple counts of conviction in which at least one of the counts is a conviction other than a conviction for 18 U.S.C. § 924(c) or § 929(a), the guideline range shall be the greater of—

    (A) the guideline range that results by adding the mandatory minimum consecutive penalty required by the 18 U.S.C. § 924(c) or § 929(a) count(s) to the minimum and the maximum of the otherwise applicable guideline range determined for the count(s) of conviction other than the 18 U.S.C. § 924(c) or § 929(a) count(s); and

    (B) the guideline range determined using the table in subsection (c)(3).

  (3) CAREER OFFENDER TABLE FOR 18 U.S.C. § 924(C) OR § 929(A) OFFENDERS

§3E1.1 REDUCTION	GUIDELINE RANGE FOR THE 18 U.S.C. § 924(C) OR § 929(A) COUNT(S)
No reduction	360–life
2-level reduction	292–365
3-level reduction	262–327.

Commentary

Application Notes:

1. **Definitions.**—"*Crime of violence*," "*controlled substance offense*," and "*two prior felony convictions*" are defined in §4B1.2.

2. **"Offense Statutory Maximum".**—"*Offense Statutory Maximum*," for the purposes of this guideline, refers to the maximum term of imprisonment authorized for the offense of conviction that is a crime of violence or controlled substance offense, including any increase in that maximum term under a sentencing enhancement provision that applies because of the defendant's prior criminal record (such sentencing enhancement provisions are contained, for example, in 21 U.S.C. § 841(b)(1)(A), (B), (C), and (D)). For example, in a case in which the statutory maximum term of imprisonment under 21 U.S.C. § 841(b)(1)(C) is increased from twenty years to thirty years because the defendant has one or more qualifying prior drug convictions, the "Offense Statutory Maximum" for that defendant for the purposes of this guideline is thirty years and not twenty years. If more than one count of conviction is of a crime of violence or controlled substance offense, use the maximum authorized term of imprisonment for the count that has the greatest offense statutory maximum.

3. **Application of Subsection (c).**—

    (A) **In General.**—Subsection (c) applies in any case in which the defendant (i) was convicted of violating 18 U.S.C. § 924(c) or § 929(a); and (ii) as a result of that conviction (alone or in addition to another offense of conviction), is determined to be a career offender under §4B1.1(a).

    (B) **Subsection (c)(2).**—To determine the greater guideline range under subsection (c)(2), the court shall use the guideline range with the highest minimum term of imprisonment.

(C) **"Otherwise Applicable Guideline Range".**—For purposes of subsection (c)(2)(A), "otherwise applicable guideline range" for the count(s) of conviction other than the 18 U.S.C. § 924(c) or 18 U.S.C. § 929(a) count(s) is determined as follows:

   (i) If the count(s) of conviction other than the 18 U.S.C. § 924(c) or 18 U.S.C. § 929(a) count(s) does not qualify the defendant as a career offender, the otherwise applicable guideline range for that count(s) is the guideline range determined using: (I) the Chapter Two and Three offense level for that count(s); and (II) the appropriate criminal history category determined under §§4A1.1 (Criminal History Category) and 4A1.2 (Definitions and Instructions for Computing Criminal History).

   (ii) If the count(s) of conviction other than the 18 U.S.C. § 924(c) or 18 U.S.C. § 929(a) count(s) qualifies the defendant as a career offender, the otherwise applicable guideline range for that count(s) is the guideline range determined for that count(s) under §4B1.1(a) and (b).

(D) **Imposition of Consecutive Term of Imprisonment.**—In a case involving multiple counts, the sentence shall be imposed according to the rules in subsection (e) of §5G1.2 (Sentencing on Multiple Counts of Conviction).

(E) **Example.**—The following example illustrates the application of subsection (c)(2) in a multiple count situation:

   The defendant is convicted of one count of violating 18 U.S.C. § 924(c) for possessing a firearm in furtherance of a drug trafficking offense (5 year mandatory minimum), and one count of violating 21 U.S.C. § 841(b)(1)(B) (5 year mandatory minimum, 40 year statutory maximum). Applying subsection (c)(2)(A), the court determines that the drug count (without regard to the 18 U.S.C. § 924(c) count) qualifies the defendant as a career offender under §4B1.1(a). Under §4B1.1(a), the otherwise applicable guideline range for the drug count is 188–235 months (using offense level 34 (because the statutory maximum for the drug count is 40 years), minus 3 levels for acceptance of responsibility, and criminal history category VI). The court adds 60 months (the minimum required by 18 U.S.C. § 924(c)) to the minimum and the maximum of that range, resulting in a guideline range of 248–295 months. Applying subsection (c)(2)(B), the court then determines the career offender guideline range from the table in subsection (c)(3) is 262–327 months. The range with the greatest minimum, 262–327 months, is used to impose the sentence in accordance with §5G1.2(e).

4. **Departure Provision for State Misdemeanors.**—In a case in which one or both of the defendant's "two prior felony convictions" is based on an offense that was classified as a misdemeanor at the time of sentencing for the instant federal offense, application of the career offender guideline may result in a guideline range that substantially overrepresents the seriousness of the defendant's criminal history or substantially overstates the seriousness of the instant offense. In such a case, a downward departure may be warranted without regard to the limitation in §4A1.3(b)(3)(A).

Background: Section 994(h) of Title 28, United States Code, mandates that the Commission assure that certain "career" offenders receive a sentence of imprisonment "at or near the maximum term authorized." Section 4B1.1 implements this directive, with the definition of a career offender tracking in large part the criteria set forth in 28 U.S.C. § 994(h). However, in accord with its general guideline promulgation authority under 28 U.S.C. § 994(a)–(f), and its amendment authority under 28 U.S.C. § 994(o) and (p), the Commission has modified this definition in several respects to focus more precisely on the class of recidivist offenders for whom a lengthy term of imprisonment is appropriate and to avoid "unwarranted sentencing disparities among defendants with similar records who have been found guilty of similar criminal conduct . . . ." 28 U.S.C. § 991(b)(1)(B). The Commission's refinement of this definition over time is consistent with Congress's choice of a directive to the Commission rather than a mandatory minimum sentencing statute ("The [Senate Judiciary] Committee believes that such a directive to the Commission will be more effective; the guidelines development process can assure consistent and rational implementation for the Committee's view that substantial prison terms should be imposed on repeat violent offenders and repeat drug traffickers." S. Rep. No. 225, 98th Cong., 1st Sess. 175 (1983)).

Subsection (c) provides rules for determining the sentence for career offenders who have been convicted of 18 U.S.C. § 924(c) or § 929(a). The Career Offender Table in subsection (c)(3) provides a sentence at or near the statutory maximum for these offenders by using guideline ranges that correspond to criminal history category VI and offense level 37 (assuming §3E.1.1 (Acceptance of Responsibility) does not apply), offense level 35 (assuming a 2-level reduction under §3E.1.1 applies), and offense level 34 (assuming a 3-level reduction under §3E1.1 applies).

Historical Note	Effective November 1, 1987. Amended effective January 15, 1988 (amendments 47 and 48); November 1, 1989 (amendments 266 and 267); November 1, 1992 (amendment 459); November 1, 1994 (amendment 506); November 1, 1995 (amendment 528); November 1, 1997 (amendments 546 and 567); November 1, 2002 (amendment 642); November 1, 2011 (amendment 758); August 1, 2016 (amendment 798).

§4B1.2. Definitions of Terms Used in Section 4B1.1

(a) The term "crime of violence" means any offense under federal or state law, punishable by imprisonment for a term exceeding one year, that—

   (1) has as an element the use, attempted use, or threatened use of physical force against the person of another, or

   (2) is murder, voluntary manslaughter, kidnapping, aggravated assault, a forcible sex offense, robbery, arson, extortion, or the use or unlawful possession of a firearm described in 26 U.S.C. § 5845(a) or explosive material as defined in 18 U.S.C. § 841(c).

(b) The term "controlled substance offense" means an offense under federal or state law, punishable by imprisonment for a term exceeding one year, that prohibits the manufacture, import, export, distribution, or dispensing of a controlled substance (or a counterfeit substance) or the possession of a controlled substance (or a counterfeit substance) with intent to manufacture, import, export, distribute, or dispense.

(c) The term "two prior felony convictions" means (1) the defendant committed the instant offense of conviction subsequent to sustaining at least two felony convictions of either a crime of violence or a controlled substance offense (*i.e.*, two felony convictions of a crime of violence, two felony convictions of a controlled substance offense, or one felony conviction of a crime of violence and one felony conviction of a controlled substance offense), and (2) the sentences for at least two of the aforementioned felony convictions are counted separately under the provisions of §4A1.1(a), (b), or (c). The date that a defendant sustained a conviction shall be the date that the guilt of the defendant has been established, whether by guilty plea, trial, or plea of *nolo contendere*.

Commentary

Application Notes:

1. **Definitions.**—For purposes of this guideline—

   "**Crime of violence**" and "**controlled substance offense**" include the offenses of aiding and abetting, conspiring, and attempting to commit such offenses.

   "**Forcible sex offense**" includes where consent to the conduct is not given or is not legally valid, such as where consent to the conduct is involuntary, incompetent, or coerced. The offenses of sexual abuse of a minor and statutory rape are included only if the sexual abuse of a minor or statutory rape was (A) an offense described in 18 U.S.C. § 2241(c) or (B) an offense under state law that would have been an offense under section 2241(c) if the offense had occurred within the special maritime and territorial jurisdiction of the United States.

   "**Extortion**" is obtaining something of value from another by the wrongful use of (A) force, (B) fear of physical injury, or (C) threat of physical injury.

   Unlawfully possessing a listed chemical with intent to manufacture a controlled substance (21 U.S.C. § 841(c)(1)) is a "controlled substance offense."

   Unlawfully possessing a prohibited flask or equipment with intent to manufacture a controlled substance (21 U.S.C. § 843(a)(6)) is a "controlled substance offense."

   Maintaining any place for the purpose of facilitating a drug offense (21 U.S.C. § 856) is a "controlled substance offense" if the offense of conviction established that the underlying offense (the offense facilitated) was a "controlled substance offense."

   Using a communications facility in committing, causing, or facilitating a drug offense (21 U.S.C. § 843(b)) is a "controlled substance offense" if the offense of conviction established that the underlying offense (the offense committed, caused, or facilitated) was a "controlled substance offense."

   A violation of 18 U.S.C. § 924(c) or § 929(a) is a "crime of violence" or a "controlled substance offense" if the offense of conviction established that the underlying offense was a "crime of violence" or a "controlled substance offense". (Note that in the case of a prior

18 U.S.C. § 924(c) or § 929(a) conviction, if the defendant also was convicted of the underlying offense, the sentences for the two prior convictions will be treated as a single sentence under §4A1.2 (Definitions and Instructions for Computing Criminal History).)

"*Prior felony conviction*" means a prior adult federal or state conviction for an offense punishable by death or imprisonment for a term exceeding one year, regardless of whether such offense is specifically designated as a felony and regardless of the actual sentence imposed. A conviction for an offense committed at age eighteen or older is an adult conviction. A conviction for an offense committed prior to age eighteen is an adult conviction if it is classified as an adult conviction under the laws of the jurisdiction in which the defendant was convicted (*e.g.*, a federal conviction for an offense committed prior to the defendant's eighteenth birthday is an adult conviction if the defendant was expressly proceeded against as an adult).

2.   **Offense of Conviction as Focus of Inquiry.**—Section 4B1.1 (Career Offender) expressly provides that the instant and prior offenses must be crimes of violence or controlled substance offenses of which the defendant was convicted. Therefore, in determining whether an offense is a crime of violence or controlled substance for the purposes of §4B1.1 (Career Offender), the offense of conviction (*i.e.*, the conduct of which the defendant was convicted) is the focus of inquiry.

3.   **Applicability of §4A1.2.**—The provisions of §4A1.2 (Definitions and Instructions for Computing Criminal History) are applicable to the counting of convictions under §4B1.1.

4.   **Upward Departure for Burglary Involving Violence.**—There may be cases in which a burglary involves violence, but does not qualify as a "crime of violence" as defined in §4B1.2(a) and, as a result, the defendant does not receive a higher offense level or higher Criminal History Category that would have applied if the burglary qualified as a "crime of violence." In such a case, an upward departure may be appropriate.

Historical Note	Effective November 1, 1987. Amended effective January 15, 1988 (amendment 49); November 1, 1989 (amendment 268); November 1, 1991 (amendment 433); November 1, 1992 (amendment 461); November 1, 1995 (amendment 528); November 1, 1997 (amendments 546 and 568); November 1, 2000 (amendment 600); November 1, 2002 (amendments 642 and 646); November 1, 2004 (amendment 674); November 1, 2007 (amendment 709); November 1, 2009 (amendment 736); November 1, 2015 (amendment 795); August 1, 2016 (amendment 798).

§4B1.3.   Criminal Livelihood

If the defendant committed an offense as part of a pattern of criminal conduct engaged in as a livelihood, his offense level shall be not less than **13**, unless §3E1.1 (Acceptance of Responsibility) applies, in which event his offense level shall be not less than **11**.

Commentary

Application Notes:

1.   "*Pattern of criminal conduct*" means planned criminal acts occurring over a substantial period of time. Such acts may involve a single course of conduct or independent offenses.

2.   "*Engaged in as a livelihood*" means that (A) the defendant derived income from the pattern of criminal conduct that in any twelve-month period exceeded 2,000 times the then existing hourly minimum wage under federal law; and (B) the totality of circumstances shows that such criminal conduct was the defendant's primary occupation in that twelve-month period (*e.g.*, the defendant engaged in criminal conduct rather than regular, legitimate employment; or the defendant's legitimate employment was merely a front for the defendant's criminal conduct).

Background: Section 4B1.3 implements 28 U.S.C. § 994(i)(2), which directs the Commission to ensure that the guidelines specify a "substantial term of imprisonment" for a defendant who committed an offense as part of a pattern of criminal conduct from which the defendant derived a substantial portion of the defendant's income.

Historical Note	Effective November 1, 1987. Amended effective June 15, 1988 (amendment 50); November 1, 1989 (amendment 269); November 1, 1990 (amendment 354); November 1, 2010 (amendment 747).

§4B1.4.   Armed Career Criminal

(a)   A defendant who is subject to an enhanced sentence under the provisions of 18 U.S.C. § 924(e) is an armed career criminal.

(b)   The offense level for an armed career criminal is the greatest of:

   (1)   the offense level applicable from Chapters Two and Three; or

   (2)   the offense level from §4B1.1 (Career Offender) if applicable; or

   (3)   (A)   **34**, if the defendant used or possessed the firearm or ammunition in connection with either a crime of violence, as defined in §4B1.2(a), or a controlled substance offense, as defined in §4B1.2(b), or if the firearm possessed by the defendant was of a type described in 26 U.S.C. § 5845(a)*; or

          (B)   **33**, otherwise.*

          *If an adjustment from §3E1.1 (Acceptance of Responsibility) applies, decrease the offense level by the number of levels corresponding to that adjustment.

(c)   The criminal history category for an armed career criminal is the greatest of:

   (1)   the criminal history category from Chapter Four, Part A (Criminal History), or §4B1.1 (Career Offender) if applicable; or

(2) Category VI, if the defendant used or possessed the firearm or ammunition in connection with either a crime of violence, as defined in §4B1.2(a), or a controlled substance offense, as defined in §4B1.2(b), or if the firearm possessed by the defendant was of a type described in 26 U.S.C. § 5845(a); or

(3) Category IV.

Commentary

Application Notes:

1. This guideline applies in the case of a defendant subject to an enhanced sentence under 18 U.S.C. § 924(e). Under 18 U.S.C. § 924(e)(1), a defendant is subject to an enhanced sentence if the instant offense of conviction is a violation of 18 U.S.C. § 922(g) and the defendant has at least three prior convictions for a "violent felony" or "serious drug offense," or both, committed on occasions different from one another. The terms "*violent felony*" and "*serious drug offense*" are defined in 18 U.S.C. § 924(e)(2). It is to be noted that the definitions of "violent felony" and "serious drug offense" in 18 U.S.C. § 924(e)(2) are not identical to the definitions of "crime of violence" and "controlled substance offense" used in §4B1.1 (Career Offender), nor are the time periods for the counting of prior sentences under §4A1.2 (Definitions and Instructions for Computing Criminal History) applicable to the determination of whether a defendant is subject to an enhanced sentence under 18 U.S.C. § 924(e).

It is also to be noted that the procedural steps relative to the imposition of an enhanced sentence under 18 U.S.C. § 924(e) are not set forth by statute and may vary to some extent from jurisdiction to jurisdiction.

2. **Application of §4B1.4 in Cases Involving Convictions Under 18 U.S.C. § 844(h), § 924(c), or § 929(a).**—If a sentence under this guideline is imposed in conjunction with a sentence for a conviction under 18 U.S.C. § 844(h), § 924(c), or § 929(a), do not apply either subsection (b)(3)(A) or (c)(2). A sentence under 18 U.S.C. § 844(h), § 924(c), or § 929(a) accounts for the conduct covered by subsections (b)(3)(A) and (c)(2) because of the relatedness of the conduct covered by these subsections to the conduct that forms the basis for the conviction under 18 U.S.C. § 844(h), § 924(c), or § 929(a).

In a few cases, the rule provided in the preceding paragraph may result in a guideline range that, when combined with the mandatory consecutive sentence under 18 U.S.C. § 844(h), § 924(c), or § 929(a), produces a total maximum penalty that is less than the maximum of the guideline range that would have resulted had there not been a count of conviction under 18 U.S.C. § 844(h), § 924(c), or § 929(a) (*i.e.*, the guideline range that would have resulted if subsections (b)(3)(A) and (c)(2) had been applied). In such a case, an upward departure may be warranted so that the conviction under 18 U.S.C. § 844(h), § 924(c), or § 929(a) does not result in a decrease in the total punishment. An upward departure under this paragraph shall not exceed the maximum of the guideline range that would have resulted had there not been a count of conviction under 18 U.S.C. § 844(h), § 924(c), or § 929(a).

Background: This section implements 18 U.S.C. § 924(e), which requires a minimum sentence of imprisonment of fifteen years for a defendant who violates 18 U.S.C. § 922(g) and has three previous convictions for a violent felony or a serious drug offense. If the offense level determined under this section is greater than the offense level otherwise applicable, the offense level determined under this section shall be applied. A minimum criminal history category

(Category IV) is provided, reflecting that each defendant to whom this section applies will have at least three prior convictions for serious offenses. In some cases, the criminal history category may not adequately reflect the defendant's criminal history; *see* §4A1.3 (Adequacy of Criminal History Category).

| *Historical Note* | Effective November 1, 1990 (amendment 355). Amended effective November 1, 1992 (amendment 459); November 1, 2002 (amendment 646); November 1, 2004 (amendment 674). |

§4B1.5. Repeat and Dangerous Sex Offender Against Minors

(a) In any case in which the defendant's instant offense of conviction is a covered sex crime, §4B1.1 (Career Offender) does not apply, and the defendant committed the instant offense of conviction subsequent to sustaining at least one sex offense conviction:

   (1) The offense level shall be the greater of:

      (A) the offense level determined under Chapters Two and Three; or

      (B) the offense level from the table below decreased by the number of levels corresponding to any applicable adjustment from §3E1.1 (Acceptance of Responsibility):

OFFENSE STATUTORY MAXIMUM	OFFENSE LEVEL
(i) Life	37
(ii) 25 years or more	34
(iii) 20 years or more, but less than 25 years	32
(iv) 15 years or more, but less than 20 years	29
(v) 10 years or more, but less than 15 years	24
(vi) 5 years or more, but less than 10 years	17
(vii) More than 1 year, but less than 5 years	12.

   (2) The criminal history category shall be the greater of: (A) the criminal history category determined under Chapter Four, Part A (Criminal History); or (B) criminal history Category V.

(b) In any case in which the defendant's instant offense of conviction is a covered sex crime, neither §4B1.1 nor subsection (a) of this guideline applies, and the defendant engaged in a pattern of activity involving prohibited sexual conduct:

   (1) The offense level shall be **5** plus the offense level determined under Chapters Two and Three. However, if the resulting offense level is less than level **22**, the offense level shall be

level **22**, decreased by the number of levels corresponding to any applicable adjustment from §3E1.1.

(2) The criminal history category shall be the criminal history category determined under Chapter Four, Part A.

Commentary

Application Notes:

1. **Definition.**—For purposes of this guideline, "***minor***" means (A) an individual who had not attained the age of 18 years; (B) an individual, whether fictitious or not, who a law enforcement officer represented to a participant (i) had not attained the age of 18 years; and (ii) could be provided for the purposes of engaging in sexually explicit conduct; or (C) an undercover law enforcement officer who represented to a participant that the officer had not attained the age of 18 years.

2. **Covered Sex Crime as Instant Offense of Conviction.**—For purposes of this guideline, the instant offense of conviction must be a covered sex crime, *i.e.*: (A) an offense, perpetrated against a minor, under (i) chapter 109A of title 18, United States Code; (ii) chapter 110 of such title, not including trafficking in, receipt of, or possession of, child pornography, or a recordkeeping offense; (iii) chapter 117 of such title, not including transmitting information about a minor or filing a factual statement about an alien individual; or (iv) 18 U.S.C. § 1591; or (B) an attempt or a conspiracy to commit any offense described in subdivisions (A)(i) through (iv) of this note.

3. **Application of Subsection (a).**—

    (A) **Definitions.**—For purposes of subsection (a):

        (i) "***Offense statutory maximum***" means the maximum term of imprisonment authorized for the instant offense of conviction that is a covered sex crime, including any increase in that maximum term under a sentencing enhancement provision (such as a sentencing enhancement provision contained in 18 U.S.C. § 2247(a) or § 2426(a)) that applies to that covered sex crime because of the defendant's prior criminal record.

        (ii) "***Sex offense conviction***" (I) means any offense described in 18 U.S.C. § 2426(b)(1)(A) or (B), if the offense was perpetrated against a minor; and (II) does not include trafficking in, receipt of, or possession of, child pornography. "***Child pornography***" has the meaning given that term in 18 U.S.C. § 2256(8).

    (B) **Determination of Offense Statutory Maximum in the Case of Multiple Counts of Conviction.**—In a case in which more than one count of the instant offense of conviction is a felony that is a covered sex crime, the court shall use the maximum authorized term of imprisonment for the count that has the greatest offense statutory maximum, for purposes of determining the offense statutory maximum under subsection (a).

4. **Application of Subsection (b).**—

    (A) **Definition.**—For purposes of subsection (b), "***prohibited sexual conduct***" means any of the following: (i) any offense described in 18 U.S.C. § 2426(b)(1)(A) or (B);

(ii) the production of child pornography; or (iii) trafficking in child pornography only if, prior to the commission of the instant offense of conviction, the defendant sustained a felony conviction for that trafficking in child pornography. It does not include receipt or possession of child pornography. "*Child pornography*" has the meaning given that term in 18 U.S.C. § 2256(8).

(B) **Determination of Pattern of Activity.—**

(i) **In General.—**For purposes of subsection (b), the defendant engaged in a pattern of activity involving prohibited sexual conduct if on at least two separate occasions, the defendant engaged in prohibited sexual conduct with a minor.

(ii) **Occasion of Prohibited Sexual Conduct.—**An occasion of prohibited sexual conduct may be considered for purposes of subsection (b) without regard to whether the occasion (I) occurred during the course of the instant offense; or (II) resulted in a conviction for the conduct that occurred on that occasion.

5. **Treatment and Monitoring.—**

(A) **Recommended Maximum Term of Supervised Release.—**The statutory maximum term of supervised release is recommended for offenders sentenced under this guideline.

(B) **Recommended Conditions of Probation and Supervised Release.—**Treatment and monitoring are important tools for supervising offenders and should be considered as special conditions of any term of probation or supervised release that is imposed.

Background: This guideline applies to offenders whose instant offense of conviction is a sex offense committed against a minor and who present a continuing danger to the public. The relevant criminal provisions provide for increased statutory maximum penalties for repeat sex offenders and make those increased statutory maximum penalties available if the defendant previously was convicted of any of several federal and state sex offenses (*see* 18 U.S.C. §§ 2247, 2426). In addition, section 632 of Public Law 102–141 and section 505 of Public Law 105–314 directed the Commission to ensure lengthy incarceration for offenders who engage in a pattern of activity involving the sexual abuse or exploitation of minors.

Section 401(i)(1)(A) of Public Law 108–21 directly amended Application Note 4(b)(i), effective April 30, 2003.

Historical Note	Effective November 1, 2001 (amendment 615). Amended effective April 30, 2003 (amendment 649); November 1, 2003 (amendment 661); November 1, 2007 (amendment 701).

CHAPTER FIVE

DETERMINING THE SENTENCE

Introductory Commentary

For certain categories of offenses and offenders, the guidelines permit the court to impose either imprisonment or some other sanction or combination of sanctions. In determining the type of sentence to impose, the sentencing judge should consider the nature and seriousness of the conduct, the statutory purposes of sentencing, and the pertinent offender characteristics. A sentence is within the guidelines if it complies with each applicable section of this chapter. The court should impose a sentence sufficient, but not greater than necessary, to comply with the statutory purposes of sentencing. 18 U.S.C. § 3553(a).

Historical Note	Effective November 1, 1987.

PART A — SENTENCING TABLE

The Sentencing Table used to determine the guideline range follows:

SENTENCING TABLE
(in months of imprisonment)

Offense Level	Criminal History Category (Criminal History Points)					
	I (0 or 1)	II (2 or 3)	III (4, 5, 6)	IV (7, 8, 9)	V (10, 11, 12)	VI (13 or more)
1	0–6	0–6	0–6	0–6	0–6	0–6
2	0–6	0–6	0–6	0–6	0–6	1–7
3	0–6	0–6	0–6	0–6	2–8	3–9
4	0–6	0–6	0–6	2–8	4–10	6–12
5	0–6	0–6	1–7	4–10	6–12	9–15
6	0–6	1–7	2–8	6–12	9–15	12–18
7	0–6	2–8	4–10	8–14	12–18	15–21
8	0–6	4–10	6–12	10–16	15–21	18–24
9	4–10	6–12	8–14	12–18	18–24	21–27
10	6–12	8–14	10–16	15–21	21–27	24–30
11	8–14	10–16	12–18	18–24	24–30	27–33
12	10–16	12–18	15–21	21–27	27–33	30–37
13	12–18	15–21	18–24	24–30	30–37	33–41
14	15–21	18–24	21–27	27–33	33–41	37–46
15	18–24	21–27	24–30	30–37	37–46	41–51
16	21–27	24–30	27–33	33–41	41–51	46–57
17	24–30	27–33	30–37	37–46	46–57	51–63
18	27–33	30–37	33–41	41–51	51–63	57–71
19	30–37	33–41	37–46	46–57	57–71	63–78
20	33–41	37–46	41–51	51–63	63–78	70–87
21	37–46	41–51	46–57	57–71	70–87	77–96
22	41–51	46–57	51–63	63–78	77–96	84–105
23	46–57	51–63	57–71	70–87	84–105	92–115
24	51–63	57–71	63–78	77–96	92–115	100–125
25	57–71	63–78	70–87	84–105	100–125	110–137
26	63–78	70–87	78–97	92–115	110–137	120–150
27	70–87	78–97	87–108	100–125	120–150	130–162
28	78–97	87–108	97–121	110–137	130–162	140–175
29	87–108	97–121	108–135	121–151	140–175	151–188
30	97–121	108–135	121–151	135–168	151–188	168–210
31	108–135	121–151	135–168	151–188	168–210	188–235
32	121–151	135–168	151–188	168–210	188–235	210–262
33	135–168	151–188	168–210	188–235	210–262	235–293
34	151–188	168–210	188–235	210–262	235–293	262–327
35	168–210	188–235	210–262	235–293	262–327	292–365
36	188–235	210–262	235–293	262–327	292–365	324–405
37	210–262	235–293	262–327	292–365	324–405	360–life
38	235–293	262–327	292–365	324–405	360–life	360–life
39	262–327	292–365	324–405	360–life	360–life	360–life
40	292–365	324–405	360–life	360–life	360–life	360–life
41	324–405	360–life	360–life	360–life	360–life	360–life
42	360–life	360–life	360–life	360–life	360–life	360–life
43	life	life	life	life	life	life

A (rows 1–8)
B (rows 9–11)
C (rows 12–13)
D (rows 14 onward)

Commentary to Sentencing Table

Application Notes:

1. The Offense Level (1–43) forms the vertical axis of the Sentencing Table. The Criminal History Category (I–VI) forms the horizontal axis of the Table. The intersection of the Offense Level and Criminal History Category displays the Guideline Range in months of imprisonment. "*Life*" means life imprisonment. For example, the guideline range applicable to a defendant with an Offense Level of 15 and a Criminal History Category of III is 24–30 months of imprisonment.

2. In rare cases, a total offense level of less than 1 or more than 43 may result from application of the guidelines. A total offense level of less than 1 is to be treated as an offense level of 1. An offense level of more than 43 is to be treated as an offense level of 43.

3. The Criminal History Category is determined by the total criminal history points from Chapter Four, Part A, except as provided in §§4B1.1 (Career Offender) and 4B1.4 (Armed Career Criminal). The total criminal history points associated with each Criminal History Category are shown under each Criminal History Category in the Sentencing Table.

Historical Note	Effective November 1, 1987. Amended effective November 1, 1989 (amendment 270); November 1, 1991 (amendment 418); November 1, 1992 (amendment 462); November 1, 2010 (amendment 738).

PART B — PROBATION

Introductory Commentary

The Comprehensive Crime Control Act of 1984 makes probation a sentence in and of itself. 18 U.S.C. § 3561. Probation may be used as an alternative to incarceration, provided that the terms and conditions of probation can be fashioned so as to meet fully the statutory purposes of sentencing, including promoting respect for law, providing just punishment for the offense, achieving general deterrence, and protecting the public from further crimes by the defendant.

Historical Note	Effective November 1, 1987.

§5B1.1. Imposition of a Term of Probation

(a) Subject to the statutory restrictions in subsection (b) below, a sentence of probation is authorized if:

(1) the applicable guideline range is in Zone A of the Sentencing Table; or

(2) the applicable guideline range is in Zone B of the Sentencing Table and the court imposes a condition or combination of conditions requiring intermittent confinement, community confinement, or home detention as provided in subsection (c)(3) of §5C1.1 (Imposition of a Term of Imprisonment).

(b) A sentence of probation may not be imposed in the event:

(1) the offense of conviction is a Class A or B felony, 18 U.S.C. § 3561(a)(1);

(2) the offense of conviction expressly precludes probation as a sentence, 18 U.S.C. § 3561(a)(2);

(3) the defendant is sentenced at the same time to a sentence of imprisonment for the same or a different offense, 18 U.S.C. § 3561(a)(3).

Commentary

Application Notes:

1. Except where prohibited by statute or by the guideline applicable to the offense in Chapter Two, the guidelines authorize, but do not require, a sentence of probation in the following circumstances:

(A) **Where the applicable guideline range is in Zone A of the Sentencing Table (*i.e.*, the minimum term of imprisonment specified in the applicable guideline range is zero months).** In such cases, a condition requiring a period of community confinement, home detention, or intermittent confinement may be imposed but is not required.

(B) **Where the applicable guideline range is in Zone B of the Sentencing Table (*i.e.*, the minimum term of imprisonment specified in the applicable guideline range is at least one but not more than nine months).** In such cases, the court may impose probation only if it imposes a condition or combination of conditions requiring a period of community confinement, home detention, or intermittent confinement sufficient to satisfy the minimum term of imprisonment specified in the guideline range. For example, where the offense level is 7 and the criminal history category is II, the guideline range from the Sentencing Table is 2–8 months. In such a case, the court may impose a sentence of probation only if it imposes a condition or conditions requiring at least two months of community confinement, home detention, or intermittent confinement, or a combination of community confinement, home detention, and intermittent confinement totaling at least two months.

2. Where the applicable guideline range is in Zone C or D of the Sentencing Table (*i.e.*, the minimum term of imprisonment specified in the applicable guideline range is ten months or more), the guidelines do not authorize a sentence of probation. *See* §5C1.1 (Imposition of a Term of Imprisonment).

Background: This section provides for the imposition of a sentence of probation. The court may sentence a defendant to a term of probation in any case unless (1) prohibited by statute, or (2) where a term of imprisonment is required under §5C1.1 (Imposition of a Term of Imprisonment). Under 18 U.S.C. § 3561(a)(3), the imposition of a sentence of probation is prohibited where the defendant is sentenced at the same time to a sentence of imprisonment for the same or a different offense. Although this provision has effectively abolished the use of "split sentences" imposable pursuant to the former 18 U.S.C. § 3651, the drafters of the Sentencing Reform Act noted that the functional equivalent of the split sentence could be "achieved by a more direct and logically consistent route" by providing that a defendant serve a term of imprisonment followed by a period of supervised release. (S. Rep. No. 225, 98th Cong., 1st Sess. 89 (1983)). Section 5B1.1(a)(2) provides a transition between the circumstances under which a "straight" probationary term is authorized and those where probation is prohibited.

Historical Note	Effective November 1, 1987. Amended effective November 1, 1989 (amendment 302); November 1, 1992 (amendment 462); November 1, 2010 (amendments 738 and 747).

§5B1.2. Term of Probation

(a) When probation is imposed, the term shall be:

(1) at least one year but not more than five years if the offense level is **6** or greater;

(2) no more than three years in any other case.

§5B1.3

Commentary

Background: This section governs the length of a term of probation. Subject to statutory restrictions, the guidelines provide that a term of probation may not exceed three years if the offense level is less than 6. If a defendant has an offense level of 6 or greater, the guidelines provide that a term of probation be at least one year but not more than five years. Although some distinction in the length of a term of probation is warranted based on the circumstances of the case, a term of probation may also be used to enforce conditions such as fine or restitution payments, or attendance in a program of treatment such as drug rehabilitation. Often, it may not be possible to determine the amount of time required for the satisfaction of such payments or programs in advance. This issue has been resolved by setting forth two broad ranges for the duration of a term of probation depending upon the offense level. Within the guidelines set forth in this section, the determination of the length of a term of probation is within the discretion of the sentencing judge.

Historical Note	Effective November 1, 1987

§5B1.3.   Conditions of Probation

(a)   MANDATORY CONDITIONS

(1)   For any offense, the defendant shall not commit another federal, state or local offense (*see* 18 U.S.C. § 3563(a)).

(2)   For a felony, the defendant shall (A) make restitution, (B) work in community service, or (C) both, unless the court has imposed a fine, or unless the court finds on the record that extraordinary circumstances exist that would make such a condition plainly unreasonable, in which event the court shall impose one or more of the discretionary conditions set forth under 18 U.S.C. § 3563(b) (*see* 18 U.S.C. § 3563(a)(2)).

(3)   For any offense, the defendant shall not unlawfully possess a controlled substance (*see* 18 U.S.C. § 3563(a)).

(4)   For a domestic violence crime as defined in 18 U.S.C. § 3561(b) by a defendant convicted of such an offense for the first time, the defendant shall attend a public, private, or non-profit offender rehabilitation program that has been approved by the court, in consultation with a State Coalition Against Domestic Violence or other appropriate experts, if an approved program is available within a 50-mile radius of the legal residence of the defendant (*see* 18 U.S.C. § 3563(a)).

(5) For any offense, the defendant shall refrain from any unlawful use of a controlled substance and submit to one drug test within 15 days of release on probation and at least two periodic drug tests thereafter (as determined by the court) for use of a controlled substance, but the condition stated in this paragraph may be ameliorated or suspended by the court for any individual defendant if the defendant's presentence report or other reliable information indicates a low risk of future substance abuse by the defendant (*see* 18 U.S.C. § 3563(a)).

(6) The defendant shall (A) make restitution in accordance with 18 U.S.C. §§ 2248, 2259, 2264, 2327, 3663, 3663A, and 3664; and (B) pay the assessment imposed in accordance with 18 U.S.C. § 3013. If there is a court-established payment schedule for making restitution or paying the assessment (*see* 18 U.S.C. § 3572(d)), the defendant shall adhere to the schedule.

(7) The defendant shall notify the court of any material change in the defendant's economic circumstances that might affect the defendant's ability to pay restitution, fines, or special assessments (*see* 18 U.S.C. § 3563(a)).

(8) If the court has imposed a fine, the defendant shall pay the fine or adhere to a court-established payment schedule (*see* 18 U.S.C. § 3563(a)).

(9) If the defendant is required to register under the Sex Offender Registration and Notification Act, the defendant shall comply with the requirements of that Act (*see* 18 U.S.C. § 3563(a)).

(10) The defendant shall submit to the collection of a DNA sample from the defendant at the direction of the United States Probation Office if the collection of such a sample is authorized pursuant to section 3 of the DNA Analysis Backlog Elimination Act of 2000 (42 U.S.C. § 14135a).

(b) DISCRETIONARY CONDITIONS

The court may impose other conditions of probation to the extent that such conditions (1) are reasonably related to (A) the nature and circumstances of the offense and the history and characteristics of the defendant; (B) the need for the sentence imposed to reflect the seriousness of the offense, to promote respect for the law, and to provide just punishment for the offense; (C) the need for the sentence imposed to afford adequate deterrence to criminal conduct;

(D) the need to protect the public from further crimes of the defendant; and (E) the need to provide the defendant with needed educational or vocational training, medical care, or other correctional treatment in the most effective manner; and (2) involve only such deprivations of liberty or property as are reasonably necessary for the purposes of sentencing indicated in 18 U.S.C. § 3553(a) (*see* 18 U.S.C. § 3563(b)).

(c)   "STANDARD" CONDITIONS (POLICY STATEMENT)

The following "standard" conditions are recommended for probation. Several of the conditions are expansions of the conditions required by statute:

(1)   The defendant shall report to the probation office in the federal judicial district where he or she is authorized to reside within 72 hours of the time the defendant was sentenced, unless the probation officer instructs the defendant to report to a different probation office or within a different time frame.

(2)   After initially reporting to the probation office, the defendant will receive instructions from the court or the probation officer about how and when to report to the probation officer, and the defendant shall report to the probation officer as instructed.

(3)   The defendant shall not knowingly leave the federal judicial district where he or she is authorized to reside without first getting permission from the court or the probation officer.

(4)   The defendant shall answer truthfully the questions asked by the probation officer.

(5)   The defendant shall live at a place approved by the probation officer. If the defendant plans to change where he or she lives or anything about his or her living arrangements (such as the people the defendant lives with), the defendant shall notify the probation officer at least 10 days before the change. If notifying the probation officer at least 10 days in advance is not possible due to unanticipated circumstances, the defendant shall notify the probation officer within 72 hours of becoming aware of a change or expected change.

(6)   The defendant shall allow the probation officer to visit the defendant at any time at his or her home or elsewhere, and the defendant shall permit the probation officer to take any items prohibited by the conditions of the defendant's supervision that he or she observes in plain view.

(7) The defendant shall work full time (at least 30 hours per week) at a lawful type of employment, unless the probation officer excuses the defendant from doing so. If the defendant does not have full-time employment he or she shall try to find full-time employment, unless the probation officer excuses the defendant from doing so. If the defendant plans to change where the defendant works or anything about his or her work (such as the position or the job responsibilities), the defendant shall notify the probation officer at least 10 days before the change. If notifying the probation officer at least 10 days in advance is not possible due to unanticipated circumstances, the defendant shall notify the probation officer within 72 hours of becoming aware of a change or expected change.

(8) The defendant shall not communicate or interact with someone the defendant knows is engaged in criminal activity. If the defendant knows someone has been convicted of a felony, the defendant shall not knowingly communicate or interact with that person without first getting the permission of the probation officer.

(9) If the defendant is arrested or questioned by a law enforcement officer, the defendant shall notify the probation officer within 72 hours.

(10) The defendant shall not own, possess, or have access to a firearm, ammunition, destructive device, or dangerous weapon (*i.e.*, anything that was designed, or was modified for, the specific purpose of causing bodily injury or death to another person, such as nunchakus or tasers).

(11) The defendant shall not act or make any agreement with a law enforcement agency to act as a confidential human source or informant without first getting the permission of the court.

(12) If the probation officer determines that the defendant poses a risk to another person (including an organization), the probation officer may require the defendant to notify the person about the risk and the defendant shall comply with that instruction. The probation officer may contact the person and confirm that the defendant has notified the person about the risk.

(13) The defendant shall follow the instructions of the probation officer related to the conditions of supervision.

(d) "SPECIAL" CONDITIONS (POLICY STATEMENT)

The following "special" conditions of probation are recommended in the circumstances described and, in addition, may otherwise be appropriate in particular cases:

(1) SUPPORT OF DEPENDENTS

(A) If the defendant has one or more dependents — a condition specifying that the defendant shall support his or her dependents.

(B) If the defendant is ordered by the government to make child support payments or to make payments to support a person caring for a child — a condition specifying that the defendant shall make the payments and comply with the other terms of the order.

(2) DEBT OBLIGATIONS

If an installment schedule of payment of restitution or a fine is imposed — a condition prohibiting the defendant from incurring new credit charges or opening additional lines of credit without approval of the probation officer unless the defendant is in compliance with the payment schedule.

(3) ACCESS TO FINANCIAL INFORMATION

If the court imposes an order of restitution, forfeiture, or notice to victims, or orders the defendant to pay a fine — a condition requiring the defendant to provide the probation officer access to any requested financial information.

(4) SUBSTANCE ABUSE

If the court has reason to believe that the defendant is an abuser of narcotics, other controlled substances or alcohol — (A) a condition requiring the defendant to participate in a program approved by the United States Probation Office for substance abuse, which program may include testing to determine whether the defendant has reverted to the use of drugs or alcohol; and (B) a condition specifying that the defendant shall not use or possess alcohol.

(5) MENTAL HEALTH PROGRAM PARTICIPATION

If the court has reason to believe that the defendant is in need of psychological or psychiatric treatment — a condition requiring that the defendant participate in a mental health program approved by the United States Probation Office.

(6) DEPORTATION

If (A) the defendant and the United States entered into a stipulation of deportation pursuant to section 238(c)(5) of the Immigration and Nationality Act (8 U.S.C. § 1228(c)(5)*); or (B) in the absence of a stipulation of deportation, if, after notice and hearing pursuant to such section, the Attorney General demonstrates by clear and convincing evidence that the alien is deportable — a condition ordering deportation by a United States district court or a United States magistrate judge.

*So in original. Probably should be 8 U.S.C. § 1228(d)(5).

(7) SEX OFFENSES

If the instant offense of conviction is a sex offense, as defined in Application Note 1 of the Commentary to §5D1.2 (Term of Supervised Release)—

(A) A condition requiring the defendant to participate in a program approved by the United States Probation Office for the treatment and monitoring of sex offenders.

(B) A condition limiting the use of a computer or an interactive computer service in cases in which the defendant used such items.

(C) A condition requiring the defendant to submit to a search, at any time, with or without a warrant, and by any law enforcement or probation officer, of the defendant's person and any property, house, residence, vehicle, papers, computer, other electronic communication or data storage devices or media, and effects, upon reasonable suspicion concerning a violation of a condition of probation or unlawful conduct by the defendant, or by any probation officer in the lawful discharge of the officer's supervision functions.

(e) ADDITIONAL CONDITIONS (POLICY STATEMENT)

The following "special conditions" may be appropriate on a case-by-case basis:

(1) COMMUNITY CONFINEMENT

Residence in a community treatment center, halfway house or similar facility may be imposed as a condition of probation. *See* §5F1.1 (Community Confinement).

(2) HOME DETENTION

Home detention may be imposed as a condition of probation but only as a substitute for imprisonment. *See* §5F1.2 (Home Detention).

(3) COMMUNITY SERVICE

Community service may be imposed as a condition of probation. *See* §5F1.3 (Community Service).

(4) OCCUPATIONAL RESTRICTIONS

Occupational restrictions may be imposed as a condition of probation. *See* §5F1.5 (Occupational Restrictions).

(5) CURFEW

A condition imposing a curfew may be imposed if the court concludes that restricting the defendant to his place of residence during evening and nighttime hours is necessary to provide just punishment for the offense, to protect the public from crimes that the defendant might commit during those hours, or to assist in the rehabilitation of the defendant. Electronic monitoring may be used as a means of surveillance to ensure compliance with a curfew order.

(6) INTERMITTENT CONFINEMENT

Intermittent confinement (custody for intervals of time) may be ordered as a condition of probation during the first year of probation. *See* §5F1.8 (Intermittent Confinement).

Commentary

Application Note:

1. **Application of Subsection (c)(4).**—Although the condition in subsection (c)(4) requires the defendant to "answer truthfully" the questions asked by the probation officer, a defendant's legitimate invocation of the Fifth Amendment privilege against self-incrimination in response to a probation officer's question shall not be considered a violation of this condition.

Historical Note	Effective November 1, 1987. Amended effective November 1, 1989 (amendments 273, 274, and 302); November 1, 1997 (amendment 569); November 1, 1998 (amendment 584); November 1, 2000 (amendment 605); November 1, 2001 (amendment 615); November 1, 2002 (amendment 644); November 1, 2004 (amendment 664); November 1, 2007 (amendments 701 and 711); November 1, 2009 (amendment 733); November 1, 2016 (amendment 803).

§5B1.4. [Deleted]

Historical Note	Effective November 1, 1987. Amended effective November 1, 1989 (amendments 271, 272, and 302), was deleted by consolidation with §§5B1.3 and 5D1.3 effective November 1, 1997 (amendment 569).

PART C — IMPRISONMENT

§5C1.1. Imposition of a Term of Imprisonment

(a) A sentence conforms with the guidelines for imprisonment if it is within the minimum and maximum terms of the applicable guideline range.

(b) If the applicable guideline range is in Zone A of the Sentencing Table, a sentence of imprisonment is not required, unless the applicable guideline in Chapter Two expressly requires such a term.

(c) If the applicable guideline range is in Zone B of the Sentencing Table, the minimum term may be satisfied by—

    (1) a sentence of imprisonment; or

    (2) a sentence of imprisonment that includes a term of supervised release with a condition that substitutes community confinement or home detention according to the schedule in subsection (e), provided that at least one month is satisfied by imprisonment; or

    (3) a sentence of probation that includes a condition or combination of conditions that substitute intermittent confinement, community confinement, or home detention for imprisonment according to the schedule in subsection (e).

(d) If the applicable guideline range is in Zone C of the Sentencing Table, the minimum term may be satisfied by—

    (1) a sentence of imprisonment; or

    (2) a sentence of imprisonment that includes a term of supervised release with a condition that substitutes community confinement or home detention according to the schedule in subsection (e), provided that at least one-half of the minimum term is satisfied by imprisonment.

(e) Schedule of Substitute Punishments:

    (1) One day of intermittent confinement in prison or jail for one day of imprisonment (each 24 hours of confinement is credited as one day of intermittent confinement, provided, however, that one day shall be credited for any calendar day during

which the defendant is employed in the community and confined during all remaining hours);

    (2) One day of community confinement (residence in a community treatment center, halfway house, or similar residential facility) for one day of imprisonment;

    (3) One day of home detention for one day of imprisonment.

(f) If the applicable guideline range is in Zone D of the Sentencing Table, the minimum term shall be satisfied by a sentence of imprisonment.

Commentary

Application Notes:

1. Subsection (a) provides that a sentence conforms with the guidelines for imprisonment if it is within the minimum and maximum terms of the applicable guideline range specified in the Sentencing Table in Part A of this Chapter. For example, if the defendant has an Offense Level of 20 and a Criminal History Category of I, the applicable guideline range is 33–41 months of imprisonment. Therefore, a sentence of imprisonment of at least thirty-three months, but not more than forty-one months, is within the applicable guideline range.

2. Subsection (b) provides that where the applicable guideline range is in Zone A of the Sentencing Table (*i.e.*, the minimum term of imprisonment specified in the applicable guideline range is zero months), the court is not required to impose a sentence of imprisonment unless a sentence of imprisonment or its equivalent is specifically required by the guideline applicable to the offense. Where imprisonment is not required, the court, for example, may impose a sentence of probation. In some cases, a fine appropriately may be imposed as the sole sanction.

3. Subsection (c) provides that where the applicable guideline range is in Zone B of the Sentencing Table (*i.e.*, the minimum term of imprisonment specified in the applicable guideline range is at least one but not more than nine months), the court has three options:

(A) It may impose a sentence of imprisonment.

(B) It may impose a sentence of probation provided that it includes a condition of probation requiring a period of intermittent confinement, community confinement, or home detention, or combination of intermittent confinement, community confinement, and home detention, sufficient to satisfy the minimum period of imprisonment specified in the guideline range. For example, where the guideline range is 4–10 months, a sentence of probation with a condition requiring at least four months of intermittent confinement, community confinement, or home detention would satisfy the minimum term of imprisonment specified in the guideline range.

(C) Or, it may impose a sentence of imprisonment that includes a term of supervised release with a condition that requires community confinement or home detention. In such case, at least one month must be satisfied by actual imprisonment and the remainder of the minimum term specified in the guideline range must be satisfied by community confinement or home detention. For example, where the guideline range is 4–10 months, a sentence of imprisonment of one month followed by a term of supervised release with a condition requiring three months of community confinement or home detention would satisfy the minimum term of imprisonment specified in the guideline range.

The preceding examples illustrate sentences that satisfy the minimum term of imprisonment required by the guideline range. The court, of course, may impose a sentence at a higher point within the applicable guideline range. For example, where the guideline range is 4–10 months, both a sentence of probation with a condition requiring six months of community confinement or home detention (under subsection (c)(3)) and a sentence of two months imprisonment followed by a term of supervised release with a condition requiring four months of community confinement or home detention (under subsection (c)(2)) would be within the guideline range.

4. Subsection (d) provides that where the applicable guideline range is in Zone C of the Sentencing Table (*i.e.*, the minimum term specified in the applicable guideline range is ten or twelve months), the court has two options:

(A) It may impose a sentence of imprisonment.

(B) Or, it may impose a sentence of imprisonment that includes a term of supervised release with a condition requiring community confinement or home detention. In such case, at least one-half of the minimum term specified in the guideline range must be satisfied by imprisonment, and the remainder of the minimum term specified in the guideline range must be satisfied by community confinement or home detention. For example, where the guideline range is 10–16 months, a sentence of five months imprisonment followed by a term of supervised release with a condition requiring five months community confinement or home detention would satisfy the minimum term of imprisonment required by the guideline range.

The preceding example illustrates a sentence that satisfies the minimum term of imprisonment required by the guideline range. The court, of course, may impose a sentence at a higher point within the guideline range. For example, where the guideline range is 10–16 months, both a sentence of five months imprisonment followed by a term of supervised release with a condition requiring six months of community confinement or home detention (under subsection (d)), and a sentence of ten months imprisonment followed by a term of supervised release with a condition requiring four months of community confinement or home detention (also under subsection (d)) would be within the guideline range.

5. Subsection (e) sets forth a schedule of imprisonment substitutes.

6. There may be cases in which a departure from the sentencing options authorized for Zone C of the Sentencing Table (under which at least half the minimum term must be satisfied by imprisonment) to the sentencing options authorized for Zone B of the Sentencing Table (under which all or most of the minimum term may be satisfied by intermittent confinement, community confinement, or home detention instead of imprisonment) is appropriate to accomplish a specific treatment purpose. Such a departure should be considered only in cases where the court finds that (A) the defendant is an abuser of narcotics, other controlled substances, or alcohol, or suffers from a significant mental illness, and (B) the defendant's criminality is related to the treatment problem to be addressed.

In determining whether such a departure is appropriate, the court should consider, among other things, (1) the likelihood that completion of the treatment program will successfully address the treatment problem, thereby reducing the risk to the public from further crimes of the defendant, and (2) whether imposition of less imprisonment than required by Zone C will increase the risk to the public from further crimes of the defendant.

Examples: The following examples both assume the applicable guideline range is 12–18 months and the court departs in accordance with this application note. Under Zone C rules, the defendant must be sentenced to at least six months imprisonment. (1) The defendant is a nonviolent drug offender in Criminal History Category I and probation is not prohibited by statute. The court departs downward to impose a sentence of probation, with twelve months of intermittent confinement, community confinement, or home detention and participation in a substance abuse treatment program as conditions of probation. (2) The defendant is convicted of a Class A or B felony, so probation is prohibited by statute (*see* §5B1.1(b)). The court departs downward to impose a sentence of one month imprisonment, with eleven months in community confinement or home detention and participation in a substance abuse treatment program as conditions of supervised release.

7. The use of substitutes for imprisonment as provided in subsections (c) and (d) is not recommended for most defendants with a criminal history category of III or above.

8. In a case in which community confinement in a residential treatment program is imposed to accomplish a specific treatment purpose, the court should consider the effectiveness of the residential treatment program.

9. Subsection (f) provides that, where the applicable guideline range is in Zone D of the Sentencing Table (*i.e.*, the minimum term of imprisonment specified in the applicable guideline range is 15 months or more), the minimum term must be satisfied by a sentence of imprisonment without the use of any of the imprisonment substitutes in subsection (e).

Historical Note	Effective November 1, 1987. Amended effective January 15, 1988 (amendment 51); November 1, 1989 (amendments 271, 275, and 302); November 1, 1992 (amendment 462); November 1, 2002 (amendment 646); November 1, 2009 (amendment 733); November 1, 2010 (amendment 738).

§5C1.2. Limitation on Applicability of Statutory Minimum Sentences in Certain Cases

(a) Except as provided in subsection (b), in the case of an offense under 21 U.S.C. § 841, § 844, § 846, § 960, or § 963, the court shall impose a sentence in accordance with the applicable guidelines without regard to any statutory minimum sentence, if the court finds that the defendant meets the criteria in 18 U.S.C. § 3553(f)(1)–(5) set forth below:

    (1) the defendant does not have more than 1 criminal history point, as determined under the sentencing guidelines before

application of subsection (b) of §4A1.3 (Departures Based on Inadequacy of Criminal History Category);

(2)   the defendant did not use violence or credible threats of violence or possess a firearm or other dangerous weapon (or induce another participant to do so) in connection with the offense;

(3)   the offense did not result in death or serious bodily injury to any person;

(4)   the defendant was not an organizer, leader, manager, or supervisor of others in the offense, as determined under the sentencing guidelines and was not engaged in a continuing criminal enterprise, as defined in 21 U.S.C. § 848; and

(5)   not later than the time of the sentencing hearing, the defendant has truthfully provided to the Government all information and evidence the defendant has concerning the offense or offenses that were part of the same course of conduct or of a common scheme or plan, but the fact that the defendant has no relevant or useful other information to provide or that the Government is already aware of the information shall not preclude a determination by the court that the defendant has complied with this requirement.

(b)   In the case of a defendant (1) who meets the criteria set forth in subsection (a); and (2) for whom the statutorily required minimum sentence is at least five years, the offense level applicable from Chapters Two (Offense Conduct) and Three (Adjustments) shall be not less than level **17**.

Commentary

Application Notes:

1.   "***More than 1 criminal history point, as determined under the sentencing guidelines***," as used in subsection (a)(1), means more than one criminal history point as determined under §4A1.1 (Criminal History Category) before application of subsection (b) of §4A1.3 (Departures Based on Inadequacy of Criminal History Category).

2.   "***Dangerous weapon***" and "***firearm***," as used in subsection (a)(2), and "***serious bodily injury***," as used in subsection (a)(3), are defined in the Commentary to §1B1.1 (Application Instructions).

3.   "***Offense***," as used in subsection (a)(2)–(4), and "***offense or offenses that were part of the same course of conduct or of a common scheme or plan***," as used in subsection (a)(5), mean the offense of conviction and all relevant conduct.

4. Consistent with §1B1.3 (Relevant Conduct), the term "*defendant*," as used in subsection (a)(2), limits the accountability of the defendant to his own conduct and conduct that he aided or abetted, counseled, commanded, induced, procured, or willfully caused.

5. "*Organizer, leader, manager, or supervisor of others in the offense, as determined under the sentencing guidelines*," as used in subsection (a)(4), means a defendant who receives an adjustment for an aggravating role under §3B1.1 (Aggravating Role).

6. "*Engaged in a continuing criminal enterprise*," as used in subsection (a)(4), is defined in 21 U.S.C. § 848(c). As a practical matter, it should not be necessary to apply this prong of subsection (a)(4) because (i) this section does not apply to a conviction under 21 U.S.C. § 848, and (ii) any defendant who "engaged in a continuing criminal enterprise" but is convicted of an offense to which this section applies will be an "organizer, leader, manager, or supervisor of others in the offense."

7. Information disclosed by the defendant with respect to subsection (a)(5) may be considered in determining the applicable guideline range, except where the use of such information is restricted under the provisions of §1B1.8 (Use of Certain Information). That is, subsection (a)(5) does not provide an independent basis for restricting the use of information disclosed by the defendant.

8. Under 18 U.S.C. § 3553(f), prior to its determination, the court shall afford the government an opportunity to make a recommendation. *See also* Fed. R. Crim. P. 32(f), (i).

9. A defendant who meets the criteria under this section is exempt from any otherwise applicable statutory minimum sentence of imprisonment and statutory minimum term of supervised release.

Background: This section sets forth the relevant provisions of 18 U.S.C. § 3553(f), as added by section 80001(a) of the Violent Crime Control and Law Enforcement Act of 1994, which limit the applicability of statutory minimum sentences in certain cases. Under the authority of section 80001(b) of that Act, the Commission has promulgated application notes to provide guidance in the application of 18 U.S.C. § 3553(f). *See also* H. Rep. No. 460, 103d Cong., 2d Sess. 3 (1994) (expressing intent to foster greater coordination between mandatory minimum sentencing and the sentencing guideline system).

Historical Note	Effective September 23, 1994 (amendment 509). Amended effective November 1, 1995 (amendment 515); November 1, 1996 (amendment 540); November 1, 1997 (amendment 570); November 1, 2001 (amendment 624); October 27, 2003 (amendment 651); November 1, 2004 (amendment 674); November 1, 2009 (amendment 736).

PART D — SUPERVISED RELEASE

§5D1.1. Imposition of a Term of Supervised Release

(a) The court shall order a term of supervised release to follow imprisonment—

    (1) when required by statute (*see* 18 U.S.C. § 3583(a)); or

    (2) except as provided in subsection (c), when a sentence of imprisonment of more than one year is imposed.

(b) The court may order a term of supervised release to follow imprisonment in any other case. *See* 18 U.S.C. § 3583(a).

(c) The court ordinarily should not impose a term of supervised release in a case in which supervised release is not required by statute and the defendant is a deportable alien who likely will be deported after imprisonment.

Commentary

Application Notes:

1. **Application of Subsection (a).**—Under subsection (a), the court is required to impose a term of supervised release to follow imprisonment when supervised release is required by statute or, except as provided in subsection (c), when a sentence of imprisonment of more than one year is imposed. The court may depart from this guideline and not impose a term of supervised release if supervised release is not required by statute and the court determines, after considering the factors set forth in Note 3, that supervised release is not necessary.

2. **Application of Subsection (b).**—Under subsection (b), the court may impose a term of supervised release to follow a term of imprisonment in any other case, after considering the factors set forth in Note 3.

3. **Factors to Be Considered.—**

(A) **Statutory Factors.**—In determining whether to impose a term of supervised release, the court is required by statute to consider, among other factors:

    (i) the nature and circumstances of the offense and the history and characteristics of the defendant;

    (ii) the need to afford adequate deterrence to criminal conduct, to protect the public from further crimes of the defendant, and to provide the defendant with needed educational or vocational training, medical care, or other correctional treatment in the most effective manner;

    (iii) the need to avoid unwarranted sentence disparities among defendants with similar records who have been found guilty of similar conduct; and

(iv)   the need to provide restitution to any victims of the offense.

See 18 U.S.C. § 3583(c).

(B)   **Criminal History.**—The court should give particular consideration to the defendant's criminal history (which is one aspect of the "history and characteristics of the defendant" in subparagraph (A)(i), above). In general, the more serious the defendant's criminal history, the greater the need for supervised release.

(C)   **Substance Abuse.**—In a case in which a defendant sentenced to imprisonment is an abuser of controlled substances or alcohol, it is highly recommended that a term of supervised release also be imposed. *See* §5H1.4 (Physical Condition, Including Drug or Alcohol Dependence or Abuse; Gambling Addiction).

(D)   **Domestic Violence.**—If the defendant is convicted for the first time of a domestic violence crime as defined in 18 U.S.C. § 3561(b), a term of supervised release is required by statute. *See* 18 U.S.C. § 3583(a). Such a defendant is also required by statute to attend an approved rehabilitation program, if available within a 50-mile radius of the legal residence of the defendant. *See* 18 U.S.C. § 3583(d); §5D1.3(a)(3). In any other case involving domestic violence or stalking in which the defendant is sentenced to imprisonment, it is highly recommended that a term of supervised release also be imposed.

4.   **Community Confinement or Home Detention Following Imprisonment.**—A term of supervised release must be imposed if the court wishes to impose a "split sentence" under which the defendant serves a term of imprisonment followed by a period of community confinement or home detention pursuant to subsection (c)(2) or (d)(2) of §5C1.1 (Imposition of a Term of Imprisonment). In such a case, the period of community confinement or home detention is imposed as a condition of supervised release.

5.   **Application of Subsection (c).**—In a case in which the defendant is a deportable alien specified in subsection (c) and supervised release is not required by statute, the court ordinarily should not impose a term of supervised release. Unless such a defendant legally returns to the United States, supervised release is unnecessary. If such a defendant illegally returns to the United States, the need to afford adequate deterrence and protect the public ordinarily is adequately served by a new prosecution. The court should, however, consider imposing a term of supervised release on such a defendant if the court determines it would provide an added measure of deterrence and protection based on the facts and circumstances of a particular case.

Historical Note	Effective November 1, 1987. Amended effective November 1, 1989 (amendment 302); November 1, 1995 (amendment 529); November 1, 2010 (amendment 747); November 1, 2011 (amendment 756); November 1, 2014 (amendment 781).

§5D1.2.   Term of Supervised Release

(a)   Except as provided in subsections (b) and (c), if a term of supervised release is ordered, the length of the term shall be:

(1) At least two years but not more than five years for a defendant convicted of a Class A or B felony. *See* 18 U.S.C. § 3583(b)(1).

(2) At least one year but not more than three years for a defendant convicted of a Class C or D felony. *See* 18 U.S.C. § 3583(b)(2).

(3) One year for a defendant convicted of a Class E felony or a Class A misdemeanor. *See* 18 U.S.C. § 3583(b)(3).

(b) Notwithstanding subdivisions (a)(1) through (3), the length of the term of supervised release shall be not less than the minimum term of years specified for the offense under subdivisions (a)(1) through (3) and may be up to life, if the offense is—

(1) any offense listed in 18 U.S.C. § 2332b(g)(5)(B), the commission of which resulted in, or created a foreseeable risk of, death or serious bodily injury to another person; or

(2) a sex offense.

(Policy Statement) If the instant offense of conviction is a sex offense, however, the statutory maximum term of supervised release is recommended.

(c) The term of supervised release imposed shall be not less than any statutorily required term of supervised release.

Commentary

Application Notes:

1. **Definitions.**—For purposes of this guideline:

"*Sex offense*" means (A) an offense, perpetrated against a minor, under (i) chapter 109A of title 18, United States Code; (ii) chapter 110 of such title, not including a recordkeeping offense; (iii) chapter 117 of such title, not including transmitting information about a minor or filing a factual statement about an alien individual; (iv) an offense under 18 U.S.C. § 1201; or (v) an offense under 18 U.S.C. § 1591; or (B) an attempt or a conspiracy to commit any offense described in subdivisions (A)(i) through (v) of this note. Such term does not include an offense under 18 U.S.C. § 2250 (Failure to register).

"*Minor*" means (A) an individual who had not attained the age of 18 years; (B) an individual, whether fictitious or not, who a law enforcement officer represented to a participant (i) had not attained the age of 18 years; and (ii) could be provided for the purposes of engaging in sexually explicit conduct; or (C) an undercover law enforcement officer who represented to a participant that the officer had not attained the age of 18 years.

2. **Safety Valve Cases.**—A defendant who qualifies under §5C1.2 (Limitation on Applicability of Statutory Minimum Sentence in Certain Cases) is not subject to any statutory minimum sentence of supervised release. *See* 18 U.S.C. § 3553(f). In such a case, the term of supervised release shall be determined under subsection (a).

3. **Substantial Assistance Cases.**—Upon motion of the Government, a defendant who has provided substantial assistance in the investigation or prosecution of another person who has committed an offense may be sentenced to a term of supervised release that is less than any minimum required by statute or the guidelines. *See* 18 U.S.C. § 3553(e), §5K1.1 (Substantial Assistance to Authorities).

4. **Factors Considered.**—The factors to be considered in determining the length of a term of supervised release are the same as the factors considered in determining whether to impose such a term. *See* 18 U.S.C. § 3583(c); Application Note 3 to §5D1.1 (Imposition of a Term of Supervised Release). The court should ensure that the term imposed on the defendant is long enough to address the purposes of imposing supervised release on the defendant.

5. **Early Termination and Extension.**—The court has authority to terminate or extend a term of supervised release. *See* 18 U.S.C. § 3583(e)(1), (2). The court is encouraged to exercise this authority in appropriate cases. The prospect of exercising this authority is a factor the court may wish to consider in determining the length of a term of supervised release. For example, the court may wish to consider early termination of supervised release if the defendant is an abuser of narcotics, other controlled substances, or alcohol who, while on supervised release, successfully completes a treatment program, thereby reducing the risk to the public from further crimes of the defendant.

6. **Application of Subsection (c).**—Subsection (c) specifies how a statutorily required minimum term of supervised release may affect the minimum term of supervised release provided by the guidelines.

    For example, if subsection (a) provides a range of two years to five years, but the relevant statute requires a minimum term of supervised release of three years and a maximum term of life, the term of supervised release provided by the guidelines is restricted by subsection (c) to three years to five years. Similarly, if subsection (a) provides a range of two years to five years, but the relevant statute requires a minimum term of supervised release of five years and a maximum term of life, the term of supervised release provided by the guidelines is five years.

    The following example illustrates the interaction of subsections (a) and (c) when subsection (b) is also involved. In this example, subsection (a) provides a range of two years to five years; the relevant statute requires a minimum term of supervised release of five years and a maximum term of life; and the offense is a sex offense under subsection (b). The effect of subsection (b) is to raise the maximum term of supervised release from five years (as provided by subsection (a)) to life, yielding a range of two years to life. The term of supervised release provided by the guidelines is then restricted by subsection (c) to five years to life. In this example, a term of supervised release of more than five years would be a guideline sentence. In addition, subsection (b) contains a policy statement recommending that the maximum — a life term of supervised release — be imposed.

Background: This section specifies the length of a term of supervised release that is to be imposed. Subsection (c) applies to statutes, such as the Anti-Drug Abuse Act of 1986, that require imposition of a specific minimum term of supervised release.

| *Historical Note* | Effective November 1, 1987. Amended effective January 15, 1988 (amendment 52); November 1, 1989 (amendment 302); November 1, 1995 (amendment 529); November 1, 1997 (amendment 570); November 1, 2001 (amendment 615); November 1, 2002 (amendments 637 and 646); November 1, 2004 (amendment 664); November 1, 2005 (amendment 679); November 1, 2007 (amendment 701); November 1, 2009 (amendment 736); November 1, 2011 (amendment 756); November 1, 2014 (amendment 786). |

---

§5D1.3.   Conditions of Supervised Release

(a)   MANDATORY CONDITIONS

   (1)   The defendant shall not commit another federal, state or local offense (*see* 18 U.S.C. § 3583(d)).

   (2)   The defendant shall not unlawfully possess a controlled substance (*see* 18 U.S.C. § 3583(d)).

   (3)   The defendant who is convicted for a domestic violence crime as defined in 18 U.S.C. § 3561(b) for the first time shall attend a public, private, or private non-profit offender rehabilitation program that has been approved by the court, in consultation with a State Coalition Against Domestic Violence or other appropriate experts, if an approved program is available within a 50-mile radius of the legal residence of the defendant (*see* 18 U.S.C. § 3583(d)).

   (4)   The defendant shall refrain from any unlawful use of a controlled substance and submit to one drug test within 15 days of release on probation and at least two periodic drug tests thereafter (as determined by the court) for use of a controlled substance, but the condition stated in this paragraph may be ameliorated or suspended by the court for any individual defendant if the defendant's presentence report or other reliable information indicates a low risk of future substance abuse by the defendant (*see* 18 U.S.C. § 3583(d)).

   (5)   If a fine is imposed and has not been paid upon release to supervised release, the defendant shall adhere to an installment schedule to pay that fine (*see* 18 U.S.C. § 3624(e)).

   (6)   The defendant shall (A) make restitution in accordance with 18 U.S.C. §§ 2248, 2259, 2264, 2327, 3663, 3663A, and 3664; and (B) pay the assessment imposed in accordance with 18 U.S.C. § 3013. If there is a court-established payment schedule for making restitution or paying the assessment (*see* 18 U.S.C. § 3572(d)), the defendant shall adhere to the schedule.

   (7)   If the defendant is required to register under the Sex Offender Registration and Notification Act, the defendant shall comply with the requirements of that Act (*see* 18 U.S.C. § 3583(d)).

(8) The defendant shall submit to the collection of a DNA sample from the defendant at the direction of the United States Probation Office if the collection of such a sample is authorized pursuant to section 3 of the DNA Analysis Backlog Elimination Act of 2000 (42 U.S.C. § 14135a).

(b) DISCRETIONARY CONDITIONS

The court may impose other conditions of supervised release to the extent that such conditions (1) are reasonably related to (A) the nature and circumstances of the offense and the history and characteristics of the defendant; (B) the need for the sentence imposed to afford adequate deterrence to criminal conduct; (C) the need to protect the public from further crimes of the defendant; and (D) the need to provide the defendant with needed educational or vocational training, medical care, or other correctional treatment in the most effective manner; and (2) involve no greater deprivation of liberty than is reasonably necessary for the purposes set forth above and are consistent with any pertinent policy statements issued by the Sentencing Commission.

(c) "STANDARD" CONDITIONS (POLICY STATEMENT)

The following "standard" conditions are recommended for supervised release. Several of the conditions are expansions of the conditions required by statute:

(1) The defendant shall report to the probation office in the federal judicial district where he or she is authorized to reside within 72 hours of release from imprisonment, unless the probation officer instructs the defendant to report to a different probation office or within a different time frame.

(2) After initially reporting to the probation office, the defendant will receive instructions from the court or the probation officer about how and when to report to the probation officer, and the defendant shall report to the probation officer as instructed.

(3) The defendant shall not knowingly leave the federal judicial district where he or she is authorized to reside without first getting permission from the court or the probation officer.

(4) The defendant shall answer truthfully the questions asked by the probation officer.

(5) The defendant shall live at a place approved by the probation officer. If the defendant plans to change where he or she lives

or anything about his or her living arrangements (such as the people the defendant lives with), the defendant shall notify the probation officer at least 10 days before the change. If notifying the probation officer at least 10 days in advance is not possible due to unanticipated circumstances, the defendant shall notify the probation officer within 72 hours of becoming aware of a change or expected change.

(6) The defendant shall allow the probation officer to visit the defendant at any time at his or her home or elsewhere, and the defendant shall permit the probation officer to take any items prohibited by the conditions of the defendant's supervision that he or she observes in plain view.

(7) The defendant shall work full time (at least 30 hours per week) at a lawful type of employment, unless the probation officer excuses the defendant from doing so. If the defendant does not have full-time employment he or she shall try to find full-time employment, unless the probation officer excuses the defendant from doing so. If the defendant plans to change where the defendant works or anything about his or her work (such as the position or the job responsibilities), the defendant shall notify the probation officer at least 10 days before the change. If notifying the probation officer in advance is not possible due to unanticipated circumstances, the defendant shall notify the probation officer within 72 hours of becoming aware of a change or expected change.

(8) The defendant shall not communicate or interact with someone the defendant knows is engaged in criminal activity. If the defendant knows someone has been convicted of a felony, the defendant shall not knowingly communicate or interact with that person without first getting the permission of the probation officer.

(9) If the defendant is arrested or questioned by a law enforcement officer, the defendant shall notify the probation officer within 72 hours.

(10) The defendant shall not own, possess, or have access to a firearm, ammunition, destructive device, or dangerous weapon (*i.e.*, anything that was designed, or was modified for, the specific purpose of causing bodily injury or death to another person, such as nunchakus or tasers).

(11) The defendant shall not act or make any agreement with a law enforcement agency to act as a confidential human source or informant without first getting the permission of the court.

(12) If the probation officer determines that the defendant poses a risk to another person (including an organization), the probation officer may require the defendant to notify the person about the risk and the defendant shall comply with that instruction. The probation officer may contact the person and confirm that the defendant has notified the person about the risk.

(13) The defendant shall follow the instructions of the probation officer related to the conditions of supervision.

(d) "SPECIAL" CONDITIONS (POLICY STATEMENT)

The following "special" conditions of supervised release are recommended in the circumstances described and, in addition, may otherwise be appropriate in particular cases:

(1) SUPPORT OF DEPENDENTS

(A) If the defendant has one or more dependents — a condition specifying that the defendant shall support his or her dependents.

(B) If the defendant is ordered by the government to make child support payments or to make payments to support a person caring for a child — a condition specifying that the defendant shall make the payments and comply with the other terms of the order.

(2) DEBT OBLIGATIONS

If an installment schedule of payment of restitution or a fine is imposed — a condition prohibiting the defendant from incurring new credit charges or opening additional lines of credit without approval of the probation officer unless the defendant is in compliance with the payment schedule.

(3) ACCESS TO FINANCIAL INFORMATION

If the court imposes an order of restitution, forfeiture, or notice to victims, or orders the defendant to pay a fine — a condition requiring the defendant to provide the probation officer access to any requested financial information.

(4) SUBSTANCE ABUSE

If the court has reason to believe that the defendant is an abuser of narcotics, other controlled substances or alcohol — (A) a condition requiring the defendant to participate in a program approved by the United States Probation Office for substance abuse, which program may include testing to determine whether the defendant has reverted to the use of drugs or alcohol; and (B) a condition specifying that the defendant shall not use or possess alcohol.

(5) MENTAL HEALTH PROGRAM PARTICIPATION

If the court has reason to believe that the defendant is in need of psychological or psychiatric treatment — a condition requiring that the defendant participate in a mental health program approved by the United States Probation Office.

(6) DEPORTATION

If (A) the defendant and the United States entered into a stipulation of deportation pursuant to section 238(c)(5) of the Immigration and Nationality Act (8 U.S.C. § 1228(c)(5)*); or (B) in the absence of a stipulation of deportation, if, after notice and hearing pursuant to such section, the Attorney General demonstrates by clear and convincing evidence that the alien is deportable — a condition ordering deportation by a United States district court or a United States magistrate judge.

*So in original. Probably should be 8 U.S.C. § 1228(d)(5).

(7) SEX OFFENSES

If the instant offense of conviction is a sex offense, as defined in Application Note 1 of the Commentary to §5D1.2 (Term of Supervised Release) —

(A) A condition requiring the defendant to participate in a program approved by the United States Probation Office for the treatment and monitoring of sex offenders.

(B) A condition limiting the use of a computer or an interactive computer service in cases in which the defendant used such items.

(C) A condition requiring the defendant to submit to a search, at any time, with or without a warrant, and by any law enforcement or probation officer, of the defendant's person and any property, house, residence, vehicle, papers, computer, other electronic communication or data storage devices or media, and effects upon reasonable suspicion concerning a violation of a condition of supervised release or unlawful conduct by the defendant, or by any probation officer in the lawful discharge of the officer's supervision functions.

(8) UNPAID RESTITUTION, FINES, OR SPECIAL ASSESSMENTS

If the defendant has any unpaid amount of restitution, fines, or special assessments, the defendant shall notify the probation officer of any material change in the defendant's economic circumstances that might affect the defendant's ability to pay.

(e) ADDITIONAL CONDITIONS (POLICY STATEMENT)

The following "special conditions" may be appropriate on a case-by-case basis:

(1) COMMUNITY CONFINEMENT

Residence in a community treatment center, halfway house or similar facility may be imposed as a condition of supervised release. *See* §5F1.1 (Community Confinement).

(2) HOME DETENTION

Home detention may be imposed as a condition of supervised release, but only as a substitute for imprisonment. *See* §5F1.2 (Home Detention).

(3) COMMUNITY SERVICE

Community service may be imposed as a condition of supervised release. *See* §5F1.3 (Community Service).

(4) OCCUPATIONAL RESTRICTIONS

Occupational restrictions may be imposed as a condition of supervised release. *See* §5F1.5 (Occupational Restrictions).

(5) CURFEW

A condition imposing a curfew may be imposed if the court concludes that restricting the defendant to his place of residence during evening and nighttime hours is necessary to protect the public from crimes that the defendant might commit during those hours, or to assist in the rehabilitation of the defendant. Electronic monitoring may be used as a means of surveillance to ensure compliance with a curfew order.

(6) INTERMITTENT CONFINEMENT

Intermittent confinement (custody for intervals of time) may be ordered as a condition of supervised release during the first year of supervised release, but only for a violation of a condition of supervised release in accordance with 18 U.S.C. § 3583(e)(2) and only when facilities are available. *See* §5F1.8 (Intermittent Confinement).

Commentary

Application Note:

1. **Application of Subsection (c)(4).**—Although the condition in subsection (c)(4) requires the defendant to "answer truthfully" the questions asked by the probation officer, a defendant's legitimate invocation of the Fifth Amendment privilege against self-incrimination in response to a probation officer's question shall not be considered a violation of this condition.

Historical Note	Effective November 1, 1987. Amended effective November 1, 1989 (amendments 276, 277, and 302); November 1, 1997 (amendment 569); November 1, 1998 (amendment 584); November 1, 2000 (amendment 605); November 1, 2001 (amendment 615); November 1, 2002 (amendments 644 and 646); November 1, 2004 (amendment 664); November 1, 2007 (amendments 701 and 711); November 1, 2009 (amendment 733); November 1, 2016 (amendment 803).

PART E — RESTITUTION, FINES, ASSESSMENTS, FORFEITURES

§5E1.1.   Restitution

(a)   In the case of an identifiable victim, the court shall—

(1)   enter a restitution order for the full amount of the victim's loss, if such order is authorized under 18 U.S.C. § 1593, § 2248, § 2259, § 2264, § 2327, § 3663, or § 3663A, or 21 U.S.C. § 853(q); or

(2)   impose a term of probation or supervised release with a condition requiring restitution for the full amount of the victim's loss, if the offense is not an offense for which restitution is authorized under 18 U.S.C. § 3663(a)(1) but otherwise meets the criteria for an order of restitution under that section.

(b)   *Provided*, that the provisions of subsection (a) do not apply—

(1)   when full restitution has been made; or

(2)   in the case of a restitution order under 18 U.S.C. § 3663; a restitution order under 18 U.S.C. § 3663A that pertains to an offense against property described in 18 U.S.C. § 3663A(c)(1)(A)(ii); or a condition of restitution imposed pursuant to subsection (a)(2) above, to the extent the court finds, from facts on the record, that (A) the number of identifiable victims is so large as to make restitution impracticable; or (B) determining complex issues of fact related to the cause or amount of the victim's losses would complicate or prolong the sentencing process to a degree that the need to provide restitution to any victim is outweighed by the burden on the sentencing process.

(c)   If a defendant is ordered to make restitution to an identifiable victim and to pay a fine, the court shall order that any money paid by the defendant shall first be applied to satisfy the order of restitution.

(d)   In a case where there is no identifiable victim and the defendant was convicted under 21 U.S.C. § 841, § 848(a), § 849, § 856, § 861, or § 863, the court, taking into consideration the amount of public harm caused by the offense and other relevant factors, shall order an amount of community restitution not to exceed the fine imposed under §5E1.2.

(e) A restitution order may direct the defendant to make a single, lump sum payment, partial payments at specified intervals, in-kind payments, or a combination of payments at specified intervals and in-kind payments. *See* 18 U.S.C. § 3664(f)(3)(A). An in-kind payment may be in the form of (1) return of property; (2) replacement of property; or (3) if the victim agrees, services rendered to the victim or to a person or organization other than the victim. *See* 18 U.S.C. § 3664(f)(4).

(f) A restitution order may direct the defendant to make nominal periodic payments if the court finds from facts on the record that the economic circumstances of the defendant do not allow the payment of any amount of a restitution order and do not allow for the payment of the full amount of a restitution order in the foreseeable future under any reasonable schedule of payments.

(g) Special Instruction

(1) This guideline applies only to a defendant convicted of an offense committed on or after November 1, 1997. Notwithstanding the provisions of §1B1.11 (Use of Guidelines Manual in Effect on Date of Sentencing), use the former §5E1.1 (set forth in Appendix C, amendment 571) in lieu of this guideline in any other case.

Commentary

Application Note:

1. The court shall not order community restitution under subsection (d) if it appears likely that such an award would interfere with a forfeiture under Chapter 46 or 96 of Title 18, United States Code, or under the Controlled Substances Act (21 U.S.C. § 801 *et seq.*). *See* 18 U.S.C. § 3663(c)(4).

   Furthermore, a penalty assessment under 18 U.S.C. § 3013 or a fine under Subchapter C of Chapter 227 of Title 18, United States Code, shall take precedence over an order of community restitution under subsection (d). *See* 18 U.S.C. § 3663(c)(5).

Background: Section 3553(a)(7) of Title 18, United States Code, requires the court, "in determining the particular sentence to be imposed," to consider "the need to provide restitution to any victims of the offense." Orders of restitution are authorized under 18 U.S.C. §§ 1593, 2248, 2259, 2264, 2327, 3663, and 3663A, and 21 U.S.C. § 853(q). For offenses for which an order of restitution is not authorized, restitution may be imposed as a condition of probation or supervised release.

Subsection (d) implements the instruction to the Commission in section 205 of the Antiterrorism and Effective Death Penalty Act of 1996. This provision directs the Commission to develop guidelines for community restitution in connection with certain drug offenses where there is no identifiable victim but the offense causes "public harm."

To the extent that any of the above-noted statutory provisions conflict with the provisions of this guideline, the applicable statutory provision shall control.

Historical Note	Effective November 1, 1987. Amended effective January 15, 1988 (amendment 53); November 1, 1989 (amendments 278, 279, and 302); November 1, 1991 (amendment 383); November 1, 1993 (amendment 501); November 1, 1995 (amendment 530); November 1, 1997 (amendment 571); May 1, 2001 (amendment 612); November 1, 2001 (amendment 627).

§5E1.2.   Fines for Individual Defendants

(a)   The court shall impose a fine in all cases, except where the defendant establishes that he is unable to pay and is not likely to become able to pay any fine.

(b)   The applicable fine guideline range is that specified in subsection (c) below. If, however, the guideline for the offense in Chapter Two provides a specific rule for imposing a fine, that rule takes precedence over subsection (c) of this section.

(c)   (1)   The minimum of the fine guideline range is the amount shown in column A of the table below.

(2)   Except as specified in (4) below, the maximum of the fine guideline range is the amount shown in column B of the table below.

(3)   FINE TABLE

OFFENSE LEVEL	A MINIMUM	B MAXIMUM
3 and below	$200	$9,500
4–5	$500	$9,500
6–7	$1,000	$9,500
8–9	$2,000	$20,000
10–11	$4,000	$40,000
12–13	$5,500	$55,000
14–15	$7,500	$75,000
16–17	$10,000	$95,000
18–19	$10,000	$100,000
20–22	$15,000	$150,000
23–25	$20,000	$200,000
26–28	$25,000	$250,000
29–31	$30,000	$300,000
32–34	$35,000	$350,000
35–37	$40,000	$400,000
38 and above	$50,000	$500,000.

        (4)   Subsection (c)(2), limiting the maximum fine, does not apply if the defendant is convicted under a statute authorizing (A) a maximum fine greater than $500,000, or (B) a fine for each day of violation. In such cases, the court may impose a fine up to the maximum authorized by the statute.

(d)   In determining the amount of the fine, the court shall consider:

        (1)   the need for the combined sentence to reflect the seriousness of the offense (including the harm or loss to the victim and the gain to the defendant), to promote respect for the law, to provide just punishment and to afford adequate deterrence;

        (2)   any evidence presented as to the defendant's ability to pay the fine (including the ability to pay over a period of time) in light of his earning capacity and financial resources;

        (3)   the burden that the fine places on the defendant and his dependents relative to alternative punishments;

        (4)   any restitution or reparation that the defendant has made or is obligated to make;

        (5)   any collateral consequences of conviction, including civil obligations arising from the defendant's conduct;

        (6)   whether the defendant previously has been fined for a similar offense;

        (7)   the expected costs to the government of any term of probation, or term of imprisonment and term of supervised release imposed; and

        (8)   any other pertinent equitable considerations.

The amount of the fine should always be sufficient to ensure that the fine, taken together with other sanctions imposed, is punitive.

(e)   If the defendant establishes that (1) he is not able and, even with the use of a reasonable installment schedule, is not likely to become able to pay all or part of the fine required by the preceding provisions, or (2) imposition of a fine would unduly burden the defendant's dependents, the court may impose a lesser fine or waive the fine. In these circumstances, the court shall consider alternative sanctions in lieu of all or a portion of the fine, and must still impose a total combined sanction that is punitive. Although any additional sanction not proscribed by the guidelines is permissible, community service is the generally preferable alternative in such instances.

(f)   If the defendant establishes that payment of the fine in a lump sum would have an unduly severe impact on him or his dependents, the court should establish an installment schedule for payment of the fine. The length of the installment schedule generally should not exceed twelve months, and shall not exceed the maximum term of probation authorized for the offense. The defendant should be required to pay a substantial installment at the time of sentencing. If the court authorizes a defendant sentenced to probation or supervised release to pay a fine on an installment schedule, the court shall require as a condition of probation or supervised release that the defendant pay the fine according to the schedule. The court also may impose a condition prohibiting the defendant from incurring new credit charges or opening additional lines of credit unless he is in compliance with the payment schedule.

(g)   If the defendant knowingly fails to pay a delinquent fine, the court shall resentence him in accordance with 18 U.S.C. § 3614.

(h)   Special Instruction

    (1)   For offenses committed prior to November 1, 2015, use the applicable fine guideline range that was set forth in the version of §5E1.2(c) that was in effect on November 1, 2014, rather than the applicable fine guideline range set forth in subsection (c) above.

Commentary

Application Notes:

1.   A fine may be the sole sanction if the guidelines do not require a term of imprisonment. If, however, the fine is not paid in full at the time of sentencing, it is recommended that the court sentence the defendant to a term of probation, with payment of the fine as a condition of probation. If a fine is imposed in addition to a term of imprisonment, it is recommended that the court impose a term of supervised release following imprisonment as a means of enforcing payment of the fine.

2.   In general, the maximum fine permitted by law as to each count of conviction is $250,000 for a felony or for any misdemeanor resulting in death; $100,000 for a Class A misdemeanor; and $5,000 for any other offense. 18 U.S.C. § 3571(b)(3)–(7). However, higher or lower limits may apply when specified by statute. 18 U.S.C. § 3571(b)(1), (e). As an alternative maximum, the court may fine the defendant up to the greater of twice the gross gain or twice the gross loss. 18 U.S.C. § 3571(b)(2), (d).

3.   The determination of the fine guideline range may be dispensed with entirely upon a court determination of present and future inability to pay any fine. The inability of a defendant to post bail bond (having otherwise been determined eligible for release) and

the fact that a defendant is represented by (or was determined eligible for) assigned counsel are significant indicators of present inability to pay any fine. In conjunction with other factors, they may also indicate that the defendant is not likely to become able to pay any fine.

4. The Commission envisions that for most defendants, the maximum of the guideline fine range from subsection (c) will be at least twice the amount of gain or loss resulting from the offense. Where, however, two times either the amount of gain to the defendant or the amount of loss caused by the offense exceeds the maximum of the fine guideline, an upward departure from the fine guideline may be warranted.

Moreover, where a sentence within the applicable fine guideline range would not be sufficient to ensure both the disgorgement of any gain from the offense that otherwise would not be disgorged (*e.g.*, by restitution or forfeiture) and an adequate punitive fine, an upward departure from the fine guideline range may be warranted.

5. Subsection (c)(4) applies to statutes that contain special provisions permitting larger fines; the guidelines do not limit maximum fines in such cases. These statutes include, among others: 21 U.S.C. §§ 841(b) and 960(b), which authorize fines up to $8 million in offenses involving the manufacture, distribution, or importation of certain controlled substances; 21 U.S.C. § 848(a), which authorizes fines up to $4 million in offenses involving the manufacture or distribution of controlled substances by a continuing criminal enterprise; 18 U.S.C. § 1956(a), which authorizes a fine equal to the greater of $500,000 or two times the value of the monetary instruments or funds involved in offenses involving money laundering of financial instruments; 18 U.S.C. § 1957(b)(2), which authorizes a fine equal to two times the amount of any criminally derived property involved in a money laundering transaction; 33 U.S.C. § 1319(c), which authorizes a fine of up to $50,000 per day for violations of the Water Pollution Control Act; 42 U.S.C. § 6928(d), which authorizes a fine of up to $50,000 per day for violations of the Resource Conservation Act; and 52 U.S.C. § 30109(d)(1)(D), which authorizes, for violations of the Federal Election Campaign Act under 52 U.S.C. § 30122, a fine up to the greater of $50,000 or 1,000 percent of the amount of the violation, and which requires, in the case of such a violation, a minimum fine of not less than 300 percent of the amount of the violation.

There may be cases in which the defendant has entered into a conciliation agreement with the Federal Election Commission under section 309 of the Federal Election Campaign Act of 1971 in order to correct or prevent a violation of such Act by the defendant. The existence of a conciliation agreement between the defendant and Federal Election Commission, and the extent of compliance with that conciliation agreement, may be appropriate factors in determining at what point within the applicable fine guideline range to sentence the defendant, unless the defendant began negotiations toward a conciliation agreement after becoming aware of a criminal investigation.

6. The existence of income or assets that the defendant failed to disclose may justify a larger fine than that which otherwise would be warranted under this section. The court may base its conclusion as to this factor on information revealing significant unexplained expenditures by the defendant or unexplained possession of assets that do not comport with the defendant's reported income. If the court concludes that the defendant willfully misrepresented all or part of his income or assets, it may increase the offense level and resulting sentence in accordance with Chapter Three, Part C (Obstruction and Related Adjustments).

7. In considering subsection (d)(7), the court may be guided by reports published by the Bureau of Prisons and the Administrative Office of the United States Courts concerning average costs.

Historical Note	Effective November 1, 1987. Amended effective January 15, 1988 (amendment 54); November 1, 1989 (amendments 280, 281, and 302); November 1, 1990 (amendment 356); November 1, 1991 (amendment 384); November 1, 1997 (amendment 572); November 1, 2002 (amendment 646); January 25, 2003 (amendment 648); November 1, 2003 (amendment 656); November 1, 2011 (amendment 758); November 1, 2015 (amendments 791 and 796).

§5E1.3. Special Assessments

A special assessment must be imposed on a convicted defendant in the amount prescribed by statute.

Commentary

Application Notes:

1. This guideline applies only if the defendant is an individual. *See* §8E1.1 for special assessments applicable to organizations.

2. The following special assessments are provided by statute (18 U.S.C. § 3013):

    FOR OFFENSES COMMITTED BY INDIVIDUALS ON OR AFTER APRIL 24, 1996:
    (A) $100, if convicted of a felony;
    (B) $25, if convicted of a Class A misdemeanor;
    (C) $10, if convicted of a Class B misdemeanor;
    (D) $5, if convicted of a Class C misdemeanor or an infraction.

    FOR OFFENSES COMMITTED BY INDIVIDUALS ON OR AFTER NOVEMBER 18, 1988 BUT PRIOR TO APRIL 24, 1996:
    (E) $50, if convicted of a felony;
    (F) $25, if convicted of a Class A misdemeanor;
    (G) $10, if convicted of a Class B misdemeanor;
    (H) $5, if convicted of a Class C misdemeanor or an infraction.

    FOR OFFENSES COMMITTED BY INDIVIDUALS PRIOR TO NOVEMBER 18, 1988:
    (I) $50, if convicted of a felony;
    (J) $25, if convicted of a misdemeanor.

3. A special assessment is required by statute for each count of conviction.

Background: Section 3013 of Title 18, United States Code, added by The Victims of Crimes Act of 1984, Pub. L. No. 98–473, Title II, Chap. XIV, requires courts to impose special assessments on convicted defendants for the purpose of funding the Crime Victims Fund established by the same legislation.

| *Historical* *Note* | Effective November 1, 1987. Amended effective November 1, 1989 (amendments 282 and 302); November 1, 1997 (amendment 573). |

§5E1.4.   Forfeiture

Forfeiture is to be imposed upon a convicted defendant as provided by statute.

Commentary

Background: Forfeiture provisions exist in various statutes. For example, 18 U.S.C. § 3554 requires the court imposing a sentence under 18 U.S.C. § 1962 (proscribing the use of the proceeds of racketeering activities in the operation of an enterprise engaged in interstate commerce) or Titles II and III of the Comprehensive Drug Abuse Prevention and Control Act of 1970 (proscribing the manufacture and distribution of controlled substances) to order the forfeiture of property in accordance with 18 U.S.C. § 1963 and 21 U.S.C. § 853, respectively. Those provisions require the automatic forfeiture of certain property upon conviction of their respective underlying offenses.

In addition, the provisions of 18 U.S.C. §§ 3681–3682 authorizes the court, in certain circumstances, to order the forfeiture of a violent criminal's proceeds from the depiction of his crime in a book, movie, or other medium. Those sections authorize the deposit of proceeds in an escrow account in the Crime Victims Fund of the United States Treasury. The money is to remain available in the account for five years to satisfy claims brought against the defendant by the victim(s) of his offenses. At the end of the five-year period, the court may require that any proceeds remaining in the account be released from escrow and paid into the Fund. 18 U.S.C. § 3681(c)(2).

| *Historical* *Note* | Effective November 1, 1987. Amended effective November 1, 1989 (amendment 302). |

§5E1.5.   Costs of Prosecution (Policy Statement)

Costs of prosecution shall be imposed on a defendant as required by statute.

Commentary

Background: Various statutes require the court to impose the costs of prosecution: 7 U.S.C. § 13 (larceny or embezzlement in connection with commodity exchanges); 21 U.S.C. § 844 (simple possession of controlled substances) (unless the court finds that the defendant lacks the ability to pay); 26 U.S.C. § 7201 (attempt to defeat or evade income tax); 26 U.S.C. § 7202 (willful failure to collect or pay tax); 26 U.S.C. § 7203 (willful failure to file income tax return, supply information, or pay tax); 26 U.S.C. § 7206 (fraud and false statements); 26 U.S.C. § 7210 (failure to obey summons); 26 U.S.C. § 7213 (unauthorized disclosure of information); 26 U.S.C. § 7215 (offenses with respect to collected taxes); 26 U.S.C. § 7216 (disclosure or use of information by preparers of returns); 26 U.S.C. § 7232 (failure to register or false statement by gasoline manufacturer or producer); 42 U.S.C. § 1320c-9 (improper FOIA disclosure); 43 U.S.C. § 942-6 (rights of way for Alaskan wagon roads).

Historical Note	Effective November 1, 1992 (amendment 463). Amended effective November 1, 2010 (amendment 747).

PART F — SENTENCING OPTIONS

§5F1.1.   Community Confinement

Community confinement may be imposed as a condition of probation or supervised release.

Commentary

Application Notes:

1.   "*Community confinement*" means residence in a community treatment center, halfway house, restitution center, mental health facility, alcohol or drug rehabilitation center, or other community facility; and participation in gainful employment, employment search efforts, community service, vocational training, treatment, educational programs, or similar facility-approved programs during non-residential hours.

2.   Community confinement generally should not be imposed for a period in excess of six months. A longer period may be imposed to accomplish the objectives of a specific rehabilitative program, such as drug rehabilitation. The sentencing judge may impose other discretionary conditions of probation or supervised release appropriate to effectuate community confinement.

Historical Note	Effective November 1, 1987. Amended effective November 1, 1989 (amendment 302); November 1, 2002 (amendment 646); November 1, 2009 (amendment 733).

§5F1.2.   Home Detention

Home detention may be imposed as a condition of probation or supervised release, but only as a substitute for imprisonment.

Commentary

Application Notes:

1.   "*Home detention*" means a program of confinement and supervision that restricts the defendant to his place of residence continuously, except for authorized absences, enforced by appropriate means of surveillance by the probation office. When an order of home detention is imposed, the defendant is required to be in his place of residence at all times except for approved absences for gainful employment, community service, religious services, medical care, educational or training programs, and such other times as may be specifically authorized. Electronic monitoring is an appropriate means of surveillance and ordinarily should be used in connection with home detention. However, alternative means of surveillance may be used so long as they are as effective as electronic monitoring.

2.   The court may impose other conditions of probation or supervised release appropriate to effectuate home detention. If the court concludes that the amenities available in the residence of a defendant would cause home detention not to be sufficiently punitive, the court may limit the amenities available.

3. The defendant's place of residence, for purposes of home detention, need not be the place where the defendant previously resided. It may be any place of residence, so long as the owner of the residence (and any other person(s) from whom consent is necessary) agrees to any conditions that may be imposed by the court, *e.g.*, conditions that a monitoring system be installed, that there will be no "call forwarding" or "call waiting" services, or that there will be no cordless telephones or answering machines.

Background: The Commission has concluded that the surveillance necessary for effective use of home detention ordinarily requires electronic monitoring. However, in some cases home detention may effectively be enforced without electronic monitoring, *e.g.*, when the defendant is physically incapacitated, or where some other effective means of surveillance is available. Accordingly, the Commission has not required that electronic monitoring be a necessary condition for home detention. Nevertheless, before ordering home detention without electronic monitoring, the court should be confident that an alternative form of surveillance will be equally effective.

In the usual case, the Commission assumes that a condition requiring that the defendant seek and maintain gainful employment will be imposed when home detention is ordered.

Historical Note	Effective November 1, 1987. Amended effective November 1, 1989 (amendments 271 and 302).

§5F1.3. Community Service

Community service may be ordered as a condition of probation or supervised release.

Commentary

Application Note:

1. Community service generally should not be imposed in excess of 400 hours. Longer terms of community service impose heavy administrative burdens relating to the selection of suitable placements and the monitoring of attendance.

Historical Note	Effective November 1, 1987. Amended effective November 1, 1989 (amendments 283 and 302); November 1, 1991 (amendment 419).

§5F1.4. Order of Notice to Victims

The court may order the defendant to pay the cost of giving notice to victims pursuant to 18 U.S.C. § 3555. This cost may be set off against any fine imposed if the court determines that the imposition of both sanctions would be excessive.

§5F1.5

Commentary

Background: In cases where a defendant has been convicted of an offense involving fraud or "other intentionally deceptive practices," the court may order the defendant to "give reasonable notice and explanation of the conviction, in such form as the court may approve" to the victims of the offense. 18 U.S.C. § 3555. The court may order the notice to be given by mail, by advertising in specific areas or through specific media, or by other appropriate means. In determining whether a notice is appropriate, the court must consider the generally applicable sentencing factors listed in 18 U.S.C. § 3553(a) and the cost involved in giving the notice as it relates to the loss caused by the crime. The court may not require the defendant to pay more than $20,000 to give notice.

If an order of notice to victims is under consideration, the court must notify the government and the defendant. 18 U.S.C. § 3553(d). Upon motion of either party, or on its own motion, the court must: (1) permit the parties to submit affidavits and memoranda relevant to the imposition of such an order; (2) provide counsel for both parties the opportunity to address orally, in open court, the appropriateness of such an order; and (3) if it issues such an order, state its reasons for doing so. The court may also order any additional procedures that will not unduly complicate or prolong the sentencing process.

Historical Note	Effective November 1, 1987. Amended effective November 1, 1989 (amendments 284 and 302).

§5F1.5.   Occupational Restrictions

    (a)   The court may impose a condition of probation or supervised release prohibiting the defendant from engaging in a specified occupation, business, or profession, or limiting the terms on which the defendant may do so, only if it determines that:

        (1)   a reasonably direct relationship existed between the defendant's occupation, business, or profession and the conduct relevant to the offense of conviction; and

        (2)   imposition of such a restriction is reasonably necessary to protect the public because there is reason to believe that, absent such restriction, the defendant will continue to engage in unlawful conduct similar to that for which the defendant was convicted.

    (b)   If the court decides to impose a condition of probation or supervised release restricting a defendant's engagement in a specified occupation, business, or profession, the court shall impose the condition for the minimum time and to the minimum extent necessary to protect the public.

Commentary

Background: The Comprehensive Crime Control Act authorizes the imposition of occupational restrictions as a condition of probation, 18 U.S.C. § 3563(b)(5), or supervised release, 18 U.S.C. § 3583(d). Pursuant to § 3563(b)(5), a court may require a defendant to:

> [R]efrain, in the case of an individual, from engaging in a specified occupation, business, or profession bearing a reasonably direct relationship to the conduct constituting the offense, or engage in such a specified occupation, business, or profession only to a stated degree or under stated circumstances.

Section 3583(d) incorporates this section by reference. The Senate Judiciary Committee Report on the Comprehensive Crime Control Act explains that the provision was "intended to be used to preclude the continuation or repetition of illegal activities while avoiding a bar from employment that exceeds that needed to achieve that result." S. Rep. No. 225, 98th Cong., 1st Sess. 96–97. The condition "should only be used as reasonably necessary to protect the public. It should not be used as a means of punishing the convicted person." *Id.* at 96. Section 5F1.5 accordingly limits the use of the condition and, if imposed, limits its scope, to the minimum reasonably necessary to protect the public.

The appellate review provisions permit a defendant to challenge the imposition of a probation condition under 18 U.S.C. § 3563(b)(5) if the sentence includes a more limiting condition of probation or supervised release than the maximum established in the guideline. *See* 18 U.S.C. § 3742(a)(3). The government may appeal if the sentence includes a less limiting condition of probation than the minimum established in the guideline. *See* 18 U.S.C. § 3742(b)(3).

Historical Note	Effective November 1, 1987. Amended effective November 1, 1989 (amendments 285 and 302); November 1, 1991 (amendment 428); November 1, 2002 (amendment 646).

---

§5F1.6. Denial of Federal Benefits to Drug Traffickers and Possessors

The court, pursuant to 21 U.S.C. § 862, may deny the eligibility for certain Federal benefits of any individual convicted of distribution or possession of a controlled substance.

Commentary

Application Note:

1. *"Federal benefit"* is defined in 21 U.S.C. § 862(d) to mean "any grant, contract, loan, professional license, or commercial license provided by an agency of the United States or by appropriated funds of the United States" but "does not include any retirement, welfare, Social Security, health, disability, veterans benefit, public housing, or other similar benefit, or any other benefit for which payments or services are required for eligibility."

Background: Subsections (a) and (b) of 21 U.S.C. § 862 provide that an individual convicted of a state or federal drug trafficking or possession offense may be denied certain federal benefits. Except for an individual convicted of a third or subsequent drug distribution offense, the period of benefit ineligibility, within the applicable maximum term set forth in 21 U.S.C. § 862(a)(1) (for distribution offenses) and (b)(1)(for possession offenses), is at the discretion of the court. In the case of an individual convicted of a third or subsequent drug distribution offense, denial of benefits is mandatory and permanent under 21 U.S.C. § 862(a)(1)(C) (unless suspended by the court under 21 U.S.C. § 862(c)).

Subsection (b)(2) of 21 U.S.C. § 862 provides that the period of benefit ineligibility that may be imposed in the case of a drug possession offense "shall be waived in the case of a person who, if there is a reasonable body of evidence to substantiate such declaration, declares himself to be an addict and submits himself to a long-term treatment program for addiction, or is deemed to be rehabilitated pursuant to rules established by the Secretary of Health and Human Services."

Subsection (c) of 21 U.S.C. § 862 provides that the period of benefit ineligibility shall be suspended "if the individual (A) completes a supervised drug rehabilitation program after becoming ineligible under this section; (B) has otherwise been rehabilitated; or (C) has made a good faith effort to gain admission to a supervised drug rehabilitation program, but is unable to do so because of inaccessibility or unavailability of such a program, or the inability of the individual to pay for such a program."

Subsection (e) of 21 U.S.C. § 862 provides that a period of benefit ineligibility "shall not apply to any individual who cooperates or testifies with the Government in the prosecution of a Federal or State offense or who is in a Government witness protection program."

| *Historical Note* | Effective November 1, 1989 (amendment 305); November 1, 1992 (amendment 464). |

§5F1.7. Shock Incarceration Program (Policy Statement)

The court, pursuant to 18 U.S.C. §§ 3582(a) and 3621(b)(4), may recommend that a defendant who meets the criteria set forth in 18 U.S.C. § 4046 participate in a shock incarceration program.

Commentary

Background: Section 4046 of title 18, United States Code, provides—

"(a) the Bureau of Prisons may place in a shock incarceration program any person who is sentenced to a term of more than 12, but not more than 30 months, if such person consents to that placement.

(b) For such initial portion of the term of imprisonment as the Bureau of Prisons may determine, not to exceed six months, an inmate in the shock incarceration program shall be required to—

(1) adhere to a highly regimented schedule that provides the strict discipline, physical training, hard labor, drill, and ceremony characteristic of military basic training; and

(2) participate in appropriate job training and educational programs (including literacy programs) and drug, alcohol, and other counseling programs.

(c)   An inmate who in the judgment of the Director of the Bureau of Prisons has successfully completed the required period of shock incarceration shall remain in the custody of the Bureau for such period (not to exceed the remainder of the prison term otherwise required by law to be served by that inmate), and under such conditions, as the Bureau deems appropriate. 18 U.S.C. § 4046."

The Bureau of Prisons has issued an operations memorandum (174-90 (5390), November 20, 1990) that outlines eligibility criteria and procedures for the implementation of this program (which the Bureau of Prisons has titled "intensive confinement program"). Under these procedures, the Bureau will not place a defendant in an intensive confinement program unless the sentencing court has approved, either at the time of sentencing or upon consultation after the Bureau has determined that the defendant is otherwise eligible. In return for the successful completion of the "intensive confinement" portion of the program, the defendant is eligible to serve the remainder of his term of imprisonment in a graduated release program comprised of community corrections center and home confinement phases.

Historical Note	Effective November 1, 1991 (amendment 424). Amended effective November 1, 2002 (amendment 646).

§5F1.8.   Intermittent Confinement

Intermittent confinement may be imposed as a condition of probation during the first year of probation. *See* 18 U.S.C. § 3563(b)(10). It may be imposed as a condition of supervised release during the first year of supervised release, but only for a violation of a condition of supervised release in accordance with 18 U.S.C. § 3583(e)(2) and only when facilities are available. *See* 18 U.S.C. § 3583(d).

Commentary

Application Note:

1.   "*Intermittent confinement*" means remaining in the custody of the Bureau of Prisons during nights, weekends, or other intervals of time, totaling no more than the lesser of one year or the term of imprisonment authorized for the offense, during the first year of the term of probation or supervised release. *See* 18 U.S.C. § 3563(b)(10).

Historical Note	Effective November 1, 2009 (amendment 733).

PART G — IMPLEMENTING THE TOTAL SENTENCE OF IMPRISONMENT

§5G1.1. Sentencing on a Single Count of Conviction

(a) Where the statutorily authorized maximum sentence is less than the minimum of the applicable guideline range, the statutorily authorized maximum sentence shall be the guideline sentence.

(b) Where a statutorily required minimum sentence is greater than the maximum of the applicable guideline range, the statutorily required minimum sentence shall be the guideline sentence.

(c) In any other case, the sentence may be imposed at any point within the applicable guideline range, provided that the sentence—

(1) is not greater than the statutorily authorized maximum sentence, and

(2) is not less than any statutorily required minimum sentence.

Commentary

This section describes how the statutorily authorized maximum sentence, or a statutorily required minimum sentence, may affect the determination of a sentence under the guidelines. For example, if the applicable guideline range is 51–63 months and the maximum sentence authorized by statute for the offense of conviction is 48 months, the sentence required by the guidelines under subsection (a) is 48 months; a sentence of less than 48 months would be a guideline departure. If the applicable guideline range is 41–51 months and there is a statutorily required minimum sentence of 60 months, the sentence required by the guidelines under subsection (b) is 60 months; a sentence of more than 60 months would be a guideline departure. If the applicable guideline range is 51–63 months and the maximum sentence authorized by statute for the offense of conviction is 60 months, the guideline range is restricted to 51–60 months under subsection (c).

Historical Note	Effective November 1, 1987. Amended effective November 1, 1989 (amendment 286).

§5G1.2. Sentencing on Multiple Counts of Conviction

(a) Except as provided in subsection (e), the sentence to be imposed on a count for which the statute (1) specifies a term of imprisonment to be imposed; and (2) requires that such term of imprisonment be imposed to run consecutively to any other term of imprisonment, shall be determined by that statute and imposed independently.

(b)   For all counts not covered by subsection (a), the court shall determine the total punishment and shall impose that total punishment on each such count, except to the extent otherwise required by law.

(c)   If the sentence imposed on the count carrying the highest statutory maximum is adequate to achieve the total punishment, then the sentences on all counts shall run concurrently, except to the extent otherwise required by law.

(d)   If the sentence imposed on the count carrying the highest statutory maximum is less than the total punishment, then the sentence imposed on one or more of the other counts shall run consecutively, but only to the extent necessary to produce a combined sentence equal to the total punishment. In all other respects, sentences on all counts shall run concurrently, except to the extent otherwise required by law.

(e)   In a case in which subsection (c) of §4B1.1 (Career Offender) applies, to the extent possible, the total punishment is to be apportioned among the counts of conviction, except that (1) the sentence to be imposed on a count requiring a minimum term of imprisonment shall be at least the minimum required by statute; and (2) the sentence to be imposed on the 18 U.S.C. § 924(c) or § 929(a) count shall be imposed to run consecutively to any other count.

Commentary

Application Notes:

1.   **In General.**—This section specifies the procedure for determining the specific sentence to be formally imposed on each count in a multiple-count case. The combined length of the sentences ("total punishment") is determined by the court after determining the adjusted combined offense level and the Criminal History Category and determining the defendant's guideline range on the Sentencing Table in Chapter Five, Part A (Sentencing Table).

Note that the defendant's guideline range on the Sentencing Table may be affected or restricted by a statutorily authorized maximum sentence or a statutorily required minimum sentence not only in a single-count case, *see* §5G1.1 (Sentencing on a Single Count of Conviction), but also in a multiple-count case. *See* Note 3, below.

Except as otherwise required by subsection (e) or any other law, the total punishment is to be imposed on each count and the sentences on all counts are to be imposed to run concurrently to the extent allowed by the statutory maximum sentence of imprisonment for each count of conviction.

This section applies to multiple counts of conviction (A) contained in the same indictment or information, or (B) contained in different indictments or informations for which sentences are to be imposed at the same time or in a consolidated proceeding.

Usually, at least one of the counts will have a statutory maximum adequate to permit imposition of the total punishment as the sentence on that count. The sentence on each of the other counts will then be set at the lesser of the total punishment and the applicable statutory maximum, and be made to run concurrently with all or part of the longest sentence. If no count carries an adequate statutory maximum, consecutive sentences are to be imposed to the extent necessary to achieve the total punishment.

2. **Mandatory Minimum and Mandatory Consecutive Terms of Imprisonment (Not Covered by Subsection (e)).—**

    (A) **In General.**—Subsection (a) applies if a statute (i) specifies a term of imprisonment to be imposed; and (ii) requires that such term of imprisonment be imposed to run consecutively to any other term of imprisonment. *See, e.g.*, 18 U.S.C. § 924(c) (requiring mandatory minimum terms of imprisonment, based on the conduct involved, and also requiring the sentence imposed to run consecutively to any other term of imprisonment) and 18 U.S.C. § 1028A (requiring a mandatory term of imprisonment of either two or five years, based on the conduct involved, and also requiring, except in the circumstances described in subdivision (B), the sentence imposed to run consecutively to any other term of imprisonment). Except for certain career offender situations in which subsection (c) of §4B1.1 (Career Offender) applies, the term of years to be imposed consecutively is the minimum required by the statute of conviction and is independent of the guideline sentence on any other count. *See, e.g.*, the Commentary to §§2K2.4 (Use of Firearm, Armor-Piercing Ammunition, or Explosive During or in Relation to Certain Crimes) and 3D1.1 (Procedure for Determining Offense Level on Multiple Counts) regarding the determination of the offense levels for related counts when a conviction under 18 U.S.C. § 924(c) is involved. Subsection (a) also applies in certain other instances in which an independently determined and consecutive sentence is required. *See, e.g.*, Application Note 3 of the Commentary to §2J1.6 (Failure to Appear by Defendant), relating to failure to appear for service of sentence.

    (B) **Multiple Convictions Under 18 U.S.C. § 1028A.**—Section 1028A of title 18, United States Code, generally requires that the mandatory term of imprisonment for a violation of such section be imposed consecutively to any other term of imprisonment. However, 18 U.S.C. § 1028A(b)(4) permits the court, in its discretion, to impose the mandatory term of imprisonment on a defendant for a violation of such section "concurrently, in whole or in part, only with another term of imprisonment that is imposed by the court at the same time on that person for an additional violation of this section, provided that such discretion shall be exercised in accordance with any applicable guidelines and policy statements issued by the Sentencing Commission . . .".

    In determining whether multiple counts of 18 U.S.C. § 1028A should run concurrently with, or consecutively to, each other, the court should consider the following non-exhaustive list of factors:

    (i) The nature and seriousness of the underlying offenses. For example, the court should consider the appropriateness of imposing consecutive, or partially consecutive, terms of imprisonment for multiple counts of 18 U.S.C. § 1028A in a case in which an underlying offense for one of the 18 U.S.C. § 1028A offenses is a crime of violence or an offense enumerated in 18 U.S.C. § 2332b(g)(5)(B).

    (ii) Whether the underlying offenses are groupable under §3D1.2 (Groups of Closely Related Counts). Generally, multiple counts of 18 U.S.C. § 1028A should run concurrently with one another in cases in which the underlying offenses are groupable under §3D1.2.

(iii) Whether the purposes of sentencing set forth in 18 U.S.C. § 3553(a)(2) are better achieved by imposing a concurrent or a consecutive sentence for multiple counts of 18 U.S.C. § 1028A.

(C) **Imposition of Supervised Release.**—In the case of a consecutive term of imprisonment imposed under subsection (a), any term of supervised release imposed is to run concurrently with any other term of supervised release imposed. *See* 18 U.S.C. § 3624(e).

3. **Application of Subsection (b).—**

(A) **In General.**—Subsection (b) provides that, for all counts not covered by subsection (a), the court shall determine the total punishment (*i.e.*, the combined length of the sentences to be imposed) and shall impose that total punishment on each such count, except to the extent otherwise required by law (such as where a statutorily required minimum sentence or a statutorily authorized maximum sentence otherwise requires).

(B) **Effect on Guidelines Range of Mandatory Minimum or Statutory Maximum.**—The defendant's guideline range on the Sentencing Table may be affected or restricted by a statutorily authorized maximum sentence or a statutorily required minimum sentence not only in a single-count case, *see* §5G1.1, but also in a multiple-count case.

In particular, where a statutorily required minimum sentence on any count is greater than the maximum of the applicable guideline range, the statutorily required minimum sentence on that count shall be the guideline sentence on all counts. *See* §5G1.1(b). Similarly, where a statutorily required minimum sentence on any count is greater than the minimum of the applicable guideline range, the guideline range for all counts is restricted by that statutorily required minimum sentence. *See* §5G1.1(c)(2) and accompanying Commentary.

However, where a statutorily authorized maximum sentence on a particular count is less than the minimum of the applicable guideline range, the sentence imposed on that count shall not be greater than the statutorily authorized maximum sentence on that count. *See* §5G1.1(a).

(C) **Examples.**—The following examples illustrate how subsection (b) applies, and how the restrictions in subparagraph (B) operate, when a statutorily required minimum sentence is involved.

Defendant A and Defendant B are each convicted of the same four counts. Counts 1, 3, and 4 have statutory maximums of 10 years, 20 years, and 2 years, respectively. Count 2 has a statutory maximum of 30 years and a mandatory minimum of 10 years.

For Defendant A, the court determines that the final offense level is 19 and the defendant is in Criminal History Category I, which yields a guideline range on the Sentencing Table of 30 to 37 months. Because of the 10-year mandatory minimum on Count 2, however, Defendant A's guideline sentence is 120 months. *See* subparagraph (B), above. After considering that guideline sentence, the court determines that the appropriate "total punishment" to be imposed on Defendant A is 120 months. Therefore, subsection (b) requires that the total punishment of 120 months be imposed on each of Counts 1, 2, and 3. The sentence imposed on Count 4 is limited to 24 months, because a statutory maximum of 2 years applies to that particular count.

For Defendant B, in contrast, the court determines that the final offense level is 30 and the defendant is in Criminal History Category II, which yields a guideline range on the Sentencing Table of 108 to 135 months. Because of the 10-year mandatory minimum on Count 2, however, Defendant B's guideline range is restricted to 120 to 135 months. *See* subparagraph (B), above. After considering that restricted guideline range, the court determines that the appropriate "total punishment" to be imposed on Defendant B is 130 months. Therefore, subsection (b) requires that the total punishment of 130 months be imposed on each of Counts 2 and 3. The sentences imposed on Counts 1 and 4 are limited to 120 months (10 years) and 24 months (2 years), respectively, because of the applicable statutory maximums.

(D) **Special Rule on Resentencing.**—In a case in which (i) the defendant's guideline range on the Sentencing Table was affected or restricted by a statutorily required minimum sentence (as described in subparagraph (B)), (ii) the court is resentencing the defendant, and (iii) the statutorily required minimum sentence no longer applies, the defendant's guideline range for purposes of the remaining counts shall be redetermined without regard to the previous effect or restriction of the statutorily required minimum sentence.

4. **Career Offenders Covered under Subsection (e).—**

(A) **Imposing Sentence.**—The sentence imposed for a conviction under 18 U.S.C. § 924(c) or § 929(a) shall, under that statute, consist of a minimum term of imprisonment imposed to run consecutively to the sentence on any other count. Subsection (e) requires that the total punishment determined under §4B1.1(c) be apportioned among all the counts of conviction. In most cases this can be achieved by imposing the statutory minimum term of imprisonment on the 18 U.S.C. § 924(c) or § 929(a) count, subtracting that minimum term of imprisonment from the total punishment determined under §4B1.1(c), and then imposing the balance of the total punishment on the other counts of conviction. In some cases covered by subsection (e), a consecutive term of imprisonment longer than the minimum required by 18 U.S.C. § 924(c) or § 929(a) will be necessary in order both to achieve the total punishment determined by the court and to comply with the applicable statutory requirements.

(B) **Examples.**—The following examples illustrate the application of subsection (e) in a multiple count situation:

(i) The defendant is convicted of one count of violating 18 U.S.C. § 924(c) for possessing a firearm in furtherance of a drug trafficking offense (5 year mandatory minimum), and one count of violating 21 U.S.C. § 841(b)(1)(C) (20 year statutory maximum). Applying §4B1.1(c), the court determines that a sentence of 300 months is appropriate (applicable guideline range of 262–327). The court then imposes a sentence of 60 months on the 18 U.S.C. § 924(c) count, subtracts that 60 months from the total punishment of 300 months and imposes the remainder of 240 months on the 21 U.S.C. § 841 count. As required by statute, the sentence on the 18 U.S.C. § 924(c) count is imposed to run consecutively.

(ii)   The defendant is convicted of one count of 18 U.S.C. § 924(c) (5 year mandatory minimum), and one count of violating 21 U.S.C. § 841(b)(1)(C) (20 year statutory maximum). Applying §4B1.1(c), the court determines that a sentence of 327 months is appropriate (applicable guideline range of 262–327). The court then imposes a sentence of 240 months on the 21 U.S.C. § 841 count and a sentence of 87 months on the 18 U.S.C. § 924(c) count to run consecutively to the sentence on the 21 U.S.C. § 841 count.

(iii)   The defendant is convicted of two counts of 18 U.S.C. § 924(c) (5 year mandatory minimum on first count, 25 year mandatory minimum on second count) and one count of violating 18 U.S.C. § 113(a)(3) (10 year statutory maximum). Applying §4B1.1(c), the court determines that a sentence of 460 months is appropriate (applicable guideline range of 460–485 months). The court then imposes (I) a sentence of 60 months on the first 18 U.S.C. § 924(c) count; (II) a sentence of 300 months on the second 18 U.S.C. § 924(c) count; and (III) a sentence of 100 months on the 18 U.S.C. § 113(a)(3) count. The sentence on each count is imposed to run consecutively to the other counts.

Historical Note   Effective November 1, 1987. Amended effective November 1, 1989 (amendments 287 and 288); November 1, 1994 (amendment 507); November 1, 1998 (amendment 579); November 1, 2000 (amendment 598); November 1, 2002 (amendment 642); November 1, 2004 (amendment 674); November 1, 2005 (amendments 677 and 680); November 1, 2010 (amendment 747); November 1, 2012 (amendments 767 and 770).

§5G1.3.   Imposition of a Sentence on a Defendant Subject to an Undischarged Term of Imprisonment or Anticipated State Term of Imprisonment

(a)   If the instant offense was committed while the defendant was serving a term of imprisonment (including work release, furlough, or escape status) or after sentencing for, but before commencing service of, such term of imprisonment, the sentence for the instant offense shall be imposed to run consecutively to the undischarged term of imprisonment.

(b)   If subsection (a) does not apply, and a term of imprisonment resulted from another offense that is relevant conduct to the instant offense of conviction under the provisions of subsections (a)(1), (a)(2), or (a)(3) of §1B1.3 (Relevant Conduct), the sentence for the instant offense shall be imposed as follows:

(1)   the court shall adjust the sentence for any period of imprisonment already served on the undischarged term of imprisonment if the court determines that such period of imprisonment will not be credited to the federal sentence by the Bureau of Prisons; and

(2)   the sentence for the instant offense shall be imposed to run concurrently to the remainder of the undischarged term of imprisonment.

(c) If subsection (a) does not apply, and a state term of imprisonment is anticipated to result from another offense that is relevant conduct to the instant offense of conviction under the provisions of subsections (a)(1), (a)(2), or (a)(3) of §1B1.3 (Relevant Conduct), the sentence for the instant offense shall be imposed to run concurrently to the anticipated term of imprisonment.

(d) (Policy Statement) In any other case involving an undischarged term of imprisonment, the sentence for the instant offense may be imposed to run concurrently, partially concurrently, or consecutively to the prior undischarged term of imprisonment to achieve a reasonable punishment for the instant offense.

Commentary

Application Notes:

1. **Consecutive Sentence — Subsection (a) Cases.** Under subsection (a), the court shall impose a consecutive sentence when the instant offense was committed while the defendant was serving an undischarged term of imprisonment or after sentencing for, but before commencing service of, such term of imprisonment.

2. **Application of Subsection (b).—**

   (A) **In General.**—Subsection (b) applies in cases in which all of the prior offense is relevant conduct to the instant offense under the provisions of subsection (a)(1), (a)(2), or (a)(3) of §1B1.3 (Relevant Conduct). Cases in which only part of the prior offense is relevant conduct to the instant offense are covered under subsection (d).

   (B) **Inapplicability of Subsection (b).**—Subsection (b) does not apply in cases in which the prior offense was not relevant conduct to the instant offense under §1B1.3(a)(1), (a)(2), or (a)(3) (*e.g.*, the prior offense is a prior conviction for which the defendant received an increase under §2L1.2 (Unlawfully Entering or Remaining in the United States), or the prior offense was a crime of violence for which the defendant received an increased base offense level under §2K2.1 (Unlawful Receipt, Possession, or Transportation of Firearms or Ammunition; Prohibited Transactions Involving Firearms or Ammunition)).

   (C) **Imposition of Sentence.**—If subsection (b) applies, and the court adjusts the sentence for a period of time already served, the court should note on the Judgment in a Criminal Case Order (i) the applicable subsection (*e.g.*, §5G1.3(b)); (ii) the amount of time by which the sentence is being adjusted; (iii) the undischarged term of imprisonment for which the adjustment is being given; and (iv) that the sentence imposed is a sentence reduction pursuant to §5G1.3(b) for a period of imprisonment that will not be credited by the Bureau of Prisons.

   (D) **Example.**—The following is an example in which subsection (b) applies and an adjustment to the sentence is appropriate:

   The defendant is convicted of a federal offense charging the sale of 90 grams of cocaine. Under §1B1.3, the defendant is held accountable for the sale of an additional 25 grams of cocaine, an offense for which the defendant has been convicted and sentenced in state court. The defendant received a nine-month sentence of imprisonment for the state offense and has served six months on that sentence at the time of sentencing on the instant federal offense. The guideline range applicable to the defendant is 12–18 months (Chapter Two offense level of level 16 for sale of 115 grams of cocaine; 3 level reduction for acceptance of responsibility; final offense level of level 13; Criminal History Category I). The court determines that a sentence of 13 months provides the appropriate total punishment. Because the defendant has already served six months on the related state charge as of the date of sentencing on the instant federal offense, a sentence of seven months, imposed to run concurrently with the three months remaining on the defendant's state sentence, achieves this result.

3. **Application of Subsection (c).**—Subsection (c) applies to cases in which the federal court anticipates that, after the federal sentence is imposed, the defendant will be sentenced in state court and serve a state sentence before being transferred to federal custody for federal imprisonment. In such a case, where the other offense is relevant conduct to the instant offense of conviction under the provisions of subsections (a)(1), (a)(2), or (a)(3) of §1B1.3 (Relevant Conduct), the sentence for the instant offense shall be imposed to run concurrently to the anticipated term of imprisonment.

4. **Application of Subsection (d).—**

   (A) **In General.**—Under subsection (d), the court may impose a sentence concurrently, partially concurrently, or consecutively to the undischarged term of imprisonment. In order to achieve a reasonable incremental punishment for the instant offense and avoid unwarranted disparity, the court should consider the following:

   (i) the factors set forth in 18 U.S.C. § 3584 (referencing 18 U.S.C. § 3553(a));

   (ii) the type (*e.g.*, determinate, indeterminate/parolable) and length of the prior undischarged sentence;

   (iii) the time served on the undischarged sentence and the time likely to be served before release;

   (iv) the fact that the prior undischarged sentence may have been imposed in state court rather than federal court, or at a different time before the same or different federal court; and

   (v) any other circumstance relevant to the determination of an appropriate sentence for the instant offense.

   (B) **Partially Concurrent Sentence.**—In some cases under subsection (d), a partially concurrent sentence may achieve most appropriately the desired result. To impose a partially concurrent sentence, the court may provide in the Judgment in a Criminal Case Order that the sentence for the instant offense shall commence on the earlier of (i) when the defendant is released from the prior undischarged sentence; or (ii) on a specified date. This order provides for a fully consecutive sentence if the defendant is released on the undischarged term of imprisonment on or before the date specified in the order, and a partially concurrent sentence if the defendant is not released on the undischarged term of imprisonment by that date.

   (C) **Undischarged Terms of Imprisonment Resulting from Revocations of Probation, Parole or Supervised Release.**—Subsection (d) applies in cases in which the defendant was on federal or state probation, parole, or supervised release at the time of the instant offense and has had such probation, parole, or supervised release revoked. Consistent with the policy set forth in Application Note 4 and subsection (f) of §7B1.3 (Revocation of Probation or Supervised Release), the Commission recommends that the sentence for the instant offense be imposed consecutively to the sentence imposed for the revocation.

(D) **Complex Situations.**—Occasionally, the court may be faced with a complex case in which a defendant may be subject to multiple undischarged terms of imprisonment that seemingly call for the application of different rules. In such a case, the court may exercise its discretion in accordance with subsection (d) to fashion a sentence of appropriate length and structure it to run in any appropriate manner to achieve a reasonable punishment for the instant offense.

(E) **Downward Departure.**—Unlike subsection (b), subsection (d) does not authorize an adjustment of the sentence for the instant offense for a period of imprisonment already served on the undischarged term of imprisonment. However, in an extraordinary case involving an undischarged term of imprisonment under subsection (d), it may be appropriate for the court to downwardly depart. This may occur, for example, in a case in which the defendant has served a very substantial period of imprisonment on an undischarged term of imprisonment that resulted from conduct only partially within the relevant conduct for the instant offense. In such a case, a downward departure may be warranted to ensure that the combined punishment is not increased unduly by the fortuity and timing of separate prosecutions and sentencings. Nevertheless, it is intended that a departure pursuant to this application note result in a sentence that ensures a reasonable incremental punishment for the instant offense of conviction.

To avoid confusion with the Bureau of Prisons' exclusive authority provided under 18 U.S.C. § 3585(b) to grant credit for time served under certain circumstances, the Commission recommends that any downward departure under this application note be clearly stated on the Judgment in a Criminal Case Order as a downward departure pursuant to §5G1.3(d), rather than as a credit for time served.

5. **Downward Departure Provision.**—In the case of a discharged term of imprisonment, a downward departure is not prohibited if the defendant (A) has completed serving a term of imprisonment; and (B) subsection (b) would have provided an adjustment had that completed term of imprisonment been undischarged at the time of sentencing for the instant offense. See §5K2.23 (Discharged Terms of Imprisonment).

Background: Federal courts generally "have discretion to select whether the sentences they impose will run concurrently or consecutively with respect to other sentences that they impose, or that have been imposed in other proceedings, including state proceedings." *See Setser v. United States*, 132 S. Ct. 1463, 1468 (2012); 18 U.S.C. § 3584(a). Federal courts also generally have discretion to order that the sentences they impose will run concurrently with or consecutively to other state sentences that are anticipated but not yet imposed. *See Setser*, 132 S. Ct. at 1468. Exercise of that discretion, however, is predicated on the court's consideration of the factors listed in 18 U.S.C. § 3553(a), including any applicable guidelines or policy statements issued by the Sentencing Commission.

Historical Note	Effective November 1, 1987. Amended effective November 1, 1989 (amendment 289); November 1, 1991 (amendment 385); November 1, 1992 (amendment 465); November 1, 1993 (amendment 494); November 1, 1995 (amendment 535); November 1, 2002 (amendment 645); November 1, 2003 (amendment 660); November 1, 2010 (amendment 747); November 1, 2013 (amendment 776).; November 1, 2014 (amendments 782, 787, and 789); November 1, 2016 (amendment 802).

PART H — SPECIFIC OFFENDER CHARACTERISTICS

Introductory Commentary

This Part addresses the relevance of certain specific offender characteristics in sentencing. The Sentencing Reform Act (the "Act") contains several provisions regarding specific offender characteristics:

First, the Act directs the Commission to ensure that the guidelines and policy statements "are entirely neutral" as to five characteristics – race, sex, national origin, creed, and socioeconomic status. *See* 28 U.S.C. § 994(d).

Second, the Act directs the Commission to consider whether eleven specific offender characteristics, "among others", have any relevance to the nature, extent, place of service, or other aspects of an appropriate sentence, and to take them into account in the guidelines and policy statements only to the extent that they do have relevance. *See* 28 U.S.C. § 994(d).

Third, the Act directs the Commission to ensure that the guidelines and policy statements, in recommending a term of imprisonment or length of a term of imprisonment, reflect the "general inappropriateness" of considering five of those characteristics – education; vocational skills; employment record; family ties and responsibilities; and community ties. *See* 28 U.S.C. § 994(e).

Fourth, the Act also directs the sentencing court, in determining the particular sentence to be imposed, to consider, among other factors, "the history and characteristics of the defendant". *See* 18 U.S.C. § 3553(a)(1).

Specific offender characteristics are taken into account in the guidelines in several ways. One important specific offender characteristic is the defendant's criminal history, *see* 28 U.S.C. § 994(d)(10), which is taken into account in the guidelines in Chapter Four (Criminal History and Criminal Livelihood). *See* §5H1.8 (Criminal History). Another specific offender characteristic in the guidelines is the degree of dependence upon criminal history for a livelihood, *see* 28 U.S.C. § 994(d)(11), which is taken into account in Chapter Four, Part B (Career Offenders and Criminal Livelihood). *See* §5H1.9 (Dependence upon Criminal Activity for a Livelihood). Other specific offender characteristics are accounted for elsewhere in this manual. *See, e.g.,* §§2C1.1(a)(1) and 2C1.2(a)(1) (providing alternative base offense levels if the defendant was a public official); 3B1.3 (Abuse of Position of Trust or Use of Special Skill); and 3E1.1 (Acceptance of Responsibility).

The Supreme Court has emphasized that the advisory guideline system should "continue to move sentencing in Congress' preferred direction, helping to avoid excessive sentencing disparities while maintaining flexibility sufficient to individualize sentences where necessary." *See United States v. Booker,* 543 U.S. 220, 264–65 (2005). Although the court must consider "the history and characteristics of the defendant" among other factors, *see* 18 U.S.C. § 3553(a), in order to avoid unwarranted sentencing disparities the court should not give them excessive weight. Generally, the most appropriate use of specific offender characteristics is to consider them not as a reason for a sentence outside the applicable guideline range but for other reasons, such as in determining the sentence within the applicable guideline range, the type of sentence (*e.g.,* probation or imprisonment) within the sentencing options available for the applicable Zone on the Sentencing Table, and various other aspects of an appropriate sentence. To avoid unwarranted sentencing disparities among defendants with similar records who have been found guilty of similar conduct, *see* 18 U.S.C. § 3553(a)(6), 28 U.S.C. § 991(b)(1)(B), the guideline range, which reflects the defendant's criminal conduct and the defendant's criminal history, should continue to be "the starting point and the initial benchmark." *Gall v. United States*, 552 U.S. 38, 49 (2007).

Accordingly, the purpose of this Part is to provide sentencing courts with a framework for addressing specific offender characteristics in a reasonably consistent manner. Using such a framework in a uniform manner will help "secure nationwide consistency," *see Gall v. United States*, 552 U.S. 38, 49 (2007), "avoid unwarranted sentencing disparities," *see* 28 U.S.C. § 991(b)(1)(B), 18 U.S.C. § 3553(a)(6), "provide certainty and fairness," *see* 28 U.S.C. § 991(b)(1)(B), and "promote respect for the law," *see* 18 U.S.C. § 3553(a)(2)(A).

This Part allocates specific offender characteristics into three general categories.

In the first category are specific offender characteristics the consideration of which Congress has prohibited (*e.g.*, §5H1.10 (Race, Sex, National Origin, Creed, Religion, and Socio-Economic Status)) or that the Commission has determined should be prohibited.

In the second category are specific offender characteristics that Congress directed the Commission to take into account in the guidelines only to the extent that they have relevance to sentencing. *See* 28 U.S.C. § 994(d). For some of these, the policy statements indicate that these characteristics may be relevant in determining whether a sentence outside the applicable guideline range is warranted (*e.g.*, age; mental and emotional condition; physical condition). These characteristics may warrant a sentence outside the applicable guideline range if the characteristic, individually or in combination with other such characteristics, is present to an unusual degree and distinguishes the case from the typical cases covered by the guidelines. These specific offender characteristics also may be considered for other reasons, such as in determining the sentence within the applicable guideline range, the type of sentence (*e.g.*, probation or imprisonment) within the sentencing options available for the applicable Zone on the Sentencing Table, and various other aspects of an appropriate sentence.

In the third category are specific offender characteristics that Congress directed the Commission to ensure are reflected in the guidelines and policy statements as generally inappropriate in recommending a term of imprisonment or length of a term of imprisonment. *See* 28 U.S.C. § 994(e). The policy statements indicate that these characteristics are not ordinarily relevant to the determination of whether a sentence should be outside the applicable guideline range. Unless expressly stated, this does not mean that the Commission views such circumstances as necessarily inappropriate to the determination of the sentence within the applicable guideline range, the type of sentence (*e.g.*, probation or imprisonment) within the sentencing options available for the applicable Zone on the Sentencing Table, or various other aspects of an appropriate sentence (*e.g.*, the appropriate conditions of probation or supervised release). Furthermore, although these circumstances are not ordinarily relevant to the determination of whether a sentence should be outside the applicable guideline range, they may be relevant to this determination in exceptional cases. They also may be relevant if a combination of such circumstances makes the case an exceptional one, but only if each such circumstance is identified as an affirmative ground for departure and is present in the case to a substantial degree. *See* §5K2.0 (Grounds for Departure).

As with the other provisions in this manual, these policy statements "are evolutionary in nature". *See* Chapter One, Part A, Subpart 2 (Continuing Evolution and Role of the Guidelines); 28 U.S.C. § 994(o). The Commission expects, and the Sentencing Reform Act contemplates, that continuing research, experience, and analysis will result in modifications and revisions.

The nature, extent, and significance of specific offender characteristics can involve a range of considerations. The Commission will continue to provide information to the courts on the relevance of specific offender characteristics in sentencing, as the Sentencing Reform Act contemplates. *See, e.g.,* 28 U.S.C. § 995(a)(12)(A) (the Commission serves as a "clearinghouse and information center" on federal sentencing). Among other things, this may include information on the use of specific offender characteristics, individually and in combination, in determining the sentence to be imposed (including, where available, information on rates of use, criteria for use, and reasons for use); the relationship, if any, between specific offender characteristics and (A) the "forbidden factors" specified in 28 U.S.C. § 994(d) and (B) the "discouraged factors" specified in 28 U.S.C. § 994(e); and the relationship, if any, between specific offender characteristics and the statutory purposes of sentencing.

Historical Note	Effective November 1, 1987. Amended effective November 1, 1990 (amendment 357); November 1, 1991 (amendment 386); November 1, 1994 (amendment 508); October 27, 2003 (amendment 651); November 1, 2010 (amendment 739).

§5H1.1.   Age (Policy Statement)

Age (including youth) may be relevant in determining whether a departure is warranted, if considerations based on age, individually or in combination with other offender characteristics, are present to an unusual degree and distinguish the case from the typical cases covered by the guidelines. Age may be a reason to depart downward in a case in which the defendant is elderly and infirm and where a form of punishment such as home confinement might be equally efficient as and less costly than incarceration. Physical condition, which may be related to age, is addressed at §5H1.4 (Physical Condition, Including Drug or Alcohol Dependence or Abuse; Gambling Addiction).

Historical Note	Effective November 1, 1987. Amended effective November 1, 1991 (amendment 386); November 1, 1993 (amendment 475); October 27, 2003 (amendment 651); November 1, 2004 (amendment 674); November 1, 2010 (amendment 739).

§5H1.2.   Education and Vocational Skills (Policy Statement)

Education and vocational skills are not ordinarily relevant in determining whether a departure is warranted, but the extent to which a defendant may have misused special training or education to facilitate criminal activity is an express guideline factor. *See* §3B1.3 (Abuse of Position of Trust or Use of Special Skill).

Education and vocational skills may be relevant in determining the conditions of probation or supervised release for rehabilitative purposes, for public protection by restricting activities that allow for the utilization of a certain skill, or in determining the appropriate type of community service.

§5H1.4

| Historical Note | Effective November 1, 1987. Amended effective November 1, 1991 (amendment 386); November 1, 2004 (amendment 674). |

§5H1.3. Mental and Emotional Conditions (Policy Statement)

Mental and emotional conditions may be relevant in determining whether a departure is warranted, if such conditions, individually or in combination with other offender characteristics, are present to an unusual degree and distinguish the case from the typical cases covered by the guidelines. *See also* Chapter Five, Part K, Subpart 2 (Other Grounds for Departure).

In certain cases a downward departure may be appropriate to accomplish a specific treatment purpose. *See* §5C1.1, Application Note 6.

Mental and emotional conditions may be relevant in determining the conditions of probation or supervised release; *e.g.*, participation in a mental health program (*see* §§5B1.3(d)(5) and 5D1.3(d)(5)).

| Historical Note | Effective November 1, 1987. Amended effective November 1, 1991 (amendment 386); November 1, 1997 (amendment 569); November 1, 2004 (amendment 674); November 1, 2010 (amendment 739). |

§5H1.4. Physical Condition, Including Drug or Alcohol Dependence or Abuse; Gambling Addiction (Policy Statement)

Physical condition or appearance, including physique, may be relevant in determining whether a departure is warranted, if the condition or appearance, individually or in combination with other offender characteristics, is present to an unusual degree and distinguishes the case from the typical cases covered by the guidelines. An extraordinary physical impairment may be a reason to depart downward; *e.g.*, in the case of a seriously infirm defendant, home detention may be as efficient as, and less costly than, imprisonment.

Drug or alcohol dependence or abuse ordinarily is not a reason for a downward departure. Substance abuse is highly correlated to an increased propensity to commit crime. Due to this increased risk, it is highly recommended that a defendant who is incarcerated also be sentenced to supervised release with a requirement that the defendant participate in an appropriate substance abuse program (*see* §5D1.3(d)(4)). If participation in a substance abuse program is required, the length of supervised release should take into account the length of time necessary for the probation office to judge the success of the program.

In certain cases a downward departure may be appropriate to accomplish a specific treatment purpose. *See* §5C1.1, Application Note 6.

In a case in which a defendant who is a substance abuser is sentenced to probation, it is strongly recommended that the conditions of probation contain a requirement that the defendant participate in an appropriate substance abuse program (*see* §5B1.3(d)(4)).

Addiction to gambling is not a reason for a downward departure.

Historical Note	Effective November 1, 1987. Amended effective November 1, 1991 (amendment 386); November 1, 1997 (amendment 569); October 27, 2003 (amendment 651); November 1, 2010 (amendment 739).

§5H1.5. Employment Record (Policy Statement)

Employment record is not ordinarily relevant in determining whether a departure is warranted.

Employment record may be relevant in determining the conditions of probation or supervised release (*e.g.*, the appropriate hours of home detention).

Historical Note	Effective November 1, 1987. Amended effective November 1, 1991 (amendment 386); November 1, 2004 (amendment 674).

§5H1.6. Family Ties and Responsibilities (Policy Statement)

In sentencing a defendant convicted of an offense other than an offense described in the following paragraph, family ties and responsibilities are not ordinarily relevant in determining whether a departure may be warranted.

In sentencing a defendant convicted of an offense involving a minor victim under section 1201, an offense under section 1591, or an offense under chapter 71, 109A, 110, or 117, of title 18, United States Code, family ties and responsibilities and community ties are not relevant in determining whether a sentence should be below the applicable guideline range.

Family responsibilities that are complied with may be relevant to the determination of the amount of restitution or fine.

Commentary

Application Note:

1. **Circumstances to Consider.—**

    (A) **In General.—**In determining whether a departure is warranted under this policy statement, the court shall consider the following non-exhaustive list of circumstances:

         (i)   The seriousness of the offense.

         (ii) The involvement in the offense, if any, of members of the defendant's family.

         (iii) The danger, if any, to members of the defendant's family as a result of the offense.

    (B) **Departures Based on Loss of Caretaking or Financial Support.—**A departure under this policy statement based on the loss of caretaking or financial support of the defendant's family requires, in addition to the court's consideration of the non-exhaustive list of circumstances in subdivision (A), the presence of the following circumstances:

         (i)   The defendant's service of a sentence within the applicable guideline range will cause a substantial, direct, and specific loss of essential caretaking, or essential financial support, to the defendant's family.

         (ii) The loss of caretaking or financial support substantially exceeds the harm ordinarily incident to incarceration for a similarly situated defendant. For example, the fact that the defendant's family might incur some degree of financial hardship or suffer to some extent from the absence of a parent through incarceration is not in itself sufficient as a basis for departure because such hardship or suffering is of a sort ordinarily incident to incarceration.

         (iii) The loss of caretaking or financial support is one for which no effective remedial or ameliorative programs reasonably are available, making the defendant's caretaking or financial support irreplaceable to the defendant's family.

         (iv) The departure effectively will address the loss of caretaking or financial support.

Background: Section 401(b)(4) of Public Law 108–21 directly amended this policy statement to add the second paragraph, effective April 30, 2003.

Historical Note	Effective November 1, 1987. Amended effective November 1, 1991 (amendment 386); April 30, 2003 (amendment 649); October 27, 2003 (amendment 651); November 1, 2004 (amendment 674).

§5H1.7. Role in the Offense (Policy Statement)

A defendant's role in the offense is relevant in determining the applicable guideline range (*see* Chapter Three, Part B (Role in the Offense)) but is not a basis for departing from that range (*see* subsection (d) of §5K2.0 (Grounds for Departures)).

Historical Note	Effective November 1, 1987. Amended effective October 27, 2003 (amendment 651).

§5H1.8. Criminal History (Policy Statement)

A defendant's criminal history is relevant in determining the applicable criminal history category. *See* Chapter Four (Criminal History and Criminal Livelihood). For grounds of departure based on the defendant's criminal history, *see* §4A1.3 (Departures Based on Inadequacy of Criminal History Category).

Historical Note	Effective November 1, 1987. Amended effective October 27, 2003 (amendment 651).

§5H1.9. Dependence upon Criminal Activity for a Livelihood (Policy Statement)

The degree to which a defendant depends upon criminal activity for a livelihood is relevant in determining the appropriate sentence. *See* Chapter Four, Part B (Career Offenders and Criminal Livelihood).

Historical Note	Effective November 1, 1987.

§5H1.10. Race, Sex, National Origin, Creed, Religion, and Socio-Economic Status (Policy Statement)

These factors are not relevant in the determination of a sentence.

Historical Note	Effective November 1, 1987.

§5H1.11. Military, Civic, Charitable, or Public Service; Employment-Related Contributions; Record of Prior Good Works (Policy Statement)

Military service may be relevant in determining whether a departure is warranted, if the military service, individually or in combination with other offender characteristics, is present to an unusual degree and distinguishes the case from the typical cases covered by the guidelines.

Civic, charitable, or public service; employment-related contributions; and similar prior good works are not ordinarily relevant in determining whether a departure is warranted.

| *Historical Note* | Effective November 1, 1991 (amendment 386). Amended effective November 1, 2004 (amendment 674); November 1, 2010 (amendment 739). |

§5H1.12. Lack of Guidance as a Youth and Similar Circumstances (Policy Statement)

Lack of guidance as a youth and similar circumstances indicating a disadvantaged upbringing are not relevant grounds in determining whether a departure is warranted.

| *Historical Note* | Effective November 1, 1992 (amendment 466). Amended effective November 1, 2004 (amendment 674). |

PART I — [NOT USED]

PART J — RELIEF FROM DISABILITY

| Historical Note | Effective November 1, 1987. Amended effective June 15, 1988 (amendment 55). |

§5J1.1. Relief from Disability Pertaining to Convicted Persons Prohibited from Holding Certain Positions (Policy Statement)

A collateral consequence of conviction of certain crimes described in 29 U.S.C. §§ 504 and 1111 is the prohibition of convicted persons from service and employment with labor unions, employer associations, employee pension and welfare benefit plans, and as labor relations consultants in the private sector. A convicted person's prohibited service or employment in such capacities without having been granted one of the following three statutory procedures of administrative or judicial relief is subject to criminal prosecution. First, a disqualified person whose citizenship rights have been fully restored to him or her in the jurisdiction of conviction, following the revocation of such rights as a result of the disqualifying conviction, is relieved of the disability. Second, a disqualified person convicted after October 12, 1984, may petition the sentencing court to reduce the statutory length of disability (thirteen years after date of sentencing or release from imprisonment, whichever is later) to a lesser period (not less than three years after date of conviction or release from imprisonment, whichever is later). Third, a disqualified person may petition either the United States Parole Commission or a United States District Court judge to exempt his or her service or employment in a particular prohibited capacity pursuant to the procedures set forth in 29 U.S.C. §§ 504(a)(B) and 1111(a)(B). In the case of a person convicted of a disqualifying crime committed before November 1, 1987, the United States Parole Commission will continue to process such exemption applications.

In the case of a person convicted of a disqualifying crime committed on or after November 1, 1987, however, a petition for exemption from disability must be directed to a United States District Court. If the petitioner was convicted of a disqualifying federal offense, the petition is directed to the sentencing judge. If the petitioner was convicted of a disqualifying state or local offense, the petition is directed to the United States District Court for the district in which the offense was committed. In such cases, relief shall not be given to aid rehabilitation, but may be granted only following a clear demonstration by the convicted person that he or she has been rehabilitated since commission of the disqualifying crime and can therefore be trusted not to endanger the organization in the position for which he or she seeks relief from disability.

| Historical Note | Effective November 1, 1987. Amended effective June 15, 1988 (amendment 56). |

PART K — DEPARTURES

1. SUBSTANTIAL ASSISTANCE TO AUTHORITIES

§5K1.1. Substantial Assistance to Authorities (Policy Statement)

Upon motion of the government stating that the defendant has provided substantial assistance in the investigation or prosecution of another person who has committed an offense, the court may depart from the guidelines.

(a) The appropriate reduction shall be determined by the court for reasons stated that may include, but are not limited to, consideration of the following:

(1) the court's evaluation of the significance and usefulness of the defendant's assistance, taking into consideration the government's evaluation of the assistance rendered;

(2) the truthfulness, completeness, and reliability of any information or testimony provided by the defendant;

(3) the nature and extent of the defendant's assistance;

(4) any injury suffered, or any danger or risk of injury to the defendant or his family resulting from his assistance;

(5) the timeliness of the defendant's assistance.

Commentary

Application Notes:

1. Under circumstances set forth in 18 U.S.C. § 3553(e) and 28 U.S.C. § 994(n), as amended, substantial assistance in the investigation or prosecution of another person who has committed an offense may justify a sentence below a statutorily required minimum sentence.

2. The sentencing reduction for assistance to authorities shall be considered independently of any reduction for acceptance of responsibility. Substantial assistance is directed to the investigation and prosecution of criminal activities by persons other than the defendant, while acceptance of responsibility is directed to the defendant's affirmative recognition of responsibility for his own conduct.

3. Substantial weight should be given to the government's evaluation of the extent of the defendant's assistance, particularly where the extent and value of the assistance are difficult to ascertain.

Background: A defendant's assistance to authorities in the investigation of criminal activities has been recognized in practice and by statute as a mitigating sentencing factor. The nature, extent, and significance of assistance can involve a broad spectrum of conduct that must be evaluated by the court on an individual basis. Latitude is, therefore, afforded the sentencing judge to reduce a sentence based upon variable relevant factors, including those listed above. The sentencing judge must, however, state the reasons for reducing a sentence under this section. 18 U.S.C. § 3553(c). The court may elect to provide its reasons to the defendant *in camera* and in writing under seal for the safety of the defendant or to avoid disclosure of an ongoing investigation.

Historical Note	Effective November 1, 1987. Amended effective November 1, 1989 (amendment 290).

§5K1.2.   Refusal to Assist (Policy Statement)

A defendant's refusal to assist authorities in the investigation of other persons may not be considered as an aggravating sentencing factor.

Historical Note	Effective November 1, 1987. Amended effective November 1, 1989 (amendment 291).

*   *   *   *   *

2.   OTHER GROUNDS FOR DEPARTURE

Historical Note	Effective November 1, 1987. Amended effective November 1, 1990 (amendment 358).

§5K2.0.   Grounds for Departure (Policy Statement)

(a)   UPWARD DEPARTURES IN GENERAL AND DOWNWARD DEPARTURES IN CRIMINAL CASES OTHER THAN CHILD CRIMES AND SEXUAL OFFENSES.—

(1)   IN GENERAL.—The sentencing court may depart from the applicable guideline range if—

(A)   in the case of offenses other than child crimes and sexual offenses, the court finds, pursuant to 18 U.S.C. § 3553(b)(1), that there exists an aggravating or mitigating circumstance; or

(B) in the case of child crimes and sexual offenses, the court finds, pursuant to 18 U.S.C. § 3553(b)(2)(A)(i), that there exists an aggravating circumstance,

of a kind, or to a degree, not adequately taken into consideration by the Sentencing Commission in formulating the guidelines that, in order to advance the objectives set forth in 18 U.S.C. § 3553(a)(2), should result in a sentence different from that described.

(2) DEPARTURES BASED ON CIRCUMSTANCES OF A KIND NOT ADEQUATELY TAKEN INTO CONSIDERATION.—

(A) IDENTIFIED CIRCUMSTANCES.—This subpart (Chapter Five, Part K, Subpart 2 (Other Grounds for Departure)) identifies some of the circumstances that the Commission may have not adequately taken into consideration in determining the applicable guideline range (*e.g.*, as a specific offense characteristic or other adjustment). If any such circumstance is present in the case and has not adequately been taken into consideration in determining the applicable guideline range, a departure consistent with 18 U.S.C. § 3553(b) and the provisions of this subpart may be warranted.

(B) UNIDENTIFIED CIRCUMSTANCES.—A departure may be warranted in the exceptional case in which there is present a circumstance that the Commission has not identified in the guidelines but that nevertheless is relevant to determining the appropriate sentence.

(3) DEPARTURES BASED ON CIRCUMSTANCES PRESENT TO A DEGREE NOT ADEQUATELY TAKEN INTO CONSIDERATION.—A departure may be warranted in an exceptional case, even though the circumstance that forms the basis for the departure is taken into consideration in determining the guideline range, if the court determines that such circumstance is present in the offense to a degree substantially in excess of, or substantially below, that which ordinarily is involved in that kind of offense.

(4) DEPARTURES BASED ON NOT ORDINARILY RELEVANT OFFENDER CHARACTERISTICS AND OTHER CIRCUMSTANCES.—An offender characteristic or other circumstance identified in Chapter Five, Part H (Offender Characteristics) or elsewhere in the guidelines as not ordinarily relevant in determining whether a departure is warranted may be relevant to this determination

only if such offender characteristic or other circumstance is present to an exceptional degree.

   (b) DOWNWARD DEPARTURES IN CHILD CRIMES AND SEXUAL OFFENSES.— Under 18 U.S.C. § 3553(b)(2)(A)(ii), the sentencing court may impose a sentence below the range established by the applicable guidelines only if the court finds that there exists a mitigating circumstance of a kind, or to a degree, that—

      (1) has been affirmatively and specifically identified as a permissible ground of downward departure in the sentencing guidelines or policy statements issued under section 994(a) of title 28, United States Code, taking account of any amendments to such sentencing guidelines or policy statements by act of Congress;

      (2) has not adequately been taken into consideration by the Sentencing Commission in formulating the guidelines; and

      (3) should result in a sentence different from that described.

The grounds enumerated in this Part K of Chapter Five are the sole grounds that have been affirmatively and specifically identified as a permissible ground of downward departure in these sentencing guidelines and policy statements. Thus, notwithstanding any other reference to authority to depart downward elsewhere in this Sentencing Manual, a ground of downward departure has not been affirmatively and specifically identified as a permissible ground of downward departure within the meaning of section 3553(b)(2) unless it is expressly enumerated in this Part K as a ground upon which a downward departure may be granted.

   (c) LIMITATION ON DEPARTURES BASED ON MULTIPLE CIRCUMSTANCES.— The court may depart from the applicable guideline range based on a combination of two or more offender characteristics or other circumstances, none of which independently is sufficient to provide a basis for departure, only if—

      (1) such offender characteristics or other circumstances, taken together, make the case an exceptional one; and

      (2) each such offender characteristic or other circumstance is—

         (A) present to a substantial degree; and

(B) identified in the guidelines as a permissible ground for departure, even if such offender characteristic or other circumstance is not ordinarily relevant to a determination of whether a departure is warranted.

(d) PROHIBITED DEPARTURES.—Notwithstanding subsections (a) and (b) of this policy statement, or any other provision in the guidelines, the court may not depart from the applicable guideline range based on any of the following circumstances:

(1) Any circumstance specifically prohibited as a ground for departure in §§5H1.10 (Race, Sex, National Origin, Creed, Religion, and Socio-Economic Status), 5H1.12 (Lack of Guidance as a Youth and Similar Circumstances), the last sentence of 5H1.4 (Physical Condition, Including Drug or Alcohol Dependence or Abuse; Gambling Addiction), and the last sentence of 5K2.12 (Coercion and Duress).

(2) The defendant's acceptance of responsibility for the offense, which may be taken into account only under §3E1.1 (Acceptance of Responsibility).

(3) The defendant's aggravating or mitigating role in the offense, which may be taken into account only under §3B1.1 (Aggravating Role) or §3B1.2 (Mitigating Role), respectively.

(4) The defendant's decision, in and of itself, to plead guilty to the offense or to enter a plea agreement with respect to the offense (*i.e.*, a departure may not be based merely on the fact that the defendant decided to plead guilty or to enter into a plea agreement, but a departure may be based on justifiable, non-prohibited reasons as part of a sentence that is recommended, or agreed to, in the plea agreement and accepted by the court. *See* §6B1.2 (Standards for Acceptance of Plea Agreement).

(5) The defendant's fulfillment of restitution obligations only to the extent required by law including the guidelines (*i.e.*, a departure may not be based on unexceptional efforts to remedy the harm caused by the offense).

(6) Any other circumstance specifically prohibited as a ground for departure in the guidelines.

(e) REQUIREMENT OF SPECIFIC WRITTEN REASONS FOR DEPARTURE.—If the court departs from the applicable guideline range, it shall state, pursuant to 18 U.S.C. § 3553(c), its specific reasons for departure in open court at the time of sentencing and, with limited exception in the case of statements received *in camera*, shall state those reasons with specificity in the statement of reasons form.

Commentary

Application Notes:

1. **Definitions.**—For purposes of this policy statement:

    "*Circumstance*" includes, as appropriate, an offender characteristic or any other offense factor.

    "*Depart*", "*departure*", "*downward departure*", and "*upward departure*" have the meaning given those terms in Application Note 1 of the Commentary to §1B1.1 (Application Instructions).

2. **Scope of this Policy Statement.**—

    (A) **Departures Covered by this Policy Statement.**—This policy statement covers departures from the applicable guideline range based on offense characteristics or offender characteristics of a kind, or to a degree, not adequately taken into consideration in determining that range. *See* 18 U.S.C. § 3553(b).

    Subsection (a) of this policy statement applies to upward departures in all cases covered by the guidelines and to downward departures in all such cases except for downward departures in child crimes and sexual offenses.

    Subsection (b) of this policy statement applies only to downward departures in child crimes and sexual offenses.

    (B) **Departures Covered by Other Guidelines.**—This policy statement does not cover the following departures, which are addressed elsewhere in the guidelines: (i) departures based on the defendant's criminal history (*see* Chapter Four (Criminal History and Criminal Livelihood), particularly §4A1.3 (Departures Based on Inadequacy of Criminal History Category)); (ii) departures based on the defendant's substantial assistance to the authorities (*see* §5K1.1 (Substantial Assistance to Authorities)); and (iii) departures based on early disposition programs (*see* §5K3.1 (Early Disposition Programs)).

3. **Kinds and Expected Frequency of Departures under Subsection (a).**—As set forth in subsection (a), there generally are two kinds of departures from the guidelines based on offense characteristics and/or offender characteristics: (A) departures based on circumstances of a kind not adequately taken into consideration in the guidelines; and (B) departures based on circumstances that are present to a degree not adequately taken into consideration in the guidelines.

    (A) **Departures Based on Circumstances of a Kind Not Adequately Taken into Account in Guidelines.**—Subsection (a)(2) authorizes the court to depart if there exists an aggravating or a mitigating circumstance in a case under 18 U.S.C. § 3553(b)(1), or an aggravating circumstance in a case under 18 U.S.C. § 3553(b)(2)(A)(i), of a kind not adequately taken into consideration in the guidelines.

        (i) **Identified Circumstances.**—This subpart (Chapter Five, Part K, Subpart 2) identifies several circumstances that the Commission may have not adequately taken into consideration in setting the offense level for certain cases. Offense guidelines in Chapter Two (Offense Conduct) and adjustments in Chapter Three (Adjustments) sometimes identify circumstances the Commission may have not adequately taken into consideration in setting the offense level for offenses covered by those guidelines. If the offense guideline in Chapter Two or an adjustment in Chapter Three does not adequately take that circumstance into consideration in setting the offense level for the offense, and only to the extent not adequately taken into consideration, a departure based on that circumstance may be warranted.

(ii) **Unidentified Circumstances.**—A case may involve circumstances, in addition to those identified by the guidelines, that have not adequately been taken into consideration by the Commission, and the presence of any such circumstance may warrant departure from the guidelines in that case. However, inasmuch as the Commission has continued to monitor and refine the guidelines since their inception to take into consideration relevant circumstances in sentencing, it is expected that departures based on such unidentified circumstances will occur rarely and only in exceptional cases.

(B) **Departures Based on Circumstances Present to a Degree Not Adequately Taken into Consideration in Guidelines.**—

(i) **In General.**—Subsection (a)(3) authorizes the court to depart if there exists an aggravating or a mitigating circumstance in a case under 18 U.S.C. § 3553(b)(1), or an aggravating circumstance in a case under 18 U.S.C. § 3553(b)(2)(A)(i), to a degree not adequately taken into consideration in the guidelines. However, inasmuch as the Commission has continued to monitor and refine the guidelines since their inception to determine the most appropriate weight to be accorded the mitigating and aggravating circumstances specified in the guidelines, it is expected that departures based on the weight accorded to any such circumstance will occur rarely and only in exceptional cases.

(ii) **Examples.**—As set forth in subsection (a)(3), if the applicable offense guideline and adjustments take into consideration a circumstance identified in this subpart, departure is warranted only if the circumstance is present to a degree substantially in excess of that which ordinarily is involved in the offense. Accordingly, a departure pursuant to §5K2.7 for the disruption of a governmental function would have to be substantial to warrant departure from the guidelines when the applicable offense guideline is bribery or obstruction of justice. When the guideline covering the mailing of injurious articles is applicable, however, and the offense caused disruption of a governmental function, departure from the applicable guideline range more readily would be appropriate. Similarly, physical injury would not warrant departure from the guidelines when the robbery offense guideline is applicable because the robbery guideline includes a specific adjustment based on the extent of any injury. However, because the robbery guideline does not deal with injury to more than one victim, departure may be warranted if several persons were injured.

(C) **Departures Based on Circumstances Identified as Not Ordinarily Relevant.**—Because certain circumstances are specified in the guidelines as not ordinarily relevant to sentencing (*see, e.g.*, Chapter Five, Part H (Specific Offender Characteristics)), a departure based on any one of such circumstances should occur only in exceptional cases, and only if the circumstance is present in the case to an exceptional degree. If two or more of such circumstances each is present in the case to a substantial degree, however, and taken together make the case an exceptional one, the court may consider whether a departure would be warranted pursuant to subsection (c). Departures based on a combination of not ordinarily relevant circumstances that are present to a substantial degree should occur extremely rarely and only in exceptional cases.

In addition, as required by subsection (e), each circumstance forming the basis for a departure described in this subdivision shall be stated with specificity in the statement of reasons form.

4. **Downward Departures in Child Crimes and Sexual Offenses.**—

(A) **Definition.**—For purposes of this policy statement, the term "*child crimes and sexual offenses*" means offenses under any of the following: 18 U.S.C. § 1201 (involving a minor victim), 18 U.S.C. § 1591, or chapter 71, 109A, 110, or 117 of title 18, United States Code.

(B) **Standard for Departure.**—

    (i) **Requirement of Affirmative and Specific Identification of Departure Ground.**—The standard for a downward departure in child crimes and sexual offenses differs from the standard for other departures under this policy statement in that it includes a requirement, set forth in 18 U.S.C. § 3553(b)(2)(A)(ii)(I) and subsection (b)(1) of this guideline, that any mitigating circumstance that forms the basis for such a downward departure be affirmatively and specifically identified as a ground for downward departure in this part (*i.e.*, Chapter Five, Part K).

    (ii) **Application of Subsection (b)(2).**—The commentary in Application Note 3 of this policy statement, except for the commentary in Application Note 3(A)(ii) relating to unidentified circumstances, shall apply to the court's determination of whether a case meets the requirement, set forth in subsection 18 U.S.C. § 3553(b)(2)(A)(ii)(II) and subsection (b)(2) of this policy statement, that the mitigating circumstance forming the basis for a downward departure in child crimes and sexual offenses be of kind, or to a degree, not adequately taken into consideration by the Commission.

5. **Departures Based on Plea Agreements.**—Subsection (d)(4) prohibits a downward departure based only on the defendant's decision, in and of itself, to plead guilty to the offense or to enter a plea agreement with respect to the offense. Even though a departure may not be based merely on the fact that the defendant agreed to plead guilty or enter a plea agreement, a departure may be based on justifiable, non-prohibited reasons for departure as part of a sentence that is recommended, or agreed to, in the plea agreement and accepted by the court. *See* §6B1.2 (Standards for Acceptance of Plea Agreements). In cases in which the court departs based on such reasons as set forth in the plea agreement, the court must state the reasons for departure with specificity in the statement of reasons form, as required by subsection (e).

Background: This policy statement sets forth the standards for departing from the applicable guideline range based on offense and offender characteristics of a kind, or to a degree, not adequately considered by the Commission. Circumstances the Commission has determined are not ordinarily relevant to determining whether a departure is warranted or are prohibited as bases for departure are addressed in Chapter Five, Part H (Offender Characteristics) and in this policy statement. Other departures, such as those based on the defendant's criminal history, the defendant's substantial assistance to authorities, and early disposition programs, are addressed elsewhere in the guidelines.

As acknowledged by Congress in the Sentencing Reform Act and by the Commission when the first set of guidelines was promulgated, "it is difficult to prescribe a single set of guidelines that encompasses the vast range of human conduct potentially relevant to a sentencing decision." (*See* Chapter One, Part A). Departures, therefore, perform an integral function in the sentencing guideline system. Departures permit courts to impose an appropriate sentence in the exceptional case in which mechanical application of the guidelines would fail to achieve the statutory purposes and goals of sentencing. Departures also help maintain "sufficient flexibility to permit individualized sentences when warranted by mitigating or aggravating factors not taken into account in the establishment of general sentencing practices." 28 U.S.C. § 991(b)(1)(B). By monitoring when courts depart from the guidelines and by analyzing their stated reasons for doing so, along with appellate cases reviewing these departures, the Commission can further refine the guidelines to specify more precisely when departures should and should not be permitted.

As reaffirmed in the Prosecutorial Remedies and Other Tools to end the Exploitation of Children Today Act of 2003 (the "PROTECT Act", Public Law 108–21), circumstances warranting departure should be rare. Departures were never intended to permit sentencing courts to substitute their policy judgments for those of Congress and the Sentencing Commission. Departure in such circumstances would produce unwarranted sentencing disparity, which the Sentencing Reform Act was designed to avoid.

In order for appellate courts to fulfill their statutory duties under 18 U.S.C. § 3742 and for the Commission to fulfill its ongoing responsibility to refine the guidelines in light of information it receives on departures, it is essential that sentencing courts state with specificity the reasons for departure, as required by the PROTECT Act.

This policy statement, including its commentary, was substantially revised, effective October 27, 2003, in response to directives contained in the PROTECT Act, particularly the directive in section 401(m) of that Act to—

> "(1) review the grounds of downward departure that are authorized by the sentencing guidelines, policy statements, and official commentary of the Sentencing Commission; and
> (2) promulgate, pursuant to section 994 of title 28, United States Code—
> (A) appropriate amendments to the sentencing guidelines, policy statements, and official commentary to ensure that the incidence of downward departures is substantially reduced;
> (B) a policy statement authorizing a departure pursuant to an early disposition program; and
> (C) any other conforming amendments to the sentencing guidelines, policy statements, and official commentary of the Sentencing Commission necessitated by the Act, including a revision of . . . section 5K2.0".

The substantial revision of this policy statement in response to the PROTECT Act was intended to refine the standards applicable to departures while giving due regard for concepts, such as the "heartland", that have evolved in departure jurisprudence over time.

Section 401(b)(1) of the PROTECT Act directly amended this policy statement to add subsection (b), effective April 30, 2003.

Historical Note	Effective November 1, 1987. Amended effective June 15, 1988 (amendment 57); November 1, 1990 (amendment 358); November 1, 1994 (amendment 508); November 1, 1997 (amendment 561); November 1, 1998 (amendment 585); April 30, 2003 (amendment 649); October 27, 2003 (amendment 651); November 1, 2008 (amendment 725); November 1, 2010 (amendment 739); November 1, 2011 (amendment 757); November 1, 2012 (amendment 770).

§5K2.1. Death (Policy Statement)

If death resulted, the court may increase the sentence above the authorized guideline range.

Loss of life does not automatically suggest a sentence at or near the statutory maximum. The sentencing judge must give consideration to matters that would normally distinguish among levels of homicide, such as the defendant's state of mind and the degree of planning or preparation. Other appropriate factors are whether multiple deaths resulted, and the means by which life was taken. The extent of the increase should depend on the dangerousness of the defendant's conduct, the extent to which death or serious injury was intended or knowingly risked, and the extent to which the offense level for the offense of conviction, as determined by the other Chapter Two guidelines, already reflects the risk of personal injury. For example, a substantial increase may be appropriate if the death was intended or knowingly risked or if the underlying offense was one for which base offense levels do not reflect an allowance for the risk of personal injury, such as fraud.

Historical Note	Effective November 1, 1987.

§5K2.2. Physical Injury (Policy Statement)

If significant physical injury resulted, the court may increase the sentence above the authorized guideline range. The extent of the increase ordinarily should depend on the extent of the injury, the degree to which it may prove permanent, and the extent to which the injury was intended or knowingly risked. When the victim suffers a major, permanent disability and when such injury was intentionally inflicted, a substantial departure may be appropriate. If the injury is less serious or if the defendant (though criminally negligent) did not knowingly create the risk of harm, a less substantial departure would be indicated. In general, the same considerations apply as in §5K2.1.

Historical Note	Effective November 1, 1987.

§5K2.3. Extreme Psychological Injury (Policy Statement)

If a victim or victims suffered psychological injury much more serious than that normally resulting from commission of the offense, the court may increase the sentence above the authorized guideline range. The extent of the increase ordinarily should depend on the severity of the psychological injury and the extent to which the injury was intended or knowingly risked.

Normally, psychological injury would be sufficiently severe to warrant application of this adjustment only when there is a substantial impairment of the intellectual, psychological, emotional, or behavioral functioning of a victim, when the impairment is likely to be of an extended or continuous duration, and when the impairment manifests itself by physical or psychological symptoms or by changes in behavior patterns. The court should consider the extent to which such harm was likely, given the nature of the defendant's conduct.

Historical Note	Effective November 1, 1987.

§5K2.4. Abduction or Unlawful Restraint (Policy Statement)

If a person was abducted, taken hostage, or unlawfully restrained to facilitate commission of the offense or to facilitate the escape from the scene of the crime, the court may increase the sentence above the authorized guideline range.

Historical Note	Effective November 1, 1987.

§5K2.5. Property Damage or Loss (Policy Statement)

If the offense caused property damage or loss not taken into account within the guidelines, the court may increase the sentence above the authorized guideline range. The extent of the increase ordinarily should depend on the extent to which the harm was intended or knowingly risked and on the extent to which the harm to property is more serious than other harm caused or risked by the conduct relevant to the offense of conviction.

| Historical Note | Effective November 1, 1987. |

§5K2.6. Weapons and Dangerous Instrumentalities (Policy Statement)

If a weapon or dangerous instrumentality was used or possessed in the commission of the offense the court may increase the sentence above the authorized guideline range. The extent of the increase ordinarily should depend on the dangerousness of the weapon, the manner in which it was used, and the extent to which its use endangered others. The discharge of a firearm might warrant a substantial sentence increase.

| Historical Note | Effective November 1, 1987. |

§5K2.7. Disruption of Governmental Function (Policy Statement)

If the defendant's conduct resulted in a significant disruption of a governmental function, the court may increase the sentence above the authorized guideline range to reflect the nature and extent of the disruption and the importance of the governmental function affected. Departure from the guidelines ordinarily would not be justified when the offense of conviction is an offense such as bribery or obstruction of justice; in such cases interference with a governmental function is inherent in the offense, and unless the circumstances are unusual the guidelines will reflect the appropriate punishment for such interference.

| Historical Note | Effective November 1, 1987. |

§5K2.8. Extreme Conduct (Policy Statement)

If the defendant's conduct was unusually heinous, cruel, brutal, or degrading to the victim, the court may increase the sentence above the guideline range to reflect the nature of the conduct. Examples of extreme conduct include torture of a victim, gratuitous infliction of injury, or prolonging of pain or humiliation.

| Historical Note | Effective November 1, 1987. |

§5K2.9. Criminal Purpose (Policy Statement)

If the defendant committed the offense in order to facilitate or conceal the commission of another offense, the court may increase the sentence above the guideline range to reflect the actual seriousness of the defendant's conduct.

Historical Note	Effective November 1, 1987.

§5K2.10. Victim's Conduct (Policy Statement)

If the victim's wrongful conduct contributed significantly to provoking the offense behavior, the court may reduce the sentence below the guideline range to reflect the nature and circumstances of the offense. In deciding whether a sentence reduction is warranted, and the extent of such reduction, the court should consider the following:

(1) The size and strength of the victim, or other relevant physical characteristics, in comparison with those of the defendant.

(2) The persistence of the victim's conduct and any efforts by the defendant to prevent confrontation.

(3) The danger reasonably perceived by the defendant, including the victim's reputation for violence.

(4) The danger actually presented to the defendant by the victim.

(5) Any other relevant conduct by the victim that substantially contributed to the danger presented.

(6) The proportionality and reasonableness of the defendant's response to the victim's provocation.

Victim misconduct ordinarily would not be sufficient to warrant application of this provision in the context of offenses under Chapter Two, Part A, Subpart 3 (Criminal Sexual Abuse). In addition, this provision usually would not be relevant in the context of non-violent offenses. There may, however, be unusual circumstances in which substantial victim misconduct would warrant a reduced penalty in the case of a non-violent offense. For example, an extended course of provocation and harassment might lead a defendant to steal or destroy property in retaliation.

| *Historical Note* | Effective November 1, 1987. Amended effective October 27, 2003 (amendment 651). |

§5K2.11. Lesser Harms (Policy Statement)

Sometimes, a defendant may commit a crime in order to avoid a perceived greater harm. In such instances, a reduced sentence may be appropriate, provided that the circumstances significantly diminish society's interest in punishing the conduct, for example, in the case of a mercy killing. Where the interest in punishment or deterrence is not reduced, a reduction in sentence is not warranted. For example, providing defense secrets to a hostile power should receive no lesser punishment simply because the defendant believed that the government's policies were misdirected.

In other instances, conduct may not cause or threaten the harm or evil sought to be prevented by the law proscribing the offense at issue. For example, where a war veteran possessed a machine gun or grenade as a trophy, or a school teacher possessed controlled substances for display in a drug education program, a reduced sentence might be warranted.

| *Historical Note* | Effective November 1, 1987. |

§5K2.12. Coercion and Duress (Policy Statement)

If the defendant committed the offense because of serious coercion, blackmail or duress, under circumstances not amounting to a complete defense, the court may depart downward. The extent of the decrease ordinarily should depend on the reasonableness of the defendant's actions, on the proportionality of the defendant's actions to the seriousness of coercion, blackmail, or duress involved, and on the extent to which the conduct would have been less harmful under the circumstances as the defendant believed them to be. Ordinarily coercion will be sufficiently serious to warrant departure only when it involves a threat of physical injury, substantial damage to property or similar injury resulting from the unlawful action of a third party or from a natural emergency. Notwithstanding this policy statement, personal financial difficulties and economic pressures upon a trade or business do not warrant a downward departure.

| *Historical Note* | Effective November 1, 1987. Amended effective October 27, 2003 (amendment 651); November 1, 2004 (amendment 674). |

§5K2.13. Diminished Capacity (Policy Statement)

A downward departure may be warranted if (1) the defendant committed the offense while suffering from a significantly reduced mental capacity; and (2) the significantly reduced mental capacity contributed substantially to the commission of the offense. Similarly, if a departure is warranted under this policy statement, the extent of the departure should reflect the extent to which the reduced mental capacity contributed to the commission of the offense.

However, the court may not depart below the applicable guideline range if (1) the significantly reduced mental capacity was caused by the voluntary use of drugs or other intoxicants; (2) the facts and circumstances of the defendant's offense indicate a need to protect the public because the offense involved actual violence or a serious threat of violence; (3) the defendant's criminal history indicates a need to incarcerate the defendant to protect the public; or (4) the defendant has been convicted of an offense under chapter 71, 109A, 110, or 117, of title 18, United States Code.

Commentary

Application Note:

1. For purposes of this policy statement—

   "*Significantly reduced mental capacity*" means the defendant, although convicted, has a significantly impaired ability to (A) understand the wrongfulness of the behavior comprising the offense or to exercise the power of reason; or (B) control behavior that the defendant knows is wrongful.

Background: Section 401(b)(5) of Public Law 108–21 directly amended this policy statement to add subdivision (4), effective April 30, 2003.

Historical Note	Effective November 1, 1987. Amended effective November 1, 1998 (amendment 583); April 30, 2003 (amendment 649); October 27, 2003 (amendment 651); November 1, 2004 (amendment 674).

§5K2.14. Public Welfare (Policy Statement)

If national security, public health, or safety was significantly endangered, the court may depart upward to reflect the nature and circumstances of the offense.

Historical Note	Effective November 1, 1987. Amended effective November 1, 2004 (amendment 674).

§5K2.15. [Deleted]

Historical Note   Effective November 1, 1989 (amendment 292), was deleted effective November 1, 1995 (amendment 526).

§5K2.16. Voluntary Disclosure of Offense (Policy Statement)

If the defendant voluntarily discloses to authorities the existence of, and accepts responsibility for, the offense prior to the discovery of such offense, and if such offense was unlikely to have been discovered otherwise, a downward departure may be warranted. For example, a downward departure under this section might be considered where a defendant, motivated by remorse, discloses an offense that otherwise would have remained undiscovered. This provision does not apply where the motivating factor is the defendant's knowledge that discovery of the offense is likely or imminent, or where the defendant's disclosure occurs in connection with the investigation or prosecution of the defendant for related conduct.

Historical Note   Effective November 1, 1991 (amendment 420). Amended effective November 1, 2004 (amendment 674).

§5K2.17. Semiautomatic Firearms Capable of Accepting Large Capacity Magazine (Policy Statement)

If the defendant possessed a semiautomatic firearm capable of accepting a large capacity magazine in connection with a crime of violence or controlled substance offense, an upward departure may be warranted. A "semiautomatic firearm capable of accepting a large capacity magazine" means a semiautomatic firearm that has the ability to fire many rounds without reloading because at the time of the offense (1) the firearm had attached to it a magazine or similar device that could accept more than 15 rounds of ammunition; or (2) a magazine or similar device that could accept more than 15 rounds of ammunition was in close proximity to the firearm. The extent of any increase should depend upon the degree to which the nature of the weapon increased the likelihood of death or injury in the circumstances of the particular case.

Commentary

Application Note:

1. "*Crime of violence*" and "*controlled substance offense*" are defined in §4B1.2 (Definitions of Terms Used in Section 4B1.1).

Historical Note	Effective November 1, 1995 (amendment 531). Amended effective November 1, 2006 (amendment 691); November 1, 2010 (amendment 746).

§5K2.18. Violent Street Gangs (Policy Statement)

If the defendant is subject to an enhanced sentence under 18 U.S.C. § 521 (pertaining to criminal street gangs), an upward departure may be warranted. The purpose of this departure provision is to enhance the sentences of defendants who participate in groups, clubs, organizations, or associations that use violence to further their ends. It is to be noted that there may be cases in which 18 U.S.C. § 521 applies, but no violence is established. In such cases, it is expected that the guidelines will account adequately for the conduct and, consequently, this departure provision would not apply.

Historical Note	Effective November 1, 1995 (amendment 532).

§5K2.19. [Deleted]

Historical Note	Section 5K2.19 (Post-Sentencing Rehabilitative Efforts) (Policy Statement), effective November 1, 2000 (amendment 602), was deleted effective November 1, 2012 (amendment 768).

§5K2.20. Aberrant Behavior (Policy Statement)

(a) IN GENERAL.—Except where a defendant is convicted of an offense involving a minor victim under section 1201, an offense under section 1591, or an offense under chapter 71, 109A, 110, or 117, of title 18, United States Code, a downward departure may be warranted in an exceptional case if (1) the defendant's criminal conduct meets the requirements of subsection (b); and (2) the departure is not prohibited under subsection (c).

(b) REQUIREMENTS.—The court may depart downward under this policy statement only if the defendant committed a single criminal occurrence or single criminal transaction that (1) was committed without significant planning; (2) was of limited duration; and (3) represents a marked deviation by the defendant from an otherwise law-abiding life.

(c) PROHIBITIONS BASED ON THE PRESENCE OF CERTAIN CIRCUM-STANCES.—The court may not depart downward pursuant to this policy statement if any of the following circumstances are present:

(1) The offense involved serious bodily injury or death.

(2) The defendant discharged a firearm or otherwise used a firearm or a dangerous weapon.

(3) The instant offense of conviction is a serious drug trafficking offense.

(4) The defendant has either of the following: (A) more than one criminal history point, as determined under Chapter Four (Criminal History and Criminal Livelihood) before application of subsection (b) of §4A1.3 (Departures Based on Inadequacy of Criminal History Category); or (B) a prior federal or state felony conviction, or any other significant prior criminal behavior, regardless of whether the conviction or significant prior criminal behavior is countable under Chapter Four.

Commentary

Application Notes:

1. **Definitions.**—For purposes of this policy statement:

   "*Dangerous weapon*," "*firearm*," "*otherwise used*," and "*serious bodily injury*" have the meaning given those terms in the Commentary to §1B1.1 (Application Instructions).

   "*Serious drug trafficking offense*" means any controlled substance offense under title 21, United States Code, other than simple possession under 21 U.S.C. § 844, that provides for a mandatory minimum term of imprisonment of five years or greater, regardless of whether the defendant meets the criteria of §5C1.2 (Limitation on Applicability of Statutory Mandatory Minimum Sentences in Certain Cases).

2. **Repetitious or Significant, Planned Behavior.**—Repetitious or significant, planned behavior does not meet the requirements of subsection (b). For example, a fraud scheme generally would not meet such requirements because such a scheme usually involves repetitive acts, rather than a single occurrence or single criminal transaction, and significant planning.

3. **Other Circumstances to Consider.**—In determining whether the court should depart under this policy statement, the court may consider the defendant's (A) mental and emotional conditions; (B) employment record; (C) record of prior good works; (D) motivation for committing the offense; and (E) efforts to mitigate the effects of the offense.

Background: Section 401(b)(3) of Public Law 108–21 directly amended subsection (a) of this policy statement, effective April 30, 2003.

Historical Note	Effective November 1, 2000 (amendment 603). Amended effective April 30, 2003 (amendment 649); October 27, 2003 (amendment 651).

---

§5K2.21. Dismissed and Uncharged Conduct (Policy Statement)

The court may depart upward to reflect the actual seriousness of the offense based on conduct (1) underlying a charge dismissed as part of a plea agreement in the case, or underlying a potential charge not pursued in the case as part of a plea agreement or for any other reason; and (2) that did not enter into the determination of the applicable guideline range.

Historical Note	Effective November 1, 2000 (amendment 604). Amended effective November 1, 2004 (amendment 674).

---

§5K2.22. Specific Offender Characteristics as Grounds for Downward Departure in Child Crimes and Sexual Offenses (Policy Statement)

In sentencing a defendant convicted of an offense involving a minor victim under section 1201, an offense under section 1591, or an offense under chapter 71, 109A, 110, or 117, of title 18, United States Code:

(1) Age may be a reason to depart downward only if and to the extent permitted by §5H1.1.

(2) An extraordinary physical impairment may be a reason to depart downward only if and to the extent permitted by §5H1.4.

(3) Drug, alcohol, or gambling dependence or abuse is not a reason to depart downward.

Commentary

Background: Section 401(b)(2) of Public Law 108–21 directly amended Chapter Five, Part K, to add this policy statement, effective April 30, 2003.

Historical Note	Effective April 30, 2003 (amendment 649). Amended effective November 1, 2004 (amendment 674).

---

§5K2.23. Discharged Terms of Imprisonment (Policy Statement)

A downward departure may be appropriate if the defendant (1) has completed serving a term of imprisonment; and (2) subsection (b) of §5G1.3 (Imposition of a Sentence on a Defendant Subject to Undischarged Term of Imprisonment or Anticipated Term of Imprisonment) would have provided an adjustment had that completed term of imprisonment been undischarged at the time of sentencing for the instant offense. Any such departure should be fashioned to achieve a reasonable punishment for the instant offense.

Historical *Note*	Effective November 1, 2003 (amendment 660). Amended effective November 1, 2004 (amendment 674); November 1, 2014 (amendment 787).

§5K2.24. Commission of Offense While Wearing or Displaying Unauthorized or Counterfeit Insignia or Uniform (Policy Statement)

If, during the commission of the offense, the defendant wore or displayed an official, or counterfeit official, insignia or uniform received in violation of 18 U.S.C. § 716, an upward departure may be warranted.

Commentary

Application Note:

1. **Definition.**—For purposes of this policy statement, "*official insignia or uniform*" has the meaning given that term in 18 U.S.C. § 716(c)(3).

Historical *Note*	Effective November 1, 2007 (amendment 700).

*   *   *   *   *

3.   EARLY DISPOSITION PROGRAMS

Historical *Note*	Effective October 27, 2003 (amendment 651).

§5K3.1.   Early Disposition Programs (Policy Statement)

Upon motion of the Government, the court may depart downward not more than **4** levels pursuant to an early disposition program authorized by the Attorney General of the United States and the United States Attorney for the district in which the court resides.

Commentary

Background: This policy statement implements the directive to the Commission in section 401(m)(2)(B) of the Prosecutorial Remedies and Other Tools to end the Exploitation of Children Today Act of 2003 (the "PROTECT Act", Public Law 108–21).

Historical Note	Effective October 27, 2003 (amendment 651).

CHAPTER SIX

SENTENCING PROCEDURES, PLEA AGREEMENTS, AND CRIME VICTIMS' RIGHTS

Historical Note	Effective November 1, 1987. Amended effective November 1, 2006 (amendment 694).

PART A — SENTENCING PROCEDURES

Introductory Commentary

This Part addresses sentencing procedures that are applicable in all cases, including those in which guilty or *nolo contendere* pleas are entered with or without a plea agreement between the parties, and convictions based upon judicial findings or verdicts. It sets forth the procedures for establishing the facts upon which the sentence will be based. Reliable fact-finding is essential to procedural due process and to the accuracy and uniformity of sentencing.

Historical Note	Effective November 1, 1987.

§6A1.1. Presentence Report (Policy Statement)

    (a)   The probation officer must conduct a presentence investigation and submit a report to the court before it imposes sentence unless—

        (1)   18 U.S.C. § 3593(c) or another statute requires otherwise; or

        (2)   the court finds that the information in the record enables it to meaningfully exercise its sentencing authority under 18 U.S.C. § 3553, and the court explains its finding on the record.

        Rule 32(c)(1)(A), Fed. R. Crim. P.

    (b)   The defendant may not waive preparation of the presentence report.

Commentary

A thorough presentence investigation ordinarily is essential in determining the facts relevant to sentencing. Rule 32(c)(1)(A) permits the judge to dispense with a presentence report in certain limited circumstances, as when a specific statute requires or when the court finds sufficient information in the record to enable it to exercise its statutory sentencing authority meaningfully and explains its finding on the record.

Historical Note	Effective November 1, 1987. Amended effective June 15, 1988 (amendment 58); November 1, 1989 (amendment 293); November 1, 1997 (amendment 574); November 1, 2004 (amendment 674).

§6A1.2. Disclosure of Presentence Report; Issues in Dispute (Policy Statement)

(a) The probation officer must give the presentence report to the defendant, the defendant's attorney, and an attorney for the government at least 35 days before sentencing unless the defendant waives this minimum period. Rule 32(e)(2), Fed. R. Crim. P.

(b) Within 14 days after receiving the presentence report, the parties must state in writing any objections, including objections to material information, sentencing guideline ranges, and policy statements contained in or omitted from the report. An objecting party must provide a copy of its objections to the opposing party and to the probation officer. After receiving objections, the probation officer may meet with the parties to discuss the objections. The probation officer may then investigate further and revise the presentence report accordingly. Rule 32(f), Fed. R. Crim. P.

(c) At least 7 days before sentencing, the probation officer must submit to the court and to the parties the presentence report and an addendum containing any unresolved objections, the grounds for those objections, and the probation officer's comments on them. Rule 32(g), Fed. R. Crim. P.

Commentary

Background: In order to focus the issues prior to sentencing, the parties are required to respond in writing to the presentence report and to identify any issues in dispute. *See* Rule 32(f), Fed. R. Crim. P.

Historical Note	Effective November 1, 1987. Amended effective June 15, 1988 (amendment 59); November 1, 1991 (amendment 425); November 1, 1997 (amendment 574); November 1, 2004 (amendment 674).

§6A1.3. Resolution of Disputed Factors (Policy Statement)

(a) When any factor important to the sentencing determination is reasonably in dispute, the parties shall be given an adequate opportunity to present information to the court regarding that factor. In resolving any dispute concerning a factor important to the sentencing determination, the court may consider relevant information without regard to its admissibility under the rules of evidence applicable at trial, provided that the information has sufficient indicia of reliability to support its probable accuracy.

(b) The court shall resolve disputed sentencing factors at a sentencing hearing in accordance with Rule 32(i), Fed. R. Crim. P.

Commentary

Although lengthy sentencing hearings seldom should be necessary, disputes about sentencing factors must be resolved with care. When a dispute exists about any factor important to the sentencing determination, the court must ensure that the parties have an adequate opportunity to present relevant information. Written statements of counsel or affidavits of witnesses may be adequate under many circumstances. *See, e.g., United States v. Ibanez*, 924 F.2d 427 (2d Cir. 1991). An evidentiary hearing may sometimes be the only reliable way to resolve disputed issues. *See, e.g., United States v. Jimenez Martinez*, 83 F.3d 488, 494–95 (1st Cir. 1996) (finding error in district court's denial of defendant's motion for evidentiary hearing given questionable reliability of affidavit on which the district court relied at sentencing); *United States v. Roberts*, 14 F.3d 502, 521(10th Cir. 1993) (remanding because district court did not hold evidentiary hearing to address defendants' objections to drug quantity determination or make requisite findings of fact regarding drug quantity); *see also, United States v. Fatico*, 603 F.2d 1053, 1057 n.9 (2d Cir. 1979), *cert. denied*, 444 U.S. 1073 (1980). The sentencing court must determine the appropriate procedure in light of the nature of the dispute, its relevance to the sentencing determination, and applicable case law.

In determining the relevant facts, sentencing judges are not restricted to information that would be admissible at trial. *See* 18 U.S.C. § 3661; *see also United States v. Watts*, 519 U.S. 148, 154 (1997) (holding that lower evidentiary standard at sentencing permits sentencing court's consideration of acquitted conduct); *Witte v. United States*, 515 U.S. 389, 399–401 (1995) (noting that sentencing courts have traditionally considered wide range of information without the procedural protections of a criminal trial, including information concerning criminal conduct that may be the subject of a subsequent prosecution); *Nichols v. United States*, 511 U.S. 738, 747–48 (1994) (noting that district courts have traditionally considered defendant's prior criminal conduct even when the conduct did not result in a conviction). Any information may be considered, so long as it has sufficient indicia of reliability to support its probable accuracy. *Watts*, 519 U.S. at 157; *Nichols*, 511 U.S. at 748; *United States v. Zuleta-Alvarez*, 922 F.2d 33 (1st Cir. 1990), *cert. denied*, 500 U.S. 927 (1991); *United States v. Beaulieu*, 893 F.2d 1177 (10th Cir.), *cert. denied*, 497 U.S. 1038 (1990). Reliable hearsay evidence may be considered. *United States v. Petty*, 982 F.2d 1365 (9th Cir. 1993), *cert. denied*, 510 U.S. 1040 (1994); *United States v. Sciarrino*, 884 F.2d 95 (3d Cir.), *cert. denied*, 493 U.S. 997 (1989). Out-of-court declarations by an unidentified informant may be considered where there is good cause for the non-disclosure of the informant's identity and there is sufficient corroboration by other means. *United States v. Rogers*, 1 F.3d 341 (5th Cir. 1993); *see also United States v. Young*, 981 F.2d 180 (5th Cir.), *cert. denied*, 508 U.S. 980 (1993); *United States v. Fatico*, 579 F.2d 707, 713 (2d Cir. 1978), *cert. denied*, 444 U.S. 1073 (1980). Unreliable allegations shall not be considered. *United States v. Ortiz*, 993 F.2d 204 (10th Cir. 1993).

The Commission believes that use of a preponderance of the evidence standard is appropriate to meet due process requirements and policy concerns in resolving disputes regarding application of the guidelines to the facts of a case.

§6A1.5

| Historical Note | Effective November 1, 1987. Amended effective November 1, 1989 (amendment 294); November 1, 1991 (amendment 387); November 1, 1997 (amendment 574); November 1, 1998 (amendment 586); November 1, 2004 (amendment 674). |

§6A1.4. Notice of Possible Departure (Policy Statement)

Before the court may depart from the applicable sentencing guideline range on a ground not identified for departure either in the presentence report or in a party's prehearing submission, the court must give the parties reasonable notice that it is contemplating such a departure. The notice must specify any ground on which the court is contemplating a departure. Rule 32(h), Fed. R. Crim. P.

Commentary

Background: The Federal Rules of Criminal Procedure were amended, effective December 1, 2002, to incorporate into Rule 32(h) the holding in *Burns v. United States*, 501 U.S. 129, 138–39 (1991). This policy statement parallels Rule 32(h), Fed. R. Crim. P.

| Historical Note | Effective November 1, 2004 (amendment 674). |

§6A1.5. Crime Victims' Rights (Policy Statement)

In any case involving the sentencing of a defendant for an offense against a crime victim, the court shall ensure that the crime victim is afforded the rights described in 18 U.S.C. § 3771 and in any other provision of Federal law pertaining to the treatment of crime victims.

Commentary

Application Note:

1. **Definition.**—For purposes of this policy statement, "*crime victim*" has the meaning given that term in 18 U.S.C. § 3771(e).

| Historical Note | Effective November 1, 2006 (amendment 694). |

PART B — PLEA AGREEMENTS

Introductory Commentary

Policy statements governing the acceptance of plea agreements under Rule 11(c), Fed. R. Crim. P., are intended to ensure that plea negotiation practices: (1) promote the statutory purposes of sentencing prescribed in 18 U.S.C. § 3553(a); and (2) do not perpetuate unwarranted sentencing disparity.

These policy statements make clear that sentencing is a judicial function and that the appropriate sentence in a guilty plea case is to be determined by the judge. The policy statements also ensure that the basis for any judicial decision to depart from the guidelines will be explained on the record.

Historical Note	Effective November 1, 1987. Amended effective November 1, 2004 (amendment 674).

§6B1.1.   Plea Agreement Procedure (Policy Statement)

(a)   The parties must disclose the plea agreement in open court when the plea is offered, unless the court for good cause allows the parties to disclose the plea agreement in camera. Rule 11(c)(2), Fed. R. Crim. P.

(b)   To the extent the plea agreement is of the type specified in Rule 11(c)(1)(B), the court must advise the defendant that the defendant has no right to withdraw the plea if the court does not follow the recommendation or request. Rule 11(c)(3)(B), Fed. R. Crim. P.

(c)   To the extent the plea agreement is of the type specified in Rule 11(c)(1)(A) or (C), the court may accept the agreement, reject it, or defer a decision until the court has reviewed the presentence report. Rule 11(c)(3)(A), Fed. R. Crim. P.

Commentary

This provision parallels the procedural requirements of Rule 11(c), Fed. R. Crim. P. Plea agreements must be fully disclosed and a defendant whose plea agreement includes a nonbinding recommendation must be advised that the court's refusal to accept the sentencing recommendation will not entitle the defendant to withdraw the plea.

Section 6B1.1(c) deals with the timing of the court's decision regarding whether to accept or reject the plea agreement. Rule 11(c)(3)(A) gives the court discretion to accept or reject the plea agreement immediately or defer a decision pending consideration of the presentence report. Given that a presentence report normally will be prepared, the Commission recommends that the court defer acceptance of the plea agreement until the court has reviewed the presentence report.

§6B1.2

| Historical Note | Effective November 1, 1987. Amended effective November 1, 2004 (amendment 674). |

§6B1.2.   Standards for Acceptance of Plea Agreements (Policy Statement)

(a)   In the case of a plea agreement that includes the dismissal of any charges or an agreement not to pursue potential charges (Rule 11(c)(1)(A)), the court may accept the agreement if the court determines, for reasons stated on the record, that the remaining charges adequately reflect the seriousness of the actual offense behavior and that accepting the agreement will not undermine the statutory purposes of sentencing or the sentencing guidelines.

However, a plea agreement that includes the dismissal of a charge or a plea agreement not to pursue a potential charge shall not preclude the conduct underlying such charge from being considered under the provisions of §1B1.3 (Relevant Conduct) in connection with the count(s) of which the defendant is convicted.

(b)   In the case of a plea agreement that includes a nonbinding recommendation (Rule 11(c)(1)(B)), the court may accept the recommendation if the court is satisfied either that:

(1)   the recommended sentence is within the applicable guideline range; or

(2)   (A) the recommended sentence is outside the applicable guideline range for justifiable reasons; and (B) those reasons are set forth with specificity in the statement of reasons form.

(c)   In the case of a plea agreement that includes a specific sentence (Rule 11(c)(1)(C)), the court may accept the agreement if the court is satisfied either that:

(1)   the agreed sentence is within the applicable guideline range; or

(2)   (A) the agreed sentence is outside the applicable guideline range for justifiable reasons; and (B) those reasons are set forth with specificity in the statement of reasons form.

Commentary

The court may accept an agreement calling for dismissal of charges or an agreement not to pursue potential charges if the remaining charges reflect the seriousness of the actual offense behavior. This requirement does not authorize judges to intrude upon the charging discretion of the prosecutor. If the government's motion to dismiss charges or statement that potential charges will not be pursued is not contingent on the disposition of the remaining charges, the judge should defer to the government's position except under extraordinary circumstances. Rule 48(a), Fed. R. Crim. P. However, when the dismissal of charges or agreement not to pursue potential charges is contingent on acceptance of a plea agreement, the court's authority to adjudicate guilt and impose sentence is implicated, and the court is to determine whether or not dismissal of charges will undermine the sentencing guidelines.

Similarly, the court should accept a recommended sentence or a plea agreement requiring imposition of a specific sentence only if the court is satisfied either that such sentence is an appropriate sentence within the applicable guideline range or, if not, that the sentence is outside the applicable guideline range for justifiable reasons and those reasons are set forth with specificity in the statement of reasons form. *See* 18 U.S.C. § 3553(c). As set forth in subsection (d) of §5K2.0 (Grounds for Departure), however, the court may not depart below the applicable guideline range merely because of the defendant's decision to plead guilty to the offense or to enter a plea agreement with respect to the offense.

A defendant who enters a plea of guilty in a timely manner will enhance the likelihood of his receiving a reduction in offense level under §3E1.1 (Acceptance of Responsibility). Further reduction in offense level (or sentence) due to a plea agreement will tend to undermine the sentencing guidelines.

The second paragraph of subsection (a) provides that a plea agreement that includes the dismissal of a charge, or a plea agreement not to pursue a potential charge, shall not prevent the conduct underlying that charge from being considered under the provisions of §1B1.3 (Relevant Conduct) in connection with the count(s) of which the defendant is convicted. This paragraph prevents a plea agreement from restricting consideration of conduct that is within the scope of §1B1.3 (Relevant Conduct) in respect to the count(s) of which the defendant is convicted; it does not in any way expand or modify the scope of §1B1.3 (Relevant Conduct). Section 5K2.21 (Dismissed and Uncharged Conduct) addresses the use, as a basis for upward departure, of conduct underlying a charge dismissed as part of a plea agreement in the case, or underlying a potential charge not pursued in the case as part of a plea agreement.

The Commission encourages the prosecuting attorney prior to the entry of a plea of guilty or *nolo contendere* under Rule 11 of the Federal Rules of Criminal Procedure to disclose to the defendant the facts and circumstances of the offense and offender characteristics, then known to the prosecuting attorney, that are relevant to the application of the sentencing guidelines. This recommendation, however, shall not be construed to confer upon the defendant any right not otherwise recognized in law.

Historical Note Effective November 1, 1987. Amended effective November 1, 1989 (amendment 295); November 1, 1992 (amendment 467); November 1, 1993 (amendment 495); November 1, 2000 (amendment 604); October 27, 2003 (amendment 651); November 1, 2011 (amendment 757).

§6B1.3.   Procedure Upon Rejection of a Plea Agreement (Policy Statement)

If the court rejects a plea agreement containing provisions of the type specified in Rule 11(c)(1)(A) or (C), the court must do the following on the record and in open court (or, for good cause, in camera)—

(a)   inform the parties that the court rejects the plea agreement;

(b)   advise the defendant personally that the court is not required to follow the plea agreement and give the defendant an opportunity to withdraw the plea; and

(c)   advise the defendant personally that if the plea is not withdrawn, the court may dispose of the case less favorably toward the defendant than the plea agreement contemplated.

Rule 11(c)(5), Fed. R. Crim. P.

Commentary

This provision implements the requirements of Rule 11(c)(5). It assures the defendant an opportunity to withdraw his plea when the court has rejected a plea agreement.

Historical Note	Effective November 1, 1987. Amended effective November 1, 2004 (amendment 674).

§6B1.4.   Stipulations (Policy Statement)

(a)   A plea agreement may be accompanied by a written stipulation of facts relevant to sentencing. Except to the extent that a party may be privileged not to disclose certain information, stipulations shall:

(1)   set forth the relevant facts and circumstances of the actual offense conduct and offender characteristics;

(2)   not contain misleading facts; and

(3)   set forth with meaningful specificity the reasons why the sentencing range resulting from the proposed agreement is appropriate.

(b)   To the extent that the parties disagree about any facts relevant to sentencing, the stipulation shall identify the facts that are in dispute.

(c) A district court may, by local rule, identify categories of cases for which the parties are authorized to make the required stipulation orally, on the record, at the time the plea agreement is offered.

(d) The court is not bound by the stipulation, but may with the aid of the presentence report, determine the facts relevant to sentencing.

Commentary

This provision requires that when a plea agreement includes a stipulation of fact, the stipulation must fully and accurately disclose all factors relevant to the determination of sentence. This provision does not obligate the parties to reach agreement on issues that remain in dispute or to present the court with an appearance of agreement in areas where agreement does not exist. Rather, the overriding principle is full disclosure of the circumstances of the actual offense and the agreement of the parties. The stipulation should identify all areas of agreement, disagreement and uncertainty that may be relevant to the determination of sentence. Similarly, it is not appropriate for the parties to stipulate to misleading or non-existent facts, even when both parties are willing to assume the existence of such "facts" for purposes of the litigation. Rather, the parties should fully disclose the actual facts and then explain to the court the reasons why the disposition of the case should differ from that which such facts ordinarily would require under the guidelines.

Because of the importance of the stipulations and the potential complexity of the factors that can affect the determination of sentences, stipulations ordinarily should be in writing. However, exceptions to this practice may be allowed by local rule. The Commission intends to pay particular attention to this aspect of the plea agreement procedure as experience under the guidelines develops. *See* Commentary to §6A1.2 (Disclosure of Presentence Report; Issues in Dispute).

Section 6B1.4(d) makes clear that the court is not obliged to accept the stipulation of the parties. Even though stipulations are expected to be accurate and complete, the court cannot rely exclusively upon stipulations in ascertaining the factors relevant to the determination of sentence. Rather, in determining the factual basis for the sentence, the court will consider the stipulation, together with the results of the presentence investigation, and any other relevant information.

| *Historical Note* | Effective November 1, 1987. |

CHAPTER SEVEN

VIOLATIONS OF PROBATION AND SUPERVISED RELEASE

PART A — INTRODUCTION TO CHAPTER SEVEN

1. Authority

Under 28 U.S.C. § 994(a)(3), the Sentencing Commission is required to issue guidelines or policy statements applicable to the revocation of probation and supervised release. At this time, the Commission has chosen to promulgate policy statements only. These policy statements will provide guidance while allowing for the identification of any substantive or procedural issues that require further review. The Commission views these policy statements as evolutionary and will review relevant data and materials concerning revocation determinations under these policy statements. Revocation guidelines will be issued after federal judges, probation officers, practitioners, and others have the opportunity to evaluate and comment on these policy statements.

2. Background

(a) Probation.

Prior to the implementation of the federal sentencing guidelines, a court could stay the imposition or execution of sentence and place a defendant on probation. When a court found that a defendant violated a condition of probation, the court could continue probation, with or without extending the term or modifying the conditions, or revoke probation and either impose the term of imprisonment previously stayed, or, where no term of imprisonment had originally been imposed, impose any term of imprisonment that was available at the initial sentencing.

The statutory authority to "suspend" the imposition or execution of sentence in order to impose a term of probation was abolished upon implementation of the sentencing guidelines. Instead, the Sentencing Reform Act recognized probation as a sentence in itself. 18 U.S.C. § 3561. Under current law, if the court finds that a defendant violated a condition of probation, the court may continue probation, with or without extending the term or modifying the conditions, or revoke probation and impose any other sentence that initially could have been imposed. 18 U.S.C. § 3565. For certain violations, revocation is required by statute.

(b) Supervised Release.

Supervised release, a new form of post-imprisonment supervision created by the Sentencing Reform Act, accompanied implementation of the guidelines. A term of supervised release may be imposed by the court as a part of the sentence of imprisonment at the time of initial sentencing. 18 U.S.C. § 3583(a). Unlike parole, a term of supervised release does not replace a portion of the sentence of imprisonment, but rather is an order of supervision in addition to any term of imprisonment imposed by the court. Accordingly, supervised release is more analogous to the additional "special parole term" previously authorized for certain drug offenses.

The conditions of supervised release authorized by statute are the same as those for a sentence of probation, except for intermittent confinement. (Intermittent confinement is available for a sentence of probation, but is available as a condition of supervised release only for a violation of a condition of supervised release.) When the court finds that the defendant violated a condition of supervised release, it may continue the defendant on supervised release, with or without extending the term or modifying the conditions, or revoke supervised release and impose a term of imprisonment. The periods of imprisonment authorized by statute for a violation of the conditions of supervised release generally are more limited, however, than those available for a violation of the conditions of probation. 18 U.S.C. § 3583(e)(3).

3. Resolution of Major Issues

(a) Guidelines versus Policy Statements.

At the outset, the Commission faced a choice between promulgating guidelines or issuing advisory policy statements for the revocation of probation and supervised release. After considered debate and input from judges, probation officers, and prosecuting and defense attorneys, the Commission decided, for a variety of reasons, initially to issue policy statements. Not only was the policy statement option expressly authorized by statute, but this approach provided greater flexibility to both the Commission and the courts. Unlike guidelines, policy statements are not subject to the May 1 statutory deadline for submission to Congress, and the Commission believed that it would benefit from the additional time to consider complex issues relating to revocation guidelines provided by the policy statement option.

Moreover, the Commission anticipates that, because of its greater flexibility, the policy statement option will provide better opportunities for evaluation by the courts and the Commission. This flexibility is important, given that supervised release as a method of post-incarceration supervision and transformation of probation from a suspension of sentence to a sentence in itself represent recent changes in federal sentencing practices. After an adequate period of evaluation, the Commission intends to promulgate revocation guidelines.

(b) Choice Between Theories.

The Commission debated two different approaches to sanctioning violations of probation and supervised release.

The first option considered a violation resulting from a defendant's failure to follow the court-imposed conditions of probation or supervised release as a "breach of trust." While the nature of the conduct leading to the revocation would be considered in measuring the extent of the breach of trust, imposition of an appropriate punishment for any new criminal conduct would not be the primary goal of a revocation sentence. Instead, the sentence imposed upon revocation would be intended to sanction the violator for failing to abide by the conditions of the court-ordered supervision, leaving the punishment for any new criminal conduct to the court responsible for imposing the sentence for that offense.

The second option considered by the Commission sought to sanction violators for the particular conduct triggering the revocation as if that conduct were being sentenced as new federal criminal conduct. Under this approach, offense guidelines in Chapters Two and Three of the Guidelines Manual would be applied to any criminal conduct that formed the basis of the violation, after which the criminal history in Chapter Four of the Guidelines Manual would be recalculated to determine the appropriate revocation sentence. This option would also address a violation not constituting a criminal offense.

After lengthy consideration, the Commission adopted an approach that is consistent with the theory of the first option; *i.e.*, at revocation the court should sanction primarily the defendant's breach of trust, while taking into account, to a limited degree, the seriousness of the underlying violation and the criminal history of the violator.

The Commission adopted this approach for a variety of reasons. First, although the Commission found desirable several aspects of the second option that provided for a detailed revocation guideline system similar to that applied at the initial sentencing, extensive testing proved it to be impractical. In particular, with regard to new criminal conduct that constituted a violation of state or local law, working groups expert in the functioning of federal criminal law noted that it would be difficult in many instances for the court or the parties to obtain the information necessary to apply properly the guidelines to this new conduct. The potential unavailability of information and witnesses necessary for a determination of specific offense characteristics or other guideline adjustments could create questions about the accuracy of factual findings concerning the existence of those factors.

In addition, the Commission rejected the second option because that option was inconsistent with its views that the court with jurisdiction over the criminal conduct leading to revocation is the more appropriate body to impose punishment for that new criminal conduct, and that, as a breach of trust inherent in the conditions of supervision, the sanction for the violation of trust should be in addition, or consecutive, to any sentence imposed for the new conduct. In contrast, the second option would have the revocation court substantially duplicate the sanctioning role of the court with jurisdiction over a defendant's new criminal conduct and would provide for the punishment imposed upon revocation to run concurrently with, and thus generally be subsumed in, any sentence imposed for that new criminal conduct.

Further, the sanctions available to the courts upon revocation are, in many cases, more significantly restrained by statute. Specifically, the term of imprisonment that may be imposed upon revocation of supervised release is limited by statute to not more than five years for persons convicted of Class A felonies, except for certain Title 21 drug offenses; not more than three years for Class B felonies; not more than two years for Class C or D felonies; and not more than one year for Class E felonies. 18 U.S.C. § 3583(e)(3).

Given the relatively narrow ranges of incarceration available in many cases, combined with the potential difficulty in obtaining information necessary to determine specific offense characteristics, the Commission felt that it was undesirable at this time to develop guidelines that attempt to distinguish, in detail, the wide variety of behavior that can lead to revocation. Indeed, with the relatively low ceilings set by statute, revocation policy statements that attempted to delineate with great particularity the gradations of conduct leading to revocation would frequently result in a sentence at the statutory maximum penalty.

Accordingly, the Commission determined that revocation policy statements that provided for three broad grades of violations would permit proportionally longer terms for more serious violations and thereby would address adequately concerns about proportionality, without creating the problems inherent in the second option.

4. The Basic Approach

The revocation policy statements categorize violations of probation and supervised release in three broad classifications ranging from serious new felonious criminal conduct to less serious criminal conduct and technical violations. The grade of the violation, together with the violator's criminal history category calculated at the time of the initial sentencing, fix the applicable sentencing range.

The Commission has elected to develop a single set of policy statements for revocation of both probation and supervised release. In reviewing the relevant literature, the Commission determined that the purpose of supervision for probation and supervised release should focus on the integration of the violator into the community, while providing the supervision designed to limit further criminal conduct. Although there was considerable debate as to whether the sanction imposed upon revocation of probation should be different from that imposed upon revocation of supervised release, the Commission has initially concluded that a single set of policy statements is appropriate.

5.   A Concluding Note

The Commission views these policy statements for revocation of probation and supervised release as the first step in an evolutionary process. The Commission expects to issue revocation guidelines after judges, probation officers, and practitioners have had an opportunity to apply and comment on the policy statements.

In developing these policy statements, the Commission assembled two outside working groups of experienced probation officers representing every circuit in the nation, officials from the Probation Division of the Administrative Office of the U.S. Courts, the General Counsel's office at the Administrative Office of the U.S. Courts, and the U.S. Parole Commission. In addition, a number of federal judges, members of the Criminal Law and Probation Administration Committee of the Judicial Conference, and representatives from the Department of Justice and federal and community defenders provided considerable input into this effort.

Historical Note	Effective November 1, 1990 (amendment 362). Amended effective November 1, 2002 (amendment 646); November 1, 2009 (amendment 733).

§§7A1.1 – 7A1.4 [Deleted]

Historical Note	Sections 7A1.1 (Reporting of Violations of Probation and Supervised Release), 7A1.2 (Revocation of Probation), 7A1.3 (Revocation of Supervised Release), and 7A1.4 (No Credit for Time Under Supervision), effective November 1, 1987, were deleted as part of an overall revision of this chapter effective November 1, 1990 (amendment 362).

PART B — PROBATION AND SUPERVISED RELEASE VIOLATIONS

Introductory Commentary

The policy statements in this chapter seek to prescribe penalties only for the violation of the judicial order imposing supervision. Where a defendant is convicted of a criminal charge that also is a basis of the violation, these policy statements do not purport to provide the appropriate sanction for the criminal charge itself. The Commission has concluded that the determination of the appropriate sentence on any new criminal conviction should be a separate determination for the court having jurisdiction over such conviction.

Because these policy statements focus on the violation of the court-ordered supervision, this chapter, to the extent permitted by law, treats violations of the conditions of probation and supervised release as functionally equivalent.

Under 18 U.S.C. § 3584, the court, upon consideration of the factors set forth in 18 U.S.C. § 3553(a), including applicable guidelines and policy statements issued by the Sentencing Commission, may order a term of imprisonment to be served consecutively or concurrently to an undischarged term of imprisonment. It is the policy of the Commission that the sanction imposed upon revocation is to be served consecutively to any other term of imprisonment imposed for any criminal conduct that is the basis of the revocation.

This chapter is applicable in the case of a defendant under supervision for a felony or Class A misdemeanor. Consistent with §1B1.9 (Class B or C Misdemeanors and Infractions), this chapter does not apply in the case of a defendant under supervision for a Class B or C misdemeanor or an infraction.

Historical Note	Effective November 1, 1990 (amendment 362).

§7B1.1.   Classification of Violations (Policy Statement)

(a)   There are three grades of probation and supervised release violations:

   (1)   GRADE A VIOLATIONS — conduct constituting (A) a federal, state, or local offense punishable by a term of imprisonment exceeding one year that (i) is a crime of violence, (ii) is a controlled substance offense, or (iii) involves possession of a firearm or destructive device of a type described in 26 U.S.C. § 5845(a); or (B) any other federal, state, or local offense punishable by a term of imprisonment exceeding twenty years;

   (2)   GRADE B VIOLATIONS — conduct constituting any other federal, state, or local offense punishable by a term of imprisonment exceeding one year;

(3) GRADE C VIOLATIONS — conduct constituting (A) a federal, state, or local offense punishable by a term of imprisonment of one year or less; or (B) a violation of any other condition of supervision.

(b) Where there is more than one violation of the conditions of supervision, or the violation includes conduct that constitutes more than one offense, the grade of the violation is determined by the violation having the most serious grade.

Commentary

Application Notes:

1. Under 18 U.S.C. §§ 3563(a)(1) and 3583(d), a mandatory condition of probation and supervised release is that the defendant not commit another federal, state, or local crime. A violation of this condition may be charged whether or not the defendant has been the subject of a separate federal, state, or local prosecution for such conduct. The grade of violation does not depend upon the conduct that is the subject of criminal charges or of which the defendant is convicted in a criminal proceeding. Rather, the grade of the violation is to be based on the defendant's actual conduct.

2. "*Crime of violence*" is defined in §4B1.2 (Definitions of Terms Used in Section 4B1.1). *See* §4B1.2(a) and Application Note 1 of the Commentary to §4B1.2.

3. "*Controlled substance offense*" is defined in §4B1.2 (Definitions of Terms Used in Section 4B1.1). *See* §4B1.2(b) and Application Note 1 of the Commentary to §4B1.2.

4. A "*firearm or destructive device of a type described in 26 U.S.C. § 5845(a)*" includes a shotgun, or a weapon made from a shotgun, with a barrel or barrels of less than 18 inches in length; a weapon made from a shotgun or rifle with an overall length of less than 26 inches; a rifle, or a weapon made from a rifle, with a barrel or barrels of less than 16 inches in length; a machine gun; a muffler or silencer for a firearm; a destructive device; and certain large bore weapons.

5. Where the defendant is under supervision in connection with a felony conviction, or has a prior felony conviction, possession of a firearm (other than a firearm of a type described in 26 U.S.C. § 5845(a)) will generally constitute a Grade B violation, because 18 U.S.C. § 922(g) prohibits a convicted felon from possessing a firearm. The term "generally" is used in the preceding sentence, however, because there are certain limited exceptions to the applicability of 18 U.S.C. § 922(g). *See, e.g.,* 18 U.S.C. § 925(c).

Historical Note	Effective November 1, 1990 (amendment 362). Amended effective November 1, 1992 (amendment 473); November 1, 1997 (amendment 568); November 1, 2002 (amendment 646).

§7B1.2. Reporting of Violations of Probation and Supervised Release (Policy Statement)

(a) The probation officer shall promptly report to the court any alleged Grade A or B violation.

(b) The probation officer shall promptly report to the court any alleged Grade C violation unless the officer determines: (1) that such violation is minor, and not part of a continuing pattern of violations; and (2) that non-reporting will not present an undue risk to an individual or the public or be inconsistent with any directive of the court relative to the reporting of violations.

Commentary

Application Note:

1. Under subsection (b), a Grade C violation must be promptly reported to the court unless the probation officer makes an affirmative determination that the alleged violation meets the criteria for non-reporting. For example, an isolated failure to file a monthly report or a minor traffic infraction generally would not require reporting.

Historical Note	Effective November 1, 1990 (amendment 362).

§7B1.3. Revocation of Probation or Supervised Release (Policy Statement)

(a) (1) Upon a finding of a Grade A or B violation, the court shall revoke probation or supervised release.

(2) Upon a finding of a Grade C violation, the court may (A) revoke probation or supervised release; or (B) extend the term of probation or supervised release and/or modify the conditions of supervision.

(b) In the case of a revocation of probation or supervised release, the applicable range of imprisonment is that set forth in §7B1.4 (Term of Imprisonment).

(c) In the case of a Grade B or C violation—

(1) Where the minimum term of imprisonment determined under §7B1.4 (Term of Imprisonment) is at least one month but not more than six months, the minimum term may be satisfied by (A) a sentence of imprisonment; or (B) a sentence of imprisonment that includes a term of supervised release with a condition that substitutes community confinement or home detention according to the schedule in §5C1.1(e) for any portion of the minimum term; and

(2) Where the minimum term of imprisonment determined under §7B1.4 (Term of Imprisonment) is more than six months but

not more than ten months, the minimum term may be satisfied by (A) a sentence of imprisonment; or (B) a sentence of imprisonment that includes a term of supervised release with a condition that substitutes community confinement or home detention according to the schedule in §5C1.1(e), provided that at least one-half of the minimum term is satisfied by imprisonment.

(3) In the case of a revocation based, at least in part, on a violation of a condition specifically pertaining to community confinement, intermittent confinement, or home detention, use of the same or a less restrictive sanction is not recommended.

(d) Any restitution, fine, community confinement, home detention, or intermittent confinement previously imposed in connection with the sentence for which revocation is ordered that remains unpaid or unserved at the time of revocation shall be ordered to be paid or served in addition to the sanction determined under §7B1.4 (Term of Imprisonment), and any such unserved period of community confinement, home detention, or intermittent confinement may be converted to an equivalent period of imprisonment.

(e) Where the court revokes probation or supervised release and imposes a term of imprisonment, it shall increase the term of imprisonment determined under subsections (b), (c), and (d) above by the amount of time in official detention that will be credited toward service of the term of imprisonment under 18 U.S.C. § 3585(b), other than time in official detention resulting from the federal probation or supervised release violation warrant or proceeding.

(f) Any term of imprisonment imposed upon the revocation of probation or supervised release shall be ordered to be served consecutively to any sentence of imprisonment that the defendant is serving, whether or not the sentence of imprisonment being served resulted from the conduct that is the basis of the revocation of probation or supervised release.

(g) (1) If probation is revoked and a term of imprisonment is imposed, the provisions of §§5D1.1–1.3 shall apply to the imposition of a term of supervised release.

(2) If supervised release is revoked, the court may include a requirement that the defendant be placed on a term of supervised release upon release from imprisonment. The length of such a term of supervised release shall not exceed the term of supervised release authorized by statute for the offense that resulted

in the original term of supervised release, less any term of imprisonment that was imposed upon revocation of supervised release. 18 U.S.C. § 3583(h).

Commentary

Application Notes:

1. Revocation of probation or supervised release generally is the appropriate disposition in the case of a Grade C violation by a defendant who, having been continued on supervision after a finding of violation, again violates the conditions of his supervision.

2. The provisions for the revocation, as well as early termination and extension, of a term of supervised release are found in 18 U.S.C. § 3583(e), (g)–(i). Under 18 U.S.C. § 3583(h) (effective September 13, 1994), the court, in the case of revocation of supervised release, may order an additional period of supervised release to follow imprisonment.

3. Subsection (e) is designed to ensure that the revocation penalty is not decreased by credit for time in official detention other than time in official detention resulting from the federal probation or supervised release violation warrant or proceeding. **Example**: A defendant, who was in pre-trial detention for three months, is placed on probation, and subsequently violates that probation. The court finds the violation to be a Grade C violation, determines that the applicable range of imprisonment is 4–10 months, and determines that revocation of probation and imposition of a term of imprisonment of four months is appropriate. Under subsection (e), a sentence of seven months imprisonment would be required because the Bureau of Prisons, under 18 U.S.C. § 3585(b), will allow the defendant three months' credit toward the term of imprisonment imposed upon revocation.

4. Subsection (f) provides that any term of imprisonment imposed upon the revocation of probation or supervised release shall run consecutively to any sentence of imprisonment being served by the defendant. Similarly, it is the Commission's recommendation that any sentence of imprisonment for a criminal offense that is imposed after revocation of probation or supervised release be run consecutively to any term of imprisonment imposed upon revocation.

5. Intermittent confinement is authorized as a condition of probation during the first year of the term of probation. 18 U.S.C. § 3563(b)(10). Intermittent confinement is authorized as a condition of supervised release during the first year of supervised release, but only for a violation of a condition of supervised release in accordance with 18 U.S.C. § 3583(e)(2) and only when facilities are available. *See* §5F1.8 (Intermittent Confinement).

Historical Note	Effective November 1, 1990 (amendment 362). Amended effective November 1, 1991 (amendment 427); November 1, 1995 (amendment 533); November 1, 2002 (amendment 646); November 1, 2004 (amendment 664); November 1, 2009 (amendment 733).

§7B1.4. Term of Imprisonment (Policy Statement)

(a) The range of imprisonment applicable upon revocation is set forth in the following table:

Revocation Table
(in months of imprisonment)

Grade of Violation	Criminal History Category*					
	I	II	III	IV	V	VI
Grade C	3–9	4–10	5–11	6–12	7–13	8–14
Grade B	4–10	6–12	8–14	12–18	18–24	21–27

Grade A (1) Except as provided in subdivision (2) below:

	I	II	III	IV	V	VI
	12–18	15–21	18–24	24–30	30–37	33–41

(2) Where the defendant was on probation or supervised release as a result of a sentence for a Class A felony:

	I	II	III	IV	V	VI
	24–30	27–33	30–37	37–46	46–57	51–63.

*The criminal history category is the category applicable at the time the defendant originally was sentenced to a term of supervision.

(b) *Provided, that*—

(1) Where the statutorily authorized maximum term of imprisonment that is imposable upon revocation is less than the minimum of the applicable range, the statutorily authorized maximum term shall be substituted for the applicable range; and

(2) Where the minimum term of imprisonment required by statute, if any, is greater than the maximum of the applicable range, the minimum term of imprisonment required by statute shall be substituted for the applicable range.

(3) In any other case, the sentence upon revocation may be imposed at any point within the applicable range, provided that the sentence—

(A) is not greater than the maximum term of imprisonment authorized by statute; and

(B) is not less than any minimum term of imprisonment required by statute.

Commentary

Application Notes:

1. The criminal history category to be used in determining the applicable range of imprisonment in the Revocation Table is the category determined at the time the defendant originally was sentenced to the term of supervision. The criminal history category is not to be recalculated because the ranges set forth in the Revocation Table have been designed to take into account that the defendant violated supervision. In the rare case in which no criminal history category was determined when the defendant originally was sentenced to the term of supervision being revoked, the court shall determine the criminal history category that would have been applicable at the time the defendant originally was sentenced to the term of supervision. (*See* the criminal history provisions of §§4A1.1–4B1.4.)

2. Departure from the applicable range of imprisonment in the Revocation Table may be warranted when the court departed from the applicable range for reasons set forth in §4A1.3 (Departures Based on Inadequacy of Criminal History Category) in originally imposing the sentence that resulted in supervision. Additionally, an upward departure may be warranted when a defendant, subsequent to the federal sentence resulting in supervision, has been sentenced for an offense that is not the basis of the violation proceeding.

3. In the case of a Grade C violation that is associated with a high risk of new felonious conduct (*e.g.*, a defendant, under supervision for conviction of criminal sexual abuse, violates the condition that the defendant not associate with children by loitering near a schoolyard), an upward departure may be warranted.

4. Where the original sentence was the result of a downward departure (*e.g.*, as a reward for substantial assistance), or a charge reduction that resulted in a sentence below the guideline range applicable to the defendant's underlying conduct, an upward departure may be warranted.

5. Upon a finding that a defendant violated a condition of probation or supervised release by being in possession of a controlled substance or firearm or by refusing to comply with a condition requiring drug testing, the court is required to revoke probation or supervised release and impose a sentence that includes a term of imprisonment. 18 U.S.C. §§ 3565(b), 3583(g).

6. In the case of a defendant who fails a drug test, the court shall consider whether the availability of appropriate substance abuse programs, or a defendant's current or past participation in such programs, warrants an exception from the requirement of mandatory revocation and imprisonment under 18 U.S.C. §§ 3565(b) and 3583(g). 18 U.S.C. §§ 3563(a), 3583(d).

Historical Note	Effective November 1, 1990 (amendment 362); November 1, 1995 (amendment 533); November 1, 2010 (amendment 747).

§7B1.5. No Credit for Time Under Supervision (Policy Statement)

(a) Upon revocation of probation, no credit shall be given (toward any sentence of imprisonment imposed) for any portion of the term of probation served prior to revocation.

(b) Upon revocation of supervised release, no credit shall be given (toward any term of imprisonment ordered) for time previously served on post-release supervision.

(c) *Provided,* that in the case of a person serving a period of supervised release on a foreign sentence under the provisions of 18 U.S.C. § 4106A, credit shall be given for time on supervision prior to revocation, except that no credit shall be given for any time in escape or absconder status.

Commentary

Application Note:

1. Subsection (c) implements 18 U.S.C. § 4106A(b)(1)(C), which provides that the combined periods of imprisonment and supervised release in transfer treaty cases shall not exceed the term of imprisonment imposed by the foreign court.

Background: This section provides that time served on probation or supervised release is not to be credited in the determination of any term of imprisonment imposed upon revocation. Other aspects of the defendant's conduct, such as compliance with supervision conditions and adjustment while under supervision, appropriately may be considered by the court in the determination of the sentence to be imposed within the applicable revocation range.

Historical Note	Effective November 1, 1990 (amendment 362).

CHAPTER EIGHT

SENTENCING OF ORGANIZATIONS

Introductory Commentary

The guidelines and policy statements in this chapter apply when the convicted defendant is an organization. Organizations can act only through agents and, under federal criminal law, generally are vicariously liable for offenses committed by their agents. At the same time, individual agents are responsible for their own criminal conduct. Federal prosecutions of organizations therefore frequently involve individual and organizational co-defendants. Convicted individual agents of organizations are sentenced in accordance with the guidelines and policy statements in the preceding chapters. This chapter is designed so that the sanctions imposed upon organizations and their agents, taken together, will provide just punishment, adequate deterrence, and incentives for organizations to maintain internal mechanisms for preventing, detecting, and reporting criminal conduct.

This chapter reflects the following general principles:

First, the court must, whenever practicable, order the organization to remedy any harm caused by the offense. The resources expended to remedy the harm should not be viewed as punishment, but rather as a means of making victims whole for the harm caused.

Second, if the organization operated primarily for a criminal purpose or primarily by criminal means, the fine should be set sufficiently high to divest the organization of all its assets.

Third, the fine range for any other organization should be based on the seriousness of the offense and the culpability of the organization. The seriousness of the offense generally will be reflected by the greatest of the pecuniary gain, the pecuniary loss, or the amount in a guideline offense level fine table. Culpability generally will be determined by six factors that the sentencing court must consider. The four factors that increase the ultimate punishment of an organization are: (i) the involvement in or tolerance of criminal activity; (ii) the prior history of the organization; (iii) the violation of an order; and (iv) the obstruction of justice. The two factors that mitigate the ultimate punishment of an organization are: (i) the existence of an effective compliance and ethics program; and (ii) self-reporting, cooperation, or acceptance of responsibility.

Fourth, probation is an appropriate sentence for an organizational defendant when needed to ensure that another sanction will be fully implemented, or to ensure that steps will be taken within the organization to reduce the likelihood of future criminal conduct.

These guidelines offer incentives to organizations to reduce and ultimately eliminate criminal conduct by providing a structural foundation from which an organization may self-police its own conduct through an effective compliance and ethics program. The prevention and detection of criminal conduct, as facilitated by an effective compliance and ethics program, will assist an organization in encouraging ethical conduct and in complying fully with all applicable laws.

Historical Note	Effective November 1, 1991 (amendment 422). Amended effective November 1, 2004 (amendment 673).

PART A — GENERAL APPLICATION PRINCIPLES

§8A1.1. Applicability of Chapter Eight

This chapter applies to the sentencing of all organizations for felony and Class A misdemeanor offenses.

Commentary

Application Notes:

1. "*Organization*" means "a person other than an individual." 18 U.S.C. § 18. The term includes corporations, partnerships, associations, joint-stock companies, unions, trusts, pension funds, unincorporated organizations, governments and political subdivisions thereof, and non-profit organizations.

2. The fine guidelines in §§8C2.2 through 8C2.9 apply only to specified types of offenses. The other provisions of this chapter apply to the sentencing of all organizations for all felony and Class A misdemeanor offenses. For example, the restitution and probation provisions in Parts B and D of this chapter apply to the sentencing of an organization, even if the fine guidelines in §§8C2.2 through 8C2.9 do not apply.

Historical Note	Effective November 1, 1991 (amendment 422).

§8A1.2. Application Instructions — Organizations

(a) Determine from Part B, Subpart 1 (Remedying Harm from Criminal Conduct) the sentencing requirements and options relating to restitution, remedial orders, community service, and notice to victims.

(b) Determine from Part C (Fines) the sentencing requirements and options relating to fines:

    (1) If the organization operated primarily for a criminal purpose or primarily by criminal means, apply §8C1.1 (Determining the Fine — Criminal Purpose Organizations).

    (2) Otherwise, apply §8C2.1 (Applicability of Fine Guidelines) to identify the counts for which the provisions of §§8C2.2 through 8C2.9 apply. For such counts:

        (A) Refer to §8C2.2 (Preliminary Determination of Inability to Pay Fine) to determine whether an abbreviated determination of the guideline fine range may be warranted.

(B)   Apply §8C2.3 (Offense Level) to determine the offense level from Chapter Two (Offense Conduct) and Chapter Three, Part D (Multiple Counts).

(C)   Apply §8C2.4 (Base Fine) to determine the base fine.

(D)   Apply §8C2.5 (Culpability Score) to determine the culpability score. To determine whether the organization had an effective compliance and ethics program for purposes of §8C2.5(f), apply §8B2.1 (Effective Compliance and Ethics Program).

(E)   Apply §8C2.6 (Minimum and Maximum Multipliers) to determine the minimum and maximum multipliers corresponding to the culpability score.

(F)   Apply §8C2.7 (Guideline Fine Range — Organizations) to determine the minimum and maximum of the guideline fine range.

(G)   Refer to §8C2.8 (Determining the Fine Within the Range) to determine the amount of the fine within the applicable guideline range.

(H)   Apply §8C2.9 (Disgorgement) to determine whether an increase to the fine is required.

For any count or counts not covered under §8C2.1 (Applicability of Fine Guidelines), apply §8C2.10 (Determining the Fine for Other Counts).

(3)   Apply the provisions relating to the implementation of the sentence of a fine in Part C, Subpart 3 (Implementing the Sentence of a Fine).

(4)   For grounds for departure from the applicable guideline fine range, refer to Part C, Subpart 4 (Departures from the Guideline Fine Range).

(c)   Determine from Part D (Organizational Probation) the sentencing requirements and options relating to probation.

(d)   Determine from Part E (Special Assessments, Forfeitures, and Costs) the sentencing requirements relating to special assessments, forfeitures, and costs.

§8A1.2

Commentary

Application Notes:

1. Determinations under this chapter are to be based upon the facts and information specified in the applicable guideline. Determinations that reference other chapters are to be made under the standards applicable to determinations under those chapters.

2. The definitions in the Commentary to §1B1.1 (Application Instructions) and the guidelines and commentary in §§1B1.2 through 1B1.8 apply to determinations under this chapter unless otherwise specified. The adjustments in Chapter Three, Parts A (Victim-Related Adjustments), B (Role in the Offense), C (Obstruction and Related Adjustments), and E (Acceptance of Responsibility) do not apply. The provisions of Chapter Six (Sentencing Procedures, Plea Agreements, and Crime Victims' Rights) apply to proceedings in which the defendant is an organization. Guidelines and policy statements not referenced in this chapter, directly or indirectly, do not apply when the defendant is an organization; *e.g.*, the policy statements in Chapter Seven (Violations of Probation and Supervised Release) do not apply to organizations.

3. The following are definitions of terms used frequently in this chapter:

    (A) "*Offense*" means the offense of conviction and all relevant conduct under §1B1.3 (Relevant Conduct) unless a different meaning is specified or is otherwise clear from the context. The term "*instant*" is used in connection with "offense," "federal offense," or "offense of conviction," as the case may be, to distinguish the violation for which the defendant is being sentenced from a prior or subsequent offense, or from an offense before another court (*e.g.*, an offense before a state court involving the same underlying conduct).

    (B) "*High-level personnel of the organization*" means individuals who have substantial control over the organization or who have a substantial role in the making of policy within the organization. The term includes: a director; an executive officer; an individual in charge of a major business or functional unit of the organization, such as sales, administration, or finance; and an individual with a substantial ownership interest. "*High-level personnel of a unit of the organization*" is defined in the Commentary to §8C2.5 (Culpability Score).

    (C) "*Substantial authority personnel*" means individuals who within the scope of their authority exercise a substantial measure of discretion in acting on behalf of an organization. The term includes high-level personnel of the organization, individuals who exercise substantial supervisory authority (*e.g.*, a plant manager, a sales manager), and any other individuals who, although not a part of an organization's management, nevertheless exercise substantial discretion when acting within the scope of their authority (*e.g.*, an individual with authority in an organization to negotiate or set price levels or an individual authorized to negotiate or approve significant contracts). Whether an individual falls within this category must be determined on a case-by-case basis.

    (D) "*Agent*" means any individual, including a director, an officer, an employee, or an independent contractor, authorized to act on behalf of the organization.

    (E) An individual "*condoned*" an offense if the individual knew of the offense and did not take reasonable steps to prevent or terminate the offense.

(F) "*Similar misconduct*" means prior conduct that is similar in nature to the conduct underlying the instant offense, without regard to whether or not such conduct violated the same statutory provision. For example, prior Medicare fraud would be misconduct similar to an instant offense involving another type of fraud.

(G) "*Prior criminal adjudication*" means conviction by trial, plea of guilty (including an *Alford* plea), or plea of *nolo contendere*.

(H) "*Pecuniary gain*" is derived from 18 U.S.C. § 3571(d) and means the additional before-tax profit to the defendant resulting from the relevant conduct of the offense. Gain can result from either additional revenue or cost savings. For example, an offense involving odometer tampering can produce additional revenue. In such a case, the pecuniary gain is the additional revenue received because the automobiles appeared to have less mileage, *i.e.*, the difference between the price received or expected for the automobiles with the apparent mileage and the fair market value of the automobiles with the actual mileage. An offense involving defense procurement fraud related to defective product testing can produce pecuniary gain resulting from cost savings. In such a case, the pecuniary gain is the amount saved because the product was not tested in the required manner.

(I) "*Pecuniary loss*" is derived from 18 U.S.C. § 3571(d) and is equivalent to the term "loss" as used in Chapter Two (Offense Conduct). *See* Commentary to §2B1.1 (Theft, Property Destruction, and Fraud), and definitions of "tax loss" in Chapter Two, Part T (Offenses Involving Taxation).

(J) An individual was "*willfully ignorant of the offense*" if the individual did not investigate the possible occurrence of unlawful conduct despite knowledge of circumstances that would lead a reasonable person to investigate whether unlawful conduct had occurred.

Historical Note	Effective November 1, 1991 (amendment 422); November 1, 1997 (amendment 546); November 1, 2001 (amendment 617); November 1, 2004 (amendment 673); November 1, 2010 (amendment 747); November 1, 2011 (amendment 758).

PART B — REMEDYING HARM FROM CRIMINAL CONDUCT, AND EFFECTIVE COMPLIANCE AND ETHICS PROGRAM

Historical Note	Effective November 1, 1991 (amendment 422). Amended effective November 1, 2004 (amendment 673).

1. REMEDYING HARM FROM CRIMINAL CONDUCT

Historical Note	Effective November 1, 2004 (amendment 673).

Introductory Commentary

As a general principle, the court should require that the organization take all appropriate steps to provide compensation to victims and otherwise remedy the harm caused or threatened by the offense. A restitution order or an order of probation requiring restitution can be used to compensate identifiable victims of the offense. A remedial order or an order of probation requiring community service can be used to reduce or eliminate the harm threatened, or to repair the harm caused by the offense, when that harm or threatened harm would otherwise not be remedied. An order of notice to victims can be used to notify unidentified victims of the offense.

Historical Note	Effective November 1, 1991 (amendment 422).

§8B1.1. Restitution — Organizations

(a) In the case of an identifiable victim, the court shall—

    (1) enter a restitution order for the full amount of the victim's loss, if such order is authorized under 18 U.S.C. § 2248, § 2259, § 2264, § 2327, § 3663, or § 3663A; or

    (2) impose a term of probation or supervised release with a condition requiring restitution for the full amount of the victim's loss, if the offense is not an offense for which restitution is authorized under 18 U.S.C. § 3663(a)(1) but otherwise meets the criteria for an order of restitution under that section.

(b) *Provided*, that the provisions of subsection (a) do not apply—

    (1) when full restitution has been made; or

    (2) in the case of a restitution order under § 3663; a restitution order under 18 U.S.C. § 3663A that pertains to an offense against property described in 18 U.S.C. § 3663A(c)(1)(A)(ii); or

a condition of restitution imposed pursuant to subsection (a)(2) above, to the extent the court finds, from facts on the record, that (A) the number of identifiable victims is so large as to make restitution impracticable; or (B) determining complex issues of fact related to the cause or amount of the victim's losses would complicate or prolong the sentencing process to a degree that the need to provide restitution to any victim is outweighed by the burden on the sentencing process.

(c) If a defendant is ordered to make restitution to an identifiable victim and to pay a fine, the court shall order that any money paid by the defendant shall first be applied to satisfy the order of restitution.

(d) A restitution order may direct the defendant to make a single, lump sum payment, partial payments at specified intervals, in-kind payments, or a combination of payments at specified intervals and in-kind payments. *See* 18 U.S.C. § 3664(f)(3)(A). An in-kind payment may be in the form of (1) return of property; (2) replacement of property; or (3) if the victim agrees, services rendered to the victim or to a person or organization other than the victim. *See* 18 U.S.C. § 3664(f)(4).

(e) A restitution order may direct the defendant to make nominal periodic payments if the court finds from facts on the record that the economic circumstances of the defendant do not allow the payment of any amount of a restitution order, and do not allow for the payment of the full amount of a restitution order in the foreseeable future under any reasonable schedule of payments.

(f) Special Instruction

(1) This guideline applies only to a defendant convicted of an offense committed on or after November 1, 1997. Notwithstanding the provisions of §1B1.11 (Use of Guidelines Manual in Effect on Date of Sentencing), use the former §8B1.1 (set forth in Appendix C, amendment 571) in lieu of this guideline in any other case.

Commentary

Background: Section 3553(a)(7) of Title 18, United States Code, requires the court, "in determining the particular sentence to be imposed," to consider "the need to provide restitution to any victims of the offense." Orders of restitution are authorized under 18 U.S.C. §§ 2248, 2259, 2264, 2327, 3663, and 3663A. For offenses for which an order of restitution is not authorized, restitution may be imposed as a condition of probation.

§8B1.2

| Historical Note | Effective November 1, 1991 (amendment 422); November 1, 1997 (amendment 571). |

§8B1.2. Remedial Orders — Organizations (Policy Statement)

(a) To the extent not addressed under §8B1.1 (Restitution — Organizations), a remedial order imposed as a condition of probation may require the organization to remedy the harm caused by the offense and to eliminate or reduce the risk that the instant offense will cause future harm.

(b) If the magnitude of expected future harm can be reasonably estimated, the court may require the organization to create a trust fund sufficient to address that expected harm.

Commentary

Background: The purposes of a remedial order are to remedy harm that has already occurred and to prevent future harm. A remedial order requiring corrective action by the organization may be necessary to prevent future injury from the instant offense, *e.g.*, a product recall for a food and drug violation or a clean-up order for an environmental violation. In some cases in which a remedial order potentially may be appropriate, a governmental regulatory agency, *e.g.*, the Environmental Protection Agency or the Food and Drug Administration, may have authority to order remedial measures. In such cases, a remedial order by the court may not be necessary. If a remedial order is entered, it should be coordinated with any administrative or civil actions taken by the appropriate governmental regulatory agency.

| Historical Note | Effective November 1, 1991 (amendment 422). |

§8B1.3. Community Service — Organizations (Policy Statement)

Community service may be ordered as a condition of probation where such community service is reasonably designed to repair the harm caused by the offense.

Commentary

Background: An organization can perform community service only by employing its resources or paying its employees or others to do so. Consequently, an order that an organization perform community service is essentially an indirect monetary sanction, and therefore generally less desirable than a direct monetary sanction. However, where the convicted organization possesses knowledge, facilities, or skills that uniquely qualify it to repair damage caused by the offense, community service directed at repairing damage may provide an efficient means of remedying harm caused.

In the past, some forms of community service imposed on organizations have not been related to the purposes of sentencing. Requiring a defendant to endow a chair at a university or to contribute to a local charity would not be consistent with this section unless such community service provided a means for preventive or corrective action directly related to the offense and therefore served one of the purposes of sentencing set forth in 18 U.S.C. § 3553(a).

Historical Note	Effective November 1, 1991 (amendment 422).

§8B1.4. Order of Notice to Victims — Organizations

Apply §5F1.4 (Order of Notice to Victims).

Historical Note	Effective November 1, 1991 (amendment 422).

*   *   *   *   *

2.   EFFECTIVE COMPLIANCE AND ETHICS PROGRAM

Historical Note	Effective November 1, 2004 (amendment 673).

§8B2.1. Effective Compliance and Ethics Program

(a) To have an effective compliance and ethics program, for purposes of subsection (f) of §8C2.5 (Culpability Score) and subsection (b)(1) of §8D1.4 (Recommended Conditions of Probation — Organizations), an organization shall—

(1) exercise due diligence to prevent and detect criminal conduct; and

(2) otherwise promote an organizational culture that encourages ethical conduct and a commitment to compliance with the law.

Such compliance and ethics program shall be reasonably designed, implemented, and enforced so that the program is generally effective in preventing and detecting criminal conduct. The failure to prevent or detect the instant offense does not necessarily mean that the program is not generally effective in preventing and detecting criminal conduct.

(b) Due diligence and the promotion of an organizational culture that encourages ethical conduct and a commitment to compliance with the law within the meaning of subsection (a) minimally require the following:

    (1) The organization shall establish standards and procedures to prevent and detect criminal conduct.

    (2) (A) The organization's governing authority shall be knowledgeable about the content and operation of the compliance and ethics program and shall exercise reasonable oversight with respect to the implementation and effectiveness of the compliance and ethics program.

        (B) High-level personnel of the organization shall ensure that the organization has an effective compliance and ethics program, as described in this guideline. Specific individual(s) within high-level personnel shall be assigned overall responsibility for the compliance and ethics program.

        (C) Specific individual(s) within the organization shall be delegated day-to-day operational responsibility for the compliance and ethics program. Individual(s) with operational responsibility shall report periodically to high-level personnel and, as appropriate, to the governing authority, or an appropriate subgroup of the governing authority, on the effectiveness of the compliance and ethics program. To carry out such operational responsibility, such individual(s) shall be given adequate resources, appropriate authority, and direct access to the governing authority or an appropriate subgroup of the governing authority.

    (3) The organization shall use reasonable efforts not to include within the substantial authority personnel of the organization any individual whom the organization knew, or should have known through the exercise of due diligence, has engaged in illegal activities or other conduct inconsistent with an effective compliance and ethics program.

    (4) (A) The organization shall take reasonable steps to communicate periodically and in a practical manner its standards and procedures, and other aspects of the compliance and ethics program, to the individuals referred to in subparagraph (B) by conducting effective training programs and otherwise disseminating information appropriate to such individuals' respective roles and responsibilities.

(B) The individuals referred to in subparagraph (A) are the members of the governing authority, high-level personnel, substantial authority personnel, the organization's employees, and, as appropriate, the organization's agents.

(5) The organization shall take reasonable steps—

(A) to ensure that the organization's compliance and ethics program is followed, including monitoring and auditing to detect criminal conduct;

(B) to evaluate periodically the effectiveness of the organization's compliance and ethics program; and

(C) to have and publicize a system, which may include mechanisms that allow for anonymity or confidentiality, whereby the organization's employees and agents may report or seek guidance regarding potential or actual criminal conduct without fear of retaliation.

(6) The organization's compliance and ethics program shall be promoted and enforced consistently throughout the organization through (A) appropriate incentives to perform in accordance with the compliance and ethics program; and (B) appropriate disciplinary measures for engaging in criminal conduct and for failing to take reasonable steps to prevent or detect criminal conduct.

(7) After criminal conduct has been detected, the organization shall take reasonable steps to respond appropriately to the criminal conduct and to prevent further similar criminal conduct, including making any necessary modifications to the organization's compliance and ethics program.

(c) In implementing subsection (b), the organization shall periodically assess the risk of criminal conduct and shall take appropriate steps to design, implement, or modify each requirement set forth in subsection (b) to reduce the risk of criminal conduct identified through this process.

Commentary

Application Notes:

1. **Definitions.**—For purposes of this guideline:

"*Compliance and ethics program*" means a program designed to prevent and detect criminal conduct.

"*Governing authority*" means the (A) the Board of Directors; or (B) if the organization does not have a Board of Directors, the highest-level governing body of the organization.

"*High-level personnel of the organization*" and "*substantial authority personnel*" have the meaning given those terms in the Commentary to §8A1.2 (Application Instructions — Organizations).

"*Standards and procedures*" means standards of conduct and internal controls that are reasonably capable of reducing the likelihood of criminal conduct.

2.   **Factors to Consider in Meeting Requirements of this Guideline.—**

(A)   **In General.—**Each of the requirements set forth in this guideline shall be met by an organization; however, in determining what specific actions are necessary to meet those requirements, factors that shall be considered include: (i) applicable industry practice or the standards called for by any applicable governmental regulation; (ii) the size of the organization; and (iii) similar misconduct.

(B)   **Applicable Governmental Regulation and Industry Practice.—**An organization's failure to incorporate and follow applicable industry practice or the standards called for by any applicable governmental regulation weighs against a finding of an effective compliance and ethics program.

(C)   **The Size of the Organization.—**

(i)   **In General.—**The formality and scope of actions that an organization shall take to meet the requirements of this guideline, including the necessary features of the organization's standards and procedures, depend on the size of the organization.

(ii)   **Large Organizations.—**A large organization generally shall devote more formal operations and greater resources in meeting the requirements of this guideline than shall a small organization. As appropriate, a large organization should encourage small organizations (especially those that have, or seek to have, a business relationship with the large organization) to implement effective compliance and ethics programs.

(iii)   **Small Organizations.—**In meeting the requirements of this guideline, small organizations shall demonstrate the same degree of commitment to ethical conduct and compliance with the law as large organizations. However, a small organization may meet the requirements of this guideline with less formality and fewer resources than would be expected of large organizations. In appropriate circumstances, reliance on existing resources and simple systems can demonstrate a degree of commitment that, for a large organization, would only be demonstrated through more formally planned and implemented systems.

Examples of the informality and use of fewer resources with which a small organization may meet the requirements of this guideline include the following: (I) the governing authority's discharge of its responsibility for oversight of the compliance and ethics program by directly managing the organization's compliance and ethics efforts; (II) training employees through informal staff meetings, and monitoring through regular "walk-arounds" or continuous observation while managing the organization; (III) using available personnel, rather than employing separate staff, to carry out the compliance and ethics program; and (IV) modeling its own compliance and ethics program on existing, well-regarded compliance and ethics programs and best practices of other similar organizations.

(D) **Recurrence of Similar Misconduct.**—Recurrence of similar misconduct creates doubt regarding whether the organization took reasonable steps to meet the requirements of this guideline. For purposes of this subparagraph, "*similar misconduct*" has the meaning given that term in the Commentary to §8A1.2 (Application Instructions — Organizations).

3. **Application of Subsection (b)(2).**—High-level personnel and substantial authority personnel of the organization shall be knowledgeable about the content and operation of the compliance and ethics program, shall perform their assigned duties consistent with the exercise of due diligence, and shall promote an organizational culture that encourages ethical conduct and a commitment to compliance with the law.

If the specific individual(s) assigned overall responsibility for the compliance and ethics program does not have day-to-day operational responsibility for the program, then the individual(s) with day-to-day operational responsibility for the program typically should, no less than annually, give the governing authority or an appropriate subgroup thereof information on the implementation and effectiveness of the compliance and ethics program.

4. **Application of Subsection (b)(3).**—

(A) **Consistency with Other Law.**—Nothing in subsection (b)(3) is intended to require conduct inconsistent with any Federal, State, or local law, including any law governing employment or hiring practices.

(B) **Implementation.**—In implementing subsection (b)(3), the organization shall hire and promote individuals so as to ensure that all individuals within the high-level personnel and substantial authority personnel of the organization will perform their assigned duties in a manner consistent with the exercise of due diligence and the promotion of an organizational culture that encourages ethical conduct and a commitment to compliance with the law under subsection (a). With respect to the hiring or promotion of such individuals, an organization shall consider the relatedness of the individual's illegal activities and other misconduct (*i.e.*, other conduct inconsistent with an effective compliance and ethics program) to the specific responsibilities the individual is anticipated to be assigned and other factors such as: (i) the recency of the individual's illegal activities and other misconduct; and (ii) whether the individual has engaged in other such illegal activities and other such misconduct.

5. **Application of Subsection (b)(6).**—Adequate discipline of individuals responsible for an offense is a necessary component of enforcement; however, the form of discipline that will be appropriate will be case specific.

6. **Application of Subsection (b)(7).**—Subsection (b)(7) has two aspects.

First, the organization should respond appropriately to the criminal conduct. The organization should take reasonable steps, as warranted under the circumstances, to remedy the harm resulting from the criminal conduct. These steps may include, where appropriate, providing restitution to identifiable victims, as well as other forms of remediation.

Other reasonable steps to respond appropriately to the criminal conduct may include self-reporting and cooperation with authorities.

Second, the organization should act appropriately to prevent further similar criminal conduct, including assessing the compliance and ethics program and making modifications necessary to ensure the program is effective. The steps taken should be consistent with subsections (b)(5) and (c) and may include the use of an outside professional advisor to ensure adequate assessment and implementation of any modifications.

7. **Application of Subsection (c).**—To meet the requirements of subsection (c), an organization shall:

(A) Assess periodically the risk that criminal conduct will occur, including assessing the following:

(i) The nature and seriousness of such criminal conduct.

(ii) The likelihood that certain criminal conduct may occur because of the nature of the organization's business. If, because of the nature of an organization's business, there is a substantial risk that certain types of criminal conduct may occur, the organization shall take reasonable steps to prevent and detect that type of criminal conduct. For example, an organization that, due to the nature of its business, employs sales personnel who have flexibility to set prices shall establish standards and procedures designed to prevent and detect price-fixing. An organization that, due to the nature of its business, employs sales personnel who have flexibility to represent the material characteristics of a product shall establish standards and procedures designed to prevent and detect fraud.

(iii) The prior history of the organization. The prior history of an organization may indicate types of criminal conduct that it shall take actions to prevent and detect.

(B) Prioritize periodically, as appropriate, the actions taken pursuant to any requirement set forth in subsection (b), in order to focus on preventing and detecting the criminal conduct identified under subparagraph (A) of this note as most serious, and most likely, to occur.

(C) Modify, as appropriate, the actions taken pursuant to any requirement set forth in subsection (b) to reduce the risk of criminal conduct identified under subparagraph (A) of this note as most serious, and most likely, to occur.

Background: This section sets forth the requirements for an effective compliance and ethics program. This section responds to section 805(a)(5) of the Sarbanes–Oxley Act of 2002, Public Law 107–204, which directed the Commission to review and amend, as appropriate, the guidelines and related policy statements to ensure that the guidelines that apply to organizations in this chapter "are sufficient to deter and punish organizational criminal misconduct."

The requirements set forth in this guideline are intended to achieve reasonable prevention and detection of criminal conduct for which the organization would be vicariously liable. The prior diligence of an organization in seeking to prevent and detect criminal conduct has a direct bearing on the appropriate penalties and probation terms for the organization if it is convicted and sentenced for a criminal offense.

Historical Note	Effective November 1, 2004 (amendment 673). Amended effective November 1, 2010 (amendment 744); November 1, 2011 (amendment 758); November 1, 2013 (amendment 778).

PART C — FINES

1. DETERMINING THE FINE — CRIMINAL PURPOSE ORGANIZATIONS

§8C1.1. Determining the Fine — Criminal Purpose Organizations

If, upon consideration of the nature and circumstances of the offense and the history and characteristics of the organization, the court determines that the organization operated primarily for a criminal purpose or primarily by criminal means, the fine shall be set at an amount (subject to the statutory maximum) sufficient to divest the organization of all its net assets. When this section applies, Subpart 2 (Determining the Fine — Other Organizations) and §8C3.4 (Fines Paid by Owners of Closely Held Organizations) do not apply.

Commentary

Application Note:

1. "*Net assets*," as used in this section, means the assets remaining after payment of all legitimate claims against assets by known innocent bona fide creditors.

Background: This guideline addresses the case in which the court, based upon an examination of the nature and circumstances of the offense and the history and characteristics of the organization, determines that the organization was operated primarily for a criminal purpose (*e.g.*, a front for a scheme that was designed to commit fraud; an organization established to participate in the illegal manufacture, importation, or distribution of a controlled substance) or operated primarily by criminal means (*e.g.*, a hazardous waste disposal business that had no legitimate means of disposing of hazardous waste). In such a case, the fine shall be set at an amount sufficient to remove all of the organization's net assets. If the extent of the assets of the organization is unknown, the maximum fine authorized by statute should be imposed, absent innocent bona fide creditors.

Historical Note	Effective November 1, 1991 (amendment 422).

*   *   *   *   *

2. DETERMINING THE FINE — OTHER ORGANIZATIONS

§8C2.1. Applicability of Fine Guidelines

The provisions of §§8C2.2 through 8C2.9 apply to each count for which the applicable guideline offense level is determined under:

    (a)   §§2B1.1, 2B1.4, 2B2.3, 2B4.1, 2B5.3, 2B6.1;
          §§2C1.1, 2C1.2, 2C1.6;
          §§2D1.7, 2D3.1, 2D3.2;
          §§2E3.1, 2E4.1, 2E5.1, 2E5.3;
          §2G3.1;
          §§2K1.1, 2K2.1;
          §2L1.1;
          §2N3.1;
          §2R1.1;
          §§2S1.1, 2S1.3;
          §§2T1.1, 2T1.4, 2T1.6, 2T1.7, 2T1.8, 2T1.9, 2T2.1, 2T2.2, 2T3.1; or

    (b)   §§2E1.1, 2X1.1, 2X2.1, 2X3.1, 2X4.1, with respect to cases in which the offense level for the underlying offense is determined under one of the guideline sections listed in subsection (a) above.

Commentary

Application Notes:

1.   If the Chapter Two offense guideline for a count is listed in subsection (a) or (b) above, and the applicable guideline results in the determination of the offense level by use of one of the listed guidelines, apply the provisions of §§8C2.2 through 8C2.9 to that count. For example, §§8C2.2 through 8C2.9 apply to an offense under §2K2.1 (an offense guideline listed in subsection (a)), unless the cross reference in that guideline requires the offense level to be determined under an offense guideline section not listed in subsection (a).

2.   If the Chapter Two offense guideline for a count is not listed in subsection (a) or (b) above, but the applicable guideline results in the determination of the offense level by use of a listed guideline, apply the provisions of §§8C2.2 through 8C2.9 to that count. For example, where the conduct set forth in a count of conviction ordinarily referenced to §2N2.1 (an offense guideline not listed in subsection (a)) establishes §2B1.1 (Theft, Property Destruction, and Fraud) as the applicable offense guideline (an offense guideline listed in subsection (a)), §§8C2.2 through 8C2.9 would apply because the actual offense level is determined under §2B1.1 (Theft, Property Destruction, and Fraud).

Background: The fine guidelines of this subpart apply only to offenses covered by the guideline sections set forth in subsection (a) above. For example, the provisions of §§8C2.2 through 8C2.9 do not apply to counts for which the applicable guideline offense level is determined under Chapter Two, Part Q (Offenses Involving the Environment). For such cases, §8C2.10 (Determining the Fine for Other Counts) is applicable.

Historical Note	Effective November 1, 1991 (amendment 422). Amended effective November 1, 1992 (amendment 453); November 1, 1993 (amendment 496); November 1, 2001 (amendments 617, 619, and 634); November 1, 2005 (amendment 679).

§8C2.2. Preliminary Determination of Inability to Pay Fine

(a) Where it is readily ascertainable that the organization cannot and is not likely to become able (even on an installment schedule) to pay restitution required under §8B1.1 (Restitution — Organizations), a determination of the guideline fine range is unnecessary because, pursuant to §8C3.3(a), no fine would be imposed.

(b) Where it is readily ascertainable through a preliminary determination of the minimum of the guideline fine range (*see* §§8C2.3 through 8C2.7) that the organization cannot and is not likely to become able (even on an installment schedule) to pay such minimum guideline fine, a further determination of the guideline fine range is unnecessary. Instead, the court may use the preliminary determination and impose the fine that would result from the application of §8C3.3 (Reduction of Fine Based on Inability to Pay).

Commentary

Application Notes:

1. In a case of a determination under subsection (a), a statement that "the guideline fine range was not determined because it is readily ascertainable that the defendant cannot and is not likely to become able to pay restitution" is recommended.

2. In a case of a determination under subsection (b), a statement that "no precise determination of the guideline fine range is required because it is readily ascertainable that the defendant cannot and is not likely to become able to pay the minimum of the guideline fine range" is recommended.

Background: Many organizational defendants lack the ability to pay restitution. In addition, many organizational defendants who may be able to pay restitution lack the ability to pay the minimum fine called for by §8C2.7(a). In such cases, a complete determination of the guideline fine range may be a needless exercise. This section provides for an abbreviated determination of the guideline fine range that can be applied where it is readily ascertainable that the fine within the guideline fine range determined under §8C2.7 (Guideline Fine Range — Organizations) would be reduced under §8C3.3 (Reduction of Fine Based on Inability to Pay).

Historical Note	Effective November 1, 1991 (amendment 422).

§8C2.3. Offense Level

(a) For each count covered by §8C2.1 (Applicability of Fine Guidelines), use the applicable Chapter Two guideline to determine the base offense level and apply, in the order listed, any appropriate adjustments contained in that guideline.

    (b)   Where there is more than one such count, apply Chapter Three, Part D (Multiple Counts) to determine the combined offense level.

Commentary

Application Notes:

1.   In determining the offense level under this section, "*defendant*," as used in Chapter Two, includes any agent of the organization for whose conduct the organization is criminally responsible.

2.   In determining the offense level under this section, apply the provisions of §§1B1.2 through 1B1.8. Do not apply the adjustments in Chapter Three, Parts A (Victim-Related Adjustments), B (Role in the Offense), C (Obstruction and Related Adjustments), and E (Acceptance of Responsibility).

Historical Note	Effective November 1, 1991 (amendment 422). Amended effective November 1, 2011 (amendment 758).

§8C2.4.　Base Fine

    (a)   The base fine is the greatest of:

        (1)   the amount from the table in subsection (d) below corresponding to the offense level determined under §8C2.3 (Offense Level); or

        (2)   the pecuniary gain to the organization from the offense; or

        (3)   the pecuniary loss from the offense caused by the organization, to the extent the loss was caused intentionally, knowingly, or recklessly.

    (b)   *Provided,* that if the applicable offense guideline in Chapter Two includes a special instruction for organizational fines, that special instruction shall be applied, as appropriate.

    (c)   *Provided, further*, that to the extent the calculation of either pecuniary gain or pecuniary loss would unduly complicate or prolong the sentencing process, that amount, *i.e.*, gain or loss as appropriate, shall not be used for the determination of the base fine.

(d) OFFENSE LEVEL FINE TABLE

Offense Level	Amount
6 or less	$8,500
7	$15,000
8	$15,000
9	$25,000
10	$35,000
11	$50,000
12	$70,000
13	$100,000
14	$150,000
15	$200,000
16	$300,000
17	$450,000
18	$600,000
19	$850,000
20	$1,000,000
21	$1,500,000
22	$2,000,000
23	$3,000,000
24	$3,500,000
25	$5,000,000
26	$6,500,000
27	$8,500,000
28	$10,000,000
29	$15,000,000
30	$20,000,000
31	$25,000,000
32	$30,000,000
33	$40,000,000
34	$50,000,000
35	$65,000,000
36	$80,000,000
37	$100,000,000
38 or more	$150,000,000.

(e) Special Instruction

(1) For offenses committed prior to November 1, 2015, use the offense level fine table that was set forth in the version of §8C2.4(d) that was in effect on November 1, 2014, rather than the offense level fine table set forth in subsection (d) above.

§8C2.4

Application Notes:

1. "*Pecuniary gain*," "*pecuniary loss*," and "*offense*" are defined in the Commentary to §8A1.2 (Application Instructions — Organizations). Note that subsections (a)(2) and (a)(3) contain certain limitations as to the use of pecuniary gain and pecuniary loss in determining the base fine. Under subsection (a)(2), the pecuniary gain used to determine the base fine is the pecuniary gain to the organization from the offense. Under subsection (a)(3), the pecuniary loss used to determine the base fine is the pecuniary loss from the offense caused by the organization, to the extent that such loss was caused intentionally, knowingly, or recklessly.

2. Under 18 U.S.C. § 3571(d), the court is not required to calculate pecuniary loss or pecuniary gain to the extent that determination of loss or gain would unduly complicate or prolong the sentencing process. Nevertheless, the court may need to approximate loss in order to calculate offense levels under Chapter Two. *See* Commentary to §2B1.1 (Theft, Property Destruction, and Fraud). If loss is approximated for purposes of determining the applicable offense level, the court should use that approximation as the starting point for calculating pecuniary loss under this section.

3. In a case of an attempted offense or a conspiracy to commit an offense, pecuniary loss and pecuniary gain are to be determined in accordance with the principles stated in §2X1.1 (Attempt, Solicitation, or Conspiracy).

4. In a case involving multiple participants (*i.e.*, multiple organizations, or the organization and individual(s) unassociated with the organization), the applicable offense level is to be determined without regard to apportionment of the gain from or loss caused by the offense. *See* §1B1.3 (Relevant Conduct). However, if the base fine is determined under subsections (a)(2) or (a)(3), the court may, as appropriate, apportion gain or loss considering the defendant's relative culpability and other pertinent factors. Note also that under §2R1.1(d)(1), the volume of commerce, which is used in determining a proxy for loss under §8C2.4(a)(3), is limited to the volume of commerce attributable to the defendant.

5. Special instructions regarding the determination of the base fine are contained in §§2B4.1 (Bribery in Procurement of Bank Loan and Other Commercial Bribery); 2C1.1 (Offering, Giving, Soliciting, or Receiving a Bribe; Extortion Under Color of Official Right; Fraud Involving the Deprivation of the Intangible Right to Honest Services of Public Officials; Conspiracy to Defraud by Interference with Governmental Functions); 2C1.2 (Offering, Giving, Soliciting, or Receiving a Gratuity); 2E5.1 (Offering, Accepting, or Soliciting a Bribe or Gratuity Affecting the Operation of an Employee Welfare or Pension Benefit Plan; Prohibited Payments or Lending of Money by Employer or Agent to Employees, Representatives, or Labor Organizations); and 2R1.1 (Bid-Rigging, Price-Fixing or Market-Allocation Agreements Among Competitors).

Background: Under this section, the base fine is determined in one of three ways: (1) by the amount, based on the offense level, from the table in subsection (d); (2) by the pecuniary gain to the organization from the offense; and (3) by the pecuniary loss caused by the organization, to the extent that such loss was caused intentionally, knowingly, or recklessly. In certain cases, special instructions for determining the loss or offense level amount apply. As a general rule, the base fine measures the seriousness of the offense. The determinants of the base fine are selected so that, in conjunction with the multipliers derived from the culpability score in §8C2.5 (Culpability Score), they will result in guideline fine ranges appropriate to deter organizational criminal conduct and to provide incentives for organizations to maintain internal mechanisms for preventing, detecting, and reporting criminal conduct. In order to deter organizations from seeking to obtain financial reward through criminal conduct, this section provides that, when greatest, pecuniary gain to the organization is used to determine the base fine. In order to ensure that organizations will seek to prevent losses intentionally, knowingly, or recklessly caused by their agents, this section provides that, when greatest, pecuniary loss is used to determine the base fine in such circumstances. Chapter Two provides special instructions for fines that include specific rules for determining the base fine in connection with certain types of offenses in which the calculation of loss or gain is difficult, *e.g.*, price-fixing. For these offenses, the special instructions tailor the base fine to circumstances that occur in connection with such offenses and that generally relate to the magnitude of loss or gain resulting from such offenses.

Historical Note	Effective November 1, 1991 (amendment 422). Amended effective November 1, 1993 (amendment 496); November 1, 1995 (amendment 534); November 1, 2001 (amendment 634); November 1, 2004 (amendments 666 and 673); November 1, 2015 (amendment 791).

§8C2.5. Culpability Score

(a) Start with **5** points and apply subsections (b) through (g) below.

(b) INVOLVEMENT IN OR TOLERANCE OF CRIMINAL ACTIVITY

If more than one applies, use the greatest:

(1) If—

(A) the organization had **5,000** or more employees and

(i) an individual within high-level personnel of the organization participated in, condoned, or was willfully ignorant of the offense; or

(ii) tolerance of the offense by substantial authority personnel was pervasive throughout the organization; or

(B) the unit of the organization within which the offense was committed had **5,000** or more employees and

(i) an individual within high-level personnel of the unit participated in, condoned, or was willfully ignorant of the offense; or

(ii) tolerance of the offense by substantial authority personnel was pervasive throughout such unit,

add **5** points; or

(2) If—

    (A) the organization had 1,000 or more employees and

        (i) an individual within high-level personnel of the organization participated in, condoned, or was willfully ignorant of the offense; or

        (ii) tolerance of the offense by substantial authority personnel was pervasive throughout the organization; or

    (B) the unit of the organization within which the offense was committed had 1,000 or more employees and

        (i) an individual within high-level personnel of the unit participated in, condoned, or was willfully ignorant of the offense; or

        (ii) tolerance of the offense by substantial authority personnel was pervasive throughout such unit,

add **4** points; or

(3) If—

    (A) the organization had 200 or more employees and

        (i) an individual within high-level personnel of the organization participated in, condoned, or was willfully ignorant of the offense; or

        (ii) tolerance of the offense by substantial authority personnel was pervasive throughout the organization; or

    (B) the unit of the organization within which the offense was committed had 200 or more employees and

        (i) an individual within high-level personnel of the unit participated in, condoned, or was willfully ignorant of the offense; or

        (ii) tolerance of the offense by substantial authority personnel was pervasive throughout such unit,

add **3** points; or

(4)   If the organization had 50 or more employees and an individual within substantial authority personnel participated in, condoned, or was willfully ignorant of the offense, add **2** points; or

(5)   If the organization had 10 or more employees and an individual within substantial authority personnel participated in, condoned, or was willfully ignorant of the offense, add **1** point.

(c)   PRIOR HISTORY

If more than one applies, use the greater:

(1)   If the organization (or separately managed line of business) committed any part of the instant offense less than 10 years after (A) a criminal adjudication based on similar misconduct; or (B) civil or administrative adjudication(s) based on two or more separate instances of similar misconduct, add **1** point; or

(2)   If the organization (or separately managed line of business) committed any part of the instant offense less than 5 years after (A) a criminal adjudication based on similar misconduct; or (B) civil or administrative adjudication(s) based on two or more separate instances of similar misconduct, add **2** points.

(d)   VIOLATION OF AN ORDER

If more than one applies, use the greater:

(1)   (A) If the commission of the instant offense violated a judicial order or injunction, other than a violation of a condition of probation; or (B) if the organization (or separately managed line of business) violated a condition of probation by engaging in similar misconduct, *i.e.*, misconduct similar to that for which it was placed on probation, add **2** points; or

(2)   If the commission of the instant offense violated a condition of probation, add **1** point.

(e)   OBSTRUCTION OF JUSTICE

If the organization willfully obstructed or impeded, attempted to obstruct or impede, or aided, abetted, or encouraged obstruction of justice during the investigation, prosecution, or sentencing of the instant offense, or, with knowledge thereof, failed to take reasonable steps to prevent such obstruction or impedance or attempted obstruction or impedance, add **3** points.

(f)   EFFECTIVE COMPLIANCE AND ETHICS PROGRAM

(1)   If the offense occurred even though the organization had in place at the time of the offense an effective compliance and ethics program, as provided in §8B2.1 (Effective Compliance and Ethics Program), subtract **3** points.

(2)   Subsection (f)(1) shall not apply if, after becoming aware of an offense, the organization unreasonably delayed reporting the offense to appropriate governmental authorities.

(3)   (A)   Except as provided in subparagraphs (B) and (C), subsection (f)(1) shall not apply if an individual within high-level personnel of the organization, a person within high-level personnel of the unit of the organization within which the offense was committed where the unit had 200 or more employees, or an individual described in §8B2.1(b)(2)(B) or (C), participated in, condoned, or was willfully ignorant of the offense.

(B)   There is a rebuttable presumption, for purposes of subsection (f)(1), that the organization did not have an effective compliance and ethics program if an individual—

(i)   within high-level personnel of a small organization; or

(ii)   within substantial authority personnel, but not within high-level personnel, of any organization,

participated in, condoned, or was willfully ignorant of, the offense.

(C)   Subparagraphs (A) and (B) shall not apply if—

(i)   the individual or individuals with operational responsibility for the compliance and ethics program (*see* §8B2.1(b)(2)(C)) have direct reporting obligations to the governing authority or an appropriate subgroup thereof (*e.g.*, an audit committee of the board of directors);

(ii)   the compliance and ethics program detected the offense before discovery outside the organization or before such discovery was reasonably likely;

(iii) the organization promptly reported the offense to appropriate governmental authorities; and

(iv) no individual with operational responsibility for the compliance and ethics program participated in, condoned, or was willfully ignorant of the offense.

(g) SELF-REPORTING, COOPERATION, AND ACCEPTANCE OF RESPONSIBILITY

If more than one applies, use the greatest:

(1) If the organization (A) prior to an imminent threat of disclosure or government investigation; and (B) within a reasonably prompt time after becoming aware of the offense, reported the offense to appropriate governmental authorities, fully cooperated in the investigation, and clearly demonstrated recognition and affirmative acceptance of responsibility for its criminal conduct, subtract **5** points; or

(2) If the organization fully cooperated in the investigation and clearly demonstrated recognition and affirmative acceptance of responsibility for its criminal conduct, subtract **2** points; or

(3) If the organization clearly demonstrated recognition and affirmative acceptance of responsibility for its criminal conduct, subtract **1** point.

Commentary

Application Notes:

1. **Definitions.**—For purposes of this guideline, "*condoned*", "*prior criminal adjudication*", "*similar misconduct*", "*substantial authority personnel*", and "*willfully ignorant of the offense*" have the meaning given those terms in Application Note 3 of the Commentary to §8A1.2 (Application Instructions — Organizations).

   "*Small Organization*", for purposes of subsection (f)(3), means an organization that, at the time of the instant offense, had fewer than 200 employees.

2. For purposes of subsection (b), "*unit of the organization*" means any reasonably distinct operational component of the organization. For example, a large organization may have several large units such as divisions or subsidiaries, as well as many smaller units such as specialized manufacturing, marketing, or accounting operations within these larger units. For purposes of this definition, all of these types of units are encompassed within the term "unit of the organization."

3. "*High-level personnel of the organization*" is defined in the Commentary to §8A1.2 (Application Instructions — Organizations). With respect to a unit with 200 or more employees, "*high-level personnel of a unit of the organization*" means agents within the unit who set the policy for or control that unit. For example, if the managing agent

of a unit with 200 employees participated in an offense, three points would be added under subsection (b)(3); if that organization had 1,000 employees and the managing agent of the unit with 200 employees were also within high-level personnel of the organization in its entirety, four points (rather than three) would be added under subsection (b)(2).

4. Pervasiveness under subsection (b) will be case specific and depend on the number, and degree of responsibility, of individuals within substantial authority personnel who participated in, condoned, or were willfully ignorant of the offense. Fewer individuals need to be involved for a finding of pervasiveness if those individuals exercised a relatively high degree of authority. Pervasiveness can occur either within an organization as a whole or within a unit of an organization. For example, if an offense were committed in an organization with 1,000 employees but the tolerance of the offense was pervasive only within a unit of the organization with 200 employees (and no high-level personnel of the organization participated in, condoned, or was willfully ignorant of the offense), three points would be added under subsection (b)(3). If, in the same organization, tolerance of the offense was pervasive throughout the organization as a whole, or an individual within high-level personnel of the organization participated in the offense, four points (rather than three) would be added under subsection (b)(2).

5. A "*separately managed line of business*," as used in subsections (c) and (d), is a subpart of a for-profit organization that has its own management, has a high degree of autonomy from higher managerial authority, and maintains its own separate books of account. Corporate subsidiaries and divisions frequently are separately managed lines of business. Under subsection (c), in determining the prior history of an organization with separately managed lines of business, only the prior conduct or criminal record of the separately managed line of business involved in the instant offense is to be used. Under subsection (d), in the context of an organization with separately managed lines of business, in making the determination whether a violation of a condition of probation involved engaging in similar misconduct, only the prior misconduct of the separately managed line of business involved in the instant offense is to be considered.

6. Under subsection (c), in determining the prior history of an organization or separately managed line of business, the conduct of the underlying economic entity shall be considered without regard to its legal structure or ownership. For example, if two companies merged and became separate divisions and separately managed lines of business within the merged company, each division would retain the prior history of its predecessor company. If a company reorganized and became a new legal entity, the new company would retain the prior history of the predecessor company. In contrast, if one company purchased the physical assets but not the ongoing business of another company, the prior history of the company selling the physical assets would not be transferred to the company purchasing the assets. However, if an organization is acquired by another organization in response to solicitations by appropriate federal government officials, the prior history of the acquired organization shall not be attributed to the acquiring organization.

7. Under subsections (c)(1)(B) and (c)(2)(B), the civil or administrative adjudication(s) must have occurred within the specified period (ten or five years) of the instant offense.

8. Adjust the culpability score for the factors listed in subsection (e) whether or not the offense guideline incorporates that factor, or that factor is inherent in the offense.

9. Subsection (e) applies where the obstruction is committed on behalf of the organization; it does not apply where an individual or individuals have attempted to conceal their misconduct from the organization. The Commentary to §3C1.1 (Obstructing or Impeding the

Administration of Justice) provides guidance regarding the types of conduct that constitute obstruction.

10. Subsection (f)(2) contemplates that the organization will be allowed a reasonable period of time to conduct an internal investigation. In addition, no reporting is required by subsection (f)(2) or (f)(3)(C)(iii) if the organization reasonably concluded, based on the information then available, that no offense had been committed.

11. For purposes of subsection (f)(3)(C)(i), an individual has "**_direct reporting obligations_**" to the governing authority or an appropriate subgroup thereof if the individual has express authority to communicate personally to the governing authority or appropriate subgroup thereof (A) promptly on any matter involving criminal conduct or potential criminal conduct, and (B) no less than annually on the implementation and effectiveness of the compliance and ethics program.

12. "**_Appropriate governmental authorities_**," as used in subsections (f) and (g)(1), means the federal or state law enforcement, regulatory, or program officials having jurisdiction over such matter. To qualify for a reduction under subsection (g)(1), the report to appropriate governmental authorities must be made under the direction of the organization.

13. To qualify for a reduction under subsection (g)(1) or (g)(2), cooperation must be both timely and thorough. To be timely, the cooperation must begin essentially at the same time as the organization is officially notified of a criminal investigation. To be thorough, the cooperation should include the disclosure of all pertinent information known by the organization. A prime test of whether the organization has disclosed all pertinent information is whether the information is sufficient for law enforcement personnel to identify the nature and extent of the offense and the individual(s) responsible for the criminal conduct. However, the cooperation to be measured is the cooperation of the organization itself, not the cooperation of individuals within the organization. If, because of the lack of cooperation of particular individual(s), neither the organization nor law enforcement personnel are able to identify the culpable individual(s) within the organization despite the organization's efforts to cooperate fully, the organization may still be given credit for full cooperation.

14. Entry of a plea of guilty prior to the commencement of trial combined with truthful admission of involvement in the offense and related conduct ordinarily will constitute significant evidence of affirmative acceptance of responsibility under subsection (g), unless outweighed by conduct of the organization that is inconsistent with such acceptance of responsibility. This adjustment is not intended to apply to an organization that puts the government to its burden of proof at trial by denying the essential factual elements of guilt, is convicted, and only then admits guilt and expresses remorse. Conviction by trial, however, does not automatically preclude an organization from consideration for such a reduction. In rare situations, an organization may clearly demonstrate an acceptance of responsibility for its criminal conduct even though it exercises its constitutional right to a trial. This may occur, for example, where an organization goes to trial to assert and preserve issues that do not relate to factual guilt (_e.g._, to make a constitutional challenge to a statute or a challenge to the applicability of a statute to its conduct). In each such instance, however, a determination that an organization has accepted responsibility will be based primarily upon pretrial statements and conduct.

15. In making a determination with respect to subsection (g), the court may determine that the chief executive officer or highest ranking employee of an organization should appear at sentencing in order to signify that the organization has clearly demonstrated recognition and affirmative acceptance of responsibility.

§8C2.6

Background: The increased culpability scores under subsection (b) are based on three inter-related principles. First, an organization is more culpable when individuals who manage the organization or who have substantial discretion in acting for the organization participate in, condone, or are willfully ignorant of criminal conduct. Second, as organizations become larger and their managements become more professional, participation in, condonation of, or willful ignorance of criminal conduct by such management is increasingly a breach of trust or abuse of position. Third, as organizations increase in size, the risk of criminal conduct beyond that reflected in the instant offense also increases whenever management's tolerance of that offense is pervasive. Because of the continuum of sizes of organizations and professionalization of management, subsection (b) gradually increases the culpability score based upon the size of the organization and the level and extent of the substantial authority personnel involvement.

| *Historical Note* | Effective November 1, 1991 (amendment 422). Amended effective November 1, 2004 (amendment 673); November 1, 2006 (amendment 695); November 1, 2010 (amendment 744). |

§8C2.6. Minimum and Maximum Multipliers

Using the culpability score from §8C2.5 (Culpability Score) and applying any applicable special instruction for fines in Chapter Two, determine the applicable minimum and maximum fine multipliers from the table below.

CULPABILITY SCORE	MINIMUM MULTIPLIER	MAXIMUM MULTIPLIER
10 or more	2.00	4.00
9	1.80	3.60
8	1.60	3.20
7	1.40	2.80
6	1.20	2.40
5	1.00	2.00
4	0.80	1.60
3	0.60	1.20
2	0.40	0.80
1	0.20	0.40
0 or less	0.05	0.20.

Commentary

Application Note:

1. A special instruction for fines in §2R1.1 (Bid-Rigging, Price-Fixing or Market-Allocation Agreements Among Competitors) sets a floor for minimum and maximum multipliers in cases covered by that guideline.

| *Historical Note* | Effective November 1, 1991 (amendment 422). |

§8C2.7. Guideline Fine Range — Organizations

(a) The minimum of the guideline fine range is determined by multiplying the base fine determined under §8C2.4 (Base Fine) by the applicable minimum multiplier determined under §8C2.6 (Minimum and Maximum Multipliers).

(b) The maximum of the guideline fine range is determined by multiplying the base fine determined under §8C2.4 (Base Fine) by the applicable maximum multiplier determined under §8C2.6 (Minimum and Maximum Multipliers).

Historical Note	Effective November 1, 1991 (amendment 422).

§8C2.8. Determining the Fine Within the Range (Policy Statement)

(a) In determining the amount of the fine within the applicable guideline range, the court should consider:

(1) the need for the sentence to reflect the seriousness of the offense, promote respect for the law, provide just punishment, afford adequate deterrence, and protect the public from further crimes of the organization;

(2) the organization's role in the offense;

(3) any collateral consequences of conviction, including civil obligations arising from the organization's conduct;

(4) any nonpecuniary loss caused or threatened by the offense;

(5) whether the offense involved a vulnerable victim;

(6) any prior criminal record of an individual within high-level personnel of the organization or high-level personnel of a unit of the organization who participated in, condoned, or was willfully ignorant of the criminal conduct;

(7) any prior civil or criminal misconduct by the organization other than that counted under §8C2.5(c);

(8) any culpability score under §8C2.5 (Culpability Score) higher than **10** or lower than **0**;

(9) partial but incomplete satisfaction of the conditions for one or more of the mitigating or aggravating factors set forth in §8C2.5 (Culpability Score);

(10) any factor listed in 18 U.S.C. § 3572(a); and

(11) whether the organization failed to have, at the time of the instant offense, an effective compliance and ethics program within the meaning of §8B2.1 (Effective Compliance and Ethics Program).

(b) In addition, the court may consider the relative importance of any factor used to determine the range, including the pecuniary loss caused by the offense, the pecuniary gain from the offense, any specific offense characteristic used to determine the offense level, and any aggravating or mitigating factor used to determine the culpability score.

Commentary

Application Notes:

1. Subsection (a)(2) provides that the court, in setting the fine within the guideline fine range, should consider the organization's role in the offense. This consideration is particularly appropriate if the guideline fine range does not take the organization's role in the offense into account. For example, the guideline fine range in an antitrust case does not take into consideration whether the organization was an organizer or leader of the conspiracy. A higher fine within the guideline fine range ordinarily will be appropriate for an organization that takes a leading role in such an offense.

2. Subsection (a)(3) provides that the court, in setting the fine within the guideline fine range, should consider any collateral consequences of conviction, including civil obligations arising from the organization's conduct. As a general rule, collateral consequences that merely make victims whole provide no basis for reducing the fine within the guideline range. If criminal and civil sanctions are unlikely to make victims whole, this may provide a basis for a higher fine within the guideline fine range. If punitive collateral sanctions have been or will be imposed on the organization, this may provide a basis for a lower fine within the guideline fine range.

3. Subsection (a)(4) provides that the court, in setting the fine within the guideline fine range, should consider any nonpecuniary loss caused or threatened by the offense. To the extent that nonpecuniary loss caused or threatened (*e.g.*, loss of or threat to human life; psychological injury; threat to national security) by the offense is not adequately considered in setting the guideline fine range, this factor provides a basis for a higher fine within the range. This factor is more likely to be applicable where the guideline fine range is determined by pecuniary loss or gain, rather than by offense level, because the Chapter Two offense levels frequently take actual or threatened nonpecuniary loss into account.

4. Subsection (a)(6) provides that the court, in setting the fine within the guideline fine range, should consider any prior criminal record of an individual within high-level personnel of the organization or within high-level personnel of a unit of the organization. Since an individual within high-level personnel either exercises substantial control over

the organization or a unit of the organization or has a substantial role in the making of policy within the organization or a unit of the organization, any prior criminal misconduct of such an individual may be relevant to the determination of the appropriate fine for the organization.

5. Subsection (a)(7) provides that the court, in setting the fine within the guideline fine range, should consider any prior civil or criminal misconduct by the organization other than that counted under §8C2.5(c). The civil and criminal misconduct counted under §8C2.5(c) increases the guideline fine range. Civil or criminal misconduct other than that counted under §8C2.5(c) may provide a basis for a higher fine within the range. In a case involving a pattern of illegality, an upward departure may be warranted.

6. Subsection (a)(8) provides that the court, in setting the fine within the guideline fine range, should consider any culpability score higher than ten or lower than zero. As the culpability score increases above ten, this may provide a basis for a higher fine within the range. Similarly, as the culpability score decreases below zero, this may provide a basis for a lower fine within the range.

7. Under subsection (b), the court, in determining the fine within the range, may consider any factor that it considered in determining the range. This allows for courts to differentiate between cases that have the same offense level but differ in seriousness (*e.g.*, two fraud cases at offense level 12, one resulting in a loss of $21,000, the other $40,000). Similarly, this allows for courts to differentiate between two cases that have the same aggravating factors, but in which those factors vary in their intensity (*e.g.*, two cases with upward adjustments to the culpability score under §8C2.5(c)(2) (prior criminal adjudications within 5 years of the commencement of the instant offense, one involving a single conviction, the other involving two or more convictions)).

Background: Subsection (a) includes factors that the court is required to consider under 18 U.S.C. §§ 3553(a) and 3572(a) as well as additional factors that the Commission has determined may be relevant in a particular case. A number of factors required for consideration under 18 U.S.C. § 3572(a) (*e.g.*, pecuniary loss, the size of the organization) are used under the fine guidelines in this subpart to determine the fine range, and therefore are not specifically set out again in subsection (a) of this guideline. In unusual cases, factors listed in this section may provide a basis for departure.

Historical Note	Effective November 1, 1991 (amendment 422). Amended effective November 1, 2004 (amendment 673); November 1, 2015 (amendment 797).

§8C2.9. Disgorgement

The court shall add to the fine determined under §8C2.8 (Determining the Fine Within the Range) any gain to the organization from the offense that has not and will not be paid as restitution or by way of other remedial measures.

Commentary

Application Note:

1. This section is designed to ensure that the amount of any gain that has not and will not be taken from the organization for remedial purposes will be added to the fine. This section typically will apply in cases in which the organization has received gain from an offense but restitution or remedial efforts will not be required because the offense did not result in harm to identifiable victims, *e.g.*, money laundering, obscenity, and regulatory reporting offenses. Money spent or to be spent to remedy the adverse effects of the offense, *e.g.*, the cost to retrofit defective products, should be considered as disgorged gain. If the cost of remedial efforts made or to be made by the organization equals or exceeds the gain from the offense, this section will not apply.

Historical Note	Effective November 1, 1991 (amendment 422).

§8C2.10. Determining the Fine for Other Counts

For any count or counts not covered under §8C2.1 (Applicability of Fine Guidelines), the court should determine an appropriate fine by applying the provisions of 18 U.S.C. §§ 3553 and 3572. The court should determine the appropriate fine amount, if any, to be imposed in addition to any fine determined under §8C2.8 (Determining the Fine Within the Range) and §8C2.9 (Disgorgement).

Commentary

Background: The Commission has not promulgated guidelines governing the setting of fines for counts not covered by §8C2.1 (Applicability of Fine Guidelines). For such counts, the court should determine the appropriate fine based on the general statutory provisions governing sentencing. In cases that have a count or counts not covered by the guidelines in addition to a count or counts covered by the guidelines, the court shall apply the fine guidelines for the count(s) covered by the guidelines, and add any additional amount to the fine, as appropriate, for the count(s) not covered by the guidelines.

Historical Note	Effective November 1, 1991 (amendment 422).

*   *   *   *   *

3.   IMPLEMENTING THE SENTENCE OF A FINE

§8C3.1. Imposing a Fine

(a)   Except to the extent restricted by the maximum fine authorized by statute or any minimum fine required by statute, the fine or fine range shall be that determined under §8C1.1 (Determining the Fine — Criminal Purpose Organizations); §8C2.7 (Guideline Fine Range — Organizations) and §8C2.9 (Disgorgement); or §8C2.10 (Determining the Fine for Other Counts), as appropriate.

(b) Where the minimum guideline fine is greater than the maximum fine authorized by statute, the maximum fine authorized by statute shall be the guideline fine.

(c) Where the maximum guideline fine is less than a minimum fine required by statute, the minimum fine required by statute shall be the guideline fine.

Commentary

Background: This section sets forth the interaction of the fines or fine ranges determined under this chapter with the maximum fine authorized by statute and any minimum fine required by statute for the count or counts of conviction. The general statutory provisions governing a sentence of a fine are set forth in 18 U.S.C. § 3571.

When the organization is convicted of multiple counts, the maximum fine authorized by statute may increase. For example, in the case of an organization convicted of three felony counts related to a $200,000 fraud, the maximum fine authorized by statute will be $500,000 on each count, for an aggregate maximum authorized fine of $1,500,000.

Historical Note	Effective November 1, 1991 (amendment 422).

§8C3.2. Payment of the Fine — Organizations

(a) If the defendant operated primarily for a criminal purpose or primarily by criminal means, immediate payment of the fine shall be required.

(b) In any other case, immediate payment of the fine shall be required unless the court finds that the organization is financially unable to make immediate payment or that such payment would pose an undue burden on the organization. If the court permits other than immediate payment, it shall require full payment at the earliest possible date, either by requiring payment on a date certain or by establishing an installment schedule.

Commentary

Application Note:

1. When the court permits other than immediate payment, the period provided for payment shall in no event exceed five years. 18 U.S.C. § 3572(d).

§8C3.3

Historical Note	Effective November 1, 1991 (amendment 422).

§8C3.3.   Reduction of Fine Based on Inability to Pay

(a)   The court shall reduce the fine below that otherwise required by §8C1.1 (Determining the Fine — Criminal Purpose Organizations), or §8C2.7 (Guideline Fine Range — Organizations) and §8C2.9 (Disgorgement), to the extent that imposition of such fine would impair its ability to make restitution to victims.

(b)   The court may impose a fine below that otherwise required by §8C2.7 (Guideline Fine Range — Organizations) and §8C2.9 (Disgorgement) if the court finds that the organization is not able and, even with the use of a reasonable installment schedule, is not likely to become able to pay the minimum fine required by §8C2.7 (Guideline Fine Range — Organizations) and §8C2.9 (Disgorgement).

Provided, that the reduction under this subsection shall not be more than necessary to avoid substantially jeopardizing the continued viability of the organization.

Commentary

Application Note:

1.   For purposes of this section, an organization is not able to pay the minimum fine if, even with an installment schedule under §8C3.2 (Payment of the Fine — Organizations), the payment of that fine would substantially jeopardize the continued existence of the organization.

Background: Subsection (a) carries out the requirement in 18 U.S.C. § 3572(b) that the court impose a fine or other monetary penalty only to the extent that such fine or penalty will not impair the ability of the organization to make restitution for the offense; however, this section does not authorize a criminal purpose organization to remain in business in order to pay restitution.

Historical Note	Effective November 1, 1991 (amendment 422).

§8C3.4.   Fines Paid by Owners of Closely Held Organizations

The court may offset the fine imposed upon a closely held organization when one or more individuals, each of whom owns at least a 5 percent interest in the organization, has been fined in a federal criminal proceeding for the same offense conduct for which the organization is being sentenced. The amount of such offset shall not exceed the amount resulting from multiplying the total fines imposed on those individuals by those individuals' total percentage interest in the organization.

Commentary

Application Notes:

1.   For purposes of this section, an organization is closely held, regardless of its size, when relatively few individuals own it. In order for an organization to be closely held, ownership and management need not completely overlap.

2.   This section does not apply to a fine imposed upon an individual that arises out of offense conduct different from that for which the organization is being sentenced.

Background: For practical purposes, most closely held organizations are the alter egos of their owner-managers. In the case of criminal conduct by a closely held corporation, the organization and the culpable individual(s) both may be convicted. As a general rule in such cases, appropriate punishment may be achieved by offsetting the fine imposed upon the organization by an amount that reflects the percentage ownership interest of the sentenced individuals and the magnitude of the fines imposed upon those individuals. For example, an organization is owned by five individuals, each of whom has a twenty percent interest; three of the individuals are convicted; and the combined fines imposed on those three equals $100,000. In this example, the fine imposed upon the organization may be offset by up to 60 percent of their combined fine amounts, *i.e.*, by $60,000.

Historical Note	Effective November 1, 1991 (amendment 422).

*   *   *   *   *

4.   DEPARTURES FROM THE GUIDELINE FINE RANGE

Introductory Commentary

The statutory provisions governing departures are set forth in 18 U.S.C. § 3553(b). Departure may be warranted if the court finds "that there exists an aggravating or mitigating circumstance of a kind, or to a degree, not adequately taken into consideration by the Sentencing Commission in formulating the guidelines that should result in a sentence different from that described." This subpart sets forth certain factors that, in connection with certain offenses, may not have been adequately taken into consideration by the guidelines. In deciding whether departure is warranted, the court should consider the extent to which that factor is adequately taken into consideration by the guidelines and the relative importance or substantiality of that factor in the particular case.

To the extent that any policy statement from Chapter Five, Part K (Departures) is relevant to the organization, a departure from the applicable guideline fine range may be warranted. Some factors listed in Chapter Five, Part K that are particularly applicable to organizations are listed in this subpart. Other factors listed in Chapter Five, Part K may be applicable in particular cases. While this subpart lists factors that the Commission believes may constitute grounds for departure, the list is not exhaustive.

| *Historical Note* | Effective November 1, 1991 (amendment 422). |

§8C4.1.   Substantial Assistance to Authorities — Organizations (Policy Statement)

(a)   Upon motion of the government stating that the defendant has provided substantial assistance in the investigation or prosecution of another organization that has committed an offense, or in the investigation or prosecution of an individual not directly affiliated with the defendant who has committed an offense, the court may depart from the guidelines.

(b)   The appropriate reduction shall be determined by the court for reasons stated on the record that may include, but are not limited to, consideration of the following:

(1)   the court's evaluation of the significance and usefulness of the organization's assistance, taking into consideration the government's evaluation of the assistance rendered;

(2)   the nature and extent of the organization's assistance; and

(3)   the timeliness of the organization's assistance.

Commentary

Application Note:

1.   Departure under this section is intended for cases in which substantial assistance is provided in the investigation or prosecution of crimes committed by individuals not directly affiliated with the organization or by other organizations. It is not intended for assistance in the investigation or prosecution of the agents of the organization responsible for the offense for which the organization is being sentenced.

| *Historical Note* | Effective November 1, 1991 (amendment 422). |

§8C4.2. Risk of Death or Bodily Injury (Policy Statement)

If the offense resulted in death or bodily injury, or involved a foreseeable risk of death or bodily injury, an upward departure may be warranted. The extent of any such departure should depend, among other factors, on the nature of the harm and the extent to which the harm was intended or knowingly risked, and the extent to which such harm or risk is taken into account within the applicable guideline fine range.

Historical Note	Effective November 1, 1991 (amendment 422).

§8C4.3. Threat to National Security (Policy Statement)

If the offense constituted a threat to national security, an upward departure may be warranted.

Historical Note	Effective November 1, 1991 (amendment 422).

§8C4.4. Threat to the Environment (Policy Statement)

If the offense presented a threat to the environment, an upward departure may be warranted.

Historical Note	Effective November 1, 1991 (amendment 422).

§8C4.5. Threat to a Market (Policy Statement)

If the offense presented a risk to the integrity or continued existence of a market, an upward departure may be warranted. This section is applicable to both private markets (*e.g.*, a financial market, a commodities market, or a market for consumer goods) and public markets (*e.g.*, government contracting).

Historical Note	Effective November 1, 1991 (amendment 422).

§8C4.6. Official Corruption (Policy Statement)

If the organization, in connection with the offense, bribed or unlawfully gave a gratuity to a public official, or attempted or conspired to bribe or unlawfully give a gratuity to a public official, an upward departure may be warranted.

Historical Note	Effective November 1, 1991 (amendment 422).

§8C4.7. Public Entity (Policy Statement)

If the organization is a public entity, a downward departure may be warranted.

Historical Note	Effective November 1, 1991 (amendment 422).

§8C4.8. Members or Beneficiaries of the Organization as Victims (Policy Statement)

If the members or beneficiaries, other than shareholders, of the organization are direct victims of the offense, a downward departure may be warranted. If the members or beneficiaries of an organization are direct victims of the offense, imposing a fine upon the organization may increase the burden upon the victims of the offense without achieving a deterrent effect. In such cases, a fine may not be appropriate. For example, departure may be appropriate if a labor union is convicted of embezzlement of pension funds.

Historical Note	Effective November 1, 1991 (amendment 422).

§8C4.9. Remedial Costs that Greatly Exceed Gain (Policy Statement)

If the organization has paid or has agreed to pay remedial costs arising from the offense that greatly exceed the gain that the organization received from the offense, a downward departure may be warranted. In such a case, a substantial fine may not be necessary in order to achieve adequate punishment and deterrence. In deciding whether departure is appropriate, the court should consider the level and extent of substantial authority personnel involvement in the offense and the degree to which the loss exceeds the gain. If an individual within high-level personnel was involved in the offense, a departure would not be appropriate under this section. The lower the level and the more limited the extent of substantial authority personnel involvement in the offense, and the greater the degree to which remedial costs exceeded or will exceed gain, the less will be the need for a substantial fine to achieve adequate punishment and deterrence.

Historical Note	Effective November 1, 1991 (amendment 422).

§8C4.10. Mandatory Programs to Prevent and Detect Violations of Law (Policy Statement)

If the organization's culpability score is reduced under §8C2.5(f) (Effective Compliance and Ethics Program) and the organization had implemented its program in response to a court order or administrative order specifically directed at the organization, an upward departure may be warranted to offset, in part or in whole, such reduction.

Similarly, if, at the time of the instant offense, the organization was required by law to have an effective compliance and ethics program, but the organization did not have such a program, an upward departure may be warranted.

Historical Note	Effective November 1, 1991 (amendment 422). Amended effective November 1, 2004 (amendment 673).

§8C4.11. Exceptional Organizational Culpability (Policy Statement)

If the organization's culpability score is greater than **10**, an upward departure may be appropriate.

If no individual within substantial authority personnel participated in, condoned, or was willfully ignorant of the offense; the organization at the time of the offense had an effective program to prevent and detect violations of law; and the base fine is determined under §8C2.4(a)(1), §8C2.4(a)(3), or a special instruction for fines in Chapter Two (Offense Conduct), a downward departure may be warranted. In a case meeting these criteria, the court may find that the organization had exceptionally low culpability and therefore a fine based on loss, offense level, or a special Chapter Two instruction results in a guideline fine range higher than necessary to achieve the purposes of sentencing. Nevertheless, such fine should not be lower than if determined under §8C2.4(a)(2).

Historical Note	Effective November 1, 1991 (amendment 422).

PART D — ORGANIZATIONAL PROBATION

Introductory Commentary

Section 8D1.1 sets forth the circumstances under which a sentence to a term of probation is required. Sections 8D1.2 through 8D1.4, and 8F1.1, address the length of the probation term, conditions of probation, and violations of probation conditions.

Historical Note	Effective November 1, 1991 (amendment 422). Amended effective November 1, 2004 (amendment 673).

§8D1.1. Imposition of Probation — Organizations

(a) The court shall order a term of probation:

(1) if such sentence is necessary to secure payment of restitution (§8B1.1), enforce a remedial order (§8B1.2), or ensure completion of community service (§8B1.3);

(2) if the organization is sentenced to pay a monetary penalty (*e.g.*, restitution, fine, or special assessment), the penalty is not paid in full at the time of sentencing, and restrictions are necessary to safeguard the organization's ability to make payments;

(3) if, at the time of sentencing, (A) the organization (i) has 50 or more employees, or (ii) was otherwise required under law to have an effective compliance and ethics program; and (B) the organization does not have such a program;

(4) if the organization within five years prior to sentencing engaged in similar misconduct, as determined by a prior criminal adjudication, and any part of the misconduct underlying the instant offense occurred after that adjudication;

(5) if an individual within high-level personnel of the organization or the unit of the organization within which the instant offense was committed participated in the misconduct underlying the instant offense and that individual within five years prior to sentencing engaged in similar misconduct, as determined by a prior criminal adjudication, and any part of the misconduct underlying the instant offense occurred after that adjudication;

(6) if such sentence is necessary to ensure that changes are made within the organization to reduce the likelihood of future criminal conduct;

(7) if the sentence imposed upon the organization does not include a fine; or

(8) if necessary to accomplish one or more of the purposes of sentencing set forth in 18 U.S.C. § 3553(a)(2).

Commentary

Background: Under 18 U.S.C. § 3561(a), an organization may be sentenced to a term of probation. Under 18 U.S.C. § 3551(c), imposition of a term of probation is required if the sentence imposed upon the organization does not include a fine.

Historical Note Effective November 1, 1991 (amendment 422). Amended effective November 1, 2004 (amendment 673).

§8D1.2. Term of Probation — Organizations

(a) When a sentence of probation is imposed—

(1) In the case of a felony, the term of probation shall be at least one year but not more than five years.

(2) In any other case, the term of probation shall be not more than five years.

Commentary

Application Note:

1. Within the limits set by the guidelines, the term of probation should be sufficient, but not more than necessary, to accomplish the court's specific objectives in imposing the term of probation. The terms of probation set forth in this section are those provided in 18 U.S.C. § 3561(c).

Historical Note Effective November 1, 1991 (amendment 422). Amended effective November 1, 2013 (amendment 778).

§8D1.3. Conditions of Probation — Organizations

(a) Pursuant to 18 U.S.C. § 3563(a)(1), any sentence of probation shall include the condition that the organization not commit another federal, state, or local crime during the term of probation.

(b) Pursuant to 18 U.S.C. § 3563(a)(2), if a sentence of probation is imposed for a felony, the court shall impose as a condition of probation at least one of the following: (1) restitution or (2) community service, unless the court has imposed a fine, or unless the court finds on the record that extraordinary circumstances exist that would make such condition plainly unreasonable, in which event the court shall impose one or more other conditions set forth in 18 U.S.C. § 3563(b).

(c) The court may impose other conditions that (1) are reasonably related to the nature and circumstances of the offense or the history and characteristics of the organization; and (2) involve only such deprivations of liberty or property as are necessary to effect the purposes of sentencing.

Historical *Note*	Effective November 1, 1991 (amendment 422). Amended effective November 1, 1997 (amendment 569); November 1, 2009 (amendment 733).

§8D1.4. Recommended Conditions of Probation — Organizations (Policy Statement)

(a) The court may order the organization, at its expense and in the format and media specified by the court, to publicize the nature of the offense committed, the fact of conviction, the nature of the punishment imposed, and the steps that will be taken to prevent the recurrence of similar offenses.

(b) If probation is imposed under §8D1.1, the following conditions may be appropriate:

(1) The organization shall develop and submit to the court an effective compliance and ethics program consistent with §8B2.1 (Effective Compliance and Ethics Program). The organization shall include in its submission a schedule for implementation of the compliance and ethics program.

(2) Upon approval by the court of a program referred to in paragraph (1), the organization shall notify its employees and shareholders of its criminal behavior and its program referred to in paragraph (1). Such notice shall be in a form prescribed by the court.

(3) The organization shall make periodic submissions to the court or probation officer, at intervals specified by the court, (A) reporting on the organization's financial condition and results of

business operations, and accounting for the disposition of all funds received, and (B) reporting on the organization's progress in implementing the program referred to in paragraph (1). Among other things, reports under subparagraph (B) shall disclose any criminal prosecution, civil litigation, or administrative proceeding commenced against the organization, or any investigation or formal inquiry by governmental authorities of which the organization learned since its last report.

(4) The organization shall notify the court or probation officer immediately upon learning of (A) any material adverse change in its business or financial condition or prospects, or (B) the commencement of any bankruptcy proceeding, major civil litigation, criminal prosecution, or administrative proceeding against the organization, or any investigation or formal inquiry by governmental authorities regarding the organization.

(5) The organization shall submit to: (A) a reasonable number of regular or unannounced examinations of its books and records at appropriate business premises by the probation officer or experts engaged by the court; and (B) interrogation of knowledgeable individuals within the organization. Compensation to and costs of any experts engaged by the court shall be paid by the organization.

(6) The organization shall make periodic payments, as specified by the court, in the following priority: (A) restitution; (B) fine; and (C) any other monetary sanction.

Commentary

Application Note:

1. In determining the conditions to be imposed when probation is ordered under §8D1.1, the court should consider the views of any governmental regulatory body that oversees conduct of the organization relating to the instant offense. To assess the efficacy of a compliance and ethics program submitted by the organization, the court may employ appropriate experts who shall be afforded access to all material possessed by the organization that is necessary for a comprehensive assessment of the proposed program. The court should approve any program that appears reasonably calculated to prevent and detect criminal conduct, as long as it is consistent with §8B2.1 (Effective Compliance and Ethics Program), and any applicable statutory and regulatory requirements.

   Periodic reports submitted in accordance with subsection (b)(3) should be provided to any governmental regulatory body that oversees conduct of the organization relating to the instant offense.

Historical Note	Effective November 1, 1991 (amendment 422). Amended effective November 1, 2004 (amendment 673); November 1, 2010 (amendment 744).

§8D1.5. [Deleted]

Historical Note	Effective November 1, 1991 (amendment 422); was moved to §8F1.1 effective November 1, 2004 (amendment 673).

PART E — SPECIAL ASSESSMENTS, FORFEITURES, AND COSTS

§8E1.1.   Special Assessments — Organizations

A special assessment must be imposed on an organization in the amount prescribed by statute.

Commentary

Application Notes:

1.   This guideline applies if the defendant is an organization. It does not apply if the defendant is an individual. *See* §5E1.3 for special assessments applicable to individuals.

2.   The following special assessments are provided by statute (*see* 18 U.S.C. § 3013):

FOR OFFENSES COMMITTED BY ORGANIZATIONS ON OR AFTER APRIL 24, 1996:
(A)	$400, if convicted of a felony;
(B)	$125, if convicted of a Class A misdemeanor;
(C)	$50, if convicted of a Class B misdemeanor; or
(D)	$25, if convicted of a Class C misdemeanor or an infraction.

FOR OFFENSES COMMITTED BY ORGANIZATIONS ON OR AFTER NOVEMBER 18, 1988 BUT PRIOR TO APRIL 24, 1996:
(E)	$200, if convicted of a felony;
(F)	$125, if convicted of a Class A misdemeanor;
(G)	$50, if convicted of a Class B misdemeanor; or
(H)	$25, if convicted of a Class C misdemeanor or an infraction.

FOR OFFENSES COMMITTED BY ORGANIZATIONS PRIOR TO NOVEMBER 18, 1988:
(I)	$200, if convicted of a felony;
(J)	$100, if convicted of a misdemeanor.

3.   A special assessment is required by statute for each count of conviction.

Background: Section 3013 of Title 18, United States Code, added by The Victims of Crimes Act of 1984, Pub. L. No. 98-473, Title II, Chap. XIV, requires courts to impose special assessments on convicted defendants for the purpose of funding the Crime Victims Fund established by the same legislation.

Historical Note	Effective November 1, 1991 (amendment 422); November 1, 1997 (amendment 573).

§8E1.2.   Forfeiture — Organizations

Apply §5E1.4 (Forfeiture).

§8E1.3.   Assessment of Costs — Organizations

As provided in 28 U.S.C. § 1918, the court may order the organization to pay the costs of prosecution. In addition, specific statutory provisions mandate assessment of costs.

PART F — VIOLATIONS OF PROBATION — ORGANIZATIONS

Historical Note	Effective November 1, 2004 (amendment 673).

§8F1.1. Violations of Conditions of Probation — Organizations (Policy Statement)

Upon a finding of a violation of a condition of probation, the court may extend the term of probation, impose more restrictive conditions of probation, or revoke probation and resentence the organization.

Commentary

Application Notes:

1. **Appointment of Master or Trustee.**—In the event of repeated violations of conditions of probation, the appointment of a master or trustee may be appropriate to ensure compliance with court orders.

2. **Conditions of Probation.**—Mandatory and recommended conditions of probation are specified in §§8D1.3 (Conditions of Probation — Organizations) and 8D1.4 (Recommended Conditions of Probation — Organizations).

Historical Note	Effective November 1, 2004 (amendment 673).

APPENDIX A

STATUTORY INDEX

INTRODUCTION

This index specifies the offense guideline section(s) in Chapter Two (Offense Conduct) applicable to the statute of conviction. If more than one guideline section is referenced for the particular statute, use the guideline most appropriate for the offense conduct charged in the count of which the defendant was convicted. For the rules governing the determination of the offense guideline section(s) from Chapter Two, and for any exceptions to those rules, *see* §1B1.2 (Applicable Guidelines).

Historical Note	Effective November 1, 1987. Amended effective November 1, 1989 (amendments 296 and 297); November 1, 1993 (amendment 496); November 1, 2000 (amendment 591); November 1, 2014 (amendment 781).

INDEX

Statute	Guideline	Statute	Guideline
2 U.S.C. § 192	2J1.1, 2J1.5	7 U.S.C. § 23	2B1.1
2 U.S.C. § 390	2J1.1, 2J1.5	7 U.S.C. § 87b	2N2.1
7 U.S.C. § 6	2B1.1	7 U.S.C. § 87f(e)	2J1.1, 2J1.5
7 U.S.C. § 6b(A)	2B1.1	7 U.S.C. § 136	2Q1.2
7 U.S.C. § 6b(B)	2B1.1	7 U.S.C. § 136j	2Q1.2
7 U.S.C. § 6b(C)	2B1.1	7 U.S.C. § 136k	2Q1.2
7 U.S.C. § 6c	2B1.1	7 U.S.C. § 136l	2Q1.2
7 U.S.C. § 6h	2B1.1	7 U.S.C. § 149	2N2.1
7 U.S.C. § 6o	2B1.1	7 U.S.C. § 150bb	2N2.1
7 U.S.C. § 13(a)(1)	2B1.1	7 U.S.C. § 150gg	2N2.1
7 U.S.C. § 13(a)(2)	2B1.1	7 U.S.C. § 154	2N2.1
7 U.S.C. § 13(a)(3)	2B1.1	7 U.S.C. § 156	2N2.1
7 U.S.C. § 13(a)(4)	2B1.1	7 U.S.C. § 157	2N2.1
7 U.S.C. § 13(c)	2C1.3	7 U.S.C. § 158	2N2.1
7 U.S.C. § 13(d)	2B1.4	7 U.S.C. § 161	2N2.1
7 U.S.C. § 13(e)	2B1.4	7 U.S.C. § 163	2N2.1

7 U.S.C. § 195	2N2.1	8 U.S.C. § 1255a(c)(6)	2L2.1, 2L2.2
7 U.S.C. § 270	2B1.1	8 U.S.C. § 1324(a)	2L1.1
7 U.S.C. § 281	2N2.1	8 U.S.C. § 1325(a)	2L1.2
7 U.S.C. § 472	2N2.1	8 U.S.C. § 1325(c)	2L2.1, 2L2.2
7 U.S.C. § 473c-1	2N2.1	8 U.S.C. § 1325(d)	2L2.1, 2L2.2
7 U.S.C. § 491	2N2.1	8 U.S.C. § 1326	2L1.2
7 U.S.C. § 499n	2N2.1	8 U.S.C. § 1327	2L1.1
7 U.S.C. § 503	2N2.1	8 U.S.C. § 1328	2G1.1, 2G1.3
7 U.S.C. § 511d	2N2.1	8 U.S.C. § 1375a(d)(5)(B)(i)	2H3.1
7 U.S.C. § 511i	2N2.1	8 U.S.C. § 1375a(d)(5)(B)(ii)	2H3.1
7 U.S.C. § 516	2N2.1	8 U.S.C. § 1375a(d)(5)(B)(iii)	2B1.1
7 U.S.C. § 610(g)	2C1.3	10 U.S.C. § 987(f)	2X5.2
7 U.S.C. § 2018(c)	2N2.1	12 U.S.C. § 631	2B1.1
7 U.S.C. § 2024(b)	2B1.1	12 U.S.C. § 1818(j)	2B1.1
7 U.S.C. § 2024(c)	2B1.1	12 U.S.C. § 1844(f)	2J1.1, 2J1.5
7 U.S.C. § 2156 (felony provisions only)	2E3.1	12 U.S.C. § 2273	2J1.1, 2J1.5
7 U.S.C. § 6810	2N2.1	12 U.S.C. § 3108(b)(6)	2J1.1, 2J1.5
7 U.S.C. § 7734	2N2.1	12 U.S.C. § 4636b	2B1.1
7 U.S.C. § 8313	2N2.1	12 U.S.C. § 4641	J1.1, 2J1.5
8 U.S.C. § 1160(b)(7)(A)	2L2.1, 2L2.2	12 U.S.C. § 5382	2H3.1
8 U.S.C. § 1185(a)(1)	2L1.2	15 U.S.C. § 1	2R1.1
8 U.S.C. § 1185(a)(2)	2L1.1	15 U.S.C. § 3(b)	2R1.1
8 U.S.C. § 1185(a)(3)	2L2.1, 2L2.2	15 U.S.C. § 50	2B1.1, 2J1.1, 2J1.5
8 U.S.C. § 1185(a)(4)	2L2.1	15 U.S.C. § 77e	2B1.1
8 U.S.C. § 1185(a)(5)	2L2.2	15 U.S.C. § 77q	2B1.1
8 U.S.C. § 1253	2L1.2	15 U.S.C. § 77x	2B1.1

15 U.S.C. § 78j	2B1.1, 2B1.4
15 U.S.C. § 78dd-1	2C1.1
15 U.S.C. § 78dd-2	2C1.1
15 U.S.C. § 78dd-3	2C1.1
15 U.S.C. § 78ff	2B1.1, 2C1.1
15 U.S.C. § 78u(c)	2J1.1, 2J1.5
15 U.S.C. § 78jjj(c)(1),(2)	2B1.1
15 U.S.C. § 78jjj(d)	2B1.1
15 U.S.C. § 80a-41(c)	2J1.1, 2J1.5
15 U.S.C. § 80b-6	2B1.1
15 U.S.C. § 80b-9(c)	2J1.1, 2J1.5
15 U.S.C. § 158	2B1.1
15 U.S.C. § 377	2T2.1, 2T2.2
15 U.S.C. § 645(a)	2B1.1
15 U.S.C. § 645(b)	2B1.1
15 U.S.C. § 645(c)	2B1.1
15 U.S.C. § 714m(a)	2B1.1
15 U.S.C. § 714m(b)	2B1.1
15 U.S.C. § 714m(c)	2B1.1
15 U.S.C. § 717m(d)	2J1.1, 2J1.5
15 U.S.C. § 1172	2E3.1
15 U.S.C. § 1173	2E3.1
15 U.S.C. § 1174	2E3.1
15 U.S.C. § 1175	2E3.1
15 U.S.C. § 1176	2E3.1
15 U.S.C. § 1192	2N2.1
15 U.S.C. § 1197(b)	2N2.1
15 U.S.C. § 1202(c)	2N2.1
15 U.S.C. § 1263	2N2.1
15 U.S.C. § 1281	2B1.1 (for offenses committed prior to July 5, 1994)
15 U.S.C. § 1644	2B1.1
15 U.S.C. § 1681q	2B1.1
15 U.S.C. § 1693n(a)	2B1.1
15 U.S.C. § 1983	2N3.1 (for offenses committed prior to July 5, 1994)
15 U.S.C. § 1984	2N3.1 (for offenses committed prior to July 5, 1994)
15 U.S.C. § 1985	2N3.1 (for offenses committed prior to July 5, 1994)
15 U.S.C. § 1986	2N3.1 (for offenses committed prior to July 5, 1994)
15 U.S.C. § 1987	2N3.1 (for offenses committed prior to July 5, 1994)
15 U.S.C. § 1988	2N3.1 (for offenses committed prior to July 5, 1994)
15 U.S.C. § 1990c	2N3.1 (for offenses committed prior to July 5, 1994)
15 U.S.C. § 2068	2N2.1
15 U.S.C. § 2614	2Q1.2
15 U.S.C. § 2615	2Q1.2
15 U.S.C. § 6821	2B1.1
15 U.S.C. § 7704(d)	2G2.5

16 U.S.C. § 114	2B1.1		16 U.S.C. § 1387	2Q2.1
16 U.S.C. § 117c	2B1.1		16 U.S.C. § 1417(a)(5),(6), (b)(2)	2A2.4
16 U.S.C. § 123	2B1.1, 2B2.3		16 U.S.C. § 1437(c)	2A2.4
16 U.S.C. § 146	2B1.1, 2B2.3		16 U.S.C. § 1540(b)	2Q2.1
16 U.S.C. § 413	2B1.1		16 U.S.C. § 1857(1)(D)	2A2.4
16 U.S.C. § 470aaa–5	2B1.1, 2B1.5		16 U.S.C. § 1857(1)(E)	2A2.4
16 U.S.C. § 470ee	2B1.5		16 U.S.C. § 1857(1)(F)	2A2.4
16 U.S.C. § 668(a)	2B1.5, 2Q2.1		16 U.S.C. § 1857(1)(H)	2A2.4
16 U.S.C. § 707(b)	2B1.5, 2Q2.1		16 U.S.C. § 1859	2A2.4
16 U.S.C. § 742j-1(a)	2Q2.1		16 U.S.C. § 2435(4)	2A2.4
16 U.S.C. § 773e (a)(2),(3),(4),(6)	2A2.4		16 U.S.C. § 2435(5)	2A2.4
16 U.S.C. § 773g	2A2.4		16 U.S.C. § 2435(6)	2A2.4
16 U.S.C. § 825f(c)	2J1.1, 2J1.5		16 U.S.C. § 2435(7)	2A2.4
16 U.S.C. § 831t(a)	2B1.1		16 U.S.C. § 2438	2A2.4
16 U.S.C. § 831t(b)	2B1.1		16 U.S.C. § 3373(d)	2Q2.1
16 U.S.C. § 831t(c)	2B1.1, 2X1.1		16 U.S.C. § 3606	2A2.4
16 U.S.C. § 916c	2Q2.1		16 U.S.C. §3637(a)(2), (3),(4),(6),(c)	2A2.4
16 U.S.C. § 916f	2Q2.1		16 U.S.C. § 4223	2Q2.1
16 U.S.C. §973c(a) (8),(10),(11),(12)	2A2.4		16 U.S.C. § 4224	2Q2.1
16 U.S.C. § 973e	2A2.4		16 U.S.C. § 4910(a)	2Q2.1
16 U.S.C. § 1029	2A2.4		16 U.S.C. § 4912(a)(2)(A)	2Q2.1
16 U.S.C. § 1030	2A2.4		16 U.S.C. § 5009(5),(6),(7),(8)	2A2.4
16 U.S.C. § 1174(a)	2Q2.1		16 U.S.C. § 5010(b)	2A2.4
16 U.S.C. § 1338(a)	2Q2.1		17 U.S.C. § 506(a)	2B5.3
16 U.S.C. § 1372	2Q2.1		17 U.S.C. § 1201	2B5.3
16 U.S.C. § 1375(b)	2Q2.1			

17 U.S.C. § 1204	2B5.3
18 U.S.C. § 2	2X2.1
18 U.S.C. § 3	2X3.1
18 U.S.C. § 4	2X4.1
18 U.S.C. § 25	2X6.1
18 U.S.C. §32(a),(b)	2A1.1, 2A1.2, 2A1.3, 2A1.4, 2A2.1, 2A2.2, 2A2.3, 2A4.1, 2A5.1, 2A5.2, 2B1.1, 2K1.4, 2X1.1
18 U.S.C. § 32(c)	2A6.1
18 U.S.C. § 33	2A2.1, 2A2.2, 2B1.1, 2K1.4
18 U.S.C. § 34	2A1.1, 2A1.2, 2A1.3, 2A1.4
18 U.S.C. § 35(b)	2A6.1
18 U.S.C. § 36	2D1.1
18 U.S.C. § 37	2A1.1, 2A1.2, 2A1.3, 2A1.4, 2A2.1, 2A2.2, 2A2.3, 2A3.1, 2A3.4, 2A4.1, 2A5.1, 2A5.2, 2B1.1, 2B3.1, 2K1.4, 2X1.1
18 U.S.C. § 38	2B1.1
18 U.S.C. § 39A	2A5.2
18 U.S.C. § 43	2B1.1
18 U.S.C. § 48	2G3.1
18 U.S.C. § 81	2K1.4
18 U.S.C. § 111	2A2.2, 2A2.4
18 U.S.C. § 112(a)	2A2.1, 2A2.2, 2A2.3, 2A4.1, 2B1.1, 2K1.4
18 U.S.C. § 113(a)	2A2.1 (for offenses committed prior to September 13, 1994)

18 U.S.C. § 113(a)(1)	2A2.1, 2A3.1
18 U.S.C. § 113(a)(2)	2A2.2, 2A3.2, 2A3.3, 2A3.4
18 U.S.C. § 113(a)(3)	2A2.2
18 U.S.C. § 113(a)(4)	2A2.3
18 U.S.C. § 113(a)(5) (Class A misdemeanor provisions only)	2A2.3
18 U.S.C. § 113(a)(6)	2A2.2
18 U.S.C. § 113(a)(7)	2A2.3
18 U.S.C. § 113(a)(8)	2A2.2
18 U.S.C. § 113(b)	2A2.2 (for offenses committed prior to September 13, 1994)
18 U.S.C. § 113(c)	2A2.2 (for offenses committed prior to September 13, 1994)
18 U.S.C. § 113(f)	2A2.2 (for offenses committed prior to September 13, 1994)
18 U.S.C. § 114	2A2.2
18 U.S.C. § 115(a)	2A1.1, 2A1.2, 2A1.3, 2A2.1, 2A2.2, 2A2.3, 2A4.1, 2A6.1, 2X1.1
18 U.S.C. § 115(b)(1)	2A2.1, 2A2.2, 2A2.3
18 U.S.C. § 115(b)(2)	2A4.1, 2X1.1
18 U.S.C. § 115(b)(3)	2A1.1, 2A1.2, 2A2.1, 2X1.1
18 U.S.C. § 115(b)(4)	2A6.1
18 U.S.C. § 117	2A6.2
18 U.S.C. § 119	2H3.1
18 U.S.C. § 152	2B1.1, 2B4.1, 2J1.3
18 U.S.C. § 153	2B1.1

18 U.S.C. § 155	2B1.1	18 U.S.C. § 226	2C1.1
18 U.S.C. § 175	2M6.1	18 U.S.C. § 227	2C1.1
18 U.S.C. § 175b	2M6.1	18 U.S.C. § 228	2J1.1
18 U.S.C. § 175c	2M6.1	18 U.S.C. § 229	2M6.1
18 U.S.C. § 201(b)(1)	2C1.1	18 U.S.C. § 241	2H1.1, 2H2.1, 2H4.1
18 U.S.C. § 201(b)(2)	2C1.1	18 U.S.C. § 242	2H1.1, 2H2.1
18 U.S.C. § 201(b)(3)	2J1.3	18 U.S.C. § 245(b)	2H1.1, 2H2.1, 2J1.2
18 U.S.C. § 201(b)(4)	2J1.3	18 U.S.C. § 246	2H1.1
18 U.S.C. § 201(c)(1)	2C1.2	18 U.S.C. § 247	2H1.1
18 U.S.C. § 201(c)(2)	2J1.9	18 U.S.C. § 248	2H1.1
18 U.S.C. § 201(c)(3)	2J1.9	18 U.S.C. § 249	2H1.1
18 U.S.C. § 203	2C1.3	18 U.S.C. § 281	2C1.3
18 U.S.C. § 204	2C1.3	18 U.S.C. § 285	2B1.1
18 U.S.C. § 205	2C1.3	18 U.S.C. § 286	2B1.1
18 U.S.C. § 207	2C1.3	18 U.S.C. § 287	2B1.1
18 U.S.C. § 208	2C1.3	18 U.S.C. § 288	2B1.1
18 U.S.C. § 209	2C1.3	18 U.S.C. § 289	2B1.1
18 U.S.C. § 210	2C1.5	18 U.S.C. § 332	2B1.1
18 U.S.C. § 211	2C1.5	18 U.S.C. § 335	2B1.1
18 U.S.C. § 212	2C1.2	18 U.S.C. § 342	2D2.3
18 U.S.C. § 213	2C1.2	18 U.S.C. § 351(a)	2A1.1, 2A1.2, 2A1.3, 2A1.4
18 U.S.C. § 214	2C1.2	18 U.S.C. § 351(b)	2A1.1, 2A4.1
18 U.S.C. § 215	2B4.1	18 U.S.C. § 351(c)	2A2.1, 2A4.1
18 U.S.C. § 217	2C1.2	18 U.S.C. § 351(d)	2A1.5, 2A4.1
18 U.S.C. § 219	2C1.3	18 U.S.C. § 351(e)	2A2.2, 2A2.3
18 U.S.C. § 224	2B4.1	18 U.S.C. § 371	2A1.5, 2C1.1 (if conspiracy to defraud by
18 U.S.C. § 225	2B1.1, 2B4.1		

	interference with governmental functions), 2T1.9, 2K2.1 (if a conspiracy to violate 18 U.S.C. § 924(c)), 2X1.1	18 U.S.C. § 488	2B1.1
		18 U.S.C. § 490	2B5.1
		18 U.S.C. § 491	2B1.1, 2B5.1
18 U.S.C. § 372	2X1.1	18 U.S.C. § 493	2B1.1, 2B5.1
18 U.S.C. § 373	2A1.5, 2X1.1	18 U.S.C. § 494	2B1.1
18 U.S.C. § 401	2J1.1	18 U.S.C. § 495	2B1.1
18 U.S.C. § 403	2J1.1	18 U.S.C. § 496	2B1.1, 2T3.1
18 U.S.C. § 440	2C1.3	18 U.S.C. § 497	2B1.1
18 U.S.C. § 442	2C1.3	18 U.S.C. § 498	2B1.1
18 U.S.C. § 470	2B1.1, 2B5.1	18 U.S.C. § 499	2B1.1
18 U.S.C. § 471	2B1.1, 2B5.1	18 U.S.C. § 500	2B1.1, 2B5.1
18 U.S.C. § 472	2B1.1, 2B5.1	18 U.S.C. § 501	2B1.1, 2B5.1
18 U.S.C. § 473	2B1.1, 2B5.1	18 U.S.C. § 502	2B1.1
18 U.S.C. § 474	2B1.1, 2B5.1	18 U.S.C. § 503	2B1.1
18 U.S.C. § 474A	2B5.1	18 U.S.C. § 505	2B1.1, 2J1.2
18 U.S.C. § 476	2B5.1	18 U.S.C. § 506	2B1.1
18 U.S.C. § 477	2B1.1, 2B5.1	18 U.S.C. § 507	2B1.1
18 U.S.C. § 478	2B1.1	18 U.S.C. § 508	2B1.1
18 U.S.C. § 479	2B1.1	18 U.S.C. § 509	2B1.1
18 U.S.C. § 480	2B1.1	18 U.S.C. § 510	2B1.1
18 U.S.C. § 481	2B1.1	18 U.S.C. § 511	2B6.1
18 U.S.C. § 482	2B1.1	18 U.S.C. § 513	2B1.1
18 U.S.C. § 483	2B1.1	18 U.S.C. § 514	2B1.1
18 U.S.C. § 484	2B1.1, 2B5.1	18 U.S.C. § 541	2B1.5, 2T3.1
18 U.S.C. § 485	2B1.1, 2B5.1	18 U.S.C. § 542	2B1.5, 2T3.1
18 U.S.C. § 486	2B1.1, 2B5.1	18 U.S.C. § 543	2B1.5, 2T3.1
18 U.S.C. § 487	2B5.1	18 U.S.C. § 544	2B1.5, 2T3.1

18 U.S.C. § 545	2B1.5, 2Q2.1, 2T3.1
18 U.S.C. § 546	2B1.5
18 U.S.C. § 547	2T3.1
18 U.S.C. § 548	2T3.1
18 U.S.C. § 549	2B1.1, 2T3.1
18 U.S.C. § 550	2T3.1
18 U.S.C. § 551	2J1.2, 2T3.1
18 U.S.C. § 552	2G3.1
18 U.S.C. § 553(a)(1)	2B1.1
18 U.S.C. § 553(a)(2)	2B1.1, 2B6.1
18 U.S.C. § 554	2B1.5, 2M5.1, 2M5.2, 2Q2.1
18 U.S.C. § 555	2X7.1
18 U.S.C. § 592	2H2.1
18 U.S.C. § 593	2H2.1
18 U.S.C. § 594	2H2.1
18 U.S.C. § 597	2H2.1
18 U.S.C. § 607	2C1.8
18 U.S.C. § 608	2H2.1
18 U.S.C. § 611	2H2.1
18 U.S.C. § 641	2B1.1, 2B1.5
18 U.S.C. § 642	2B1.1, 2B5.1
18 U.S.C. § 643	2B1.1
18 U.S.C. § 644	2B1.1
18 U.S.C. § 645	2B1.1
18 U.S.C. § 646	2B1.1
18 U.S.C. § 647	2B1.1
18 U.S.C. § 648	2B1.1

18 U.S.C. § 649	2B1.1
18 U.S.C. § 650	2B1.1
18 U.S.C. § 651	2B1.1
18 U.S.C. § 652	2B1.1
18 U.S.C. § 653	2B1.1
18 U.S.C. § 654	2B1.1
18 U.S.C. § 655	2B1.1
18 U.S.C. § 656	2B1.1
18 U.S.C. § 657	2B1.1
18 U.S.C. § 658	2B1.1
18 U.S.C. § 659	2B1.1
18 U.S.C. § 660	2B1.1
18 U.S.C. § 661	2B1.1, 2B1.5
18 U.S.C. § 662	2B1.1, 2B1.5
18 U.S.C. § 663	2B1.1
18 U.S.C. § 664	2B1.1
18 U.S.C. § 665(a)	2B1.1
18 U.S.C. § 665(b)	2B3.3, 2C1.1
18 U.S.C. § 665(c)	2J1.2
18 U.S.C. § 666(a)(1)(A)	2B1.1, 2B1.5
18 U.S.C. § 666(a)(1)(B)	2C1.1, 2C1.2
18 U.S.C. § 666(a)(2)	2C1.1, 2C1.2
18 U.S.C. § 667	2B1.1
18 U.S.C. § 668	2B1.5
18 U.S.C. § 669	2B1.1

18 U.S.C. § 670	2B1.1	18 U.S.C. § 844(d)	2K1.3
18 U.S.C. § 709	2B1.1	18 U.S.C. § 844(e)	2A6.1
18 U.S.C. § 712	2B1.1	18 U.S.C. § 844(f)	2K1.4, 2X1.1
18 U.S.C. § 751	2P1.1	18 U.S.C. § 844(g)	2K1.3
18 U.S.C. § 752	2P1.1, 2X3.1	18 U.S.C. § 844(h)	2K2.4 (2K1.4 for offenses committed prior to November 18, 1988)
18 U.S.C. § 753	2P1.1		
18 U.S.C. § 755	2P1.1	18 U.S.C. § 844(i)	2K1.4
18 U.S.C. § 756	2P1.1	18 U.S.C. § 844(m)	2K1.3
18 U.S.C. § 757	2P1.1, 2X3.1	18 U.S.C. § 844(n)	2X1.1
18 U.S.C. § 758	2A2.4	18 U.S.C. § 844(o)	2K2.4
18 U.S.C. § 793(a)–(c)	2M3.2	18 U.S.C. § 871	2A6.1
18 U.S.C. § 793(d),(e)	2M3.2, 2M3.3	18 U.S.C. § 872	2C1.1
18 U.S.C. § 793(f)	2M3.4	18 U.S.C. § 873	2B3.3
18 U.S.C. § 793(g)	2M3.2, 2M3.3	18 U.S.C. § 874	2B3.2, 2B3.3
18 U.S.C. § 794	2M3.1	18 U.S.C. § 875(a)	2A4.2, 2B3.2
18 U.S.C. § 798	2M3.3	18 U.S.C. § 875(b)	2B3.2
18 U.S.C. § 831	2M6.1	18 U.S.C. § 875(c)	2A6.1
18 U.S.C. § 832	2M6.1	18 U.S.C. § 875(d)	2B3.2, 2B3.3
18 U.S.C. § 842(a)–(e)	2K1.3	18 U.S.C. § 876	2A4.2, 2A6.1, 2B3.2, 2B3.3
18 U.S.C. § 842(f)	2K1.6		
18 U.S.C. § 842(g)	2K1.6	18 U.S.C. § 877	2A4.2, 2A6.1, 2B3.2, 2B3.3
18 U.S.C. § 842(h),(i)	2K1.3	18 U.S.C. § 878(a)	2A6.1
18 U.S.C. § 842(j)	2K1.1	18 U.S.C. § 878(b)	2B3.2
18 U.S.C. § 842(k)	2K1.1	18 U.S.C. § 879	2A6.1
18 U.S.C. § 842(l)–(o)	2K1.3	18 U.S.C. § 880	2B1.1
18 U.S.C. § 842(p)(2)	2K1.3, 2M6.1	18 U.S.C. § 892	2E2.1
18 U.S.C. § 844(b)	2K1.1	18 U.S.C. § 893	2E2.1

18 U.S.C. § 894	2E2.1	18 U.S.C. § 970(a)	2B1.1, 2K1.4
18 U.S.C. § 911	2B1.1, 2L2.2	18 U.S.C. § 1001	2B1.1, 2J1.2 (when the statutory maximum term of eight years' imprisonment applies because the matter relates to international terrorism or domestic terrorism, or to sex offenses under 18 U.S.C. § 1591 or chapters 109A, 109B, 110, or 117 of title 18, United States Code)
18 U.S.C. § 912	2J1.4		
18 U.S.C. § 913	2J1.4		
18 U.S.C. § 914	2B1.1		
18 U.S.C. § 915	2B1.1		
18 U.S.C. § 917	2B1.1		
18 U.S.C. § 922(a)–(p)	2K2.1		
18 U.S.C. § 922(q)	2K2.5	18 U.S.C. § 1002	2B1.1
18 U.S.C. § 922(r)–(w)	2K2.1	18 U.S.C. § 1003	2B1.1, 2B5.1
18 U.S.C. § 922(x)(1)	2K2.1	18 U.S.C. § 1004	2B1.1
18 U.S.C. § 923	2K2.1	18 U.S.C. § 1005	2B1.1
18 U.S.C. § 924(a)	2K2.1	18 U.S.C. § 1006	2B1.1, 2S1.3
18 U.S.C. § 924(b)	2K2.1	18 U.S.C. § 1007	2B1.1, 2S1.3
18 U.S.C. § 924(c)	2K2.4	18 U.S.C. § 1010	2B1.1
18 U.S.C. § 924(e)	2K2.1 (see also 4B1.4)	18 U.S.C. § 1011	2B1.1
18 U.S.C. § 924(f)	2K2.1	18 U.S.C. § 1012	2B1.1, 2C1.3
18 U.S.C. § 924(g)	2K2.1	18 U.S.C. § 1013	2B1.1
18 U.S.C. § 924(h)	2K2.1	18 U.S.C. § 1014	2B1.1
18 U.S.C. § 924(i)	2K2.1	18 U.S.C. § 1015(a)–(e)	2B1.1, 2J1.3, 2L2.1, 2L2.2
18 U.S.C. § 924(j)(1)	2A1.1, 2A1.2		
18 U.S.C. § 924(j)(2)	2A1.3, 2A1.4	18 U.S.C. § 1015(f)	2H2.1
18 U.S.C. § 924(k)–(o)	2K2.1	18 U.S.C. § 1016	2B1.1
18 U.S.C. § 929(a)	2K2.4	18 U.S.C. § 1017	2B1.1
18 U.S.C. § 930	2K2.5	18 U.S.C. § 1018	2B1.1
18 U.S.C. § 931	2K2.6	18 U.S.C. § 1019	2B1.1
18 U.S.C. § 956	2A1.5, 2X1.1	18 U.S.C. § 1020	2B1.1

18 U.S.C. § 1021	2B1.1	18 U.S.C. § 1071	2X3.1
18 U.S.C. § 1022	2B1.1	18 U.S.C. § 1072	2X3.1
18 U.S.C. § 1023	2B1.1	18 U.S.C. § 1073	2J1.5, 2J1.6
18 U.S.C. § 1024	2B1.1	18 U.S.C. § 1082	2E3.1
18 U.S.C. § 1025	2B1.1	18 U.S.C. § 1084	2E3.1
18 U.S.C. § 1026	2B1.1	18 U.S.C. § 1091	2H1.1
18 U.S.C. § 1027	2E5.3	18 U.S.C. § 1111(a)	2A1.1, 2A1.2
18 U.S.C. § 1028	2B1.1, 2L2.1, 2L2.2	18 U.S.C. § 1112	2A1.3, 2A1.4
18 U.S.C. § 1028A	2B1.6	18 U.S.C. § 1113	2A2.1, 2A2.2
18 U.S.C. § 1029	2B1.1	18 U.S.C. § 1114	2A1.1, 2A1.2, 2A1.3, 2A1.4, 2A2.1
18 U.S.C. § 1030(a)(1)	2M3.2	18 U.S.C. § 1115	2A1.4
18 U.S.C. § 1030(a)(2)	2B1.1	18 U.S.C. § 1116	2A1.1, 2A1.2, 2A1.3, 2A1.4, 2A2.1
18 U.S.C. § 1030(a)(3)	2B2.3		
18 U.S.C. § 1030(a)(4)	2B1.1	18 U.S.C. § 1117	2A1.5
18 U.S.C. § 1030(a)(5)	2B1.1	18 U.S.C. § 1118	2A1.1, 2A1.2
18 U.S.C. § 1030(a)(6)	2B1.1	18 U.S.C. § 1119	2A1.1, 2A1.2, 2A1.3, 2A1.4, 2A2.1
18 U.S.C. § 1030(a)(7)	2B3.2		
18 U.S.C. § 1030(b)	2X1.1	18 U.S.C. § 1120	2A1.1, 2A1.2, 2A1.3, 2A1.4
18 U.S.C. § 1031	2B1.1	18 U.S.C. § 1121	2A1.1, 2A1.2
18 U.S.C. § 1032	2B1.1, 2B4.1	18 U.S.C. § 1158	2B1.1, 2B5.3
18 U.S.C. § 1033	2B1.1, 2J1.2	18 U.S.C. § 1159	2B1.1
18 U.S.C. § 1035	2B1.1	18 U.S.C. § 1163	2B1.1, 2B1.5
18 U.S.C. § 1036	2B2.3	18 U.S.C. § 1167	2B1.1
18 U.S.C. § 1037	2B1.1	18 U.S.C. § 1168	2B1.1
18 U.S.C. § 1038	2A6.1	18 U.S.C. § 1170	2B1.5
18 U.S.C. § 1039	2H3.1	18 U.S.C. § 1201(a)	2A4.1
18 U.S.C. § 1040	2B1.1	18 U.S.C. § 1201(c),(d)	2X1.1

18 U.S.C. § 1202	2A4.2	18 U.S.C. § 1366	2B1.1
18 U.S.C. § 1203	2A4.1, 2X1.1	18 U.S.C. § 1369	2B1.1, 2B1.5
18 U.S.C. § 1204	2J1.2	18 U.S.C. § 1389	2A2.2, 2A2.3, 2B1.1
18 U.S.C. § 1301	2E3.1	18 U.S.C. § 1422	2B1.1, 2C1.2
18 U.S.C. § 1302	2E3.1	18 U.S.C. § 1423	2L2.2
18 U.S.C. § 1303	2E3.1	18 U.S.C. § 1424	2L2.2
18 U.S.C. § 1304	2E3.1	18 U.S.C. § 1425	2L2.1, 2L2.2
18 U.S.C. § 1306	2E3.1	18 U.S.C. § 1426	2L2.1, 2L2.2
18 U.S.C. § 1341	2B1.1, 2C1.1	18 U.S.C. § 1427	2L2.1
18 U.S.C. § 1342	2B1.1, 2C1.1	18 U.S.C. § 1428	2L2.5
18 U.S.C. § 1343	2B1.1, 2C1.1	18 U.S.C. § 1429	2J1.1
18 U.S.C. § 1344	2B1.1	18 U.S.C. § 1460	2G3.1
18 U.S.C. § 1347	2B1.1	18 U.S.C. § 1461	2G3.1
18 U.S.C. § 1348	2B1.1	18 U.S.C. § 1462	2G3.1
18 U.S.C. § 1349	2X1.1	18 U.S.C. § 1463	2G3.1
18 U.S.C. § 1350	2B1.1	18 U.S.C. § 1464	2G3.2
18 U.S.C. § 1351	2B1.1	18 U.S.C. § 1465	2G3.1
18 U.S.C. § 1361	2B1.1, 2B1.5	18 U.S.C. § 1466	2G3.1
18 U.S.C. § 1362	2B1.1, 2K1.4	18 U.S.C. § 1466A	2G2.2
18 U.S.C. § 1363	2B1.1, 2K1.4	18 U.S.C. § 1468	2G3.2
18 U.S.C. § 1364	2K1.4	18 U.S.C. § 1470	2G3.1
18 U.S.C. § 1365(a)	2N1.1	18 U.S.C. § 1501	2A2.2, 2A2.4
18 U.S.C. § 1365(b)	2N1.3	18 U.S.C. § 1502	2A2.4
18 U.S.C. § 1365(c)	2N1.2	18 U.S.C. § 1503	2J1.2
18 U.S.C. § 1365(d)	2N1.2	18 U.S.C. § 1505	2J1.2
18 U.S.C. § 1365(e)	2N1.1	18 U.S.C. § 1506	2J1.2
18 U.S.C. § 1365(f)	2X5.2	18 U.S.C. § 1507	2J1.2

18 U.S.C. § 1508	2J1.2		18 U.S.C. § 1585	2H4.1
18 U.S.C. § 1509	2J1.2		18 U.S.C. § 1586	2H4.1
18 U.S.C. § 1510	2J1.2		18 U.S.C. § 1587	2H4.1
18 U.S.C. §.1511	2E3.1, 2J1.2		18 U.S.C. § 1588	2H4.1
18 U.S.C. § 1512(a)	2A1.1, 2A1.2, 2A1.3, 2A2.1, 2A2.2, 2A2.3, 2J1.2		18 U.S.C. § 1589	2H4.1
			18 U.S.C. § 1590	2H4.1
18 U.S.C. § 1512(b)	2J1.2		18 U.S.C. § 1591	2G1.1, 2G2.1, 2G1.3
18 U.S.C. § 1512(c)	2J1.2		18 U.S.C. § 1592	2H4.1
18 U.S.C. § 1512(d)	2J1.2		18 U.S.C. § 1593A	2H4.1
18 U.S.C. § 1513	2A1.1, 2A1.2, 2A1.3, 2A2.1, 2A2.2, 2A2.3, 2B1.1, 2J1.2		18 U.S.C. § 1597	2X5.2
			18 U.S.C. § 1621	2J1.3
18 U.S.C. § 1514(c)	2J1.2		18 U.S.C. § 1622	2J1.3
18 U.S.C. § 1516	2J1.2		18 U.S.C. § 1623	2J1.3
18 U.S.C. § 1517	2J1.2		18 U.S.C. § 1700	2H3.3
18 U.S.C. § 1518	2J1.2		18 U.S.C. § 1702	2B1.1, 2H3.3
18 U.S.C. § 1519	2J1.2		18 U.S.C. § 1703	2B1.1, 2H3.3
18 U.S.C. § 1520	2E5.3		18 U.S.C. § 1704	2B1.1
18 U.S.C. § 1521	2A6.1		18 U.S.C. § 1705	2B1.1
18 U.S.C. § 1541	2L2.1		18 U.S.C. § 1706	2B1.1
18 U.S.C. § 1542	2L2.1, 2L2.2		18 U.S.C. § 1707	2B1.1
18 U.S.C. § 1543	2L2.1, 2L2.2		18 U.S.C. § 1708	2B1.1
18 U.S.C. § 1544	2L2.1, 2L2.2		18 U.S.C. § 1709	2B1.1
18 U.S.C. § 1546	2L2.1, 2L2.2		18 U.S.C. § 1710	2B1.1
18 U.S.C. § 1581	2H4.1		18 U.S.C. § 1711	2B1.1
18 U.S.C. § 1582	2H4.1		18 U.S.C. § 1712	2B1.1
18 U.S.C. § 1583	2H4.1		18 U.S.C. § 1715	2K2.1
18 U.S.C. § 1584	2H4.1		18 U.S.C. § 1716 (felony provisions only)	2K1.3, 2K3.2

18 U.S.C. § 1716C	2B1.1
18 U.S.C. § 1716D	2Q2.1
18 U.S.C. § 1716E	2T2.2
18 U.S.C. § 1720	2B1.1
18 U.S.C. § 1721	2B1.1
18 U.S.C. § 1728	2B1.1
18 U.S.C. § 1735	2G3.1
18 U.S.C. § 1737	2G3.1
18 U.S.C. § 1751(a)	2A1.1, 2A1.2, 2A1.3, 2A1.4
18 U.S.C. § 1751(b)	2A4.1
18 U.S.C. § 1751(c)	2A2.1, 2A4.1, 2X1.1
18 U.S.C. § 1751(d)	2A1.5, 2A4.1, 2X1.1
18 U.S.C. § 1751(e)	2A2.2, 2A2.3
18 U.S.C. § 1752	2A2.4, 2B2.3
18 U.S.C. § 1791	2P1.2
18 U.S.C. § 1792	2P1.3
18 U.S.C. § 1801	2X5.2
18 U.S.C. § 1831	2B1.1
18 U.S.C. § 1832	2B1.1
18 U.S.C. § 1841(a)(1)	2X5.1
18 U.S.C. § 1841(a)(2)(C)	2A1.1, 2A1.2, 2A1.3, 2A1.4, 2A2.1, 2A2.2
18 U.S.C. § 1851	2B1.1
18 U.S.C. § 1852	2B1.1
18 U.S.C. § 1853	2B1.1
18 U.S.C. § 1854	2B1.1
18 U.S.C. § 1855	2K1.4
18 U.S.C. § 1857	2B1.1, 2B2.3
18 U.S.C. § 1860	2R1.1
18 U.S.C. § 1861	2B1.1
18 U.S.C. § 1864	2Q1.6
18 U.S.C. § 1901	2C1.3
18 U.S.C. § 1902	2B1.4
18 U.S.C. § 1903	2C1.3
18 U.S.C. § 1905	2H3.1
18 U.S.C. § 1909	2C1.3
18 U.S.C. § 1915	2T3.1
18 U.S.C. § 1919	2B1.1
18 U.S.C. § 1920	2B1.1
18 U.S.C. § 1923	2B1.1
18 U.S.C. § 1951	2B3.1, 2B3.2, 2B3.3, 2C1.1
18 U.S.C. § 1952	2E1.2
18 U.S.C. § 1952A	2E1.4
18 U.S.C. § 1952B	2E1.3
18 U.S.C. § 1953	2E3.1
18 U.S.C. § 1954	2E5.1
18 U.S.C. § 1955	2E3.1
18 U.S.C. § 1956	2S1.1
18 U.S.C. § 1957	2S1.1
18 U.S.C. § 1958	2E1.4
18 U.S.C. § 1959	2E1.3
18 U.S.C. § 1960	2S1.1, 2S1.3
18 U.S.C. § 1962	2E1.1

18 U.S.C. § 1963	2E1.1
18 U.S.C. § 1991	2A2.1, 2X1.1
18 U.S.C. § 1992(a)(1)	2A5.2, 2B1.1, 2K1.4, 2X1.1
18 U.S.C. § 1992(a)(2)	2K1.4, 2M6.1, 2X1.1
18 U.S.C. § 1992(a)(3)	2M6.1, 2X1.1
18 U.S.C. § 1992(a)(4)	2A5.2, 2K1.4, 2M6.1, 2X1.1
18 U.S.C. § 1992(a)(5)	2A5.2, 2B1.1, 2X1.1
18 U.S.C. § 1992(a)(6)	2A5.2, 2X1.1
18 U.S.C. § 1992(a)(7)	2A1.1, 2A2.1, 2A2.2, 2X1.1
18 U.S.C. § 1992(a)(8)	2X1.1
18 U.S.C. § 1992(a)(9)	2A6.1, 2X1.1
18 U.S.C. § 1992(a)(10)	2A6.1, 2X1.1
18 U.S.C. § 2071	2B1.1
18 U.S.C. § 2072	2B1.1
18 U.S.C. § 2073	2B1.1
18 U.S.C. § 2111	2B3.1
18 U.S.C. § 2112	2B3.1
18 U.S.C. § 2113(a)	2B1.1, 2B2.1, 2B3.1, 2B3.2
18 U.S.C. § 2113(b)	2B1.1
18 U.S.C. § 2113(c)	2B1.1
18 U.S.C. § 2113(d)	2B3.1
18 U.S.C. § 2113(e)	2A1.1, 2B3.1
18 U.S.C. § 2114(a)	2B3.1
18 U.S.C. § 2114(b)	2B1.1
18 U.S.C. § 2115	2B2.1
18 U.S.C. § 2116	2A2.2, 2A2.3, 2B2.1, 2B3.1
18 U.S.C. § 2117	2B2.1
18 U.S.C. § 2118(a)	2B3.1
18 U.S.C. § 2118(b)	2B2.1
18 U.S.C. § 2118(c)(1)	2A2.1, 2A2.2, 2B3.1
18 U.S.C. § 2118(c)(2)	2A1.1
18 U.S.C. § 2118(d)	2X1.1
18 U.S.C. § 2119	2B3.1
18 U.S.C. § 2153	2M2.1
18 U.S.C. § 2154	2M2.1
18 U.S.C. § 2155	2M2.3
18 U.S.C. § 2156	2M2.3
18 U.S.C. § 2197	2B1.1
18 U.S.C. § 2199	2A1.1, 2A1.2, 2A1.3, 2A1.4, 2A2.1, 2A2.2, 2A2.3, 2B1.1, 2B2.3
18 U.S.C. § 2231	2A2.2, 2A2.3
18 U.S.C. § 2232	2B1.5, 2J1.2
18 U.S.C. § 2233	2B1.1, 2B3.1
18 U.S.C. § 2237(a)(1), (a)(2)(A)	2A2.4
18 U.S.C. § 2237(a)(2)(B)	2B1.1
18 U.S.C. § 2237(b)(2)(B)(i)	2A1.3, 2A1.4
18 U.S.C. § 2237(b)(2)(B)(ii)(I)	2A2.1, 2A2.2
18 U.S.C. § 2237(b)(2)(B)(ii)(II)	2A4.1

18 U.S.C. § 2237(b)(2)(B)(ii)(III)	2A3.1
18 U.S.C. § 2237(b)(3)	2A2.2
18 U.S.C. § 2237(b)(4)	2A2.1, 2A2.2, 2G1.1, 2G1.3, 2G2.1, 2H4.1, 2L1.1
18 U.S.C. § 2241	2A3.1
18 U.S.C. § 2242	2A3.1
18 U.S.C. § 2243(a)	2A3.2
18 U.S.C. § 2243(b)	2A3.3
18 U.S.C. § 2244	2A3.4
18 U.S.C. § 2245	2A1.1
18 U.S.C. § 2250(a)	2A3.5
18 U.S.C. § 2250(c)	2A3.6
18 U.S.C. § 2251(a),(b)	2G2.1
18 U.S.C. § 2251(c)	2G2.1
18 U.S.C. § 2251(d)(1)(A)	2G2.2
18 U.S.C. § 2251(d)(1)(B)	2G2.1
18 U.S.C. § 2251A	2G2.3
18 U.S.C. § 2252	2G2.2
18 U.S.C. § 2252A(a),(b)	2G2.2
18 U.S.C. § 2252A(g)	2G2.6
18 U.S.C. § 2252B	2G3.1
18 U.S.C. § 2252C	2G3.1
18 U.S.C. § 2257	2G2.5
18 U.S.C. § 2257A	2G2.5
18 U.S.C. § 2260(a)	2G2.1

18 U.S.C. § 2260(b)	2G2.2
18 U.S.C. § 2260A	2A3.6
18 U.S.C. § 2261	2A6.2
18 U.S.C. § 2261A	2A6.2
18 U.S.C. § 2262	2A6.2
18 U.S.C. § 2271	2X1.1
18 U.S.C. § 2272	2B1.1
18 U.S.C. § 2275	2B1.1, 2K1.4
18 U.S.C. § 2276	2B1.1, 2B2.1
18 U.S.C. § 2280	2A1.1, 2A1.2, 2A1.3, 2A1.4, 2A2.1, 2A2.2, 2A2.3, 2A4.1, 2A6.1, 2B1.1, 2B3.1, 2B3.2, 2K1.4, 2X1.1
18 U.S.C. § 2280a	2A1.1, 2A1.2, 2A1.3, 2A1.4, 2A2.1, 2A2.2, 2A2.3, 2A6.1, 2B1.1, 2B3.2, 2K1.3, 2K1.4, 2M5.2, 2M5.3, 2M6.1, 2Q1.1, 2Q1.2, 2X1.1, 2X2.1, 2X3.1
18 U.S.C. § 2281	2A1.1, 2A1.2, 2A1.3, 2A1.4, 2A2.1, 2A2.2, 2A2.3, 2A4.1, 2B1.1, 2B3.1, 2B3.2, 2K1.4, 2X1.1
18 U.S.C. § 2281a	2A1.1, 2A1.2, 2A1.3, 2A1.4, 2A2.1, 2A2.2, 2A2.3, 2A6.1, 2B1.1, 2B3.2, 2K1.4, 2M6.1, 2Q1.1, 2Q1.2, 2X1.1
18 U.S.C. § 2282A	2A1.1, 2A1.2, 2B1.1, 2K1.4, 2X1.1
18 U.S.C. § 2282B	2B1.1, 2K1.4, 2X1.1
18 U.S.C. § 2283	2K1.3, 2M5.3, 2M6.1
18 U.S.C. § 2284	2M5.3, 2X2.1, 2X3.1

18 U.S.C. § 2285	2X7.2	18 U.S.C. § 2332d	2M5.1
18 U.S.C. § 2291	2A1.1, 2A1.2, 2A1.3, 2A1.4, 2A2.1, 2A2.2, 2A2.3, 2A6.1, 2B1.1, 2K1.4, 2M6.1	18 U.S.C. § 2332f	2K1.4, 2M6.1
		18 U.S.C. § 2332g	2K2.1
		18 U.S.C. § 2332h	2M6.1
18 U.S.C. § 2292	2A6.1	18 U.S.C. § 2332i	2A6.1, 2K1.4, 2M2.1, 2M2.3, 2M6.1
18 U.S.C. § 2312	2B1.1		
18 U.S.C. § 2313	2B1.1	18 U.S.C. § 2339	2M5.3, 2X2.1, 2X3.1
18 U.S.C. § 2314	2B1.1, 2B1.5	18 U.S.C. § 2339A	2X2.1, 2X3.1
18 U.S.C. § 2315	2B1.1, 2B1.5	18 U.S.C. § 2339B	2M5.3
18 U.S.C. § 2316	2B1.1	18 U.S.C. § 2339C(a)(1)(A)	2X2.1
18 U.S.C. § 2317	2B1.1		
18 U.S.C. § 2318	2B5.3	18 U.S.C. § 2339C(a)(1)(B)	2M5.3
18 U.S.C. § 2319	2B5.3	18 U.S.C. § 2339C(c)(2)(A)	2X3.1
18 U.S.C. § 2319A	2B5.3		
18 U.S.C. § 2319B	2B5.3	18 U.S.C. § 2339C(c)(2)(B)	2M5.3, 2X3.1
18 U.S.C. § 2320	2B5.3	18 U.S.C. § 2340A	2A1.1, 2A1.2, 2A2.1, 2A2.2, 2A4.1
18 U.S.C. § 2321	2B6.1		
18 U.S.C. § 2322	2B6.1	18 U.S.C. § 2342(a)	2E4.1
18 U.S.C. § 2332(a)	2A1.1, 2A1.2, 2A1.3, 2A1.4	18 U.S.C. § 2344(a)	2E4.1
		18 U.S.C. § 2381	2M1.1
18 U.S.C. § 2332(b)(1)	2A2.1	18 U.S.C. § 2421	2G1.1, 2G1.3
18 U.S.C. § 2332(b)(2)	2A1.5	18 U.S.C. § 2422	2G1.1, 2G1.3
18 U.S.C. § 2332(c)	2A2.2	18 U.S.C. § 2423(a)–(d)	2G1.3
18 U.S.C. § 2332a	2A6.1, 2K1.4, 2M6.1		
		18 U.S.C. § 2425	2G1.3
18 U.S.C. § 2332b(a)(1)	2A1.1, 2A1.2, 2A1.3, 2A1.4, 2A2.1, 2A2.2, 2A4.1, 2B1.1	18 U.S.C. § 2441	2X5.1
		18 U.S.C. § 2442	2H4.1
18 U.S.C. § 2332b(a)(2)	2A6.1	18 U.S.C. § 2511	2B5.3, 2H3.1
		18 U.S.C. § 2512	2H3.2

Appendix A

18 U.S.C. § 2701	2B1.1	21 U.S.C. § 102	2N2.1
18 U.S.C. § 3056(d)	2A2.4	21 U.S.C. § 103	2N2.1
18 U.S.C. § 3146(b)(1)(A)	2J1.6	21 U.S.C. § 104	2N2.1
		21 U.S.C. § 105	2N2.1
18 U.S.C. § 3146(b)(1)(B)	2J1.5	21 U.S.C. § 111	2N2.1
19 U.S.C. § 283	2T3.1	21 U.S.C. § 115	2N2.1
19 U.S.C. § 1304	2T3.1	21 U.S.C. § 117	2N2.1
19 U.S.C. § 1433	2T3.1	21 U.S.C. § 120	2N2.1
19 U.S.C. § 1434	2B1.1, 2T3.1	21 U.S.C. § 121	2N2.1
19 U.S.C. § 1435	2B1.1, 2T3.1	21 U.S.C. § 122	2N2.1
19 U.S.C. § 1436	2B1.1, 2T3.1	21 U.S.C. § 124	2N2.1
19 U.S.C. § 1464	2T3.1	21 U.S.C. § 126	2N2.1
19 U.S.C. § 1465	2T3.1	21 U.S.C. § 134a–e	2N2.1
19 U.S.C. § 1586(e)	2T3.1	21 U.S.C. § 135a	2N2.1
19 U.S.C. § 1590(d)(1)	2T3.1	21 U.S.C. § 141	2N2.1
19 U.S.C. § 1590(d)(2)	2D1.1	21 U.S.C. § 143	2N2.1
19 U.S.C. § 1707	2T3.1	21 U.S.C. § 144	2N2.1
19 U.S.C. § 1708(b)	2T3.1	21 U.S.C. § 145	2N2.1
19 U.S.C. § 1919	2B1.1	21 U.S.C. § 151	2N2.1
19 U.S.C. § 2316	2B1.1	21 U.S.C. § 152	2N2.1
19 U.S.C. § 2401f	2B1.1	21 U.S.C. § 153	2N2.1
19 U.S.C. § 3907	2T3.1	21 U.S.C. § 154	2N2.1
20 U.S.C. § 1097(a)	2B1.1	21 U.S.C. § 155	2N2.1
20 U.S.C. § 1097(b)	2B1.1	21 U.S.C. § 156	2N2.1
20 U.S.C. § 1097(c)	2B4.1	21 U.S.C. § 157	2N2.1
20 U.S.C. § 1097(d)	2B1.1	21 U.S.C. § 158	2N2.1
21 U.S.C. § 101	2N2.1	21 U.S.C. § 331	2N2.1

21 U.S.C. § 333(a)(1)	2N2.1
21 U.S.C. § 333(a)(2)	2B1.1, 2N2.1
21 U.S.C. § 333(b)(1)–(6)	2N2.1
21 U.S.C. § 333(b)(7)	2N1.1
21 U.S.C. § 458	2N2.1
21 U.S.C. § 459	2N2.1
21 U.S.C. § 460	2N2.1
21 U.S.C. § 461	2N2.1
21 U.S.C. § 463	2N2.1
21 U.S.C. § 466	2N2.1
21 U.S.C. § 610	2N2.1
21 U.S.C. § 611	2N2.1
21 U.S.C. § 614	2N2.1
21 U.S.C. § 617	2N2.1
21 U.S.C. § 619	2N2.1
21 U.S.C. § 620	2N2.1
21 U.S.C. § 622	2C1.1
21 U.S.C. § 642	2N2.1
21 U.S.C. § 643	2N2.1
21 U.S.C. § 644	2N2.1
21 U.S.C. § 675	2A1.1, 2A1.2, 2A1.3, 2A1.4, 2A2.1, 2A2.2, 2A2.3
21 U.S.C. § 676	2N2.1
21 U.S.C. § 841(a)	2D1.1
21 U.S.C. § 841(b)(1)–(3)	2D1.1
21 U.S.C. § 841(b)(4)	2D2.1

21 U.S.C. § 841(b)(7)	2D1.1
21 U.S.C. § 841(c)(1),(2)	2D1.11
21 U.S.C. § 841(c)(3)	2D1.13
21 U.S.C. § 841(d)	2D1.9
21 U.S.C. § 841(f)(1)	2D1.11, 2D1.13
21 U.S.C. § 841(g)	2D1.1
21 U.S.C. § 841(h)	2D1.1
21 U.S.C. § 842(a)(1)	2D3.1
21 U.S.C. § 842(a)(2),(9),(10)	2D3.2
21 U.S.C. § 842(b)	2D3.2
21 U.S.C. § 843(a)(1),(2)	2D3.1
21 U.S.C. § 843(a)(3)	2D2.2
21 U.S.C. § 843(a)(4)(A)	2D1.13
21 U.S.C. § 843(a)(4)(B)	2D1.13
21 U.S.C. § 843(a)(6),(7)	2D1.12
21 U.S.C. § 843(a)(8)	2D1.13
21 U.S.C. § 843(a)(9)	2D3.1
21 U.S.C. § 843(b)	2D1.6
21 U.S.C. § 843(c)	2D3.1
21 U.S.C. § 844(a)	2D2.1
21 U.S.C. § 845	2D1.2
21 U.S.C. § 845a	2D1.2
21 U.S.C. § 845b	2D1.2

21 U.S.C. § 846	2D1.1, 2D1.2, 2D1.5, 2D1.6, 2D1.7, 2D1.8, 2D1.9, 2D1.10, 2D1.11, 2D1.12, 2D1.13, 2D2.1, 2D2.2, 2D3.1, 2D3.2
21 U.S.C. § 848(a)	2D1.5
21 U.S.C. § 848(b)	2D1.5
21 U.S.C. § 848(e)	2A1.1
21 U.S.C. § 849	2D1.2
21 U.S.C. § 854	2S1.1
21 U.S.C. § 856	2D1.8
21 U.S.C. § 857	2D1.7
21 U.S.C. § 858	2D1.10
21 U.S.C. § 859	2D1.2
21 U.S.C. § 860	2D1.2
21 U.S.C. § 860a	2D1.1
21 U.S.C. § 861	2D1.2
21 U.S.C. § 863	2D1.7
21 U.S.C. § 864	2D1.12
21 U.S.C. § 865	2D1.1, 2D1.11
21 U.S.C. § 952	2D1.1
21 U.S.C. § 953	2D1.1
21 U.S.C. § 954	2D3.2
21 U.S.C. § 955	2D1.1
21 U.S.C. § 955a(a)–(d)	2D1.1
21 U.S.C. § 959	2D1.1, 2D1.11
21 U.S.C. § 960(a),(b)	2D1.1
21 U.S.C. § 960(d)(1),(2)	2D1.11
21 U.S.C. § 960(d)(3),(4)	2D1.11
21 U.S.C. § 960(d)(5)	2D1.13
21 U.S.C. § 960(d)(6)	2D3.1
21 U.S.C. § 960(d)(7)	2D1.11
21 U.S.C. § 960a	2D1.14
21 U.S.C. § 961	2D3.2
21 U.S.C. § 963	2D1.1, 2D1.2, 2D1.5, 2D1.6, 2D1.7, 2D1.8, 2D1.9, 2D1.10, 2D1.11, 2D1.12, 2D1.13, 2D2.1, 2D2.2, 2D3.1, 2D3.2
22 U.S.C. § 1980(g)	2B1.1
22 U.S.C. § 2197(n)	2B1.1
22 U.S.C. § 2778	2M5.2
22 U.S.C. § 2780	2M5.2
22 U.S.C. § 4217	2B1.1
22 U.S.C. § 4221	2B1.1
22 U.S.C. § 8512	2M5.1, 2M5.2, 2M5.3
25 U.S.C. § 450d	2B1.1
26 U.S.C. § 5148(1)	2T2.1
26 U.S.C. § 5214(a)(1)	2T2.1
26 U.S.C. § 5273(b)(2)	2T2.1
26 U.S.C. § 5273(c)	2T2.1
26 U.S.C. § 5291(a)	2T2.1, 2T2.2
26 U.S.C. § 5601(a)	2T2.1, 2T2.2
26 U.S.C. § 5602	2T2.1
26 U.S.C. § 5603	2T2.1, 2T2.2
26 U.S.C. § 5604(a)	2T2.1, 2T2.2

26 U.S.C. § 5605	2T2.1, 2T2.2
26 U.S.C. § 5607	2T2.1
26 U.S.C. § 5608	2T2.1
26 U.S.C. § 5661	2T2.1, 2T2.2
26 U.S.C. § 5662	2T2.2
26 U.S.C. § 5671	2T2.1, 2T2.2
26 U.S.C. § 5684	2T2.1
26 U.S.C. § 5685	2K1.3, 2K2.1
26 U.S.C. § 5691(a)	2T2.1
26 U.S.C. § 5751(a)(1),(2)	2T2.1
26 U.S.C. § 5752	2T2.2
26 U.S.C. § 5762(a)(1), (2),(4),(5),(6)	2T2.2
26 U.S.C. § 5762(a)(3)	2T2.1
26 U.S.C. § 5861(a)–(l)	2K2.1
26 U.S.C. § 5871	2K2.1
26 U.S.C. § 7201	2T1.1
26 U.S.C. § 7202	2T1.6
26 U.S.C. § 7203	2S1.3, 2T1.1
26 U.S.C. § 7204	2T1.8
26 U.S.C. § 7205	2T1.8
26 U.S.C. § 7206(1),(3),(4),(5)	2S1.3, 2T1.1
26 U.S.C. § 7206(2)	2S1.3, 2T1.4
26 U.S.C. § 7207	2T1.1
26 U.S.C. § 7208	2B1.1
26 U.S.C. § 7210	2J1.1, 2J1.5
26 U.S.C. § 7211	2T1.1
26 U.S.C. § 7212(a)	2A2.4
26 U.S.C. § 7212(a) (omnibus clause)	2J1.2, 2T1.1
26 U.S.C. § 7212(b)	2B1.1, 2B2.1, 2B3.1
26 U.S.C. § 7213(a)(1)	2H3.1
26 U.S.C. § 7213(a)(2)	2H3.1
26 U.S.C. § 7213(a)(3)	2H3.1
26 U.S.C. § 7213(a)(5)	2H3.1
26 U.S.C. § 7213(d)	2H3.1
26 U.S.C. § 7213A	2H3.1
26 U.S.C. § 7214	2B1.1, 2C1.1, 2C1.2
26 U.S.C. § 7215	2T1.7
26 U.S.C. § 7216	2H3.1
26 U.S.C. § 7232	2B1.1
26 U.S.C. § 7512(b)	2T1.7
26 U.S.C. § 9012(e)	2B4.1
26 U.S.C. § 9042(d)	2B4.1
28 U.S.C. § 1826(c)	2P1.1
28 U.S.C. § 2902(e)	2P1.1
29 U.S.C. § 186	2E5.1
29 U.S.C. § 431	2E5.3
29 U.S.C. § 432	2E5.3
29 U.S.C. § 433	2E5.3
29 U.S.C. § 439	2E5.3
29 U.S.C. § 461	2E5.3
29 U.S.C. § 501(c)	2B1.1
29 U.S.C. § 530	2B3.2

29 U.S.C. § 1131(a)	2E5.3	1319(c)(1),(2),(4)	2Q1.2, 2Q1.3
29 U.S.C. § 1141	2B1.1, 2B3.2	33 U.S.C. § 1319(c)(3)	2Q1.1
29 U.S.C. § 1149	2B1.1	33 U.S.C. § 1321	2Q1.2, 2Q1.3
29 U.S.C. § 1851	2H4.2	33 U.S.C. § 1342	2Q1.2, 2Q1.3
30 U.S.C. § 1461(a)(3), (4),(5),(7)	2A2.4	33 U.S.C. § 1415(b)	2Q1.2, 2Q1.3
30 U.S.C. § 1463	2A2.4	33 U.S.C. § 1517	2Q1.2, 2Q1.3
31 U.S.C. § 5311 note (section 329 of the USA PATRIOT Act of 2001)	2C1.1	33 U.S.C. § 1907	2Q1.3
		33 U.S.C. § 1908	2Q1.3
		33 U.S.C. § 3851	2Q1.2
31 U.S.C. § 5313	2S1.3	38 U.S.C. § 787	2B1.1
31 U.S.C. § 5314	2S1.3	38 U.S.C. § 2413	2B2.3
31 U.S.C. § 5316	2S1.3	38 U.S.C. § 3501(a)	2B1.1
31 U.S.C. § 5318	2S1.3	38 U.S.C. § 3502	2B1.1
31 U.S.C. § 5318A(b)	2S1.3	40 U.S.C. § 5104(e)(1)	2K2.5
31 U.S.C. § 5322	2S1.3	40 U.S.C. § 14309(a),(b)	2C1.3
31 U.S.C. § 5324	2S1.3	41 U.S.C. § 2102	2B1.1, 2C1.1
31 U.S.C. § 5326	2S1.3, 2T2.2	41 U.S.C. § 2105	2B1.1, 2C1.1
31 U.S.C. § 5331	2S1.3	41 U.S.C. § 8702	2B4.1
31 U.S.C. § 5332	2S1.3	41 U.S.C. § 8707	2B4.1
31 U.S.C. § 5363	2E3.1	42 U.S.C. § 261(a)	2D1.1
33 U.S.C. § 403	2Q1.3	42 U.S.C. § 262	2N2.1
33 U.S.C. § 406	2Q1.3	42 U.S.C. § 300h-2	2Q1.2
33 U.S.C. § 407	2Q1.3	42 U.S.C. § 300i-1	2Q1.4
33 U.S.C. § 411	2Q1.3	42 U.S.C. § 408	2B1.1
33 U.S.C. § 1227(b)	2J1.1, 2J1.5	42 U.S.C. § 1011	2B1.1
33 U.S.C. § 1232(b)(2)	2A2.4	42 U.S.C. § 1307(a)	2B1.1
33 U.S.C. §		42 U.S.C. § 1307(b)	2B1.1

42 U.S.C. § 1320a-7b	2B1.1, 2B4.1
42 U.S.C. § 1320a-8b	2X5.1, 2X5.2
42 U.S.C. § 1383(d)(2)	2B1.1
42 U.S.C. § 1383a(a)	2B1.1
42 U.S.C. § 1383a(b)	2B1.1
42 U.S.C. § 1395nn(a)	2B1.1
42 U.S.C. § 1395nn(b)(1)	2B4.1
42 U.S.C. § 1395nn(b)(2)	2B4.1
42 U.S.C. § 1395nn(c)	2B1.1
42 U.S.C. § 1396h(a)	2B1.1
42 U.S.C. § 1396h(b)(1)	2B4.1
42 U.S.C. § 1396h(b)(2)	2B4.1
42 U.S.C. § 1396w–2	2H3.1
42 U.S.C. § 1713	2B1.1
42 U.S.C. § 1760(g)	2B1.1
42 U.S.C. § 1761(o)(1)	2B1.1
42 U.S.C. § 1761(o)(2)	2B1.1
42 U.S.C. § 2000e-13	2A1.1, 2A1.2, 2A1.3, 2A1.4, 2A2.1, 2A2.2, 2A2.3
42 U.S.C. § 2077	2M6.1
42 U.S.C. § 2122	2M6.1
42 U.S.C. § 2131	2M6.1
42 U.S.C. § 2272	2M6.1
42 U.S.C. § 2273	2M6.2
42 U.S.C. §	
2274(a),(b)	2M3.1
42 U.S.C. § 2275	2M3.1
42 U.S.C. § 2276	2M3.5
42 U.S.C. § 2278a(c)	2B2.3
42 U.S.C. § 2283(a)	2A1.1, 2A1.2, 2A1.3, 2A1.4
42 U.S.C. § 2283(b)	2A2.2, 2A2.3
42 U.S.C. § 2284(a)	2M2.1, 2M2.3
42 U.S.C. § 3220(a)	2B1.1
42 U.S.C. § 3220(b)	2B1.1
42 U.S.C. § 3426	2B1.1
42 U.S.C. § 3611(f)	2J1.1, 2J1.5
42 U.S.C. § 3631	2H1.1
42 U.S.C. § 3791	2B1.1
42 U.S.C. § 3792	2B1.1
42 U.S.C. § 3795	2B1.1
42 U.S.C. § 5157(a)	2B1.1
42 U.S.C. § 5409	2N2.1
42 U.S.C. § 6928(d)	2Q1.2
42 U.S.C. § 6928(e)	2Q1.1
42 U.S.C. § 7270b	2B2.3
42 U.S.C. § 7413(c)(1)–(4)	2Q1.2, 2Q1.3
42 U.S.C. § 7413(c)(5)	2Q1.1
42 U.S.C. § 9151(2),(3),(4),(5)	2A2.4
42 U.S.C. § 9152(d)	2A2.4
42 U.S.C. § 9603(b)	2Q1.2
42 U.S.C. § 9603(c)	2Q1.2

APPENDIX A

42 U.S.C. § 9603(d)	2Q1.2	47 U.S.C. § 605	2B5.3, 2H3.1
42 U.S.C. § 14133	2X5.2	49 U.S.C. § 121	2B1.1 (for offenses committed prior to July 5, 1994)
42 U.S.C. § 14905	2B1.1		
42 U.S.C. § 16962	2H3.1	49 U.S.C. § 1809(b)	2Q1.2 (for offenses committed prior to July 5, 1994)
42 U.S.C. § 16984	2H3.1		
43 U.S.C. § 1350	2Q1.2	49 U.S.C. § 5124	2Q1.2
43 U.S.C. § 1733(a) (43 C.F.R. 4140.1(b)(1)(i)	2B2.3	49 U.S.C. § 11902	2B4.1
		49 U.S.C. § 11903	2B1.1
43 U.S.C. § 1816(a)	2Q1.2	49 U.S.C. § 11904	2B1.1 (2B4.1 for offenses committed prior to January 1, 1996)
43 U.S.C. § 1822(b)	2Q1.2		
45 U.S.C. § 359(a)	2B1.1	49 U.S.C. § 11907(a)	2B4.1 (for offenses committed prior to January 1, 1996)
46 U.S.C. § 1276	2B1.1		
46 U.S.C. § 3718(b)	2Q1.2	49 U.S.C. § 11907(b)	2B4.1 (for offenses committed prior to January 1, 1996)
46 U.S.C. App. § 1707a(f)(2)	2B1.1		
46 U.S.C. App. § 1903(a)	2D1.1	49 U.S.C. § 14103(b)	2B1.1
		49 U.S.C. § 14905(b)	2B1.1
46 U.S.C. App. § 1903(g)	2D1.1	49 U.S.C. § 14909	2J1.1, 2J1.5
46 U.S.C. App. § 1903(j)	2D1.1	49 U.S.C. § 14912	2B1.1
		49 U.S.C. § 14915	2B1.1
47 U.S.C. § 223(a)(1)(C)	2A6.1	49 U.S.C. § 16102	2B1.1
47 U.S.C. § 223(a)(1)(D)	2A6.1	49 U.S.C. § 16104	2J1.1, 2J1.5
47 U.S.C. § 223(a)(1)(E)	2A6.1	49 U.S.C. § 30170	2B1.1
		49 U.S.C. § 31310	2X5.2
47 U.S.C. § 223(b)(1)(A)	2G3.2	49 U.S.C. § 32703	2N3.1
47 U.S.C. § 409(m)	2J1.1, 2J1.5	49 U.S.C. § 32704	2N3.1
47 U.S.C. § 553(b)(2)	2B5.3	49 U.S.C. § 32705	2N3.1
		49 U.S.C. § 32709(b)	2N3.1

49 U.S.C. § 46308	2A5.2
49 U.S.C. § 46312	2Q1.2
49 U.S.C. § 46317(a)	2B1.1
49 U.S.C. § 46317(b)	2D1.1
49 U.S.C. § 46502(a),(b)	2A5.1, 2X1.1
49 U.S.C. § 46503	2A5.2
49 U.S.C. § 46504	2A5.2
49 U.S.C. § 46505	2K1.5
49 U.S.C. § 46506	2A5.3
49 U.S.C. § 46507	2A6.1
49 U.S.C. § 60123(b)	2B1.1, 2K1.4, 2M2.1, 2M2.3
49 U.S.C. § 60123(d)	2B1.1
49 U.S.C. § 80116	2B1.1
49 U.S.C. § 80501	2B1.1
49 U.S.C. App. § 1687(g)	2B1.1 (for offenses committed prior to July 5, 1994)
50 U.S.C. § 783	2M3.3
50 U.S.C. § 1705	2M5.1, 2M5.2, 2M5.3
50 U.S.C. § 3121	2M3.9
50 U.S.C. App. § 462	2M4.1
50 U.S.C. App. § 527(e)	2X5.2
50 U.S.C. App. § 2410	2M5.1
52 U.S.C. § 10307(c)	2H2.1
52 U.S.C. § 10307(d)	2H2.1
52 U.S.C. § 10307(e)	2H2.1
52 U.S.C. § 10308(a)	2H2.1
52 U.S.C. § 10308(b)	2H2.1
52 U.S.C. § 10308(c)	2X1.1
52 U.S.C. § 10501	2H2.1
52 U.S.C. § 10502	2H2.1
52 U.S.C. § 10503	2H2.1
52 U.S.C. § 10505	2H2.1
52 U.S.C. § 10701	2H2.1
52 U.S.C. § 20511	2H2.1
52 U.S.C. § 30109(d)	2C1.8
52 U.S.C. § 30114	2C1.8
52 U.S.C. § 30116	2C1.8
52 U.S.C. § 30117	2C1.8
52 U.S.C. § 30118	2C1.8
52 U.S.C. § 30119	2C1.8
52 U.S.C. § 30120	2C1.8
52 U.S.C. § 30121	2C1.8
52 U.S.C. § 30122	2C1.8
52 U.S.C. § 30123	2C1.8
52 U.S.C. § 30124(a)	2C1.8
52 U.S.C. § 30125	2C1.8
52 U.S.C. § 30126	2C1.8

APPENDIX A

Historical Note	Effective November 1, 1987. Amended effective January 15, 1988 (amendments 60 and 61); June 15, 1988 (amendments 62 and 63); October 15, 1988 (amendments 64 and 65); November 1, 1989 (amendments 297–301); November 1, 1990 (amendment 359); November 1, 1991 (amendment 421); November 1, 1992 (amendment 468); November 1, 1993 (amendment 496); November 1, 1995 (amendment 534); November 1, 1996 (amendment 540); November 1, 1997 (amendment 575); November 1, 1998 (amendment 589); November 1, 2000 (amendment 592); May 1, 2001 (amendment 612); November 1, 2001 (amendments 617, 622, 626, 627, 628, 633, and 634); November 1, 2002 (amendments 637, 638, 639, and 646); January 25, 2003 (amendments 647 and 648); November 1, 2003 (amendments 653, 654, 655, 656, 658, and 661); November 1, 2004 (amendments 664, 665, 666, 667, 669, and 674); October 24, 2005 (amendments 675 and 676); November 1, 2005 (amendments 677, 679, and 680); November 1, 2006 (amendments 685, 686, 687, 689, and 690); May 1, 2007 (amendment 697); November 1, 2007 (amendments 699, 700, 701, 703, 704, 705, 707, 708, and 711); February 6, 2008 (amendment 714); November 1, 2008 (amendments 718, 720, 721, 724 and 725); November 1, 2009 (amendments 727, 728, 729, 730, 731, 733, 736, and 737); November 1, 2010 (amendments 743, 745, and 746); November 1, 2011 (amendments 749, 753, and 757); November 1, 2012 (amendments 765 and 769); November 1, 2013 (amendments 772, 773, and 777); November 1, 2014 (amendment 781); November 1, 2015 (amendment 796); November 1, 2016 (amendments 800 and 804).

INDEX TO GUIDELINES MANUAL

This index provides an alphabetical list of topics addressed in the Guidelines Manual and refers the reader to provisions that may be relevant to those topics. This index is unofficial and is provided only as a convenience to the reader.

Note that this index generally does not refer the reader to provisions in Chapter Two offense guidelines. This is by design, because this index is not to be used in determining the offense guideline section in Chapter Two (Offense Conduct) that applies in a particular case. Such determinations are made based on the statute of conviction. *See* §1B1.2 (Applicable Guidelines) and Appendix A (Statutory Index).

For example, this index contains an entry for "kidnapping" which refers the reader to the Chapter Three adjustment at §3A1.3 (Restraint of Victim) and the upward departure provision at §5K2.4 (Abduction or Unlawful Restraint), each of which may be relevant to kidnapping. This index does not, however, refer the reader to any of the Chapter Two offense guidelines with provisions that may be relevant to kidnapping. The Chapter Two offense guideline that applies in a case involving a kidnapping is determined by identifying the statute of conviction and consulting §1B1.2 (Applicable Guidelines) and Appendix A (Statutory Index).

LIST OF DEPARTURE PROVISIONS

This list identifies provisions in the Guidelines Manual that indicate when a departure based on a specific ground may be warranted.

In the list that follows, the guideline provision is printed in **bold type** if it involves a downward departure and *italic type* if it involves an upward departure. (Where the guideline provision could involve either an upward departure or a downward departure, depending on the circumstances, the guideline provision is printed in normal, roman type.)

For departures generally, including provisions setting forth the standards that apply in determining whether a departure is warranted, provisions indicating certain factors that are not relevant (or not ordinarily relevant) in determining whether a departure is warranted, and provisions indicating certain circumstances that are prohibited as grounds for departure, see Chapter Five, Parts H (Specific Offender Characteristics) and K (Departures). For departures with regard to organizations, *see* Chapter 8, Part C, Subpart 4 (Departures from the Guideline Fine Range).

For the definition of "departure" and related terms, *see* §1B1.1 (Application Instructions), Application Note 1(E).

For the use of departures in determining the sentence, *see* §1B1.1(b). For the information to be used in determining whether a departure is warranted, *see* §§1B1.4 (Information to be Used in Imposing Sentence (Selecting a Point Within the Guideline Range or Departing from the Guideline) and 1B1.8 (Use of Certain Information). Other procedural provisions applicable to departures include §§5K2.0(e) (Requirement of Specific Written Reasons for Departure), 6A1.4 (Notice of Possible Departure), and 6B1.2 (Standards for Acceptance of Plea Agreements).

As an aid to understanding the role of departures in the guidelines, *see* Chapter One, Part A, Subpart 1(4)(b) (Departures).

The list is as follows:

CHAPTER ONE
1B1.3, comment. (n.3(B))
1B1.3, comment. (n.6(B))

CHAPTER TWO
2A1.1, comment. (n.2(B))
2A1.2, comment. (n.1)
2A2.1, comment. (n.2)
2A2.4, comment. (n.3)
2A3.1, comment. (n.6)
2A3.2, comment. (n.6)
2A3.6, comment. (n.4)
2A5.3, comment. (n.2)
2A6.1, comment. (n.4(B))
2A6.2, comment. (n.5)
2B1.1, comment. (n.8(A))
2B1.1, comment. (n.20(A))
2B1.1, comment. (n.20(B))

2B1.1, comment. (n.20(C))
2B1.1, comment. (n.20(D))
2B1.5, comment. (n.9)
2B2.1, comment. (backg'd.)
2B3.1, comment. (n.5)
2B3.2, comment. (n.7)
2B3.2, comment. (n.8)
2B5.3, comment. (n.5)
2C1.1, comment. (n.7)
2C1.1, comment. (n.7)
2C1.8, comment. (n.4)
2D1.1, comment. (n.1)
2D1.1, comment. (n.10)
2D1.1, comment. (n.18(A))
2D1.1, comment. (n.22(B))
2D1.1, comment. (n.27(A))
2D1.1, comment. (n.27(B))
2D1.1, comment. (n.27(C))

UNITED STATES SENTENCING COMMISSION
GUIDELINES MANUAL
2016

APPENDIX B

PATTI B. SARIS
Chair

CHARLES R. BREYER
Vice Chair

DABNEY L. FRIEDRICH
Commissioner

RACHEL E. BARKOW
Commissioner

WILLIAM H. PRYOR, JR.
Commissioner

MICHELLE MORALES
Commissioner, *Ex-officio*

J. PATRICIA WILSON SMOOT
Commissioner, *Ex-officio*

This document contains the principal statutory provisions governing sentencing, the Sentencing Commission, and the drafting of sentencing guidelines, as of May 1, 2016.

SELECTED SENTENCING STATUTES

This appendix sets forth the principal statutory provisions governing sentencing, the Sentencing Commission, and the drafting of sentencing guidelines, **as of May 1, 2016**, as follows:

Title 18. First, it sets forth relevant provisions of title 18, United States Code (Crimes and Criminal Procedure), as extracted from the following chapters of title 18:

- Chapter 227 (Sentences);
- Chapter 229 (Postsentence Administration);
- Chapter 232 (Miscellaneous Sentencing Provisions); and
- Chapter 235 (Appeal).

Title 28. Second, it sets forth relevant provisions of title 28, United States Code (Judiciary and Judicial Procedure), as extracted from the following chapter of title 28:

- Chapter 58 (United States Sentencing Commission).

Public Laws Governing the Commission and the Drafting of Sentencing Guidelines. Third, it sets forth other relevant provisions of freestanding public laws governing the Commission and the drafting of sentencing guidelines (*e.g.*, congressional directives). These provisions ordinarily appear in the United States Code in the notes following 28 U.S.C. § 994. This appendix sets them forth separately and in fuller detail for ease of reference.

The legal authority for the Commission and the related authority and procedures for sentencing in federal courts have their legislative foundation in the Sentencing Reform Act of 1984 (Chapter II of the Comprehensive Crime Control Act of 1984, Pub. L. 98–473, October 12, 1984).

These statutory provisions are presented in this appendix solely for the purpose of providing a reference to federal sentencing law as it stands as of **May 1, 2016**. For the sake of brevity, certain miscellaneous provisions are omitted. The Commission makes no representations concerning the accuracy of these provisions and recommends that authoritative sources be consulted where legal reliance is necessary.

CONTENTS

Page

Title 18

CRIMES AND CRIMINAL PROCEDURE

—

CHAPTER 227–SENTENCES

SUBCHAPTER A–GENERAL PROVISIONS

§ 3551. Authorized sentences

(a) In general.—Except as otherwise specifically provided, a defendant who has been found guilty of an offense described in any Federal statute, including sections 13 and 1153 of this title, other than an Act of Congress applicable exclusively in the District of Columbia or the Uniform Code of Military Justice, shall be sentenced in accordance with the provisions of this chapter so as to achieve the purposes set forth in subparagraphs (A) through (D) of section 3553(a)(2) to the extent that they are applicable in light of all the circumstances of the case.

(b) Individuals.—An individual found guilty of an offense shall be sentenced, in accordance with the provisions of section 3553, to—

(1) a term of probation as authorized by subchapter B;

(2) a fine as authorized by subchapter C; or

(3) a term of imprisonment as authorized by subchapter D.

A sentence to pay a fine may be imposed in addition to any other sentence. A sanction authorized by section 3554, 3555, or 3556 may be imposed in addition to the sentence required by this subsection.

(c) Organizations.—An organization found guilty of an offense shall be sentenced, in accordance with the provisions of section 3553, to—

(1) a term of probation as authorized by subchapter B; or

(2) a fine as authorized by subchapter C.

A sentence to pay a fine may be imposed in addition to a sentence to probation. A sanction authorized by section 3554, 3555, or 3556 may be imposed in addition to the sentence required by this subsection.

(Added Pub.L. 98–473, Title II, § 212(a)(2), Oct. 12, 1984, 98 Stat. 1988, and amended Pub.L. 101–647, Title XVI, § 1602, Nov. 29, 1990, 104 Stat. 4843.)

EDITORIAL NOTES

Effective Date and Savings Provisions of Sentencing Reform Act of 1984 (Pub.L. 98–473, Title II, c. II, §§ 211 to 239); Terms of Members of U.S. Sentencing Commission and U.S. Parole Commission; Parole Release Dates; Membership of National Institute of Corrections, Advisory Corrections Council, and U.S. Sentencing Commission. Section 235 of Pub.L. 98–473, Title II, c. II, Oct. 12, 1984, 98 Stat. 2031, as amended by Pub.L. 99–217, §§ 2, 4, Dec. 26, 1985, 99 Stat. 1728; Pub.L. 99–646, § 35, Nov. 10, 1986, 100 Stat. 3599; Pub.L. 100–182, § 2, Dec. 7, 1987, 101 Stat. 1266; Pub.L. 104–232, § 4, Oct. 2, 1996, 110 Stat. 3056, provided:

"**(a)(1)** This chapter [chapter II, §§ 211–239, of Title II of Pub.L. 98–473] shall take effect on the first day of the first calendar month beginning 36 months after the date of enactment [Oct. 12, 1984] and shall apply only to offenses committed after the taking effect of this chapter, except that—

(A) the repeal of chapter 402 of title 18, United States Code, shall take effect on the date of enactment;

(B)(i) chapter 58 of title 28, United States Code, shall take effect on the date of enactment of this Act or October 1, 1983, whichever occurs later, and the United States Sentencing Commission shall submit the initial sentencing guidelines promulgated under section 994(a)(1) of title 28 to the Congress within 30 months of the effective date of such chapter 58; and

(ii) the sentencing guidelines promulgated pursuant to section 994(a)(1) shall not go into effect until—

(I) the United States Sentencing Commission has submitted the initial set of sentencing guidelines to the Congress pursuant to subparagraph (B)(i), along with a report stating the reasons for the Commission's recommendations;

(II) the General Accounting Office has undertaken a study of the guidelines, and their potential impact in comparison with the operation of the existing sentencing and parole release system, and has, within one hundred and fifty days of submission of the guidelines, reported to the Congress the results of its study; and

(III) the day after the Congress has had six months after the date described in subclause (I) in which to examine the guidelines and consider the reports; and

(IV) section 212(a)(2) [enacting chapter 227, sentences, comprised of sections 3551 to 3559, 3561 to 3566, 3571 to 3574, and 3581 to 3586; and chapter 229, postsentence administration, comprised of sections 3601 to 3607, 3611 to 3615, and 3621 to 3625 of this title; and repealing former chapter 227, sentence, judgment, and execution, comprised of sections 3561 to 3580; former chapter 229, fines, penalties, and forfeitures, comprised of sections 3611 to 3620; and former chapter 231, probation, comprised of sections 3651 to 3656 of this title] takes effect, in the case of the initial sentencing guidelines so promulgated.

(2) For the purposes of section 992(a) of title 28, the terms of the first members of the United States Sentencing Commission shall not begin to run until the sentencing guidelines go into effect pursuant to paragraph (1)(B)(ii).

(b)(1) The following provisions of law in effect on the day before the effective date of this Act shall remain in effect for five years after the effective date as to an individual who committed an offense or an act of juvenile delinquency before the effective date and as to a term of imprisonment during the period described in subsection (a)(1)(B):

(A) Chapter 311 of title 18, United States Code.

(B) Chapter 309 of title 18, United States Code.

(C) Sections 4251 through 4255 of title 18, United States Code.

(D) Sections 5041 and 5042 of title 18, United States Code.

(E) Sections 5017 through 5020 of title 18, United States Code, as to a sentence imposed before the date of enactment.

(F) The maximum term of imprisonment in effect on the effective date for an offense committed before the effective date.

(G) Any other law relating to a violation of a condition of release or to arrest authority with regard to a person who violates a condition of release.

[(2) Repealed. Pub.L. 104–232, § 4, Oct. 2, 1996, 110 Stat. 3056.]

(3) The United States Parole Commission shall set a release date, for an individual who will be in its jurisdiction the day before the expiration of five years after the effective date of this Act, pursuant to section 4206 of title 18, United States Code. A release date set pursuant to this paragraph shall be set early enough to permit consideration of an appeal of the release date, in accordance with Parole Commission procedures, before the expiration of five years following the effective date of this Act.

(4) Notwithstanding the other provisions of this subsection, all laws in effect on the day before the effective date of this Act pertaining to an individual who is—

(A) released pursuant to a provision listed in paragraph (1); and

(B)(i) subject to supervision on the day before the expiration of the five-year period following the effective date of this Act; or

(ii) released on a date set pursuant to paragraph (3);

including laws pertaining to terms and conditions of release, revocation of release, provision of counsel, and payment of transportation costs, shall remain in effect as to the individual until the expiration of his sentence, except that the district court shall determine, in accord with the Federal Rules of Criminal Procedure, whether release should be revoked or the conditions of release amended for violation of a condition of release.

(5) Notwithstanding the provisions of section 991 of title 28, United States Code, and sections 4351 and 5002 of title 18, United States Code, the Chairman of the United States Parole Commission or his designee shall be a member of the National Institute of Corrections, and the Chairman of the United States Parole Commission shall be a member of the Advisory Corrections Council and a nonvoting member of the United States Sentencing Commission, ex officio, until the expiration of the five-year period following the effective date of this Act. Notwithstanding the provisions of section 4351 of title 18, during the five-year period the National Institute of Corrections shall have seventeen members, including seven ex officio members. Notwithstanding the provisions of section

991 of title 28, during the five-year period the United States Sentencing Commission shall consist of nine members, including two ex officio, nonvoting members."

[Pub.L. 113–47, § 2, Oct. 31, 2013, 127 Stat. 572, provided that: "For purposes of section 235(b) of the Sentencing Reform Act of 1984 (18 U.S.C. 3551 note; Public Law 98–473; 98 Stat. 2032), as such section relates to chapter 311 of title 18, United States Code, and the United States Parole Commission, each reference in such section to '26 years' or '26-year period' shall be deemed a reference to '31 years' or '31-year period', respectively."]

[Pub.L. 112–44, § 2, Oct. 21, 2011, 125 Stat. 532, provided that: "For purposes of section 235(b) of the Sentencing Reform Act of 1984 (18 U.S.C. 3551 note; Public Law 98–473; 98 Stat. 2032), as such section relates to chapter 311 of title 18, United States Code, and the United States Parole Commission, each reference in such section to '24 years' or '24-year period' shall be deemed a reference to '26 years' or '26-year period', respectively."]

[Pub.L. 110–312, § 2, Aug. 12, 2008, 122 Stat. 3013, provided that: "For purposes of section 235(b) of the Sentencing Reform Act of 1984 (18 U.S.C. 3551 note; Public Law 98–473; 98 Stat. 2032) [set out in an Effective and Applicability Provisions note under this section], as such section relates to chapter 311 of title 18, United States Code [18 U.S.C.A. § 4201 et seq.], and the United States Parole Commission, each reference in such section to '21 years' or '21-year period' shall be deemed a reference to '24 years' or '24-year period', respectively."]

[Pub.L. 109–76, § 2, Sept. 29, 2005, 119 Stat. 2035, provided that: "For purposes of section 235(b) of the Sentencing Reform Act of 1984 (98 Stat. 2032) [Pub.L. 98–473, Title II, § 235, Oct. 12, 1984, 98 Stat. 2032, as amended, set out as a note under this section] as such section relates to chapter 311 of title 18, United States Code, [18 U.S.C.A. § 4201 et seq.] and the United States Parole Commission, each reference in such section to 'eighteen years' or 'eighteen-year period' shall be deemed a reference to '21 years' or '21-year period', respectively."]

[Pub.L. 107–273, Div. C, Title I, § 11017(a), Nov. 2, 2002, 116 Stat. 1824, provided that: "For purposes of section 235(b) of the Sentencing Reform Act of 1984 (98 Stat. 2032) [section 235(b) of Pub.L. 98–473, set out as a note under this section], as such section

relates to chapter 311 of title 18, United States Code [18 U.S.C.A. § 4201 et seq. (repealed)], and the Parole Commission, each reference in such section to 'fifteen years' or 'fifteen-year period' shall be deemed to be a reference to 'eighteen years' or 'eighteen-year period', respectively." See also section 11017(b) and (c) of Pub.L. 107–273, set out as a note under 18 U.S.C.A. § 4202]

[Pub.L. 104–232, § 3(b)(2), Oct. 2, 1996, 110 Stat. 3056, provided that: "Effective on the date such plan [an alternative plan by the Attorney General for the transfer of the United States Parole Commission's functions to another entity within the Department of Justice pursuant to section 3 of Pub.L. 104–232, set out as a note under section 4201 of this title] takes effect, paragraphs (3) and (4) of section 235(b) of the Sentencing Reform Act of 1984 (98 Stat. 2032) [section 235(b)(3) and (4) of Pub.L. 98–473, set out above] are repealed."]

[Pub.L. 104–232, § 2(a), Oct. 2, 1996, 110 Stat. 3055, provided that: "For purposes of section 235(b) of the Sentencing Reform Act of 1984 (98 Stat. 2032) [section 235(b) of Pub.L. 98–473, set out as a note under this section], as it related to chapter 311 of title 18, United States Code [section 4201 et seq. of this title], and the Parole Commission, each reference in such section to 'ten years' or 'ten-year period' shall be deemed to be a reference to 'fifteen years' or 'fifteen-year period', respectively."]

[Pub.L. 101–650, Title III, § 316, Dec. 1, 1990, 104 Stat. 5115, provided that: "For the purposes of section 235(b) of Public Law 98–473 [set out as a note under this section] as it relates to chapter 311 of title 18, United States Code [section 4201 et seq. of this title], and the United States Parole Commission, each reference in such section to 'five years' or a 'five-year period' shall be deemed a reference to 'ten years' or a 'ten-year period', respectively."]

Sentencing Considerations Prior to Enactment of Guidelines. Section 239 of Pub.L. 98–473, Title II, c. II, Oct. 12, 1984, 98 Stat. 2039, provided:

"Since, due to an impending crisis in prison over-crowding, available Federal prison space must be treated as a scarce resource in the sentencing of criminal defendants;
"Since, sentencing decisions should be designed to ensure that prison resources are, first and foremost,

reserved for those violent and serious criminal offenders who pose the most dangerous threat to society;

"Since, in cases of nonviolent and nonserious offenders, the interests of society as a whole as well as individual victims of crime can continue to be served through the imposition of alternative sentences, such as restitution and community service;

"Since, in the two years preceding the enactment of sentencing guidelines, Federal sentencing practice should ensure that scarce prison resources are available to house violent and serious criminal offenders by the increased use of restitution, community service, and other alternative sentences in cases of nonviolent and nonserious offenders: Now, therefore, be it

"Declared, That it is the sense of the Senate that in the two years preceding the enactment of the sentencing guidelines, Federal judges, in determining the particular sentence to be imposed, consider—

(1) the nature and circumstances of the offense and the history and characteristics of the defendant;

(2) the general appropriateness of imposing a sentence other than imprisonment in cases in which the defendant has not been convicted of a crime of violence or otherwise serious offense; and

(3) the general appropriateness of imposing a sentence of imprisonment in cases in which the defendant has been convicted of a crime of violence or otherwise serious offense."

§ 3552. Presentence reports

(a) Presentence investigation and report by probation officer.—A United States probation officer shall make a presentence investigation of a defendant that is required pursuant to the provisions of Rule 32(c) of the Federal Rules of Criminal Procedure, and shall, before the imposition of sentence, report the results of the investigation to the court.

(b) Presentence study and report by bureau of prisons.—If the court, before or after its receipt of a report specified in subsection (a) or (c), desires more information than is otherwise available to it as a basis for determining the sentence to be imposed on a defendant found guilty of a misdemeanor or felony, it may order a study of the defendant. The study shall be con-

ducted in the local community by qualified consultants unless the sentencing judge finds that there is a compelling reason for the study to be done by the Bureau of Prisons or there are no adequate professional resources available in the local community to perform the study. The period of the study shall be no more than sixty days. The order shall specify the additional information that the court needs before determining the sentence to be imposed. Such an order shall be treated for administrative purposes as a provisional sentence of imprisonment for the maximum term authorized by section 3581(b) for the offense committed. The study shall inquire into such matters as are specified by the court and any other matters that the Bureau of Prisons or the professional consultants believe are pertinent to the factors set forth in section 3553(a). The period of the study may, in the discretion of the court, be extended for an additional period of not more than sixty days. By the expiration of the period of the study, or by the expiration of any extension granted by the court, the United States marshal shall, if the defendant is in custody, return the defendant to the court for final sentencing. The Bureau of Prisons or the professional consultants shall provide the court with a written report of the pertinent results of the study and make to the court whatever recommendations the Bureau or the consultants believe will be helpful to a proper resolution of the case. The report shall include recommendations of the Bureau or the consultants concerning the guidelines and policy statements, promulgated by the Sentencing Commission pursuant to 28 U.S.C. 994(a), that they believe are applicable to the defendant's case. After receiving the report and the recommendations, the court shall proceed finally to sentence the defendant in accordance with the sentencing alternatives and procedures available under this chapter.

(c) Presentence examination and report by psychiatric or psychological examiners.—If the court, before or after its receipt of a report specified in subsection (a) or (b) desires more information than is otherwise available to it as a basis for determining the mental condition of the defendant, the court may order the same psychiatric or psychological examination and report thereon as may be ordered under section 4244(b) of this title.

(d) Disclosure of presentence reports.— The court shall assure that a report filed pursuant to this section is disclosed to the defendant, the counsel for the defendant, and the attorney for the Government at least ten days prior to the date set for sentencing, unless this minimum period is waived by the defendant. The court shall provide a copy of the presentence report to the attorney for the Government to use in collecting an assessment, criminal fine, forfeiture or restitution imposed.

(Added Pub.L. 98–473, Title II, § 212(a)(2), Oct. 12, 1984, 98 Stat. 1988, and amended Pub.L. 99–646, § 7(a), Nov. 10, 1986, 100 Stat. 3593; Pub.L. 101–647, Title XXXVI, § 3625, Nov. 29, 1990, 104 Stat. 4965).

EDITORIAL NOTES

Use of Certain Technology to Facilitate Criminal Conduct. Pub.L. 104–294, Title V, § 501, Oct. 11, 1996, 110 Stat. 3497, provided that:

"**(a) Information.**—The Administrative Office of the United States courts shall establish policies and procedures for the inclusion in all presentence reports of information that specifically identifies and describes any use of encryption or scrambling technology that would be relevant to an enhancement under section 3C1.1 (dealing with Obstructing or Impeding the Administration of Justice) of the Sentencing Guidelines [set out in this title] or to offense conduct under the Sentencing Guidelines.

(b) Compiling and report.—The United States Sentencing Commission shall—

(1) compile and analyze any information contained in documentation described in subsection (a) relating to the use of encryption or scrambling technology to facilitate or conceal criminal conduct; and

(2) based on the information compiled and analyzed under paragraph (1), annually report to the Congress on the nature and extent of the use of encryption or scrambling technology to facilitate or conceal criminal conduct."

§ 3553. Imposition of a sentence

(a) Factors to be considered in imposing a sentence.—The court shall impose a sentence sufficient, but not greater than necessary, to comply with the purposes set forth in paragraph (2) of this subsection. The court, in determining the particular sentence to be imposed, shall consider—

(1) the nature and circumstances of the offense and the history and characteristics of the defendant;

(2) the need for the sentence imposed—

(A) to reflect the seriousness of the offense, to promote respect for the law, and to provide just punishment for the offense;

(B) to afford adequate deterrence to criminal conduct;

(C) to protect the public from further crimes of the defendant; and

(D) to provide the defendant with needed educational or vocational training, medical care, or other correctional treatment in the most effective manner;

(3) the kinds of sentences available;

(4) the kinds of sentence and the sentencing range established for—

(A) the applicable category of offense committed by the applicable category of defendant as set forth in the guidelines—

(i) issued by the Sentencing Commission pursuant to section 994(a)(1) of title 28, United States Code, subject to any amendments made to such guidelines by act of Congress (regardless of whether such amendments have yet to be incorporated by the Sentencing Commission into amendments issued under section 994(p) of title 28); and

(ii) that, except as provided in section 3742(g), are in effect on the date the defendant is sentenced; or

(B) in the case of a violation of probation or supervised release, the applicable guidelines or policy statements issued by the Sentencing Commission pursuant to section 994(a)(3) of title 28, United States Code, taking into account any amendments made to such guidelines or policy statements by act of Congress (regardless of whether such amendments have yet to be incorporated by the Sentencing Commission into amendments issued under section 994(p) of title 28);

(5) any pertinent policy statement—

(A) issued by the Sentencing Commission pursuant to section 994(a)(2) of title 28, United States Code , subject to any amendments made to such policy statement by act of Congress (regardless of whether such amendments have yet to be incorporated by the Sentencing Commission into amendments issued under section 994(p) of title 28); and

(B) that, except as provided in section 3742(g), is in effect on the date the defendant is sentenced.

(6) the need to avoid unwarranted sentence disparities among defendants with similar records who have been found guilty of similar conduct; and

(7) the need to provide restitution to any victims of the offense.

(b) Application of guidelines in imposing a sentence.—(1) In general.—Except as provided in paragraph (2), the court shall impose a sentence of the kind, and within the range, referred to in subsection (a)(4) unless the court finds that there exists an aggravating or mitigating circumstance of a kind, or to a degree, not adequately taken into consideration by the Sentencing Commission in formulating the guidelines that should result in a sentence different from that described. In determining whether a circumstance was adequately taken into consideration, the court shall consider only the sentencing guidelines, policy statements, and official commentary of the Sentencing Commission. In the absence of an applicable sentencing guideline, the court shall impose an appropriate sentence, having due regard for the purposes set forth in subsection (a)(2). In the absence of an applicable sentencing guideline in the case of an offense other than a petty offense, the court shall also have due regard for the relationship of the sentence imposed to sentences

prescribed by guidelines applicable to similar offenses and offenders, and to the applicable policy statements of the Sentencing Commission.

(2) Child crimes and sexual offenses.—

(A) Sentencing.—In sentencing a defendant convicted of an offense under section 1201 involving a minor victim, an offense under section 1591, or an offense under chapter 71, 109A, 110, or 117, the court shall impose a sentence of the kind, and within the range, referred to in subsection (a)(4) unless—

(i) the court finds that there exists an aggravating circumstance of a kind, or to a degree, not adequately taken into consideration by the Sentencing Commission in formulating the guidelines that should result in a sentence greater than that described;

(ii) the court finds that there exists a mitigating circumstance of a kind or to a degree, that—

(I) has been affirmatively and specifically identified as a permissible ground of downward departure in the sentencing guidelines or policy statements issued under section 994(a) of title 28, taking account of any amendments to such sentencing guidelines or policy statements by Congress;

(II) has not been taken into consideration by the Sentencing Commission in formulating the guidelines; and

(III) should result in a sentence different from that described; or

(iii) the court finds, on motion of the Government, that the defendant has provided substantial assistance in the investigation or prosecution of another person who has committed an offense and that this assistance established a mitigating circumstance of a kind, or to a degree, not adequately taken into consideration by the Sentencing Commission in formulating the guidelines that should result in a sentence lower than that described.

In determining whether a circumstance was adequately taken into consideration, the court shall consider only the sentencing guidelines, policy statements, and official commentary of the Sentencing Commission, together with any amendments thereto by act of Congress. In the absence of an applicable sentencing guideline, the court shall impose an appropriate sentence, having due regard for the purposes set forth in subsection (a)(2). In the absence of an applicable sentencing guideline in the case of an offense other than a petty offense, the court shall also have due regard for the relationship of the sentence imposed to sentences prescribed by guidelines applicable to similar offenses and offenders, and to the applicable policy statements of the Sentencing Commission, together with any amendments to such guidelines or policy statements by act of Congress.

(c) Statement of reasons for imposing a sentence.—The court, at the time of sentencing, shall state in open court the reasons for its imposition of the particular sentence, and, if the sentence—

(1) is of the kind, and within the range, described in subsection (a)(4), and that range exceeds 24 months, the reason for imposing a sentence at a particular point within the range; or

(2) is not of the kind, or is outside the range, described in subsection (a)(4), the specific reason for the imposition of a sentence different from that described, which reasons must also be stated with specificity in a statement of reasons form issued under section 994(w)(1)(B) of title 28, except to the extent that the court relies upon statements received in camera in accordance with Federal Rule of Criminal Procedure 32. In the event that the court relies upon statements received in camera in accordance with Federal Rule of Criminal Procedure 32 the court shall state that such statement were so received and that it relied upon the content of such statements.

If the court does not order restitution, or orders only partial restitution, the court shall include in the statement the reason therefor. The court shall provide a transcription or other appropri-ate public record of the court's statement of reasons, together with the order of judgement and commitment, to the Probation System and to the Sentencing Commission,[1] and, if the sentence includes a term of imprisonment, to the Bureau of Prisons.

(d) Presentence procedure for an order of notice.—Prior to imposing an order of notice pursuant to section 3555, the court shall give notice to the defendant and the Government that it is considering imposing such an order. Upon motion of the defendant or the Government, or on its own motion, the court shall—

(1) permit the defendant and the Government to submit affidavits and written memoranda addressing matters relevant to the imposition of such an order;

(2) afford counsel an opportunity in open court to address orally the appropriateness of the imposition of such an order; and

(3) include in its statement of reasons pursuant to subsection (c) specific reasons underlying its determinations regarding the nature of such an order.

Upon motion of the defendant or the Government, or on its own motion, the court may in its discretion employ any additional procedures that it concludes will not unduly complicate or prolong the sentencing process.

(e) Limited authority to impose a sentence below a statutory minimum.—Upon motion of the Government, the court shall have the authority to impose a sentence below a level established by statute as a minimum sentence so as to reflect a defendant's substantial assistance in the investigation or prosecution of another person who has committed an offense. Such sentence shall be imposed in accordance with the guidelines and policy statements issued by the Sentencing Commission pursuant to section 994 of title 28, United States Code.

(f) Limitation on applicability of statutory minimums in certain cases.—Notwithstanding any other provision of law, in the case of an offense under section 401, 404, or 406 of the Controlled Substances Act (21 U.S.C. 841,

---

[1]   So in original. The second comma probably should not appear.

844, 846) or section 1010 or 1013 of the Controlled Substances Import and Export Act (21 U.S.C. 960, 963), the court shall impose a sentence pursuant to guidelines promulgated by the United States Sentencing Commission under section 994 of title 28 without regard to any statutory minimum sentence, if the court finds at sentencing, after the Government has been afforded the opportunity to make a recommendation, that—

(1) the defendant does not have more than 1 criminal history point, as determined under the sentencing guidelines;

(2) the defendant did not use violence or credible threats of violence or possess a firearm or other dangerous weapon (or induce another participant to do so) in connection with the offense;

(3) the offense did not result in death or serious bodily injury to any person;

(4) the defendant was not an organizer, leader, manager, or supervisor of others in the offense, as determined under the sentencing guidelines and was not engaged in a continuing criminal enterprise, as defined in section 408 of the Controlled Substances Act; and

(5) not later than the time of the sentencing hearing, the defendant has truthfully provided to the Government all information and evidence the defendant has concerning the offense or offenses that were part of the same course of conduct or of a common scheme or plan, but the fact that the defendant has no relevant or useful other information to provide or that the Government is already aware of the information shall not preclude a determination by the court that the defendant has complied with this requirement.

(Added Pub.L. 98–473, Title II, § 212(a)(2), Oct. 12, 1984, 98 Stat. 1989, and amended Pub.L. 99–570, Title I, § 1007(b), Oct. 27, 1986, 100 Stat. 3707–7; Pub.L. 99–646, §§ 8(a), 9(a), 80(a), 81(a), Nov. 10, 1986, 100 Stat. 3593, 3619; Pub.L. 100–182, §§ 3, 16(a), (17), Dec. 7, 1987, 101 Stat. 1266, 1269, 1270; Pub.L. 100–690, Title VII, § 7102, Nov. 18, 1988, 102 Stat. 4416; Pub.L. 103–322, Title VIII, § 80001(a), Title XXVIII, § 280001, Sept. 13, 1994, 108 Stat. 1985, 2095; Pub.L. 104–294, Title VI, § 601(b)(5), (6), (h), Oct. 11, 1996, 110 Stat. 3499, 3500; Pub.L. 107–273, Div. B, Title IV, §4002(a)(8), Nov. 2, 2002, 116 Stat. 1807; Pub.L. 107–273, Div. B, Title IV, § 4002(a)(8), Nov. 2, 2002, 116 Stat. 1807; Pub.L. 108–21, Title IV, § 401(a), (c), (j)(5), Apr. 30, 2003, 117 Stat. 667, 669, 673; Pub.L. 111–174, § 4, May 27, 2010, 124 Stat. 1216.)

EDITORIAL NOTES

Unconstitutionality of Subsection (b). Mandatory aspect of subsection (b) of this section held unconstitutional by *United States v. Booker*, 543 U.S. 220, 125 S. Ct. 738 (2005).

Authority to Lower Sentences Below Statutory Minimum for Old Offenses. Section 24 of Pub.L. 100–182 provided that: "Notwithstanding section 235 of the Comprehensive Crime Control Act of 1984 [section 235 of Pub.L. 98–473, set out as a note under section 3551 of this title]—

(1) section 3553(e) of title 18, United States Code [subsec. (e) of this section];

(2) rule 35(b) of the Federal Rules of Criminal Procedure as amended by section 215(b) of such Act; and

(3) rule 35(b) as in effect before the taking effect of the initial set of guidelines promulgated by the United States Sentencing Commission pursuant to chapter 58 of title 28, United States Code [sections 991 et seq. of Title 28, Judiciary and Judicial Procedure],

shall apply in the case of an offense committed before the taking effect of such guidelines."

§ 3554. Order of criminal forfeiture

The court, in imposing a sentence on a defendant who has been found guilty of an offense described in section 1962 of this title or in title II or III of the Comprehensive Drug Abuse Prevention and Control Act of 1970 shall order, in addition to the sentence that is imposed pursuant to the provisions of section 3551, that the defendant forfeit property to the United States in accordance with the provisions of section 1963 of this title or section 413 of the Comprehensive Drug Abuse and Control Act of 1970.

(Added Pub.L. 98–473, Title II, § 212(a)(2), Oct. 12, 1984, 98 Stat. 1990.)

EDITORIAL NOTES

References in Text. Title II or III of the Comprehensive Drug Abuse Prevention and Control Act of 1970, referred to in text, are Titles II and III of Pub.L. 91–513, Oct. 27, 1970, 84 Stat. 1242, which are principally classified to subchapters I and II of chapter 13 of Title 21, Food and Drugs.

Section 413 of such Act, referred to in text, is section 413 of Pub.L. 91–513, added Pub.L. 98–473, Title II, c. III, part B, § 303, Oct. 12, 1984, 98 Stat. 2044, which is classified to section 853 of Title 21.

§ 3555. Order of notice to victims

The court, in imposing a sentence on a defendant who has been found guilty of an offense involving fraud or other intentionally deceptive practices, may order, in addition to the sentence that is imposed pursuant to the provisions of section 3551, that the defendant give reasonable notice and explanation of the conviction, in such form as the court may approve, to the victims of the offense. The notice may be ordered to be given by mail, by advertising in designated areas or through designated media, or by other appropriate means. In determining whether to require the defendant to give such notice, the court shall consider the factors set forth in section 3553(a) to the extent that they are applicable and shall consider the cost involved in giving the notice as it relates to the loss caused by the offense, and shall not require the defendant to bear the costs of notice in excess of $20,000.

(Added Pub.L. 98–473, Title II, § 212(a)(2), Oct. 12, 1984, 98 Stat. 1991.)

§ 3556. Order of restitution

The court, in imposing a sentence on a defendant who has been found guilty of an offense shall order restitution in accordance with section 3663A, and may order restitution in accordance with section 3663. The procedures under section 3664 shall apply to all orders of restitution under this section.

(Added Pub.L. 98–473, Title II, § 212(a)(2), Oct. 12, 1984, 98 Stat. 1991, and amended Pub.L. 99–646, § 20(b), Nov. 10, 1986, 100 Stat. 3596; Pub.L. 104–132, Title II, § 202, Apr. 24, 1996, 110 Stat. 1227.)

§ 3557. Review of a sentence

The review of a sentence imposed pursuant to section 3551 is governed by the provisions of section 3742.

(Added Pub.L. 98–473, Title II, § 212(a)(2), Oct. 12, 1984, 98 Stat. 1991.)

§ 3558. Implementation of a sentence

The implementation of a sentence imposed pursuant to section 3551 is governed by the provisions of chapter 229.

(Added Pub.L. 98–473, Title II, § 212(a)(2), Oct. 12, 1984, 98 Stat. 1991.)

§ 3559. Sentencing classification of offenses

(a) Classification.—An offense that is not specifically classified by a letter grade in the section defining it, is classified if the maximum term of imprisonment authorized is—

(1) life imprisonment, or if the maximum penalty is death, as a Class A felony;

(2) twenty-five years or more, as a Class B felony;

(3) less than twenty-five years but ten or more years, as a Class C felony;

(4) less than ten years but five or more years, as a Class D felony;

(5) less than five years but more than one year, as a Class E felony;

(6) one year or less but more than six months, as a Class A misdemeanor;

(7) six months or less but more than thirty days, as a Class B misdemeanor;

(8) thirty days or less but more than five days, as a Class C misdemeanor; or

(9) five days or less, or if no imprisonment is authorized, as an infraction.

(b) Effect of classification.—Except as provided in subsection (c), an offense classified under subsection (a) carries all the incidents assigned to the applicable letter designation, except that the maximum term of imprisonment is the term authorized by the law describing the offense.

(c) Imprisonment of certain violent felons.—

(1) Mandatory life imprisonment.— Notwithstanding any other provision of law, a person who is convicted in a court of the United States of a serious violent felony shall be sentenced to life imprisonment if—

(A) the person has been convicted (and those convictions have become final) on separate prior occasions in a court of the United States or of a State of—

(i) 2 or more serious violent felonies; or

(ii) one or more serious violent felonies and one or more serious drug offenses; and

(B) each serious violent felony or serious drug offense used as a basis for sentencing under this subsection, other than the first, was committed after the defendant's conviction of the preceding serious violent felony or serious drug offense.

(2) Definitions.— For purposes of this subsection—

(A) the term "assault with the intent to commit rape" means an offense that has as its elements engaging in physical contact with another person or using or brandishing a weapon against another person with intent to commit aggravated sexual abuse or sexual abuse (as described in sections 2241 and 2242);

(B) the term "arson" means an offense that has as its elements maliciously damaging or destroying any building, inhabited structure, vehicle, vessel, or real property by means of fire or an explosive;

(C) the term "extortion" means an offense that has as its elements the extraction of anything of value from another person by threatening or placing that person in fear of injury to any person or kidnapping of any person;

(D) the term "firearms use" means an offense that has as its elements those described in section 924(c) or 929(a), if the firearm was brandished, discharged, or otherwise used as a weapon and the crime of violence or drug trafficking crime during and relation[1] to which the firearm was used was subject to prosecution in a court of the United States or a court of a State, or both;

(E) the term "kidnapping" means an offense that has as its elements the abduction, restraining, confining, or carrying away of another person by force or threat of force;

(F) the term "serious violent felony" means—

(i) a Federal or State offense, by whatever designation and wherever committed, consisting of murder (as described in section 1111); manslaughter other than involuntary manslaughter (as described in section 1112); assault with intent to commit murder (as described in section 113(a)); assault with intent to commit rape; aggravated sexual abuse and sexual abuse (as described in sections 2241 and 2242); abusive sexual contact (as described in sections 2244 (a)(1) and (a)(2)); kidnapping; aircraft piracy (as described in section 46502 of Title 49); robbery (as described in section 2111, 2113, or 2118); carjacking (as described in section 2119); extortion; arson; firearms use; firearms possession (as described in section 924(c)); or attempt, conspiracy, or solicitation to commit any of the above offenses; and

(ii) any other offense punishable by a maximum term of imprisonment of 10 years or more that has as an element the use, attempted use, or threatened use of physical force against the person of another or that, by its nature, involves a substantial risk that physical force against the person of another may

---

[1] So in original. Probably should be "in relation".

be used in the course of committing the offense;

(G) the term "State" means a State of the United States, the District of Columbia, and a commonwealth, territory, or possession of the United States; and

(H) the term "serious drug offense" means—

(i) an offense that is punishable under section 401(b)(1)(A) or 408 of the Controlled Substances Act (21 U.S.C. 841(b)(1)(A), 848) or section 1010(b)(1)(A) of the Controlled Substances Import and Export Act (21 U.S.C. § 960(b)(1)(A)); or

(ii) an offense under State law that, had the offense been prosecuted in a court of the United States, would have been punishable under section 401(b)(1)(A) or 408 of the Controlled Substances Act (21 U.S.C. 841(b)(1)(A), 848) or section 1010(b)(1)(A) of the Controlled Substances Import and Export Act (21 U.S.C. 960(b)(1)(A)).

(3) Nonqualifying felonies.—

(A) Robbery in certain cases.—Robbery, an attempt, conspiracy, or solicitation to commit robbery; or an offense described in paragraph (2)(F)(ii) shall not serve as a basis for sentencing under this subsection if the defendant establishes by clear and convincing evidence that—

(i) no firearm or other dangerous weapon was used in the offense and no threat of use of a firearm or other dangerous weapon was involved in the offense; and

(ii) the offense did not result in death or serious bodily injury (as defined in section 1365) to any person.

(B) Arson in certain cases.—Arson shall not serve as a basis for sentencing under this subsection if the defendant establishes by clear and convincing evidence that—

(i) the offense posed no threat to human life; and

(ii) the defendant reasonably believed the offense posed no threat to human life.

(4) Information filed by United States Attorney.—The provisions of section 411(a) of the Controlled Substances Act (21 U.S.C. § 851(a)) shall apply to the imposition of sentence under this subsection.

(5) Rule of construction.—This subsection shall not be construed to preclude imposition of the death penalty.

(6) Special provision for Indian country.—No person subject to the criminal jurisdiction of an Indian tribal government shall be subject to this subsection for any offense for which Federal jurisdiction is solely predicated on Indian country (as defined in section 1151) and which occurs within the boundaries of such Indian country unless the governing body of the tribe has elected that this subsection have effect over land and persons subject to the criminal jurisdiction of the tribe.

(7) Resentencing upon overturning of prior conviction.—If the conviction for a serous violent felony or serious drug offense that was a basis for sentencing under this subsection is found, pursuant to any appropriate State or Federal procedure, to be unconstitutional or is vitiated on the explicit basis of innocence, or if the convicted person is pardoned on the explicit basis of innocence, the person serving a sentence imposed under this subsection shall be resentenced to any sentence that was available at the time of the original sentencing.

(d) Death or imprisonment for crimes against children.—

(1) In general.— Subject to paragraph (2) and notwithstanding any other provision of law, a person who is convicted of a federal offense that is a serious violent felony (as defined in subsection (c)) or a violation of section 2422, 2423, or 2251 shall, unless the sentence of death is imposed, be sentenced to imprisonment for life, if—

(A) the victim of the offense has not attained the age of 14 years;

(B) the victim dies as a result of the offense; and

(C) the defendant, in the course of the offense, engages in conduct described in section 3591(a)(2).

(2) Exception.—With respect to a person convicted of a federal offense described in paragraph (1), the court may impose any lesser sentence that is authorized by law to take into account any substantial assistance provided by the defendant in the investigation or prosecution of another person who has committed an offense, in accordance with the federal sentencing guidelines and the policy statements of the federal sentencing commission pursuant to section 994(p) of title 28, or for other good cause.

(e) Mandatory life imprisonment for repeated sex offenses against children.—

(1) In general.—A person who is convicted of a Federal sex offense in which a minor is the victim shall be sentenced to life imprisonment if the person has a prior sex conviction in which a minor was the victim, unless the sentence of death is imposed.

(2) Definitions.—For the purposes of this subsection—

(A) the term "Federal sex offense" means an offense under section 1591 (relating to sex trafficking of children), 2241 (relating to aggravated sexual abuse), 2242 (relating to sexual abuse), 2244(a)(1) (relating to abusive sexual contact), 2245 (relating to sexual abuse resulting in death), 2251 (relating to sexual exploitation of children), 2251A (relating to selling or buying of children), 2422(b) (relating to coercion and enticement of a minor into prostitution), or 2423(a) (relating to transportation of minors);

(B) the term "State sex offense" means an offense under State law that is punishable by more than one year in prison and consists of conduct that would be a Federal sex offense if, to the extent or in the manner specified in the applicable provision of this title—

(i) the offense involved interstate or foreign commerce, or the use of the mails; or

(ii) the conduct occurred in any commonwealth, territory, or possession of the United States, within the special maritime and territorial jurisdiction of the United States, in a Federal prison, on any land or building owned by, leased to, or otherwise used by or under the control of the Government of the United States, or in the Indian country (as defined in section 1151);

(C) the term "prior sex conviction" means a conviction for which the sentence was imposed before the conduct occurred constituting the subsequent Federal sex offense, and which was for a Federal sex offense or a State sex offense;

(D) the term "minor" means an individual who has not attained the age of 17 years; and

(E) the term "state" has the meaning given that term in subsection (c)(2).

(3) Nonqualifying felonies.—An offense described in section 2422(b) or 2423(a) shall not serve as a basis for sentencing under this subsection if the defendant establishes by clear and convincing evidence that—

(A) the sexual act or activity was consensual and not for the purpose of commercial or pecuniary gain;

(B) the sexual act or activity would not be punishable by more than one year in prison under the law of the State in which it occurred; or

(C) no sexual act or activity occurred.

(f) Mandatory Minimum Terms of Imprisonment for Violent Crimes Against Children.—A person who is convicted of a Federal offense that is a crime of violence against the person of an individual who has not attained the age of 18 years shall, unless a greater mandatory minimum sentence of imprisonment is otherwise provided by law and regardless of any maximum term of imprisonment otherwise provided for the offense—

(1) if the crime of violence is murder, be imprisoned for life or for any term of years not less than 30, except that such person shall be punished by death or life imprisonment if the circumstances satisfy any of subparagraphs

(A) through (D) of section 3591(a)(2) of this title;

(2) if the crime of violence is kidnapping (as defined in section 1201) or maiming (as defined in section 114), be imprisoned for life or any term of years not less than 25; and

(3) if the crime of violence results in serious bodily injury (as defined in section 1365), or if a dangerous weapon was used during and in relation to the crime of violence, be imprisoned for life or for any term of years not less than 10.

(g)(1) If a defendant who is convicted of a felony offense (other than offense of which an element is the false registration of a domain name) knowingly falsely registered a domain name and knowingly used that domain name in the course of that offense, the maximum imprisonment otherwise provided by law for that offense shall be doubled or increased by 7 years, whichever is less.

(2) As used in this section—

(A) the term "falsely registers" means registers in a manner that prevents the effective identification of or contact with the person who registers; and

(B) the term "domain name" has the meaning given that term is section 45 of the Act entitled "An Act to provide for the registration and protection of trademarks used in commerce, to carry out the provisions of certain international conventions, and for other purposes" approved July 5, 1946 (commonly referred to as the "Trademark Act of 1946") (15 U.S.C. 1127).

(Added Pub.L. 98–473, Title II, § 212(a)(2), Oct. 12, 1984, 98 Stat. 1991, and amended Pub.L. 100–185, § 5, Dec. 11, 1987, 101 Stat. 1279; Pub.L. 100–690, Title VII, § 7041, Nov. 18, 1988, 102 Stat. 4399); Pub.L. 103–322, Title VII § 70001, Sept. 13, 1994, 108 Stat. 1982; Pub.L. 105–314, Title V, § 501, Oct. 30, 1998, 112 Stat. 2980; Pub.L. 105–386, § 1(b), Nov. 13, 1998, 112 Stat. 3470; Pub.L. 108–21, Title I, § 106(a), Apr. 30, 2003, 117 Stat. 654; Pub.L. 108–482, Title II, § 204(a), Dec. 23, 2004, 118 Stat. 3917; Pub.L. 109–248, Title II, §§ 202, 206(c), July 27, 2006, 120 Stat. 612, 614.)

SUBCHAPTER B–PROBATION

§ 3561. Sentence of probation

(a) In general.—A defendant who has been found guilty of an offense may be sentenced to a term of probation unless—

(1) the offense is a Class A or Class B felony and the defendant is an individual;

(2) the offense is an offense for which probation has been expressly precluded; or

(3) the defendant is sentenced at the same time to a term of imprisonment for the same or a different offense that is not a petty offense.

(b) Domestic violence offenders.—A defendant who has been convicted for the first time of a domestic violence crime shall be sentenced to a term of probation if not sentenced to a term of imprisonment. The term "domestic violence crime" means a crime of violence for which the defendant may be prosecuted in a court of the United States in which the victim or intended victim is the spouse, former spouse, intimate partner, former intimate partner, child, or former child of the defendant, or any other relative of the defendant.

(c) Authorized terms.—The authorized terms of probation are—

(1) for a felony, not less than one nor more than five years;

(2) for a misdemeanor, not more than five years; and

(3) for an infraction, not more than one year.

(Added Pub.L. 98–473, Title II, § 212(a)(2), Oct. 12, 1984, 98 Stat. 1992, and amended Pub.L. 99–646, § 10(a), Nov. 10, 1986, 100 Stat. 3593; Pub.L. 100–182, § 7, Dec. 7, 1987, 101 Stat. 1267; Pub.L. 103–322, Title XXVIII, § 280004, Title XXXII, § 320921(a), Sept. 13, 1994, 108 Stat. 2096, 2130; Pub.L. 104–294, Title VI, § 604(c)(1), Oct. 11, 1996, 110 Stat. 3509.)

§ 3562. Imposition of a sentence of probation

(a) Factors to be considered in imposing a term of probation.—The court, in determining whether to impose a term of probation, and, if a term of probation is to be imposed, in determining the length of the term and the conditions of probation, shall consider the factors set forth in section 3553(a) to the extent that they are applicable.

(b) Effect of finality of judgment.—Notwithstanding the fact that a sentence of probation can subsequently be—

(1) modified or revoked pursuant to the provisions of section 3564 or 3565;

(2) corrected pursuant to the provisions of rule 35 of the Federal Rules of Criminal Procedure and section 3742; or

(3) appealed and modified, if outside the guideline range, pursuant to the provisions of section 3742;

a judgment of conviction that includes such a sentence constitutes a final judgment for all other purposes.

(Added Pub.L. 98–473, Title II, § 212(a)(2), Oct. 12, 1984, 98 Stat. 1992, and amended Pub.L. 101–647, Title XXXV, § 3583, Nov. 29, 1990, 104 Stat. 4930.)

§ 3563. Conditions of probation

(a) Mandatory conditions.—The court shall provide, as an explicit condition of a sentence of probation—

(1) for a felony, a misdemeanor, or an infraction, that the defendant not commit another Federal, State, or local crime during the term of probation;

(2) for a felony, that the defendant also abide by at least one condition set forth in subsection (b)(2) or (b)(12), unless the court has imposed a fine under this chapter, or unless the court finds on the record that extraordinary circumstances exist that would make such a condition plainly unreasonable, in which event the court shall impose one or more of the other conditions set forth under subsection (b);

(3) for a felony, a misdemeanor, or an infraction, that the defendant not unlawfully possess a controlled substance;

(4) for a domestic violence crime as defined in section 3561(b) by a defendant convicted of such an offense for the first time that the defendant attend a public, private, or private non-profit offender rehabilitation program that has been approved by the court, in consultation with a State Coalition Against Domestic Violence or other appropriate experts, if an approved program is readily available within a 50-mile radius of the legal residence of the defendant; and

(5) for a felony, a misdemeanor, or an infraction, that the defendant refrain from any unlawful use of a controlled substance and submit to one drug test within 15 days of release on probation and at least 2 periodic drug tests thereafter (as determined by the court) for use of a controlled substance, but the condition stated in this paragraph may be ameliorated or suspended by the court for any individual defendant if the defendant's presentence report or other reliable sentencing information indicates a low risk of future substance abuse by the defendant;

(6) that the defendant—

(A) make restitution in accordance with sections 2248, 2259, 2264, 2327, 3663, 3663A, and 3664; and

(B) pay the assessment imposed in accordance with section 3013; and

(7) that the defendant will notify the court of any material change in the defendant's economic circumstances that might affect the defendant's ability to pay restitution, fines, or special assessments;

(8) for a person required to register under the Sex Offender Registration and Notification Act, that the person comply with the requirements of that Act; and

(9) that the defendant cooperate in the collection of a DNA sample from the defendant if the collection of such a sample is authorized pursuant to section 3 of the DNA Analysis Backlog Elimination Act of 2000.

If the court has imposed and ordered execution of a fine and placed the defendant on probation, payment of the fine or adherence to the court-established installment schedule shall be a condition of the probation.

(b) Discretionary conditions.—The court may provide, as further conditions of a sentence of probation, to the extent that such conditions are reasonably related to the factors set forth in section 3553(a)(1) and (a)(2) and to the extent that such conditions involve only such deprivations of liberty or property as are reasonably necessary for the purposes indicated in section 3553(a)(2), that the defendant—

(1) support his dependents and meet other family responsibilities;

(2) make restitution to a victim of the offense under section 3556 (but not subject to the limitation of section 3663(a) or 3663A(c)(1)(A));

(3) give to the victims of the offense the notice ordered pursuant to the provisions of section 3555;

(4) work conscientiously at suitable employment or pursue conscientiously a course of study or vocational training that will equip him for suitable employment;

(5) refrain, in the case of an individual, from engaging in a specified occupation, business, or profession bearing a reasonably direct relationship to the conduct constituting the offense, or engage in such a specified occupation, business, or profession only to a stated degree or under stated circumstances;

(6) refrain from frequenting specified kinds of places or from associating unnecessarily with specified persons;

(7) refrain from excessive use of alcohol, or any use of a narcotic drug or other controlled substance, as defined in section 102 of the Controlled Substances Act (21 U.S.C. 802), without a prescription by a licensed medical practitioner;

(8) refrain from possessing a firearm, destructive device, or other dangerous weapon;

(9) undergo available medical, psychiatric, or psychological treatment, including treatment for drug or alcohol dependency, as specified by the court, and remain in a specified institution if required for that purpose;

(10) remain in the custody of the Bureau of Prisons during nights, weekends, or other intervals of time, totaling no more than the lesser of one year or the term of imprisonment authorized for the offense, during the first year of the term of probation or supervised release;

(11) reside at, or participate in the program of, a community corrections facility (including a facility maintained or under contract to the Bureau of Prisons) for all or part of the term of probation;

(12) work in community service as directed by the court;

(13) reside in a specified place or area, or refrain from residing in a specified place or area;

(14) remain within the jurisdiction of the court, unless granted permission to leave by the court or a probation officer;

(15) report to a probation officer as directed by the court or the probation officer;

(16) permit a probation officer to visit him at his home or elsewhere as specified by the court;

(17) answer inquiries by a probation officer and notify the probation officer promptly of any change in address or employment;

(18) notify the probation officer promptly if arrested or questioned by a law enforcement officer;

(19) remain at his place of residence during nonworking hours and, if the court finds it appropriate, that compliance with this condition be monitored by telephonic or electronic signaling devices, except that a condition under this paragraph may be imposed only as an alternative to incarceration;

(20) comply with the terms of any court order or order of an administrative process pursuant to the law of a State, the District of Columbia, or any other possession or territory of the United States, requiring payments by the defendant for the support and maintenance of a child or of a child and the parent with whom the child is living;

(21) be ordered deported by a United States district court, or United States magistrate judge, pursuant to a stipulation entered into by the defendant and the United States under section 238(d)(5) of the Immigration and Nationality Act, except that, in the absence of a stipulation, the United States district court or a United States magistrate judge, may order deportation as a condition of probation, if, after notice and hearing pursuant to such section, the Attorney General demonstrates by clear and convincing evidence that the alien is deportable;

(22) satisfy such other conditions as the court may impose; or

(23) if required to register under the Sex Offender Registration and Notification Act, submit his person, and any property, house, residence, vehicle, papers, computer, other electronic communication or data storage devices or media, and effects to search at any time, with or without a warrant, by any law enforcement or probation officer with reasonable suspicion concerning a violation of a condition of probation or unlawful conduct by the person, and by any probation officer in the lawful discharge of the officer's supervision functions.

(c) Modifications of conditions.—The court may modify, reduce, or enlarge the conditions of a sentence of probation at any time prior to the expiration or termination of the term of probation, pursuant to the provisions of the Federal Rules of Criminal Procedure relating to the modification of probation and the provisions applicable to the initial setting of the conditions of probation.

(d) Written statement of conditions.— The court shall direct that the probation officer provide the defendant with a written statement that sets forth all the conditions to which the sentence is subject, and that is sufficiently clear and specific to serve as a guide for the defendant's conduct and for such supervision as is required.

(e) Results of Drug Testing.—The results of a drug test administered in accordance with subsection (a)(5) shall be subject to confirmation only if the results are positive, the defendant is subject to possible imprisonment for such failure, and either the defendant denies the accuracy of such test or there is some other reason to question the results of the test. A defendant who tests positive may be detained pending verification of a positive drug test result. A drug test confirmation shall be a urine drug test confirmed using gas chromatography/mass spectrometry techniques or such test as the Director of the Administrative Office of the United States Courts after consultation with the Secretary of Health and Human Services may determine to be of equivalent accuracy. The court shall consider whether the availability of appropriate substance abuse treatment programs, or an individual's current or past participation in such programs, warrants an exception in accordance with United States Sentencing Commission guidelines from the rule of section 3565(b), when considering any action against a defendant who fails a drug test administered in accordance with subsection (a)(5).

(Added Pub.L. 98–473, Title II, § 212(a)(2), Oct. 12, 1984, 98 Stat. 1993, and amended Pub.L. 99–646, §§ 11(a), 12(a), Nov. 10, 1986, 100 Stat. 3594; Pub.L. 100–182, §§ 10, 18, Dec. 7, 1987, 101 Stat. 1267, 1270; Pub.L. 100–690, Title VII, §§ 7086, 7110, 7303(a)(1), 7305(a), Nov. 18, 1988, 102 Stat. 4408, 4419, 4464, 4465; Pub.L. 101–647, Title XXXV, § 3584, Nov. 29, 1990, 104 Stat. 4430; Pub.L. 102–521, § 3, Oct. 25, 1992, 106 Stat. 3404; Pub.L. 103–322, Title II, § 20414(b), Title XXVIII, § 280002, Title XXXII, § 320921(b), Sept. 13, 1994, 108 Stat. 1830, 2096, 2130; Pub.L. 104–132, Title II, § 203, Apr. 24, 1996, 110 Stat. 1227; Pub.L. 104–208, Div. C, Title III, §§ 308(g)(10)(E), 374(b), Sept 30, 1996, 110 Stat. 3009–625, 3009–647; Pub.L. 104–294, Title VI, § 601(k), Oct. 11, 1996, 110 Stat. 3501; Pub.L. 105–119, Title I, § 115(a)(8)(B), Nov. 26, 1997, 111 Stat. 2465; Pub.L. 106–546, § 7 (a), Dec. 19, 2000, 114 Stat. 2734; Pub. L. 107–273, Div. B, Title IV, § 4002(c)(1), (e)(12), Nov. 2, 2002, 116 Stat. 1802, 1811; Pub.L. 109–248, Title I, § 141(d), Title II, § 210(a), July 27, 2006, 120 Stat. 603, 615; Pub.L. 110–406, § 14(a), (c), Oct. 13, 2008, 122 Stat. 4294.)

§ 3564. Running of a term of probation

(a) Commencement.—A term of probation commences on the day that the sentence of probation is imposed, unless otherwise ordered by the court.

(b) Concurrence with other sentences.— Multiple terms of probation, whether imposed at the same time or at different times, run concurrently with each other. A term of probation runs concurrently with any Federal, State, or local term of probation, supervised release, or parole for another offense to which the defendant is subject or becomes subject during the term of probation. A term of probation does not run while the defendant is imprisoned in connection with a conviction for a Federal, State, or local crime unless the imprisonment is for a period of less than thirty consecutive days.

(c) Early termination.—The court, after considering the factors set forth in section 3553(a) to the extent that they are applicable, may, pursuant to the provisions of the Federal Rules of Criminal Procedure relating to the modification of probation, terminate a term of probation previously ordered and discharge the defendant at any time in the case of a misdemeanor or an infraction or at any time after the expiration of one year of probation in the case of a felony, if it is satisfied that such action is warranted by the conduct of the defendant and the interest of justice.

(d) Extension.—The court may, after a hearing, extend a term of probation, if less than the maximum authorized term was previously imposed, at any time prior to the expiration or termination of the term of probation, pursuant to the provisions applicable to the initial setting of the term of probation.

(e) Subject to revocation.—A sentence of probation remains conditional and subject to revocation until its expiration or termination.

(Added Pub.L. 98–473, Title II, § 212(a)(2), Oct. 12, 1984, 98 Stat. 1994, and amended Pub.L. 99–646, § 13(a), Nov. 10, 1986, 100 Stat. 3594; Pub.L. 100–182, § 11, Dec. 7, 1987, 101 Stat. 1268.)

§ 3565. Revocation of probation

(a) Continuation or revocation.—If the defendant violates a condition of probation at any time prior to the expiration or termination of the term of probation, the court may, after a hearing pursuant to Rule 32.1 of the Federal Rules of Criminal Procedure, and after considering the factors set forth in section 3553(a) to the extent that they are applicable—

(1) continue him on probation, with or without extending the term or modifying or enlarging the conditions; or

(2) revoke the sentence of probation and resentence the defendant under subchapter A.

(b) Mandatory revocation for possession of controlled substance or firearm or refusal to comply with drug testing.—If the defendant—

(1) possesses a controlled substance in violation of the condition set forth in section 3563(a)(3);

(2) possesses a firearm, as such term is defined in section 921 of this title, in violation of Federal law, or otherwise violates a condition of probation prohibiting the defendant from possessing a firearm;

(3) refuses to comply with drug testing, thereby violating the condition imposed by section 3563(a)(4); or

(4) as a part of drug testing, tests positive for illegal controlled substances more than 3 times over the course of 1 year;

the court shall revoke the sentence of probation and resentence the defendant under subchapter A to a sentence that includes a term of imprisonment.

(c) Delayed revocation.—The power of the court to revoke a sentence of probation for violation of a condition of probation, and to impose another sentence, extends beyond the expiration of the term of probation for any period reasonably necessary for the adjudication of matters arising before its expiration if, prior to its expiration, a warrant or summons has been issued on the basis of an allegation of such a violation.

(Added Pub.L. 98–473, Title II, § 212(a)(2), Oct. 12, 1984, 98 Stat. 1995, amended Pub.L. 100–690, Title VI, § 6214, Title VII, § 7303(a)(2), Nov. 18, 1988, 102 Stat. 4361, 4464; Pub.L. 101–647, Title XXXV, § 3585, Nov. 29, 1990, 104 Stat. 4930; Pub.L. 103–322, Title XI § 110506, Sept. 13, 1994, 108 Stat. 2017; Pub.L. 107–273, Div. B, Title II, § 2103(a), Nov. 2, 2002, 116 Stat. 1793.)

§ 3566. Implementation of a sentence of probation

The implementation of a sentence of probation is governed by the provisions of subchapter A of chapter 229.

(Added Pub.L. 98–473, Title II, § 212(a)(2), Oct. 12, 1984, 98 Stat. 1995.)

SUBCHAPTER C – FINES

Section
3571. Sentence of fine.
3572. Imposition of a sentence of fine and related matters.
3573. Petition of the Government for modification or remission.
3574. Implementation of a sentence of fine.

§ 3571. Sentence of fine

(a) In general.—A defendant who has been found guilty of an offense may be sentenced to pay a fine.

(b) Fines for individuals.—Except as provided in subsection (e) of this section, an individual who has been found guilty of an offense may be fined not more than the greatest of—

(1) the amount specified in the law setting forth the offense;

(2) the applicable amount under subsection (d) of this section;

(3) for a felony, not more than $250,000;

(4) for a misdemeanor resulting in death, not more than $250,000;

(5) for a Class A misdemeanor that does not result in death, not more than $100,000;

(6) for a Class B or C misdemeanor that does not result in death, not more than $5,000; or

(7) for an infraction, not more than $5,000.

(c) Fines for organizations.—Except as provided in subsection (e) of this section, an organization that has been found guilty of an offense may be fined not more than the greatest of—

(1) the amount specified in the law setting forth the offense;

(2) the applicable amount under subsection (d) of this section;

(3) for a felony, not more than $500,000;

(4) for a misdemeanor resulting in death, not more than $500,000;

(5) for a Class A misdemeanor that does not result in death, not more than $200,000;

(6) for a Class B or C misdemeanor that does not result in death, not more than $10,000; and

(7) for an infraction, not more than $10,000.

(d) Alternative fine based on gain or loss.—If any person derives pecuniary gain from the offense, or if the offense results in pecuniary loss to a person other than the defendant, the defendant may be fined not more than the greater of twice the gross gain or twice the gross loss, unless imposition of a fine under this subsection would unduly complicate or prolong the sentencing process.

(e) Special rule for lower fine specified in substantive provision.—If a law setting forth an offense specifies no fine or a fine that is lower than the fine otherwise applicable under this section and such law, by specific reference, exempts the offense from the applicability of the fine otherwise applicable under this section, the defendant may not be fined more than the amount specified in the law setting forth the offense.

(Added Pub.L. 98–473, Title II, § 212(a)(2), Oct. 12, 1984, 98 Stat. 1995, and amended Pub.L. 100–185, § 6, Dec. 11, 1987, 101 Stat. 1280.)

§ 3572. Imposition of a sentence of fine and related matters

(a) Factors to be considered.—In determining whether to impose a fine, and the amount, time for payment, and method of payment of a fine, the court shall consider, in addition to the factors set forth in section 3553(a)—

(1) the defendant's income, earning capacity, and financial resources;

(2) the burden that the fine will impose upon the defendant, any person who is financially dependent on the defendant, or any other person (including a government) that would be responsible for the welfare of any person financially dependent on the defendant, relative to the burden that alternative punishments would impose;

(3) any pecuniary loss inflicted upon others as a result of the offense;

(4) whether restitution is ordered or made and the amount of such restitution;

(5) the need to deprive the defendant of illegally obtained gains from the offense;

(6) the expected costs to the government of any imprisonment, supervised release, or probation component of the sentence;

(7) whether the defendant can pass on to consumers or other persons the expense of the fine; and

(8) if the defendant is an organization, the size of the organization and any measure taken by the organization to discipline any officer, director, employee, or agent of the organization responsible for the offense and to prevent a recurrence of such an offense.

(b) Fine not to impair ability to make restitution.—If, as a result of a conviction, the defendant has the obligation to make restitution to a victim of the offense, other than the United States, the court shall impose a fine or other monetary penalty only to the extent that such fine or penalty will not impair the ability of the defendant to make restitution.

(c) Effect of finality of judgment.—Notwithstanding the fact that a sentence to pay a fine can subsequently be—

(1) modified or remitted under section 3573;

(2) corrected under rule 35 of the Federal Rules of Criminal Procedure and section 3742; or

(3) appealed and modified under section 3742;

a judgment that includes such a sentence is a final judgment for all other purposes.

(d) Time, method of payment, and related items.—(1) A person sentenced to pay a fine or other monetary penalty, including restitution, shall make such payment immediately, unless, in the interest of justice, the court provides for payment on a date certain or in installments. If the court provides for payment in installments, the installments shall be in equal monthly payments over the period provided by the court, unless the court establishes another schedule.

(2) If the judgment, or, in the case of a restitution order, the order, permits other than immediate payment, the length of time over which scheduled payments will be made shall be set by the court, but shall be the shortest time in which full payment can reasonably be made.

(3) A judgment for a fine which permits payments in installments shall include a requirement that the defendant will notify the court of any material change in the defendant's economic circumstances that might affect the defendant's ability to pay the fine. Upon receipt of such notice the court may, on its own motion or the motion of any party, adjust the payment schedule, or require immediate payment in full, as the interests of justice require.

(e) Alternative sentence precluded.—At the time a defendant is sentenced to pay a fine, the court may not impose an alternative sentence to be carried out if the fine is not paid.

(f) Responsibility for payment of monetary obligation relating to organization.—If a sentence includes a fine, special assessment, restitution or other monetary obligation (including interest) with respect to an organization, each individual authorized to make disbursements for the organization has a duty to pay the obligation from assets of the organization. If such an obligation is imposed on a director, officer, shareholder, employee, or agent of an organization, payments may not be made, directly or indirectly, from assets of the organization, unless the court finds that such payment is expressly permissible under applicable State law.

(g) Security for stayed fine.—If a sentence imposing a fine is stayed, the court shall, absent exceptional circumstances (as determined by the court)—

(1) require the defendant to deposit, in the registry of the district court, any amount of the fine that is due;

(2) require the defendant to provide a bond or other security to ensure payment of the fine; or

(3) restrain the defendant from transferring or dissipating assets.

(h) Delinquency.—A fine or payment of restitution is delinquent if a payment is more than 30 days late.

(i) Default.—A fine or payment of restitution is in default if a payment is delinquent for more than 90 days. Notwithstanding any installment schedule, when a fine or payment of restitution is in default, the entire amount of the fine or restitution is due within 30 days after notification of the default, subject to the provisions of section 3613A.

(Added Pub.L. 98–473, Title II, § 212(a)(2), Oct. 12, 1984, 98 Stat. 1995, and amended Pub.L. 100–185, § 7, Dec. 11, 1987, 101 Stat. 1280; Pub.L. 101–647, Title XXXV, § 3587, Nov. 29, 1990, 104 Stat. 4930; Pub.L. 103–322, Title II, § 20403(a), Sept. 13, 1994, 108 Stat. 1825; Pub.L. 104–132, Title II, § 207(b), Apr. 24, 1996, 110 Stat. 1236.)

§ 3573. Petition of the Government for modification or remission

Upon petition of the Government showing that reasonable efforts to collect a fine or assessment are not likely to be effective, the court may, in the interest of justice—

(1) remit all or part of the unpaid portion of the fine or special assessment, including interest and penalties;

(2) defer payment of the fine or special assessment to a date certain or pursuant to an installment schedule; or

(3) extend a date certain or an installment schedule previously ordered.

A petition under this subsection shall be filed in the court in which sentence was originally imposed, unless the court transfers jurisdiction to another court. This section shall apply to all fines and assessments irrespective of the date of imposition.

(Added Pub.L. 98–473, Title II, § 212(a)(2), Oct. 12, 1984, 98 Stat. 1997, and amended Pub.L. 100–185, § 8(a), Dec. 11, 1987, 101 Stat. 1282; Pub.L. 100–690, Title VII, § 7082(a), Nov. 18, 1988, 102 Stat. 4407.)

§ 3574. Implementation of a sentence of fine

The implementation of a sentence to pay a fine is governed by the provisions of subchapter B of chapter 229.

(Added Pub.L. 98–473, Title II, § 212(a)(2), Oct. 12, 1984, 98 Stat. 1997.)

SUBCHAPTER D–IMPRISONMENT

§ 3581. Sentence of imprisonment

(a) In general.—A defendant who has been found guilty of an offense may be sentenced to a term of imprisonment.

(b) Authorized terms.—The authorized terms of imprisonment are—

(1) for a Class A felony, the duration of the defendant's life or any period of time;

(2) for a Class B felony, not more than twenty-five years;

(3) for a Class C felony, not more than twelve years;

(4) for a Class D felony, not more than six years;

(5) for a Class E felony, not more than three years;

(6) for a Class A misdemeanor, not more than one year;

(7) for a Class B misdemeanor, not more than six months;

(8) for a Class C misdemeanor, not more than thirty days; and

(9) for an infraction, not more than five days.

(Added Pub.L. 98–473, Title II, § 212(a)(2), Oct. 12, 1984, 98 Stat. 1998.)

§ 3582. Imposition of a sentence of imprisonment

(a) Factors to be considered in imposing a term of imprisonment.—The court, in determining whether to impose a term of imprisonment, and, if a term of imprisonment is to be imposed, in determining the length of the term, shall consider the factors set forth in section 3553(a) to the extent that they are applicable, recognizing that imprisonment is not an appropriate means of promoting correction and rehabilitation. In determining whether to make a recommendation concerning the type of prison facility appropriate for the defendant, the court shall consider any pertinent policy statements issued by the Sentencing Commission pursuant to 28 U.S.C. 994(a)(2).

(b) Effect of finality of judgment.—Notwithstanding the fact that a sentence to imprisonment can subsequently be—

(1) modified pursuant to the provisions of subsection (c);

(2) corrected pursuant to the provisions of rule 35 of the Federal Rules of Criminal Procedure and section 3742; or

(3) appealed and modified, if outside the guideline range, pursuant to the provisions of section 3742;

a judgment of conviction that includes such a sentence constitutes a final judgment for all other purposes.

(c) Modification of an imposed term of imprisonment.—The court may not modify a term of imprisonment once it has been imposed except that—

(1) in any case—

(A) the court, upon motion of the Director of the Bureau of Prisons, may reduce the term of imprisonment (and may impose a term of probation or supervised release with or without conditions that does not exceed the unserved portion of the original term of imprisonment), after considering the factors set forth in section 3553(a) to the extent that they are applicable, if it finds that—

(i) extraordinary and compelling reasons warrant such a reduction; or

(ii) the defendant is at least 70 years of age, has served at least 30 year in prison, pursuant to a sentence imposed under section 3559(c), for the offense or offenses for which the defendant is currently imprisoned, and a determination has been made by the Director of the Bureau of Prisons that the defendant is not a danger to the safety of any other person or the community, as provided under section 3142(g);

and that such a reduction is consistent with applicable policy statements issued by the Sentencing Commission; and

(B) the court may modify an imposed term of imprisonment to the extent otherwise expressly permitted by statute or by Rule 35 of the Federal Rules of Criminal Procedure; and

(2) in the case of a defendant who has been sentenced to a term of imprisonment based on a sentencing range that has subsequently been lowered by the Sentencing Commission pursuant to 28 U.S.C. 994(o), upon motion of the defendant or the Director of the Bureau of Prisons, or on its own motion, the court may reduce the term of imprisonment, after considering the factors set forth in section 3553(a) to the extent that they are applicable, if such a reduction is consistent with applicable policy statements issued by the Sentencing Commission.

(d) Inclusion of an order to limit criminal association of organized crime and drug offenders.—The court, in imposing a sentence to a term of imprisonment upon a defendant convicted of a felony set forth in chapter 95 (racketeering) or 96 (racketeer influenced and corrupt organizations) of this title or in the Comprehensive Drug Abuse Prevention and Control Act of 1970 (21 U.S.C. 801 et seq.), or at any time thereafter upon motion by the Director of the Bureau of Prisons or a United States attorney, may include as a part of the sentence an order that requires that the defendant not associate or communicate with a specified person, other than his attorney, upon a showing of probable cause to believe that association or communication with such person is for the purpose of enabling the defendant to control, manage, direct, finance, or otherwise participate in an illegal enterprise.

(Added Pub.L. 98–473, Title II, § 212(a)(2), Oct. 12, 1984, 98 Stat. 1998, amended Pub.L. 100–690, Title VII, § 7107, Nov. 18, 1988, 102 Stat. 4418; Pub.L. 101–647, Title XXXV, § 3588, Nov. 29, 1990, 104 Stat. 4930; Pub.L. 103–322, Title VII, § 70002, Sept. 13, 1994, 108 Stat. 1984; Pub.L. 104–294, Title VI, § 604(b)(3), Oct. 11, 1996, 110 Stat. 3506; Pub.L. 107–273, Div. B, Title III, § 3006, Nov. 2, 2002, 116 Stat. 1806.)

§ 3583. Inclusion of a term of supervised release after imprisonment

(a) In general.—The court, in imposing a sentence to a term of imprisonment for a felony or a misdemeanor, may include as a part of the sentence a requirement that the defendant be placed on a term of supervised release after imprisonment, except that the court shall include as a part of the sentence a requirement that the defendant be placed on a term of supervised release if such a term is required by statute or if the defendant has been convicted for the first time of a domestic violence crime as defined in section 3561(b).

(b) Authorized terms of supervised release.—Except as otherwise provided, the authorized terms of supervised release are—

    (1) for a Class A or Class B felony, not more than five years;

    (2) for a Class C or Class D felony, not more than three years; and

    (3) for a Class E felony, or for a misdemeanor (other than a petty offense), not more than one year.

(c) Factors to be considered in including a term of supervised release.—The court, in determining whether to include a term of supervised release, and, if a term of supervised release is to be included, in determining the length of the term and the conditions of supervised release, shall consider the factors set forth in section 3553(a)(1), (a)(2)(B), (a)(2)(C), (a)(2)(D), (a)(4), (a)(5), (a)(6), and (a)(7).

(d) Conditions of supervised release.—The court shall order, as an explicit condition of supervised release, that the defendant not commit another Federal, State, or local crime during the term of supervision and that the defendant not unlawfully possess a controlled substance. The court shall order as an explicit condition of supervised release for a defendant convicted for the first time of a domestic violence crime as defined in section 3561(b) that the defendant attend a public, private, or private nonprofit offender rehabilitation program that has been approved by the court, in consultation with a State Coalition Against Domestic Violence or other appropriate experts, if an approved program is readily available within a 50-mile radius of the legal residence of the defendant. The court shall order, as an explicit condition of supervised release for a person required to register under the Sex Offender Registration and Notification Act, that the person comply with the requirements of that Act. The court shall order, as an explicit condition of supervised release, that the defendant cooperate in the collection of a DNA sample from the defendant, if the collection of such a sample is authorized pursuant to section 3 of the DNA Analysis Backlog Elimination Act of 2000. The court shall also order, as an explicit condition of supervised release, that the defendant refrain from any unlawful use of a controlled substance and submit to a drug test within 15 days of release on supervised release and at least 2 periodic drug tests thereafter (as determined by the court) for use of a controlled substance. The condition stated in the preceding sentence may be ameliorated or suspended by the court as provided in section 3563(a)(4). The results of a drug test administered in accordance with the preceding subsection shall be subject to confirmation only if the results are positive, the defendant is subject to possible imprisonment for such failure, and either the defendant denies the accuracy of such test or there is some other reason to question the results of the test. A drug test confirmation shall be a urine drug test confirmed using gas chromatography/mass spectrometry techniques or such test as the Director of the Administrative Office of the United States Courts after consultation with the Secretary of Health and Human Services may determine to be of equivalent accuracy. The court shall consider whether the availability of appropriate substance abuse treatment programs, or an individual's current or past participation in such programs, warrants an exception in accordance with United States Sentencing Commission guidelines from the rule of section 3583(g) when considering any action against a defendant who fails a drug test. The court may order, as a further condition of supervised release, to the extent that such condition—

(1) is reasonably related to the factors set forth in section 3553(a)(1), (a)(2)(B), (a)(2)(C), and (a)(2)(D);

(2) involves no greater deprivation of liberty than is reasonably necessary for the purposes set forth in section 3553(a)(2)(B), (a)(2)(C), and (a)(2)(D); and

(3) is consistent with any pertinent policy statements issued by the Sentencing Commission pursuant to 28 U.S.C. 994(a);

any condition set forth as a discretionary condition of probation in section 3563(b) and any other condition it considers to be appropriate, provided, however that a condition set forth in subsection 3563(b)(10) shall be imposed only for a violation of a condition of supervised release in accordance with section 3583(e)(2) and only when facilities are available. If an alien defendant is subject to deportation, the court may provide, as a condition of supervised release, that he be deported and remain outside the United States, and may order that he be delivered to a duly authorized immigration official for such deportation. The court may order, as an explicit condition of supervised release for a person who is a felon and required to register under the Sex Offender Registration and Notification Act, that the person submit his person, and any property, house, residence, vehicle, papers, computer, other electronic communications or data storage devices or media, and effects to search at any time, with or without a warrant, by any law enforcement or probation officer with reasonable suspicion concerning a violation of a condition of supervised release or unlawful conduct by the person, and by any probation officer in the lawful discharge of the officer's supervision functions.

(e) Modification of conditions or revocation.—The court may, after considering the factors set forth in section 3553(a)(1), (a)(2)(B), (a)(2)(C), (a)(2)(D), (a)(4), (a)(5), (a)(6), and (a)(7)—

(1) terminate a term of supervised release and discharge the defendant released[1] at any time after the expiration of one year of supervised release, pursuant to the provisions of the Federal Rules of Criminal Procedure relating to the modification of probation, if it is satisfied that such action is warranted by the conduct of the defendant released[1] and the interest of justice;

(2) extend a term of supervised release if less than the maximum authorized term was previously imposed, and may modify, reduce, or enlarge the conditions of supervised release, at any time prior to the expiration or termination of the term of supervised release, pursuant to the provisions of the Federal Rules of Criminal Procedure relating to the modification of probation and the provisions applicable to the initial setting of the terms and conditions of post-release supervision;

(3) revoke a term of supervised release, and require the defendant to serve in prison all or part of the term of supervised release authorized by statute for the offense that resulted in such term of supervised release without credit for time previously served on postrelease supervision, if the court, pursuant to the Federal Rules of Criminal Procedure applicable to revocation of probation or supervised release, finds by a preponderance of the evidence that the defendant violated a condition of supervised release, except that a defendant whose term is revoked under this paragraph may not be required to serve on any such revocation more than 5 years in prison if the offense that resulted in the term of supervised release is a class A felony, more

---

[1] So in original. Probably "defendant released" should be "defendant".

than 3 years in prison if such offense is a class B felony, more than 2 years in prison if such offense is a class C or D felony, or more than one year in any other case; or

(4) order the defendant to remain at his place of residence during nonworking hours and, if the court so directs, to have compliance monitored by telephone or electronic signaling devices, except that an order under this paragraph may be imposed only as an alternative to incarceration.

(f) Written statement of conditions.—The court shall direct that the probation officer provide the defendant with a written statement that sets forth all the conditions to which the term of supervised release is subject, and that is sufficiently clear and specific to serve as a guide for the defendant's conduct and for such supervision as is required.

(g) Mandatory revocation for possession of controlled substance or firearm or for refusal to comply with drug testing.—If the defendant—

(1) possesses a controlled substance in violation of the condition set forth in subsection (d);

(2) possesses a firearm, as such term is defined in section 921 of this title, in violation of Federal law, or otherwise violates a condition of supervised release prohibiting the defendant from possessing a firearm;

(3) refuses to comply with drug testing imposed as a condition of supervised release; or

(4) as a part of drug testing, tests positive for illegal controlled substances more than 3 times over the course of 1 year;

the court shall revoke the term of supervised release and require the defendant to serve a term of imprisonment not to exceed the maximum term of imprisonment authorized under subsection (e)(3).

(h) Supervised release following revocation.—When a term of supervise release is revoked and the defendant is required to serve a term of imprisonment, the court may include a requirement that the defendant be placed on a term of supervised release after imprisonment. The length of such a term of supervised release shall not exceed the term of supervised release

authorized by statute for the offense that resulted in the original term of supervised release, less any term of imprisonment that was imposed upon revocation of supervised release.

(i) Delayed revocation.—The power of the court to revoke a term of supervised release for violation for a condition of supervised release, and to order the defendant to serve a term of imprisonment and, subject to the limitations in subsection (h), a further term of supervised release, extends beyond the expiration of the term of supervised release for any period reasonably necessary for the adjudication of matters arising before its expiration if, before its expiration, a warrant or summons has been issued on the basis of an allegation of such a violation.

(j) Supervised Release Terms for Terrorism Predicates.—Notwithstanding subsection (b), the authorized term of supervised release for any offense listed in section 2332b(g)(5)(B), is any term of years or life.

(k) Notwithstanding subsection (b), the authorized term of supervised release for any offense under section 1201 involving a minor victim, and for any offense under section 1591, 1594(c), 2241, 2242, 2243, 2244, 2245, 2250, 2251, 2251A, 2252, 2252A, 2260, 2421, 2422, 2423, or 2425, is any term of years not less than 5, or life. If a defendant required to register under the Sex Offender Registration and Notification Act commits any criminal offense under chapter 109A, 110, or 117, or section 1201 or 1591, for which imprisonment for a term longer than 1 year can be imposed, the court shall revoke the term of supervised release and require the defendant to serve a term of imprisonment under subsection (e)(3) without regard to the exception contained therein. Such term shall be not less than 5 years.

(Added Pub.L. 98–473, Title II, § 212(a)(2), Oct. 12, 1984, 98 Stat. 1999, and amended Pub.L. 99–570, Title I, § 1006(a), Oct. 27, 1986, 100 Stat. 3207–6, 3207–7; Pub.L. 99–646, § 14(a), Nov. 10, 1986, 100 Stat. 3594; Pub.L. 100–182, §§ 8, 9, 12, 25, Dec. 7, 1987, 101 Stat. 1267, 1268, 1272; Pub.L. 100–690, Title VII, §§ 7108, 7303(b), 7305(b), Nov. 18, 1988, 102 Stat. 4418, 4419, 4464–4466; Pub.L. 101–647, Title XXXV, § 3589, Nov. 29, 1990, 104 Stat. 4930; Pub.L. 103–322, Title II, § 20414(c), Title XI, § 110505, Title XXXII, § 320921(c), Sept. 13, 1994, 108 Stat. 1831, 2016, 2130; Pub.L. 105–119, Title I, § 115(a)(8)(B), Nov. 26, 1997, 111 Stat. 2465; Pub.L. 106–546, § 7(b), Dec. 19, 2000, 114

Stat. 2734; Pub.L. 107–56, Title VIII, § 812, Oct. 26, 2001, 115 Stat. 382; Pub.L. 107–273, Div. B, Title II, § 2103(b), Title III, § 3007, Nov. 2, 2002, 116 Stat. 1793, 1806; Pub.L. 108–21, Title I, § 101, Apr. 30, 2003, 117 Stat. 651; Pub.L. 109–177, Title II, § 212, Mar. 9, 2006, 120 Stat. 230; Pub.L. 109–248, Title I, § 141(e), Title II, § 201(b), July 27, 2006, 120 Stat. 603, 615; Pub.L. 110–406, § 14(b), Oct. 13, 2008, 122 Stat. 4294; Pub.L. 114–22, title I, §114(d), May 29, 2015, 129 Stat. 242.)

EDITORIAL NOTES

Codification. Amendment by section 7108(a)(2) of Pub.L. 100–690 to subsec. (d)(2), which directed that "(a)(2)(C)," be inserted after "(a)(2)(B),", was executed by inserting "(a)(2)(C)," after "(a)(2)(B)" since no comma appeared after "(a)(2)(B)".

Amendment by section 7305(b)(2) of Pub.L. 100–690 to subsec. (e) which struck out "or" at the end of par. (3), struck out the period at the end of par. (4) and inserted "; or", and added par. (5) could not be completely executed in view of prior amendment to such provision by section 7108(b) of Pub.L. 100–690 which redesignated former par. (4) as (3) thereby resulting in no par. (4) amended.

Amendment by section 14(a)(1) of Pub.L. 99–646 to subsec. (e) catchline duplicates amendment to such subsection catchline made by Pub.L. 99–570, § 1006(a)(3)(A).

§ 3584. Multiple sentences of imprisonment

(a) Imposition of concurrent or consecutive terms.—If multiple terms of imprisonment are imposed on a defendant at the same time, or if a term of imprisonment is imposed on a defendant who is already subject to an undischarged term of imprisonment, the terms may run concurrently or consecutively, except that the terms may not run consecutively for an attempt and for another offense that was the sole objective of the attempt. Multiple terms of imprisonment imposed at the same time run concurrently unless the court orders or the statute mandates that the terms are to run consecutively. Multiple terms of imprisonment imposed at different times run consecutively unless the court orders that the terms are to run concurrently.

(b) Factors to be considered in imposing concurrent or consecutive terms.—The court, in determining whether the terms imposed are to be ordered to run concurrently or consecutively, shall consider, as to each offense for which a term of imprisonment is being imposed, the factors set forth in section 3553(a).

(c) Treatment of multiple sentence as an aggregate.—Multiple terms of imprisonment ordered to run consecutively or concurrently shall be treated for administrative purposes as a single, aggregate term of imprisonment.

(Added Pub.L. 98–473, Title II, § 212(a)(2), Oct. 12, 1984, 98 Stat. 2000.)

§ 3585. Calculation of a term of imprisonment

(a) Commencement of sentence.—A sentence to a term of imprisonment commences on the date the defendant is received in custody awaiting transportation to, or arrives voluntarily to commence service of sentence at, the official detention facility at which the sentence is to be served.

(b) Credit for prior custody.—A defendant shall be given credit toward the service of a term of imprisonment for any time he has spent in official detention prior to the date the sentence commences—

    (1) as a result of the offense for which the sentence was imposed; or

    (2) as a result of any other charge for which the defendant was arrested after the commission of the offense for which the sentence was imposed;

that has not been credited against another sentence.

(Added Pub.L. 98–473, Title II, § 212(a)(2), Oct. 12, 1984, 98 Stat. 2001.)

§ 3586. Implementation of a sentence of imprisonment

The implementation of a sentence of imprisonment is governed by the provisions of subchapter C of chapter 229 and, if the sentence includes a term of supervised release, by the provisions of subchapter A of chapter 229.

(Added Pub.L. 98–473, Title II, § 212(a)(2), Oct. 12, 1984, 98 Stat. 2001.)

* * *

CHAPTER 229—POSTSENTENCE ADMINISTRATION

* * *

SUBCHAPTER C –IMPRISONMENT

* * *

§ 3621. Imprisonment of a convicted person

(a) Commitment to custody of Bureau of Prisons.—A person who has been sentenced to a term of imprisonment pursuant to the provisions of subchapter D of chapter 227 shall be committed to the custody of the Bureau of Prisons until the expiration of the term imposed, or until earlier released for satisfactory behavior pursuant to the provisions of section 3624.

(b) Place of imprisonment.—The Bureau of Prisons shall designate the place of the prisoner's imprisonment. The Bureau may designate any available penal or correctional facility that meets minimum standards of health and habitability established by the Bureau, whether maintained by the Federal Government or otherwise and whether within or without the judicial district in which the person was convicted, that the Bureau determines to be appropriate and suitable, considering—

(1) the resources of the facility contemplated;

(2) the nature and circumstances of the offense;

(3) the history and characteristics of the prisoner;

(4) any statement by the court that imposed the sentence—

(A) concerning the purposes for which the sentence to imprisonment was determined to be warranted; or

(B) recommending a type of penal or correctional facility as appropriate; and

(5) any pertinent policy statement issued by the Sentencing Commission pursuant to section 994(a)(2) of title 28.

In designating the place of imprisonment or making transfers under this subsection, there shall be no favoritism given to prisoners of high social or economic status. The Bureau may at any time, having regard for the same matters, direct the transfer of a prisoner from one penal or correctional facility to another. The Bureau shall make available appropriate substance abuse treatment for each prisoner the Bureau determines has a treatable condition of substance addiction or abuse. Any order, recommendation, or request by a sentencing court that a convicted person serve a term of imprisonment in a community corrections facility shall have no binding effect on the authority of the Bureau under this section to determine or change the place of imprisonment of that person.

(c) Delivery of order of commitment.— When a prisoner, pursuant to a court order, is placed in the custody of a person in charge of a penal or correctional facility, a copy of the order shall be delivered to such person as evidence of this authority to hold the prisoner, and the original order, with the return endorsed thereon, shall be returned to the court that issued it.

(d) Delivery of prisoner for court appearances.—The United States marshal shall, without charge, bring a prisoner into court or return him to a prison facility on order of a court of the United States or on written request of an attorney for the Government.

(e) Substance abuse treatment.—

(1) Phase-in.—In order to carry out the requirement of the last sentence of subsection (b) of this section, that every prisoner with a substance abuse problem have the opportunity to participate in appropriate substance abuse treatment, the Bureau of Prisons shall, subject to the availability of appropriations, provide residential substance abuse treatment (and make arrangements for appropriate aftercare)—

(A) for not less than 50 percent of eligible prisoners by the end of fiscal year 1995, with priority for such treatment accorded based on an eligible prisoner's proximity to release date;

(B) for not less than 75 percent of eligible prisoners by the end of fiscal year 1996, with priority for such treatment accorded based on an eligible prisoner's proximity to release date; and

(C) for all eligible prisoners by the end of fiscal year 1997 and thereafter, with priority for such treatment accorded based on an eligible prisoner's proximity to release date.

(2) Incentive for prisoners' successful completion of treatment program.—

(A) Generally.—Any prisoner who, in the judgment of the Director of the Bureau of Prisons, has successfully completed a program of residential substance abuse treatment provided under paragraph (1) of this subsection, shall remain in the custody of the Bureau under such conditions as the Bureau deems appropriate. If the conditions of confinement are different from those the prisoner would have experienced absent the successful completion of the treatment, the Bureau shall periodically test the prisoner for substance abuse and discontinue such conditions on determining that substance abuse has recurred.

(B) Period of custody.—The period a prisoner convicted of a nonviolent offense remains in custody after successfully completing a treatment program may be reduced by the Bureau of Prisons, but such reduction may not be more than one year from the term the prisoner must otherwise serve.

(3) Report.—The Bureau of Prisons shall transmit to the Committees on the Judiciary of the Senate and the House of Representatives on January 1, 1995, and on January 1 of each year thereafter, a report. Such report shall contain—

(A) a detailed quantitative and qualitative description of each substance abuse treatment program, residential or not, operated by the Bureau;

(B) a full explanation of how eligibility for such programs is determined, with complete information on what proportion of prisoners with substance abuse problems are eligible; and

(C) a complete statement of to what extent the Bureau has achieved compliance with the requirements of this title.

(4) Authorization of Appropriations.—There are authorized to carry out this subsection such sums as may be necessary for each of fiscal years 2007 through 2011.

(5) Definitions.—As used in this subsection—

(A) the term "residential substance abuse treatment" means a course of individual and group activities and treatment, lasting at least 6 months, in residential treatment facilities set apart from the general prison population (which may include the use of pharmocotherapies, where appropriate, that may extend beyond the 6-month period);

(B) the term "eligible prisoner" means a prisoner who is—

(i) determined by the Bureau of Prisons to have a substance abuse problem; and

(ii) willing to participate in a residential substance abuse treatment program; and

(C) the term "aftercare" means placement, case management and monitoring of the participants in a community-based substance abuse treatment program when the participant leaves the custody of the Bureau of Prisons.

(6) Coordination of Federal assistance.—The Bureau of Prisons shall consult with the Department of Health and Human Services concerning substance abuse treatment and related services and the incorporation of applicable components existing comprehensive approaches including relapse prevention and aftercare services.

(f) Sex Offender Management.—

(1) In General.—The Bureau of Prisons shall make available appropriate treatment to sex offenders who are in need of and suitable for treatment, as follows:

(A) Sex Offender Management Programs.—The Bureau of Prisons shall establish non-residential sex offender management programs to provide appropriate treatment, monitoring, and supervision of sex offenders and to provide aftercare during pre-release custody.

(B) Residential Sex Offender Treatment Programs.—The Bureau of Prisons shall establish residential sex offender treatment programs to provide treatment to sex offenders who volunteer for such programs and are deemed by the Bureau of Prisons to be in need of and suitable for residential treatment.

(2) Regions.—At least 1 sex offender management program under paragraph (1)(A), and at least one residential sex offender treatment program under paragraph (1)(B), shall be established in each region within the Bureau of Prisons.

(3) Authorization of Appropriations.—There are authorized to be appropriated to the Bureau of Prisons for each fiscal year such sums as may be necessary to carry out this subsection.

(g) Continued access to medical care.—

(1) In general.—In order to ensure a minimum standard of health and habitability, the Bureau of Prisons should ensure that each prisoner in a community confinement facility has access to necessary medical care, mental health care, and medicine through partnerships with local health service providers and transition planning.

(2) Definition.—In this subsection, the term "community confinement" has the meaning given that term in the application notes under section 5F1.1 of the Federal Sentencing Guidelines Manual, as in effect on the

date of the enactment of the Second Chance Act of 2007.

(Added Pub.L. 98–473, Title II, § 212(a)(2), Oct. 12, 1984, 98 Stat. 2007, and amended Pub.L. 101–647, Title XXIX, § 2903, Nov. 29, 1990, 104 Stat. 4913; Pub.L. 103–322, Title II, § 20401, Title III § 32001, Sept. 13, 1994,108 Stat. 1824, 1896; Pub.L. 109–162, Title XI, § 1146, Jan. 5, 2006, 119 Stat. 3112; Pub.L. 109–248, Title VI, § 622, July 7, 2006, 120 Stat. 634; Pub.L. 110–199, Title II, §§ 231(f), 251(b), 252, Apr. 9, 2008, 122 Stat. 687, 693.)

EDITORIAL NOTES

References in Text. The date of the enactment of the Second Chance Act of 2007, referred to in subsec. (g)(2), is April 9, 2008, the approval date of Pub.L. 110–199, 122 Stat. 657.

§ 3622. Temporary release of a prisoner

The Bureau of Prisons may release a prisoner from the place of his imprisonment for a limited period if such release appears to be consistent with the purpose for which the sentence was imposed and any pertinent policy statement issued by the Sentencing Commission pursuant to 28 U.S.C. 994(a)(2), if such release otherwise appears to be consistent with the public interest and if there is reasonable cause to believe that a prisoner will honor the trust to be imposed in him, by authorizing him, under prescribed conditions, to—

(a) visit a designated place for a period not to exceed thirty days, and then return to the same or another facility, for the purpose of—

(1) visiting a relative who is dying;

(2) attending a funeral of a relative;

(3) obtaining medical treatment not otherwise available;

(4) contacting a prospective employer;

(5) establishing or reestablishing family or community ties; or

(6) engaging in any other significant activity consistent with the public interest;

(b) participate in a training or educational program in the community while continuing in official detention at the prison facility; or

(c) work at paid employment in the community while continuing in official detention at the penal or correctional facility if—

(1) the rates of pay and other conditions of employment will not be less than those paid or provided for work of a similar nature in the community; and

(2) the prisoner agrees to pay to the Bureau such costs incident to official detention as the Bureau finds appropriate and reasonable under all the circumstances, such costs to be collected by the Bureau and deposited in the Treasury to the credit of the appropriation available for such costs at the time such collections are made.

(Added Pub.L. 98–473, Title II, § 212(a)(2), Oct. 12, 1984, 98 Stat. 2007.)

§ 3623. Transfer of a prisoner to State authority

The Director of the Bureau of Prisons shall order that a prisoner who has been charged in an indictment or information with, or convicted of, a State felony, be transferred to an official detention facility within such State prior to his release from a Federal prison facility if—

(1) the transfer has been requested by the Governor or other executive authority of the State;

(2) the State has presented to the Director a certified copy of the indictment, information, or judgment of conviction; and

(3) the Director finds that the transfer would be in the public interest.

If more than one request is presented with respect to a prisoner, the Director shall determine which request should receive preference. The expenses of such transfer shall be borne by the State requesting the transfer.

(Added Pub.L. 98–473, Title II, § 212(a)(2), Oct. 12, 1984, 98 Stat. 2008.)

§ 3624. Release of a prisoner

(a) Date of release.—A prisoner shall be released by the Bureau of Prisons on the date of the expiration of the prisoner's term of imprisonment, less any time credited toward the service of the prisoner's sentence as provided in subsection (b). If the date for a prisoner's release falls on a Saturday, a Sunday, or a legal holiday at the place of confinement, the prisoner may be released by the Bureau on the last preceding weekday.

(b) Credit toward service of sentence for satisfactory behavior.—**(1)** Subject to paragraph (2), a prisoner who is serving a term of imprisonment of more than 1 year, other than a term of imprisonment for the duration of the prisoner's life, may receive credit toward the service of the prisoner's sentence, beyond the time served, of up to 54 days at the end of each year of the prisoner's term of imprisonment, beginning at the end of the first year of the term, subject to determination by the Bureau of Prisons that, during that year, the prisoner has displayed exemplary compliance with institutional disciplinary regulations. Subject to paragraph (2), if the Bureau determines that, during that year, the prisoner has not satisfactorily complied with such institutional regulations, the prisoner shall receive no such credit toward service of the prisoner's sentence or shall receive such lesser credit as the Bureau determines to be appropriate. In awarding credit under this section, the Bureau shall consider whether the prisoner, during the relevant period, has earned, or is making satisfactory progress toward earning, a high school diploma or an equivalent degree. Credit that has not been earned may not later be granted. Subject to paragraph (2), credit for the last year or portion of a year of the term of imprisonment shall be prorated and credited within the last six weeks of the sentence.

(2) Notwithstanding any other law, credit awarded under this subsection after the date of enactment of the Prison Litigation Reform Act shall vest on the date the prisoner is released from custody.

(3) The Attorney General shall ensure that the Bureau of Prisons has in effect an optional General Educational Development program for inmates who have not earned a high school diploma or its equivalent.

(4) Exemptions to the General Educational Development requirement may be made as deemed appropriate by the Director of the Federal Bureau of Prisons.

(c) Pre-release custody.—(1) In general.—The Director of the Bureau of Prisons shall, to the extent practicable, ensure that a prisoner serving a term of imprisonment spends a portion of the final months of that term (not to exceed 12 months), under conditions that will afford that prisoner a reasonable opportunity to adjust to and prepare for the reentry of that prisoner into the community. Such conditions may include a community correctional facility.

(2) Home confinement authority.—The authority under this subsection may be used to place a prisoner in home confinement for the shorter of 10 percent of the term of imprisonment of that prisoner or 6 months.

(3) Assistance.—The United States Probation System shall, to the extent practicable, offer assistance to a prisoner during prerelease custody under this subsection.

(4) No limitations.—Nothing in this subsection shall be construed to limit or restrict the authority of the Director of the Bureau of Prisons under section 3621.

(5) Reporting.—Not later than 1 year after the date of the enactment of the Second Chance Act of 2007 (and every year thereafter), the Director of the Bureau of Prisons shall transmit to the Committee on the Judiciary of the Senate and the Committee on the Judiciary of the House of Representatives a report describing the Bureau's utilization of community corrections facilities. Each report under this paragraph shall set forth the number and percentage of Federal prisoners placed in community corrections facilities during the preceding year, the average length of such placements, trends in such utilization, the reasons some prisoners are not placed in community corrections facilities, and any other information that may be useful to the committees in determining if the Bureau is utilizing community corrections facilities in an effective manner.

(6) Issuance of regulations.—The Director of the Bureau of Prisons shall issue regulations pursuant to this subsection not later than 90 days after the date of the enactment of the Second Chance Act of 2007, which shall ensure that placement in a community correctional facility by the Bureau of Prisons is—

(A) conducted in a manner consistent with section 3621(b) of this title;

(B) determined on an individual basis; and

(C) of sufficient duration to provide the greatest likelihood of successful reintegration into the community.

(d) Allotment of clothing, funds, and transportation.—Upon the release of a prisoner on the expiration of the prisoner's term of imprisonment, the Bureau of Prisons shall furnish the prisoner with—

(1) suitable clothing;

(2) an amount of money, not more than $500, determined by the Director to be consistent with the needs of the offender and the public interest, unless the Director determines that the financial position of the offender is such that no sum should be furnished; and

(3) transportation to the place of the prisoner's conviction, to the prisoner's bona fide residence within the United States, or to such other place within the United States as may be authorized by the Director.

(e) Supervision after release.—A prisoner whose sentence includes a term of supervised release after imprisonment shall be released by the Bureau of Prisons to the supervision of a probation officer who shall, during the term imposed, supervise the person released to the degree warranted by the conditions specified by the sentencing court. The term of supervised release commences on the day the person is released from imprisonment and runs concurrently with any Federal, State, or local term of probation or supervised release or parole for another offense to which the person is subject or becomes subject during the term of supervised release. A term of supervised release does not run during any period in which the person is imprisoned in connection with a conviction for a Federal, State, or local crime unless the imprisonment is for a period of less than 30 consecutive days. Upon the release of a prisoner by the Bureau of Prisons to supervised release, the Bureau of Prisons shall notify such prisoner, verbally and in writing, of the requirement that the prisoner adhere to an installment schedule, not to exceed 2 years except in special circumstances, to pay for any fine imposed for the offense committed by such prisoner, and of the consequences of failure to pay such fines under sections 3611 through 3614 of this title.

(f) Mandatory functional literacy requirement.—

(1) The Attorney General shall direct the Bureau of Prisons to have in effect a mandatory functional literacy program for all mentally capable inmates who are not functionally literate in each Federal correctional institution within 6 months from the date of the enactment of this Act.

(2) Each mandatory functional literacy program shall include a requirement that each inmate participate in such program for a mandatory period sufficient to provide the inmate with an adequate opportunity to achieve functional literacy, and appropriate incentives which lead to successful completion of such programs shall be developed and implemented.

(3) As used in this section, the term "functional literacy" means—

(A) an eighth grade equivalence in reading and mathematics on a nationally recognized standardized test;

(B) functional competency or literacy on a nationally recognized criterion–referenced test; or

(C) a combination of subparagraphs (A) and (B).

(4) Non-English speaking inmates shall be required to participate in an English-As-A-Second-Language program until they function at the equivalence of the eighth grade on a nationally recognized educational achievement test.

(5) The Chief Executive Officer of each institution shall have authority to grant waivers for good cause as determined and documented on an individual basis.

[**(6) Repealed.** Pub.L. 104–66, Title I, § 1091(c), Dec. 21, 1995, 109 Stat. 722.]

(Added Pub.L. 98–473, Title II, § 212(a)(2), Oct. 12, 1984, 98 Stat. 2008, and amended Pub.L. 99–646, §§ 16(a), 17(a), Nov. 10, 1986, 100 Stat. 3595; Pub.L. 101–647, Title XXIX, §§ 2902(a), 2904, Nov. 29, 1990, 104 Stat. 4913; Pub.L. 103–322, Title II, §§ 20405, 20412, Sept. 13, 1994, 108 Stat. 1825, 1828; Pub.L. 104–66, Title I, § 1091(c), Dec. 21, 1995, 109 Stat. 722; Pub.L. 104–134, Title I, § 101[(a)] [Title VIII § 809(c)], Apr. 26, 1996, 110 Stat. 1321–76, renumbered Title I, Pub.L. 104–140, § 1(a), May 2, 1996, 110 Stat. 1327; Pub.L. 110–177, Title V, § 505, Jan. 7, 2008, 121 Stat. 2542; Pub.L. 110–199, Title II, § 251(a), Apr. 9, 2008, 122 Stat. 692.)

EDITORIAL NOTES

References in Text. The date of enactment of the Prison Litigation Reform Act, referred to in subsec. (b)(2), is the date of enactment of Title VIII of Pub.L. 104–134, which was approved Apr. 26, 1996.

The date of the enactment of the Second Chance Act of 2007, referred to in subsec. (c)(5), (6), is April 9, 2008, the approval date of Pub.L. 110–199, 122 Stat. 657.

The date of enactment of this Act, referred to in subsec. (f)(1), probably means the date of enactment of Pub.L. 101–647, Nov. 29, 1990, 104 Stat. 4789, which was approved Nov. 29, 1990.

* * *

CHAPTER 232–MISCELLANEOUS SENTENCING PROVISIONS

* * *

§ 3661. Use of information for sentencing

No limitation shall be placed on the information concerning the background, character, and conduct of a person convicted of an offense which a court of the United States may receive and consider for the purpose of imposing an appropriate sentence.

(Added Pub.L. 91–452, Title X, § 1001(a), Oct. 15, 1970, 84 Stat. 951, § 3577, and renumbered Pub.L. 98–473, Title II, § 212(a)(1), Oct. 12, 1984, 98 Stat. 1987.)

* * *

§ 3663. Order of restitution

(a)(1)(A) The court, when sentencing a defendant convicted of an offense under this title, section 401, 408(a), 409, 416, 420, or 422(a) of the Controlled Substances Act (21 U.S.C. 841, 848(a), 849, 856, 861, 863) (but in no case shall a participant in an offense under such sections be considered a victim of such offense under this section), or section 5124, 46312, 46502, or 46504 of title 49, other than an offense described in section 3663A(c), may order, in addition to or, in the case of a misdemeanor, in lieu of any other penalty authorized by law, that the defendant make restitution to any victim of such offense, or if the victim is deceased, to the victim's estate. The court may also order, if agreed to by the parties in a plea agreement, restitution to persons other than the victim of the offense.

(B)(i) The court, in determining whether to order restitution under this section, shall consider—

(I) the amount of the loss sustained by each victim as a result of the offense; and

(II) the financial resources of the defendant, the financial needs and earning ability of the defendant and the defendant's dependents, and such other factors as the court deems appropriate.

(ii) To the extent that the court determines that the complication and prolongation of the sentencing process resulting from the fashioning of an order of restitution under this section outweighs the need to provide restitution to any victims, the court may decline to make such an order.

(2) For the purposes of this section, the term "victim" means a person directly and proximately harmed as a result of the commission of an offense for which restitution may be ordered including, in the case of an offense that involves as an element a scheme, conspiracy, or pattern of criminal activity, any person directly harmed by the defendant's criminal conduct in the course of the scheme, conspiracy, or pattern. In the case of a victim who is under 18 years of age, incompetent, incapacitated, or deceased, the legal guardian of the victim or representative of the victim's estate, another family member, or any other person appointed as suitable by the court, may assume the victim's rights under this section, but in no event shall the defendant be named as such representative or guardian.

(3) The court may also order restitution in any criminal case to the extent agreed to by the parties in a plea agreement.

(b) The order may require that such defendant—

(1) in the case of an offense resulting in damage to or loss or destruction of property of a victim of the offense—

(A) return the property to the owner of the property or someone designated by the owner; or

(B) if return of the property under subparagraph (A) is impossible, impractical, or inadequate, pay an amount equal to the greater of—

(i) the value of the property on the date of the damage, loss, or destruction, or

(ii) the value of the property on the date of sentencing,

less the value (as of the date the property is returned) of any part of the property that is returned;

(2) in the case of an offense resulting in bodily injury to a victim including an offense under chapter 109A or chapter 110—

(A) pay an amount equal to the cost of necessary medical and related professional services and devices relating to physical, psychiatric, and psychological care, including nonmedical care and treatment rendered in accordance with a method of healing recognized by the law of the place of treatment;

(B) pay an amount equal to the cost of necessary physical and occupational therapy and rehabilitation; and

(C) reimburse the victim for income lost by such victim as a result of such offense;

(3) in the case of an offense resulting in bodily injury also results in the death of a victim, pay an amount equal to the cost of necessary funeral and related services;

(4) in any case, reimburse the victim for lost income and necessary child care, transportation, and other expenses related to participation in the investigation or prosecution of the offense or attendance at proceedings related to the offense;

(5) in any case, if the victim (or if the victim is deceased, the victim's estate) consents, make restitution in services in lieu of money, or make restitution to a person or organization designated by the victim or the estate; and

(6) in the case of an offense under sections 1028(a)(7) or 1028A(a) of this title, pay an amount equal to the value of the time reasonably spent by the victim in an attempt to remediate the intended or actual harm incurred by the victim from the offense.

(c)(1) Notwithstanding any other provision of law (but subject to the provisions of subsections (a)(1)(B) (i)(II) and (ii), when sentencing a defendant convicted of an offense described in section 401, 408(a), 409, 416, 420, or 422(a) of the Controlled Substances Act (21 U.S.C. 841, 848(a), 849, 856, 861, 863), in which there is no identifiable victim, the court may order that the defendant make restitution in accordance with this subsection.

(2)(A) An order of restitution under this subsection shall be based on the amount of public harm caused by the offense, as determined by the court in accordance with guidelines promulgated by the United States Sentencing Commission.

(B) In no case shall the amount of restitution ordered under this subsection exceed the amount of the fine which may be ordered for the offense charged in the case.

(3) Restitution under this subsection shall be distributed as follows:

(A) 65 percent of the total amount of restitution shall be paid to the State entity designated to administer crime victim assistance in the State in which the crime occurred.

(B) 35 percent of the total amount of restitution shall be paid to the State entity designated to receive Federal substance abuse block grant funds.

(4) The court shall not make an award under this subsection if it appears likely that such award would interfere with a forfeiture under chapter 46 or chapter 96 of this title or under the Controlled Substances Act (21 U.S.C. 801 et seq.).

(5) Notwithstanding section 3612(c) or any other provision of law, a penalty assessment under section 3013 or a fine under subchapter C of chapter 227 shall take precedence over an order of restitution under this subsection.

(6) Requests for community restitution under this subsection may be considered in all plea agreements negotiated by the United States.

(7)(A) The United States Sentencing Commission shall promulgate guidelines to assist courts in determining the amount of restitution that may be ordered under this subsection.

(B) No restitution shall be ordered under this subsection until such time as the Sentencing Commission promulgates guidelines pursuant to this paragraph.

(d) An order of restitution made pursuant to this section shall be issued and enforced in accordance with section 3664.

(Added Pub.L. 97–291, § 5(a), Oct. 12, 1982, 96 Stat. 1253, § 3579 renumbered and amended Pub.L. 98–473, Title II, § 212(a)(1), (3), Oct. 12, 1984, 98 Stat. 1987, 2010; Pub.L. 98–596, § 9, Oct. 30, 1984, 98 Stat. 3138; Nov. 10, 1986, Pub.L. 99–646, §§ 8(b), 20(a), 77(a), 78(a), 79(a), 100 Stat. 3593, 3596, 3618, 3619; Pub.L. 100–182, § 13, Dec. 7, 1987, 101 Stat. 1268; Pub.L. 100–185, § 12, Dec. 11, 1987, 101 Stat. 1285; Pub.L. 100–690, Title VII, § 7042, Nov. 18, 1988, 102 Stat. 4399; Pub.L. 101–647, Title XXV, § 2509, Title XXXV, § 3595, Nov. 29, 1990, 104 Stat. 4863, 4931; Pub.L. 103–272, § 5(e)(12), July 5, 1994, 108 Stat. 1374; Pub.L. 103–322, Title IV, §§ 40504, 40505, Sept. 13, 1994, 108 Stat. 1947; Pub.L. 104–132, Title II, § 205(a), Apr. 24, 1996, 110 Stat. 1229; Pub.L. 104–294, Title VI, §§ 601(r)(1)(2), 605(l), Oct. 11, 1996, 110 Stat. 3502, 3510; Pub.L. 106–310, Div. B, Title XXXVI, § 3613(c), Oct. 17, 2000, 114 Stat. 1230; Pub.L. 109–59, Title VII, § 7128(b), Aug. 10, 2005, 109 Stat. 1910; Sept. 26, 2008, Pub.L. 110–326, Title II, § 202, 122 Stat. 3561.)

§ 3663A. Mandatory restitution to victims of certain crimes

(a)(1) Notwithstanding any other provision of law, when sentencing a defendant convicted of an offense described in subsection (c), the court shall order, in addition to, or in the case of a misdemeanor, in addition to or in lieu of, any other penalty authorized by law, that the defendant make restitution to the victim of the offense or, if the victim is deceased, to the victim's estate.

(2) For the purposes of this section, the term "victim" means a person directly and proximately harmed as a result of the commission of an offense for which restitution may be ordered including, in the case of an offense that involves as an element a scheme, conspiracy, or pattern of criminal activity, any person directly harmed by the defendant's criminal conduct in the course of the scheme, conspiracy, or pattern. In the case of a victim who is under 18 years of age, incompetent, incapacitated, or deceased, the legal guardian of the victim or representative of the victim's estate, another family member, or any other person appointed as suitable by the court, may assume the victim's rights under this section, but in no event shall the defendant be named as such representative or guardian.

(3) The court shall also order, if agreed to by the parties in a plea agreement, restitution to persons other than the victim of the offense.

(b) The order of restitution shall require that such defendant—

(1) in the case of an offense resulting in damage to or loss or destruction of property of a victim of the offense—

(A) return the property to the owner of the property or someone designated by the owner; or

(B) if return of the property under subparagraph (A) is impossible, impracticable, or inadequate, pay an amount equal to—

(i) the greater of—

(I) the value of the property on the date of the damage, loss, or destruction; or

(II) the value of the property on the date of sentencing, less

(ii) the value (as of the date the property is returned) of any part of the property that is returned;

(2) in the case of an offense resulting in bodily injury to a victim—

(A) pay an amount equal to the cost of necessary medical and related professional services and devices relating to physical, psychiatric, and psychological care, including nonmedical care and treatment rendered in accordance with a method of healing recognized by the law of the place of treatment;

(B) pay an amount equal to the cost of necessary physical and occupational therapy and rehabilitation; and

(C) reimburse the victim for income lost by such victim as a result of such offense;

(3) in the case of an offense resulting in bodily injury that results in the death of the victim, pay an amount equal to the cost of necessary funeral and related services; and

(4) in any case, reimburse the victim for lost income and necessary child care, transportation, and other expenses incurred during participation in the investigation or prosecution of the offense or attendance at proceedings related to the offense.

(c)(1) This section shall apply in all sentencing proceedings for convictions of, or plea agreements relating to charges for, any offense—

(A) that is—

(i) a crime of violence, as defined in section 16;

(ii) an offense against property under this title, or under section 416(a) of the Controlled Substance Act (21 U.S.C. 856(a)), including any offense committed by fraud or deceit;

(iii) an offense described in section 1365 (relating to tampering with consumer products); or

(iv) an offense under section 670 (relating to theft of medical products); and

(B) in which an identifiable victim or victims has suffered a physical injury or pecuniary loss.

(2) In the case of a plea agreement that does not result in a conviction for an offense described in paragraph (1), this section shall apply only if the plea specifically states that an offense listed under such paragraph gave rise to the plea agreement.

(3) This section shall not apply in the case of an offense described in paragraph (1)(A)(ii) if the court finds, from facts on the record, that—

    (A) the number of identifiable victims is so large as to make restitution impracticable; or

    (B) determining complex issues of fact related to the cause or amount of the victim's losses would complicate or prolong the sentencing process to a degree that the need to provide restitution to any victim is outweighed by the burden on the sentencing process.

(d) An order of restitution under this section shall be issued and enforced in accordance with section 3664.

(Added Pub.L. 104–132, Title II, § 204(a), Apr. 24, 1996, 110 Stat. 1227; amended Pub.L. 106–310, Div. B, Title XXXVI, § 3613(d), Oct. 17, 2000, 114 Stat. 1230; Pub.L. 112–186, § 6, Oct. 5, 2012, 126 Stat. 1430.)

§ 3664. Procedure for issuance and enforcement of order of restitution

(a) For orders of restitution under this title, the court shall order the probation officer to obtain and include in its presentence report, or in a separate report, as the court may direct, information sufficient for the court to exercise its discretion in fashioning a restitution order. The report shall include, to the extent practicable, a complete accounting of the losses to each victim, any restitution owed pursuant to a plea agreement, and information relating to the economic circumstances of each defendant. If the number or identity of victims cannot be reasonably ascertained, or other circumstances exist that make this requirement clearly impracticable, the probation officer shall so inform the court.

(b) The court shall disclose to both the defendant and the attorney for the Government all portions of the presentence or other report pertaining to the matters described in subsection (a) of this section.

(c) The provisions of this chapter, chapter 227, and Rule 32(c) of the Federal Rules of Criminal Procedure shall be the only rules applicable to proceedings under this section.

(d)(1) Upon the request of the probation officer, but not later than 60 days prior to the date initially set for sentencing, the attorney for the Government, after consulting, to the extent practicable, with all identified victims, shall promptly provide the probation officer with a listing of the amounts subject to restitution.

(2) The probation officer shall, prior to submitting the presentence report under subsection (a), to the extent practicable—

    (A) provide notice to all identified victims of—

        (i) the offense or offenses of which the defendant was convicted;

        (ii) the amounts subject to restitution submitted to the probation officer;

        (iii) the opportunity of the victim to submit information to the probation officer concerning the amount of the victim's losses;

        (iv) the scheduled date, time, and place of the sentencing hearing;

        (v) the availability of a lien in favor of the victim pursuant to subsection (m)(1)(B); and

        (vi) the opportunity of the victim to file with the probation officer a separate affidavit relating to the amount of the victim's losses subject to restitution; and

    (B) provide the victim with an affidavit form to submit pursuant to subparagraph (A)(vi).

(3) Each defendant shall prepare and file with the probation officer an affidavit fully describing the financial resources of the defendant, including a complete listing of all assets owned or controlled by the defendant as of the date on which the defendant was arrested, the financial needs and earning ability of the defendant and the defendant's dependents, and such other information that the court requires relating to such other factors as the court deems appropriate.

(4) After reviewing the report of the probation officer, the court may require additional documentation or hear testimony. The privacy of any records filed, or testimony heard, pursuant to this section shall be maintained to the greatest extent possible, and such records may be filed or testimony heard in camera.

(5) If the victim's losses are not ascertainable by the date that is 10 days prior to sentencing, the attorney for the Government or the probation officer shall so inform the court, and the court shall set a date for the final determination of the victim's losses, not to exceed 90 days after sentencing. If the victim subsequently discovers further losses, the victim shall have 60 days after discovery of those losses in which to petition the court for an amended restitution order. Such order may be granted only upon a showing of good cause for the failure to include such losses in the initial claim for restitutionary relief.

(6) The court may refer any issue arising in connection with a proposed order of restitution to a magistrate judge or special master for proposed findings of fact and recommendations as to disposition, subject to a de novo determination of the issue by the court.

(e) Any dispute as to the proper amount or type of restitution shall be resolved by the court by the preponderance of the evidence. The burden of demonstrating the amount of the loss sustained by a victim as a result of the offense shall be on the attorney for the Government. The burden of demonstrating the financial resources of the defendant and the financial needs of the defendant's dependents, shall be on the defendant. The burden of demonstrating such other matters as the court deems appropriate shall be upon the party designated by the court as justice requires.

(f)(1)(A) In each order of restitution, the court shall order restitution to each victim in the full amount of each victim's losses as determined by the court and without consideration of the economic circumstances of the defendant.

(B) In no case shall the fact that a victim has received or is entitled to receive compensation with respect to a loss from insurance or any other source be considered in determining the amount of restitution.

(2) Upon determination of the amount of restitution owed to each victim, the court shall, pursuant to section 3572, specify in the restitution order the manner in which, and the schedule according to which, the restitution is to be paid, in consideration of—

(A) the financial resources and other assets of the defendant, including whether any of these assets are jointly controlled;

(B) projected earnings and other income of the defendant; and

(C) any financial obligations of the defendant; including obligations to dependents.

(3)(A) A restitution order may direct the defendant to make a single, lump-sum payment, partial payments at specified intervals, in-kind payments, or a combination of payments at specified intervals and in-kind payments.

(B) A restitution order may direct the defendant to make nominal periodic payments if the court finds from facts on the record that the economic circumstances of the defendant do not allow the payment of any amount of a restitution order, and do not allow for the payment of the full amount of a restitution order in the foreseeable future under any reasonable schedule of payments.

(4) An in-kind payment described in paragraph (3) may be in the form of—

(A) return of property;

(B) replacement of property; or

(C) if the victim agrees, services rendered to the victim or a person or organization other than the victim.

(g)(1) No victim shall be required to participate in any phase of a restitution order.

(2) A victim may at any time assign the victim's interest in restitution payments to the Crime Victims Fund in the Treasury without in any way impairing the obligation of the defendant to make such payments.

(h) If the court finds that more than 1 defendant has contributed to the loss of a victim, the court may make each defendant liable for payment of the full amount of restitution or may apportion liability among the defendants to reflect the level of contribution to the victim's loss and economic circumstances of each defendant.

(i) If the court finds that more than 1 victim has sustained a loss requiring restitution by a defendant, the court may provide for a different payment schedule for each victim based on the type and amount of each victim's loss and accounting for the economic circumstances of each victim. In any case in which the United States is a victim, the court shall ensure that all other victims receive full restitution before the United States receives any restitution.

(j)(1) If a victim has received compensation from insurance or any other source with respect to a loss, the court shall order that restitution be paid to the person who provided or is obligated to provide the compensation, but the restitution order shall provide that all restitution of victims required by the order be paid to the victims before any restitution is paid to such a provider of compensation.

(2) Any amount paid to a victim under an order of restitution shall be reduced by any amount later recovered as compensatory damages for the same loss by the victim in—

(A) any Federal civil proceeding; and

(B) any State civil proceeding, to the extent provided by the law of the State.

(k) A restitution order shall provide that the defendant shall notify the court and the Attorney General of any material change in the defendant's economic circumstances that might affect the defendant's ability to pay restitution. The court may also accept notification of a material change in the defendant's economic circumstances from the United States or from the victim. The Attorney General shall certify to the court that the victim or victims owed restitution by the defendant have been notified of the change in circumstances. Upon receipt of the notification, the court may, on its own motion, or the motion of any party, including the victim, adjust the payment schedule, or require immediate payment in full, as the interests of justice require.

(l) A conviction of a defendant for an offense involving the act giving rise to an order of restitution shall estop the defendant from denying the essential allegations of that offense in any subsequent Federal civil proceeding or State civil proceeding, to the extent consistent with State law, brought by the victim.

(m)(1)(A)(i) An order of restitution may be enforced by the United States in the manner provided for in subchapter C of chapter 227 and subchapter B of chapter 229 of this title; or

(ii) by all other available and reasonable means.

(B) At the request of a victim named in a restitution order, the clerk of the court shall issue an abstract of judgment certifying that a judgment has been entered in favor of such victim in the amount specified in the restitution order. Upon registering, recording, docketing, or indexing such abstract in accordance with the rules and requirements relating to judgments of the court of the State where the district court is located, the abstract of judgment shall be a lien on the property of the defendant located in such State in the same manner and to the same extent and under the same conditions as a judgment of a court of general jurisdiction in that State.

(2) An order of in-kind restitution in the form of services shall be enforced by the probation officer.

(n) If a person obligated to provide restitution, or pay a fine, receives substantial resources from any source, including inheritance, settlement, or other judgment, during a period of incarceration, such person shall be required to apply the value of such resources to any restitution or fine still owed.

(o) A sentence that imposes an order of restitution is a final judgment notwithstanding the fact that—

(1) such a sentence can subsequently be—

(A) corrected under Rule 35 of the Federal Rules of Criminal Procedure and section 3742 of chapter 235 of this title;

(B) appealed and modified under section 3742;

(C) amended under subsection (d)(5); or

(D) adjusted under section 3664(k), 3572, or 3613A; or

(2) the defendant may be resentenced under section 3565 or 3614.

(p) Nothing in this section or sections 2248, 2259, 2264, 2327, 3663, and 3663A and arising out of the application of such sections, shall be construed to create a cause of action not otherwise authorized in favor of any person against the United States or any officer or employee of the United States.

(Added Pub.L. 97–291, § 5(a), Oct. 12, 1982, 96 Stat. 1255, § 3580, renumbered Pub.L. 98–473, Title II, § 212(a)(1), Oct. 12, 1984; 98 Stat. 1987; Pub.L. 101–647, Title XXXV, § 3596, Nov. 29, 1990, 104 Stat. 4931; Pub.L. 104–132, Title II, § 206(a), Apr. 24, 1996, 110 Stat. 1232; Pub.L. 107–273, Div. B, Title IV, § 4002(e)(1), Nov. 2, 2002, 116 Stat. 1810.)

* * *

CHAPTER 235–APPEAL

* * *

§ 3742. Review of a sentence

(a) Appeal by a defendant.—A defendant may file a notice of appeal in the district court for review of an otherwise final sentence if the sentence—

(1) was imposed in violation of law;

(2) was imposed as a result of an incorrect application of the sentencing guidelines; or

(3) is greater than the sentence specified in the applicable guideline range to the extent that the sentence includes a greater fine or term of imprisonment, probation, or supervised release than the maximum established in the guideline range, or includes a more limiting condition of probation or supervised release under section 3563(b)(6) or (b)(11) than the maximum established in the guideline range; or

(4) was imposed for an offense for which there is no sentencing guideline and is plainly unreasonable.

(b) Appeal by the Government.—The Government may file a notice of appeal in the district court for review of an otherwise final sentence if the sentence—

(1) was imposed in violation of law;

(2) was imposed as a result of an incorrect application of the sentencing guidelines;

(3) is less than the sentence specified in the applicable guideline range to the extent that the sentence includes a lesser fine or term of imprisonment, probation, or supervised release than the minimum established in the guideline range, or includes a less limiting condition of probation or supervised release under section 3563(b)(6) or (b)(11) than the minimum established in the guideline range; or

(4) was imposed for an offense for which there is no sentencing guideline and is plainly unreasonable.

The Government may not further prosecute such appeal without the personal approval of the Attorney General, the Solicitor General, or a deputy solicitor general designated by the Solicitor General.

(c) Plea agreements.—In the case of a plea agreement that includes a specific sentence under rule 11(e)(1)(C) of the Federal Rules of Criminal Procedure—

(1) a defendant may not file a notice of appeal under paragraph (3) or (4) of subsection (a) unless the sentence imposed is greater than the sentence set forth in such agreement; and

(2) the Government may not file a notice of appeal under paragraph (3) or (4) of subsection (b) unless the sentence imposed is less than the sentence set forth in such agreement.

(d) Record on review.—If a notice of appeal is filed in the district court pursuant to subsection (a) or (b), the clerk shall certify to the court of appeals—

(1) that portion of the record in the case that is designated as pertinent by either of the parties;

(2) the presentence report; and

(3) the information submitted during the sentencing proceeding.

(e) Consideration.—Upon review of the record, the court of appeals shall determine whether the sentence—

(1) was imposed in violation of law;

(2) was imposed as a result of an incorrect application of the sentencing guidelines;

(3) is outside the applicable guideline range, and

(A) the district court failed to provide the written statement of reasons required by section 3553(c);

(B) the sentence departs from the applicable guideline range based on a factor that—

    (i) does not advance the objectives set forth in section 3553(a)(2); or

    (ii) is not authorized under section 3553(b); or

    (iii) is not justified by the facts of the case; or

(C) the sentence departs to an unreasonable degree from the applicable guidelines range, having regard for the factors to be considered in imposing a sentence, as set forth in section 3553(a) of this title and the reasons for the imposition of the particular sentence, as stated by the district court pursuant to the provisions of section 3553(c); or

(4) was imposed for an offense for which there is no applicable sentencing guideline and is plainly unreasonable.

The court of appeals shall give due regard to the opportunity of the district court to judge the credibility of the witnesses, and shall accept the findings of fact of the district court unless they are clearly erroneous and, except with respect to determinations under subsection (3)(A) or (3)(B), shall give due deference to the district court's application of the guidelines to the facts. With respect to determinations under subsection (3)(A) or (3)(B), the court of appeals shall review de novo the district court's application of the guidelines to the facts.

(f) Decision and disposition.—If the court of appeals determines that—

(1) the sentence was imposed in violation of law or imposed as a result of an incorrect application of the sentencing guidelines, the court shall remand the case for further sentencing proceedings with such instructions as the court considers appropriate;

(2) the sentence is outside the applicable guideline range and the district court failed to provide the required statement of reasons in the order of judgment and commitment, or the departure is based on an impermissible

factor, or is to an unreasonable degree, or the sentence was imposed for an offense for which there is no applicable sentencing guideline and is plainly unreasonable, it shall state specific reasons for its conclusions and—

(A) if it determines that the sentence is too high and the appeal has been filed under subsection (a), it shall set aside the sentence and remand the case for further sentencing proceedings with such instructions as the court considers appropriate, subject to subsection (g);

(B) if it determines that the sentence is too low and the appeal has been filed under subsection (b), it shall set aside the sentence and remand the case for further sentencing proceedings with such instructions as the court considers appropriate, subject to subsection (g);

(3) the sentence is not described in paragraph (1) or (2), it shall affirm the sentence.

(g) Sentencing upon remand.—A district court to which a case is remanded pursuant to subsection (f)(1) or (f)(2) shall resentence a defendant in accordance with section 3553 and with such instructions as may have been given by the court of appeals, except that—

(1) In determining the range referred to in subsection 3553(a)(4), the court shall apply the guidelines issued by the Sentencing Commission pursuant to section 994(a)(1) of title 28, United States Code, and that were in effect on the date of the previous sentencing of the defendant prior to the appeal, together with any amendments thereto by any act of Congress that was in effect on such date; and

(2) The court shall not impose a sentence outside the applicable guidelines range except upon a ground that—

(A) was specifically and affirmatively included in the written statement of reasons required by section 3553(c) in connection with the previous sentencing of the defendant prior to the appeal; and

(B) was held by the court of appeals, in remanding the case, to be a permissible ground of departure.

(h) Application to a sentence by a magistrate.—An appeal of an otherwise final sentence imposed by a United States magistrate may be taken to a judge of the district court, and this section shall apply (except for the requirement of approval by the Attorney General or the Solicitor General in the case of a Government appeal) as though the appeal were to a court of appeals from a sentence imposed by a district court.

(i) Guideline not expressed as a range.—For the purpose of this section, the term "guideline range" includes a guideline range having the same upper and lower limits.

(j) Definitions.—For purposes of this section—

(1) a factor is a "permissible" ground of departure if it—

(A) advances the objectives set forth in section 3553(a)(2); and

(B) is authorized under section 3553(b); and

(C) is justified by the facts of the case; and

(2) a factor is an "impermissible" ground of departure if it is not a permissible factor within the meaning of subsection (j)(1).

(Added Pub.L. 98–473, Title II, § 213(a), Oct. 12, 1984, 98 Stat. 2011, and amended Pub.L. 99–646, § 73(a), Nov. 10, 1986, 100 Stat. 3617; Pub.L. 100–182, §§ 4–6, Dec. 7, 1987, 101 Stat. 1266, 1267; Pub.L. 100–690, Title VII, § 7103(a), Nov. 18, 1988, 102 Stat. 4416, 4417; Pub.L. 101–647, Title XXXV, §§ 3501, 3503, Nov. 29, 1990, 104 Stat. 4921; Pub.L. 103–322, Title XXXIII, § 330002(k), Sept. 13, 1994, 108 Stat. 2140; Pub.L. 108–21, Title IV, § 401(d)–(f), Apr. 30, 2003, 117 Stat. 670, 671.)

EDITORIAL NOTES

Unconstitutionality of Subsection (e). Mandatory aspect of subsection (e) of this section held unconstitutional by *United States v. Booker*, 543 U.S. 220, 125 S. Ct. 738 (2005).

Change of Name of United States Magistrates. United States magistrates appointed under section 631 of the Title 28, Judiciary and Judicial Procedure, to be known as United States magistrate judge after Dec. 1, 1990, with any reference to any United States magistrate or magistrate contained in Title 28, in any other Federal statute, etc., deemed to refer to a United States magistrate judge appointed under section 631 of Title 28, see section 321 of Pub.L. 101–650.

* * *

Title 28

JUDICIARY AND JUDICIAL
PROCEDURE

—

CHAPTER 58–UNITED STATES
SENTENCING COMMISSION

§ 991. United States Sentencing Commission; establishment and purposes

(a) There is established as an independent commission in the judicial branch of the United States a United States Sentencing Commission which shall consist of seven voting members and one nonvoting member. The President, after consultation with representatives of judges, prosecuting attorneys, defense attorneys, law enforcement officials, senior citizens, victims of crime, and others interested in the criminal justice process, shall appoint the voting members of the Commission, by and with the advice and consent of the Senate, one of whom shall be appointed, by and with the advice and consent of the Senate, as the Chair and three of whom shall be designated by the President as Vice Chairs. At least 3 of the members shall be Federal judges selected after considering a list of six judges recommended to the President by the Judicial Conference of the United States. Not more than four of the members of the Commission shall be members of the same political party, and of the three Vice Chairs, no more than two shall be members of the same political party. The Attorney General, or the Attorney General's

designee, shall be an ex officio, nonvoting member of the Commission. The Chair, Vice Chairs, and members of the Commission shall be subject to removal from the Commission by the President only for neglect of duty or malfeasance in office or for other good cause shown.

(b) The purposes of the United States Sentencing Commission are to—

(1) establish sentencing policies and practices for the Federal criminal justice system that—

(A) assure the meeting of the purposes of sentencing as set forth in section 3553(a)(2) of title 18, United States Code;

(B) provide certainty and fairness in meeting the purposes of sentencing, avoiding unwarranted sentencing disparities among defendants with similar records who have been found guilty of similar criminal conduct while maintaining sufficient flexibility to permit individualized sentences when warranted by mitigating or aggravating factors not taken into account in the establishment of general sentencing practices; and

(C) reflect, to the extent practicable, advancement in knowledge of human behavior as it relates to the criminal justice process; and

(2) develop means of measuring the degree to which the sentencing, penal, and correctional practices are effective in meeting the purposes of sentencing as set forth in section 3553(a)(2) of title 18, United States Code.

(Added Pub.L. 98–473, Title II, § 217(a), Oct. 12, 1984, 98 Stat. 2017, and amended Pub.L. 99–22, § 1(1), Apr. 15, 1985, 99 Stat. 46; Pub.L. 103–322, Title XXVIII, § 280005(a), (c)(1), (2), Sept. 13, 1994, 108 Stat. 2096, 2097; Pub.L. 104–294, Title VI, § 604(b)(11), Oct. 11, 1996, 110 Stat. 3507; Pub.L. 108–21, Title IV, § 401(n)(1), Apr. 30, 2003, 117 Stat. 676; Pub.L. 110–406, § 16, Oct. 13, 2008, 122 Stat. 4295.)

§ 992. Terms of office; compensation

(a) The voting members of the United States Sentencing Commission shall be appointed for six-year terms, except that the initial terms of the first members of the Commission shall be staggered so that—

(1) two members, including the Chair, serve terms of six years;

(2) three members serve terms of four years; and

(3) two members serve terms of two years.

(b)(1) Subject to paragraph (2)—

(A) no voting member of the Commission may serve more than two full terms; and

(B) a voting member appointed to fill a vacancy that occurs before the expiration of the term for which a predecessor was appointed shall be appointed only for the remainder of such term.

(2) A voting member of the Commission whose term has expired may continue to serve until the earlier of—

(A) the date on which a successor has taken office; or

(B) the date on which the Congress adjourns sine die to end the session of Congress that commences after the date on which the member's term expired.

(c) The Chair and Vice Chairs of the Commission shall hold full-time positions and shall be compensated during their terms of office at the annual rate at which judges of the United States courts of appeals are compensated. The voting members of the Commission, other than the Chair and Vice Chair, shall hold full-time positions until the end of the first six years after the sentencing guidelines go into effect pursuant to section 235(a)(1)(B)(ii) of the Sentencing Reform Act of 1984, and shall be compensated at the annual rate at which judges of the United States courts of appeals are compensated. Thereafter, the voting members of the commission, other than the Chair and Vice Chairs, shall hold part-time positions and shall be paid at the daily rate at which judges of the United States courts of appeals are compensated. A Federal judge may serve as a member of the Commission without resigning the judge's appointment as a Federal judge.

(d) Sections 44(c) and 134(b) of this title (relating to the residence of judges) do not apply to any judge holding a full-time position on the Commission under subsection (c) of this section.

(Added Pub.L. 98–473, Title II, § 217(a), Oct. 12, 1984, 98 Stat. 2018, and amended Pub.L. 99–646, §§ 4, 6(a), Nov. 10, 1986; 100 Stat. 3592; Pub.L. 102–349, § 1, Aug. 26, 1992, 106 Stat. 933; Pub.L. 103–322, Tittle XXVIII, § 280005(b), (c)(1), (3), Sept. 13, 1994, 108 Stat. 2096, 2097.)

EDITORIAL NOTES

References in Text. Section 235(a)(1)(B)(ii) of the Sentencing Reform Act of 1984, referred to in subsec. (c), is section 235(a)(1)(B)(ii) of Pub.L. 98–473, which is set out as a note under section 3551 of Title 18, Crimes and Criminal Procedure.

Commencement of Terms of First Members of Commission. For provisions directing that, for purposes of subsec. (a) of this section, the terms of the first members of the United States Sentencing Commission shall not begin to run until the sentencing guidelines go into effect pursuant to section 235(a)(1)(B)(ii) of Pub.L. 98–473, set out as a note under section 994 of this title, see section 235(a)(2) of Pub.L. 98–473, set out as a note under section 3551 of Title 18, Crimes and Criminal Procedure.

§ 993. Powers and duties of Chair

The Chair shall—

(a) call and preside at meetings of the Commission, which shall be held for at least two weeks in each quarter after the members of the Commission hold part-time positions; and

(b) direct—

(1) the preparation of requests for appropriations for the Commission; and

(2) the use of funds made available to the Commission.

(Added Pub.L. 98–473, Title II, § 217(a), Oct. 12, 1984, 98 Stat. 2019, and amended Pub.L. 99–22, § 1(2), Apr. 15, 1985, 99 Stat. 46; Pub.L. 99–646, § 5, Nov. 10, 1986, 100 Stat. 3592; Pub.L. 103–322, Title XXVIII, § 280005(c)(1), Sept. 13, 1994, 108 Stat. 2097.)

§ 994. Duties of the Commission

(a) The Commission, by affirmative vote of at least four members of the Commission, and pursuant to its rules and regulations and consistent with all pertinent provisions of any Federal statute shall promulgate and distribute to all courts of the United States and to the United States Probation System—

(1) guidelines, as described in this section, for use of a sentencing court in determining the sentence to be imposed in a criminal case, including—

(A) a determination whether to impose a sentence to probation, a fine, or a term of imprisonment;

(B) a determination as to the appropriate amount of a fine or the appropriate length of a term of probation or a term of imprisonment;

(C) a determination whether a sentence to a term of imprisonment should include a requirement that the defendant be placed on a term of supervised release after imprisonment, and, if so, the appropriate length of such a term;

(D) a determination whether multiple sentences to terms of imprisonment should be ordered to run concurrently or consecutively; and

(E) a determination under paragraphs (6) and (11) of section 3563(b) of title 18;

(2) general policy statements regarding application of the guidelines or any other aspect of sentencing or sentence implementation that in the view of the Commission would further the purposes set forth in section 3553(a)(2) of title 18, United States Code, including the appropriate use of—

(A) the sanctions set forth in sections 3554, 3555, and 3556 of title 18;

(B) the conditions of probation and supervised release set forth in sections 3563(b) and 3583(d) of title 18;

(C) the sentence modification provisions set forth in sections 3563(c), 3564, 3573, and 3582(c) of title 18;

(D) the fine imposition provisions set forth in section 3572 of title 18;

(E) the authority granted under rule 11(e)(2) of the Federal Rules of Criminal Procedure to accept or reject a plea agreement entered into pursuant to rule 11(e)(1); and

(F) the temporary release provisions set forth in section 3622 of title 18, and the prerelease custody provisions set forth in section 3624(c) of title 18; and

(3) guidelines or general policy statements regarding the appropriate use of the provisions for revocation of probation set forth in section 3565 of title 18, and the provisions for modification of the term or conditions of supervised release and revocation of supervised release set forth in section 3583(e) of title 18.

(b)(1) The Commission, in the guidelines promulgated pursuant to subsection (a)(1), shall, for each category of offense involving each category of defendant, establish a sentencing range that is consistent with all pertinent provisions of title 18, United States Code.

(2) If a sentence specified by the guidelines includes a term of imprisonment, the maximum of the range established for such a term shall not exceed the minimum of that range by more than the greater of 25 percent or 6 months, except that, if the minimum term of the range is 30 years or more, the maximum may be life imprisonment.

(c) The Commission, in establishing categories of offenses for use in the guidelines and policy statements governing the imposition of sentences of probation, a fine, or imprisonment, governing the imposition of other authorized sanctions, governing the size of a fine or the length of a term of probation, imprisonment, or supervised release, and governing the conditions of probation, supervised release, or imprisonment, shall consider whether the following matters, among others, have any relevance to the nature, extent, place of service, or other incidents of an appropriate sentence, and shall take them into account only to the extent that they do have relevance—

(1) the grade of the offense;

(2) the circumstances under which the offense was committed which mitigate or aggravate the seriousness of the offense;

(3) the nature and degree of the harm caused by the offense, including whether it involved property, irreplaceable property, a person, a number of persons, or a breach of public trust;

(4) the community view of the gravity of the offense;

(5) the public concern generated by the offense;

(6) the deterrent effect a particular sentence may have on the commission of the offense by others; and

(7) the current incidence of the offense in the community and in the Nation as a whole.

(d) The Commission in establishing categories of defendants for use in the guidelines and policy statements governing the imposition of sentences of probation, a fine, or imprisonment, governing the imposition of other authorized sanctions, governing the size of a fine or the length of a term of probation, imprisonment, or supervised release, and governing the conditions of probation, supervised release, or imprisonment, shall consider whether the following matters, among others with respect to a defendant, have any relevance to the nature, extent, place of service, or other incidents of an appropriate sentence, and shall take them into account only to the extent that they do have relevance—

(1) age;

(2) education;

(3) vocational skills;

(4) mental and emotional condition to the extent that such condition mitigates the defendant's culpability or to the extent that such condition is otherwise plainly relevant;

(5) physical condition, including drug dependence;

(6) previous employment record;

(7) family ties and responsibilities;

(8) community ties;

(9) role in the offense;

(10) criminal history; and

(11) degree of dependence upon criminal activity for a livelihood.

The Commission shall assure that the guidelines and policy statements are entirely neutral as to the race, sex, national origin, creed, and socioeconomic status of offenders.

(e) The Commission shall assure that the guidelines and policy statements, in recommending a term of imprisonment or length of a term of imprisonment, reflect the general inappropriateness of considering the education, vocational skills, employment record, family ties and responsibilities, and community ties of the defendant.

(f) The Commission, in promulgating guidelines pursuant to subsection (a)(1), shall promote the purposes set forth in section 991(b)(1), with particular attention to the requirements of subsection 991(b)(1)(B) for providing certainty and fairness in sentencing and reducing unwarranted sentence disparities.

(g) The Commission, in promulgating guidelines pursuant to subsection (a)(1) to meet the purposes of sentencing as set forth in section 3553(a)(2) of title 18, United States Code, shall take into account the nature and capacity of the penal, correctional, and other facilities and services available, and shall make recommendations concerning any change or expansion in the nature or capacity of such facilities and services that might become necessary as a result of the guidelines promulgated pursuant to the provisions of this chapter. The sentencing guidelines prescribed under this chapter shall be formulated to minimize the likelihood that the Federal prison population will exceed the capacity of the Federal prisons, as determined by the Commission.

(h) The Commission shall assure that the guidelines specify a sentence to a term of imprisonment at or near the maximum term authorized for categories of defendants in which the defendant is eighteen years old or older and—

(1) has been convicted of a felony that is—

(A) a crime of violence; or

(B) an offense described in section 401 of the Controlled Substances Act (21 U.S.C. 841), sections 1002(a), 1005, and 1009 of the Controlled Substances Import and Export Act (21 U.S.C. 952(a), 955, and 959), and chapter 705 of title 46; and

(2) has previously been convicted of two or more prior felonies, each of which is—

(A) a crime of violence; or

(B) an offense described in section 401 of the Controlled Substances Act (21 U.S.C. 841), sections 1002(a), 1005, and 1009 of the Controlled Substances Import and Export Act (21 U.S.C. 952(a), 955, and 959), and chapter 705 of title 46.

(i) The Commission shall assure that the guidelines specify a sentence to a substantial term of imprisonment for categories of defendants in which the defendant—

(1) has a history of two or more prior Federal, State, or local felony convictions for offenses committed on different occasions;

(2) committed the offense as part of a pattern of criminal conduct from which the defendant derived a substantial portion of the defendant's income;

(3) committed the offense in furtherance of a conspiracy with three or more persons engaging in a pattern of racketeering activity in which the defendant participated in a managerial or supervisory capacity;

(4) committed a crime of violence that constitutes a felony while on release pending trial, sentence, or appeal from a Federal, State, or local felony for which he was ultimately convicted; or

(5) committed a felony that is set forth in section 401 or 1010 of the Comprehensive Drug Abuse Prevention and Control Act of 1970 (21 U.S.C. 841 and 960), and that involved trafficking in a substantial quantity of a controlled substance.

(j) The Commission shall insure that the guidelines reflect the general appropriateness of imposing a sentence other than imprisonment in cases in which the defendant is a first offender who has not been convicted of a crime of violence or an otherwise serious offense, and the general appropriateness of imposing a term of imprisonment on a person convicted of a crime of violence that results in serious bodily injury.

(k) The Commission shall insure that the guidelines reflect the inappropriateness of imposing a sentence to a term of imprisonment for the purpose of rehabilitating the defendant or providing the defendant with needed educational or vocational training, medical care, or other correctional treatment.

(l) The Commission shall insure that the guidelines promulgated pursuant to subsection (a)(1) reflect—

(1) the appropriateness of imposing an incremental penalty for each offense in a case in which a defendant is convicted of—

(A) multiple offenses committed in the same course of conduct that result in the exercise of ancillary jurisdiction over one or more of the offenses; and

(B) multiple offenses committed at different times, including those cases in which the subsequent offense is a violation of section 3146 (penalty for failure to appear) or is committed while the person is released pursuant to the provisions of section 3147 (penalty for an offense committed while on release) of title 18; and

(2) the general inappropriateness of imposing consecutive terms of imprisonment for an offense of conspiring to commit an offense or soliciting commission of an offense and for an offense that was the sole object of the conspiracy or solicitation.

(m) The Commission shall insure that the guidelines reflect the fact that, in many cases, current sentences do not accurately reflect the seriousness of the offense. This will require that, as a starting point in its development of the initial sets of guidelines for particular categories of cases, the Commission ascertain the average sentences imposed in such categories of cases prior to the creation of the Commission, and in cases involving sentences to terms of imprisonment, the length of such terms actually served. The Commission shall not be bound by such average sentences, and shall independently develop a sentencing range that is consistent with the purposes of sentencing described in section 3553(a)(2) of Title 18, United States Code.

(n) The Commission shall assure that the guidelines reflect the general appropriateness of imposing a lower sentence than would otherwise be imposed, including a sentence that is lower than that established by statute as a minimum sentence, to take into account a defendant's substantial assistance in the investigation or prosecution of another person who has committed an offense.

(o) The Commission periodically shall review and revise, in consideration of comments and data coming to its attention, the guidelines promulgated pursuant to the provisions of this section. In fulfilling its duties and in exercising its powers, the Commission shall consult with authorities on, and individual and institutional representatives of, various aspects of the Federal criminal justice system. The United States Probation System, the Bureau of Prisons, the Judicial Conference of the United States, the Criminal Division of the United States Department of Justice, and a representative of the Federal Public Defenders shall submit to the Commission any observations, comments, or questions pertinent to the work of the Commission whenever they believe such communication would be useful, and shall, at least annually, submit to the Commission a written report commenting on the operation of the Commission's guidelines, suggesting changes in the guidelines that appear to be warranted, and otherwise assessing the Commission's work.

(p) The Commission, at or after the beginning of a regular session of Congress, but not later than the first day of May, may promulgate under subsection (a) of this section and submit to Congress amendments to the guidelines and modifications to previously submitted amendments that have not taken effect, including modifications to the effective dates of such amendments. Such an amendment or modification shall be accompanied by a statement of the reasons therefor and shall take effect on a date specified by the Commission, which shall be no earlier than 180 days after being so submitted and no later than the first day of November of the calendar year in which the amendment or modification is submitted, except to the extent that the effective date is revised or the amendment is otherwise modified or disapproved by Act of Congress.

(q) The Commission and the Bureau of Prisons shall submit to Congress an analysis and recommendations concerning maximum utilization of resources to deal effectively with the Federal prison population. Such report shall be based upon consideration of a variety of alternatives, including—

(1) modernization of existing facilities;

(2) inmate classification and periodic review of such classification for use in placing inmates in the least restrictive facility necessary to ensure adequate security; and

(3) use of existing Federal facilities, such as those currently within military jurisdiction.

(r) The Commission, not later than two years after the initial set of sentencing guidelines promulgated under subsection (a) goes into effect, and thereafter whenever it finds it advisable, shall recommend to the Congress that it raise or lower the grades, or otherwise modify the maximum penalties, of those offenses for which such an adjustment appears appropriate.

(s) The Commission shall give due consideration to any petition filed by a defendant requesting modification of the guidelines utilized in the sentencing of such defendant, on the basis of changed circumstances unrelated to the defendant, including changes in—

(1) the community view of the gravity of the offense;

(2) the public concern generated by the offense; and

(3) the deterrent effect particular sentences may have on the commission of the offense by others.

(t) The Commission, in promulgating general policy statements regarding the sentencing modification provisions in section 3582(c)(1)(A) of title 18, shall describe what should be considered extraordinary and compelling reasons for sentence reduction, including the criteria to be applied and a list of specific examples. Rehabilitation of the defendant alone shall not be considered an extraordinary and compelling reason.

(u) If the Commission reduces the term of imprisonment recommended in the guidelines applicable to a particular offense or category of offenses, it shall specify in what circumstances and by what amount the sentences of prisoners serving terms of imprisonment for the offense may be reduced.

(v) The Commission shall ensure that the general policy statements promulgated pursuant to subsection (a)(2) include a policy limiting consecutive terms of imprisonment for an offense involving a violation of a general prohibition and for an offense involving a violation of a specific prohibition encompassed within the general prohibition.

(w)(1) The Chief Judge of each district court shall ensure that, within 30 days following entry of judgment in every criminal case, the sentencing court submits to the Commission, in a format approved and required by the Commission, a written report of the sentence, the offense for which it is imposed, the age, race, sex of the offender, and information regarding factors made relevant by the guidelines. The report shall also include—

(A) the judgment and commitment order;

(B) the written statement of reasons for the sentence imposed (which shall include the reason for any departure from the otherwise applicable guideline range and which shall be stated on the written statement of reasons form issued by the Judicial Conference and approved by the United States Sentencing Commission);

(C) any plea agreement;

(D) the indictment or other charging document;

(E) the presentence report; and

(F) any other information as the Commission finds appropriate.

The information referred to in subparagraphs (A) through (F) shall be submitted by the sentencing court in a format approved and required by the Commission.

(2) The Commission shall, upon request, make available to the House and Senate Committees on the Judiciary, the written reports and all underlying records accompanying those reports described in this section, as well as other records received from courts.

(3) The Commission shall submit to Congress at least annually an analysis of these documents, any recommendations for legislation that the Commission concludes is warranted by that analysis, and an accounting of those districts that the Commission believes have not submitted the appropriate information and documents required by this section.

(4) The Commission shall make available to the Attorney General, upon request, such data files as the Commission itself may assemble or maintain in electronic form as a result of the information submitted under paragraph (1). Such data files shall be made available in electronic form and shall include all data fields requested, including the identity of the sentencing judge.

(x) The provisions of section 553 of title 5, relating to publication in the Federal Register and public hearing procedure, shall apply to the promulgation of guidelines pursuant to this section.

(y) The Commission, in promulgating guidelines pursuant to subsection (a)(1), may include, as a component of a fine, the expected costs to the Government of any imprisonment, supervised release, or probation sentence that is ordered.

(Added Pub.L. 98–473, Title II, § 217(a), Oct. 12, 1984, 98 Stat. 2019, and amended Pub.L. 99–217, § 3, Dec. 26, 1985, 99 Stat. 1728; Pub.L. 99–363, § 2, July 11, 1986, 100 Stat. 770; Pub.L. 99–570, Title I, §§ 1006(b), 1008, Oct. 27, 1986, 100 Stat. 3214; Pub.L. 99–646, §§ 6(b), 56, Nov. 10, 1986, 100 Stat. 3592, 3611; Pub.L. 100–182, §§ 16(b), 23, Dec. 7, 1987, 101 Stat. 1269, 1271; Pub.L. 100–690, Title VII, §§ 7083, 7103(b), 7109, Nov. 18, 1988, 102 Stat. 4408, 4418, 4419; Pub.L. 103–322, Title II § 20403(b) Title XXVII, § 280005(c)(4), Title XXXIII, § 330003(f)(1), Sept. 13, 1994, 108 Stat. 1825, 2097, 2141; Pub.L. 108–21, Title IV, § 401(h), (k), Apr. 30, 2003, 117 Stat. 672, 674; Pub.L. 109–177, Title VII, § 735, March 9, 2006, 120 Stat. 192, 271; Pub.L. 109–304, § 17(f)(1), Oct. 6, 2006, 120 Stat. 1708.)

EDITORIAL NOTES

Codification. Amendment by Pub.L. 99–646 to subsec. (t) of this section has been executed to subsec. (u) as the probable intent of Congress in view of redesignation of subsec. (t) as (u) by Pub.L. 99–570.

Emergency Guidelines Promulgation Authority. Pub.L. 100–182, § 21, Dec. 7, 1987, 101 Stat. 1271, provided that:

"**Sec. 21. Emergency Guidelines Promulgation Authority.**

(a) In General.—In the case of—

(1) an invalidated sentencing guideline;

(2) the creation of a new offense or amendment of an existing offense; or

(3) any other reason relating to the application of a previously established sentencing guideline, and determined by the United States Sentencing Commission to be urgent and compelling;

the Commission, by affirmative vote of at least four members of the Commission, and pursuant to its rules and regulations and consistent with all pertinent provisions of title 28 and title 18, United States Code, shall promulgate and distribute to all courts of the United States and to the United States Probation System a temporary guideline or amendment to an existing guideline, to remain in effect until and during the pendency of the next report to Congress under section 994(p) of title 28, United States Code.

(b) Expiration of Authority.—The authority of the Commission under paragraphs (1) and (2) of subsection (a) shall expire on November 1, 1989. The authority of the Commission to promulgate and distribute guidelines under paragraph (3) of subsection (a) shall expire on May 1, 1988."

Initial Sentencing Guidelines. For provisions directing that the United States Sentencing Commission submit to Congress within 30 months of Oct. 12, 1984, the initial sentencing guidelines promulgated pursuant to subsec. (a)(1) of this section, see section 235(a)(1)(B)(i) of Pub.L. 98–473, as amended, set out as a note under section 3551 of Title 18, Crimes and Criminal Procedure.

Effective Date of Sentencing Guidelines. For provisions directing that the sentencing guidelines promulgated pursuant to subsec. (a)(1) of this section not go into effect until—

(I) the United States Sentencing Commission has submitted the initial set of sentencing guidelines to the Congress, along with a report stating the reasons for the Commission's recommendations;

(II) the General Accounting Office has undertaken a study of the guidelines, and their potential impact in comparison with the operation of the existing sentencing and parole release system, and has, within one hundred and fifty days of submission of the guidelines, reported to the Congress the results of its study; and

(III) the day after the Congress has had six months after the date described in subclause (I) in which to examine the guidelines and consider the reports, and

(IV) certain other provisions take effect, see section 235(a)(1)(B)(ii) of Pub.L. 98–473, as amended, set out as a note under section 3551 of Title 18, Crimes and Criminal Procedure.

General Accounting Office Study of Impact and Operation of Sentencing Guideline System. Pub.L. 98–473, Title II, § 236, Oct. 12, 1984, 98 Stat. 2033, provided that:

"**(a)(1)** Four years after the sentencing guidelines promulgated pursuant to section 994(a)(1), and the provisions of section 3581, 3583, and 3624 of title 18, United States Code, go into effect, the General Accounting Office shall undertake a study of the guidelines in order to determine their impact and compare the guideline system with the operation of the previous sentencing and parole release system, and within six months of the undertaking of such study, report to the Congress the results of its study.

(2) Within one month of the start of the study required under subsection (a), the United States Sentencing Commission shall submit a report to the General Accounting Office, all appropriate courts, the Department of Justice, and the Congress detailing the operation of the sentencing guideline system and discussing any problems with the system or reforms needed. The report shall include an evaluation of the impact of the sentencing guidelines on prosecutorial discretion, plea bargaining, disparities in sentencing, and the use of incarceration, and shall be issued by affirmative vote of a majority of the voting members of the Commission.

(b) The Congress shall review the study submitted pursuant to subsection (a) in order to determine—

(1) whether the sentencing guideline system has been effective;

(2) whether any changes should be made in the sentencing guideline system; and

(3) whether the parole system should be reinstated in some form and the life of the Parole Commission extended."

§ 995. Powers of the Commission

(a) The Commission, by vote of a majority of the members present and voting, shall have the power to—

(1) establish general policies and promulgate such rules and regulations for the Commission as are necessary to carry out the purposes of this chapter;

(2) appoint and fix the salary and duties of the Staff Director of the Sentencing Commission, who shall serve at the discretion of the Commission and who shall be compensated at a rate not to exceed the highest rate now or hereafter prescribed for Level 6 of the Senior Executive Service Schedule (5 U.S.C. 5382);

(3) deny, revise, or ratify any request for regular, supplemental, or deficiency appropriations prior to any submission of such request to the Office of Management and Budget by the Chair;

(4) procure for the Commission temporary and intermittent services to the same extent as is authorized by section 3109(b) of title 5, United States Code;

(5) utilize, with their consent, the services, equipment, personnel, information, and facilities of other Federal, State, local, and private agencies and instrumentalities with or without reimbursement therefor;

(6) without regard to 31 U.S.C. 3324, enter into and perform such contracts, leases, cooperative agreements, and other transactions as may be necessary in the conduct of the functions of the Commission, with any public agency, or with any person, firm, association, corporation, educational institution, or nonprofit organization;

(7) accept and employ, in carrying out the provisions of this title, voluntary and uncompensated services, notwithstanding the provisions of 31 U.S.C. 1342, however, individuals providing such services shall not be considered Federal employees except for purposes of chapter 81 of title 5, United States Code, with respect to job-incurred disability and title 28, United States Code, with respect to tort claims;

(8) request such information, data, and reports from any Federal agency or judicial officer as the Commission may from time to time require and as may be produced consistent with other law;

(9) monitor the performance of probation officers with regard to sentencing recommendations, including application of the Sentencing Commission guidelines and policy statements;

(10) issue instructions to probation officers concerning the application of Commission guidelines and policy statements;

(11) arrange with the head of any other Federal agency for the performance by such agency of any function of the Commission, with or without reimbursement;

(12) establish a research and development program within the Commission for the purpose of—

(A) serving as a clearinghouse and information center for the collection, preparation, and dissemination of information on Federal sentencing practices; and

(B) assisting and serving in a consulting capacity to Federal courts, departments, and agencies in the development, maintenance, and coordination of sound sentencing practices;

(13) collect systematically the data obtained from studies, research, and the empirical experience of public and private agencies concerning the sentencing process;

(14) publish data concerning the sentencing process;

(15) collect systematically and disseminate information concerning sentences actually imposed, and the relationship of such sentences to the factors set forth in section 3553(a) of title 18, United States Code;

(16) collect systematically and disseminate information regarding effectiveness of sentences imposed;

(17) devise and conduct, in various geographical locations, seminars and workshops providing continuing studies for persons engaged in the sentencing field;

(18) devise and conduct periodic training programs of instruction in sentencing techniques for judicial and probation personnel and other persons connected with the sentencing process;

(19) study the feasibility of developing guidelines for the disposition of juvenile delinquents;

(20) make recommendations to Congress concerning modification or enactment of statutes relating to sentencing, penal, and correctional matters that the Commission finds to be necessary and advisable to carry out an effective, humane and rational sentencing policy;

(21) hold hearings and call witnesses that might assist the Commission in the exercise of its powers or duties;

(22) perform such other functions as are required to permit Federal courts to meet their responsibilities under section 3553(a) of title 18, United States Code, and to permit others involved in the Federal criminal justice system to meet their related responsibilities;

(23) retain private attorneys to provide legal advice to the Commission in the conduct of its work, or to appear for or represent the Commission in any case in which the Commission is authorized by law to represent itself, or in which the Commission is representing itself with the consent of the Department of Justice; and the Commission may in its discretion pay reasonable attorney's fees to private attorneys employed by it out of its appropriated funds. When serving as officers or employees of the United States, such private attorneys shall be considered special government employees as defined in section 202(a) of title 18; and

(24) grant incentive awards to its employees pursuant to chapter 45 of title 5, United States Code.

(b) The Commission shall have such other powers and duties and shall perform such other functions as may be necessary to carry out the purposes of this chapter, and may delegate to any member or designated person such powers as may be appropriate other than the power to establish general policy statements and guidelines pursuant to section 994(a)(1) and (2), the issuance of general policies and promulgation of rules and regulations pursuant to subsection (a)(1) of this section, and the decisions as to the factors to be considered in establishment of categories of offenses and offenders pursuant to section 994(b). The Commission shall, with respect to its activities under subsections (a)(9), (a)(10), (a)(11), (a)(12), (a)(13), (a)(14), (a)(15), (a)(16), (a)(17), and (a)(18), to the extent practicable, utilize existing resources of the Administrative Office of the United States Courts and the Federal Judicial Center for the purpose of avoiding unnecessary duplication.

(c) Upon the request of the Commission, each Federal agency is authorized and directed to make its services, equipment, personnel, facilities, and information available to the greatest practicable extent to the Commission in the execution of its functions.

(d) A simple majority of the membership then serving shall constitute a quorum for the conduct of business. Other than for the promulgation of guidelines and policy statements pursuant to section 994, the Commission may exercise its powers and fulfill its duties by the vote of a simple majority of the members present.

(e) Except as otherwise provided by law, the Commission shall maintain and make available for public inspection a record of the final vote of each member on any action taken by it.

(f) The Commission may—

(1) use available funds to enter into contracts for the acquisition of severable services for a period that begins in 1 fiscal year and ends in the next fiscal year, to the same extent as executive agencies may enter into such contracts under the authority of section 303L of the Federal Property and Administrative Services Act of 1949 (41 U.S.C. 253l);

(2) enter into multi-year contracts for the acquisition of property or services to the same extent as executive agencies may enter into such contracts under the authority of section 304B of the Federal Property and Administrative Services Act of 1949 (41 U.S.C. 254c); and

(3) make advance, partial, progress, or other payments under contracts for property or services to the same extent as executive agencies may make such payments under the authority of section 305 of the Federal Property and Administrative Services Act of 1949 (41 U.S.C. 255).

(Added Pub.L. 98–473, Title II, § 217(a), Oct. 12, 1984, 98 Stat. 2024; amended Pub.L. 100–690, Title VII, §§ 7104, 7105, 7106(b), Nov. 18, 1988, 102 Stat. 4418; Pub.L. 101–650, Title III, § 325(b)(5), Dec. 1, 1990, 104 Stat. 5121; Pub.L. 103–322, Title XXVIII, § 280005(c)(1), Sept. 13, 1994, 108 Stat. 2097; Pub.L. 110–177, Title V, § 501(a), Jan. 7, 2008, 121 Stat. 2541.)

EDITORIAL NOTES

References in Text. The provisions of title 28, United States Code, with respect to tort claims, referred to in subsec. (a)(7), are classified generally to section 1346(b) and chapter 171 (section 2671 et seq.) of this title.

Sunset Provision. Pub.L. 110–177, Title V, § 501(b), Jan. 7, 2008, 121 Stat. 2542, provided that: "The amendment made by subsection (a) [enacting subsec. (f) of this section] shall cease to have force and effect on September 30, 2010.".

§ 996. Director and staff

(a) The Staff Director shall supervise the activities of persons employed by the Commission and perform other duties assigned to the Staff Director by the Commission.

(b) The Staff Director shall, subject to the approval of the Commission, appoint such officers and employees as are necessary in the execution of the functions of the Commission. The officers and employees of the Commission shall be exempt from the provisions of part III of title 5 except the following: chapters 45 (Incentive Awards), 63 (Leave), 81 (Compensation for Work Injuries), 83 (Retirement), 85 (Unemployment Compensation), 87 (Life Insurance), and 89 (Health Insurance), and subchapter VI of chapter 55 (Payment for accumulated and accrued leave).

(Added Pub.L. 98–473, Title II, § 217(a), Oct. 12, 1984, 98 Stat. 2026, and amended Pub.L. 100–690, Title VII, § 7106(c), Nov. 18, 1988, 102 Stat. 4418; Pub.L. 101–650, Title III, § 325(b)(6), Dec. 1, 1990, 104 Stat. 5121; Pub.L. 103–322, Title XXVIII, § 280005(c)(5), Sept. 13, 1994, 108 Stat. 2097; Pub.L. 106–518, Title III, § 302(a), Nov. 13, 2000, 114 Stat. 2416.)

EDITORIAL NOTES

Accrued or Accumulated Leave. Pub. L. 106–518, § 302(b), Nov. 13, 2000, 114 Stat. 2417, provided that: "Any leave that an individual accrued or accumulated (or that otherwise became available to such individual) under the leave system of the United States Sentencing Commission and that remains unused as of the date of the enactment of this Act shall, on and after such date, be treated as leave accrued or accumulated (or that otherwise became available to such individual) under chapter 63 of title 5, United States Code."

§ 997. Annual report

The Commission shall report annually to the Judicial Conference of the United States, the Congress, and the President of the United States on the activities of the Commission.

(Added Pub.L. 98–473, Title II, § 217(a), Oct. 12, 1984, 98 Stat. 2026.)

§ 998. Definitions

As used in this chapter—

(a) "Commission" means the United States Sentencing Commission;

(b) "Commissioner" means a member of the United States Sentencing Commission;

(c) "guidelines" means the guidelines promulgated by the Commission pursuant to section 994(a) of this title; and

(d) "rules and regulations" means rules and regulations promulgated by the Commission pursuant to section 995 of this title.

(Added Pub.L. 98–473, Title II, § 217(a), Oct. 12, 1984, 98 Stat. 2026.)

* * *

PROVISIONS OF PUBLIC LAWS
GOVERNING THE COMMISSION
AND THE DRAFTING
OF SENTENCING GUIDELINES
(classified at 28 U.S.C. § 994 notes)

* * *

ANTI-DRUG ABUSE ACT OF 1988
(PUB. L. 100–690)

IMPORTATION OF CONTROLLED SUBSTANCES BY AIRCRAFT AND OTHER VESSELS. Pub.L. 100–690, Title VI, § 6453, Nov. 18, 1988, 102 Stat. 4371, provided:

"Sec. 6453. Penalties for Importation by Aircraft and Other Vessels.

(a) In General.—Pursuant to its authority under section 994(p) of title 28, United States Code, and section 21 of the Sentencing Act of 1987 [28 U.S.C. 994 note], the United States Sentencing Commission shall promulgate guidelines, or shall amend existing guidelines, to provide that a defendant convicted of violating section 1010(a) of the Controlled Substances Import and Export Act (21 U.S.C. 960(a)) under circumstances in which—

(1) an aircraft other than a regularly scheduled commercial air carrier was used to import the controlled substance; or

(2) the defendant acted as a pilot, copilot, captain, navigator, flight officer, or any other operation officer aboard any craft of vessel carrying a controlled substance,

shall be assigned an offense level under chapter 2 of the sentencing guidelines that is—

(A) two levels greater than the level that would have been assigned had the offense not been committed under circumstances set forth in (A) or (B) above; and

(B) in no event less than level 26.

(b) Effect of Amendment.—If the sentencing guidelines are amended after the effective date of this section [probably means date of enactment of this section, Nov. 18, 1988], the Sentencing Commission shall implement the instruction set forth in subsection (a) so as to achieve a comparable result."

CONTROLLED SUBSTANCE OFFENSES INVOLVING CHILDREN. Pub.L. 100–690, Title VI, § 6454, Nov. 18, 1988, 102 Stat. 4372, provided:

"Sec. 6454. Enhanced Penalties for Offenses Involving Children.

(a) In General.—Pursuant to its authority under section 994(p) of title 28, United States Code, and section 21 of the Sentencing Act of 1987 [28 U.S.C. 994 note], the United States Sentencing Commission shall promulgate guidelines, or shall amend existing guidelines, to provide that a defendant convicted of violating sections 405, 405A, or 405B of the Controlled Substances Act (21 U.S.C. 845, 845a or 845b) [redesignated as sections 418, 419, and 420, respectively (21 U.S.C. §§ 859, 860, and 861) by section 1002 of Pub.L. 101–647] involving a person under 18 years of age shall be assigned an offense level under chapter 2 of the sentencing guidelines that is—

(1) two levels greater than the level that would have been assigned for the underlying controlled substance offense; and

(2) in no event less than level 26.

(b) Effects of Amendment.—If the sentencing guidelines are amended after the effective date of this section [probably means date of enactment of this section, Nov. 18, 1988], the Sentencing Commission shall implement the instruction set forth in subsection (a) so as to achieve a comparable result.

(c) Multiple Enhancements.—The guidelines referred to in subsection (a), as promulgated or amended under such subsection, shall provide that an offense that could be subject to multiple enhancements pursuant to such subsection is subject to not more than one such enhancement."

CONTRABAND IN PRISON. Pub.L. 100–690, Title VI, § 6468(c), (d), Nov. 18, 1988, 102 Stat. 4376, provided:

"(c) Pursuant to its authority under section 994(p) of title 28, United States Code, and section 21 of the Sentencing Act of 1987 [28 U.S.C.

994 note], the United States Sentencing Commission shall promulgate guidelines, or shall amend existing guidelines, to provide that a defendant convicted of violating section 1791(a)(1) of title 18, United States Code, and punishable under section 1791(b)(1) of that title as so redesignated, shall be assigned an offense level under chapter 2 of the sentencing guidelines that is—

(1) two levels greater than the level that would have been assigned had the offense not been committed in prison; and

(2) in no event less than level 26.

(d) If the sentencing guidelines are amended after the effective date of this section [probably means the date of enactment of this section, Nov. 18, 1988], the Sentencing Commission shall implement the instruction set forth in subsection (c) so as to achieve a comparable result."

COMMON CARRIER OPERATION UNDER INFLUENCE OF ALCOHOL OR DRUGS. Pub.L. 100–690, Title VI, § 6482(c), Nov. 18, 1988, 102 Stat. 4382, provided:

"**(c) Sentencing Guidelines.—(1)** Pursuant to its authority under section 994(p) of title 28, United States Code, and section 21 of the Sentencing Act of 1987 [28 U.S.C. 994 note], the United States Sentencing Commission shall promulgate guidelines, or shall amend existing guidelines, to provide that—

(A) a defendant convicted of violating section 342 of title 18, United States Code, under circumstances in which death results, shall be assigned an offense level under chapter 2 of the sentencing guidelines that is not less than level 26; and

(B) a defendant convicted of violating section 342 of title 18, United States Code, under circumstances in which serious bodily injury results, shall be assigned an offense level under chapter 2 of the sentencing guidelines that is not less than level 21.

(2) If the sentencing guidelines are amended after the effective date of this section [probably means date of enactment of this section, Nov. 18, 1988], the Sentencing Commission shall implement the instruction set forth in paragraph (1) so as to achieve a comparable result."

* * *

MAJOR FRAUD ACT OF 1988
(PUB. L. 100–700)

PERSONAL INJURY RESULTING FROM FRAUD. Pub.L. 100–700, Chapter 47, § 2(b), Nov. 19, 1988, 102 Stat. 4632, provided:

"**(b) Sentencing Guidelines.—**Pursuant to its authority under section 994(p) of title 28, United States Code and section 21 of the Sentencing Act of 1987 [28 U.S.C. 994 note], the United States Sentencing Commission shall promulgate guidelines, or shall amend existing guidelines, to provide for appropriate penalty enhancements, where conscious or reckless risk of serious personal injury resulting from the fraud has occurred. The Commission shall consider the appropriateness of assigning to such a defendant an offense level under Chapter Two of the sentencing guidelines that is at least two levels greater than the level that would have been assigned had conscious or reckless risk of serious personal injury not resulted from the fraud."

* * *

FINANCIAL INSTITUTIONS REFORM, RECOVERY, AND ENFORCEMENT ACT OF 1989
(PUB. L. 101–73)

CRIMES THAT JEOPARDIZE FEDERALLY INSURED FINANCIAL INSTITUTIONS. Pub.L. 101–73, Title IX, § 961(m), Aug. 9, 1989, 103 Stat. 501, provided:

"**(m) Sentencing Guidelines.—**Pursuant to section 994 of title 28, United States Code, and section 21 of the Sentencing Act of 1987 [28 U.S.C. 994 note], the United States Sentencing Commission shall promulgate guidelines, or amend existing guidelines, to provide for a substantial period of incarceration for a violation of, or a conspiracy to violate, section 215, 656, 657, 1005, 1006, 1007, 1014, 1341, 1343, or 1344 of title 18, United States Code, that substantially jeopardizes the safety and soundness of a federally insured financial institution."

* * *

CRIME CONTROL ACT OF 1990
(PUB. L. 101–647)

SEXUAL CRIMES AGAINST CHILDREN. Pub.L. 101–647, Title III, § 321, Nov. 29, 1990, 104 Stat. 4817, provided:

"Sec. 321. Sentencing Commission Guidelines.

The United States Sentencing Commission shall amend existing guidelines for sentences involving sexual crimes against children, including offenses contained in chapter 109A of title 18, so that more substantial penalties may be imposed if the Commission determines current penalties are inadequate."

KIDNAPPING, ABDUCTION, OR UNLAWFUL RESTRAINT. Pub.L. 101–647, Title IV, § 401, Nov. 29, 1990, 104 Stat. 4819, amended 18 U.S.C. § 1201by adding the following new subsection:

"(g) Special Rule for Certain Offenses Involving Children.—
(1) To Whom Applicable.—If—
(A) the victim of an offense under this section has not attained the age of eighteen years; and
(B) the offender—
(i) has attained such age; and
(ii) is not—
(I) a parent;
(II) a grandparent;
(III) a brother;
(IV) a sister;
(V) an aunt;
(VI) an uncle; or
(VII) an individual having legal custody of the victim;
the sentence under this section for such offense shall be subject to paragraph (2) of this subsection.

(2) Guidelines.—The United States Sentencing Commission is directed to amended the existing guidelines for the offense of 'kidnapping, abduction, or unlawful restraint,' by including the following additional specific offense characteristics: If the victim was intentionally maltreated (i.e., denied either food or medical care) to a life-threatening degree, increase by 4 levels; if the victim was sexually exploited (i.e., abused, used involuntarily for pornographic purposes) increase by 3 levels; if the victim was placed in the care or custody of another person who does not have a legal right to such care or custody of the child either in exchange for money or other consideration, increase by 3 levels; if the defendant allowed the child to be subjected to any of the conduct specified in this section by another person, then increase by 2 levels."

REPORT ON MANDATORY MINIMUM SENTENCING PROVISIONS. Pub.L. 101–647, Title XVII, § 1703, Nov. 29, 1990, 104 Stat. 4845, provided:

"Sec. 1703. Report on Mandatory Minimum Sentencing Provisions.
(a) **Report.**—Not less than six months after the date of enactment of this Act, the United States Sentencing Commission shall transmit to the respective Judiciary Committees of the Senate and House of Representatives a report on mandatory minimum sentencing provisions in Federal law.
(b) **Components of Report.**—The report mandated by subsection (a) shall included:
(1) a compilation of all mandatory minimum sentencing provisions in Federal law;
(2) an assessment of the effect of mandatory minimum sentencing provisions on the goal of eliminating unwarranted sentencing disparity;
(3) a projection of the impact of mandatory minimum sentencing provisions on the Federal prison population;
(4) an assessment of the compatibility of mandatory minimum sentencing provisions and the sentencing guidelines system established by the Sentencing Reform Act of 1984;

(5) a description of the interaction between mandatory minimum sentencing provisions and plea agreements;

(6) a detailed empirical research study of the effect of mandatory minimum penalties in the Federal system;

(7) a discussion of mechanisms other than mandatory minimum sentencing laws by which Congress can express itself with respect to sentencing policy, such as:

　(A) specific statutory instructions to the Sentencing Commission;

　(B) general statutory instructions to the Sentencing Commission;

　(C) increasing or decreasing the maximum sentence authorized for particular crimes;

　(D) Sense of Congress resolutions; and

(8) any other information that the Commission would contribute to a thorough assessment of mandatory minimum sentencing provisions.

(c) Amendment of Report.—The Commission may amend or update the report mandated by subsection (a) at any time after its transmittal."

OFFENSES AFFECTING FINANCIAL INSTITUTIONS. Pub.L. 101–647, Title XXV, § 2507, Nov. 29, 1990, 104 Stat. 4862, provided:

"Sec. 2507. Increased Penalties in Major Bank Crime Cases.

(a) Increased Penalties.—Pursuant to section 994 of title 28, United States Code, and section 21 of the Sentencing Act of 1987 [28 U.S.C. 994 note] the United States Sentencing Commission shall promulgate guidelines, or amend existing guidelines, to provide that a defendant convicted of violating, or conspiring to violate, section 215, 656, 657, 1005, 1006, 1007, 1014, 1032, or 1344 of title 18, United States Code, or section 1341 or 1343 affecting a financial institution (as defined in section 20 of title 18, United States Code) shall be assigned not less than offense level 24 under chapter 2 of the sentencing guidelines if the defendant derives more than $1,000,000 in gross receipts from the offense.

(b) Amendments to Sentencing Guidelines.—If the sentencing guidelines are amended after the effective date of this section, the Sentencing Commission shall implement the instruction set forth in subsection (a) so as to achieve a comparable result."

SMOKABLE CRYSTAL METHAMPHETAMINE. Pub.L. 101–647, Title XXVII, § 2701, Nov. 29, 1990, 104 Stat. 4912, provided:

"Sec. 2701. Sentencing Commission Guidelines.

"The United States Sentencing Commission is instructed to amend the existing guidelines for offenses involving smokable crystal methamphetamine under section 401(b) of the Controlled Substances Act (21 U.S.C. § 841(b)) so that convictions for offenses involving smokable crystal methamphetamine will be assigned an offense level under the guidelines which is two levels above that which would have been assigned to the same offense involving other forms of methamphetamine."

* * *

TREASURY, POSTAL SERVICE AND GENERAL GOVERNMENT APPROPRIATIONS ACT, 1992 (PUB. L. 102–141)

SEXUAL ABUSE AND EXPLOITATION OF MINORS; CHILD PORNOGRAPHY; OBSCENITY. Pub.L. 102–141, Title VI, § 632, Oct. 28, 1991, 105 Stat. 876, provided:

"Sec. 632. (1) Pursuant to its authority under section 994 of title 28, United States Code, the Sentencing Commission shall promulgate guidelines, or amend existing or proposed guidelines as follows:

　(A) Guideline 2G2.2 to provide a base offense level of not less than 15 and to provide at least a 5 level increase for offenders who have engaged in a pattern of activity involving the sexual abuse or exploitation of a minor.

(B) Guideline 2G2.4 to provide that such guideline shall apply only to offense conduct that involves the simple possession of materials proscribed by chapter 110 of title 18, United States Code and guideline 2G2.2 to provide that such guideline shall apply to offense conduct that involves receipt or trafficking (including, but not limited to transportation, distribution, or shipping).

(C) Guideline 2G2.4 to provide a base offense level of not less than 13, and to provide at least a 2 level increase for possessing 10 or more books, magazines, periodicals, films, video tapes or other items containing a visual depiction involving the sexual exploitation of a minor.

(D) Section 2G3.1 to provide a base offense level of not less than 10.

(2)(A) Notwithstanding any other provision of law, the Sentencing Commission shall promulgate the amendments mandated in subsection (1) by November 1, 1991, or within 30 days after enactment [probably means date of enactment of Pub.L. 102–141, which was approved Oct. 28, 1991], whichever is later. The amendments to the guidelines promulgated under subsection (1) shall take effect November 1, 1991, or 30 days after enactment, and shall supersede any amendment to the contrary contained in the amendments to the sentencing guidelines submitted to the Congress by the Sentencing Commission on or about May 1, 1991.

(B) The provisions of section 944(x) of title 28, United States Code, shall not apply to the promulgation or amendment of guidelines under this section."

* * *

VIOLENT CRIME CONTROL AND LAW ENFORCEMENT ACT OF 1994 (PUB. L. 103–322)

SEXUAL OFFENSES BY REPEAT OFFENDERS. Pub.L. 103–322, Title IV, § 40111(b), Sept. 13, 1994, 108 Stat. 1903, provided:

"(b) Amendment of Sentencing Guidelines.—The Sentencing Commission shall implement the amendment made by subsection (a)[of this section (pertaining to repeat sexual offenders)] by promulgating amendments, if appropriate, in the sentencing guidelines applicable to chapter 109A [of title 18] offenses."

SEXUAL ABUSE; AGGRAVATED SEXUAL ABUSE. Pub.L. 103–322, Title IV, § 40112, Sept. 13, 1994, 108 Stat. 1903, provided:

"Sec. 40112. Federal Penalties.

(a) Amendment of Sentencing Guidelines.—Pursuant to its authority under section 994(p) of title 28, United States Code, the United States Sentencing Commission shall review and amend, where necessary, its sentencing guidelines on aggravated sexual abuse under section 2241 of title 18, United States Code, or sexual abuse under section 2242 of title 18 United States Code, as follows:

(1) The Commission shall review and promulgate amendments to the guidelines, if appropriate, to enhance penalties if more than 1 offender is involved in the offense.

(2) The Commission shall review and promulgate amendments to the guidelines, if appropriate, to reduce unwarranted disparities between the sentences for sex offenders who are known to the victim and sentences for sex offenders who are not known to the victim.

(3) The Commission shall review and promulgate amendments to the guidelines to enhance penalties, if appropriate, to render Federal penalties on Federal territory commensurate with penalties for similar offenses in the States.

(4) The Commission shall review and promulgate amendments to the guidelines, if appropriate, to account for the general problem of recidivism in cases of sex offenses, the severity of the offense, and its devastating effects on survivors.

(b) Report.—Not later than 180 days after the date of enactment of this Act, the United States Sentencing Commission shall review and submit to Congress a report containing an analysis of Federal rape sentencing, accompanied by comment from independent experts in the field, describing—

(1) comparative Federal sentences for cases in which the rape victim is known to the defendant and cases in which the rape victim is not known to the defendant;

(2) comparative Federal sentences for cases on Federal territory and sentences in surrounding States; and

(3) an analysis of the effect of rape sentences on populations residing primarily on Federal territory relative to the impact of other Federal offenses in which the existence of Federal jurisdiction depends upon the offense's being committed on Federal territory."

INTENTIONAL TRANSMISSION OF HIV. Pub.L. 103–322, Title IV, § 40503(c), Sept. 13, 1994, 108 Stat. 1947, provided:

"**(c) Penalties for Intentional Transmission of HIV.**—Not later than 6 months after the date of enactment of this Act, the United States Sentencing Commission shall conduct a study and prepare and submit to the committees on the Judiciary of the Senate and the House of Representatives a report concerning recommendations for the revision of sentencing guidelines that relate to offenses in which an HIV infected individual engages in sexual activity if the individual knows that he or she is infected with HIV and intends, through such sexual activity, to expose another to HIV."

LIMITATION ON APPLICABILITY OF MANDATORY MINIMUM PENALTIES IN CERTAIN CASES; SENTENCING COMMISSION AUTHORITY. Pub.L. 103–322, Title VIII, § 80001, Sept. 13, 1994, 108 Stat. 1986, provided:

"**(a) [enacted 18 U.S.C. § 3553(f) (Limitation on applicability of statutory minimums in certain cases)]**
(b) Sentencing Commission Authority.—

(1) In general.—**(A)** The United States Sentencing Commission (referred to in this subsection as the 'Commission'), under section 994(a)(1) and (p) of title 28—

(i) shall promulgate guidelines, or amendments to guidelines, to carry out the purposes of this section and the amendment made by this section; and

(ii) may promulgate policy statements, or amendments to policy statements, to assist in the application of this section and that amendment.

(B) In the case of a defendant for whom the statutorily required minimum sentence of 5 years, such guidelines and amendments to guidelines issued under subparagraph (A) shall call for a guideline range in which the lowest term of imprisonment is at least 24 months.

(2) Procedures.—If the Commission determines that it is necessary to do so in order that the amendments made under paragraph (1) may take effect on the effective date of the amendment made by subsection (a), the Commission may promulgate the amendments made under paragraph (1) in accordance with the procedures set forth in section 21(a) of the Sentencing Act of 1987, as though the authority under that section had not expired."

DRUG DEALING IN "DRUG-FREE" ZONES. Pub.L. 103–322, Title IX, § 90102, Sept. 13, 1994, 108 Stat. 1987, provided:

"**Sec. 90102. Increased Penalties for Drug-Dealing in 'Drug-Free' Zones.**

"Pursuant to its authority under section 994 of title 28, United States Code, the United States Sentencing Commission shall amend its sentencing guidelines to provide an appropriate enhancement for a defendant convicted of violating section 419 of the Controlled Substances Act (21 U.S.C. 860)."

ILLEGAL DRUG USE IN FEDERAL PRISONS; SMUGGLING DRUGS INTO FEDERAL PRISONS. Pub.L. 103–322, Title IX, § 90103, Sept. 13, 1994, 108 Stat. 1987, provided:

"Sec. 90103. Enhanced Penalties for Illegal Drug Use in Federal Prisons and for Smuggling Drugs into Federal Prisons.

(a) Declaration of Policy.—It is the policy of the Federal Government that the use or distribution of illegal drugs in the Nation's Federal prisons will not be tolerated and that such crimes shall be prosecuted to the fullest extent of the law.

(b) Sentencing Guidelines.—Pursuant to its authority under section 994 of title 28, United States Code, the United States Sentencing Commission shall amend its sentencing guidelines to appropriately enhance the penalty for a person convicted of an offense—

(1) under section 404 of the Controlled Substances Act involving simple possession of a controlled substance within a Federal prison or other Federal detention facility; or

(2) under section 401(b) of the Controlled Substances Act involving the smuggling of a controlled substance into a Federal prison or other Federal detention facility or the distribution or intended distribution of a controlled substance within a Federal prison or other Federal detention facility.

(c) No Probation.—Notwithstanding any other law, the court shall not sentence a person convicted of an offense described in subsection (b) to probation."

USE OF A SEMIAUTOMATIC FIREARM DURING A CRIME OF VIOLENCE OR A DRUG TRAFFICKING CRIME. Pub.L. 103–322, Title XI, § 110501, Sept. 13, 1994, 108 Stat. 2015, provided:

"Sec. 110501. Enhanced Penalty for Use of a Semiautomatic Firearm During a Crime of Violence or a Drug Trafficking Crime.

(a) Amendment to Sentencing Guidelines.—Pursuant to its authority under section 994 of title 28, United States Code, the United States Sentencing Commission shall amend its sentencing guidelines to provide an appropriate enhancement of the punishment for a crime of violence (as defined in section 924(c)(3) of title 18, United States Code) or a drug trafficking crime (as defined in section 924(c)(2) of title 18,

United States Code) if a semiautomatic firearm is involved.

(b) Semiautomatic Firearm.—In subsection (a), 'semiautomatic firearm' means any repeating firearm that utilizes a portion of the energy of a firing cartridge to extract the fired cartridge case and chamber the next round and that requires a separate pull of the trigger to fire each cartridge."

SECOND OFFENSE OF USING AN EXPLOSIVE TO COMMIT A FELONY. Pub.L. 103–322, Title XI, § 110502, Sept. 13, 1994, 108 Stat. 2015, provided:

"Sec. 110502. Enhanced Penalty for Second Offense of Using an Explosive to Commit a Felony.

Pursuant to its authority under section 994 of title 28, United States Code, the United States Sentencing Commission shall promulgate amendments to the sentencing guidelines to appropriately enhance penalties in a case in which a defendant convicted under section 844(h) of title 18, United States Code, has previously been convicted under that section."

USING A FIREARM IN COUNTERFEITING OR FORGERY. Pub.L. 103–322, Title XI, § 110512, Sept. 13, 1994, 108 Stat. 2019, provided:

"Sec. 110512. Using a Firearm in the Commission of Counterfeiting or Forgery.

Pursuant to its authority under section 994 of title 28, United States Code, the United States Sentencing Commission shall amend its sentencing guidelines to provide an appropriate enhancement of the punishment for a defendant convicted of a felony under chapter 25 of title 18, United States Code, if the defendant used or carried a firearm (as defined in section 921(a)(3) of title 18, United States Code) during and in relation to the felony."

FIREARMS POSSESSION BY VIOLENT FELONS AND SERIOUS DRUG OFFENDERS. Pub.L. 103–322, Title XI, § 110513, Sept. 13, 1994, 108 Stat. 2019, provided:

"Sec. 110513. Enhanced Penalties for Firearms Possession by Violent Felons and Serious Drug Offenders.

Pursuant to its authority under section 994 of title 28, United States Code, the United States Sentencing Commission shall amend its sentencing guidelines to—

(1) appropriately enhance penalties in cases in which a defendant convicted under section 922(g) of title 18, United States Code, has 1 prior conviction by any court referred to in section 922(g)(1) of title 18 for a violent felony (as defined in section 924(e)(2)(B) of that title) or a serious drug offense (as defined in section 924(e)(2)(A) of that title); and

(2) appropriately enhance penalties in cases in which such a defendant has 2 prior convictions for a violent felony (as so defined) or a serious drug offense (as so defined)."

PROMOTING INTERNATIONAL TERRORISM. Pub.L. 103–322, Title XII, § 120004, Sept. 13, 1994, 108 Stat. 2022, provided:

"Sec. 120004. Sentencing Guidelines Increase for Terrorist Crimes.

The United States Sentencing Commission is directed to amend its sentencing guidelines to provide an appropriate enhancement for any felony, whether committed within or outside the United States, that involves or is intended to promote international terrorism, unless such involvement or intent is itself an element of the crime."

INVOLVING A MINOR IN THE COMMISSION OF THE OFFENSE. Pub.L. 103–322, Title XIV, § 140008, Sept. 13, 1994, 108 Stat. 2033, provided:

"Sec. 140008. Solicitation of Minor to Commit Crime.

(a) Directive to Sentencing Commission.—(1) The United States Sentencing Commission shall promulgate guidelines or amend existing guidelines to provide that a defendant 21 years of age or older who has been convicted of an offense shall receive an appropriate sentence enhancement if the defendant involved a minor in the commission of the offense.

(2) The Commission shall provide that the guidelines enhancement promulgated pursuant to paragraph (1) shall apply for any offense in relation to which the defendant has solicited, procured, recruited, counseled, encouraged, trained, directed, commanded, intimidated, or otherwise used or attempted to use any person less than 18 years of age with the intent that the minor would commit a Federal offense.

(b) Relevant Considerations.—In implementing the directive in subsection (a), the Sentencing Commission shall consider—

(1) the severity of the crime that the defendant intended the minor to commit;

(2) the number of minors that the defendant used or attempted to use in relation to the offense;

(3) the fact that involving a minor in a crime of violence is frequently of even greater seriousness than involving a minor in a drug trafficking offense, for which the guidelines already provide a two-level enhancement; and

(4) the possible relevance of the proximity in age between the offender and the minor(s) involved in the offense."

DRUG FREE TRUCK STOPS AND SAFETY REST AREAS. Pub.L. 103–322, Title XVIII, § 180201(c), Sept. 13, 1994, 108 Stat. 2047, provided:

"(c) Sentencing Guidelines.—Pursuant to its authority under section 994 of title 28, United States Code, and section 21 of the Sentencing Act of 1987 (28 U.S.C. 994 note), the United States Sentencing Commission shall promulgate guidelines, or shall amend existing guidelines, to provide an appropriate enhancement of punishment for a defendant convicted of violating section 409 of the Controlled Substances Act [21 U.S.C. § 849], as added by subsection (b) [of this section]."

CRIMES OF VIOLENCE AGAINST ELDERLY VICTIMS. Pub.L. 103–322, Title XXIV, § 240002, Sept. 13, 1994, 108 Stat. 2081, provided:

"**Sec. 240002. Crimes Against the Elderly.**

(a) **In General.**—Pursuant to its authority under the Sentencing Reform Act of 1984 and section 21 of the Sentencing Act of 1987 (including its authority to amend the sentencing guidelines and policy statements) and its authority to make such amendments on an emergency basis, the United States Sentencing Commission shall ensure that the applicable guideline range for a defendant convicted of a crime of violence against an elderly victim is sufficiently stringent to deter such a crime, to protect the public from additional crimes of such a defendant, and to adequately reflect the heinous nature of such an offense.

(b) **Criteria.**—In carrying out subsection (a), the United States Sentencing Commission shall ensure that—

(1) the guidelines provide for increasingly severe punishment for a defendant commensurate with the degree of physical harm caused to the elderly victim;

(2) the guidelines take appropriate account of the vulnerability of the victim; and

(3) the guidelines provide enhanced punishment for a defendant convicted of a crime of violence against an elderly victim who has previously been convicted of a crime of violence against an elderly victim, regardless of whether the conviction occurred in Federal or State court.

(c) **Definitions.**—In this section—

(1) 'crime of violence' means an offense under section 113, 114, 1111, 1112, 1113, 1117, 2241, 2242, or 2244 of title 18, United States Code.

(2) 'elderly victim' means a victim who is 65 years of age or older at the time of an offense."

FRAUD AGAINST OLDER VICTIMS. Pub.L. 103–322, Title XXV, § 250003, Sept. 13, 1994, 108 Stat. 2085, provided:

"**Sec. 250003. Increased Penalties for Fraud Against Older Victims.**

(a) **Review.**—The United States Sentencing Commission shall review and, if necessary, amend the sentencing guidelines to ensure that victim related adjustments for fraud offenses against older victims over the age of 55 are adequate.

(b) **Report.**—Not later than 180 days after the date of enactment of this Act, the Sentencing Commission shall report to Congress the result of its review under subsection (a)."

HATE CRIMES. Pub.L. 103–322, Title XXVIII, § 280003, Sept. 13, 1994, 108 Stat. 2096, as amended by Pub. L. 111–84, Div. E, § 4703(a), Oct. 28, 2009, 123 Stat. 2836, provided:

"**Sec. 280003. Direction to United States Sentencing Commission Regarding Sentencing Enhancements for Hate Crimes.**

(a) **Definition.**—In this section, 'hate crime' means a crime in which the defendant intentionally selects a victim, or in the case of a property crime, the property that is the object of the crime, because of the actual or perceived race, color, religion, national origin, ethnicity, gender, gender identity, disability, or sexual orientation of any person.

(b) **Sentencing Enhancement.**—Pursuant to section 994 of title 28, United States Code, the United States Sentencing Commission shall promulgate guidelines or amend existing guidelines to provide sentencing enhancements of not less than 3 offense levels for offenses that the finder of fact at trial determines beyond a reasonable doubt are hate crimes. In carrying out this section, the United States Sentencing Commission shall ensure that there is reasonable consistency with other guidelines, avoid duplicative punishments for substantially the same offense, and take into account any mitigating circumstances that might justify exceptions."

REPORT ON COCAINE PENALTIES. Pub.L. 103–322, Title XXVIII, § 280006, Sept. 13, 1994, 108 Stat. 2097, provided:

"Sec. 280006. Cocaine Penalty Study.

Not later than December 31, 1994, the United States Sentencing Commission shall submit a report to Congress on issues relating to sentences applicable to offenses involving the possession or distribution of all forms of cocaine. The report shall address the differences in penalty levels that apply to different forms of cocaine and include any recommendations that the Commission may have for retention or modification of such differences in penalty levels."

* * *

ACT TO DISAPPROVE OF AMENDMENTS TO THE FEDERAL SENTENCING GUIDELINES RELATING TO LOWERING OF CRACK SENTENCES AND SENTENCES FOR MONEY LAUNDERING AND TRANSACTIONS IN PROPERTY DERIVED FROM UNLAWFUL ACTIVITY (PUB. L. 104–38)

DISAPPROVAL OF AMENDMENTS; RECOMMENDATIONS ON COCAINE OFFENSES; STUDY AND COMMENTS ON MONEY LAUNDERING. Pub.L. 104–38, §§ 1–2, Oct. 30, 1995, 109 Stat. 334, provided:

"Section 1. Disapproval of Amendments Relating to Lowering of Crack Sentences and Sentences for Money Laundering and Transactions in Property Derived from Unlawful Activity.

In accordance with section 994(p) of title 28, United States Code, amendments numbered 5 and 18 of the "Amendments to the Sentencing Guidelines, Policy Statements, and Official Commentary", submitted by the United States Sentencing Commission to Congress on May 1, 1995, are hereby disapproved and shall not take effect.

"Sec. 2. Reduction of Sentencing Disparity.
    (a) Recommendations.—
        (1) In general.—The United States Sentencing Commission shall submit to Congress recommendations (and an explanation therefor), regarding changes to the statutes and sentencing guidelines governing sentences for unlawful manufacturing, importing, exporting, and trafficking of cocaine, and like offenses, including unlawful possession, possession with intent to commit any of the forgoing offenses, and attempt and conspiracy to commit any of the forgoing offenses. The recommendations shall reflect the following considerations—

        (A) the sentence imposed for trafficking in a quantity of crack cocaine should generally exceed the sentence imposed for trafficking in a like quantity of powder cocaine;

        (B) high-level wholesale cocaine traffickers, organizers, and leaders of criminal activities should generally receive longer sentences than low-level retail cocaine traffickers and those who played a minor or minimal role in such criminal activity;

        (C) if the Government establishes that a defendant who traffics in powder cocaine has knowledge that such cocaine will be converted into crack cocaine prior to its distribution to individual users, the defendant should be treated at sentencing as though the defendant had trafficked in crack cocaine; and

        (D) an enhanced sentence should generally be imposed on a defendant who, in the course of an offense described in this subsection—
            (i) murders or causes serious bodily injury to an individual;
            (ii) uses a dangerous weapon;
            (iii) uses or possesses a firearm;
            (iv) involves a juvenile or a woman who the defendant knows or should know to be pregnant;
            (v) engages in a continuing criminal enterprise or commits other criminal offenses in order to facilitate his drug trafficking activities;
            (vi) knows, or should know, that he is involving an unusually vulnerable person;
            (vii) restrains a victim;

(viii) traffics in cocaine within 500 feet of a school;

(ix) obstructs justice;

(x) has a significant prior criminal record; or

(xi) is an organizer or leader of drug trafficking activities involving five or more persons.

(2) Ratio.—The recommendations described in the preceding subsection shall propose revision of the drug quantity ratio of crack cocaine to powder cocaine under the relevant statutes and guidelines in a manner consistent with the ratios set for other drugs and consistent with the objectives set forth in section 3553(a) of title 28 United States Code.

(b) Study.—No later than May 1, 1996, the Department of Justice shall submit to the Judiciary Committees of the Senate and House of Representatives a report on the charging and plea practices of Federal prosecutors with respect to the offense of money laundering. Such study shall include an account of the steps taken or to be taken by the Justice Department to ensure consistency and appropriateness in the use of the money laundering statute. The Sentencing Commission shall submit to the Judiciary Committees comments on the study prepared by the Department of Justice."

* * *

SEX CRIMES AGAINST CHILDREN PREVENTION ACT OF 1995 (PUB. L. 104–71)

SEXUAL EXPLOITATION OF CHILDREN; CHILD PORNOGRAPHY. Pub.L. 104–71, § 2, Dec. 23, 1995, 109 Stat. 774, provided:

"Sec. 2. Increased Penalties for Certain Conduct Involving the Sexual Exploitation of Children.

The United States Sentencing Commission shall amend the sentencing guidelines to—

(1) increase the base offense level for an offense under section 2251 of title 18, United States Code, by at least 2 levels; and

(2) increase the base offense level for an offense under section 2252 of title 18, United States Code, by at least 2 levels."

USE OF COMPUTERS IN SEXUAL EXPLOITATION OF CHILDREN. Pub.L. 104–71, § 3, Dec. 23, 1995, 109 Stat. 774, provided:

"Sec. 3. Increased Penalties for Use of Computers in Sexual Exploitation of Children.

The United States Sentencing Commission shall amend the sentencing guidelines to increase the base offense level by at least 2 levels for an offense committed under section 2251(c)(1)(A) or 2252(a) of title 18, United States Code, if a computer was used to transmit the notice or advertisement to the intended recipient or to transport or ship the visual depiction."

TRANSPORTATION OF MINORS WITH INTENT TO ENGAGE IN CRIMINAL SEXUAL ACTIVITY. Pub.L. 104–71, § 4, Dec. 23, 1995, 109 Stat. 774, provided:

"Sec. 4. Increased Penalties for Transportation of Children With Intent to Engage in Criminal Sexual Activity.

The United States Sentencing Commission shall amend the sentencing guidelines to increase the base offense level for an offense under section 2423(a) of title 18, United States Code, by at least 3 levels."

REPORT ON CHILD PORNOGRAPHY AND OTHER SEX OFFENSES AGAINST CHILDREN. Pub.L. 104–71, § 6, Dec. 23, 1995, 109 Stat. 774, provided:

"Sec. 6. Report by the United States Sentencing Commission.

Not later than 180 days after the date of the enactment of this Act, the United States Sentencing Commission shall submit a report to Congress concerning offenses involving child pornography and other sex offenses against children. The Commission shall include in the report—

(1) an analysis of the sentences imposed for offenses under sections 2251, 2252, and

2423 of title 18, United States Code, and recommendations regarding any modifications to the sentencing guidelines that may be appropriate with respect to those offenses;

(2) an analysis of the sentences imposed for offenses under sections 2241, 2242, and 2243, and 2244 of title 18, United States Code, in cases in which the victim was under the age of 18 years, and recommendations regarding any modifications to the sentencing guidelines that may be appropriate with respect to those offenses;

(3) an analysis of the type of substantial assistance that courts have recognized as warranting a downward departure from the sentencing guidelines relating to offenses under section 2251 or 2252 of title 18, United States Code;

(4) a survey of the recidivism rate for offenders convicted of committing sex crimes against children, an analysis of the impact on recidivism of sexual abuse treatment provided during or after incarceration or both, and an analysis of whether increased penalties would reduce recidivism for those crimes; and

(5) such other recommendations with respect to the offenses described in this section as the Commission deems appropriate."

* * *

ANTITERRORISM AND EFFECTIVE DEATH PENALTY ACT OF 1996
or
MANDATORY VICTIMS RESTITUTION ACT OF 1996
(PUB. L. 104–132)

COMMUNITY RESTITUTION. Pub.L. 104–132, Title II, § 205(a)(3), Apr. 24, 1996, 110 Stat. 1230, amended 18 U.S.C. § 3663 by adding new subsection (c)(7), which provided:

"**(7)(A)** The United States Sentencing Commission shall promulgate guidelines to assist courts in determining the amount of restitution

that may be ordered under this subsection [subsection (c) of 18 U.S.C. § 3663, pertaining to community restitution].

(B) No restitution shall be ordered under this subsection until such time as the Sentencing Commission promulgates guidelines pursuant to this paragraph."

MANDATORY VICTIMS RESTITUTION. Pub.L. 104–132, § 208, April 24, 1996, 110 Stat. 1240, provided:

"Sec. 208. Instruction to Sentencing Commission.

Pursuant to section 994 of title 28, United States Code, the United States Sentencing Commission shall promulgate guidelines or amend existing guidelines to reflect this subtitle ['Mandatory Victims Restitution Act of 1996'] and the amendments made by this subtitle."

INTERNATIONAL TERRORISM. Pub.L. 104–132, § 730, April 24, 1996, 110 Stat. 1303, provided:

"Sec. 730. Directions to Sentencing Commission.

The United States Sentencing Commission shall forthwith, in accordance with the procedures set forth in section 21(a) of the Sentencing Act of 1987, as though the authority under that section had not expired, amend the sentencing guidelines so that the chapter 3 adjustment relating to international terrorism only applies to Federal crimes of terrorism, as defined in section 2332b(g) of title 18, United States Code."

FRAUD AND DAMAGE INVOLVING PROTECTED COMPUTERS (SECTION 1030 OFFENSES). Pub.L. 104–132, § 805, April 24, 1996, 110 Stat. 1305, provided:

"Sec. 805. Deterrent Against Terrorist Activity Damaging a Federal Interest Computer.

(a) Review.—Not later than 60 calendar days after the dates of enactment of this Act, the United States Sentencing Commission shall review the deterrent effect of existing guideline levels as they apply to paragraphs (4) and (5) of section 1030(a) of title 18, United States Code.

(b) Report.—The United States Sentencing Commission shall prepare and transmit a report to the Congress on the findings under the study conducted under subsection (a).

(c) Amendment of Sentencing Guidelines.— Pursuant to its authority under section 994(p) of title 28, United States Code, the United States Sentencing Commission shall amend the sentencing guidelines to ensure any individual convicted of a violation of paragraph (4) or (5) of section 1030(a) of title 18, United States Code, is imprisoned for not less than 6 months."

INTERNATIONAL COUNTERFEITING (SECTION 470 OFFENSES). Pub.L. 104–132, § 807(h), April 24, 1996, 110 Stat. 1310, provided:

"**(h) Enhanced Penalties for International Counterfeiting of United States Currency.**—Pursuant to the authority of the United States Sentencing Commission under section 994 of title 28, United States Code, the Commission shall amend the sentencing guidelines prescribed by the Commission to provide an appropriate enhancement of the punishment for a defendant convicted under section 470 of title 18 of such Code."

* * *

NATIONAL DEFENSE AUTHORIZATION ACT FOR FISCAL YEAR 1997 (PUB. L. 104–201)

NUCLEAR, BIOLOGICAL, AND CHEMICAL WEAPONS MATERIALS. Pub.L. 104–201, Title XIV, § 1423, Sept. 23, 1996, 110 Stat 2725 [which is classified both to 28 U.S.C. § 994 note and to 50 U.S.C. § 2332] provided:

"**Sec. 1423. Sense of Congress Concerning Criminal Penalties.**

(a) Sense of Congress Concerning Inadequacy of Sentencing Guidelines.—It is the sense of Congress that the sentencing guidelines prescribed by the United States Sentencing Commission for the offenses of importation, attempted importation, exportation, and attempted exportation of nuclear, biological, and chemical weapons materials constitute inadequate punishment for such offenses.

(b) Urging of Revision to Guidelines.— Congress urges the United States Sentencing Commission to revise the relevant sentencing guidelines to provide for increased penalties for offenses relating to importation, attempted importation, exportation, and attempted exportation of nuclear, biological, or chemical weapons or related materials or technologies under the following provisions of law:

(1) Section 11 of the Export Administration Act of 1979 (50 U.S.C.App. 2410).

(2) Sections 38 and 40 of the Arms Export Control Act (22 U.S.C. 2778 and 2780).

(3) The International Emergency Economic Powers Act (50 U.S.C. 1701 et seq.).

(4) Section 309(c) of the Nuclear Non-Proliferation Act of 1978 (22 U.S.C. 2156a(c))."

* * *

OMNIBUS CONSOLIDATED APPROPRIATIONS ACT, 1997 or ILLEGAL IMMIGRATION REFORM AND IMMIGRANT RESPONSIBILITY ACT OF 1996 (PUB. L. 104–208)

ALIEN SMUGGLING. Pub.L. 104–208, Div. C, Title II, § 203(e), Sept. 30, 1996, 110 Stat. 3009–566, provided:

"**(e) Sentencing Guidelines.**—

(1) In general.—Pursuant to its authority under section 994(p) of title 28, United States Code, the United States Sentencing Commission shall promulgate sentencing guidelines or amend existing sentencing guidelines for offenders convicted of offenses related to smuggling, transporting, harboring, or inducing aliens in violation of section

274(a)(1)(A) or (2) of the Immigration and Nationality Act (8 U.S.C. 1324(a)(1)(A), (2)(B)) in accordance with this subsection.

(2) Requirements.—In carrying out this subsection, the Commission shall, with respect to the offenses described in paragraph (1)—

(A) increase the base offense level for such offenses at least 3 offense levels above the applicable level in effect on the date of the enactment of this Act;

(B) review the sentencing enhancement for the number of aliens involved (U.S.S.G. 2L1.1(b)(2)), and increase the sentencing enhancement by at least 50 percent above the applicable enhancement in effect on the date of the enactment of this Act;

(C) impose an appropriate sentencing enhancement upon an offender with 1 prior felony conviction arising out of a separate and prior prosecution for an offense that involved the same or similar underlying conduct as the current offense, to be applied in addition to any sentencing enhancement that would otherwise apply pursuant to the calculation of the defendant's criminal history category;

(D) impose an additional appropriate sentencing enhancement upon an offender with 2 or more prior felony convictions arising out of separate and prior prosecutions for offenses that involved the same or similar underling conduct as the current offense, to be applied in addition to any sentencing enhancement that would otherwise apply pursuant to the calculation of the defendant's criminal history category;

(E) impose an appropriate sentencing enhancement on a defendant who, in the course of committing an offense described in this subsection—

(i) murders or otherwise causes death, bodily injury, or serious bodily injury to an individual;

(ii) uses or brandishes a firearm or other dangerous weapon; or

(iii) engages in conduct that consciously or recklessly places another in serious danger of death or serious bodily injury;

(F) consider whether a downward adjustment is appropriate if the offense is a first offense and involves the smuggling only of the alien's spouse or child; and

(G) consider whether any other aggravating or mitigating circumstances warrant upward or downward sentencing adjustments.

(3) Emergency Authority to Sentencing Commission.—The Commission shall promulgate the guidelines or amendments provided for under this subsection as soon as practicable in accordance with the procedure set forth in section 21(a) of the Sentencing Act of 1987, as though the authority under that Act had not expired."

FRAUD IN CONNECTION WITH IDENTIFICATION, NATURALIZATION, AND IMMIGRATION DOCUMENTS. Pub.L. 104–208, Div. C, Title II, § 211(b), Sept. 30, 1996, 110 Stat. 3009–569, provided:

"(b) Changes to the Sentencing Levels.—

(1) In general.—Pursuant to the Commission's authority under section 994(p) of title 28, United States Code, the United States Sentencing Commission shall promulgate sentencing guidelines or amend existing sentencing guidelines for offenders convicted of violating, or conspiring to violate, sections 1028(b)(1), 1425 through 1427, 1541 through 1544, and 1546(a) of title 18, United States Code, in accordance with this subsection.

(2) Requirements.—In carrying out this subsection, the Commission shall, with respect to the offenses referred to in paragraph (1)—

(A) increase the base offense level for such offenses at least 2 offense levels above the level in effect on the date of the enactment of this Act;

(B) review the sentencing enhancement for number of documents or passports involved (U.S.S.G. 2L2.1(b)(2)), and increase the upward adjustment by at least 50 percent above the applicable enhancement in effect on the date of the enactment of this Act;

(C) impose an appropriate sentencing enhancement upon an offender with 1 prior felony conviction arising out of a separate and prior prosecution for an offense that involved the same or similar underlying conduct as the current offense, to be applied in addition to any sentencing enhancement that would otherwise apply pursuant to the calculation of the defendant's criminal history category;

(D) impose an additional appropriate sentencing enhancement upon an offender with 2 or more prior felony convictions arising out of separate and prior prosecutions for offenses that involved the same or similar underlying conduct as the current offense, to be applied in addition to any sentencing enhancement that would otherwise apply pursuant to the calculation of the defendant's criminal history category; and

(E) consider whether any other aggravating or mitigating circumstances warrant upward or downward sentencing adjustments.

(3) Emergency Authority to Sentencing Commission.—The Commission shall promulgate the guidelines or amendments provided for under this subsection as soon as practicable in accordance with the procedure set forth in section 21(a) of the Sentencing Act of 1987, as though the authority under that Act had not expired."

PEONAGE, INVOLUNTARY SERVITUDE, AND SLAVE TRADE OFFENSES. Pub.L. 104–208, Div. C, Title II, § 218(b), (c), Sept. 30, 1996, 110 Stat. 3009–573, provided:

"**(b) Review of Sentencing Guidelines.**— The United States Sentencing Commission shall ascertain whether there exists an unwarranted disparity—

(1) between the sentences for peonage, involuntary servitude, and slave trade offenses, and the sentences for kidnapping offenses in effect on the date of the enactment of this Act; and

(2) between the sentences for peonage, involuntary servitude, and slave trade offenses, and the sentences for alien smuggling offenses in effect on the date of the enactment of this Act and after the amendment made by subsection (a).

(c) Amendment of Sentencing Guidelines.—

(1) In general.—Pursuant to its authority under section 994(p) of title 28, United States Code, the United States Sentencing Commission shall review its guidelines on sentencing for peonage, involuntary servitude, and slave trade offenses under sections 1581 through 1588 of title 18, United States Code, and shall amend such guidelines as necessary to—

(A) reduce or eliminate any unwarranted disparity found under subsection (b) that exists between the sentences for peonage, involuntary servitude, and slave trade offenses, and the sentences for kidnapping offenses and alien smuggling offenses;

(B) ensure that the applicable guidelines for defendants convicted of peonage, involuntary servitude, and slave trade offenses are sufficiently stringent to deter such offenses and adequately reflect the heinous nature of such offenses; and

(C) ensure that the guidelines reflect the general appropriateness of enhanced sentences for defendants whose peonage, involuntary servitude, or slave trade offenses involve—

(i) a large number of victims;

(ii) the use or threatened use of a dangerous weapon; or

(iii) a prolonged period of peonage or involuntary servitude.

(2) Emergency Authority to Sentencing Commission.—The Commission shall promulgate the guidelines or amendments provided for under this subsection as soon as practicable in accordance with the procedure set forth in section 21(a) of the Sentencing

Act of 1987, as though the authority under that Act had not expired."

CONSPIRING WITH OR ASSISTING AN ALIEN TO COMMIT AN OFFENSE UNDER THE CONTROLLED SUBSTANCES IMPORT AND EXPORT ACT. Pub.L. 104–208, Div. C, Title III, § 333, Sept. 30, 1996, 110 Stat. 3009–634, provided:

"Sec. 333. Penalties for Conspiring with or Assisting an Alien to Commit an Offense Under the Controlled Substances Import and Export Act.

(a) Review of Guidelines.—Not later than 6 months after the date of the enactment of this Act, the United States Sentencing Commission shall conduct a review of the guidelines applicable to an offender who conspires with, or aids or abets, a person who is not a citizen or national of the United States in committing any offense under section 1010 of the Controlled Substance Import and Export Act (21 U.S.C. 960).

(b) Revision of Guidelines.—Following such review, pursuant to section 994(p) of title 28, United States Code, the Commission shall promulgate sentencing guidelines or amend existing sentencing guidelines to ensure an appropriately stringent sentence for such offenders."

FAILURE TO DEPART, ILLEGAL REENTRY, AND PASSPORT AND VISA FRAUD. Pub. L. 104–208, Div. C, Title III, § 334, Sept. 30, 1996, 110 Stat. 3009–635, provided:

"Sec. 334. Enhanced Penalties for Failure to Depart, Illegal Reentry, and Passport and Visa Fraud.

(a) Failing to Depart.—The United States Sentencing Commission shall promptly promulgate, pursuant to section 994 of title 28, United States Code, amendments to the sentencing guidelines to make appropriate increases in the base offense level for offenses under section 242(e) and 276(b) of the Immigration and Nationality Act (8 U.S.C. 1252(e) and 1326(b)) to reflect the amendments made by section 130001 of the Violent Crime Control and Law Enforcement Act of 1994.

(b) Passport and Visa Offenses.—The United States Sentencing Commission shall promptly promulgate, pursuant to section 994 of title 28, United States Code, amendments to the sentencing guidelines to make appropriate increases in the base offense level for offenses under chapter 75 of title 18, United States Code, to reflect the amendments made by section 130009 of the Violent Crime Control and Law Enforcement Act of 1994."

* * *

COMPREHENSIVE METHAMPHETAMINE CONTROL ACT OF 1996 (PUB. L. 104–237)

METHAMPHETAMINE MANUFACTURING. Pub.L. 104–237, Title II, § 203(b), Oct. 3, 1996, 110 Stat. 3102, provided:

"(b) Sentencing Commission.—The United States Sentencing Commission shall amend the sentencing guidelines to ensure that the manufacture of methamphetamine in violation of section 403(d)(2) of the Controlled Substances Act [21 U.S.C. § 843(d)(2)], as added by subsection (a), is treated as a significant violation."

METHAMPHETAMINE OFFENSES. Pub.L. 104–237, Title II, § 301, Oct. 3, 1996, 110 Stat. 3105, provided:

"Sec. 301. Penalty Increases for Trafficking in Methamphetamine.

(a) Directive to the United States Sentencing Commission.—Pursuant to its authority under section 994 of title 28, United States Code, the United States Sentencing Commission shall review and amend its guidelines and its policy statements to provide for increased penalties for unlawful manufacturing, importing, exporting, and trafficking of methamphetamine, and other similar offenses, including unlawful possession with intent to commit any of those offenses, and attempt and conspiracy to commit any of those offenses. The

Commission shall submit to Congress explanations therefor and any additional policy recommendations for combating methamphetamine offenses.

(b) In General.—In carrying out this section, the Commission shall ensure that the sentencing guidelines and policy statements for offenders convicted of offenses described in subsection (a) and any recommendations submitted under such subsection reflect the heinous nature of such offenses, the need for aggressive law enforcement action to fight such offenses, and the extreme dangers associated with unlawful activity involving methamphetamine, including—

> **(1)** the rapidly growing incidence of methamphetamine abuse and the threat to public safety such abuse poses;

> **(2)** the high risk of methamphetamine addiction;

> **(3)** the increased risk of violence associated with methamphetamine trafficking and abuse; and

> **(4)** the recent increase in the illegal importation of methamphetamine and precursor chemicals."

LIST I CHEMICAL OFFENSES. Pub.L. 104–237, Title II, § 302(c), Oct. 3, 1996, 110 Stat. 3105, provided:

"**(c) Sentencing Guidelines.**—

(1) In General.—The United States Sentencing Commission shall, in accordance with the procedures set forth in section 21(a) of the Sentencing Act of 1987, as though the authority of that section had not expired, amend the sentencing guidelines to increase by at least two levels the offense level for offenses involving list I chemicals under—

> **(A)** section 401(d)(1) and (2) of the Controlled Substances Act (21 U.S.C. 841(d)(1) and (2)); and

> **(B)** section 1010(d)(1) and (3) of the Controlled Substance Import and Export Act (21 U.S.C. 960(d)(1) and (3)).

(2) Requirement.—In carrying out this subsection, the Commission shall ensure that the offense levels for offenses referred to in paragraph (1) are calculated proportionally on the basis of the quantity of controlled substance that reasonably could have been manufactured in a clandestine setting using the quantity of the list I chemical possessed, distributed, imported, or exported."

DANGEROUS HANDLING OF CONTROLLED SUBSTANCES. Pub.L. 104–237, Title III, § 303, Oct. 3, 1996, 110 Stat. 3106, provided:

"**Sec. 303. Enhanced Penalty for Dangerous Handling of Controlled Substances; Amendment of Sentencing Guidelines.**

(a) In General.—Pursuant to its authority under section 994 of title 28, United States Code, the United States Sentencing Commission shall determine whether the Sentencing Guidelines adequately punish the offenses described in subsection (b) and, if not, promulgate guidelines or amend existing guidelines to provide an appropriate enhancement of the punishment for a defendant convicted of such an offense.

(b) Offense.—The offense referred to in subsection (a) is a violation of section 401(d), 401(g)(1), 403(a)(6), or 403(a)(7) of the Controlled Substances Act (21 U.S.C. 841(d), 841(g)(1), 843(a)(6), and 843(a)(7)), in cases in which in the commission of the offense the defendant violated—

> **(1)** subsection (d) or (e) of section 3008 of the Solid Waste Disposal Act (relating to handling hazardous waste in a manner inconsistent with Federal or applicable State law);

> **(2)** section 103(b) of the Comprehensive Environmental Response, Compensation and Liability Act (relating to failure to notify as to the release of a reportable quantity of a hazardous substance into the environment);

> **(3)** section 301(a), 307(d), 309(c)(2), 309(c)(3), 311(b)(3), or 311(b)(5) of the Federal Water Pollution Control Act (relating to the unlawful discharge of pollutants or hazardous substances, the operation of a source in violation of a pretreatment standard, and the failure to notify as to the release of a reportable quantity of a hazardous substance into the water); or

(4) section 5124 of title 49, United States Code (relating to violations of laws and regulations enforced by the Department of Transportation with respect to the transportation of hazardous material)."

* * *

ECONOMIC ESPIONAGE ACT OF 1996 (PUB. L. 104–294)

ANNUAL REPORT ON USE OF CERTAIN TECHNOLOGY TO FACILITATE CRIMINAL CONDUCT. Pub.L. 104–294, Title V, § 501, Oct. 11, 1996, 110 Stat. 3497 [also classified to 18 U.S.C. § 3552 note], provided:

"Sec. 501. Use of Certain Technology to Facilitate Criminal Conduct.

(a) Information.—The Administrative Office of the United States courts shall establish policies and procedures for the inclusion in all presentence reports of information that specifically identifies and describes any use of encryption or scrambling technology that would be relevant to an enhancement under section 3C1.1 (dealing with Obstructing or Impeding the Administration of Justice) of the Sentencing Guidelines or to offense conduct under the Sentencing Guidelines.

(b) Compiling and Report.—The United States Sentencing Commission shall—

(1) compile and analyze any information contained in documentation described in subsection (a) relating to the use of encryption or scrambling technology to facilitate or conceal criminal conduct; and

(2) based on the information compiled and analyzed under paragraph (1), annually report to the Congress on the nature and extent of the use of encryption or scrambling technology to facilitate or conceal criminal conduct."

* * *

DRUG-INDUCED RAPE PREVENTION AND PUNISHMENT ACT OF 1996 (PUB. L. 104–305)

FLUNITRAZEPAM OFFENSES. Pub. L. 104– 305, § 2(b)(3), Oct. 13, 1996, 110 Stat. 3808, provided:

"(3) Sentencing guidelines.—

(A) Amendment of sentencing guidelines.—Pursuant to its authority under section 994 of title 28, United States Code, the United States Sentencing Commission shall review and amend, as appropriate, the sentencing guidelines for offenses involving flunitrazepam.

(B) Summary.—The United States Sentencing Commission shall submit to the Congress—

(i) a summary of its review under subparagraph (A); and

(ii) an explanation for any amendment to the sentencing guidelines made under subparagraph (A).

(C) Serious nature of offenses.—In carrying out this paragraph, the United States Sentencing Commission shall ensure that the sentencing guidelines for offenses involving flunitrazepam reflect the serious nature of such offenses."

* * *

VETERANS' CEMETERY PROTECTION ACT OF 1997 (PUB. L. 105–101)

NATIONAL CEMETERY PROPERTY OFFENSES. Pub.L. 105–101, § 2, November 19, 1997, 111 Stat. 2202, provided:

"Sec. 2. Sentencing for Offenses Against Property at National Cemeteries.

(a) In General.—Pursuant to its authority under section 994 of title 28, United States Code, the United States Sentencing Commission shall review and amend the Federal sentencing guidelines to provide a sentencing enhancement of not less than 2 levels for any offense against the property of a national cemetery.

(b) Commission Duties.—In carrying out subsection (a), the Sentencing Commission shall ensure that the sentences, guidelines, and policy statements for offenders convicted of an offense described in that subsection are—

(1) appropriately severe; and

(2) reasonably consistent with other relevant directives and with other Federal sentencing guidelines."

* * *

NO ELECTRONIC THEFT (NET) ACT
(PUB. L. 105–147)

INTELLECTUAL PROPERTY OFFENSES. Pub. L. 105–147, § 2(g), Dec. 16, 1997, 111 Stat. 2678, provided:

"**(g) Directive to Sentencing Commission.—(1)** Under the authority of the Sentencing Reform Act of 1984 (Public Law 98–473; 98 Stat.1987) and section 21 of the Sentencing Act of 1987 (Public Law 100–182; 101 Stat. 1271; 18 U.S.C. 994 note) (including the authority to amend the sentencing guidelines and policy statements), the United States Sentencing Commission shall ensure that the applicable guideline range for a defendant convicted of a crime against intellectual property (including offenses set forth at section 506(a) of title 17, United States Code, and sections 2319, 2319A, and 2320 of title 18, United States Code) is sufficiently stringent to deter such a crime and to adequately reflect the additional considerations set forth in paragraph (2) of this subsection.

(2) In implementing paragraph (1), the Sentencing Commission shall ensure that the guidelines provide for consideration of the retail value and quantity of the items with respect to which the crime against intellectual property was committed."

* * *

WIRELESS TELEPHONE PROTECTION ACT
(PUB. L. 105–172)

WIRELESS TELEPHONE CLONING. Pub.L. 105–172, § 2(e), Apr. 24, 1998, 112 Stat. 55, provided:

"**(e) Amendment of Federal Sentencing Guidelines for Wireless Telephone Cloning.—**

(1) In general.—Pursuant to its authority under section 994 of title 28, United States Code, the United States Sentencing Commission shall review and amend the Federal sentencing guidelines and the policy statements of the Commission, if appropriate, to provide an appropriate penalty for offenses involving the cloning of wireless telephones (including offenses involving an attempt or conspiracy to clone a wireless telephone).

(2) Factors for consideration.— In carrying out this subsection, the Commission shall consider, with respect to the offenses described in paragraph (1)—

(A) the range of conduct covered by the offenses;

(B) the existing sentences for the offenses;

(C) the extent to which the value of the loss caused by the offenses (as defined in the Federal sentencing guidelines) is an adequate measure for establishing penalties under the Federal sentencing guidelines;

(D) the extent to which sentencing enhancements within the Federal sentencing guidelines and the court's authority to sentence above the applicable guideline range are adequate to ensure punishment at or near the maximum penalty for the most egregious conduct covered by the offenses;

(E) the extent to which the Federal sentencing guideline sentences for the offenses have been constrained by statutory maximum penalties;

(F) the extent to which Federal sentencing guidelines for the offenses adequately achieve the purposes of sentencing set forth in section 3553(a)(2) of title 18, United States Code;

(G) the relationship of Federal sentencing guidelines for the offenses to the Federal sentencing guidelines for other offenses of comparable seriousness; and

(H) any other factor that the Commission considers to be appropriate."

* * *

TELEMARKETING FRAUD PROTECTION ACT OF 1998 (PUB. L. 105–184)

TELEMARKETING FRAUD (SECTION 2326 OFFENSES). Pub.L. 105–184, § 6, June 23, 1998, 112 Stat. 520, provided:

"**Sec. 6. Amendment of Federal Sentencing Guidelines.**

(a) Definition of Telemarketing.—In this section, the term "telemarketing" has the meaning given that term in section 2326 of title 18, United States Code.

(b) Directive to Sentencing Commission.—Pursuant to its authority under section 994(p) of title 28, United States Code, and in accordance with this section, the United States Sentencing Commission shall–

(1) promulgate Federal sentencing guidelines or amend existing sentencing guidelines (and policy statements, if appropriate) to provide for substantially increased penalties for persons convicted of offenses described in section 2326 of title 18, United States Code, as amended by this Act, in connection with the conduct of telemarketing; and

(2) submit to Congress an explanation of each action taken under paragraph (1) and any additional policy recommendations for combating the offenses described in that paragraph.

(c) Requirements.—In carrying out this section, the Commission shall—

(1) ensure that the guidelines and policy statements promulgated or amended pursuant to subsection (b)(1) and any recommendations submitted thereunder reflect the serious nature of the offenses;

(2) provide an additional appropriate sentencing enhancement, if the offense involved sophisticated means, including but not limited to sophisticated concealment efforts, such as perpetrating the offense from outside the United States;

(3) provide an additional appropriate sentencing enhancement for cases in which a large number of vulnerable victims, including but not limited to victims described in section 2326(2) of title 18, United States Code, are affected by a fraudulent scheme or schemes;

(4) ensure that guidelines and policy statements promulgated or amended pursuant to subsection (b)(1) are reasonably consistent with other relevant statutory directives to the Commission and with other guidelines;

(5) account for any aggravating or mitigating circumstances that might justify upward or downward departures;

(6) ensure that the guidelines adequately meet the purposes of sentencing as set forth in section 3553(a)(2) of title 18, United States Code; and

(7) take any other action the Commission considers necessary to carry out this section.

(d) Emergency Authority.—The Commission shall promulgate the guidelines or amendments provided for under this subsection as soon as practicable, and in any event not later than 120 days after the date of the enactment of the Telemarketing Fraud Prevention Act of 1998, in accordance with the procedures set forth in section 21(a) of the Sentencing Reform Act of 1987, as though the authority under that authority had not expired, except that the Commission shall submit to Congress the emergency guidelines or amendments promulgated under this section, and shall set an effective date for those guidelines or amendments not earlier than 30 days after their submission to Congress."

* * *

PROTECTION OF CHILDREN FROM SEXUAL PREDATORS ACT OF 1998 (PUB. L. 105–314)

SEXUAL OFFENSES AGAINST CHILDREN AND REPEAT SEXUAL OFFENDERS. Pub.L. 105–314, Title V, Oct. 30, 1998, 112 Stat. 2980 provided:

"TITLE V—INCREASED PENALTIES FOR OFFENSES AGAINST CHILDREN AND FOR REPEAT OFFENDERS

"Sec. 501. Death or Life in Prison for Certain Offenses Whose Victims Are Children.

[omitted]

"Sec. 502. Sentencing Enhancement for Chapter 117 Offenses.

(a) In General.—Pursuant to its authority under section 994(p) of title 28, United States Code, the United States Sentencing Commission shall review and amend the Federal Sentencing Guidelines to provide a sentencing enhancement for offenses under chapter 117 [18 U.S.C.A. § 2421 et seq.] of title 18, United States Code.

(b) Instruction to Commission.—In carrying out subsection (a), the United States Sentencing Commission shall ensure that the sentences, guidelines, and policy statements for offenders convicted of offenses described in subsection (a) are appropriately severe and reasonably consistent with other relevant directives and with other Federal Sentencing Guidelines.

"Sec. 503. Increased Penalties for Use of a Computer in the Sexual Abuse or Exploitation of a Child.

Pursuant to its authority under section 994(p) of title 28, United States Code, the United States Sentencing Commission shall—

(1) review the Federal Sentencing Guidelines for—

(A) aggravated sexual abuse under section 2241 of title 18, United States Code;

(B) sexual abuse under section 2242 of title 18, United States Code;

(C) sexual abuse of a minor or ward under section 2243 of title 18, United States Code; and

(D) coercion and enticement of a minor under section 2422(b) of title 18, United States Code, contacting a minor under section 2422(c) of title 18, United States Code, and transportation of minors and travel under section 2423 of title 18, United States Code; and

(2) upon completion of the review under paragraph (1), promulgate amendments to the Federal Sentencing Guidelines to provide appropriate enhancement if the defendant used a computer with the intent to persuade, induce, entice, coerce, or facilitate the transport of a child of an age specified in the applicable provision of law referred to in paragraph (1) to engage in any prohibited sexual activity.

"Sec. 504. Increased Penalties for Knowing Misrepresentation in the Sexual Abuse or Exploitation of a Child.

Pursuant to its authority under section 994(p) of title 28, United States Code, the United States Sentencing Commission shall—

(1) review the Federal Sentencing Guidelines on aggravated sexual abuse under section 2241 of title 18, United States Code, sexual abuse under section 2242 of title 18, United States Code, sexual abuse of a minor or ward under section 2243 of title 18, United States Code, coercion and enticement of a minor under section 2422(b) of title 18, United States Code, contacting a minor under section 2422(c) of title 18, United States Code, and transportation of minors and travel under section 2423 of title 18, United States Code; and

(2) upon completion of the review under paragraph (1), promulgate amendments to the Federal Sentencing Guidelines to provide appropriate enhancement if the defendant knowingly misrepresented the actual identity of the defendant with the intent to persuade, induce, entice, coerce, or facilitate the transport of a child of an age specified in the applicable provision of law referred to in paragraph (1) to engage in a prohibited sexual activity.

"Sec. 505. Increased Penalties for Pattern of Activity of Sexual Exploitation of Children.

Pursuant to its authority under section 994(p) of title 28, United States Code, the United States Sentencing Commission shall—

(1) review the Federal Sentencing Guidelines on aggravated sexual abuse under section 2241 of title 18, United States Code, sexual abuse under section 2242 of title 18, United States Code, sexual abuse of a minor or ward under section 2243 of title 18, United States Code, coercion and enticement of a minor under section 2422(b) of title 18, United States Code, contacting a minor under section 2422(c) of title 18, United States Code, and transportation of minors and travel under section 2423 of title 18, United States Code; and

(2) upon completion of the review under paragraph (1), promulgate amendments to the Federal Sentencing Guidelines to increase penalties applicable to the offenses referred to in paragraph (1) in any case in which the defendant engaged in a pattern of activity involving the sexual abuse or exploitation of a minor.

"Sec. 506. Clarification of Definition of Distribution of Pornography.

Pursuant to its authority under section 994(p) of title 28, United States Code, the United States Sentencing Commission shall—

(1) review the Federal Sentencing Guidelines relating to the distribution of pornography covered under chapter 110 of title 18, United States Code [18 U.S.C.A. § 2251 et seq.], relating to the sexual exploitation and other abuse of children; and

(2) upon completion of the review under paragraph (1), promulgate such amendments to the Federal Sentencing Guidelines as are necessary to clarify that the term 'distribution of pornography' applies to the distribution of pornography—

(A) for monetary remuneration; or
(B) for a nonpecuniary interest.

"Sec. 507. Directive to the United States Sentencing Commission.

In carrying out this title, the United States Sentencing Commission shall—

(1) with respect to any action relating to the Federal Sentencing Guidelines subject to this title, ensure reasonable consistency with other guidelines of the Federal Sentencing Guidelines; and

(2) with respect to an offense subject to the Federal Sentencing Guidelines, avoid duplicative punishment under the Federal Sentencing Guidelines for substantially the same offense."

* * *

IDENTITY THEFT AND ASSUMPTION DETERRENCE ACT OF 1998 (PUB. L. 105–318)

IDENTITY THEFT AND DOCUMENT FRAUD (SECTION 1028 OFFENSES). Pub.L. 105–318, § 4, Oct. 30, 1998, 112 Stat. 3009, provided:

"Sec. 4. Amendment of Federal Sentencing Guidelines for Offenses Under Section 1028.

(a) In general.—Pursuant to its authority under section 994(p) of title 28, United States Code, the United States Sentencing Commission shall review and amend the Federal sentencing guidelines and the policy statements of the Commission, as appropriate, to provide an appropriate penalty for each offense under section 1028 of title 18, United States Code, as amended by this Act.

(b) Factors for consideration.—In carrying out subsection (a), the United States Sentencing Commission shall consider, with respect to each offense described in subsection (a)—

(1) the extent to which the number of victims (as defined in section 3663A(a) of title 18, United States Code) involved in the offense, including harm to reputation, inconvenience, and other difficulties resulting from the offense, is an adequate measure for establishing penalties under the Federal sentencing guidelines;

(2) the number of means of identification, identification documents, or false identification documents (as those terms are defined in section 1028(d) of title 18, United States Code, as amended by this Act) involved in the offense, is an adequate measure for establishing penalties under the Federal sentencing guidelines;

(3) the extent to which the value of the loss to any individual caused by the offense is an adequate measure for establishing penalties under the Federal sentencing guidelines;

(4) the range of conduct covered by the offense;

(5) the extent to which sentencing enhancements within the Federal sentencing guidelines and the court's authority to sentence above the applicable guideline range are adequate to ensure punishment at or near the maximum penalty for the most egregious conduct covered by the offense;

(6) the extent to which Federal sentencing guidelines sentences for the offense have been constrained by statutory maximum penalties;

(7) the extent to which Federal sentencing guidelines for the offense adequately achieve the purposes of sentencing set forth in section 3553(a)(2) of title 18, United States Code; and

(8) any other factor that the United States Sentencing Commission considers to be appropriate."

* * *

DIGITAL THEFT DETERRENCE AND COPYRIGHT DAMAGES IMPROVEMENT ACT OF 1999
(PUB. L. 106–160)

INTELLECTUAL PROPERTY OFFENSES. Pub. L. 106–160, § 3, Dec. 9, 1999, 113 Stat. 1774, provided:

"Sec. 3. Sentencing Commission Guidelines.

Within 120 days after the date of the enactment of this Act [Dec. 9, 1999], or within 120 days after the first date on which there is a sufficient number of voting members of the Sentencing Commission to constitute a quorum, whichever is later, the Commission shall promulgate emergency guideline amendments to implement section 2(g) of the No Electronic Theft (NET) Act (29 U.S.C. 994 note[1]) in accordance with the procedures set forth in section 21(a) of the Sentencing Act of 1987 [28 U.S.C. 994 note], as though the authority under that Act had not expired."

* * *

CHILDREN'S HEALTH ACT OF 2000
or
METHAMPHETAMINE ANTI-PROLIFERATION ACT OF 2000
(PUB. L. 106–310)

AMPHETAMINE OFFENSES. Pub. L. 106–310, Div. B, Title XXXVI, § 3611, Oct. 17, 2000, 114 Stat. 1228, provided:

"Sec. 3611. Enhanced Punishment of Amphetamine Laboratory Operators.

(a) Amendment to Federal Sentencing Guidelines.—Pursuant to its authority under section 994(p) of title 28, United States Code, the United States Sentencing Commission shall amend the Federal sentencing guidelines in accordance with this section with respect to any offense relating to the manufacture, importation, exportation, or trafficking in amphetamine

---

[1]   So in original. Probably should be 28 U.S.C. note.

(including an attempt or conspiracy to do any of the foregoing) in violation of—

(1) the Controlled Substances Act (21 U.S.C. 801 et seq.);

(2) the Controlled Substances Import and Export Act (21 U.S.C. 951 et seq.); or

(3) the Maritime Drug Law Enforcement Act (46 U.S.C. App. 1901 et seq.).

(b) General Requirement.—In carrying out this section, the United States Sentencing Commission shall, with respect to each offense described in subsection (a) relating to amphetamine—

(1) review and amend its guidelines to provide for increased penalties such that those penalties are comparable to the base offense level for methamphetamine; and

(2) take any other action the Commission considers necessary to carry out this subsection.

(c) Additional requirements.—In carrying out this section, the United States Sentencing Commission shall ensure that the sentencing guidelines for offenders convicted of offenses described in subsection (a) reflect the heinous nature of such offenses, the need for aggressive law enforcement action to fight such offenses, and the extreme dangers associated with unlawful activity involving amphetamines, including—

(1) the rapidly growing incidence of amphetamine abuse and the threat to public safety that such abuse poses;

(2) the high risk of amphetamine addiction;

(3) the increased risk of violence associated with amphetamine trafficking and abuse; and

(4) the recent increase in the illegal importation of amphetamine and precursor chemicals.

(d) Emergency Authority to Sentencing Commission.—The United States Sentencing Commission shall promulgate amendments pursuant to this section as soon as practicable after the date of the enactment of this Act in accordance with the procedure set forth in section 21(a) of the Sentencing Act of 1987 (Public Law 100–182), as though the authority under that Act had not expired."

MANUFACTURE OF AMPHETAMINE OR METHAMPHETAMINE. Pub. L. 106–310, Div. B, Title XXXVI, § 3612, Oct. 12, 2000, 114 Stat. 1228, provided:

"Sec. 3612. Enhanced Punishment of Amphetamine or Methamphetamine Laboratory Operators.

(a) Federal Sentencing Guidelines.—

(1) In General.—Pursuant to its authority under section 994(p) of title 28, United States Code, the United States Sentencing Commission shall amend the Federal sentencing guidelines in accordance with paragraph (2) with respect to any offense relating to the manufacture, attempt to manufacture, or conspiracy to manufacture amphetamine or methamphetamine in violation of—

(A) the Controlled Substances Act (21 U.S.C. 801 et seq.);

(B) the Controlled Substances Import and Export Act (21 U.S.C. 951 et seq.); or

(C) the Maritime Drug Law Enforcement Act (46 U.S.C. App. 1901 et seq.).

(2) Requirements.—In carrying out this paragraph, the United States Sentencing Commission shall—

(A) if the offense created a substantial risk of harm to human life (other than a life described in subparagraph (B)) or the environment, increase the base offense level for the offense—

(i) by not less than 3 offense levels above the applicable level in effect on the date of the enactment of this Act; or

(ii) if the resulting base offense level after an increase under clause (i) would be less than level 27, to not less than level 27; or

(B) if the offense created a substantial risk of harm to the life of a minor or incompetent, increase the base offense level for the offense—

(i) by not less than 6 offense levels above the applicable level in effect on the date of the enactment of this Act; or

(ii) if the resulting base offense level after an increase under clause (i) would be less than level 30, to not less than level 30.

(3) Emergency authority to Sentencing Commission.—The United States Sentencing Commission shall promulgate amendments pursuant to this subsection as soon as practicable after the date of the enactment of this Act in accordance with the procedure set forth in section 21(a) of the Sentencing Act of 1987 (Public Law 100–182), as though the authority under that Act had not expired.

(b) Effective date.—The amendments made pursuant to this section shall apply with respect to any offense occurring on or after the date that is 60 days after the date of the enactment of this Act."

TRAFFICKING IN LIST I CHEMICALS. Pub. L. 106–310, Div. B, Title XXXVI, § 3651, Oct. 17, 2000, 1143 Stat. 1238, provided:

"Sec. 3651. Enhanced Punishment for Trafficking in List I Chemicals.

(a) Amendments to Federal Sentencing Guidelines.—Pursuant to its authority under section 994(p) of title 28, United States Code, the United States Sentencing Commission shall amend the Federal sentencing guidelines in accordance with this section with respect to any violation of paragraph (1) or (2) of section 401(d) of the Controlled Substances Act (21 U.S.C. 841(d)) involving a list I chemical and any violation of paragraph (1) or (3) of section 1010(d) of the Controlled Substance Import and Export Act (21 U.S.C. 960(d)) involving a list I chemical.

(b) Ephedrine, Phenylpropanolamine, and Pseudoephedrine.—

(1) In general.—In carrying this section, the United States Sentencing Commission shall, with respect to each offense described in subsection (a) involving ephedrine, phenylpropanolamine, or pseudoephedrine (including their salts, optical isomers, and salts of optical isomers), review and amend its guidelines to provide for increased penalties such that those penalties corresponded to the quantity of controlled substance that could reasonably have been manufactured using the quantity of ephedrine, phenylpropanolamine, or pseudoephedrine possessed or distributed.

(2) Conversion ratios.—For the purposes of the amendments made by this subsection, the quantity of controlled substance that could reasonably have been manufactured shall be determined by using a table of manufacturing conversion ratios for ephedrine, phenylpropanolamine, and pseudoephedrine, which table shall be established by the Sentencing Commission based on scientific, law enforcement, and other data the Sentencing Commission considers appropriate.

(c) Other List I Chemicals.—In carrying this section, the United States Sentencing Commission shall, with respect to each offense described in subsection (a) involving any list I chemical other than ephedrine, phenylpropanolamine, or pseudoephedrine, review and amend its guidelines to provide for increased penalties such that those penalties reflect the dangerous nature of such offenses, the need for aggressive law enforcement action to fight such offenses, and the extreme dangers associated with unlawful activity involving methamphetamine and amphetamine, including—

(1) the rapidly growing incidence of controlled substance manufacturing;

(2) the extreme danger inherent in manufacturing controlled substances;

(3) the threat to public safety posed by manufacturing controlled substances; and

(4) the recent increase in the importation, possession, and distribution of list I chemicals for the purpose of manufacturing controlled substances.

(d) Emergency Authority to Sentencing Commission.—The United States Sentencing Commission shall promulgate amendments pursuant to this section as soon as practicable after the date of the enactment of this Act in accordance with the procedure set forth in section 21(a) of the Sentencing Act of 1987 (Public Law 100–182), as though the authority under that Act had not expired."

ECSTASY OFFENSES. Pub. L. 106–310, Div. B, Title XXXVI, § 3661, 3663, 3664, Oct. 17, 2000, 114 Stat. 1242, provided:

"Subtitle C—Ecstasy Anti-Proliferation Act of 2000
"Sec. 3661. Short title.

This subtitle may be cited as the 'Ecstasy Anti-Proliferation Act of 2000'.

"Sec. 3662. Findings.

[omitted]

"Sec. 3663. Enhanced Punishment of Ecstasy Traffickers.

(a) Amendment to Federal Sentencing Guidelines.—Pursuant to its authority under section 994(p) of title 28, United States Code, the United States Sentencing Commission (referred to in this section as the 'Commission') shall amend the Federal sentencing guidelines regarding any offense relating to the manufacture, importation, or exportation of, or trafficking in—

(1) 3,4-methylenedioxy methamphetamine;

(2) 3,4-methylenedioxy amphetamine;

(3) 3,4-methylenedioxy-N-ethylamphetamine;

(4) paramethoxymethamphetamine (PMA); or

(5) any other controlled substance, as determined by the Commission in consultation with the Attorney General, that is marketed as Ecstasy and that has either a chemical structure substantially similar to that of 3,4-methylenedioxy methamphetamine or an effect on the central nervous system substantially similar to or greater than that of 3,4-methylenedioxy methamphetamine, including an attempt or conspiracy to commit an offense described in paragraph (1), (2), (3), (4), or (5) in violation of the Controlled Substances Act (21 U.S.C. 801 et seq.), the Controlled Substances Import and Export Act (21 U.S.C. 951 et seq.), or the Maritime Drug Law Enforcement Act (46 U.S.C. 1901 et seq.).

(b) General Requirements.—In carrying out this section, the Commission shall, with respect to each offense described in subsection (a)—

(1) review and amend the Federal sentencing guidelines to provide for increased penalties such that those penalties reflect the seriousness of these offenses and the need to deter them; and

(2) take any other action the Commission considers to be necessary to carry out this section.

(c) Additional Requirements.—In carrying out this section, the Commission shall ensure that the Federal sentencing guidelines for offenders convicted of offenses described in subsection (a) reflect—

(1) the need for aggressive law enforcement action with respect to offenses involving the controlled substances described in subsection (a); and

(2) the dangers associated with unlawful activity involving such substances, including—

(A) the rapidly growing incidence of abuse of the controlled substances described in subsection (a) and the threat to public safety that such abuse poses;

(B) the recent increase in the illegal importation of the controlled substances described in subsection (a);

(C) the young age at which children are beginning to use the controlled substances described in subsection (a);

(D) the fact that the controlled substances described in subsection (a) are frequently marketed to youth;

(E) the large number of doses per gram of the controlled substances described in subsection (a); and

(F) any other factor that the Commission determines to be appropriate.

(d) Sense of the Congress.—It is the sense of the Congress that—

(1) the base offense levels for Ecstasy are too low, particularly for high-level traffickers, and should be increased, such that they are comparable to penalties for other drugs of abuse; and

(2) based on the fact that importation of Ecstasy has surged in the past few years, the traffickers are targeting the Nation's youth, and the use of Ecstasy among youth in the United States is increasing even as other drug use among this population appears to be leveling off, the base offense levels for importing and trafficking the controlled substances described in subsection (a) should be increased.

(e) Report.—Not later than 60 days after the amendments pursuant to this section have been promulgated, the Commission shall—

(1) prepare a report describing the factors and information considered by the Commission in promulgating amendments pursuant to this section; and

(2) submit the report to—

(A) the Committee on the Judiciary, the Committee on Health, Education, Labor, and Pensions, and the Committee on Appropriations of the Senate; and

(B) the Committee on the Judiciary, the Committee on Commerce, and the Committee on Appropriations of the House of Representatives.

"Sec. 3664. Emergency Authority to United States Sentencing Commission.

The United States Sentencing Commission shall promulgate amendments under this subtitle as soon as practicable after the date of the enactment of this Act [Oct. 17, 2000] in accordance with the procedure set forth in section 21(a) of the Sentencing Act of 1987 (Public Law 100–182) [28 U.S.C. 994 note], as though the authority under that Act had not expired."

* * *

VICTIMS OF TRAFFICKING AND VIOLENCE PROTECTION ACT OF 2000 (PUB. L. 106–386)

PEONAGE, INVOLUNTARY SERVITUDE, SLAVE TRADE OFFENSES, AND OTHER HUMAN TRAFFICKING OFFENSES. Pub. L. 106–386, Div. A, § 112(b), Oct. 28, 2000, 114 Stat. 1489, provided:

"(b) Amendment to the Sentencing Guidelines.—

(1) Pursuant to its authority under section 994 of title 28, United States Code, and in accordance with this section, the United States Sentencing Commission shall review and, if appropriate, amend the sentencing guidelines and policy statements applicable to persons convicted of offenses involving the trafficking of persons including component or related crimes of peonage, involuntary servitude, slave trade offenses, and possession, transfer or sale of false immigration documents in furtherance of trafficking, and the Fair Labor Standards Act and the Migrant and Seasonal Agricultural Worker Protection Act.

(2) In carrying out this subsection, the Sentencing Commission shall—

(A) take all appropriate measures to ensure that these sentencing guidelines and policy statements applicable to the offenses described in paragraph (1) of this subsection are sufficiently stringent to deter and adequately reflect the heinous nature of such offenses;

(B) consider conforming the sentencing guidelines applicable to offenses involving trafficking in persons to the guidelines applicable to peonage, involuntary servitude, and slave trade offenses; and

(C) consider providing sentencing enhancements for those convicted of the offenses described in paragraph (1) of this subsection that—

(i) involve a large number of victims;

(ii) involve a pattern of continued and flagrant violations;

(iii) involve the use or threatened use of a dangerous weapon; or

(iv) result in the death or bodily injury of any person.

(3) The Commission may promulgate the guidelines or amendments under this subsection in accordance with the procedures set forth in section 21(a) of the Sentencing Act of 1987, as though the authority under that Act had not expired.".

INTERSTATE STALKING (SECTION 2261A OFFENSES). Pub. L. 106–386, Div. B, Title I, § 1107(b), Oct. 28, 2000, 114 Stat. 1498, provided:

"(b) Interstate Stalking.—

(1) In general.—[amended 18 U.S.C. § 2261A (Stalking); omitted]

(2) Amendment of federal sentencing guidelines.—

(A) In general.—Pursuant to its authority under section 994 of title 28, United States Code, the United States Sentencing Commission shall amend the Federal Sentencing Guidelines to reflect the amendment made by this subsection.

(B) Factors for consideration.—In carrying out subparagraph (A), the Commission shall consider—

(i) whether the Federal Sentencing Guidelines relating to stalking offenses should be modified in light of the amendment made by this subsection; and

(ii) whether any changes the Commission may make to the Federal Sentencing Guidelines pursuant to clause (i) should also be made with respect to offenses under chapter 110A of title 18, United States Code."

* * *

COLLEGE SCHOLARSHIP FRAUD PREVENTION ACT OF 2000 (PUB. L. 106–420)

HIGHER EDUCATION FINANCIAL ASSISTANCE FRAUD. Pub. L. 106–420, § 3, Nov. 1, 2000, 114 Stat. 1868, provided:

"Sec. 3. Sentencing Enhancement for Higher Education Financial Assistance Fraud.

Pursuant to its authority under section 994(p) of title 28, United States Code, the United States Sentencing Commission shall amend the Federal sentencing guidelines in or-der to provide for enhanced penalties for any offense involving fraud or misrepresentation in connection with the obtaining or providing of, or the furnishing of information to a consumer on, any scholarship, grant, loan, tuition, discount, award, or other financial assistance for purposes of financing an education at an institution of higher education, such that those penalties are comparable to the base offense level for misrepresentation that the defendant was acting on behalf of a charitable, educational, religious, or political organization, or a government agency."

* * *

UNITING AND STRENGTHENING AMERICA BY PROVIDING APPROPRIATE TOOLS REQUIRED TO INTERCEPT AND OBSTRUCT TERRORISM ACT OF 2001 or USA PATRIOT ACT (PUB. L. 107–56)

COMPUTER FRAUD AND ABUSE (SECTION 1030 OFFENSES). Pub. L. 107–56, Title VIII, § 814(f), Oct. 26, 2001, 115 Stat. 384, provided:

"(f) Amendment of Sentencing Guidelines Relating to Certain Computer Fraud and Abuse.—Pursuant to its authority under section 994(p) of title 28, United States Code, the United States Sentencing Commission shall amend the Federal sentencing guidelines to ensure that any individual convicted of a violation of section 1030 of title 18, United States Code, can be subjected to appropriate penalties, without regard to any mandatory minimum term of imprisonment."

* * *

BIPARTISAN CAMPAIGN REFORM ACT OF 2002 (PUB. L. 107–155)

ELECTION LAW VIOLATIONS. Pub. L. 107–155, § 314, Mar. 27, 2002, 116 Stat. 107, provided:

"Sec. 314. Sentencing Guidelines.

(a) In General.—The United States Sentencing Commission shall—

(1) promulgate a guideline, or amend an existing guideline under section 994 of title 28, United States Code, in accordance with paragraph (2), for penalties for violations of the Federal Election Campaign Act of 1971 and related election laws; and

(2) submit to Congress an explanation of any guidelines promulgated under paragraph (1) and any legislative or administrative recommendations regarding enforcement of the Federal Election Campaign Act of 1971 and related election laws.

(b) Considerations.—The Commission shall provide guidelines under subsection (a) taking into account the following considerations:

(1) Ensure that the sentencing guidelines and policy statements reflect the serious nature of such violations and the need for aggressive and appropriate law enforcement action to prevent such violations.

(2) Provide a sentencing enhancement for any person convicted of such violation if such violation involves—

(A) a contribution, donation, or expenditure from a foreign source;

(B) a large number of illegal transactions;

(C) a large aggregate amount of illegal contributions, donations, or expenditures;

(D) the receipt or disbursement of governmental funds; and

(E) an intent to achieve a benefit from the Federal Government.

(3) Assure reasonable consistency with other relevant directives and guidelines of the Commission.

(4) Account for aggravating or mitigating circumstances that might justify exceptions, including circumstances for which the sentencing guidelines currently provide sentencing enhancements.

(5) Assure the guidelines adequately meet the purposes of sentencing under section 3553(a)(2) of title 18, United States Code.

(c) Effective Date; Emergency Authority to Promulgate Guidelines.—

(1) Effective date.—Notwithstanding section 402, the United States Sentencing Commission shall promulgate guidelines under this section not later than the later of—

(A) 90 days after the effective date of this Act; or

(B) 90 days after the date on which at least a majority of the members of the Commission are appointed and holding office.

(2) Emergency authority to promulgate guidelines.—The Commission shall promulgate guidelines under this section in accordance with the procedures set forth in section 21(a) of the Sentencing Reform Act of 1987, as though the authority under such Act has not expired."

* * *

SARBANES–OXLEY ACT OF 2002
(PUB. L. 107–204)

OBSTRUCTION OF JUSTICE; FRAUD; ORGANIZATIONAL GUIDELINES. Pub. L. 107–204, Title VIII, § 805, July 30, 2002, 116 Stat. 802, provided:

"Sec. 805. Review of Federal Sentencing Guidelines for Obstruction of Justice and Extensive Criminal Fraud.

(a) Enhancement of Fraud and Obstruction of Justice Sentences.—Pursuant to section 994 of title 28, United States Code, and in accordance with this section, the United States Sentencing Commission shall review and amend, as appropriate, the Federal Sentencing Guidelines and related policy statements to ensure that—

(1) the base offense level and existing enhancements contained in United States Sentencing Guideline 2J1.2 relating to obstruction of justice are sufficient to deter and punish that activity;

(2) the enhancements and specific offense characteristics relating to obstruction of justice are adequate in cases where—

(A) the destruction, alteration, or fabrication of evidence involves—

(i) a large amount of evidence, a large number of participants, or is otherwise extensive;

(ii) the selection of evidence that is particularly probative or essential to the investigation; or

(iii) more than minimal planning; or

(B) the offense involved abuse of a special skill or a position of trust;

(3) the guideline offense levels and enhancements for violations of section 1519 or 1520 of title 18, United States Code, as added by this title, are sufficient to deter and punish that activity;

(4) a specific offense characteristic enhancing sentencing is provided under United States Sentencing Guideline 2B1.1 (as in effect on the date of enactment of this Act) for a fraud offense that endangers the solvency or financial security of a substantial number of victims; and

(5) the guidelines that apply to organizations in United States Sentencing Guidelines, chapter 8, are sufficient to deter and punish organizational criminal misconduct.

(b) Emergency Authority and Deadline for Commission Action.—The United States Sentencing Commission is requested to promulgate the guidelines or amendments provided for under this section as soon as practicable, and in any event not later than 180 days after the date of enactment of this Act, in accordance with the procedures set forth in section 219(a) of the Sentencing Reform Act of 1987, as though the authority under that Act had not expired.".

FRAUD AND CERTAIN OTHER WHITE-COLLAR OFFENSES. Pub. L. 107–204, Title IX, § 905, July 30, 2002, 116 Stat. 805, provided:

"**Sec. 905. Amendment to Sentencing Guidelines Relating to Certain White-Collar Offenses.**

(a) Directive to the United States Sentencing Commission.—Pursuant to its authority under section 994(p) of title 18, United States Code, and in accordance with this section, the United States Sentencing Commission shall review and, as appropriate, amend the Federal Sentencing Guidelines and related policy statements to implement the provisions of this Act.

(b) Requirements.—In carrying out this section, the Sentencing Commission shall—

(1) ensure that the sentencing guidelines and policy statements reflect the serious nature of the offenses and the penalties set forth in this Act, the growing incidence of serious fraud offenses which are identified above, and the need to modify the sentencing guidelines and policy statements to deter, prevent, and punish such offenses;

(2) consider the extent to which the guidelines and policy statements adequately address whether the guideline offense levels and enhancements for violations of the sections amended by this Act are sufficient to deter and punish such offenses, and specifically, are adequate in view of the statutory increases in penalties contained in this Act;

(3) assure reasonable consistency with other relevant directives and sentencing guidelines;

(4) account for any additional aggravating or mitigating circumstances that might justify exceptions to the generally applicable sentencing ranges;

(5) make any necessary conforming changes to the sentencing guidelines; and

(6) assure that the guidelines adequately meet the purposes of sentencing, as set forth in section 3553(a)(2) of title 18, United States Code.

(c) Emergency Authority and Deadline for Commission Action.—The United States Sentencing Commission is requested to promulgate the guidelines or amendments provided for under this section as soon as practicable, and in any event not later than 180 days after the date of enactment of this Act, in accordance with the procedures set forth in section 219(a) of the Sentencing Reform Act of 1987, as though the authority under that Act had not expired.".

SECURITIES, PENSION, AND ACCOUNTING FRAUD; ENHANCEMENT FOR OFFICERS AND DIRECTORS OF PUBLICLY TRADED CORPORATIONS. Pub. L. 107–204, Title XI, § 1104, July 30, 2002, 116 Stat. 808, provided:

"Sec. 1104. Amendment to the Federal Sentencing Guidelines.

(a) Request for Immediate Consideration by the United States Sentencing Commission.—Pursuant to its authority under section 994(p) of title 28, United States Code, and in accordance with this section, the United States Sentencing Commission is requested to—

(1) promptly review the sentencing guidelines applicable to securities and accounting fraud and related offenses;

(2) expeditiously consider the promulgation of new sentencing guidelines or amendments to existing sentencing guidelines to provide an enhancement for officers or directors of publicly traded corporations who commit fraud and related offenses; and

(3) submit to Congress an explanation of actions taken by the Sentencing Commission pursuant to paragraph (2) and any additional policy recommendations the Sentencing Commission may have for combating offenses described in paragraph (1).

(b) Considerations in Review.—In carrying out this section, the Sentencing Commission is requested to—

(1) ensure that the sentencing guidelines and policy statements reflect the serious nature of securities, pension, and accounting fraud and the need for aggressive and appropriate law enforcement action to prevent such offenses;

(2) assure reasonable consistency with other relevant directives and with other guidelines;

(3) account for any aggravating or mitigating circumstances that might justify exceptions, including circumstances for which the sentencing guidelines currently provide sentencing enhancements;

(4) ensure that guideline offense levels and enhancements for an obstruction of justice offense are adequate in cases where documents or other physical evidence are actually destroyed or fabricated;

(5) ensure that the guideline offense levels and enhancements under United States Sentencing Guideline 2B1.1 (as in effect on the date of enactment of this Act) are sufficient for a fraud offense when the number of victims adversely involved is significantly greater than 50;

(6) make any necessary conforming changes to the sentencing guidelines; and

(7) assure that the guidelines adequately meet the purposes of sentencing as set forth in section 3553 (a)(2) of title 18, United States Code.

(c) Emergency Authority and Deadline for Commission Action.—The United States Sentencing Commission is requested to promulgate the guidelines or amendments provided for under this section as soon as practicable, and in any event not later than the 180 days after the date of enactment of this Act, in accordance with the procedures sent forth in section 21(a) of the Sentencing Reform Act of 1987, as though the authority under that Act had not expired."

* * *

21ST CENTURY DEPARTMENT OF JUSTICE APPROPRIATIONS AUTHORIZATION ACT (PUB. L. 107–273)

ASSAULTS, THREATS, AND OTHER OFFENSES AGAINST FEDERAL JUDGES AND OTHER CERTAIN FEDERAL OFFICERS AND EMPLOYEES. Pub. L. 107–273, Div. C, Title I, § 11008(a), (e), Nov. 2, 2002, 116 Stat. 1819, provided:

"(a) Short Title.—This section may be cited as the 'Federal Judiciary Protection Act of 2002'.

(b)–(d) [omitted]

(e) Amendment of the Sentencing Guidelines for Assaults and Threats Against Federal Judges and Certain Other Federal Officials and Employees.—

(1) In General.— Pursuant to its authority under section 994 of title 28, United States Code, the United States Sentencing Commission shall review and amend the Federal sentencing guidelines and the policy statements of the commission, if appropriate, to provide an appropriate sentencing enhancement for offenses involving influencing, assaulting, resisting, impeding, retaliating against, or threatening a Federal judge, magistrate judge, or any other official described in section 111 or 115 of title 18, United States Code.

(2) Factors for Consideration.—In carrying out this section, the United States Sentencing Commission shall consider, with respect to each offense described in paragraph (1)—

(A) any expression of congressional intent regarding the appropriate penalties for the offense;

(B) the range of conduct covered by the offense;

(C) the existing sentences for the offense;

(D) the extent to which sentencing enhancements within the Federal sentencing guidelines and the authority of the court to impose a sentence in excess of the applicable guideline range are adequate to ensure punishment at or near the maximum penalty for the most egregious conduct covered by the offense;

(E) the extent to which the Federal sentencing guideline sentences for the offense have been constrained by statutory maximum penalties;

(F) the extent to which the Federal sentencing guidelines for the offense adequately achieve the purposes of sentencing as set forth in section 3553(a)(2) of title 18, United States Code;

(G) the relationship of the Federal sentencing guidelines for the offense to the Federal sentencing guidelines for other offenses of comparable seriousness; and

(H) any other factors that the Commission considers to be appropriate.".

CRIMES OF VIOLENCE AND DRUG TRAFFICKING CRIMES IN WHICH THE DEFENDANT USED BODY ARMOR. Pub. L. 107–273, Div. C, Title I, § 11009(a), (d), Nov. 2, 2002, 116 Stat. 1819, provided:

"**(a) Short Title.**—This section may be cited as the 'James Guelff and Chris McCurley Body Armor Act of 2002'.

(b)–(c) [omitted]

(d) Amendment of Sentencing Guidelines with Respect to Body Armor.—

(1) In General.—Pursuant to its authority under section 994(p) of title 28, United States Code, the United States Sentencing Commission shall review and amend the Federal sentencing guidelines and the policy statements of the Commission, as appropriate, to provide an appropriate sentencing enhancement for any crime of violence (as defined in section 16 of title 18, United States Code) or drug trafficking crime (as defined in section 924(c) of title 18, United States Code) (including a crime of violence or drug trafficking crime that provides for an enhanced punishment if committed by the use of a deadly or dangerous weapon or device) in which the defendant used body armor.

(2) Sense of Congress.—It is the sense of Congress that any sentencing enhancement under this subsection should be at least 2 levels.".

* * *

HOMELAND SECURITY ACT OF 2002
or
CYBER SECURITY ENHANCEMENT ACT OF 2002
(PUB. L. 107–296)

COMPUTER CRIMES (SECTION 1030 OFFENSES). Pub. L. 107–296, Title II, § 225(b), (c), Nov. 25, 2002, 116 Stat. 2156, provided:

"**(b) Amendment of Sentencing Guidelines Relating to Certain Computer Crimes.—**

(1) Directive to the United States Sentencing Commission.—Pursuant to its authority under section 994(p) of title 28, United States Code, and in accordance with this subsection, the United States Sentencing Commission shall review and, if appropriate, amend its guidelines and its policy statements applicable to persons convicted of an offense under section 1030 of title 18, United States Code.

(2) Requirements.—In carrying out this subsection, the Sentencing Commission shall—

(A) ensure that the sentencing guidelines and policy statements reflect the serious nature of the offenses described in paragraph (1), the growing incidence of such offenses, and the need for an effective deterrent and appropriate punishment to prevent such offenses;

(B) consider the following factors and the extent to which the guidelines may or may not account for them—

(i) the potential and actual loss resulting from the offense;

(ii) the level of sophistication and planning involved in the offense;

(iii) whether the offense was committed for purposes of commercial advantage or private financial benefit;

(iv) whether the defendant acted with malicious intent to cause harm in committing the offense;

(v) the extent to which the offense violated the privacy rights of individuals harmed;

(vi) whether the offense involved a computer used by the government in furtherance of national defense, national security, or the administration of justice;

(vii) whether the violation was intended to or had the effect of significantly interfering with or disrupting a critical infrastructure; and

(viii) whether the violation was intended to or had the effect of creating a threat to public health or safety, or injury to any person;

(C) assure reasonable consistency with other relevant directives and with other sentencing guidelines;

(D) account for any additional aggravating or mitigating circumstances that might justify exceptions to the generally applicable sentencing ranges;

(E) make any necessary conforming changes to the sentencing guidelines; and

(F) assure that the guidelines adequately meet the purposes of sentencing as set forth in section 3553(a)(2) of title 18, United States Code.

(c) Study and Report on Computer Crimes.—Not later than May 1, 2003, the United States Sentencing Commission shall submit a brief report to Congress that explains any actions taken by the Sentencing Commission in response to this section and includes any recommendations the Commission may have regarding statutory penalties for offenses under section 1030 of title 18, United States Code."

* * *

PROSECUTORIAL REMEDIES AND OTHER TOOLS TO END THE EXPLOITATION OF CHILDREN TODAY ACT OF 2003
or
THE PROTECT ACT
(PUB. L. 108–21)

KIDNAPPING OFFENSES. Pub. L. 108–21, Title I, § 104(a), Apr. 30, 2003, 117 Stat. 653, provided:

"Sec. 104. Stronger Penalties Against Kidnapping.

(a) Sentencing Guidelines.—Notwithstanding any other provision of law regarding the amendment of Sentencing Guidelines, the United States Sentencing Commission is directed to amend the Sentencing Guidelines, to take effect on the date that is 30 days after the date of the enactment of this Act—

(1) so that the base offense level for kidnapping in section 2A4.1(a) is increased from level 24 to level 32;

(2) so as to delete section 2A4.1(b)(4)(C); and

(3) so that the increase provided by section 2A4.1(b)(5) is 6 levels instead of 3.

(b) [omitted]".

CHILD CRIMES AND SEX OFFENSES; DOWNWARD DEPARTURES; ACCEPTANCE OF RESPONSIBILITY. Pub. L. 108–21, Title IV, § 401, Apr. 30, 2003, 117 Stat. 668, provided:

"Sec. 401. Sentencing Reform.

(a) [omitted]

(b) Conforming Amendments to Guidelines Manual.—The Federal Sentencing Guidelines are amended—

(1) in section 5K2.0—

(A) by striking 'Under' and inserting the following:

'(a) DOWNWARD DEPARTURES IN CRIMINAL CASES OTHER THAN CHILD CRIMES AND SEXUAL OFFENSES—Under'; and

(B) by adding at the end the following:

'(b) DOWNWARD DEPARTURES IN CHILD CRIMES AND SEXUAL OFFENSES—Under 18 U.S.C. Sec. 3553(b)(2), the sentencing court may impose a sentence below the range established by the applicable guidelines only if the court finds that there exists a mitigating circumstance of a kind, or to a degree, that—

(1) has been affirmatively and specifically identified as a permissible ground of downward departure in the sentencing guidelines or policy statements issued under section 994(a) of title 28, United States Code, taking account of any amendments to such sentencing guidelines or policy statements by act of Congress;

(2) has not adequately been taken into consideration by the Sentencing Commission in formulating the guidelines; and

(3) should result in a sentence different from that described.

'The grounds enumerated in this Part K of chapter 5 are the sole grounds that have been affirmatively and specifically identified as a permissible ground of downward departure in these sentencing guidelines and policy statements. Thus, notwithstanding any other reference to authority to depart downward elsewhere in this Sentencing Manual, a ground of downward departure has not been affirmatively and specifically identified as a permissible ground of downward departure within the meaning of section 3553(b)(2) unless it is expressly enumerated in this Part K as a ground upon which a downward departure may be granted.'.

(2) At the end of part K of chapter 5, add the following:

'Sec. 5K2.22 Specific Offender Characteristics as Grounds for Downward Departure in child crimes and sexual offenses (Policy Statement)

'In sentencing a defendant convicted of an offense under section 1201 involving a minor victim, an offense under section 1591, or an offense under chapter 71, 109A, 110, or 117 of title 18, United States Code, age may be a reason to impose a sentence below the applicable guideline range only if and to the extent permitted by Sec. 5H1.1.

'An extraordinary physical impairment may be a reason to impose a sentence below the applicable guideline range only if and to the extent permitted by Sec. 5H1.4. Drug, alcohol, or gambling dependence or abuse is not a reason for imposing a sentence below the guidelines.'

(3) Section 5K2.20 is amended by striking 'A' and inserting 'Except where a defendant is convicted of an offense under section 1201 involving a minor victim, an offense under section 1591, or an offense under chapter 71, 109A, 110, or 117 of title 18, United States Code, a'.

(4) Section 5H1.6 is amended by inserting after the first sentence the following: 'In sentencing a defendant convicted of an offense under section 1201 involving a minor victim, an offense under section 1591, or an offense under chapter 71, 109A, 110, or 117 of title 18, United States Code, family ties and responsibilities and community ties are not relevant in determining whether a sentence

should be below the applicable guideline range.'.

(5) Section 5K2.13 is amended by—

(A) striking 'or' before '(3)'; and

(B) replacing 'public' with 'public; or (4) the defendant has been convicted of an offense under chapter 71, 109A, 110, or 117 of title 18, United States Code.'

(c)–(f) [omitted]

(g) Reform of Guidelines Governing Acceptance of Responsibility.—Subject to subsection (j), the Guidelines Manual promulgated by the Sentencing Commission pursuant to section 994(a) of title 28, United States Code, is amended—

(1) in section 3E1.1(b)—

(A) by inserting 'upon motion of the government stating that' immediately before 'the defendant has assisted authorities'; and

(B) by striking 'taking one or more' and all that follows through and including 'additional level' and insert 'timely notifying authorities of his intention to enter a plea of guilty, thereby permitting the government to avoid preparing for trial and permitting the government and the court to allocate their resources efficiently, decrease the offense level by 1 additional level';

(2) in the Application Notes to the Commentary to section 3E1.1, by amending Application Note 6—

(A) by striking 'one or both of'; and

(B) by adding the following new sentence at the end: 'Because the Government is in the best position to determine whether the defendant has assisted authorities in a manner that avoids preparing for trial, an adjustment under subsection (b) may only be granted upon a formal motion by the Government at the time of sentencing.'; and

(3) in the Background to section 3E1.1, by striking 'one or more of.'".

(h) [omitted]

(i) Sentencing Guidelines Amendments.—**(1)** Subject to subsection (j), the Guidelines Manual promulgated by the Sentencing Commission pursuant to section 994(a) of title 28, United States Code, is amended as follows:

(A) Application Note 4(b)(i) to section 4B1.5 is amended to read as follows:

'(i) IN GENERAL—For purposes of subsection (b), the defendant engaged in a pattern of activity involving prohibited sexual conduct if on at least two separate occasions, the defendant engaged in prohibited sexual conduct with a minor.'.

(B) Section 2G2.4(b) is amended by adding at the end the following:

'(4) If the offense involved material that portrays sadistic or masochistic conduct or other depictions of violence, increase by 4 levels.

'(5) If the offense involved—

'(A) at least 10 images, but fewer than 150, increase by 2 levels;

'(B) at least 150 images, but fewer than 300, increase by 3 levels;

'(C) at least 300 images, but fewer than 600, increase by 4 levels; and

'(D) 600 or more images, increase by 5 levels.'.

(C) Section 2G2.2(b) is amended by adding at the end the following:

'(6) If the offense involved—

'(A) at least 10 images, but fewer than 150, increase by 2 levels;

'(B) at least 150 images, but fewer than 300, increase by 3 levels;

'(C) at least 300 images, but fewer than 600, increase by 4 levels; and

'(D) 600 or more images, increase by 5 levels.'.

(2) The Sentencing Commission shall amend the Sentencing Guidelines to ensure that the Guidelines adequately reflect the seriousness of the offenses under sections 2243(b), 2244(a)(4), and 2244(b) of title 18, United States Code.

(j) Conforming Amendments.—

(1) Upon enactment of this Act, the Sentencing Commission shall forthwith distribute to all courts of the United States and to the United States Probation System the amendments made by subsections (b), (g), and (i) of this section to the sentencing guidelines, policy statements, and official commentary of the Sentencing Commission. These amendments shall take effect upon the date of enactment of this Act, in accordance with paragraph (5).

(2) On or before May 1, 2005, the Sentencing Commission shall not promulgate any amendment to the sentencing guidelines, policy statements, or official commentary of the Sentencing Commission that is inconsistent with any amendment made by subsection (b) or that adds any new grounds of downward departure to Part K of chapter 5.

(3) With respect to cases covered by the amendments made by subsection (i) of this section, the Sentencing Commission may make further amendments to the sentencing guidelines, policy statements, or official commentary of the Sentencing Commission, except that the Commission shall not promulgate any amendments that, with respect to such cases, would result in sentencing ranges that are lower than those that would have applied under such subsection.

(4) At no time may the Commission promulgate any amendment that would alter or repeal the amendments made by subsection (g) of this section.

(k)–(l) [omitted]

(m) Reform of Existing Permissible Grounds of Downward Departures.—Not later than 180 days after the enactment of this Act, the United States Sentencing Commission shall—

(1) review the grounds of downward departure that are authorized by the sentencing guidelines, policy statements, and official commentary of the Sentencing Commission; and

(2) promulgate, pursuant to section 994 of title 28, United States Code—

(A) appropriate amendments to the sentencing guidelines, policy statements, and official commentary to ensure that the incidence of downward departures are substantially reduced;

(B) a policy statement authorizing a downward departure of not more than 4 levels if the Government files a motion for

such departure pursuant to an early disposition program authorized by the Attorney General and the United States Attorney; and

(C) any other conforming amendments to the sentencing guidelines, policy statements, and official commentary of the Sentencing Commission necessitated by this Act, including a revision of paragraph 4(b) of part A of chapter 1 and a revision of section 5K2.0.".

OBSCENE VISUAL REPRESENTATIONS OF SEXUAL ABUSE OF CHILDREN. (SECTION 1466A OFFENSES). Pub. L. 108–21, Title V, § 504(c), Apr. 30, 2003, 117 Stat. 682, provided:

"(c) Sentencing Guidelines.—

(1) Category.—Except as provided in paragraph (2), the applicable category of offense to be used in determining the sentencing range referred to in section 3553(a)(4) of title 18, United States Code, with respect to any person convicted under section 1466A of such title, shall be the category of offenses described in section 2G2.2 of the Sentencing Guidelines.

(2) Ranges.—The Sentencing Commission may promulgate guidelines specifically governing offenses under section 1466A of title 18, United States Code, if such guidelines do not result in sentencing ranges that are lower than those that would have applied under paragraph (1).".

TRANSPORTATION TO ENGAGE IN SEXUAL ACT WITH A MINOR (SECTION 2423 OFFENSES). Pub. L. 108–21, Title V, § 512, Apr. 30, 2003, 117 Stat. 685, provided:

"Sec. 512. Sentencing Enhancements for Interstate Travel to Engage in Sexual Act with a Juvenile.

Pursuant to its authority under section 994(p) of title 28, United States Code, and in accordance with this section, the United States Sentencing Commission shall review and, as appropriate, amend the Federal Sentencing Guidelines and policy statements to ensure that guideline penalties are adequate in cases that involve interstate travel with the intent to engage in a sexual act with a juvenile in violation of section 2423 of title 18, United States Code, to deter and punish such conduct."

DISTRIBUTING MATERIAL CONSTITUTING OR CONTAINING CHILD PORNOGRAPHY (SECTION 2252A OFFENSES). Pub L. 108–21, Title V, § 513(c), Apr. 30, 2003, 117 Stat. 685, provided:

"**(c) Sentencing Guidelines.**—Pursuant to its authority under section 994(p) of title 28, United States Code, and in accordance with this section, the United States Sentencing Commission shall review and, as appropriate, amend the Federal Sentencing Guidelines and policy statements to ensure that the guidelines are adequate to deter and punish conduct that involves a violation of paragraph (3)(B) or (6) of section 2252A(a) of title 18, United States Code, as created by this Act. With respect to the guidelines for section 2252A(a)(3)(B), the Commission shall consider the relative culpability of promoting, presenting, describing, or distributing material in violation of that section as compared with solicitation of such material.".

GHB (GAMMA HYDROXYBUTYRIC ACID) OFFENSES. Pub. L. 108–21, Title VI, § 608(e), Apr. 30, 2003, 117 Stat. 691, provided:

"**(e) Sentencing Commission Guidelines.**—The United States Sentencing Commission shall—

(1) review the Federal sentencing guidelines with respect to offenses involving gamma hydroxybutyric acid (GHB);

(2) consider amending the Federal sentencing guidelines to provide for increased penalties such that those penalties reflect the seriousness of offenses involving GHB and the need to deter them; and

(3) take any other action the Commission considers necessary to carry out this section."

* * *

CONTROLLING THE ASSAULT OF NON-SOLICITED PORNOGRAPHY AND MARKETING ACT OF 2003
or
CAN-SPAM ACT OF 2003
(PUB. L. 108–187)

ELECTRONIC MAIL FRAUD (SECTION 1037 OFFENSES). Pub. L. 108–187, § 4(b), Dec. 16, 2003, 117 Stat. 2705, provided:

"**(b) United States Sentencing Commission.**—

(1) Directive.—Pursuant to its authority under section 994(p) of title 28, United States Code, and in accordance with this section, the United States Sentencing Commission shall review and, as appropriate, amend the sentencing guidelines and policy statements to provide appropriate penalties for violations of section 1037 of title 18, United States Code, as added by this section, and other offenses that may be facilitated by the sending of large quantities of unsolicited electronic mail.

(2) Requirements.—In carrying out this subsection, the Sentencing Commission shall consider providing sentencing enhancements for—

(A) those convicted under section 1037 of title 18, United States Code, who—

(i) obtained electronic mail addresses through improper means, including—

(I) harvesting electronic mail addresses of the users of a website, proprietary service, or other online public forum operated by another person, without the authorization of such person; and

(II) randomly generating electronic mail addresses by computer; or

(ii) knew that the commercial electronic mail messages involved in the offense contained or advertised an Internet domain for which the registrant of the domain had provided false registration information; and

(B) those convicted of other offenses, including offenses involving fraud, identity theft, obscenity, child pornography, and the sexual exploitation of children, if such offenses involved the sending of large quantities of electronic mail."

* * *

IDENTITY THEFT PENALTY ENHANCEMENT ACT (PUB. L. 108–275)

IDENTITY THEFT OFFENSES INVOLVING AN ABUSE OF POSITION. Pub. L. 108–275, § 5, July 15, 2004, 118 Stat. 833, provided:

"Sec. 5. Directive to the United States Sentencing Commission.

(a) In General.—Pursuant to its authority under section 994(p) of title 28, United States Code, and in accordance with this section, the United States Sentencing Commission shall review and amend its guidelines and its policy statements to ensure that the guideline offense levels and enhancements appropriately punish identity theft offenses involving an abuse of position.

(b) Requirements.—In carrying out this section, the United States Sentencing Commission shall do the following:

(1) Amend U.S.S.G. section 3B1.3 (Abuse of Position of Trust of Use of Special Skill) to apply to and punish offenses in which the defendant exceeds or abuses the authority of his or her position in order to obtain unlawfully or use without authority any means of identification, as defined section 1028(d)(4) of title 18, United States Code.

(2) Ensure reasonable consistency with other relevant directives, other sentencing guidelines, and statutory provisions.

(3) Make any necessary and conforming changes to the sentencing guidelines.

(4) Ensure that the guidelines adequately meet the purposes of sentencing set forth in section 3553(a)(2) of title 18, United States Code."

* * *

ANABOLIC STEROID CONTROL ACT OF 2004 (PUB. L. 108–358)

ANABOLIC STEROID OFFENSES. Pub. L. 108–358, § 3, Oct. 22, 2004, 118 Stat. 1664, provided:

"Sec. 3. Sentencing Commission Guidelines.

The United States Sentencing Commission shall—

(1) review the Federal sentencing guidelines with respect to offenses involving anabolic steroids;

(2) consider amending the Federal sentencing guidelines to provide for increased penalties with respect to offenses involving anabolic steroids in a manner that reflects the seriousness of such offenses and the need to deter anabolic steroid trafficking and use; and

(3) take such other action that the Commission considers necessary to carry out this section."

* * *

INTELLIGENCE REFORM AND TERRORISM PREVENTION ACT OF 2004 or STOP TERRORIST AND MILITARY HOAXES ACT OF 2004 (PUB. L. 108–458)

OFFENSES INVOLVING INTERNATIONAL OR DOMESTIC TERRORISM. Pub. L. 108–458, Title VI, § 6703(b), Dec. 17, 2004, 118 Stat. 3766, provided:

"(b) Sentencing Guidelines.—Not later than 30 days of the enactment of this section, the United States Sentencing Commission shall amend the Sentencing Guidelines to provide for an increased offense level for an offense under sections 1001(a) and 1505 of title 18, United States Code, if the offense involves international or domestic terrorism, as defined in section 2331 of such title."

* * *

INTELLECTUAL PROPERTY PROTECTION AND COURTS AMENDMENTS ACT OF 2004
or
FRAUDULENT ONLINE IDENTITY SANCTIONS ACT
(PUB. L. 108–482)

FELONY OFFENSES COMMITTED ONLINE INVOLVING FALSE DOMAIN NAMES. Pub. L. 108–482, Title II, § 204(b), Dec. 23, 2004, 118 Stat. 3917, provided:

"**(b) United States Sentencing Commission.**—

(1) **Directive.**—Pursuant to its authority under section 994(p) of title 28, United States Code, and in accordance with this section, the United States Sentencing Commission shall review and amend the sentencing guidelines and policy statements to ensure that the applicable guideline range for a defendant convicted of any felony offense carried out online that may be facilitated through the use of a domain name registered with materially false contact information is sufficiently stringent to deter commission of such acts.

(2) **Requirements.**—In carrying out this subsection, the Sentencing Commission shall provide sentencing enhancements for anyone convicted of any felony offense furthered through knowingly providing or knowingly causing to be provided materially false contact information to a domain name registrar, domain name registry, or other domain name registration authority in registering, maintaining, or renewing a domain name used in connection with the violation.

(3) **Definition.**—For purposes of this subsection, the term 'domain name' has the meaning given that term in section 45 of the

Act entitled 'An Act to provide for the registration and protection of trademarks used in commerce, to carry out the provisions of certain international conventions, and for other purposes', approved July 5, 1946 (commonly referred to as the 'Trademark Act of 1946'; 15 U.S.C. 1127)."

* * *

FAMILY ENTERTAINMENT AND COPYRIGHT ACT OF 2005
or
ARTISTS' RIGHTS AND THEFT PREVENTION ACT OF 2005 (ART ACT)
(PUB. L. 109–9)

INTELLECTUAL PROPERTY OFFENSES. Pub. L. 109–9, Title I, § 105, Apr. 27, 2005, 119 Stat. 218, provided:

"**Sec. 105. Federal Sentencing Guidelines.**

(a) **Review and Amendment.**—Not later than 180 days after the date of enactment of this Act, the United States Sentencing Commission, pursuant to its authority under section 994 of title 28, United States Code, and in accordance with this section, shall review and, if appropriate, amend the Federal sentencing guidelines and policy statements applicable to persons convicted of intellectual property rights crimes, including any offense under—

(1) section 506, 1201, or 1202 of title 17, United States Code; or

(2) section 2318, 2319, 2319A, 2319B, or 2320 of title 18, United States Code.

(b) **Authorization.**—The United States Sentencing Commission may amend the Federal sentencing guidelines in accordance with the procedures set forth in section 21(a) of the Sentencing Act of 1987 (28 U.S.C. 994 note) as though the authority under that section had not expired.

(c) **Responsibilities of United States Sentencing Commission.**—In carrying out this section, the United States Sentencing Commission shall—

(1) take all appropriate measures to ensure that the Federal sentencing guidelines and

policy statements described in subsection (a) are sufficiently stringent to deter, and adequately reflect the nature of, intellectual property rights crimes;

(2) determine whether to provide a sentencing enhancement for those convicted of the offenses described in subsection (a), if the conduct involves the display, performance, publication, reproduction, or distribution of a copyrighted work before it has been authorized by the copyright owner, whether in the media format used by the infringing party or in any other media format;

(3) determine whether the scope of "uploading" set forth in application note 3 of section 2B5.3 of the Federal sentencing guidelines is adequate to address the loss attributable to people who, without authorization, broadly distribute copyrighted works over the Internet; and

(4) determine whether the sentencing guidelines and policy statements applicable to the offenses described in subsection (a) adequately reflect any harm to victims from copyright infringement if law enforcement authorities cannot determine how many times copyrighted material has been reproduced or distributed."

* * *

UNITED STATES PAROLE COMMISSION EXTENSION AND SENTENCING COMMISSION AUTHORITY ACT OF 2005 (PUB. L. 109–76)

EMERGENCY AMENDMENT AUTHORITY PERTAINING TO THE INTELLIGENCE REFORM AND TERRORISM PREVENTION ACT OF 2004 AND THE ANABOLIC STEROID CONTROL ACT OF 2004. Pub. L. 109–76, § 3, Sept. 29, 2005, 119 Stat. 2035, provided:

"Sec. 3. Provision of Emergency Amendment Authority for Sentencing Commission.

In accordance with the procedure set forth in section 21(a) of the Sentencing Act of 1987 (Public Law 100–182), as though the authority under that Act had not expired, the United States Sentencing Commission shall—

(1) not later than 60 days after the date of the enactment of this Act, amend the Federal sentencing guidelines, commentary, and policy statements to implement section 6703 of the Intelligence Reform and Terrorism Prevention Act of 2004 (Public Law 108–458); and

(2) not later than 180 days after the date of the enactment of this Act, amend the Federal sentencing guidelines, commentary, and policy statements to implement section 3 of the Anabolic Steroid Control Act of 2004 (Public Law 108–358)."

* * *

VIOLENCE AGAINST WOMEN AND DEPARTMENT OF JUSTICE REAUTHORIZATION ACT OF 2005 (PUB. L. 109–162)

PUBLIC EMPLOYEE UNIFORMS (SECTION 716 OFFENSES). Pub. L. 109–162, § 1191(c), Jan. 5, 2006, 119 Stat. 2960, provided:

"(c) Direction to Sentencing Commission.—The United States Sentencing Commission is directed to make appropriate amendments to sentencing guidelines, policy statements, and official commentary to assure that the sentence imposed on a defendant who is convicted of a Federal offense while wearing or displaying insignia and uniform received in violation of section 716 of title 18, United States Code, reflects the gravity of this aggravating factor."

* * *

USA PATRIOT IMPROVEMENT AND REAUTHORIZATION ACT OF 2005 (PUB. L. 109–177)

THEFT OF INTERSTATE OR FOREIGN SHIPMENTS OR VESSELS (SECTION 659 OR 2311 OFFENSES). Pub. L. 109–177, § 307(c), March 9, 2006, 120 Stat. 192, provided:

"(c) Review of Sentencing Guidelines.— Pursuant to section 994 of title 28, United States Code, the United States Sentencing Commission shall review the Federal Sentencing Guidelines to determine whether sentencing enhancement is appropriate for any offense under section 659 or 2311 of title 18, United States Code, as amended by this title."

* * *

STOP COUNTERFEITING IN MANUFACTURED GOODS ACT (PUB. L. 109–181)

TRAFFICKING IN COUNTERFEIT LABELS, GOODS, OR SERVICES (SECTION 2318 OR 2320 OFFENSES). Pub. L. 109–181, § 1(c), March 16, 2006, 120 Stat. 285, provided:

"(c) Sentencing Guidelines.—
(1) Review and Amendment.—Not later than 180 days after the date of enactment of this Act, the United States Sentencing Commission, pursuant to its authority under section 994 of title 28, United States Code, and in accordance with this subsection, shall review and, if appropriate, amend the Federal sentencing guidelines and policy statements applicable to persons convicted of any offense under section 2318 or 2320 of title 18, United States Code.
(2) Authorization.—The United States Sentencing Commission may amend the Federal sentencing guidelines in accordance with the procedures set forth in section 21(a) of the Sentencing Act of 1987 (28 U.S.C. 994 note) as though the authority under that section had not expired.
(3) Responsibilities of United States Sentencing Commission.—In carrying out this subsection, the United States Sentencing Commission shall determine whether the definition of 'infringement amount' set forth in application note 2 of section 2B5.3 of the Federal sentencing guidelines is adequate to address situations in which the defendant has been convicted of one of the offenses listed in

paragraph (1) and the item in which the defendant trafficked was not an infringing item but rather was intended to facilitate infringement, such as an anti-circumvention device, or the item in which the defendant trafficked was infringing and also was intended to facilitate infringement in another good or service, such as a counterfeit label, documentation, or packaging, taking into account cases such as U.S. v. Sung, 87 F.3d 194 (7th Cir. 1996)."

* * *

ADAM WALSH CHILD PROTECTION AND SAFETY ACT OF 2006 or SEX OFFENDER REGISTRATION AND NOTIFICATION ACT (PUB. L. 109–248)

SEX OFFENDER REGISTRATION (SECTION 2250 OFFENSES). Pub. L. 109–248, § 141(b), July 27, 2006, 120 Stat. 587, provided:

"Sec. 141. Amendments to Title 18, United States Code, Relating to Sex Offender Registration.
(a) [omitted; enacted 18 U.S.C. § 2250 (Failure to register)]
(b) Directive to the United States Sentencing Commission.—In promulgating guidelines for use of a sentencing court in determining the sentence to be imposed for the offense specified in subsection (a), the United States Sentencing Commission shall consider the following matters, in addition to the matters specified in section 994 of title 28, United States Code:
(1) Whether the person committed another sex offense in connection with, or during, the period for which the person failed to register.
(2) Whether the person committed an offense against a minor in connection with, or during, the period for which the person failed to register.
(3) Whether the person voluntarily attempted to correct the failure to register.

(4) The seriousness of the offense which gave rise to the requirement to register, including whether such offense is a tier I, tier II, or tier III offense, as those terms are defined in section 111.

(5) Whether the person has been convicted or adjudicated delinquent for any offense other than the offense which gave rise to the requirement to register."

* * *

DEPARTMENT OF HOMELAND SECURITY APPROPRIATIONS ACT, 2007 (PUB. L. 109–295)

OFFENSES INVOLVING BORDER TUNNELS AND SUBTERRANEAN PASSAGES (SECTION 554 OFFENSES). Pub. L. 109–295, § 551(d), Oct. 4, 2006, 120 Stat. 1390, provided:

"(d) Directive to the United States Sentencing Commission.—

(1) In general.—Pursuant to its authority under section 994 of title 28, United States Code, and in accordance with this subsection, the United States Sentencing Commission shall promulgate or amend sentencing guidelines to provide for increased penalties for persons convicted of offenses described in section 554 of title 18, United States Code, as added by subsection (a).

(2) Requirements.—In carrying out this subsection, the United States Sentencing Commission shall—

(A) ensure that the sentencing guidelines, policy statements, and official commentary reflect the serious nature of the offenses described in section 554 of title 18, United States Code, and the need for aggressive and appropriate law enforcement action to prevent such offenses;

(B) provide adequate base offense levels for offenses under such section;

(C) account for any aggravating or mitigating circumstances that might justify exceptions, including—

(i) the use of a tunnel or passage described in subsection (a) of such section to facilitate other felonies; and

(ii) the circumstances for which the sentencing guidelines currently provide applicable sentencing enhancements;

(D) ensure reasonable consistency with other relevant directives, other sentencing guidelines, and statutes;

(E) make any necessary and conforming changes to the sentencing guidelines and policy statements; and

(F) ensure that the sentencing guidelines adequately meet the purposes of sentencing set forth in section 3553(a)(2) of title 18, United States Code."

* * *

TELEPHONE RECORDS AND PRIVACY PROTECTION ACT OF 2006 (PUB. L. 109–476)

FRAUD IN OBTAINING CONFIDENTIAL PHONE RECORDS INFORMATION (SECTION 1039 OFFENSES). Pub. L. 109–476, § 4, Jan. 12, 2007, 120 Stat. 3571, provided:

"Sec. 4. Sentencing Guidelines.

(a) Review and Amendment.—Not later than 180 days after the date of enactment of this Act, the United States Sentencing Commission, pursuant to its authority under section 994 of title 28, United States Code, and in accordance with this section, shall review and, if appropriate, amend the Federal sentencing guidelines and policy statements applicable to persons convicted of any offense under section 1039 of title 18, United States Code.

(b) Authorization.—The United States Sentencing Commission may amend the Federal sentencing guidelines in accordance with the procedures set forth in section 21(a) of the Sentencing Act of 1987 (28 U.S.C. 994 note) as though the authority under that section had not expired."

* * *

COURT SECURITY IMPROVEMENT ACT
OF 2007
(PUB. L. 110–177)

THREATS OVER THE INTERNET AGAINST FEDERAL OFFICIALS (SECTION 115 OFFENSES). Pub. L. 110–177, § 209, Jan. 7, 2008, 121 Stat. 2538, provided:

"Sec. 209. Direction to the Sentencing Commission.

The United States Sentencing Commission is directed to review the Sentencing Guidelines as they apply to threats punishable under section 115 of title 18, United States Code, that occur over the Internet, and determine whether and by how much that circumstance should aggravate the punishment pursuant to section 994 of title 28, United States Code. In conducting the study, the Commission shall take into consideration the number of such threats made, the intended number of recipients of such threats, and whether the initial senders of such threats were acting in an individual capacity or as part of a larger group."

* * *

EMERGENCY AND DISASTER
ASSISTANCE FRAUD PENALTY
ENHANCEMENT ACT
OF 2007
(PUB. L. 110–179)

DISASTER ASSISTANCE FRAUD. Pub. L. 110–179, § 5, Jan. 7, 2008, 121 Stat. 2557, provided:

"Sec. 5. Directive to Sentencing Commission.

(a) In General.—Pursuant to its authority under section 994(p) of title 28, United States Code, and in accordance with this section, the United States Sentencing Commission forthwith shall—

(1) promulgate sentencing guidelines or amend existing sentencing guidelines to provide for increased penalties for persons convicted of fraud or theft offenses in connection with a major disaster declaration under section 401 of the Robert T. Stafford Disaster Relief and Emergency Assistance Act (42 U.S.C. 5170) or an emergency declaration under section 501 of the Robert T. Stafford Disaster Relief and Emergency Assistance Act (42 U.S.C. 5191); and

(2) submit to the Committee on the Judiciary of the Senate and the Committee on the Judiciary of the House of Representatives an explanation of actions taken by the Commission pursuant to paragraph (1) and any additional policy recommendations the Commission may have for combating offenses described in that paragraph.

(b) Requirements.—In carrying out this section, the Sentencing Commission shall—

(1) ensure that the sentencing guidelines and policy statements reflect the serious nature of the offenses described in subsection (a) and the need for aggressive and appropriate law enforcement action to prevent such offenses;

(2) assure reasonable consistency with other relevant directives and with other guidelines;

(3) account for any aggravating or mitigating circumstances that might justify exceptions, including circumstances for which the sentencing guidelines currently provide sentencing enhancements;

(4) make any necessary conforming changes to the sentencing guidelines; and

(5) assure that the guidelines adequately meet the purposes of sentencing as set forth in section 3553(a)(2) of title 18, United States Code.

(c) Emergency Authority and Deadline for Commission Action.—The Commission shall promulgate the guidelines or amendments provided for under this section as soon as practicable, and in any event not later than the 30 days after the date of enactment of this Act, in accordance with the procedures set forth in section 21(a) of the Sentencing Reform Act of 1987, as though the authority under that Act had not expired."

* * *

FORMER VICE PRESIDENT
PROTECTION ACT OF 2008
or
IDENTITY THEFT ENFORCEMENT AND
RESTITUTION ACT OF 2008
(PUB. L. 110–326)

COMPUTER CRIME; THEFT OR MISUSE OF PERSONALLY IDENTIFIABLE DATA (SECTION 1028, 1028A, 1030, 2511, AND 2701 OFFENSES). Pub.L. 110–326, Title II, § 209, Sept. 26, 2008, 122 Stat. 3564, provided:

"**Sec. 209. Directive to United States Sentencing Commission.**

(a) Directive.—Pursuant to its authority under section 994(p) of title 28, United States Code, and in accordance with this section, the United States Sentencing Commission shall review its guidelines and policy statements applicable to persons convicted of offenses under sections 1028, 1028A, 1030, 2511, and 2701 of title 18, United States Code, and any other relevant provisions of law, in order to reflect the intent of Congress that such penalties be increased in comparison to those currently provided by such guidelines and policy statements.

(b) Requirements.—In determining its guidelines and policy statements on the appropriate sentence for the crimes enumerated in subsection (a), the United States Sentencing Commission shall consider the extent to which the guidelines and policy statements may or may not account for the following factors in order to create an effective deterrent to computer crime and the theft or misuse of personally identifiable data:

(1) The level of sophistication and planning involved in such offense.

(2) Whether such offense was committed for purpose of commercial advantage or private financial benefit.

(3) The potential and actual loss resulting from the offense including—

(A) the value of information obtained from a protected computer, regardless of whether the owner was deprived of use of the information; and

(B) where the information obtained constitutes a trade secret or other proprietary information, the cost the victim incurred developing or compiling the information.

(4) Whether the defendant acted with intent to cause either physical or property harm in committing the offense.

(5) The extent to which the offense violated the privacy rights of individuals.

(6) The effect of the offense upon the operations of an agency of the United States Government, or of a State or local government.

(7) Whether the offense involved a computer used by the United States Government, a State, or a local government in furtherance of national defense, national security, or the administration of justice.

(8) Whether the offense was intended to, or had the effect of, significantly interfering with or disrupting a critical infrastructure.

(9) Whether the offense was intended to, or had the effect of, creating a threat to public health or safety, causing injury to any person, or causing death.

(10) Whether the defendant purposefully involved a juvenile in the commission of the offense.

(11) Whether the defendant's intent to cause damage or intent to obtain personal information should be disaggregated and considered separately from the other factors set forth in USSG 2B1.1(b)(14).

(12) Whether the term "victim" as used in USSG 2B1.1, should include individuals whose privacy was violated as a result of the offense in addition to individuals who suffered monetary harm as a result of the offense.

(13) Whether the defendant disclosed personal information obtained during the commission of the offense.

(c) Additional Requirements.—In carrying out this section, the United States Sentencing Commission shall—

(1) assure reasonable consistency with other relevant directives and with other sentencing guidelines;

(2) account for any additional aggravating or mitigating circumstances that might justify exceptions to the generally applicable sentencing ranges;

(3) make any conforming changes to the sentencing guidelines; and

(4) assure that the guidelines adequately meet the purposes of sentencing as set forth in section 3553(a)(2) of title 18, United States Code."

* * *

LET OUR VETERANS REST IN PEACE ACT OF 2008 (PUB. L. 110–384)

VETERANS' GRAVE MARKERS. Pub.L. 110–384, § 3, Oct. 10, 2008, 122 Stat. 4094, provided:

"Sec. 3. Direction to the Sentencing Commission.

(a) In General.—Pursuant to its authority under section 994 of title 28, United States Code, the United States Sentencing Commission shall review and, if appropriate, amend the Federal sentencing guidelines and policy statements to ensure the guidelines and policy statements provide adequate sentencing enhancements for any offense involving the desecration, theft, or trafficking in, a grave marker, headstone, monument, or other object, intended to permanently mark a veteran's grave.

(b) Commission Duties.—In carrying out this section, the Sentencing Commission shall—

(1) ensure that the sentences, guidelines, and policy statements relating to offenders convicted of these offenses are appropriately severe and reasonably consistent with other relevant directives and other Federal sentencing guidelines and policy statements;

(2) make any necessary conforming changes to the Federal sentencing guidelines; and

(3) assure that the guidelines adequately meet the purposes of sentencing as set forth in section 3553(a)(2) of title 18, United States Code."

* * *

DRUG TRAFFICKING VESSEL INTERDICTION ACT OF 2008 (PUB. L. 110–407)

SUBMERSIBLE VESSELS (SECTION 2285 OFFENSES). Pub.L. 110–407, Title I, § 103, Oct. 13, 2008, 122 Stat. 4298, provided:

"Sec. 103. Sentencing Guidelines.

(a) In General.—Pursuant to its authority under section 994(p) of title 28, United States Code, and in accordance with this section, the United States Sentencing Commission shall promulgate sentencing guidelines (including policy statements) or amend existing sentencing guidelines (including policy statements) to provide adequate penalties for persons convicted of knowingly operating by any means or embarking in any submersible vessel or semi-submersible vessel in violation of section 2285 of title 18, United States Code.

(b) Requirements.—In carrying out this section, the United States Sentencing Commission shall—

(1) ensure that the sentencing guidelines and policy statements reflect the serious nature of the offense described in section 2285 of title 18, United States Code, and the need for deterrence to prevent such offenses;

(2) account for any aggravating or mitigating circumstances that might justify exceptions, including—

(A) the use of a submersible vessel or semi-submersible vessel described in section 2285 of title 18, United States Code, to facilitate other felonies;

(B) the repeated use of a submersible vessel or semi-submersible vessel described in section 2285 of title 18, United States Code, to facilitate other felonies, including whether such use is part of an ongoing criminal organization or enterprise;

(C) whether the use of such a vessel involves a pattern of continued and flagrant violations of section 2285 of title 18, United States Code;

(D) whether the persons operating or embarking in a submersible vessel or semi-submersible vessel willfully caused, attempted to cause, or permitted the destruction or damage of such vessel or failed to heave to when directed by law enforcement officers; and

(E) circumstances for which the sentencing guidelines (and policy statements) provide sentencing enhancements;

(3) ensure reasonable consistency with other relevant directives, other sentencing guidelines and policy statements, and statutory provisions;

(4) make any necessary and conforming changes to the sentencing guidelines and policy statements; and

(5) ensure that the sentencing guidelines and policy statements adequately meet the purposes of sentencing set forth in section 3553(a)(2) of title 18, United States Code."

* * *

RYAN HAIGHT ONLINE PHARMACY CONSUMER PROTECTION ACT OF 2008 (PUB. L. 110–425)

DELIVERY OF CONTROLLED SUBSTANCES BY MEANS OF THE INTERNET. Pub.L. 110–425, § 3(k)(2), Oct. 15, 2008, 122 Stat. 4833, provided:

"**(2) Sentencing guidelines.**—The United States Sentencing Commission, in determining whether to amend, or establish new, guidelines or policy statements, to conform the Federal sentencing guidelines and policy statements to this Act and the amendments made by this Act, should not construe any change in the maximum penalty for a violation involving a controlled substance in a particular schedule as being the sole reason to amend, or establish a new, guideline or policy statement."

* * *

WILLIAM WILBERFORCE TRAFFICKING VICTIMS PROTECTION REAUTHORIZATION ACT OF 2008 (PUB. L. 110–457)

ALIEN HARBORING. Pub.L. 110–457, Title II, § 222(g), Dec. 23, 2008, 122 Stat. 5071, provided:

"**(g) Amendment to Sentencing Guidelines.**—Pursuant to its authority under section 994 of title 28, United States Code, the United States Sentencing Commission shall review and, if appropriate, amend the sentencing guidelines and policy statements applicable to persons convicted of alien harboring to ensure conformity with the sentencing guidelines applicable to persons convicted of promoting a commercial sex act if—

(1) the harboring was committed in furtherance of prostitution; and

(2) the defendant to be sentenced is an organizer, leader, manager, or supervisor of the criminal activity."

* * *

NATIONAL DEFENSE AUTHORIZATION ACT FOR FISCAL YEAR 2010 or MATTHEW SHEPARD AND JAMES BYRD, JR. HATE CRIMES PREVENTION ACT (PUB. L. 111–84)

REPORT ON MANDATORY MINIMUM SENTENCING PROVISIONS. Pub.L. 111–84, Div. E, § 4713, Oct. 28, 2009, 123 Stat. 2843, provided:

"**Sec. 4713. Report on Mandatory Minimum Sentencing Provisions.**

(a) Report.—Not later than 1 year after the date of enactment of this Act, the United States Sentencing Commission shall submit to the Committee on the Judiciary of the Senate and the Committee on the Judiciary of the House of Representatives a report on mandatory minimum sentencing provisions under Federal law.

(b) Contents of Report.—The report submitted under subsection (a) shall include—

(1) a compilation of all mandatory minimum sentencing provisions under Federal law;

(2) an assessment of the effect of mandatory minimum sentencing provisions under Federal law on the goal of eliminating unwarranted sentencing disparity and other goals of sentencing;

(3) an assessment of the impact of mandatory minimum sentencing provisions on the Federal prison population;

(4) an assessment of the compatibility of mandatory minimum sentencing provisions under Federal law and the sentencing guidelines system established under the Sentencing Reform Act of 1984 (Public Law 98–473; 98 Stat. 1987) and the sentencing guidelines system in place after Booker v. United States, 543 U.S. 220 (2005);

(5) a description of the interaction between mandatory minimum sentencing provisions under Federal law and plea agreements;

(6) a detailed empirical research study of the effect of mandatory minimum penalties under Federal law;

(7) a discussion of mechanisms other than mandatory minimum sentencing laws by which Congress can take action with respect to sentencing policy; and

(8) any other information that the Commission determines would contribute to a thorough assessment of mandatory minimum sentencing provisions under Federal law."

* * *

PATIENT PROTECTION AND AFFORDABLE CARE ACT (PUB. L. 111–148)

FEDERAL HEALTH CARE OFFENSES. Pub.L. 111–148, § 10606(a), Mar. 23, 2010, 124 Stat. 1006, provided:

"(a) Fraud Sentencing Guidelines.—
(1) Definition.—In this subsection, the term 'Federal health care offense' has the meaning given that term in section 24 of title 18, United States Code, as amended by this Act.

(2) Review and amendments.—Pursuant to the authority under section 994 of title 28, United States Code, and in accordance with this subsection, the United States Sentencing Commission shall—

(A) review the Federal Sentencing Guidelines and policy statements applicable to persons convicted of Federal health care offenses;

(B) amend the Federal Sentencing Guidelines and policy statements applicable to persons convicted of Federal health care offenses involving Government health care programs to provide that the aggregate dollar amount of fraudulent bills submitted to the Government health care program shall constitute prima facie evidence of the amount of the intended loss by the defendant; and

(C) amend the Federal Sentencing Guidelines to provide—

(i) a 2-level increase in the offense level for any defendant convicted of a Federal health care offense relating to a Government health care program which involves a loss of not less than $1,000,000 and less than $7,000,000;

(ii) a 3-level increase in the offense level for any defendant convicted of a Federal health care offense relating to a Government health care program which involves a loss of not less than $7,000,000 and less than $20,000,000;

(iii) a 4-level increase in the offense level for any defendant convicted of a Federal health care offense relating to a Government health care program which involves a loss of not less than $20,000,000; and

(iv) if appropriate, otherwise amend the Federal Sentencing Guidelines and policy statements applicable to persons convicted of Federal health care offenses involving Government health care programs.

(3) Requirements.—In carrying this subsection, the United States Sentencing Commission shall—

(A) ensure that the Federal Sentencing Guidelines and policy statements—

(i) reflect the serious harms associated with health care fraud and the need for aggressive and appropriate law enforcement action to prevent such fraud; and

(ii) provide increased penalties for persons convicted of health care fraud offenses in appropriate circumstances;

(B) consult with individuals or groups representing health care fraud victims, law enforcement officials, the health care industry, and the Federal judiciary as part of the review described in paragraph (2);

(C) ensure reasonable consistency with other relevant directives and with other guidelines under the Federal Sentencing Guidelines;

(D) account for any aggravating or mitigating circumstances that might justify exceptions, including circumstances for which the Federal Sentencing Guidelines, as in effect on the date of enactment of this Act, provide sentencing enhancements;

(E) make any necessary conforming changes to the Federal Sentencing Guidelines; and

(F) ensure that the Federal Sentencing Guidelines adequately meet the purposes of sentencing."

* * *

DODD–FRANK WALL STREET REFORM AND CONSUMER PROTECTION ACT (PUB. L. 111–203)

OFFENSES RELATING TO SECURITIES FRAUD, FINANCIAL INSTITUTION FRAUD, OR FEDERALLY RELATED MORTGAGE LOAN FRAUD. Pub.L. 111–203, § 1079A(a), July 21, 2010, 124 Stat. 2077–78, provided:

"(a) Sentencing Guidelines.—
(1) Securities fraud.—

(A) Directive.—Pursuant to its authority under section 994 of title 28, United States Code, and in accordance with this paragraph, the United States Sentencing Commission shall review and, if appropriate, amend the Federal Sentencing Guidelines and policy statements applicable to persons convicted of offenses relating to securities fraud or any other similar provision of law, in order to reflect the intent of Congress that penalties for the offenses under the guidelines and policy statements appropriately account for the potential and actual harm to the public and the financial markets from the offenses.

(B) Requirements.—In making any amendments to the Federal Sentencing Guidelines and policy statements under subparagraph (A), the United States Sentencing Commission shall—

(i) ensure that the guidelines and policy statements, particularly section 2B1.1(b)(14) and section 2B1.1(b)(17) (and any successors thereto), reflect—

(I) the serious nature of the offenses described in subparagraph (A);

(II) the need for an effective deterrent and appropriate punishment to prevent the offenses; and

(III) the effectiveness of incarceration in furthering the objectives described in subclauses (I) and (II);

(ii) consider the extent to which the guidelines appropriately account for the potential and actual harm to the public and the financial markets resulting from the offenses;

(iii) ensure reasonable consistency with other relevant directives and guidelines and Federal statutes;

(iv) make any necessary conforming changes to guidelines; and

(v) ensure that the guidelines adequately meet the purposes of sentencing, as set forth in section 3553(a)(2) of title 18, United States Code.

(2) Financial institution fraud.—

(A) Directive.—Pursuant to its authority under section 994 of title 28, United States Code, and in accordance with this paragraph, the United States Sentencing Commission shall review and, if appropriate, amend the Federal Sentencing Guidelines and policy statements applicable to persons convicted of fraud offenses relating to financial institutions or federally related mortgage loans and any other similar provisions of law, to reflect the intent of Congress that the penalties for the offenses under the guidelines and policy statements ensure appropriate terms of imprisonment for offenders involved in substantial bank frauds or other frauds relating to financial institutions.

(B) Requirements.—In making any amendments to the Federal Sentencing Guidelines and policy statements under subparagraph (A), the United States Sentencing Commission shall—

(i) ensure that the guidelines and policy statements reflect—

(I) the serious nature of the offenses described in subparagraph (A);

(II) the need for an effective deterrent and appropriate punishment to prevent the offenses; and

(III) the effectiveness of incarceration in furthering the objectives described in subclauses (I) and (II);

(ii) consider the extent to which the guidelines appropriately account for the potential and actual harm to the public and the financial markets resulting from the offenses;

(iii) ensure reasonable consistency with other relevant directives and guidelines and Federal statutes;

(iv) make any necessary conforming changes to guidelines; and

(v) ensure that the guidelines adequately meet the purposes of sentencing, as set forth in section 3553(a)(2) of title 18, United States Code."

* * *

FAIR SENTENCING ACT OF 2010
(PUB. L. 111–220)

ENHANCEMENTS FOR ACTS OF VIOLENCE DURING DRUG TRAFFICKING OFFENSE; INCREASED EMPHASIS ON DEFENDANT'S ROLE AND CERTAIN AGGRAVATING AND MITIGATING FACTORS; EMERGENCY AUTHORITY; REPORT TO CONGRESS. Pub.L. 111–220, §§ 5 to 8, 10, Aug. 3, 2010, 124 Stat. 2373, provided:

"Sec. 5. Enhancements for Acts of Violence During the Course of a Drug Trafficking Offense.

Pursuant to its authority under section 994 of title 28, United States Code, the United States Sentencing Commission shall review and amend the Federal sentencing guidelines to ensure that the guidelines provide an additional penalty increase of at least 2 offense levels if the defendant used violence, made a credible threat to use violence, or directed the use of violence during a drug trafficking offense.

"Sec. 6. Increased Emphasis on Defendant's Role and Certain Aggravating Factors.

Pursuant to its authority under section 994 of title 28, United States Code, the United States Sentencing Commission shall review and amend the Federal sentencing guidelines to ensure an additional increase of at least 2 offense levels if—

(1) the defendant bribed, or attempted to bribe, a Federal, State, or local law enforcement official in connection with a drug trafficking offense;

(2) the defendant maintained an establishment for the manufacture or distribution of a controlled substance, as generally described in section 416 of the Controlled Substances Act (21 U.S.C. 856); or

(3)(A) the defendant is an organizer, leader, manager, or supervisor of drug trafficking activity subject to an aggravating role enhancement under the guidelines; and

(B) the offense involved 1 or more of the following super-aggravating factors:

(i) The defendant—

(I) used another person to purchase, sell, transport, or store controlled substances;

(II) used impulse, fear, friendship, affection, or some combination thereof to involve such person in the offense; and

(III) such person had a minimum knowledge of the illegal enterprise and was to receive little or no compensation from the illegal transaction.

(ii) The defendant—

(I) knowingly distributed a controlled substance to a person under the age of 18 years, a person over the age of 64 years, or a pregnant individual;

(II) knowingly involved a person under the age of 18 years, a person over the age of 64 years, or a pregnant individual in drug trafficking;

(III) knowingly distributed a controlled substance to an individual who was unusually vulnerable due to physical or mental condition, or who was particularly susceptible to criminal conduct; or

(IV) knowingly involved an individual who was unusually vulnerable due to physical or mental condition, or who was particularly susceptible to criminal conduct, in the offense.

(iii) The defendant was involved in the importation into the United States of a controlled substance.

(iv) The defendant engaged in witness intimidation, tampered with or destroyed evidence, or otherwise obstructed justice in connection with the investigation or prosecution of the offense.

(v) The defendant committed the drug trafficking offense as part of a pattern of criminal conduct engaged in as a livelihood.

"Sec. 7. Increased Emphasis on Defendant's Role and Certain Mitigating Factors.

Pursuant to its authority under section 994 of title 28, United States Code, the United States Sentencing Commission shall review and amend the Federal sentencing guidelines and policy statements to ensure that—

(1) if the defendant is subject to a minimal role adjustment under the guidelines, the base offense level for the defendant based solely on drug quantity shall not exceed level 32; and

(2) there is an additional reduction of 2 offense levels if the defendant—

(A) otherwise qualifies for a minimal role adjustment under the guidelines and had a minimum knowledge of the illegal enterprise;

(B) was to receive no monetary compensation from the illegal transaction; and

(C) was motivated by an intimate or familial relationship or by threats or fear when the defendant was otherwise unlikely to commit such an offense.

"Sec. 8. Emergency Authority for United States Sentencing Commission.

The United States Sentencing Commission shall—

(1) promulgate the guidelines, policy statements, or amendments provided for in this Act as soon as practicable, and in any event not later than 90 days after the date of enactment of this Act, in accordance with the procedure set forth in section 21(a) of the Sentencing Act of 1987 (28 U.S.C. 994 note), as though the authority under that Act had not expired; and

(2) pursuant to the emergency authority provided under paragraph (1), make such conforming amendments to the Federal sentencing guidelines as the Commission determines necessary to achieve consistency with other guideline provisions and applicable law.

"Sec. 9. Report [by Comptroller General] on Effectiveness of Drug Courts.
[omitted]

"Sec. 10. United States Sentencing Commission Report on Impact of Changes to Federal Cocaine Sentencing Law.

Not later than 5 years after the date of enactment of this Act, the United States Sentencing Commission, pursuant to the authority under sections 994 and 995 of title 28, United States Code, and the responsibility of the United States Sentencing Commission to advise Congress on sentencing policy under section 995(a)(20) of title 28, United States Code, shall study and submit to Congress a report regarding the impact of the changes in Federal sentencing law under this Act and the amendments made by this Act."

* * *

SECURE AND RESPONSIBLE DRUG DISPOSAL ACT
(PUB. L. 111–273)

DRUG OFFENSES RESULTING FROM AUTHORIZATION TO RECEIVE SCHEDULED SUBSTANCES FROM ULTIMATE USERS OR LONG-TERM CARE FACILITIES. Pub.L. 111–273, § 4, Oct. 12, 2010, 124 Stat. 2860, provided:

"Sec. 4. Directive to the United States Sentencing Commission.

Pursuant to its authority under section 994 of title 28, United States Code, the United States Sentencing Commission shall review and, if appropriate, amend the Federal sentencing guidelines and policy statements to ensure that the guidelines and policy statements provide an appropriate penalty increase of up to 2 offense levels above the sentence otherwise applicable in Part D of the Guidelines Manual if a person is convicted of a drug offense resulting from the authorization of that person to receive scheduled substances from an ultimate user or long-term care facility as set forth in the amendments made by section 3 [adding subsection (g) to 21 U.S.C. § 822 and paragraph (3) to 21 U.S.C. § 828(b)]."

* * *

FOOD AND DRUG ADMINISTRATION SAFETY AND INNOVATION ACT
(PUB. L. 112–144)

COUNTERFEIT DRUG TRAFFICKING. Pub. L. 112–144, title VII, § 717(b), July 9, 2012, 126 Stat. 1076, provided:

"(b) Sentencing Commission Directive.—

(1) Directive to Sentencing Commission.—Pursuant to its authority under section 994(p) of title 28, United States Code, and in accordance with this subsection, the United States Sentencing Commission shall review and amend, if appropriate, its guidelines and its policy statements applicable to persons convicted of an offense described in section 2320(a)(4) of title 18, United States Code, as amended by subsection (a), in order to reflect the intent of Congress that such penalties be increased in comparison to those currently provided by the guidelines and policy statements.

(2) Requirements.—In carrying out this subsection, the Commission shall—

(A) ensure that the sentencing guidelines and policy statements reflect the intent of Congress that the guidelines and policy statements reflect the serious nature of the offenses described in paragraph (1) and the need for an effective deterrent and appropriate punishment to prevent such offenses;

(B) consider the extent to which the guidelines may or may not appropriately account for the potential and actual harm to the public resulting from the offense;

(C) assure reasonable consistency with other relevant directives and with other sentencing guidelines;

(D) account for any additional aggravating or mitigating circumstances that might justify exceptions to the generally applicable sentencing ranges;

(E) make any necessary conforming changes to the sentencing guidelines; and

(F) assure that the guidelines adequately meet the purposes of sentencing as set forth in section 3553(a)(2) of title 18, United States Code."

* * *

STRENGTHENING AND FOCUSING ENFORCEMENT TO DETER ORGANIZED STEALING AND ENHANCE SAFETY ACT OF 2012
or
SAFE DOSES ACT
(PUB. L. 112–186)

THEFT OF PRE-RETAIL MEDICAL PRODUCTS. Pub. L. 112–186, § 7, Oct. 5, 2012, 126 Stat. 1430, provided:

"Sec. 7. Directive to United States Sentencing Commission.

(a) In General.—Pursuant to its authority under section 994 of title 28, United States Code, and in accordance with this section, the United States Sentencing Commission shall review and, if appropriate, amend the Federal sentencing guidelines and policy statements applicable to persons convicted of offenses under section 670 of title 18, United States Code, as added by this Act, section 2118 of title 18, United States Code, or any another section of title 18, United States Code, amended by this Act, to reflect the intent of Congress that penalties for such offenses be sufficient to deter and punish such offenses, and appropriately account for the actual harm to the public from these offenses.

(b) Requirements.—In carrying out this section, the United States Sentencing Commission shall—

(1) consider the extent to which the Federal sentencing guidelines and policy statements appropriately reflect—

(A) the serious nature of such offenses;

(B) the incidence of such offenses; and

(C) the need for an effective deterrent and appropriate punishment to prevent such offenses;

(2) consider establishing a minimum offense level under the Federal sentencing guidelines and policy statements for offenses covered by this Act;

(3) account for any additional aggravating or mitigating circumstances that might justify exceptions to the generally applicable sentencing ranges;

(4) ensure reasonable consistency with other relevant directives, Federal sentencing guidelines and policy statements;

(5) make any necessary conforming changes to the Federal sentencing guidelines and policy statements; and

(6) ensure that the Federal sentencing guidelines and policy statements adequately meet the purposes of sentencing set forth in section 3553(a)(2) of title 18, United States Code."

* * *

CHILD PROTECTION ACT OF 2012
(PUB. L. 112–206)

PROTECTION OF CHILD WITNESSES. Pub. L. 112–206, § 3(b), Dec. 7, 2012, 126 Stat. 1492, provided:

"(b) Sentencing Guidelines.—Pursuant to its authority under section 994 of title 28, United States Code, and in accordance with this section, the United States Sentencing Commission shall review and, if appropriate, amend the Federal sentencing guidelines and policy statements to ensure—

(1) that the guidelines provide an additional penalty increase above the sentence otherwise applicable in Part J of Chapter 2 of the Guidelines Manual if the defendant was convicted of a violation of section 1591 of title 18, United States Code, or chapters 109A, 109B, 110, or 117 of title 18, United States Code; and

(2) if the offense described in paragraph (1) involved causing or threatening to cause physical injury to a person under 18 years of age, in order to obstruct the administration of justice, an additional penalty increase above the sentence otherwise applicable in Part J of Chapter 2 of the Guidelines Manual."

* * *

FOREIGN AND ECONOMIC ESPIONAGE PENALTY ENHANCEMENT ACT OF 2012 (PUB. L. 112–269)

TRADE SECRETS AND ECONOMIC ESPIONAGE. Pub. L. 112–269, § 3, Jan. 14, 2013, 126 Stat. 2442, provided:

"Sec. 3. Review by the United States Sentencing Commission.

(a) In General.—Pursuant to its authority under section 994(p) of title 28, United States Code, the United States Sentencing Commission shall review and, if appropriate, amend the Federal sentencing guidelines and policy statements applicable to persons convicted of offenses relating to the transmission or attempted transmission of a stolen trade secret outside of the United States or economic espionage, in order to reflect the intent of Congress that penalties for such offenses under the Federal sentencing guidelines and policy statements appropriately, reflect the seriousness of these offenses, account for the potential and actual harm caused by these offenses, and provide adequate deterrence against such offenses.

(b) Requirements.—In carrying out this section, the United States Sentencing Commission shall—

(1) consider the extent to which the Federal sentencing guidelines and policy statements appropriately account for the simple misappropriation of a trade secret, including the sufficiency of the existing enhancement for these offenses to address the seriousness of this conduct;

(2) consider whether additional enhancements in the Federal sentencing guidelines and policy statements are appropriate to account for—

(A) the transmission or attempted transmission of a stolen trade secret outside of the United States; and

(B) the transmission or attempted transmission of a stolen trade secret outside of the United States that is committed or attempted to be committed for the benefit of a foreign government, foreign instrumentality, or foreign agent;

(3) ensure the Federal sentencing guidelines and policy statements reflect the seriousness of these offenses and the need to deter such conduct;

(4) ensure reasonable consistency with other relevant directives, Federal sentencing guidelines and policy statements, and related Federal statutes;

(5) make any necessary conforming changes to the Federal sentencing guidelines and policy statements; and

(6) ensure that the Federal sentencing guidelines adequately meet the purposes of sentencing as set forth in section 3553(a)(2) of title 18, United States Code.

(c) Consultation.—In carrying out the review required under this section, the Commission shall consult with individuals or groups representing law enforcement, owners of trade secrets, victims of economic espionage offenses, the United States Department of Justice, the United States Department of Homeland Security, the United States Department of State and the Office of the United States Trade Representative.

(d) Review.—Not later than 180 days after the date of enactment of this Act, the Commission shall complete its consideration and review under this section."